PHILOSOPHY
The Quest for Truth

Louis P. Pojman

University of Mississippi

Wadsworth Publishing Company

Belmont, California ★ A Division of Wadsworth, Inc.

Philosophy Editor: *Kenneth King*
Editorial Assistant: *Cynthia Campbell*
Production Editor: *Carol Dondrea, Bookman Productions*
Print Buyer: *Martha Branch*
Designer: *Polly Christensen, Christensen & Son Design*
Copy Editor: *Dennis Marshall*
Compositor: *G&S Typesetters, Inc.*
Cover Designer: *Jill Turney*
Cover Photo: *© Costa Manos–Magnum*

Printed in the United States of America

1 2 3 4 5 6 7 8 9 10—96 95 94 93 92

Library of Congress Cataloging-in-Publication Data

Philosophy : the quest for truth / [collected by] Louis P. Pojman.—2nd ed.
    p. cm.
    Includes bibliographical references.
    ISBN 0-534-16530-3
    1. Philosophy—Introductions.   I. Pojman, Louis P.
BD21.P48 1992
100—dc20
                                     91-9056
                                      CIP

Preface

I AM GRATEFUL for the wide use the first edition of this introductory textbook received and am happy to set forth an improved edition. Many instructors sent in constructive suggestions for this edition. I have given them serious consideration and incorporated many of them without sacrificing the central focus and methodology.

This anthology was designed for lower-division (freshman and sophomore) students in Introduction to Philosophy courses. After several years of using some of the more comprehensive anthologies, and rejecting spoon-fed introductory texts, I came to the conclusion that the more rigorous anthologies are simply too hard for the average undergraduate non-philosophy major. There was a need for an anthology with more modest ambitions—but one that concentrated on the classic texts and raised the classic issues: the nature of philosophy, the existence of God, immortality, knowledge, the mind/body question, personal identity, free will and determinism, ethics, the justification of the State, and the meaning of life.

I have sought to provide such a middle way between the heavy-duty textbooks and those that seem trendy and simplistic. Although other good anthologies are available, few are centered in classic texts, as this book is. My book raises some questions not usually covered. It provides more and different readings to discuss all the questions and, at the end of each reading, it provides reflective questions. In this way *Philosophy: The Quest for Truth* fills a need and establishes a niche of its own.

Organization

Each of the eighteen questions considered in this book has a substantial introduction; in addition, individual introductions, including biographical sketches, are provided for each of the sixty-four readings. Each reading is preceded by a set of study questions and followed by a set of reflective questions that challenge the student to analyze, critique, and develop the argument presented in the reading. A short bibliography follows each major part of the book. There are two appendices, one on how to read and write a philosophy paper and one on logic. A glossary appears at the end.

Teachers will use the two sets of questions in different ways. The study questions, at the beginning of the reading, center on the content of the article and highlight material important for understanding the text. Some instructors may want students to write out answers to these questions as homework assignments. Others may simply use them as informal guides, leaving the students to use them as they see fit. Not every student needs auxiliary questions to the same degree, but most seem to find them helpful. My suggestion is to use an SQ2R approach: survey, question, read, reflect. That is, first read the article quickly, not worrying about whether you grasp all the important ideas; then go over the study questions and read the article more carefully with them in mind. Finally, look at the reflective questions and try to answer them. It may help to write out your responses.

The book is organized in a traditional way. After a set of readings on the question What is philosophy? I move to the classic question about which probably more philosophy has been written than any other: Is there a God? Can we prove that a Supreme Being exists? I follow the tradition of beginning with this question for two traditional reasons. First, it may be the most important question that philosophy asks. This is arguable, of course, as is almost everything in philosophy, but it can be supported with plausible reasons. Second, the theme provides us with some of the clearest examples in philosophy of deductive argument, and thus enables students to develop their reasoning skills.

The question of God's existence leads directly to Part III, on the theory of knowledge: What can we know and how do we know? In Part IV we study philosophy of mind, considering the mind/body problem, personal identity, and the implications of the problem of personal identity for the possibility of immortality. Part V treats various responses to the question of whether we have freedom of the will.

Part VI deals with ethics and includes such questions as What is ethics? Are there any moral absolutes? Why should I be moral? Which ethical theory (if any) is the correct one? This is followed by a Part VII, on political philosophy, and Part VIII, which asks What is the meaning of life? A new section, Part IX, is on applied ethics, and includes pro and con articles on abortion, capital punishment, and animal rights.

There is nothing sacred about this order. Each part is independent of the others, and the instructor is free to treat these topics in any order desired. I seldom cover more than five major topics. The only part I invariably use and begin with is Part I, What Is Philosophy?

The Readings

The readings have been chosen for their clearness and cogency of argument, classical expression of the position, and accessibility to intelligent college students. They are, for the most part, classical readings, raising classic questions and trying to solve them or shed light on them. There are several selections by Plato, René Descartes, John Locke, David Hume, Immanuel Kant, John Stuart Mill, Bertrand Russell, and John Hick—as well as single articles by Aristotle, Aquinas, Pascal, Thomas Hobbes, George Berkeley, William James, Nietzsche, Gilbert Ryle, Alvin Plantinga, and other imaginative and important writers. Where a classic writing on a topic was not available or suitable to my needs, I have used a less well known article to fill the bill.

The articles are generally presented in chronological order within the given section, but this sometimes conflicts with the dialogic nature of this work, in which case, I have sacrificed chronology to development of the argument. For example, I've tried to present readings with opposing viewpoints in every part, but David Hume's classic critique of the argument from design was actually written before Paley's classic exposition of the argument.

New Material for the Second Edition

Responding to several users of this textbook I have made a number of changes from the first edition, especially in Parts II, IV, and VI, and I've added a new part to the work, Part IX, Ethics in Action. In Part II I have added Paul Edwards' "A Critique of the Cosmological Argument," Alvin Plantinga's "Religious Belief Without Evidence," and a recent debate between J. P. Moreland and Kai Nielsen on the existence of God. I have also substituted a more accessible article by John Hick on the problem of evil. In Part IV I have added J. P. Moreland's defense of dualism, and in Part VI, my paper on relativism as well as Ayn Rand's and James Rachels' readings on ethical egoism. In Part VII I have added John Stuart Mill's defense of liberty. The new part, Part IX, on applied ethics, covers three contemporary moral issues: abortion, capital punishment, and animal rights.

Finally, two appendices have been added, one on how to read and write a philosophy paper and one introducing elementary logic.

Acknowledgments and Dedication

I would like to thank the reviewers who prompted these improvements: Robert Barford, Eastern Illinois University; Marjorie Clay, Bloomsburg University; Andrew Schoedinger, Boise State University; Francis Beckwith, University of Nevada-Las Vegas; Donald Zeyl, University of Rhode Island; Albert Studdard, Pembroke State University; James Magruder, Stephen F. Austin State University; Michael Critelli, Los Angeles City College. Ken King, senior editor for Wadsworth Publishing Company, both prompted this work and supported me every step of the way. I am deeply indebted to him for so much. Hal Humphrey and Carol Dondrea, as production editors, did an excellent job seeing this book through production, and I am grateful to the proofreader Beverly Zegarski for improving the manuscript at several places. My wife, Trudy, was an invaluable critic and supporter, as always.

Philosophy is an exciting subject. Indeed, I start out by arguing that it has revolutionary possibilities. Every intelligent young person should be exposed to and challenged by the questions it asks and the attempts it makes to respond to these questions, searching for truth and learning to enjoy the process of growing in wisdom. In order for that challenge to be effective, it is important to have teachers dedicated to teaching philosophy, for, perhaps more than any other subject, philosophy needs a mediator for its communication. The competent teacher is vital. I have sought to put together a set of readings with accompanying resources to help competent teachers carry on that process in the college classroom. To them this book is dedicated.

Louis P. Pojman
New York City
April 4, 1991

*Dedicated to Teachers who themselves are
dedicated to opening the hearts of the young
to the love of wisdom and the quest for truth*

Contents

Part III. *Knowledge*

Part IV. *The Mind/Body Problem*

Part I

What Is Philosophy?

The unexamined life is not worth living.

SOCRATES

If God held all Truth in His right hand and in His left hand the eternal Quest for Truth, and said to me, "Choose!" I would with courage touch His left and say, "Father, Give me this! The pure Truth is fit for you alone."

G. E. LESSING, *Werke,* vol. X, p. 53; my translation

PHILOSOPHY IS REVOLUTIONARY and vitally important to the good life. This book starts from an assumption which I hope you will be convinced of by the time you have completed this course: namely, that the unexamined life is not worth living, and that while philosophy disturbs, it also consoles. Philosophy, as Aristotle said over two thousand years ago, begins with wonder at the marvels and mysteries of the world. It begins in wonder in the pursuit of truth and wisdom and ends in life lived in passionate moral and intellectual integrity. At least this is the classical philosophical ideal and the faith—a rational faith, I hope. Of course, this thesis about the worth of philosophy is to be subject to rational scrutiny. Perhaps it is wrong, but it's one which I deeply believe. Let me expand on it.

The term "philosophy" literally means the love of wisdom (etymologically from the Greek *philos* = love and *sophia* = wisdom), but it is a wisdom that results from a pursuit of knowledge of the most important parts of reality. Hence the title of this book, the quest for truth. It is the contemplation or study of the most important questions in existence with the end of promoting illumination and understanding, a vision of the whole. It uses reason, sense perception, the imagination and intuitions in its activity of analyzing and constructing arguments and theories as possible answers to these perennial questions. It is revolutionary because its deliverances often disturb our common sense or our received tradition. Philosophy usually goes against the stream or the majority, since the majority opinion is often·a composite of past intellectual struggles or "useful" biases. There is often deeper truth, better and new evidence which disturbs the status quo and which forces us to revise or reject some of our beliefs. This experience can be as painful as it is exciting.

The pain may lead us to give up philosophical inquiry and may require a great deal of emotional health to persevere in it. We may retreat into unreason and obey the commandment of Ignorance, "Think not, lest Thou be confounded!" Truth (or what we seem justified in believing) may not always be edifying. But in the end, the philosopher's faith is that the Truth is good and worth pursuing for its own sake and for its secondary benefits. Intelligent inquiry, which philosophy promotes, is liberating, freeing us from prejudice, self-deceptive notions, and half-truths. As Bertrand Russell says in our second reading,

> The [person] who has no tincture of philosophy goes through life imprisoned in the prejudices derived from common sense, from the habitual beliefs of his age or his nation, and from convictions which have grown up in his mind without the co-operation or consent of his deliberate reason. . . . While diminishing our feeling of certainty as to what things are, [philosophy] greatly increases our knowledge as to what they may be; it removes the somewhat arrogant dogmatism of those who have never travelled into the region of liberating doubt, and it keeps alive the sense of wonder by showing familiar things in an unfamiliar light.

Philosophy should result in a wider vision of life in which the impartial use of reason results in an appreciation of other viewpoints and other people's rights and needs. There is no guarantee that this will occur. Some become radical skeptics with accompanied behavioral patterns, and some nasty people seem to be able to do philosophy quite well without being transformed by it. But for the most part those who have had the vision of a better life and have worked through arguments on substantive issues relating to the nature and destiny of humanity have been positively affected by the perennial pilgrimage. They march to a different drummer and show in their lives the fruits of their travail. This ability to live by reflective principle in spite of and in the midst of the noise of the masses is a special virtue of philosophy. It is illustrated by one of its heroes, Socrates (470–399 B.C.), in our first reading from Plato's work the *Apology*.

The hallmark of philosophy is centered in the argument. Philosophers clarify concepts, analyze and test propositions and beliefs, but the major task is to analyze and construct arguments. Philosophical reasoning is closely allied to scientific reasoning in that both look for evidence and build hypotheses which are tested with the hope of coming closer to the truth. However, scientific experiments take place in laboratories and have testing procedures through which to record objective or empirically verifiable results. The laboratory of the philosopher is the domain of ideas: the mind, where imaginative thought-experiments take place; the study, where ideas are written down and examined; and wherever conversation or debate about the perennial questions takes place, where thesis and counter-example and counter-thesis are considered. There is a joke which compares the equipment needs of the scientist, the mathematician, and the philosopher. The scientist needs an expensive laboratory with all sorts of experimental equipment. The mathematician needs only a pencil, paper, and a wastepaper basket. The philosopher needs only a pencil and paper! The truth embodied in this bit of humor is that it is not as easy to test philosophical theories as it is to test a mathematical theorem or a scientific hypothesis. Because philosophical questions are more speculative and metaphysical, one cannot prove or disprove most of the important theses. The relationship of philosophy to science is more complicated than the above suggests, for some of what theoretical scientists do could with justice be called philosophy. In general, the sciences have one by one made their way out of the family fold of philosophy to independence as they systematized their decision-making procedures. In the words of Jeffrey Olen:

> The history of philosophy reads like a long family saga. In the beginning there were the great patriarch and matriarch, the searches for knowledge and wisdom, who bore a large number of children. Mathematics, physics, ethics, psychology, logic, political thought, metaphysics, . . . and epistemology . . .—all belonged to the same family. Philosophers were not *just* philosophers, but mathematicians and physicists and psychologists as well. Indeed, in the beginning of the family's history, no distinction was made between philosophy and these other disciplines. . . .
>
> In the beginning, then, all systematic search for knowledge was philosophy. This fact is still reflected in the modern university, where the highest degree granted in all of the sciences and humanities is the Ph.D.—the doctor of philosophy.

> But the children gradually began to leave home. First to leave were physics and astronomy, as they began to develop experimental techniques of their own. This exodus, led by Galileo (1564–1642), Isaac Newton (1642–1727), and Johannes Kepler (1571–1630), created the first of many great family crises. . . . Eventually, psychology left home. [*Persons and Their World,* Random House, 1983, p. 3f]

Although many of her children have left home, not all have, and some seem permanent residents. The major areas of philosophy today are metaphysics (regarding the nature of ultimate reality), epistemology (regarding the nature of knowledge and justification), logic, philosophy of religion, ethics, and political philosophy. But there are also secondary areas of philosophy which work on conceptual and/or theoretical problems arising within first-order nonphilosophical disciplines. Examples of these are philosophy of science, philosophy of psychology, philosophy of mathematics, philosophy of language, and philosophy of art. Wherever conceptual analysis or justification of a theoretical schema is needed, philosophical expertise is appropriate. More recently, as technology creates new possibilities and problems, applied ethics (e.g., biomedical ethics, business ethics, environmental ethics, and legal ethics) has arisen. History plays a dialectical role with regard to philosophy, for not only do philosophers do philosophy while teaching the history of philosophy, but they also involve themselves in the critical examination of the principles that underlie historical investigation itself, creating a philosophy of history.

We will touch on many of these areas in this work: philosophy of religion; epistemology; metaphysics, and within metaphysics the mind-body problem, personal identity, immortality, and free will and determinism; ethics; and political philosophy. These are more than enough for an introduction to philosophy.

Philosophical study is dialectic, proceeding as an intellectual conversation in which thesis and counter-thesis, hypothesis and counter-example continue in a way that shows up the weaknesses of proposed solutions to the puzzles of existence and leaves some answers as more or less plausible. In this conversation all sides of an issue should receive a fair hearing, and then the reader is left to make up his or her own mind on the issue. Hence, in this work at least two opposing views are set forth on every issue.

Although a clearer understanding of the nature of philosophy will only emerge while working through the arguments on the various issues you are going to study, I want to end this introduction with a set of guidelines for philosophical inquiry, "Ten Commandments of Philosophy" which I hope will aid you in your own pilgrimage as you build your own philosophy of life. They embody what I take to be the classical philosophical perspective, but they are set forth as hypothetical. You should test them, refine them, and possibly reject some of them or add better ones as you proceed on your own Quest for Truth.

Ten Commandments of Philosophy

1. *Allow the spirit of Wonder to flourish in your breast.* Philosophy begins with deep wonder about the universe and about who we are and where we came from and where we are going. What is this life all about?

2. *Doubt every claim you encounter until the evidence convinces you of its Truth.* Be reasonably cautious, a moderate skeptic, suspicious of those who claim to have the Truth. Doubt is the soul's purgative. Do not fear intellectual inquiry. As Goethe said, "The masses fear the intellectual, but it is stupidity that they should fear, if they only realized how dangerous it really is."

3. *Love the Truth.* "Philosophy is the eternal search for truth, a search which inevitably fails and yet is never defeated; which continually eludes us, but which always guides us. This free, intellectual life of the mind is the noblest inheritance of the Western World; it is also the hope of our future." (W. T. Jones)

4. *Divide and Conquer.* Divide each problem and theory into its smallest essential components in order to analyze each unit carefully. This is the analytic method.

5. *Collect and Construct.* Build a coherent argument or theory from component parts. One should move from the simple, secure foundations to the complex and comprehensive. Bertrand Russell once said that the aim of philosophical argument was to move from simple propositions so obvious that no one would think of doubting them via a method of valid argument to conclusions so preposterous that no one could help but doubt them.

6. *Conjecture and Refute.* Make a complete survey of possible objections to your position, looking for counter-examples and subtle mistakes. As Karl Popper has insisted, philosophy is a system of conjecture and refutation. Seek bold hypotheses and seek to find disconfirmations of your favorite positions. In this way, by a process of elimination, you will negatively and indirectly and asymptotically approach the Truth.

7. *Revise and Rebuild.* Be willing to revise, reject, and modify your beliefs and the degree with which you hold any belief. Acknowledge that you probably have many false beliefs and be grateful to those who correct you. This is the Principle of Fallibilism, the thesis that we are very likely incorrect in many of our beliefs and have a tendency towards self-deception when considering objections to our position.

8. *Seek Simplicity.* Prefer the Simpler Explanation to the more complex, all things being equal. This is the Principle of Parsimony, sometimes known as "Occam's Razor."

9. *Live the Truth!* Appropriate your ideas in a personal way, so that even as the Objective Truth is a correspondence of the thought to the world, this Lived-Truth will be a correspondence of the life to the thought. As Kierkegaard said, "Here is a definition of [subjective] truth: holding fast to an objective uncertainty in an appropriation process of the most passionate inwardness is the truth, the highest truth available for an existing individual."

10. *Live the Good!* Let the practical conclusions of a philosophical reflection on the moral life inspire and motivate you to action. Let moral Truth transform your life so that you shine like a jewel in its light amidst the darkness of global ignorance.

We turn to our two readings on the nature and task of philosophy.

I.1   Socratic Wisdom

PLATO

Plato (427–347 B.C.) is one of the most important philosophers who ever lived and the first to write systematically on philosophical subjects. He lived in Athens, the great Greek democratic city-state, in the aftermath of its glory under its illustrious leader, Pericles. During much of Plato's life, Athens was at war with Sparta, the Greek city-state to the south. He was Socrates' disciple, the founder of the first school of philosophy (the Academy in Athens), Aristotle's teacher, and an advisor to emperors. Among his important works are the *Republic,* the *Apology, Phaedo,* and *Timaeus.* Alfred North Whitehead calls the whole history of Western philosophy "a series of footnotes to Plato."

Socrates (470–399 B.C.) is one of the most impressive human beings to have lived, and a paradigm of a philosopher. He is considered the father of moral philosophy (see Part VI). Living in Athens under Pericles, he enjoyed the freedoms of a democratic society. He spent much of his life in the marketplace of Athens, questioning and arguing with his contemporaries on philosophical issues (e.g., what is justice, friendship, self-control, piety, virtue?; how do we teach virtue?; does anyone do evil voluntarily?; and so forth). He saw himself as the gadfly of the Greek city-state, serving his fellow citizens without pay, but many of its leading citizens saw him as a nuisance and, eventually, brought him to trial. It is this trial that our reading is about. Three Athenians—Meletus, Anytus, and Lycon—have brought charges against Socrates that he has corrupted the youth and doesn't believe in the Greek gods. The real cause of the trial is probably that Socrates had made a number of enemies in high places. He defied the authorities when they ordered him to arrest naval officers against what Socrates took to be the law. He embarrassed many of the leading citizens, politicians, artisans, poets, and orators—often before their sons—in exposing their pretenses to knowledge. The accumulated ire erupted and caused one of the most famous trials of all time, if not the most famous trial of all time. The following is Plato's rendition of it.

Study Questions

1. What was the message of the Oracle of Delphi to Chaerephon about Socrates?
2. What was Socrates' response and how did he go about trying to disprove the oracle? What was the effect of his probing on his fellow citizens?
3. How did Socrates finally interpret the message of the oracle?
4. What were the charges brought against Socrates? What were Socrates' responses to the charges?
5. What should be our only concern when we deliberate on what to do?
6. Why doesn't Socrates plead for his life? What does he propose as the counter-penalty?

7. What penalty does the jury decide on? Do you notice anything peculiar when comparing the numbers voting for the original verdict and the numbers voting for the penalty? What accounts for this?

8. What kind of life does Socrates think is worth living?

9. Does Socrates believe that his fellow citizens are doing him enormous harm?

From the Apology

HOW YOU, O ATHENIANS , have been affected by my accusers, I cannot tell; but I know that they almost made me forget who I was—so persuasively did they speak; and yet they have hardly uttered a word of truth. But of the many falsehoods told by them, there was one which quite amazed me;—I mean when they said that you should be upon your guard and not allow yourselves to be deceived by the force of my eloquence. To say this, when they were certain to be detected as soon as I opened my lips and proved myself to be anything but a great speaker, did indeed appear to me most shameless—unless by the force of eloquence they mean the force of truth; for if such is their meaning, I admit that I am eloquent. But in how different a way from theirs! Well, as I was saying, they have scarcely spoken the truth at all; but from me you shall hear the whole truth: not, however, delivered after their manner in a set oration duly ornamented with words and phrases. No, by heaven! but I shall use the words and arguments which occur to me at the moment; for I am confident in the justice of my cause*: at my time of life I ought not to be appearing before you, O men of Athens, in the character of a juvenile orator—let no one expect it of me. And I must beg of you to grant me a favour:—If I defend myself in my accustomed manner, and you hear me using the words which I have been in the habit of using in the [market], at the tables of the money-changers, or anywhere else, I would ask you not to be surprised, and not to interrupt me on this account. For I am more than seventy years of age, and appearing now for the first time in a court of law, I am quite a stranger to the language of the place; and therefore I would have you regard me as if I were really a stranger, whom you would excuse if he spoke in his native tongue, and after the fashion of his country:—Am I making an unfair request of you? Never mind the manner, which may or may not be good; but think only of the truth of my words, and give heed to that: let the speaker speak truly and the judge decide justly. . . .

Well, then, I must make my defence, and endeavor to clear away in a short time, a slander which has lasted a long time. May I succeed, if to succeed be for my good and yours, or likely to avail me in my cause! The task is not an easy one; I quite understand the nature of it. And so leaving the event with God, in obedience to the law I will now make my defence.

I will begin at the beginning, and ask what is the accusation which has given rise to the slander of me, and in fact has encouraged Meletus to prefer this charge against me. Well, what do the slanderers say? They shall be my prosecutors, and I will sum up their words in an affidavit: 'Socrates is an evil-doer, and a curious person, who searches into things under the earth and in heaven, and he makes the worse appear the better cause; and he teaches the aforesaid doctrines to others.' Such is the nature of the accusation: it is just what you have yourselves seen in the comedy of Aristophanes, who has introduced a man whom he calls Socrates, going about and saying that he walks in air, and talking a deal of nonsense concerning matters of which I do not pretend to know either much or little—not that I mean to speak disparagingly of any one who is a student of natural philosophy. I should

* Or, I am certain that I am right in taking this course.

Reprinted from Dialogues of Plato, *trans. Benjamin Jowett, Oxford, 1896.*

be very sorry if Meletus could bring so grave a charge against me. But the simple truth is, O Athenians, that I have nothing to do with physical speculations. Very many of those here present are witnesses to the truth of this, and to them I appeal. Speak then, you who have heard me, and tell your neighbours whether any of you have ever known me hold forth in few words or in many upon such matters. . . . You hear their answer. And from what they say of this part of the charge you will be able to judge of the truth of the rest.

As little foundation is there for the report that I am a teacher, and take money; this accusation has no more truth in it than the other. Although, if a man were really able to instruct mankind, to receive money for giving instruction would, in my opinion, be an honour to him. There is Gorgias of Leontium, and Prodicus of Ceos, and Hippias of Elis, who go the round of the cities, and are able to persuade the young men to leave their own citizens by whom they might be taught for nothing, and come to them whom they not only pay, but are thankful if they may be allowed to pay them. . . .

I dare say, Athenians, that some one among you will reply, 'Yes, Socrates, but what is the origin of these accusations which are brought against you; there must have been something strange which you have been doing? All these rumours and this talk about you would never have arisen if you had been like other men: tell us, then, what is the cause of them, for we should be sorry to judge hastily of you.' Now I regard this as a fair challenge, and I will endeavour to explain to you the reason why I am called wise and have such an evil fame. Please to attend then. And although some of you may think that I am joking, I declare that I will tell you the entire truth. Men of Athens, this reputation of mine has come of a certain sort of wisdom which I possess. If you ask me what kind of wisdom, I reply, wisdom such as may perhaps be attained by man, for to that extent I am inclined to believe that I am wise; whereas the persons of whom I was speaking have a superhuman wisdom, which

I may fail to describe, because I have it not myself; and he who says that I have, speaks falsely, and is taking away my character. And here, O men of Athens, I must beg you not to interrupt me, even if I seem to say something extravagant. For the word which I will speak is not mine. I will refer you to a witness who is worthy of credit; that witness shall be the God of Delphi—he will tell you about my wisdom, if I have any, and of what sort it is. You must have known Chaerephon; he was early a friend of mine, and also a friend of yours, for he shared in the recent exile of the people, and returned with you. Well, Chaerephon, as you know, was very impetuous in all his doings, and he went to Delphi and boldly asked the oracle to tell him whether—as I was saying, I must beg you not to interrupt—he asked the oracle to tell him whether any one was wiser than I was, and the Pythian prophetess answered, that there was no man wiser. Chaerephon is dead himself; but his brother, who is in court, will confirm the truth of what I am saying.

Why do I mention this? Because I am going to explain to you why I have such an evil name. When I heard the answer, I said to myself, What can the god mean? and what is the interpretation of his riddle? for I know that I have no wisdom, small or great. What then can he mean when he says that I am the wisest of men? And yet he is a god, and cannot lie; that would be against his nature. After long consideration, I thought of a method of trying the question. I reflected that if I could only find a man wiser than myself, then I might go to the god with a refutation in my hand. I should say to him, 'Here is a man who is wiser than I am; but you said that I was the wisest.' Accordingly I went to one who had the reputation of wisdom, and observed him—his name I need not mention; he was a politician whom I selected for examination—and the result was as follows: When I began to talk with him, I could not help thinking that he was not really wise, although he was thought wise by many, and still wiser by himself; and thereupon I tried to explain to him that he thought himself wise, but was not really wise; and the consequence was that he hated me, and his enmity was shared by several who were present and heard me. So I left him, saying to myself, as I went away: Well, although I do not suppose that either of us knows anything really beautiful and good, I am better off than he is—for he knows nothing, and thinks that he knows; I neither know nor think that I know. In this latter particular, then, I seem to have slightly the advantage of him. Then I went to another who had still higher pretensions to wisdom, and my conclusion was exactly the same. Whereupon I made another enemy of him, and of many others besides him.

Then I went to one man after another, being not unconscious of the enmity which I provoked, and I lamented and feared this: But necessity was laid upon me,—the word of God, I thought, ought to be considered first. And I said to myself, Go I must to all who appear to know, and find out the meaning of the oracle. And I swear to you, Athenians, by the dog I swear!— for I must tell you the truth—the result of my mission was just this: I found that the men most in repute were all but the most foolish; and that others less esteemed were really wiser and better. I will tell you the tale of my wanderings and of the 'Herculean' labours, as I may call them, which I endured only to find at last the oracle irrefutable. After the politicians, I went to the poets; tragic, dithyrambic, and all sorts. And there, I said to myself, you will be instantly detected; now you will find out that you are more ignorant than they are. Accordingly, I took them some of the most elaborate passages in their own writings, and asked what was the meaning of them—thinking that they would teach me something. Will you believe me? I am almost ashamed to confess the truth, but I must say that there is hardly a person present who would not have talked better about their poetry than they did themselves. Then I knew that not by wisdom do poets write poetry, but by a sort of genius and inspiration; they are like diviners or soothsayers who also say many fine things, but do not understand the meaning of them. The poets appeared

to me to be much in the same case; and I further observed that upon the strength of their poetry they believed themselves to be the wisest of men in other things in which they were not wise. So I departed, conceiving myself to be superior to them for the same reason that I was superior to the politicians.

At last I went to the artisans, for I was conscious that I knew nothing at all, as I may say, and I was sure that they knew many fine things; and here I was not mistaken, for they did know many things of which I was ignorant, and in this they certainly were wiser than I was. But I observed that even the good artisans fell into the same error as the poets;—because they were good workmen they thought that they also knew all sorts of high matters, and this defect in them overshadowed their wisdom; and therefore I asked myself on behalf of the oracle, whether I would like to be as I was, neither having their knowledge nor their ignorance, or like them in both; and I made answer to myself and to the oracle that I was better off as I was.

This inquisition has led to my having many enemies of the worst and most dangerous kind, and has given occasion also to many calumnies. And I am called wise, for my hearers always imagine that I myself possess the wisdom which I find wanting in others: but the truth is, O men of Athens, that God only is wise; and by his answer he intends to show that the wisdom of men is worth little or nothing; he is not speaking of Socrates, he is only using my name by way of illustration, as if he said, He, O men, is the wisest, who, like Socrates, knows that his wisdom is in truth worth nothing. And so I go about the world, obedient to the god, and search and make enquiry into the wisdom of any one, whether citizen or stranger, who appears to be wise; and if he is not wise, then in vindication of the oracle I show him that he is not wise; and my occupation quite absorbs me, and I have no time to give either to any public matter of interest or to any concern of my own, but I am in utter poverty by reason of my devotion to the god.

There is another thing:—young men of the

richer classes, who have not much to do, come about me of their own accord; they like to hear the pretenders examined, and they often imitate me, and proceed to examine others; there are plenty of persons, as they quickly discover, who think that they know something, but really know little or nothing; and then those who are examined by them instead of being angry with themselves are angry with me: This confounded Socrates, they say; this villainous misleader of youth!—and then if somebody asks them, Why, what evil does he practise or teach? they do not know, and cannot tell; but in order that they may not appear to be at a loss, they repeat the ready-made charges which are used against all philosophers about teaching things up in the clouds and under the earth, and having no gods, and making the worse appear the better cause; for they do not like to confess that their pretence of knowledge has been detected—which is the truth; and as they are numerous and ambitious and energetic, and are drawn up in battle array and have persuasive tongues, they have filled your ears with their loud and inveterate calumnies. And this is the reason why my three accusers, Meletus and Anytus and Lycon, have set upon me; Meletus, who has a quarrel with me on behalf of the poets; Anytus, on behalf of the craftsmen and politicians; Lycon, on behalf of the rhetoricians: and as I said at the beginning, I cannot expect to get rid of such a mass of calumny all in a moment. And this, O men of Athens, is the truth and the whole truth; I have concealed nothing, I have dissembled nothing. And yet, I know that my plainness of speech makes them hate me, and what is their hatred but a proof that I am speaking the truth?—Hence has arisen the prejudice against me; and this is the reason of it, as you will find out either in this or in any future enquiry.

I have said enough in my defence against the first class of my accusers; I turn to the second class. They are headed by Meletus, that good man and true lover of his country, as he calls himself. . . . He says that I am a doer of evil, and corrupt the youth; but I say, O men of Athens, that Meletus is a doer of evil, in that he pretends to be in earnest when he is only in jest, and is so eager to bring men to trial from a pretended zeal and interest about matters in which he really never had the smallest interest. And the truth of this I will endeavour to prove to you.

Come hither, Meletus, and let me ask a question of you. You think a great deal about the improvement of youth?

Yes, I do.

Tell the judges, then, who is their improver; for you must know, as you have taken the pains to discover their corrupter, and are citing and accusing me before them. Speak, then, and tell the judges who their improver is.—Observe, Meletus, that you are silent, and have nothing to say. But is not this rather disgraceful, and a very considerable proof of what I was saying, that you have no interest in the matter? Speak up, friend, and tell us who their improver is.

The laws.

But that, my good sir, is not my meaning. I want to know who the person is, who, in the first place, knows the laws.

The judges, Socrates, who are present in court.

What, do you mean to say, Meletus, that they are able to instruct and improve youth?

Certainly they are.

What, all of them, or some only and not others?

All of them.

By the goddess Herè, that is good news! There are plenty of improvers, then. And what do you say of the audience,—do they improve them?

Yes, they do.

And the senators?

Yes, the senators improve them.

But perhaps the members of the assembly corrupt them?—or do they too improve them?

They improve them.

Then every Athenian improves and elevates them; all with the exception of myself; and I alone am their corrupter? Is that what you affirm?

That is what I stoutly affirm.

I am very unfortunate if you are right. But suppose I ask you a question: How about horses? Does one man do them harm and all the world good? Is not the exact opposite the truth? One man is able to do them good, or at least not many;—the trainer of horses, that is to say, does them good, and others who have to do with them rather injure them? Is not that true, Meletus, of horses, or of any other animals? Most assuredly it is; whether you and Anytus say yes or no. Happy indeed would be the condition of youth if they had one corrupter only, and all the rest of the world were their improvers. But you, Meletus, have sufficiently shown that you never had a thought about the young: your carelessness is seen in your not caring about the very things which you bring against me.

And now, Meletus, I will ask you another question—by Zeus I will: Which is better, to live among bad citizens, or among good ones? Answer, friend, I say; the question is one which may be easily answered. Do not the good do their neighbours good, and the bad do them evil?

Certainly.

And is there any one who would rather be injured than benefited by those who live with him? Answer, my good friend, the law requires you to answer—does any one like to be injured?

Certainly not.

And when you accuse me of corrupting and deteriorating the youth, do you allege that I corrupt them intentionally or unintentionally?

Intentionally, I say.

But you have just admitted that the good do their neighbours good, and evil do them evil. Now, is that a truth which your superior wisdom has recognized thus early in life, and am I, at my age, in such darkness and ignorance as not to know that if a man with whom I have to live is corrupted by me, I am very likely to be harmed by him; and yet I corrupt him, and intentionally, too—so you say, although neither I nor any other human being is ever likely to be convinced by you. But either I do not corrupt them, or I corrupt them unintentionally; and on either view of the case you lie. If my offence is unintentional, the law has no cognizance of unintentional offences: you ought to have taken me privately, and warned and admonished me; for if I had been better advised, I should have left off doing what I only did unintentionally—no doubt I should; but you would have nothing to say to me and refused to teach me. And now you bring me up in this court, which is a place not of instruction, but of punishment.

It will be very clear to you, Athenians, as I was saying, that Meletus has no care at all, great or small, about the matter. But still I should like to know, Meletus, in what I am affirmed to corrupt the young. I suppose you mean, as I infer from your indictment, that I teach them not to acknowledge the gods which the state acknowledges, but some other new divinities or spiritual agencies in their stead. These are the lessons by which I corrupt the youth, as you say.

Yes, that I say emphatically.

Then, by the gods, Meletus, of whom we are speaking, tell me and the court, in somewhat plainer terms, what you mean! for I do not as yet understand whether you affirm that I teach other men to acknowledge some gods, and therefore that I do believe in gods, and am not an entire atheist—this you do not lay to my charge,—but only you say that they are not the same gods which the city recognizes—the charge is that they are different gods. Or, do you mean that I am an atheist simply, and a teacher of atheism?

I mean the latter—that you are a complete atheist.

What an extraordinary statement! Why do you think so, Meletus? Do you mean that I do not believe in the godhead of the sun or moon, like other men?

I assure you, judges, that he does not: for he says that the sun is stone, and the moon earth.

Friend Meletus, you think that you are accusing Anaxagoras: and you have but a bad opinion of the judges, if you fancy them illiterate to such a degree as not to know that these doctrines are found in the books of Anaxagoras the Clazomenian, which are full of them. And so, forsooth, the youth are said to be taught them by Socrates, when there are not unfrequently exhibitions of them at the theatre (price of admission one drachma at the most); and they might pay their money, and laugh at Socrates if he pretends to father these extraordinary views. And so, Meletus, you really think that I do not believe in any god?

I swear by Zeus that you believe absolutely in none at all.

Nobody will believe you, Meletus, and I am pretty sure that you do not believe yourself. I cannot help thinking, men of Athens, that Meletus is reckless and impudent, and that he has written this indictment in a spirit of mere wantonness and youthful bravado. Has he not compounded a riddle, thinking to try me? He said to himself:—I shall see whether the wise Socrates will discover my facetious contradiction, or whether I shall be able to deceive him and the rest of them. For he certainly does appear to me to contradict himself in the indictment as much as if he said that Socrates is guilty of not believing in the gods, and yet of believing in them—but this is not like a person who is in earnest.

I should like you, O men of Athens, to join me in examining what I conceive to be his inconsistency; and do you, Meletus, answer. And I must remind the audience of my request that they would not make a disturbance if I speak in my accustomed manner:

Did ever man, Meletus, believe in the existence of human things, and not of human beings? . . . I wish, men of Athens, that he would answer, and not be always trying to get up an interruption. Did ever any man believe in horsemanship, and not in horses? or in flute-playing, and not in flute-players? No, my friend; I will answer to you and to the court, as you refuse to answer for yourself. There is no man who ever did. But now please to answer the next question: Can a man believe in spiritual and divine agencies, and not in spirits or demigods?

He cannot.

How lucky I am to have extracted that answer, by the assistance of the court! But then you swear in the indictment that I teach and believe in divine or spiritual agencies (new or old, no matter for that); at any rate, I believe in spiritual agencies,—so you say and swear in the affidavit; and yet if I believe in divine beings, how can I help believing in spirits or demigods;—must I not? To be sure I must; and therefore I may assume that your silence gives consent. Now what are spirits or demigods? are they not either gods or the sons of gods?

Certainly they are.

But this is what I call the facetious riddle invented by you: the demigods or spirits are gods, and you say first that I do not believe in gods, and then again that I do believe in gods; that is, if I believe in demigods. For if the demigods are the illegitimate sons of gods, whether by the nymphs or by any other mothers, of whom they are said to be the sons—what human being will ever believe that there are no gods if they are the sons of gods? You might as well affirm the existence of mules, and deny that of horses and asses. Such nonsense, Meletus, could only have been intended by you to make trial of me. You have put this into the indictment because you had nothing real of which to accuse me. But no one who has a particle of understanding will ever be convinced by you that the same men can believe in divine and superhuman things, and yet not believe that there are gods and demigods and heroes.

I have said enough in answer to the charge of Meletus: any elaborate defence is unnecessary; but I know only too well how many are the enmities which I have incurred, and this is what will be my destruction if I am destroyed;—not Meletus, nor yet Anytus, but the envy and detraction of the world, which has been the death of many good men, and will probably be the death of many more; there is no danger of my being the last of them.

Some one will say: And are you not ashamed,

Socrates, of a course of life which is likely to bring you to an untimely end? To him I may fairly answer: There you are mistaken: a man who is good for anything ought not to calculate the chance of living or dying; he ought only to consider whether in doing anything he is doing right or wrong—acting the part of a good man or of a bad. . . .

Strange, indeed, would be my conduct, O men of Athens, if I who, when I was ordered by the generals whom you chose to command me at Potidaea and Amphipolis and Delium, remained where they placed me, like any other man, facing death—if now, when, as I conceive and imagine, God orders me to fulfil the philosopher's mission of searching into myself and other men, I were to desert my post through fear of death, or any other fear; that would indeed be strange, and I might justly be arraigned in court for denying the existence of the gods, if I disobeyed the oracle because I was afraid of death, fancying that I was wise when I was not wise. For the fear of death is indeed the pretence of wisdom, and not real wisdom, being a pretence of knowing the unknown; and no one knows whether death, which men in their fear apprehend to be the greatest evil, may not be the greatest good. Is not this ignorance of a disgraceful sort, the ignorance which is the conceit that man knows what he does not know? And in this respect only I believe myself to differ from men in general, and may perhaps claim to be wiser than they are:— that whereas I know but little of the world below, I do not suppose that I know: but I do know that injustice and disobedience to a better, whether God or man, is evil and dishonourable, and I will never fear or avoid a possible good rather than a certain evil. And therefore if you let me go now, and are not convinced by Anytus, who said that since I had been prosecuted I must be put to death . . .—if you say to me, Socrates, this time we will not mind Anytus, and you shall be let off, but upon one condition, that you are not to enquire and speculate in this way any more, and that if you are caught doing so again

you shall die;—if this was the condition on which you let me go, I should reply: Men of Athens, I honour and love you; but I shall obey God rather than you, and while I have life and strength I shall never cease from the practice and teaching of philosophy, exhorting any one whom I meet and saying to him after my manner: You, my friend,—a citizen of the great and mighty and wise city of Athens,—are you not ashamed of heaping up the greatest amount of money and honour and reputation, and caring so little about wisdom and truth and the greatest improvement of the soul, which you never regard or heed at all? And if the person with whom I am arguing, says: Yes, but I do care; then I do not leave him or let him go at once; but I proceed to interrogate and examine and cross-examine him, and if I think that he has no virtue in him, but only says that he has, I reproach him with undervaluing the greater, and overvaluing the less. And I shall repeat the same words to every one whom I meet, young and old, citizen and alien, but especially to the citizens, inasmuch as they are my brethren. For know that this is the command of God; and I believe that no greater good has ever happened in the state than my service to the God. For I do nothing but go about persuading you all, old and young alike, not to take thought for your persons or your properties, but first and chiefly to care about the greatest improvement of the soul. I tell you that virtue is not given by money, but that from virtue comes money and every other good of man, public as well as private. This is my teaching, and if this is the doctrine which corrupts the youth, I am a mischievous person. But if any one says that this is not my teaching, he is speaking an untruth. Wherefore, O men of Athens, I say to you, do as Anytus bids or not as Anytus bids, and either acquit me or not; but whichever you do, understand that I shall never alter my ways, not even if I have to die many times. . . .

And now, Athenians, I am not going to argue for my own sake, as you may think, but for yours, that you may not sin against the God by condemning me, who am his gift to you. For if you kill me you will not easily find a successor to me, who, if I may use such a ludicrous figure of speech, am a sort of gadfly, given to the state by God; and the state is a great and noble steed who is tardy in his motions owing to his very size, and requires to be stirred into life. I am that gadfly which God has attached to the state, and all day long and in all places am always fastening upon you, arousing and persuading and reproaching you. You will not easily find another like me, and therefore I would advise you to spare me. . . .

Perhaps it may seem strange to you that, though I go about giving this advice privately and meddling in others' affairs, yet I do not venture to come forward in the assembly and advise the state. You have often heard me speak of my reason for this, and in many places: it is that I have a certain divine sign, which is what Meletus has caricatured in his indictment. I have had it from childhood. It is a kind of voice which, whenever I hear it, always turns me back from something which I was going to do, but never urges me to act. It is this which forbids me to take part in politics. And I think it does well to forbid me. For, Athenians, it is quite certain that, if I had attempted to take part in politics, I should have perished at once and long ago without doing any good either to you or to myself. And do not be indignant with me for telling the truth. There is no man who will preserve his life for long, either in Athens or elsewhere, if he firmly opposes the multitude, and tries to prevent the commission of much injustice and illegality in the state. He who would really fight for justice must do so as a private citizen, not as an office-holder, if he is to preserve his life, even for a short time.

I will prove to you that this is so by very strong evidence, not by mere words, but by what you value highly, actions, Listen then to what has happened to me, that you may know that there is no man who could make me consent to do wrong from the fear of death, but that I would perish at once rather than give way. What I am going to tell you may be a commonplace in the law court; nevertheless it is true. The only office that I ever held in the state, Athenians, was that of Senator. When you wished to try the ten generals who did not rescue their men after the battle of Arginusae, as a group, which was illegal, as you all came to think afterwards, the tribe Antiochis, to which I belong, held the presidency. On that occasion I alone of all the presidents opposed your illegal action and gave my vote against you. The speakers were ready to suspend me and arrest me; and you were clamoring against me, and crying out to me to submit. But I thought that I ought to face the danger, with law and justice on my side, rather than join with you in your unjust proposal, from fear of imprisonment or death. That was when the state was democratic. When the oligarchy came in, the Thirty sent for me, with four others, to the council-chamber, and ordered us to bring Leon the Salaminian from Salamis, that they might put him to death. They were in the habit of frequently giving similar orders, to many others, wishing to implicate as many as possible in their crimes. But, then, I again proved, not by mere words, but by my actions, that, if I may speak bluntly, I do not care a straw for death; but that I do care very much indeed about not doing anything unjust or impious. That government with all its powers did not terrify me into doing anything unjust; but when we left the council-chamber, the other four went over to Salamis and brought Leon across to Athens; and I went home. And if the rule of the Thirty had not been destroyed soon afterwards, I should very likely have been put to death for what I did then. Many of you will be my witnesses in this matter.

Now do you think that I could have remained alive all these years if I had taken part in public affairs, and had always maintained the cause of justice like an honest man, and had held it a paramount duty, as it is, to do so? Certainly not, Athenians, nor could any other man. But throughout my whole life, both in private and in public, whenever I have had to take part in public affairs, you will find I have always been the same and have never yielded unjustly to anyone; no, not to those whom my enemies falsely assert to have been my pupils. But I was never anyone's teacher. I have never withheld myself from anyone, young or old, who was anxious to hear me discuss while I was making my investigation; neither do I discuss for payment, and refuse to discuss without payment. I am ready to ask questions of rich and poor alike, and if any man wishes to answer me, and then listen to what I have to say, he may. . . .

I believe in the gods as no one of my accusers believes in them: and to you and to God I commit my cause to be decided as is best for you and for me.

[The vote is taken and he is found guilty by 281 votes to 220.]

There are many reasons why I am not grieved, O men of Athens, at the vote of condemnation. I expected it, and am only surprised that the votes are so nearly equal; for I had thought that the majority against me would have been far larger; but now, had thirty votes gone over to the other side, I should have been acquitted. And I may say, I think, that I have escaped Meletus. I may say more; for without the assistance of Anytus and Lycon, any one may see that he would not have had a fifth part of the votes, as the law requires, in which case he would have incurred a fine of a thousand drachmae.

And so he proposes death as the penalty. And what shall I propose on my part, O men of Athens? Clearly that which is my due. And what is my due? What return shall be made to the man who has never had the wit to be idle during his whole life; but has been careless of what the many care for—wealth, and family interests, and military offices, and speaking in the assembly, and magistracies, and plots, and parties. Reflecting that I was really too honest a man to be a politician and live, I did not go where I could do

no good to you or to myself; but where I could do the greatest good privately to every one of you, thither I went, and sought to persuade every man among you that he must look to himself, and seek virtue and wisdom before he looks to his private interests, and look to the state before he looks to the interests of the state; and that this should be the order which he observes in all his actions. What shall be done to such an one? Doubtless some good thing, O men of Athens, if he has his reward; and the good should be of a kind suitable to him. What would be a reward suitable to a poor man who is your benefactor, and who desires leisure that he may instruct you? There can be no reward so fitting as maintenance in the Prytaneum, O men of Athens, a reward which he deserves far more than the citizen who has won the prize at Olympia in the horse or chariot race, whether the chariots were drawn by two horses or by many. For I am in want, and he has enough; and he only gives you the appearance of happiness, and I give you the reality. And if I am to estimate the penalty fairly, I should say that maintenance in the Prytaneum is the just return.

Perhaps you think that I am braving you in what I am saying now, as in what I said before about the tears and prayers. But this is not so. I speak rather because I am convinced that I never intentionally wronged any one, although I cannot convince you—the time has been too short; if there were a law at Athens, as there is in other cities, that a capital cause should not be decided in one day, then I believe that I should have convinced you. But I cannot in a moment refute great slanders; and, as I am convinced that I never wronged another, I will assuredly not wrong myself. I will not say of myself that I deserve any evil, or propose any penalty. Why should I? Because I am afraid of the penalty of death which Meletus proposes? When I do not know whether death is a good or an evil, why should I propose a penalty which would certainly be an evil? Shall I say imprisonment? And why should I live in prison, and be the slave of the magistrates of the year—of the Eleven? Or shall the penalty be a fine, and imprisonment until the fine is paid? There is the same objection. I should have to lie in prison, for money I have none, and cannot pay. And if I say exile (and this may possibly be the penalty which you will affix), I must indeed be blinded by the love of life, if I am so irrational as to expect that when you, who are my own citizens, cannot endure my discourses and words, and have found them so grievous and odious that you will have no more of them, others are likely to endure me. No indeed, men of Athens, that is not very likely. And what a life should I lead, at my age, wandering from city to city, ever changing my place of exile, and always being driven out! For I am quite sure that wherever I go, there, as here, the young men will flock to me; and if I drive them away, their elders will drive me out at their request; and if I let them come, their fathers and friends will drive me out for their sakes.

Some one will say: Yes, Socrates, but cannot you hold your tongue, and then you may go into a foreign city, and no one will interfere with you? Now I have great difficulty in making you understand my answer to this. For if I tell you that to do as you say would be a disobedience to the God, and therefore that I cannot hold my tongue, you will not believe that I am serious; and if I say again that daily to discourse about virtue, and of those other things about which you hear me examining myself and others, is the greatest good of man, and that the unexamined life is not worth living, you are still less likely to believe me. Yet I say what is true, although a thing of which it is hard for me to persuade you. Also, I have never been accustomed to think that I deserve to suffer any harm. Had I money I might have estimated the offence at what I was able to pay, and not have been much the worse. But I have none, and therefore I must ask you to proportion the fine to my means. Well, perhaps I could afford a mina, and therefore I propose that penalty: Plato, Crito, Critobulus, and

Apollodorus, my friends here, bid me say thirty minae, and they will be the sureties. Let thirty minae be the penalty; for which sum they will be ample security to you.

[2nd vote: The jury decides for the death penalty by a vote of 360 to 141.]

Not much time will be gained, O Athenians, in return for the evil name which you will get from the detractors of the city, who will say that you killed Socrates, a wise man; for they will call me wise, even although I am not wise, when they want to reproach you. If you had waited a little while, your desire would have been fulfilled in the course of nature. For I am far advanced in years, as you may perceive, and not far from death. . . . The difficulty, my friends, is not to avoid death, but to avoid unrighteousness; for that runs faster than death. I am old and move slowly, and the slower runner has overtaken me, and my accusers are keen and quick, and the faster runner, who is unrighteousness, has overtaken them. And now I depart hence condemned by you to suffer the penalty of death,—they too go their ways condemned by the truth to suffer the penalty of villainy and wrong; and I must abide by my award—let them abide by theirs. I suppose that these things may be regarded as fated,—and I think that they are well. . . .

Friends, who would have acquitted me, I would like also to talk with you about the thing which has come to pass, while the magistrates are busy, and before I go to the place at which I must die. Stay then a little, for we may as well talk with one another while there is time. You are my friends, and I should like to show you the meaning of this event which has happened to me. O my judges—for you I may truly call judges—I should like to tell you of a wonderful circumstance. Hitherto the divine faculty of which the internal oracle is the source has constantly been in the habit of opposing me even about trifles, if I was going to make a slip or error in any matter; and now as you see there has come upon me that which may be thought, and is generally believed to be, the last and worst evil. But the oracle made no sign of opposition, either when I was leaving my house in the morning, or when I was on my way to the court, or while I was speaking, at anything which I was going to say; and yet I have often been stopped in the middle of a speech, but now in nothing I either said or did touching the matter in hand has the oracle opposed me. What do I take to be the explanation of this silence? I will tell you. It is an intimation that what has happened to me is a good, and that those of us who think that death is an evil are in error. For the customary sign would surely have opposed me had I been going to evil and not to good.

Let us reflect in another way, and we shall see that there is great reason to hope that death is a good; for one of two things—either death is a state of nothingness and utter unconsciousness, or, as men say, there is a change and migration of the soul from this world to another. Now if you suppose that there is no consciousness, but a sleep like the sleep of him who is undisturbed even by dreams, death will be an unspeakable gain. For if a person were to select the night in which his sleep was undisturbed even by dreams, and were to compare with this the other days and nights of his life, and then were to tell us how many days and nights he had passed in the course of his life better and more pleasantly than this one, I think that any man, I will not say a private man, but even the great king will not find many such days or nights, when compared with the others. Now if death be of such a nature, I say that to die is gain; for eternity is then only a single night. But if death is the journey to another place, and there, as men say, all the dead abide, what good, O my friends and judges, can be greater than this? If indeed when the pilgrim arrives in the world below, he is delivered from the professors of justice in this world, and finds the true judges who are said to give judgment there, Minos and Rhadamanthus and Aeacus and Triptolemus, and other sons of God who were righteous in their own life, that pilgrimage will be worth making. What would not a man give if he might converse with Orpheus and Musaeus and Hesiod and Homer? Nay, if this be true, let me die again and again. I myself, too, shall have a wonderful interest in there meeting and conversing with Palamedes, and Ajax the son of Telamon, and any other ancient hero who has suffered death through an unjust judgment; and there will be no small pleasure, as I think, in comparing my own sufferings with theirs. Above all, I shall then be able to continue my search into true and false knowledge; as in this world, so also in the next; and I shall find out who is wise, and who pretends to be wise, and is not. What would not a man give, O judges, to be able to examine the leader of the great Trojan expedition; or Odysseus or Sisyphus, or numberless others, men and women too! What infinite delight would there be in conversing with them and asking them questions! In another world they do not put a man to death for asking questions: assuredly not. For besides being happier than we are, they will be immortal, if what is said is true.

Wherefore, O judges, be of good cheer about death, and know of a certainty, that no evil can happen to a good man, either in life or after death. He and his are not neglected by the gods; nor has my own approaching end happened by mere chance. But I see clearly that the time had arrived when it was better for me to die and be released from trouble; wherefore the oracle gave no sign. For which reason, also, I am not angry with my condemners, or with my accusers; they have done me no harm, although they did not mean to do me any good; and for this I may gently blame them.

Still I have a favour to ask of them. When my sons are grown up, I would ask you, O my friends, to punish them; and I would have you trouble them, as I have troubled you, if they seem to care about riches, or anything, more than about virtue; or if they pretend to be something when they are really nothing,—then reprove them, as I have reproved you, for not caring about that for which they ought to care, and thinking that they are something when they are really nothing. And if you do this, both I and my sons will have received justice at your hands.

The hour of departure has arrived, and we go our ways—I to die, and you to live. Which is better God only knows.

For Further Reflection

1. Describe Socrates. What kind of man was he? What were his deepest beliefs?
2. Some have found a note of arrogance and insensitivity in Socrates and argue that he deserved what he got. Does this reading lend any support to that thesis?
3. Does Socrates think that we do evil voluntarily? Why do we do evil?
4. Can the good be harmed by the bad? How do we harm ourselves?
5. What does Socrates mean when he says that "the unexamined life is not worth living"? We will return to Socrates in Parts IV and VI.

I.2   The Value of Philosophy

BERTRAND RUSSELL

Bertrand Russell (1872–1970) is one of the most important philosophers of the twentieth century. His works cover almost every area of philosophy from logic and philosophy of mathematics (*Principia Mathematica* [1910], written with Alfred North Whitehead) to philosophy of religion ("Mysticism" and "Why I Am Not a Christian") and ethics ("Science and Ethics"). Russell's concern to live out his philosophy in his life led him to found a special school on his philosophy of education, become a leader in Britain's "Ban the Bomb" (the atom bomb) Movement, and speak out on moral and political issues, sometimes at personal risk.

In this reading, coming at the end of his brilliant essay *The Problems of Philosophy* (1912), Russell argues that the value of philosophy is not in any ability to produce material goods ("philosophy bakes no bread") or arrive at definitive conclusions about the nature of reality, but is its effect upon the lives of those who take it seriously. In its contemplation of the perennial questions of life it enlarges our understanding and results in spiritual liberation.

Study Questions

1. What do many scientific and practical people think of philosophy?
2. What is Russell's assessment of their views of philosophy? Why does he think that their prejudice occurs?
3. What are the aims of philosophy? Has it been successful in attaining them? Explain.
4. Where does Russell think that the value of philosophy is to be sought?

5. What effect can philosophy have on the instinctive person? What are the fruits of philosophical contemplation?

6. How does Russell define knowledge? What does he mean by this?

7. What does Russell think of the view that "man is the measure of all things"?

HAVING NOW COME TO THE END of our brief and very incomplete review of the problems of philosophy, it will be well to consider, in conclusion, what is the value of philosophy and why it ought to be studied. It is the more necessary to consider this question, in view of the fact that many men, under the influence of science or of practical affairs, are inclined to doubt whether philosophy is anything better than innocent but useless trifling, hair-splitting distinctions, and controversies on matters concerning which knowledge is impossible.

This view of philosophy appears to result, partly from a wrong conception of the ends of life, partly from a wrong conception of the kind of goods which philosophy strives to achieve. Physical science, through the medium of inventions, is useful to innumerable people who are wholly ignorant of it; thus the study of physical science is to be recommended, not only, or primarily, because of the effect on the student, but rather because of the effect on mankind in general. Thus utility does not belong to philosophy. If the study of philosophy has any value at all for others than students of philosophy, it must be only indirectly, through its effects upon the lives of those who study it. It is in these effects, therefore, if anywhere, that the value of philosophy must be primarily sought.

But further, if we are not to fail in our endeavour to determine the value of philosophy, we must first free our minds from the prejudices of what are wrongly called "practical" men. The "practical" man, as this word is often used, is one who recognizes only material needs, who realizes that men must have food for the body, but is oblivious of the necessity of providing food for the mind. If all men were well off, if poverty and disease had been reduced to their lowest possible point, there would still remain much to be done to produce a valuable society; and even in the existing world the goods of the mind are at least as important as the goods of the body. It is exclusively among the goods of the mind that the value of philosophy is to be found; and only those who are not indifferent to these goods can be persuaded that the study of philosophy is not a waste of time.

Philosophy, like all other studies, aims primarily at knowledge. The knowledge it aims at is the kind of knowledge which gives unity and system to the body of the sciences, and the kind which results from a critical examination of the grounds of our convictions, prejudices, and beliefs. But it cannot be maintained that philosophy has had any very great measure of success in its attempts to provide definite answers to its questions. If you ask a mathematician, a mineralogist, a historian, or any other man of learning, what definite body of truths has been ascertained by his science, his answer will last as long as you are willing to listen. But if you put the same question to a philosopher, he will, if he is candid, have to confess that his study has not achieved positive results such as have been achieved by other sciences. It is true that this is partly accounted for by the fact that, as soon as definite knowledge concerning any subject becomes possible, this subject ceases to be called philosophy, and becomes a separate science. The whole study of the heavens, which now belongs to astronomy, was once included in philosophy;

From The Problems of Philosophy *(New York: Oxford University Press, 1969), pp. 153–61. Reprinted by permission of Oxford University Press.*

Newton's great work was called "the mathematical principles of natural philosophy." Similarly, the study of the human mind, which was a part of philosophy, has now been separated from philosophy and has become the science of psychology. Thus, to a great extent, the uncertainty of philosophy is more apparent than real: those questions which are already capable of definite answers are placed in the sciences, while those only to which, at present, no definite answer can be given, remain to form the residue which is called philosophy.

This is, however, only a part of the truth concerning the uncertainty of philosophy. There are many questions—and among them those that are of the profoundest interest to our spiritual life—which, so far as we can see, must remain insoluble to the human intellect unless its powers become of quite a different order from what they are now. Has the universe any unity of plan or purpose, or is it a fortuitous concourse of atoms? Is consciousness a permanent part of the universe, giving hope of indefinite growth in wisdom, or is it a transitory accident on a small planet on which life must ultimately become impossible? Are good and evil of importance to the universe or only to man? Such questions are asked by philosophy, and variously answered by various philosophers. But it would seem that, whether answers be otherwise discoverable or not, the answers suggested by philosophy are none of them demonstrably true. Yet, however slight may be the hope of discovering an answer, it is part of the business of philosophy to continue the consideration of such questions, to make us aware of their importance, to examine all the approaches to them, and to keep alive that speculative interest in the universe which is apt to be killed by confining ourselves to definitely ascertainable knowledge.

Many philosophers, it is true, have held that philosophy could establish the truth of certain answers to such fundamental questions. They have supposed that what is of most importance in religious beliefs could be proved by strict demonstration to be true. In order to judge of such attempts, it is necessary to take a survey of human knowledge, and to form an opinion as to its methods and its limitations. On such a subject it would be unwise to pronounce dogmatically; but if the investigations of our previous chapters have not led us astray, we shall be compelled to renounce the hope of finding philosophical proofs of religious beliefs. We cannot, therefore, include as part of the value of philosophy any definite set of answers to such questions. Hence, once more, the value of philosophy must not depend upon any supposed body of definitely ascertainable knowledge to be acquired by those who study it.

The value of philosophy is, in fact, to be sought largely in its very uncertainty. The man who has no tincture of philosophy goes through life imprisoned in the prejudices derived from common sense, from the habitual beliefs of his age or his nation, and from convictions which have grown up in his mind without the cooperation or consent of his deliberate reason. To such a man the world tends to become definite, finite, obvious; common objects rouse no questions, and unfamiliar possibilities are contemptuously rejected. As soon as we begin to philosophize, on the contrary, we find, as we saw in our opening chapters, that even the most everyday things lead to problems to which only very incomplete answers can be given. Philosophy, though unable to tell us with certainty what is the true answer to the doubts which it raises, is able to suggest many possibilities which enlarge our thoughts and free them from the tyranny of custom. Thus, while diminishing our feeling of certainty as to what things are, it greatly increases our knowledge as to what they may be; it removes the somewhat arrogant dogmatism of those who have never travelled into the region of liberating doubt, and it keeps alive our sense of wonder by showing familiar things in an unfamiliar aspect.

Apart from its utility in showing unsuspected possibilities, philosophy has a value—perhaps its chief value—through the greatness of the objects which it contemplates, and the freedom from narrow and personal aims resulting from this contemplation. The life of the instinctive man is shut up within the circle of his private interests: family and friends may be included, but the outer world is not regarded except as it may help or hinder what comes within the circle of instinctive wishes. In such a life there is something feverish and confined, in comparison with which the philosophic life is calm and free. The private world of instinctive interests is a small one, set in the midst of a great and powerful world which must, sooner or later, lay our private world in ruins. Unless we can so enlarge our interests as to include the whole outer world, we remain like a garrison in a beleaguered fortress, knowing that the enemy prevents escape and that ultimate surrender is inevitable. In such a life there is no peace, but a constant strife between the insistence of desire and the powerlessness of will. In one way or another, if our life is to be great and free, we must escape this prison and this strife.

One way of escape is by philosophic contemplation. Philosophic contemplation does not, in its widest survey, divide the universe into two hostile camps—friends and foes, helpful and hostile, good and bad—it views the whole impartially. Philosophic contemplation, when it is unalloyed, does not aim at proving that the rest of the universe is akin to man. All acquisition of knowledge is an enlargement of the Self, but this enlargement is best attained when it is not directly sought. It is obtained when the desire for knowledge is alone operative, by a study which does not wish in advance that its objects should have this or that character, but adapts the Self to the characters which it finds in its objects. This enlargement of Self is not obtained when, taking the Self as it is, we try to show that the world is so similar to this Self that knowledge of it is possible without any admission of what seems alien. The desire to prove this is a form of self-assertion and, like all self-assertion, it is an obstacle to the growth of Self which it desires, and of which the Self knows that it is capable. Self-assertion, in philosophic speculation as elsewhere, views the world as a means to its own ends; thus it makes the world of less account than Self, and the Self sets bounds to the greatness of its goods. In contemplation, on the contrary, we start from the not-Self, and through its greatness the boundaries of Self are enlarged; through the infinity of the universe the mind which contemplates it achieves some share in infinity.

For this reason greatness of soul is not fostered by those philosophies which assimilate the universe to Man. Knowledge is a form of union of Self and not-Self; like all union, it is impaired by dominion, and therefore by any attempt to force the universe into conformity with what we find in ourselves. There is a widespread philosophical tendency towards the view which tells us that Man is the measure of all things, that truth is manmade, that space and time and the world of universals are properties of the mind, and that, if there be anything not created by the mind, it is unknowable and of no account for us. This view, if our previous discussions were correct, is untrue; but in addition to being untrue, it has the effect of robbing philosophic contemplation of all that gives it value, since it fetters contemplation to Self. What it calls knowledge is not a union with the not-Self, but a set of prejudices, habits, and desires, making an impenetrable veil between us and the world beyond. The man who finds pleasure in such a theory of knowledge is like the man who never leaves the domestic circle for fear his word might not be law.

The true philosophic contemplation, on the contrary, finds its satisfaction in every enlargement of the not-Self, in everything that magnifies the objects contemplated, and thereby the subject contemplating. Everything, in contemplation, that is personal or private, everything that depends upon habit, self-interest, or desire, distorts the object, and hence impairs the union which the intellect seeks. By thus making a barrier between subject and object, such personal and private things become a prison to the intellect. The free intellect will see as God might see, without a *here* and *now,* without hopes and fears, without the trammels of customary beliefs and traditional prejudices, calmly, dispassionately, in the sole and exclusive desire of knowledge—knowledge as impersonal, as purely contemplative, as it is possible for man to attain. Hence also the free intellect will value more the abstract and universal knowledge into which the accidents of private history do not enter, than the knowledge brought by the senses, and dependent, as such knowledge must be, upon an exclusive and personal point of view and a body whose sense-organs distort as much as they reveal.

The mind which has become accustomed to the freedom and impartiality of philosophic contemplation will preserve something of the same freedom and impartiality in the world of action and emotion. It will view its purposes and desires as parts of the whole, with the absence of insistence that results from seeing them as infinitesimal fragments in a world of which all the rest is unaffected by any one man's deeds. The impartiality which, in contemplation, is the unalloyed desire for truth, is the very same quality of mind which, in action, is justice, and in emotion is that universal love which can be given to all, and not only to those who are judged useful or admirable. Thus contemplation enlarges not only the objects of our thoughts, but also the objects of our actions and our affections: it makes us citizens of the universe, not only of one walled city at war with all the rest. In this citizenship of the universe consists man's true freedom, and his liberation from the thraldom of narrow hopes and fears.

Thus, to sum up our discussion of the value of philosophy; Philosophy is to be studied, not for the sake of any definite answers to its questions, since no definite answers can, as a rule, be known to be true, but rather for the sake of the questions themselves; because these questions enlarge our conception of what is possible, enrich our intellectual imagination and diminish the dogmatic assurance which closes the mind against speculation; but above all because, through the greatness of the universe which philosophy contemplates, the mind also is rendered great, and becomes capable of that union with the universe which constitutes its highest good.

For Further Reflection

1. Compare Russell's essay with Socrates' thought.

2. Evaluate Russell's contention: "The man who has no tincture of philosophy goes through life imprisoned in its prejudice derived from common sense, from habitual beliefs of his age or his nation, and from convictions which have grown up in his mind without the cooperation or consent of his deliberate reason. . . . Through the greatness of the universe which philosophers contemplate, the mind also is rendered great, and becomes capable of that union with the universe which constitutes the highest good."

3. A particularly poignant vignette of his view of the significance of philosophy is recorded in his autobiography, where he relates the experience of seeing Mrs. Whitehead in severe pain. (See the last article in Part VIII.) What sort of view of philosophy do you see in this experience? Is it identical with what you read in Russell's essay or does it add a new dimension? If you think it does bring in something new, what is that?

Suggestions for Further Reading

Copleston, F. C. *History of Philosophy*. Westminster, MD: Newman Press, 1966. This eight-volume set is the most comprehensive contemporary work in the history of philosophy.

Cornman, James and Keith Lehrer. *Philosophical Problems and Arguments*. New York: Macmillan, 1982. A contemporary paradigm of the analytic method.

Edwards, Paul, ed. *Encyclopedia of Philosophy*. New York: Macmillan, 1967. Many of the articles in this eight-volume set are excellent introductions to various aspects of philosophy.

Jones, W. T. *History of Western Philosophy*. New York: Harper & Row, 1976. A lucid, accessible five-volume set.

Miller, Ed. *Questions That Matter*. New York: McGraw-Hill, 1987.

Olen, Jeffrey. *Persons and Their World*. New York: Random House, 1983. One of the best single-authored introductory works in philosophy.

Russell, Bertrand. *The Problems of Philosophy*. Oxford: Oxford University Press, 1912. Although the perspective is a little dated, this is a well-written, well-thought-out little book from which much can be learned.

Woodhouse, Mark. *A Preface to Philosophy*. Belmont, CA: Wadsworth, 1984. This little gem is useful in discussing the purposes and methods of philosophical inquiry. It contains lively discussions of informal logic, reading philosophy, and writing philosophical papers.

Part II

Philosophy of Religion

If there is no God, then God is incalculably the greatest single creation of the human imagination. No other creation of the imagination has been so fertile of ideas, so great an inspiration to philosophy, to literature, to painting, sculpture, architecture, and drama. Set beside the idea of God, the most original inventions of mathematicians and the most unforgettable characters in drama are minor products of the imagination: Hamlet and the square root of minus one pale into insignificance by comparison.

ANTHONY KENNY, *Faith and Reason*, p. 59

QUESTIONS CONNECTED WITH THE EXISTENCE OF GOD may be the most important that we can ask and try to answer. If God, an omnibenevolent, supremely powerful being who interacts with the world, exists, then it is of the utmost importance that we come to know that fact and as much as possible about God and his plan. Implications follow that affect our understanding of the world and ourselves. If God exists, the world is not accidental, a product of mere chance and necessity, but a home which has been designed for rational and sentient beings. The universe is his handiwork, a place of personal purposefulness. We are not alone in the world to struggle for justice, but are working together with one whose plan is to redeem the world from evil. Most importantly, there is someone to whom we are responsible and to whom we owe absolute devotion and worship. Other implications follow for our self-understanding, the way we ought to live our lives and prospects for continued life after death.

Of course, it may be false that a supreme being exists, and many people have lived well without believing in God. La Place, when asked about his faith, is reported to have replied, "I have no need of that hypothesis." But the testimony of humankind is against him. Millions have needed and been inspired by this notion. So great is the inspiration issuing from the idea of God that we could say that if God doesn't exist, the idea is the greatest invention of the human mind. What are all the world's works of literature, art, music, drama, architecture, science, and philosophy compared to this simple concept?

The field of philosophy of religion documents a significant part of the history of humanity's quest for a supreme being. Even if God does not exist, philosophy of religion retains importance for this documentation. The arguments centered around such a quest are interesting in their own right, for their ingenuity and subtlety, even apart from their possible soundness. It may be argued that the Judeo-Christian tradition has informed our self-understanding to such a degree that it is imperative for every would-be well-informed person to come to grips with the arguments and counter-arguments surrounding its claims. Hence, even if the assertions of religion are rejected as misguided or superstitious left-overs from darker ages, an understanding of what is being rejected and why it is to be rejected is important.

The readings that follow center on three questions: (1) Are there arguments that demonstrate the existence of a supreme being? (2) Does the existence of evil provide evidence against the thesis that there is a God? and (3) What is the relationship between faith and reason? Is it rational to believe in God?

Can We Prove That God Exists?
Arguments for the Existence of God

Can the existence of God be demonstrated or made probable by argument? The debate between those who believe that reason can demonstrate that God exists and those who do not has an ancient lineage, going back to Protagoras (ca. 450 B.C.) and Plato (427–347 B.C.). The Roman Catholic Church has traditionally held that the existence of God is demonstrable by human reason. The strong statement of the First Vatican Council (1870) indicates that human reason is adequate to arrive at a state of knowledge of God's existence:

> If anyone says that the one and true God, our creator and Lord, cannot be known with certainty with the natural light of human reason by means of the things that have been made: let him be anathema.

Many others—theists and nontheists, including Catholics—have denied that human reason is adequate to arrive at knowledge or demonstrate the existence of God.

Arguments for the existence of God divide into two main groups: *a priori* and *a posteriori* arguments. An *a posteriori* argument is based on premises that can be known only by means of experience of the world (e.g., that there is a world, events have causes, and so forth). An *a priori* argument depends on no such premises. Rather, it rests on premises which can be known to be true independently of experience of the world: One need only clearly conceive of the proposition in order to see that it is true.

In this section we shall consider two types of *a posteriori* arguments for the existence of God and one *a priori* argument. The *a posteriori* arguments are the cosmological argument and the teleological argument. The *a priori* argument is the ontological argument.

The questions before us are: What do the arguments for the existence of God establish? Do any of them demonstrate beyond reasonable doubt the existence of a supreme being or deity? Do any of them make it probable (given the evidence at hand) that such a being exists?

A. The Cosmological Argument for the Existence of God

All the versions of the cosmological argument begin with the *a posteriori* assumptions that the universe exists and that something outside the universe is required to explain its existence. That is, it is *contingent,* depending on something outside of itself for its existence. That "something else" is logically prior to the universe. It constitutes the reason for the existence of the universe. Such a being is God.

One version of the cosmological argument is called the "First Cause Argument." The first two arguments given by St. Thomas Aquinas in our readings serve as examples of it. The general outline goes something like this:

1. Everything in the universe has a cause. That is, for everything that exists (E), there is some other thing (C), which existed before E existed; and C produced

E—that is, without C, E would not have existed. But C itself was caused by a prior cause, C_1, and C_1 by still another cause before it, C_2, and so on.

2. An infinite regress is impossible. The series of causes and effects cannot go on indefinitely but must have a beginning.

3. So there must be a first cause outside of the universe capable of producing everything besides itself (which is not produced but a necessary being).

4. Such a being must be an infinite, necessary being, i.e., God.

This sort of argument can be challenged at every point, and you will find many of these challenges in Paul Edwards' article, "A Critique of the Cosmological Argument." You will decide whether the challenges are successful. First of all, we may challenge the first premise. Must everything have a cause? A significant number of physicists would deny that the principle of causality applies to some behavior of subatomic particles. These particles seem to behave randomly and can be predicted only statistically. Their noncausal thesis has been confirmed by certain experiments, though the issue is controversial. Some physicists offer other explanations. In any case, the question should be raised: How do we know that everything must have a cause?

The second premise may be challenged with the question, how do we know that an infinite regress of causes is impossible? We have infinite series in mathematics, why not in physics too? Do we understand enough about the world to rule out such a series? If we can imagine an infinite series into the future, why not allow its possibility into the past?

Regarding the third premise, in using the notion of an infinite being to explain the world, have we really solved anything? For don't we still have to explain what an infinite being is? Isn't this simply a case of explaining the obscure with the even more obscure? And do we help our argument any by calling this unknown being God (the fourth premise)? Does the notion of a necessary being make any sense? We usually apply the notion of "necessity" to logically necessary propositions (such as that a contradiction is necessarily false or that it is necessarily true that $2 + 2 = 4$). What sense does it make to say that a being must necessarily exist?

There are responses to these challenges, some of which are located in J. P. Moreland's "Yes, God Exists" (reading II.11). You may want to look at that debate after reading Aquinas and Edwards. But first let us turn to Aquinas' Five Ways.

II.1   The Five Ways

THOMAS AQUINAS

The Dominican monk Thomas Aquinas (1225–1274) is considered by many to be the greatest theologian in Western religion. The five arguments given here are a posteriori arguments, already described in the introduction. Put simply, their strategies are as follows. The first argument begins with the fact that there is change and argues that there must be an Unmoved Mover which originates all change (or motion) but itself is not moved. The second argument is from causation and argues that there must be a first cause to explain the existence of cause. The third argument is from contingency. It argues that since there are dependent beings (e.g., humans), there must be an independent or necessary being on whom the dependent beings rely for their subsistence. The fourth argument is from excellence, and it argues that since there are degrees of excellence, there must be a perfect being from whence come all excellences. The final argument is from the harmony of things. There is a harmony of nature which calls for an explanation. The only sufficient explanation is that there is a divine designer who planned such harmony.

Study Questions

1. What are the two objections that people give to deny the existence of God?
2. What are Aquinas' solutions to these two objections (stated at the end of his exposition)?
3. Identify the central idea in each of the five arguments.
4. Outline the second argument in your own words and analyze it. After this, try to sum up the other arguments.

[Aquinas first identifies two objections to the thesis that God exists]

OBJECTION 1. It seems that God does not exist; because if one of two contraries be infinite, the other would be altogether destroyed. But the name *God* means that He is infinite goodness. If, therefore, God existed, there would be no evil discoverable; but there is evil in the world. Therefore God does not exist.

Objection 2. Further, it is superfluous to suppose that what can be accounted for by a few principles has been produced by many. But it seems that everything we see in the world can be accounted for by other principles, supposing God did not exist. For all natural things can be reduced to one principle, which is nature; and all voluntary things can be reduced to one principle, which is human reason, or will. Therefore there is no need to suppose God's existence.

On the Contrary, It is said in the person of God: *I am Who I am* (Ex iii.14).

I answer that, The existence of God can be proved in five ways.

The First Way: The Argument from Change

The first and clearest [way] is taken from the idea of motion. (1) Now it is certain, and our senses corroborate it, that some things in this world are in motion. (2) But everything which is in motion is moved by something else. (3) For nothing is in motion except in so far as it is in potentiality in relation to that towards which it is in motion. (4) Now a thing causes movement in so far as it is in actuality. For to cause movement is nothing else than to bring something from potentiality to actuality; but a thing cannot

Reprinted from Thomas Aquinas, Summa Theologica, *Laurence Shapcote (London: O. P. Benziger Brothers, 1911).*

be brought from potentiality to actuality except by something which exists in actuality, as, for example, that which is hot in actuality, like fire, makes wood, which is only hot in potentiality, to be hot in actuality, and thereby causes movement in it and alters it. (5) But it is not possible that the same thing should be at the same time in actuality and potentiality in relation to the same thing, but only in relation to different things; for what is hot in actuality cannot at the same time be hot in potentiality, though it is at the same time cold in potentiality. (6) It is impossible, therefore, that in relation to the same thing and in the same way anything should both cause movement and be caused, or that it should cause itself to move. (7) Everything therefore that is in motion must be moved by something else. If therefore the thing which causes it to move be in motion, this too must be moved by something else, and so on. (8) But we cannot proceed to infinity in this way, because in that cause there would be no first mover, and in consequence, neither would there be any other mover; for secondary movers do not cause movement except they be moved by a first mover, as, for example, a stick cannot cause movement unless it is moved by the hand. Therefore it is necessary to stop at some first mover which is moved by nothing else. And this is what we all understand God to be.

The Second Way:
The Argument from Causation

The Second Way is taken from the idea of the Efficient Cause. (1) For we find that there is among material things a regular order of efficient causes. (2) But we do not find, nor indeed is it possible, that anything is the efficient cause of itself, for in that case it would be prior to itself, which is impossible. (3) Now it is not possible to proceed to infinity in efficient causes. (4) For if we arrange in order all efficient causes, the first is the cause of the intermediate, and the intermediate the cause of the last, whether the

intermediate be many or only one. (5) But if we remove a cause the effect is removed; therefore, if there is no *first* among efficient causes, neither will there be a last or an intermediate. (6) But if we proceed to infinity in efficient causes there will be no first efficient cause, and thus there will be no ultimate effect, nor any intermediate efficient causes, which is clearly false. Therefore it is necessary to suppose the existence of some first efficient cause, and this men call God.

The Third Way:
The Argument from Contingency

The Third Way rests on the idea of the "contingent" and the "necessary" and is as follows: (1) Now we find that there are certain things in the Universe which are capable of existing and of not existing, for we find that some things are brought into existence and then destroyed, and consequently are capable of being or not being. (2) But it is impossible for all things which exist to be of this kind, because anything which is capable of not existing, at some time or other does not exist. (3) If therefore *all* things are capable of not existing, there was a time when nothing existed in the Universe. (4) But if this is true there would also be nothing in existence now; because anything that does not exist cannot begin to exist except by the agency of something which has existence. If therefore there was once nothing which existed, it would have been impossible for anything to begin to exist, and so nothing would exist now. (5) This is clearly false. Therefore all things are not contingent, and there must be something which is necessary in the Universe. (6) But everything which is necessary either has or has not the cause of its necessity from an outside source. Now it is not possible to proceed to infinity in necessary things which have a cause of their necessity, as has been proved in the case of efficient causes. Therefore it is necessary to suppose the existence of something which is necessary in itself, not having the cause of its necessity from any outside source, but which is the cause of necessity in others. And this "something" we call God.

The Fourth Way: The Argument from Degrees of Excellence

The Fourth Way is taken from the degrees which are found in things. (1) For among different things we find that one is more or less good or true or noble; and likewise in the case of other things of this kind. (2) But the words "more" or "less" are used of different things in proportion as they approximate in their different ways to something which has the particular quality in the highest degree—e.g., we call a thing hotter when it approximates more nearly to that which is hot in the highest degree. There is therefore something which is true in the highest degree, good in the highest degree and noble in the highest degree; (3) and consequently there must be also something which has being in the highest degree. For things which are true in the highest degree also have being in the highest degree (see Aristotle, *Metaphysics*, 2). (4) But anything which has a certain quality of any kind in the highest degree is also the cause of all the things of that kind, as, for example, fire which is hot in the highest degree is the cause of all hot things (as is said in the same book). (5) Therefore there exists something which is the cause of being, and goodness, and of every perfection in all existing things; and this we call God.

The Fifth Way: The Argument from Harmony

The Fifth Way is taken from the way in which nature is governed. (1) For we observe that certain things which lack knowledge, such as natural bodies, work for an End. This is obvious, because they always, or at any rate very frequently, operate in the same way so as to attain the best possible result. (2) Hence it is clear that they do not arrive at their goal by chance, but by purpose. (3) But those things which have no knowledge do not move towards a goal unless they are guided by someone or something which does possess knowledge and intelligence—e.g., an arrow by an archer. Therefore, there does exist something which possesses intelligence by which all natural things are directed to their goal; and this we call God.

Reply Obj. 1. As Augustine says: *Since God is the highest good, He would not allow any evil to exist in His works, unless His omnipotence and goodness were such as to bring good even out of evil.* This is part of the infinite goodness of God, that He should allow evil to exist, and out of it produce good.

Reply Obj. 2. Since nature works for a determinate end under the direction of a higher agent, whatever is done by nature must be traced back to God as to its first cause. So likewise whatever is done voluntarily must be traced back to some higher cause other than human reason and will, since these can change and fail; for all things that are changeable and capable of defect must be traced back to an immovable and self-necessary first principle, as has been shown.

For Further Reflection

1. Has Aquinas proved the existence of God? Why or why not? What do you think the value of these arguments is?

2. Do you agree that an infinite regress of causes is repugnant to reason?

3. Consider this question asked by John Stuart Mill: If God caused everything, what caused God? Is that a valid question? How would Aquinas respond to it? How would you respond to it?

II.2   A Critique of the Cosmological Argument

PAUL EDWARDS

Paul Edwards (1923–) is professor of philosophy at Brooklyn College, City University of New York, and the author of several books and articles, including *The Logic of Moral Discourse*. He is the editor of the *Encyclopedia of Philosophy*. In this article he attacks the cosmological argument, specifically Aquinas' second and third arguments, at several different points, holding that the argument fails at each of these points.

Study Questions

1. Even if the cosmological argument is sound, would it show that God is all-good and/or all-powerful? What is Edwards' view?

2. According to Aquinas, the idea of an infinite regress of causes would imply that nothing exists. Why does Aquinas hold this view? What mistake does Edwards accuse him of making?

3. Could there be more than one first cause?

4. Distinguish between causes *in fieri* and causes *in esse*. Given an illustration of this distinction.

5. Illustrate the difference between the cause of a whole series and the cause of individuals in the series.

6. State the argument from contingency.

7. What does Edwards say about the possibility of the universe being uncaused? What is his view about the universe being a "brute fact," something that is unexplainable?

Introduction

THE SO-CALLED "cosmological proof" is one of the oldest and most popular arguments for the existence of God. It was forcibly criticized by Hume, Kant, and Mill, but it would be inaccurate to consider the argument dead or even moribund. Catholic philosophers, with hardly any exception, appear to believe that it is as solid and conclusive as ever. Thus Father F. C. Copleston confidently championed it in his Third Programme debate* with Bertrand Russell, and in America, where Catholic writers are more san-

*BBC, 1948—ED.

Reprinted from The Rationalist Annual, *1959, edited by Hector Hawton. Reprinted by permission of Paul Edwards. Notes [at end of reading] were edited.*

guine, we are told by a Jesuit professor of physics that "the existence of an intelligent being as the First Cause of the universe can be established by *rational scientific inference*."[1]

> I am absolutely convinced [the same writer continues] that any one who would give the same consideration to that proof (the cosmological argument), as outlined for example in William Brosnan's *God and Reason*, as he would give to a line of argumentation found in the *Physical Review* or the *Proceedings of the Royal Society* would be forced to admit that the cogency of this argument for the existence of God far outstrips that which is found in the reasoning which Chadwick uses to prove the existence of the neutron, which today is accepted as certain as any conclusion in the physical sciences.

Mild theists like the late Professor Dawes Hicks and Dr. [A. C.] Ewing, who concede many of Hume's and Kant's criticisms, nevertheless contend that the argument possesses a certain core of truth. In popular discussions it also crops up again and again—for example, when believers address atheists with such questions as "You tell me where the universe came from!" Even philosophers who reject the cosmological proof sometimes embody certain of its confusions in the formulation of their own position. In the light of all this, it may be worth while to undertake a fresh examination of the argument with special attention to the fallacies that were not emphasized by the older critics.

Analysis of the Causal Argument

The cosmological proof has taken a number of forms, the most important of which are known as the "causal argument" and "the argument from contingency," respectively. In some writers, in Samuel Clarke for example, they are combined, but it is best to keep them apart as far as possible. The causal argument is the second of the "five ways" of Aquinas and roughly proceeds as follows: we find that the things around us come into being as the result of the activity of other things. These causes are themselves the result of the activity of other things. But such a causal series cannot "go back to infinity." Hence there must be a first member, a member which is not itself caused by any preceding member—an uncaused or "first" cause.

It has frequently been pointed out that even if this argument were sound it would not establish the existence of *God*. It would not show that the first cause is all-powerful or all-good or that it is in any sense personal. Somebody believing in the eternity of atoms, or of matter generally, could quite consistently accept the conclusion. Defenders of the causal argument usually concede this and insist that the argument is not in itself meant to prove the existence of God. Supplementary arguments are required to show that the first cause must have the attributes assigned to the deity. They claim, however, that the argument, if valid, would at least be an important step towards a complete proof of the existence of God.

Does the argument succeed in proving so much as a first cause? This will depend mainly on the soundness of the premise that an infinite series of causes is impossible. Aquinas supports this premise by maintaining that the opposite belief involves a plain absurdity. To suppose that there is an infinite series of causes logically implies that nothing exists now; but we know that plenty of things do exist now; and hence any theory which implies that nothing exists now must be wrong. Let us take some causal series and refer to its members by the letters of the alphabet:

$$A \rightarrow B \ldots W \rightarrow X \rightarrow Y \rightarrow Z$$

Z stands here for something presently existing, e.g. Margaret Truman. Y represents the cause or part of the cause of Z, say Harry Truman. X designates the cause or part of the cause of Y, say Harry Truman's father, etc. Now, Aquinas reasons, whenever we take away the cause, we also take away the effect: if Harry Truman had never lived, Margaret Truman would never have been born. If Harry Truman's father had never lived, Harry Truman and Margaret Truman would never have been born. If *A* had never existed, none of the subsequent members of the series would have come into existence. But it is precisely *A* that the believer in the infinite series is "taking away." For in maintaining that the series is infinite he is denying that it has a first member; he is denying that there is such a thing as a first cause; he is in other words denying the existence of *A*. Since without *A*, *Z* could not have existed, his position implies that *Z* does not exist now; and that is plainly false.

This argument fails to do justice to the supporter of the infinite series of causes. Aquinas has failed to distinguish between the two statements:

1. *A* did not exist, and
2. *A* is not uncaused.

To say that the series is infinite implies (2), but it does not imply (1). The following parallel may be helpful here: Suppose Captain Spaulding had said, "I am the greatest explorer who ever lived," and somebody replied, "No, you are not." This answer would be denying that the Captain possessed the exalted attribute he had claimed for himself, but it would not be denying his existence. It would not be "taking him away." Similarly, the believer in the infinite series is not "taking *A* away." He is taking away the privileged status of *A*; he is taking away its "first causiness." He does not deny the *existence* of *A* or of any particular member of the series. He denies that *A* or anything else *is the first member* of the series. Since he is not taking *A* away, he is not taking *B* away, and thus he is also not taking *X*, *Y*, or *Z* away. His view, then, does not commit him to the absurdity that nothing exists now, or more specifically, that Margaret Truman does not exist now. It may be noted in this connection that a believer in the infinite series is not necessarily denying the existence of supernatural beings. He is merely committed to denying that such a being, if it exists, is uncaused. He is committed to holding that whatever other impressive attributes a supernatural being might possess, the attribute of being a first cause is not among them.

The causal argument is open to several other objections. Thus, even if otherwise valid, the argument, would not prove a *single* first cause. For there does not seem to be any good ground for supposing that the various causal series in the universe ultimately merge. Hence even if it is granted that no series of causes can be infinite the possibility of a plurality of first members has not been ruled out. Nor does the argument establish the *present* existence of the first cause. It does not prove this, since experience clearly shows that an effect may exist long after its cause has been destroyed.

Originating vs. Sustaining Causes

Many defenders of the causal argument would contend that at least some of these criticisms rest on a misunderstanding. They would probably go further and contend that the argument was not quite fairly stated in the first place—or at any rate that if it was fair to some of its adherents it was not fair to others. They would in this connection distinguish between two types of causes—what they call "causes *in fieri*" and what they call "causes *in esse*." A cause *in fieri* is a factor which brought or helped to bring an effect into existence. A cause *in esse* is a factor which "sustains" or helps to sustain the effect "in being." The parents of a human being would be an example of a cause *in fieri*. If somebody puts a book in my hand and I keep holding it up, his putting it there would be the cause *in fieri*, and my holding it would be the cause *in esse* of the book's position. To quote Father [G. H.] Joyce:

> If a smith forges a horse-shoe, he is only a cause *in fieri* of the shape given to the iron. That shape persists after his action has ceased. So, too, a builder is a cause *in fieri* of the house which he builds. In both cases the substances employed act as causes *in esse* as regards the continued existence of the effect produced. Iron, in virtue of its natural rigidity, retains in being the shape which it has once received; and,

similarly, the materials employed in building retain in being the order and arrangement which constitute them into a house.[2]

Using this distinction, the defender of the argument now reasons in the following way. To say that there is an infinite series of causes *in fieri* does not lead to any absurd conclusions. But Aquinas is concerned only with causes *in esse* and an infinite series of *such* causes is impossible. In the words of the contemporary American Thomist, R. P. Phillips:

Each member of the series of causes possesses being solely by virtue of the actual present operation of a superior cause. . . . Life is dependent, *inter alia,* on a certain atmospheric pressure, this again on the continual operation of physical forces, whose being and operation depends on the position of the earth in the solar system, which itself must endure relatively unchanged, a state of being which can only be continuously produced by a definite—if unknown—constitution of the material universe. This constitution, however, cannot be its own cause. That a thing should cause itself is impossible: for in order that it may cause it is necessary for it to exist, which it cannot do, on the hypothesis, until it has been caused. So it must *be* in order to cause itself. Thus, not being uncaused nor yet its own cause, it must be caused by another, which produces and preserves it. It is plain, then, that as no member of this series possesses being except in virtue of the actual present operation of a superior cause, if there be no first cause actually operating none of the dependent causes could operate either. We are thus irresistibly led to posit a first efficient cause which, while itself uncaused, shall impart causality to a whole series. . . .

The series of cause which we are considering is not one which stretches back into the past; so that we are not demanding a beginning of the world at some definite moment reckoning back from the present, but an actual cause now operating, to account for the present being of things.[3]

Professor Phillips offers the following parallel to bring out his point:

In a goods train each truck is moved and moves by the action of the one immediately in front of it. If then we suppose the train to be infinite, i.e. that there is no end to it, and so no engine which starts the motion, it is plain that no truck will move. To lengthen it out to infinity will not give it what no member of it possesses of itself, viz. the power of drawing the truck behind it. If then we see any truck in motion we know there must be an end to the series of trucks which gives causality to the whole.[4]

Father Joyce introduces an illustration from Aquinas to explain how the present existence of things may be compatible with an infinite series of causes *in fieri* but not with an infinite series of causes *in esse*.

When a carpenter is at work, the series of efficient causes on which his work depends is necessarily limited. The final effect, e.g. the fastening of a nail is caused by a hammer: the hammer is moved by the arm: and the motion of his arm is determined by the motor-impulses communicated from the nerve centres of the brain. Unless the subordinate causes were limited in number, and were connected with a starting-point of motion, the hammer must remain inert; and the nail will never be driven in. If the series be supposed infinite, no work will ever take place. But if there is question of causes on which the work is not essentially dependent, we cannot draw the same conclusion. We may suppose the carpenter to have broken an infinite number of hammers, and as often to have replaced the broken tool by a fresh one. There is nothing in such a supposition which excludes the driving home of the nail.

The supporter of the infinite series of causes, Joyce also remarks, is

. . . asking us to believe that although each link in a suspended chain is prevented from falling simply because it is attached to the one above it, yet if only the chain be long enough, it will, taken as a whole, need no support, but will hang loose in the air suspended from nothing.

This formulation of the causal argument unquestionably circumvents one of the objections mentioned previously. If Y is the cause *in esse* of an effect, Z, then it must exist as long as Z exists. If the argument were valid in this form it would therefore prove the present and not merely the past existence of a first cause. In this form the argument is, however, less convincing in another respect. To maintain that all "natural" or "phenomenal" objects—things like tables and mountains and human beings—require a cause *in fieri* is not implausible, though even here Mill and others have argued that strictly speaking only *changes* require a causal explanation. It is far from plausible, on the other hand, to claim that all natural objects require a cause *in esse*. It may be granted that the air around us is a cause *in esse* of human life and further that certain gravitational forces are among the causes *in esse* of the air being where it is. But when we come to gravitational forces or, at any rate, to material particles like atoms or electrons it is difficult to see what cause *in esse* they require. To those not already convinced of the need for a supernatural First Cause some of the remarks by Professor Phillips in this connection appear merely dogmatic and question-begging. Most people would grant that such particles as atoms did not cause themselves, since, as Professor Phillips observes, they would in that event have had to exist before they began existing. It is not at all evident, however, that these particles cannot be uncaused. Professor Phillips and all other supporters of the causal argument immediately proceed to claim that there is something else which needs no cause *in esse*. They themselves admit thus, that there is nothing self-evident about the proposition that everything must have a cause *in esse*. Their entire procedure here lends substance to Schopenhauer's gibe that supporters of the cosmological argument treat the law of universal causation like "a hired cab which we dismiss when we have reached our destination."

But waiving this and all similar objections, the restatement of the argument in terms of causes *in esse* in no way avoids the main difficulty which was previously mentioned. A believer in the infinite series would insist that his position was just as much misrepresented now as before. He is no more removing the member of the series which is supposed to be the first cause *in esse* than he was removing the member which had been declared to be the first cause *in fieri*. He is again merely denying a privileged status to it. He is not denying the reality of the cause *in esse* labelled "A." He is not even necessarily denying that it possesses supernatural attributes. He is again merely taking away its "first causiness."

The advocates of the causal argument in either form seem to confuse an infinite series with one which is long but finite. If a book, Z, is to remain in its position, say 100 miles up in the air, there must be another object, say another book, Y, underneath it to serve as its support. If Y is to remain where it is, it will need another support, X, beneath it. Suppose that this series of supports, one below the other, continues for a long time, but eventually, say after 100,000 members, comes to a first book which is not resting on any other book or indeed on any other support. In that event the whole collection would come crashing down. What we seem to need is a first member of the series, a first support (such as the earth) which does not need another member as *its* support, which in other words is "self-supporting."

This is evidently the sort of picture that supporters of the First Cause argument have before their minds when they rule out the possibility of an infinite series. But such a picture is not a fair representation of the theory of the infinite series. A *finite* series of books would indeed come crashing down, since the first or lowest member would not have a predecessor on which it could be supported. If the series, however, were infinite this would not be the case. In that event every member *would* have a predecessor to support itself on and there would be no crash. That is to say: a crash can be avoided either by a finite series with a first self-supporting member or by an infinite series. Similarly, the present existence of motion is equally compatible with the theory of a first unmoved mover and with the theory of an infinite series of moving objects; and the present existence of causal activity is compatible with the theory of a first cause *in esse* as much as with the theory of an infinite series of such causes.

The illustrations given by Joyce and Phillips are hardly to the point. It is true that a carpenter would not, in a *finite* time-span, succeed in driving in a nail if he had to carry out an infinite number of movements. For that matter, he would not accomplish this goal in a finite time if he broke an infinite number of hammers. However, to make the illustrations relevant we must suppose that he has infinite time at his disposal. In that case he would succeed in driving in the nail even if he required an infinite number of movements for this purpose. As for the goods train, it may be granted that the trucks do not move unless the train has an engine. But this illustration is totally irrelevant as it stands. A relevant illustration would be that of engines, each moved by the one in front of it. Such a train would move if it were infinite. For every member of this series there would be one in front capable of drawing it along. The advocate of the infinite series of causes does not, as the original illustration suggests, believe in a series whose members are not really causally connected with one another. In the series he believes in every member is genuinely the cause of the one that follows it.

Causes of Series and of Individuals

No staunch defender of the cosmological argument would give up at this stage. Even if there were an infinite series of causes *in fieri* or *in esse*, he would contend, this still would not do away with the need for an ultimate, a first cause. As Father Copleston put it in his debate with Bertrand Russell:

> Every object has a phenomenal cause, if you insist on the infinity of the series. But the series of phenomenal causes is an insufficient explanation of the series. Therefore, the series has

not a phenomenal cause, but a transcendent cause. . . .

> An infinite series of contingent beings will be, to my way of thinking, as unable to cause itself as one contingent being.

The demand to find the cause of the series as a whole rests on the erroneous assumption that the series is something over and above the members of which it is composed. It is tempting to suppose this, at least by implication, because the word "series" is a noun like "dog" or "man." Like the expression "this dog" or "this man" the phrase "this series" is easily taken to designate an individual object. But reflection shows this to be an error. If we have explained the individual members there is nothing additional left to be explained. Supposing I see a group of five Eskimos standing on the corner of Sixth Avenue and 50th Street and I wish to explain why the group came to New York. Investigation reveals the following stories:

- Eskimo No. 1 did not enjoy the extreme cold in the polar region and decided to move to a warmer climate.
- No. 2 is the husband of Eskimo No. 1. He loves her dearly and did not wish to live without her.
- No. 3 is the son of Eskimos 1 and 2. He is too small and too weak to oppose his parents.
- No. 4 saw an advertisement in the *New York Times* for an Eskimo to appear on television.
- No. 5 is a private detective engaged by the Pinkerton Agency to keep an eye on Eskimo No. 4.

Let us assume that we have now explained in the case of each of the five Eskimos why he or she is in New York. Somebody then asks: "All right, but what about the group as a whole; why is *it* in New York?" This would plainly be an absurd question. There is no group over and above the five members, and if we have explained why each of the five members is in New York we have *ipso facto* explained why the group is there. It is just as absurd to ask for the cause of the series as a whole as distinct from asking for the causes of individual members.

The Argument from Contingency

It is most unlikely that a determined defender of the cosmological line of reasoning would surrender even here. He would probably admit that the series is not a thing over and above its members and that it does not make sense to ask for the cause of the series if the cause of each member has already been found. He would insist, however, that when he asked for the explanation of the entire series, he was not asking for its *cause*. He was really saying that a series, finite or infinite, is not "intelligible" or "explained" if it consists of nothing but "contingent" members. To quote Father Copleston once more:

> What we call the world is intrinsically unintelligible apart from the existence of God. The infinity of the series of events, if such an infinity could be proved, would not be in the slightest degree relevant to the situation. If you add up chocolates, you get chocolates after all, and not a sheep. If you add up chocolates to infinity, you presumably get an infinite number of chocolates. So, if you add up contingent beings to infinity, you still get contingent beings, not a necessary being.

This last quotation is really a summary of the "contingency argument," the other main form of the cosmological proof and the third of the five ways of Aquinas. It may be stated more fully in these words: All around us we perceive contingent beings. This includes all physical objects and also all human minds. In calling them "contingent" we mean that they might not have existed. We mean that the universe can be *conceived* without this or that physical object, without this or that human being, however certain their actual existence may be. These contingent beings we can trace back to other contingent beings— e.g. a human being to his parents. However, since these other beings are also contingent, they do not provide a real or full explanation. The

contingent beings we originally wanted explained have not yet become intelligible, since the beings to which they have been traced back are no more necessary than they were. It is just as true of our parents, for example, as it is of ourselves, that they might not have existed. We can then properly explain the contingent beings around us only by tracing them back ultimately to some necessary being, to something which exists necessarily, which has "the reason for its existence within itself." The existence of contingent beings, in other words, implies the existence of a necessary being.

This form of cosmological argument is even more beset with difficulties than the causal variety. In the first place, there is the objection, stated with great force by Kant, that it really commits the same error as the ontological argument in tacitly regarding existence as an attribute or characteristic. To say that there is a necessary being is to say that it would be a self-contradiction to deny its existence. This would mean that at least one existential statement is a necessary truth; and this in turn presupposes that in at least one case existence is contained in a concept. But only a characteristic can be contained in a concept and it has seemed plain to most philosophers since Kant that existence is not a characteristic, that it can hence never be contained in a concept, and that hence no existential statement can ever be a necessary truth. To talk about anything "existing necessarily" is in their view about as sensible as to talk about round squares, and they have concluded that the contingency-argument is quite absurd.

It would lead too far to discuss here the reasons for denying that existence is a characteristic. I will assume that this difficulty can somehow be surmounted and that the expression "necessary being," as it is intended by the champions of the contingency-argument, might conceivably apply to something. There remain other objections which are of great weight. I shall try to state these by first quoting again from the debate between Bertrand Russell and Father Copleston:

Russell: . . . It all turns on this question of sufficient reason, and I must say you haven't defined "sufficient reason" in a way that I can understand—what do you mean by sufficient reason? You don't mean cause?

Copleston: Not necessarily. Cause is a kind of sufficient reason. Only contingent being can have a cause. God is his own sufficient reason; and he is not cause of himself. By sufficient reason in the full sense I mean an explanation adequate for the existence of some particular being.

Russell: But when is an explanation adequate? Suppose I am about to make a flame with a match. You may say that the adequate explanation of that is that I rub it on the box.

Copleston: Well for practical purposes—but theoretically, that is only a partial explanation. An adequate explanation must ultimately be a total explanation, to which nothing further can be added.

Russell: Then I can only say that you're looking for something which can't be got, and which one ought not to expect to get.

Copleston: To say that one has not found it is one thing; to say that one should not look for it seems to me rather dogmatic.

Russell: Well, I don't know. I mean, the explanation of one thing is another thing which makes the other thing dependent on yet another, and you have to grasp this sorry scheme of things entire to do what you want, and that we can't do.

Russell's main point here may be expanded in the following way. The contingency-argument rests on a misconception of what an explanation is and does, and similarly on what it is that makes phenomena "intelligible." Or else it involves an obscure and arbitrary redefinition of "explanation," "intelligible," and related terms. Normally, we are satisfied that we have explained a phenomenon if we have found its cause or if we have exhibited some other uniform or near-uniform connection between it and something else. Confining ourselves to the former case, which is probably the most common, we might say that a phenomenon, Z, has been explained if it has been traced back to a group of factors, a, b, c, d, etc., which are its cause. These factors are the full and real explanation of Z, quite regardless of whether they are pleasing or displeasing, admirable or contemptible, necessary or contingent. The explanation would not be adequate only if the factors listed are not really the cause of Z. If they are the cause of Z, the explanation would be adequate, even though each of the factors is merely a "contingent" being.

Let us suppose that we have been asked to explain why General Eisenhower won the elections of 1952. "He was an extremely popular general," we might answer, "while Stevenson was relatively little known; moreover there was a great deal of resentment over the scandals in the Truman Administration." If somebody complained that this was only a partial explanation we might mention additional antecedents, such as the widespread belief that the Democrats had allowed communist agents to infiltrate the State Department, that Eisenhower was a man with a winning smile, and that unlike Stevenson he had shown the good sense to say one thing on race relations in the North and quite another in the South. Theoretically, we might go further and list the motives of all American voters during the weeks or months preceding the elections. If we could do this we would have explained Eisenhower's victory. We would have made it intelligible. We would "understand" why he won and why Stevenson lost. Perhaps there is a sense in which we might make Eisenhower's victory even more intelligible if we went further back and discussed such matters as the origin of American views on Communism or of racial attitudes in the North and South. However, to explain the outcome of the election in any ordinary sense, loose or strict, it would not be necessary to go back to prehistoric days or to the amoeba or to a first cause, if such a first cause exists. Nor would our explanation be considered in any way defective because each of the factors mentioned was a "contingent" and not a necessary being. The only thing that matters is whether the factors were really the cause of Eisenhower's election. If they were, then it has been explained although they are contingent beings. If they were not the cause of Eisenhower's victory, we would have failed to explain it even if each of the factors were a necessary being.

If it is granted that, in order to explain a phenomenon or to make it intelligible, we need not bring in a necessary being, then the contingency-argument breaks down. For a series, as was already pointed out, is not something over and above its members; and every contingent member of it could in that case be explained by reference to other contingent beings. But I should wish to go further than this and it is evident from Russell's remarks that he would do so also. Even if it were granted, both that the phrase "necessary being" is meaningful and that all explanations are defective unless the phenomena to be explained are traced back to a necessary being, the conclusion would still not have been established. The conclusion follows from this premise together with the additional premise that *there are* explanations of phenomena in the special sense just mentioned. It is this further premise which Russell (and many other philosophers) would question. They do not merely question, as Copleston implies, whether human beings can ever obtain explanations in this sense, but whether they *exist*. To assume without further ado that phenomena have explanations or an explanation in this sense is to beg the very point at issue. The use of the same word "explanation" in two crucially different ways lends the additional premise a plausibility it does not really possess. It may indeed be highly plausible to assert that phenomena have explanations, whether we have found them or not, in the ordinary sense in which this usually means that they have causes. It is then tempting to suppose, because of the use of the same word, that they also have explanations in a sense in which this implies dependence on a necessary thing. But this is a gross *non sequitur*.

Could the Universe Be Uncaused?

It is necessary to add a few words about the proper way of formulating the position of those who reject the main premise of the cosmological argument, in either of the forms we have considered. It is sometimes maintained in this connection that in order to reach a "self-existing" entity it is not necessary to go beyond the universe: the universe itself (or "Nature") is "self-existing." And this in turn is sometimes expanded into the statement that while all individual things "within" the universe are caused, the universe itself is uncaused. Statements of this kind are found in Büchner, Bradlaugh, Haeckel, and other freethinkers of the nineteenth and early twentieth century. Sometimes the assertion that the universe is "self-existing" is elaborated to mean that *it* is the "necessary being." Some eighteenth-century unbelievers, apparently accepting the view that there is a necessary being, asked why Nature or the material universe could not fill the bill as well or better than God.

> "Why," asks one of the characters in Hume's *Dialogues,* "may not the material universe be the necessarily existent Being? . . . We dare not affirm that we know all the qualities of matter; and for aught we can determine, it may contain some qualities, which, were they known, would make its nonexistence appear as great a contradiction as that twice two is five."

Similar remarks can be found in Holbach and several of the Encyclopedists.

The former of these formulations immediately invites the question why the universe, alone of all "things," is exempted from the universal sway of causation. "The strong point of the cosmological argument," writes Dr. Ewing, "is that after all it does remain incredible that the physical universe should just have happened . . . It calls out for some further explanation of some kind." The latter formulation is exposed to the criticism that there is nothing any more "necessary" about the existence of the universe or Nature as a whole than about any particular thing within the universe.

I hope some of the earlier discussions in this article have made it clear that in rejecting the cosmological argument one is not committed to either of these propositions. If I reject the view that there is a supernatural first cause, I am not thereby committed to the proposition that there is a *natural* first cause, and even less to the proposition that a mysterious "thing" called "the universe" qualifies for this title. I may hold that there is no "universe" over and above individual things of various sorts; and, accepting the causal principle, I may proceed to assert that all these things are caused by other things, and these other things by yet other things, and so on, *ad infinitum*. In this way no arbitrary exception is made to the principle of causation. Similarly, if I reject the assertion that God is a "necessary being," I am not committed to the view that the universe is such an entity. I may hold that it does not make sense to speak of anything as a "necessary being" and that even if there were such a thing as the universe it could not be properly considered a necessary being.

However, in saying that nothing is uncaused or that there is no necessary being, one is not committed to the view that everything, or for that matter anything, is merely a "brute fact." Dr. Ewing laments that "the usual modern philosophical views opposed to theism do not try to give any rational explanation of the world at all, but just take it as a brute fact not to be explained." They thus fail to "rationalize" the universe. Theism, he concedes, cannot completely rationalize things either since it does not show "how God can be his own cause or how it is that he does not need a cause." Now, if one means by "brute fact" something for which there *exists* no explanation (as distinct from something for which no explanation is in our possession), then the theists have at least one brute fact on their hands, namely God. Those who adopt Büchner's formulation also have one brute fact on their hands, namely "the universe." Only the position I have been supporting dispenses with brute facts altogether. I don't know if this is any special virtue, but the defenders of the cosmological argument seem to think so.

NOTES

1. J. S. O'Connor, "A Scientific Approach to Religion," *The Scientific Monthly* (1940), p. 369; my italics.
2. *The Principles of Natural Theology*, p. 58.
3. *Modern Thomistic Philosophy*, Vol. II, pp. 284–85.
4. Ibid., p. 278.

For Further Reflection

1. Consider the question, "Why is there something rather than nothing?" Is it a question that we should try to answer? What would Aquinas say about this question? What does Edwards think? What do you think?

2. How successful has Edwards been in criticizing the two forms of the cosmological argument? How might a theist respond to him?

B. The Teleological Argument for the Existence of God

The teleological argument for the existence of God begins with the premise that the world exhibits intelligent purpose or order and proceeds to the conclusion that there must be or probably is a divine intelligence, a supreme designer to account for the observed or perceived intelligent purpose or order. Although the argument has been cited by Plato, by St. Paul in the Epistle to the Romans (ch. 1), and by Cicero, the clearest sustained treatment is found in William Paley's *Natural Theology* (1802), our first selection.

Paley argues that just as we infer an intelligent designer to account for the purpose-revealing watch, we must analogously infer an intelligent grand designer to account for the purpose-revealing world. "Every indication of contrivance, every manifestation of design, which existed in the watch, exists in the works of nature; with the difference, on the side of nature, of being greater and more, and that in a degree which exceeds all computation." The skeleton of the argument looks like this:

1. Human artifacts are products of intelligent design (purpose).
2. The universe resembles these human artifacts.
3. Therefore, the universe is (probably) a product of intelligent design (purpose).
4. But the universe is vastly more complex and gigantic than a human artifact.
5. Therefore, there probably is a powerful and vastly intelligent designer who designed the universe.

Ironically, Paley's argument was attacked even before Paley had set it down, for David Hume (1711–1776) had long before written his famous *Dialogues Concerning Natural Religion* (published posthumously in 1779), which constitutes the classic critique of the teleological argument. Paley seems to have been unaware of it. A selection of the *Dialogues* constitutes our second reading. In it, the natural theologian, Cleanthes, debates the orthodox believer, Demea, and the skeptic or critic, Philo, who does most of the serious arguing.

Hume, through Philo, attacks the argument from several different angles. First, he argues that the universe is not sufficiently like the productions of human design to support the argument.

Philo's second objection is that the analogy from artifact to divine designer fails because we have no other universe with which to compare this one, which would be necessary in order to decide if it were the kind of universe designed or simply the kind that developed on its own. As C. S. Peirce put it, "Universes are not as plentiful as blackberries." Since there is only one of them, we have no standard of comparison by which to judge it. Paley's answer to this would be that if we can find one clear instance of purposeness in nature (e.g., the eye), we have a sufficient instance enabling us to conclude that there is probably an intelligent designer.

A third objection is that on the analogy from artifact to designer, we should infer a grand anthropomorphic designer, a human writ large, who has all the properties that we have. "Why not become a perfect anthropomorphite? Why not assert the Deity or Deities to be corporeal, and to have eyes, a nose, mouth, ears, etc.?"

Hume makes several other points against the design argument. The universe resembles in some ways an animal and in other ways a plant, in which case the argument fails since it depends on our seeing the world as a grand machine. The world might well be the result of mere chance. And, finally, the argument is weak because the world exhibits not merely order but much disorder. The question is whether the theist can answer enough of Hume's objections to make use of this argument.

The Watch and the Watchmaker   II.3

WILLIAM PALEY

William Paley (1743–1805), archdeacon of Carlisle, was a leading evangelical apologist. His most important work is *Natural Theology, or Evidences of the Existence and Attributes of the Deity Collected from the Appearances of Nature* (1802), the first chapter of which is reprinted here. Paley argues that just as we infer an intelligent designer to account for the purpose-revealing watch, so likewise we must infer an intelligent grand designer to account for the purpose-revealing world.

Study Questions

1. What does Paley think are the inherent differences between a stone and a watch? What inferences does each permit about its origins?

2. What is the analogy between the watch and the world, according to Paley? Describe his argument.

3. How does Paley respond to objections to the analogy?

Statement of the Argument

IN CROSSING A HEATH , suppose I pitched my foot against a *stone,* and were asked how the stone came to be there, I might possibly answer, that, for anything I knew to the contrary, it had lain there for ever; nor would it, perhaps, be very easy to show the absurdity of this answer. But suppose I found a *watch* upon the ground, and it should be inquired how the watch happened to be in that place, I should hardly think of the answer which I had given—that, for anything I knew, the watch might have always been there. Yet why should not this answer serve for the watch as well as for the stone? why is it not as admissible in the second case as in the first? For this reason, and for no other; viz., that, when we come to inspect the watch, we perceive (what we could not discover in the stone) that its several parts are framed and put together for a purpose, e.g. that they are so formed and adjusted as to produce motion, and that motion so regulated as to point out the hour of the day; that, if the different parts had been differently shaped from what they are, if a different size from what they are, or placed after any other manner, or in any other order than that in which they are placed, either no motion at all would have been carried on in the machine, or none which would have answered the use that is now served by it. To reckon up a few of the plainest of these parts, and of their offices, all tending to one result:— We see a cylindrical box containing a coiled elastic spring, which, by its endeavor to relax itself, turns round the box. We next observe a flexible chain (artificially wrought for the sake of flexure) communicating the action of the spring from the box to the fusee. We then find a series of wheels,

From William Paley, Natural Theology, or Evidences of the Existence and Attributes of the Deity Collected from the Appearances of Nature *(1802).*

the teeth of which catch in, and apply to, each other, conducting the motion from the fusee to the balance, and from the balance to the pointer, and, at the same time, by the size and shape of those wheels, so regulating that motion as to terminate in causing an index, by an equable and measured progression, to pass over a given space in a given time. We take notice that the wheels are made of brass, in order to keep them from rust; the springs of steel, no other metal being so elastic; that over the face of the watch there is placed a glass, a material employed in no other part of the work, but in the room of which, if there had been any other than a transparent substance, the hour could not be seen without opening the case. This mechanism being observed, (it requires indeed an examination of the instrument, and perhaps some previous knowledge of the subject, to perceive and understand it; but being once, as we have said, observed and understood,) the inference, we think, is inevitable, that the watch must have had a maker; that there must have existed, at some time, and at some place or other, an artificer or artificers who formed it for the purpose which we find it actually to answer; who comprehended its construction, and designed its use.

I. Nor would it, I apprehend, weaken the conclusion, that we had never seen a watch made; that we had never known an artist capable of making one; that we were altogether incapable of executing such a piece of workmanship ourselves, or of understanding in what manner it was performed; all this being no more than what is true of some exquisite remains of ancient art, of some lost arts, and, to the generality of mankind, of the more curious productions of modern manufacture. Does one man in a million know how oval frames are turned? Ignorance of this kind exalts our opinion of the unseen and unknown artist's skill, if he be unseen and unknown, but raises no doubt in our minds of the existence and agency of such an artist, at some former time, and in some place or other. Nor can I perceive that it varies at all the inference, whether the question arise concerning a human agent, or concerning an agent of a different species, or an agent possessing, in some respect, a different nature.

II. Neither, secondly, would it invalidate our conclusion, that the watch sometimes went wrong, or that it seldom went exactly right. The purpose of the machinery, the design, and the designer, might be evident, and, in the case supposed, would be evident, in whatever way we accounted for the irregularity of the movement, or whether we could account for it or not. It is not necessary that a machine be perfect, in order to show with what design it was made; still less necessary, where the only question is, whether it were made with any design at all.

III. Nor, thirdly, would it bring any uncertainty into the argument, if there were a few parts of the watch, concerning which we could not discover, or had not yet discovered, in what manner they conduced to the general effect; or even some parts, concerning which we could not ascertain whether they conduced to that effect in any manner whatever. For, as to the first branch of the case, if by the loss, or disorder, or decay of the parts in question, the movement of the watch were found in fact to be stopped, or disturbed, or retarded, no doubt would remain in our minds as to the utility or intention of these parts, although we should be unable to investigate the manner according to which, or the connection by which, the ultimate effect depended upon their action or assistance; and the more complex is the machine, the more likely is this obscurity to arise. Then, as to the second thing supposed, namely, that there were parts which might be spared without prejudice to the movement of the watch, and that he had proved this by experiment, these superfluous parts, even if we were completely assured that they were such, would not vacate the reasoning which we had instituted concerning other parts. The indication of contrivance remained, with respect to them, nearly as it was before.

IV. Nor, fourthly, would any man in his senses

think the existence of the watch, with its various machinery, accounted for, by being told that it was one out of possible combinations of material forms; that whatever he had found in the place where he found the watch, must have contained some internal configuration or other; and that this configuration might be the structure now exhibited, viz., of the works of a watch, as well as a different structure.

V. Nor, fifthly, would it yield his inquiry more satisfaction, to be answered, that there existed in things a principle of order, which had disposed the parts of the watch into their present form and situation. He never knew a watch made by the principle of order; nor can he even form to himself an idea of what is meant by a principle of order, distinct from the intelligence of the watchmaker.

VI. Sixthly, he would be surprised to hear that the mechanism of the watch was no proof of contrivance, only a motive to induce the mind to think so:

VII. And not less surprised to be informed, that the watch in his hand was nothing more than the result of the laws of *metallic* nature. It is a perversion of language to assign any law as the efficient, operative cause of anything. A law presupposes an agent; for it is only the mode according to which an agent proceeds; it implies a power; for it is the order according to which that power acts. Without this agent, without this power, which are both distinct from itself, the *law* does nothing, is nothing. The expression, "the law of metallic nature," may sound strange and harsh to a philosophic ear; but it seems quite as justifiable as some others which are more familiar to him such as "the law of vegetable nature," "the law of animal nature," or, indeed, as "the law of nature" in general, when assigned as the cause of phenomena in exclusion of agency and power, or when it is substituted into the place of these.

VIII. Neither, lastly, would our observer be driven out of his conclusion, or from his confidence in its truth, by being told that he knew nothing at all about the matter. He knows enough for his argument: he knows the utility of the end: he knows the subserviency and adaptation of the means to the end. These points being known, his ignorance of other points, his doubts concerning other points, affect not the certainty of his reasoning. The consciousness of knowing little need not beget a distrust of that which he does know. . . .

Application of the Argument

Every indication of contrivance, every manifestation of design, which existed in the watch, exists in the works of nature; with the difference, on the side of nature, of being greater and more, and that in a degree which exceeds all computation. I mean that the contrivances of nature surpass the contrivances of art, in the complexity, subtilty, and curiosity of the mechanism; and still more, if possible, do they go beyond them in number and variety; yet in a multitude of cases, are not less evidently mechanical, not less evidently contrivances, not less evidently accommodated to their end, or suited to their office, than are the most perfect productions of human ingenuity. . . .

For Further Reflection

1. Do you think that Paley's argument is cogent? Do you think that the universe does reveal design or order? Is there a significant difference between the concepts of design and order?

2. Can you think of possible objections to Paley's argument? How might Paley respond to them?

II.4   A Critique of the Teleological Argument

DAVID HUME

The Scottish empiricist and skeptic David Hume (1711–1776) is one of the most important philosophers. The *Dialogues Concerning Natural Religion* (published posthumously in 1779) contains the classic critique of the argument from design. Our reading is from Parts 2 and 5 of this dialogue. Cleanthes, who opens our selection, is a natural theologian, the Paley of his time, who opposes both the orthodox believer, Demea, and the skeptic, Philo. It is Philo who puts forth the major criticisms against the argument from design.

Study Questions

1. How does the natural theologian Cleanthes argue for the existence of God?
2. What are (the orthodox believer) Demea's objections to Cleanthes' way of arguing for the existence of God?
3. What does the agnostic Philo say is his chief scruple about Cleanthes' argument?
4. In Philo's second main speech, what distinction does he make between order and arrangement, on the one hand, and design, on the other? What is his purpose in this?
5. What is Philo's contention about arguing from parts to wholes?
6. Why does Philo accuse Cleanthes of anthropomorphism?
7. List six objections that Philo makes to the design argument. Are they plausible objections?
8. What is Cleanthes' response to Hume's objections?

CLEANTHES: LOOK ROUND THE WORLD: Contemplate the whole and every part of it: You will find it to be nothing but one great machine, subdivided into an infinite number of lesser machines, which again admit of subdivisions to a degree beyond what human senses and faculties can trace and explain. All these various machines, and even their most minute parts, are adjusted to each other with an accuracy which ravishes into admiration all men who have ever contemplated them. The curious adapting of means to ends, throughout all nature, resembles exactly, though it much exceeds, the productions of human contrivance; of human design, thought, wisdom, and intelligence. Since therefore the effects resemble each other, we are led to infer, by all the rules of analogy, that the causes also resemble, and that the Author of Nature is somewhat similar to the mind of man, though possessed of much larger faculties, proportioned to the grandeur of the work which he has executed. By this argument *a posteriori,* and by this argument alone, do we prove at once the existence of a Deity and his similarity to human mind and intelligence.

Demea: I shall be so free, *Cleanthes,* said *Demea,* as to tell you that from the beginning I could not approve of your conclusion concern-

From David Hume, Dialogues Concerning Natural Religion *(1779).*

ing the similarity of the Deity to men; still less can I approve of the mediums by which you endeavor to establish it. What! No demonstration of the Being of God! No abstract arguments! No proofs *a priori!* Are these which have hitherto been so much insisted on by philosophers all fallacy, all sophism? Can we reach no farther in this subject than experience and probability? I will say not that this is betraying the cause of a Deity; but surely, by this affected candor, you give advantages to atheists which they never could obtain by the mere dint of argument and reasoning.

Philo: What I chiefly scruple in this subject, said *Philo,* is not so much that all religious arguments are by *Cleanthes* reduced to experience, as that they appear not to be even the most certain and irrefragable of that inferior kind. That a stone will fall, that fire will burn, that the earth has solidity, we have observed a thousand and a thousand times; and when any new instance of this nature is presented, we draw without hesitation the accustomed inference. The exact similarity of the cases gives us a perfect assurance of a similar event, and a stronger evidence is never desired nor sought after. But wherever you depart, in the least, from the similarity of the cases, you diminish proportionably the evidence; and may at last bring it to a very weak *analogy,* which is confessedly liable to error and uncertainty. After having experienced the circulation of the blood in human creatures, we make no doubt that it takes place in *Titius* and *Maevius;* but from its circulation in frogs and fishes it is only a presumption, though a strong one, from analogy that it takes place in men and other animals. The analogical reasoning is much weaker when we infer the circulation of the sap in vegetables from our experience that the blood circulates in animals; and those who hastily followed that imperfect analogy are found, by more accurate experiments to have been mistaken.

If we see a house, *Cleanthes,* we conclude, with the greatest certainty, that it had an architect or builder because this is precisely that species of effect which we have experienced to proceed from that species of cause. But surely you will not affirm that the universe bears such a resemblance to a house that we can with the same certainty infer a similar cause, or that the analogy is here entire and perfect. The dissimilitude is so striking that the utmost you can here pretend to is a guess, a conjecture, a presumption concerning a similar cause; and how that pretension will be received in the world, I leave you to consider.

Cleanthes: It would surely be very ill received, replied *Cleanthes;* and I should be deservedly blamed and detested did I allow that the proofs of a Deity amounted to no more than a guess or conjecture. But is the whole adjustment of means to ends in a house and in the universe so slight a resemblance? The economy of final causes? The order, proportion, and arrangement of every part? Steps of a stair are plainly contrived that human legs may use them in mounting; and this inference is certain and infallible. Human legs are also contrived for walking and mounting; and this inference, I allow, is not altogether so certain because of the dissimilarity which you remark; but does it, therefore, deserve the name only of presumption or conjecture?

Demea: Good God! cried *Demea,* interrupting him, where are we? Zealous defenders of religion allow that the proofs of a Deity fall short of perfect evidence! And you, *Philo,* on whose assistance I depended in proving the adorable mysteriousness of the Divine Nature, do you assent to all these extravagant opinions of *Cleanthes?* For what other name can I give them? or, why spare my censure when such principles are advanced, supported by such an authority, before so young a man as *Pamphilus?*

Philo: You seem not to apprehend, replied *Philo,* that I argue with *Cleanthes* in his own way, and, by showing him the dangerous consequences of his tenets, hope at last to reduce him to our opinion. But what sticks most with you, I observe, is the representation which *Cleanthes* has made of the argument *a posteriori;* and, finding that that argument is likely to escape your hold and vanish into air, you think it so disguised that you can scarcely believe it to be set in its true light. Now, however much I may dissent, in other respects, from the dangerous principle of *Cleanthes,* I must allow that he has fairly represented that argument, and I shall endeavor so to state the matter to you that you will entertain no further scruples with regard to it.

Were a man to abstract from everything which he knows or has seen, he would be altogether incapable, merely from his own ideas, to determine what kind of scene the universe must be, or to give the preference to one state or situation of things above another. For as nothing which he clearly conceives could be esteemed impossible or implying a contradiction, every chimera of his fancy would be upon an equal footing; nor could he assign any just reason why he adheres to one idea or system, and rejects the others which are equally possible.

Again, after he opens his eyes and contemplates the world as it really is, it would be impossible for him at first to assign the cause of any one event, much less of the whole of things, or of the universe. He might set his fancy a rambling, and she might bring him in an infinite variety of reports and representations. These would all be possible; but, being all equally possible, he would never of himself give a satisfactory account for his preferring one of them to the rest. Experience alone can point out to him the true cause of any phenomenon.

Now, according to this method of reasoning, *Demea,* it follows (and is, indeed, tacitly allowed by *Cleanthes* himself) that order, arrangement, or the adjustment of final causes, is not of itself any proof of design, but only so far as it has been experienced to proceed from that principle. For aught we can know *a priori,* matter may contain the source or spring of order originally within itself, as well as mind does; and there is no more difficulty in conceiving that the several elements, from an internal unknown cause, may fall into the most exquisite arrangement, than to conceive that their ideas, in the great universal mind, from a like internal unknown cause, fall into that arrangement. The equal possibility of both these suppositions is allowed. But, by experience, we find, according to *Cleanthes,* that there is a difference between them. Throw several pieces of steel together, without shape or form; they will never arrange themselves so as to compose a watch. Stone and mortar and wood, without an architect, never erect a house. But the ideas in a human mind, we see, by an unknown, inexplicable economy, arrange themselves so as to form the plan of a watch or house. Experience, therefore, proves that there is an original principle of order in mind, not in matter. From similar effects we infer similar causes. The adjustment of means to ends is alike in the universe, as in a machine of human contrivance. The causes, therefore, must be resembling.

I was from the beginning scandalized, I must own, with this resemblance which is asserted between the Deity and human creatures, and must conceive it to imply such a degradation of the Supreme Being as no sound theist could endure. With your assistance, therefore, *Demea,* I shall endeavor to defend what you justly call the adorable mysteriousness of the Divine Nature, and shall refute this reasoning of *Cleanthes,* provided he allows that I have made a fair representation of it.

When *Cleanthes* had assented, *Philo,* after a short pause, proceeded in the following manner.

That all inferences, *Cleanthes,* concerning fact are founded on experience, and that all experimental reasonings are founded on the supposition that similar causes prove similar effects, and similar effects similar causes, I shall not at present much dispute with you. But observe, I entreat you, with what extreme caution all just reasoners proceed in the transferring of experiments to similar cases. Unless the cases be exactly similar, they repose no perfect confidence in applying their past observation to any particular phenomenon. Every alteration of circumstances occasions a doubt concerning the event; and it requires new experiments to prove certainly that the new circumstances are of no moment or importance. A change in bulk, situation, arrangement, age, disposition of the air, or surrounding bodies; any of these particulars may be attended with the most unexpected consequences. And unless the objects be quite familiar to us, it is the highest temerity to expect with assurance, after any of these changes, an event similar to that which before fell under our observation. The slow and deliberate steps of philosophers here, if anywhere, are distinguished from the precipitate march of the vulgar, who, hurried on by the smallest similitude, are incapable of all discernment or consideration.

But can you think, *Cleanthes,* that your usual phlegm and philosophy have been preserved in so wide a step as you have taken when you compared to the universe houses, ships, furniture, machines; and, from their similarity in some circumstances, inferred a similarity in their causes? Thought, design, intelligence, such as we discover in men and other animals, is no more than one of the springs and principles of the universe, as well as heat or cold, attraction or repulsion, and a hundred others which fall under daily observation. It is an active cause by which some particular parts of nature, we find, produce alterations on other parts. But can a conclusion, with any propriety, be transferred from parts to the whole? Does not the great disproportion bar all comparison and inference? From observing the growth of a hair, can we learn anything concerning the generation of a man? Would the manner of a leaf's blowing, even though perfectly known, afford us any instruction concerning the vegetation of a tree?

But allowing that we were to take the *operations* of one part of nature upon another for the foundation of our judgment concerning the *origin* of the whole (which never can be admitted), yet why select so minute, so weak, so bounded a principle as the reason and design of animals is found to be upon this planet? What peculiar privilege has this little agitation of the brain which we call "thought", that we must thus

make it the model of the whole universe? Our partiality in our own favor does indeed present it on all occasions, but sound philosophy ought carefully to guard against so natural an illusion.

So far from admitting, continued *Philo,* that the operations of a part can afford us any just conclusion concerning the origin of the whole, I will not allow any one part to form a rule for another part if the latter be very remote from the former. Is there any reasonable ground to conclude that the inhabitants of other planets possess thought, intelligence, reason, or anything similar to these faculties in men? When nature has so extremely diversified her manner of operation in this small globe, can we imagine that she incessantly copies herself throughout so immense a universe? And if thought, as we may well suppose, be confined merely to this narrow corner, and has even there so limited a sphere of action, with what propriety can we assign it for the original cause of all things? The narrow views of a peasant who makes his domestic economy the rule for the government of kingdoms is in comparison a pardonable sophism.

But were we ever so much assured that a thought and reason resembling the human were to be found throughout the whole universe, and were its activity elsewhere vastly greater and more commanding than it appears in this globe; yet I cannot see why the operations of a world constituted, arranged, adjusted, can with any propriety be extended to a world which is in its embryostate, and is advancing towards that constitution and arrangement. By observation we know somewhat of the economy, action, and nourishment of a finished animal; but we must transfer with great caution that observation to the growth of a foetus in the womb, and still more to the formation of an animalcule in the loins of its male parent. Nature, we find, even from our limited experience, possesses an infinite number of springs and principles which incessantly discover themselves on every change of her position and situation. And what new and unknown principles would actuate her in so new and unknown a situation as that of the formation of a universe, we cannot, without the utmost temerity, pretend to determine.

A very small part of this great system, during a very short time, is very imperfectly discovered to us; and do we thence pronounce decisively concerning the origin of the whole?

Admirable conclusion! Stone, wood, brick, iron, brass, have not, at this time, in this minute globe of earth, an order or arrangement without human art and contrivance; therefore, the universe could not originally attain its order and arrangement without something similar to human art. But is a part of nature a rule for another part very wide of the former? Is it a rule for the whole? Is a very small part a rule for the universe? Is nature in one situation a certain rule for nature in another situation vastly different from the former?

And can you blame me, *Cleanthes*, if I here imitate the prudent reserve of *Simonides*, who, according to the noted story, being asked by *Hiero, What God was?* desired a day to think of it, and then two days more; and after that manner continually prolonged the term, without ever bringing in his definition or description? Could you even blame me if I had answered, at first, *that I did not know,* and was sensible that this subject lay vastly beyond the reach of my faculties? You might cry out skeptic and raillier, as much as you pleased; but, having found in so many other subjects much more familiar the imperfections and even contradictions of human reason, I never should expect any success from its feeble conjectures in a subject so sublime and so remote from the sphere of our observation. When two *species* of objects have always been observed to be conjoined together, I can *infer,* by custom, the existence of one wherever I see the existence of the other; and this I call an argument from experience. But how this argument can have place where the objects, as in the present case, are single, individual, without parallel or specific resemblance, may be difficult to explain. And will any man tell me with a serious

countenance that an orderly universe must arise from some thought and art like the human because we have experience of it? To ascertain this reasoning it were requisite that we had experience of the origin of worlds; and it is not sufficient, surely, that we have seen ships and cities arise from human art and contrivance. . . .

Philo: But to show you still more inconveniences, continued *Philo,* in your anthropomorphism, please to take a new survey of your principles. *Like effects prove like causes.* This is the experimental argument; and this, you say too, is the sole theological argument. Now it is certain that the liker the effects are which are seen and the liker the causes which are inferred, the stronger is the argument. Every departure on either side diminishes the probability and renders the experiment less conclusive. You cannot doubt of the principle; neither ought you to reject its consequences.

All the new discoveries in astronomy which prove the immense grandeur and magnificence of the works of nature are so many additional arguments for a Deity, according to the true system of theism; but, according to your hypothesis of experimental theism, they become so many objections, by removing the effect still farther from all resemblance to the effects of human art and contrivance. For if *Lucretius,* even following the old system of the world, could exclaim:

> Who is strong enough to rule the sum, who to hold in hand and control the mighty bridle of the unfathomable deep? who to turn about all the heavens at one time, and warm the fruitful worlds with ethereal fires, or to be present in all places and at all times.[1]

If Tully[2] esteemed this reasoning so natural as to put it into the mouth of his Epicurean:

> What power of mental vision enabled your master Plato to descry the vast and elaborate architectural process which, as he makes out, the deity adopted in building the structure of the universe? What method of engineering was em-

ployed? What tools and levers and derricks? What agents carried out so vast an understanding? And how were air, fire, water, and earth enabled to obey and execute the will of the architect?

If this argument, I say, had any force in former ages, how much greater must it have at present when the bounds of nature are so infinitely enlarged and such a magnificent scene is opened to us? It is still more unreasonable to form our idea of so unlimited a cause from our experience of the narrow productions of human design and invention.

The discoveries by microscopes, as they open a new universe in miniature, are still objections, according to you; arguments, according to me. The farther we push our researches of this kind, we are still led to infer the universal cause of all to be vastly different from mankind, or from any object of human experience and observation.

And what say you to the discoveries in anatomy, chemistry, botany? . . . *Cleanthes:* These surely are no objections, replied *Cleanthes;* they only discover new instances of art and contrivance. It is still the image of mind reflected on us from innumerable objects. *Philo:* Add a mind *like the human,* said *Philo. Cleanthes:* I know of no other, replied *Cleanthes. Philo:* And the liker, the better, insisted *Philo. Cleanthes:* To be sure, said *Cleanthes.*

Philo: Now, *Cleanthes,* said *Philo,* with an air of alacrity and triumph, mark the consequences. *First,* by this method of reasoning you renounce all claim to infinity in any of the attributes of the Deity. For, as the cause ought only to be proportioned to the effect, and the effect, so far as it falls under our cognizance, is not infinite: What pretensions have we, upon your suppositions, to ascribe that attribute to the Divine Being? You will still insist that, by removing him so much from all similarity to human creatures, we give in to the most arbitrary hypothesis, and at the same time weaken all proofs of his existence.

Secondly, you have no reason, on your theory, for ascribing perfection to the Deity, even in his finite capacity; or for supposing him free from every error, mistake, or incoherence, in his undertakings. There are many inexplicable difficulties in the works of Nature which, if we allow a perfect author to be proved *a priori,* are easily solved, and become only seeming difficulties from the narrow capacity of man, who cannot trace infinite relations. But according to your method of reasoning, these difficulties become all real; and, perhaps, will be insisted on as new instances of likeness to human art and contrivance. At least, you must acknowledge that it is impossible for us to tell, from our limited views, whether this system contains any great faults or deserves any considerable praise if compared to other possible and even real systems. Could a peasant, if the *Aeneid* were read to him, pronounce that poem to be absolutely faultless, or even assign to it its proper rank among the productions of human wit, he who had never seen any other production?

But were this world ever so perfect a production, it must still remain uncertain whether all the excellences of the work can justly be ascribed to the workman. If we survey a ship, what an exalted idea must we form of the ingenuity of the carpenter who framed so complicated, useful, and beautiful a machine? And what surprise must we feel when we find him a stupid mechanic who imitated others, and copied an art which, through a long succession of ages, after multiplied trials, mistakes, corrections, deliberations, and controversies, had been gradually improving? Many worlds might have been botched and bungled, throughout an eternity, ere this system was struck out; much labor lost; many fruitless trials made; and a slow but continued improvement carried on during infinite ages in the art of world-making. In such subjects, who can determine where the truth, nay, who can conjecture where the probability lies, amidst a great number of hypotheses which may be proposed, and a still greater which may be imagined?

And what shadow of an argument, continued Philo, can you produce from your hypothesis to prove the unity of the Deity? A great number of men join in building a house or ship, in rearing a city, in framing a commonwealth; why may not several deities combine in contriving and framing a world? This is only so much greater similarity to human affairs. By sharing the work among several, we may so much further limit the attributes of each, and get rid of that extensive power and knowledge which must be supposed in one deity, and which, according to you, can only serve to weaken the proof of his existence. And if such foolish, such vicious creatures as man can yet often unite in framing and executing one plan, how much more those deities or demons, whom we may suppose several degrees more perfect?

To multiply causes without necessity is indeed contrary to true philosophy, but this principle applies not to the present case. Were one deity antecedently proved by your theory who were possessed of every attribute requisite to the production of the universe, it would be needless, I own (though not absurd), to suppose any other deity existent. But while it is still a question whether all these attributes are united in one subject or dispersed among several independent beings; by what phenomena in nature can we pretend to decide the controversy? Where we see a body raised in a scale, we are sure that there is in the opposite scale, however concealed from sight, some counterpoising weight equal to it; but it is still allowed to doubt whether that weight be an aggregate of several distinct bodies or one uniform united mass. And if the weight requisite very much exceeds anything which we have ever seen conjoined in any single body, the former supposition becomes still more probable and natural. And intelligent being of such vast power and capacity as is necessary to produce a universe, or, to speak in the language of ancient philosophy, so prodigious an animal, exceeds all analogy and even comprehension.

But further, *Cleanthes,* men are mortal, and renew their species by generation; and this is common to all living creatures. The two great sexes of male and female, says *Milton,* animate the world. Why must this circumstance, so universal, so essential, be excluded from those numerous and limited deities? Behold, then, the theogeny of ancient times brought back upon us.

And why not become a perfect anthropomorphite? Why not assert the deity or deities to be corporeal, and to have eyes, a nose, mouth, ears, etc.? *Epicurus* maintained that no man had ever seen reason but in a human figure; therefore, the gods must have a human figure. And this argument, which is deservedly so much ridiculed by *Cicero,* becomes, according to you, solid and philosophical.

In a word, *Cleanthes,* a man who follows your hypothesis is able, perhaps, to assert or conjecture that the universe sometime arose from something like design: But beyond that position he cannot ascertain one single circumstance, and is left afterwards to fix every point of his theology by the utmost license of fancy and hypothesis. This world, for aught he knows, is very faulty and imperfect, compared to a superior standard; and was only the first rude essay of some infant deity who afterwards abandoned it, ashamed of his lame performance: It is the work only of some dependent, inferior deity, and is the object of derision to his superiors: It is the production of old age and dotage in some superannuated deity; and ever since his death has run on at adventures, from the first impulse and active force which it received from him. . . . You justly give signs of horror, *Demea,* at these strange suppositions; but these, and a thousand more of the same kind, are *Cleanthes'* suppositions, not mine. From the moment the attributes of the Deity are supposed finite, all these have place. And I cannot, for my part, think that so wild and unsettled a system of theology is, in any respect, preferable to none at all.

Cleanthes: These suppositions I absolutely disown, cried *Cleanthes:* They strike me, however, with no horror, especially when proposed in that rambling way in which they drop from you. On the contrary, they give me pleasure when I see

that, by the utmost indulgence of your imagination, you never get rid of the hypothesis of design in the universe, but are obliged at every turn
to have recourse to it. To this concession I adhere steadily; and this I regard as a sufficient
foundation for religion.

NOTES

1. *On the Nature of Things*, II, 1096–1099 (trans. by
W. D. Rouse).
2. Tully was a common name for the Roman lawyer and philosopher Marcus Tullius Cicero, 106–43
B.C. The excerpt is from *The Nature of the Gods*, I, viii,
19 (trans. by H. Rackham).

For Further Reflection

1. The teleological argument has had a long and distinguished career, but is it plausible?
How probable does it make the existence of a God?

2. How effective are Hume's criticisms? Consider his contention that we can't argue from
the part to a whole. Is that always true? Can't we sometimes make valid inferences from a part
to the whole? For example, if I discover that the salt water from the Atlantic Ocean that is by
my home in Long Island is undrinkable, can't I infer that the rest of the water in the Atlantic
Ocean is likely undrinkable? This may be a weak argument, but doesn't the part lend some
probability to conclusions about the whole?

3. Examine each of Hume's objections in order to determine their strength. What might
Paley reply to them?

C. The Ontological Argument for the Existence of God

The ontological argument for the existence of God is the most intriguing of all the
arguments for theism. It is one of the most remarkable arguments ever set forth. First
set forth by St. Anselm (1033–1109), in the eleventh century, the argument has continued to puzzle and fascinate philosophers ever since.

The argument is not only important because it claims to be an *a priori* proof for the
existence of God, but it also is the primary locus of such philosophical problems as
whether existence is a property and whether the notion of necessary existence is intelligible. Furthermore, it has special religious significance because it is the only one of
the traditional arguments which clearly concludes to the necessary properties of God,
i.e., his omnipotence, omniscience, omnibenevolence, and so on.

Although there are many versions of the ontological argument and many inter-
pretations of some of these, most philosophers agree on the essential form of Anselm's
version in the second chapter of his *Proslogium*. Anselm believes that God's existence is
absolutely certain, so that only a fool would doubt or deny it. Yet he desires understanding to fulfill his faith.

The argument that follows may be treated as a *reductio ad absurdum* argument.
That is, it begins with a supposition (S: suppose that the greatest conceivable being
exists in the mind alone) that is contradictory to what one desires to prove and then
one goes about showing that (S) together with other certain or self-evident assumptions (A_1 and A_2) yields a contradiction, which in turn demonstrates that the contradictory of (S) must be true. A greatest possible being must exist in reality; I shall leave
it to you to work out the details of the argument.

Anselm's contemporary, Gaunilo, sets forth the first objection to Anselm's argument. Accusing Anselm of pulling rabbits out of hats, he tells the story of a delectable lost island, one that is more excellent than all lands. Since it is better that such a perfect island exists in reality than simply in the mind alone, this Isle of the Blest must necessarily exist. Anselm's reply is that the analogy fails, for unlike the greatest possible being, the greatest possible island can be conceived as not existing. Recently, Alvin Plantinga has clarified Anselm's point. There simply are some properties that do have intrinsic maximums and some properties that don't have them. No matter how wonderful you make the Isle of the Blest, we can conceive of a more wonderful island. The greatness of islands is like the greatness of numbers in this respect. There is no greatest natural number, for no matter how large the number you choose, we can always conceive of one twice as large. On the other hand, the properties of God have intrinsic maximums. For example, we can define perfect knowledge this way. For any proposition an omniscient being knows whether it is true or false.

II.5 The Ontological Argument

ST. ANSELM AND GAUNILO

St. Anselm (c. 1033–1109) was Abbot of Bec and later Archbishop of Canterbury. He wrote several important treatises on theological subjects, including *Cur Deus Homo* (*Why God Became Man*). In this selection from his *Proslogium,* he begins with the definition of God as "that than which nothing greater can be conceived." Today we might translate that as "the greatest possible being." From that definition he proceeds to argue for the necessary existence of God.

Gaunilo was an eleventh-century Benedictine monk who first criticized Anselm's argument. Little is known about him.

Study Questions

1. Note that St. Anselm begins his argument with a prayer to God. Is this significant for understanding the argument? What does his request show about Anselm's assumptions?

2. What is the significance of the analogy with the painter?

3. After an initial reading, attempt to outline the argument. Do you agree with Anselm that it proves the existence of God?

4. What is Gaunilo's criticism of the argument? Is it plausible?

5. Evaluate Anselm's rejoinder.

St. Anselm's Presentation

Truly there is a God, although the fool hath said in his heart, There is no God.

AND SO, LORD, DO THOU, who dost give understanding to faith, give me, so far as thou knowest it to be profitable, to understand that thou art as we believe; and that thou art that which we believe. And, indeed, we believe that thou art a being than which nothing greater can be conceived. Or is there no such nature, since the fool hath said in his heart, there is no God? (Psalms xiii, 1). But, at any rate, this very fool, when he hears of this being of which I speak—a being than which nothing greater can be conceived—understands what he hears, and what he understands is in his understanding; although he does not understand it to exist.

For, it is one thing for an object to be in the understanding, and another to understand that the object exists. When a painter first conceives of what he will afterwards perform, he has it in his understanding, but he does not yet understand it to be, because he has not yet performed it. But after he has made the painting, he both has it in his understanding, and he understands that it exists, because he has made it.

Hence, even the fool is convinced that something exists in the understanding, at least, than which nothing greater can be conceived. For, when he hears of this, he understands it. And whatever is understood, exists in the understanding. And assuredly that, than which nothing greater can be conceived, cannot exist in the understanding alone. For, suppose it exists in the understanding alone: then it can be conceived to exist in reality; which is greater.

Therefore, if that, than which nothing greater can be conceived, exists in the understanding alone, the very being, than which nothing greater can be conceived, is one, than which a greater can be conceived. But obviously this is impossible. Hence, there is no doubt that there exists a being, than which nothing greater can be conceived, and it exists both in the understanding and in reality.

God cannot be conceived not to exist.—God is that, than which nothing greater can be conceived.— That which can be conceived not to exist is not God.

And it assuredly exists so truly, that it cannot be conceived not to exist. For, it is possible to conceive of a being which cannot be conceived not to exist; and this is greater than one which can be conceived not to exist. Hence, if that, than which nothing greater can be conceived, can be conceived not to exist, it is not that, than which nothing greater can be conceived. But this is an irreconcilable contradiction. There is, then, so truly a being than which nothing greater can be conceived to exist, that it cannot even be conceived not to exist; and this being thou art, O Lord, our God.

So truly, therefore, dost thou exist, O Lord, my God, that thou canst not be conceived not to exist; and rightly. For, if a mind could conceive of a being better than thee, the creature would rise above the Creator; and this is most absurd. And, indeed, whatever else there is, except thee alone, can be conceived not to exist. To thee alone, therefore, it belongs to exist more truly than all other beings, and hence in a higher degree than all others. For, whatever else exists does not exist so truly, and hence in a less degree it belongs to it to exist. Why, then, has the fool said in his heart, there is no God (Psalms xiii, 1), since it is so evident, to a rational mind, that thou dost exist in the highest degree of all? Why, except that he is dull and a fool?

How the fool has said in his heart what cannot be conceived.—A thing may be conceived in two ways:

These extracts are from Anselm's Proslogium, *Gaunilo's* In Behalf of the Fool, *and Anselm's* "Apologetic." *Reprinted from St. Anselm,* Basic Writings, *trans. S. W. Deane, by permission of The Open Court Publishing Company. Copyrighted by The Open Court Publishing Co. 1903. Second copyright © by The Open Court Publishing Co. 1962.*

(1) when the word signifying it is conceived; (2) when the thing itself is understood. As far as the word goes, God can be conceived not to exist; in reality he cannot.

But how has the fool said in his heart what he could not conceive; or how is it that he could not conceive what he said in his heart? since it is the same to say in the heart, and to conceive.

But, if really, nay, since really, he both conceived, because he said in his heart; and did not say in his heart, because he could not conceive; there is more than one way in which a thing is said in the heart or conceived. For, in one sense, an object is conceived, when the word signifying it is conceived; and in another, when the very entity, which the object is, is understood.

In the former sense, then, God can be conceived not to exist; but in the latter, not at all. For no one who understands what fire and water are can conceive fire to be water, in accordance with the nature of the facts themselves, although this is possible according to the words. So, then, no one who understands what God is can conceive that God does not exist; although he says these words in his heart, either without any or with some foreign, signification. For, God is that than which a greater cannot be conceived. And he who thoroughly understands this, assuredly understands that this being so truly exists, that not even in concept can it be nonexistent. Therefore, he who understands that God so exists, cannot conceive that he does not exist.

I thank thee, gracious Lord, I thank thee; because what I formerly believed by thy bounty, I now so understand by thine illumination, that if I were unwilling to believe that thou dost exist, I should not be able not to understand this to be true.

Gaunilo's Criticism

For example: it is said that somewhere in the ocean is an island, which, because of the difficulty, or rather the impossibility, of discovering what does not exist, is called the lost island. And they say that this island has an inestimable wealth of all manner of riches and delicacies in greater abundance than is told of the Islands of the Blest; and that having no owner or inhabitant, it is more excellent than all other countries, which are inhabited by mankind, in the abundance with which it is stored.

Now if some one should tell me that there is such an island, I should easily understand his words, in which there is no difficulty. But suppose that he went on to say, as if by a logical inference: "You can no longer doubt that this island which is more excellent than all lands exists somewhere, since you have no doubt that it is in your understanding. And since it is more excellent not to be in the understanding alone, but to exist both in the understanding and in reality, for this reason it must exist. For if it does not exist, any land which really exists will be more excellent than it; and so the island already understood by you to be more excellent will not be more excellent."

If a man should try to prove to me by such reasoning that this island truly exists, and that its existence should no longer be doubted, either I should believe that he was jesting, or I know not which I ought to regard as the greater fool: myself, supposing that I should allow this proof; or him, if he should suppose that he had established with any certainty the existence of this island. For he ought to show first that the hypothetical excellence of this island exists as a real and indubitable fact, and in no wise as any unreal object, or one whose existence is uncertain, in my understanding.

St. Anselm's Rejoinder

A criticism of Gaunilo's example, in which he tries to show that in this way the real existence of a lost island might be inferred from the fact of its being conceived.

But, you say, it is as if one should suppose an island in the ocean, which surpasses all lands in its fertility, and which, because of the difficulty, or rather the impossibility, of discovering what does not exist, is called a lost island; and should say that there can be no doubt that this island truly exists in reality, for this reason, that one who hears it described easily understands what he hears.

Now I promise confidently that if any man shall devise anything existing either in reality or in concept alone (except that than which a greater cannot be conceived) to which he can adapt the sequence of my reasoning, I will discover that thing, and will give him his lost island, not to be lost again.

But it now appears that this being than which a greater is inconceivable cannot be conceived not to be, because it exists on so assured a ground of truth; for otherwise it would not exist at all.

Hence, if any one says that he conceives this being not to exist, I say that at the time when he conceives of this either he conceives of a being than which a greater is inconceivable, or he does not conceive at all. If he does not conceive, he does not conceive of the non-existence of that of which he does not conceive. But if he does conceive, he certainly conceives of a being which cannot be even conceived not to exist. For if it could be conceived not to exist, it could be conceived to have a beginning and an end. But this is impossible.

He, then, who conceives of this being conceives of a being which cannot be even conceived not to exist; but he who conceives of this being does not conceive that it does not exist; else he conceives what is inconceivable. The non-existence, then, of that than which a greater cannot be conceived is inconceivable.

For Further Reflection

1. Some philosophers have objected that Anselm misunderstands the concept of "being." Being is not an ordinary concept like "red" or "horse," but an instantiating concept which asserts that these other concepts are exemplified (e.g., the concept unicorn is not exemplified, but the concept of horse is). It makes no sense, they contend, to say that being is exemplified. Are they correct?

2. Is it greater to exist than not to exist, as Anselm argues? Or is the term "greater" ambiguously or wrongly used here?

3. Could a similar argument as Anselm's be used to prove that a perfectly powerful devil exists as the supreme being and creator of all things?

Why Is There Evil?

Is he willing to prevent evil, but not able? then he is impotent. Is he able, but not willing? then he is malevolent. Is he both able and willing? whence then is evil? [Epicurus 341–270 B.C.]

We have been looking at arguments in favor of God's existence. The agnostic and atheist usually base their case on the *absence* of evidence for God's existence. But they have one arrow in their own quiver, an argument for disbelief. It is the problem of evil. From it the "atheologian" (one who argues against the existence of God) hopes either to neutralize any positive evidence for God's existence based on whatever in the traditional arguments survives their criticism or to demonstrate that it is unreasonable to believe in God.

The problem of evil arises because of the paradox of an omnibenevolent, omnipotent deity allowing the existence of evil. The Judeo-Christian tradition has affirmed these three propositions:

1. God is all-powerful (including omniscience).
2. God is perfectly good.
3. Evil exists.

But if he is perfectly good, why does he allow evil to exist? Why didn't he create a better world, if not with no evil, at least with substantially less evil than in this world? Many have contended that this paradox, first schematized by Epicurus, is worse than a paradox. It is an implicit contradiction for it contains premises that are inconsistent with one another. They argue something like the following:

4. If God (an all-powerful, omniscient, omnibenevolent being) exists, there would be no (or no unnecessary) evil in the world.
5. There is evil (or unnecessary evil) in the world.
6. Therefore, God does not exist.

You will want to examine each of these premises carefully. A few words are in order. Generally, Western thought has distinguished between two types of evil: moral and natural. "Moral evil" covers all those bad things for which humans are morally responsible. "Natural evil" or "surd evil" stands for all those terrible events that nature does of her own accord, e.g., hurricanes, tornados, earthquakes, volcano eruptions, natural diseases, which bring on suffering to humans and animals. However, some defenses of theism affirm that all evil is essentially moral evil. Here the devil is brought in as the cause of natural evil.

The main defense of theism in the light of evil is the *free will defense,* going back as far as St. Augustine (354–430) and receiving modern treatment in the work of John Hick, Alvin Plantinga, and Richard Swinburne. The free will defense adds a fourth premise to Epicurus' paradox in order to show that premises 1–3 are consistent and not contradictory. This premise is:

7. It is logically impossible for God to create free creatures and guarantee that they will never do evil.

The proponent of the free will defense claims that all moral evil derives from creature freedom of the will. But what about natural evil? How does the theist account for it? There are two different ways. The first one, suggested by Alvin Plantinga (cf. bibliography), is to attribute natural evil to the work of the devil and his angels. Disease and tornados are caused by the devil and his minion. The second way, favored by Hick and Swinburne, argues that natural evil is part and parcel of the nature of things: a result of the combination of deterministic physical laws which are necessary for consistent action and the responsibility given to humans to exercise their freedom.

There is one further distinction necessary to work through this problem. Some theists attempt to answer the charge of inconsistency by simply showing that there is no formal contradiction between propositions 1–3, so that the nontheist hasn't proved his point. But others want to go beyond this negative function and offer a plausible account of evil. These latter are called "theodicists," for they attempt to justify the ways of God before humankind. They endeavor to show that God allows the temporary evil in order to bring out greater good. In our reading, John Hick represents the theodicist position.

The Problem of Evil Counts Against God   II.6

FYODOR DOSTOEVSKI

Fyodor Dostoevski (1822–1881) was one of the greatest Russian novelists. He was born in Moscow. His revolutionary sympathies and a penchant for gambling managed to keep him in constant danger. Among his famous writings are *Crime and Punishment* (1866), *The Idiot* (1868), and *The Brothers Karamazov* (1880), from which our reading is taken.

In this scene from Dostoevski's most famous work, Ivan Karamazov is relating to his pious brother, Alyosha, a Christian monk, why he cannot accept God.

Study Questions

1. Does Ivan believe that God exists? What does he think of the hypothesis that humanity invented the notion of God?

2. Does Ivan think that we can understand God? Why or why not?

3. What is Ivan's creed? Has he stated his position very clearly or consistently? How can he speak of God as holy and yet admit that God is the cause of children's suffering?

4. What does Ivan mean in saying that there can be solidarity with the suffering and guilt of humanity (or other adults) but not with children?

5. What is Ivan's response to the proposal that the solution of the problem of evil is to be found in an eternal harmony?

6. What does he mean when he says, "I most respectfully return Him the ticket"?

"WELL, TELL ME WHERE TO BEGIN, give your orders. The existence of God, eh?"

"Begin where you like. You declared yesterday at father's that there was no God." Alyosha looked searchingly at his brother.

"I said that yesterday at dinner on purpose to tease you and I saw your eyes glow. But now I've no objection to discussing with you, and I say so very seriously. I want to be friends with you, Alyosha, for I have no friends and want to try it. Well, only fancy, perhaps I too accept God," laughed Ivan, "that's a surprise for you, isn't it?"

From Fyodor Dostoevski, The Brothers Karamazov, *trans. by Constance Garnett (London: Heinemann, 1912).*

"Yes of course, if you are not joking now."

"Joking? I was told at the elder's yesterday that I was joking. You know, dear boy, there was an old sinner in the eighteenth century who declared that, if there were no God, he would have to be invented. . . . And man has actually invented God. And what's strange, what would be marvelous, is not that God should really exist; the marvel is that such an idea, the idea of the necessity of God, could enter the head of such a savage, vicious beast as man. So holy it is, so touching, so wise and so great a credit it does to man. As for me, I've long resolved not to think whether man created God or God man. . . . For what are we aiming at now? I am trying to explain as quickly as possible my essential nature, that is what manner of man I am, what I believe in, and for what I hope, that's it, isn't it? And therefore I tell you that I accept God simply. But you must note this: if God exists and if He really did create the world, then, as we all know, He created it according to the geometry of Euclid and the human mind with the conception of only three dimensions in space. Yet there have been and still are geometricians and philosophers, and even some of the most distinguished, who doubt whether the whole universe, or to speak more widely the whole of being, was only created in Euclid's geometry; they even dare to dream that two parallel lines, which according to Euclid can never meet on earth, may meet somewhere in infinity. I have come to the conclusion that, since I can't understand even that, I can't expect to understand about God. I acknowledge humbly that I have no faculty for settling such questions. I have a Euclidian earthly mind, and how could I solve problems that are not of this world? And I advise you never to think about it either, my dear Alyosha, especially about God, whether He exists or not. All such questions are utterly inappropriate for a mind created with an idea of only three dimensions. And so I accept God and am glad to, and what's more I accept His wisdom, His purpose—which are utterly beyond our ken; I believe in the underlying order and the meaning of life; I believe in the eternal harmony in which they say we shall one day be blended. I believe in the Word to Which the universe is striving, and Which Itself was 'with God,' and Which Itself is God and so on, and so on, to infinity. There are all sorts of phrases for it. I seem to be on the right path, don't I? Yet would you believe it, in the final result I don't accept this world of God's, and, although I know it exists, I don't accept it at all. It's not that I don't accept God, you must understand, it's the world created by Him I don't and cannot accept. Let me make it plain. I believe like a child that suffering will be healed and made up for, that all the humiliating absurdity of human contradictions will vanish like a pitiful mirage, like the despicable fabrication of the impotent and infinitely small Euclidian mind of man, that in the world's finale, at the moment of eternal harmony, something so precious will come to pass that it will suffice for all hearts, for the comforting of all resentments, for the atonement of all the crimes of humanity, of all the blood they've shed; that it will make it not only possible to forgive but to justify all that has happened with men—but though all that may come to pass, I don't accept it. I won't accept it. Even if parallel lines do meet and I see it myself, I shall see it and say that they've met, but still I won't accept it. That's what's at the root of me, Alyosha; that's my creed.

". . . Do you understand why this infamy must be and is permitted? Without it, I am told, man could not have known good and evil. Why should he know that diabolical good and evil when it costs so much? Why, the whole world of knowledge is not worth that child's prayer to 'dear, Kind God'! I say nothing of the sufferings of grown-up people, they have eaten the apple, damn them, and the devil take them all! But these little ones! I am making you suffer, Alyosha, you are not yourself. I'll leave off if you like."

"Never mind. I want to suffer too," muttered Alyosha.

"One picture, only one more, because it's so

curious, so characteristic, and I have only just read it in some collection of Russian antiquities. I've forgotten the name. I must look it up. It was in the darkest days of serfdom at the beginning of the century, and long live the Liberator of the People! There was in those days a general of aristocratic connections, the owner of great estates, one of these men—somewhat exceptional, I believe, even then—who, retiring from the service into a life of leisure, are convinced that they've earned absolute power over the lives of their subjects. There were such men then. So our general, settled on his property of two thousand souls, lives in pomp and domineers over his poor neighbors as though they were dependents and buffoons. He has kennels of hundreds of hounds and nearly a hundred dog-boys—all mounted, and in uniform. One day a serf boy, a little child of eight, threw a stone in play and hurt the paw of the general's favorite hound. 'Why is my favorite dog lame?' He is told that the boy threw a stone that hurt the dog's paw. 'So you did it.' The general looked the child up and down. 'Take him.' He was taken—taken from his mother and kept shut up all night. Early that morning the general comes out on horseback, with the hounds, his dependents, dog-boys, and huntsmen, all mounted around him in full hunting parade. The servants are summoned for their edification, and in front of them all stands the mother of the child. The child is brought from the lockup. It's a gloomy, cold, foggy autumn day, a capital day for hunting. The general orders the child to be undressed; the child is stripped naked. He shivers, numb with terror not daring to cry. . . . 'Make him run,' commands the general. 'Run! run!' shout the dog-boys. The boy runs. . . . 'At him!' yells the general, and he sets the whole pack of hounds on the child. The hounds catch him, and tear him to pieces before his mother's eyes! . . . I believe the general was afterwards declared incapable of administering his estates. Well—what did he deserve? To be shot? to be shot for the satisfaction of our moral feelings? Speak, Alyosha!"

"To be shot," murmured Alyosha, lifting his eyes to Ivan with a pale twisted smile.

"Bravo!" cried Ivan delighted. "If even you say so . . . You're a pretty monk! So there is a little devil sitting in your heart, Alyosha Karamazov!"

"What I said was absurd, but—"

"That's just the point that 'but'!" cried Ivan. "Let me tell you, novice, that the absurd is only too necessary on earth. The world stands on absurdities, and perhaps nothing would have come to pass in it without them. We know what we know!"

"What do you know?"

"I understand nothing," Ivan went on, as though in delirium. "I don't want to understand anything now. I want to stick to the fact. I made up my mind long ago not to understand. If I try to understand anything, I shall be false to the fact and I have determined to stick to the fact."

"Why are you trying me?" Alyosha cried, with sudden distress. "Will you say what you mean at last?"

"Of course, I will; that's what I've been leading up to. You are dear to me, I don't want to let you go, and I won't give you up to your Zossima."

Ivan for a minute was silent, his face became all at once very sad.

"Listen! I took the case of the children only to make my case clearer. Of the other tears of humanity with which the earth is soaked from its crust to its center, I will say nothing. I have narrowed my subject on purpose. I am a bug, and I recognize in all humility that I cannot understand why the world is arranged as it is. Men are themselves to blame, I suppose; they were given paradise, they wanted freedom, and stole fire from heaven, though they knew they would become unhappy, so there is no need to pity them. With my pitiful, earthly, Euclidian understanding, all I know is that there is suffering and that there are none guilty; that cause follows effect, simply and directly; that everything flows and finds its level—but that's only Euclidian nonsense, I know that, and I can't consent to live by it! What comfort is it to me that there are none guilty and that cause follows effect simply and directly, and that I know it—I must have justice, or I will destroy myself. And not justice in some remote infinite time and space, but here on earth, and that I could see myself. I have believed in it. I want to see it, and if I am dead by then, let me rise again, for if it all happens without me, it will be too unfair. Surely I haven't suffered, simply that I, my crimes and my sufferings, may manure the soil of the future harmony for somebody else. I want to see with my own eyes the hind lie down with the lion and the victim rise up and embrace his murderer. I want to be there when everyone suddenly understands what it has all been for. All the religions of the world are built on this longing, and I am a believer. But then there are the children, and what am I to do about them? That's a question I can't answer. For the hundredth time I repeat, there are numbers of questions, but I've only taken the children, because in their case what I mean is so unanswerably clear. Listen! If all must suffer to pay for the eternal harmony, what have children to do with it, tell me, please? It's beyond all comprehension why they should suffer, and why they should pay for the harmony. Why should they, too, furnish material to enrich the soil for the harmony of the future? I understand solidarity in sin among men. I understand solidarity in retribution, too; but there can be no such solidarity with children. And if it is really true that they must share responsibility for all their fathers' crimes, such a truth is not of this world and is beyond my comprehension. Some jester will say, perhaps, that the child would have grown up and have sinned, but you see he didn't grow up, he was torn to pieces by the dogs, at eight years old. Oh, Alyosha, I am not blaspheming! I understand, of course, what an upheaval of the universe it will be, when everything in heaven and earth blends in one hymn of praise and everything that lives and has lived cries aloud: 'Thou art just, O Lord, for Thy ways are revealed,' when the mother embraces the fiend who threw

her child to the dogs, and all three cry aloud with tears, 'Thou are just, O Lord!' then, of course, the crown of knowledge will be reached and all will be made clear. But what pulls me up here is that I can't accept that harmony. And while I am on earth, I make haste to take my own measures. You see, Alyosha, perhaps it really may happen that if I live to that moment, or rise again to see it, I, too, perhaps, may cry aloud with the rest, looking at the mother embracing the child's torturer, 'Thou art just, O Lord!' but I don't want to cry aloud then. While there is still time, I hasten to protect myself and so I renounce the higher harmony altogether. It's not worth the tears of that one tortured child who beat itself on the breast with its little fist and prayed in its stinking outhouse, with its unexpiated tears to 'dear, kind God'! It's not worth it, because those tears are unatoned for. They must be atoned for, or there can be no harmony. But how? How are you going to atone for them? Is it possible? By their being avenged? But what do I care for avenging them? What do I care for a hell for oppressors? What good can hell do, since those children have already been tortured? And what becomes of harmony, if there is hell? I want to forgive. I want to embrace. I don't want more suffering. And if the sufferings of children go to swell the sum of sufferings which was necessary to pay for truth, then I protest that the truth is not worth such a price. I don't want the mother to embrace the oppressor who threw her son to the dogs! She dare not forgive him! Let her forgive him for herself, if she will, let her forgive the torturer for the immeasurable suffering of her mother's heart. But the sufferings of her tortured child she has no right to forgive; she dare not forgive the torturer, even if the child were to forgive him! And if that is so, if they dare not forgive, what becomes of harmony? Is there in the whole world a being who would have the right to forgive and could forgive? I don't want harmony. From love for humanity I don't want it. I would rather be left with the unavenged suffering. I would rather remain with my unavenged suffering and un- satisfied indignation, *even if I were wrong*. Be- sides, too high a price is asked for harmony; it's beyond our means to pay so much to enter on it. And so I hasten to give back my entrance ticket, and if I am an honest man I am bound to give it back as soon as possible. And that I am doing. It's not God that I don't accept, Alyosha, only I most respectfully return Him the ticket."

"That's rebellion," murmured Alyosha, look- ing down.

"Rebellion? I am sorry you call it that," said Ivan earnestly. "One can hardly live in rebellion, and I want to live. Tell me yourself, I challenge you—answer. Imagine that you are creating a fabric of human destiny with the object of making men happy in the end, giving them peace and rest at last, but that it was essential and inevitable to torture to death only one tiny creature—that baby beating its breast with its fist, for instance—and to found that edifice on its unavenged tears, would you consent to be the architect on those conditions? Tell me, and tell the truth."

"No, I wouldn't consent," said Alyosha softly.

For Further Reflection

1. There are three propositions involved in the traditional formulation of the problem of evil: a. God is all-powerful (including omniscience); b. God is perfectly good; and c. Evil exists. How would Ivan deal with them?

2. Do you think that the fact of evil counts against the proposition that God exists? Ex- plain why or why not.

3. Some people believe that we are completely causally determined, a subject that will be discussed in Part V. What will they make of the free will defense?

There Is a Reason Why God Allows Evil   II.7

JOHN HICK

John Hick (1922–) was for many years professor of theology at the University of Bir- mingham in England. He is now professor of philosophy at Claremont Graduate School. His book *Evil and the God of Love* (1966) is considered one of the most thor- ough treatises on the problem of evil. Our reading is a shorter version of some of the ideas presented there. Hick presents a *theodicy,* a justification of God's creation in the face of evil. Theodicies can be of two types, depending on how they justify the ways of God. The Augustinian position is that God created humans without sin and set them in a sinless, paradisical world. However, humanity fell into sin through misuse of its free will. God's grace will save some of us, but others will perish everlastingly. The second type of theodicy stems from the thinking of Irenaeus (120–202), of the Greek church. The Irenaean tradition views Adam not as a free agent rebelling against God, but as a child. The fall is humanity's first faulty step in the direction of freedom. God is still working with humanity in order to bring it from undeveloped life (*bios:* biological life) to a state of self-realization in divine love, spiritual life (*zoe*). This life is a vale of soul-making.

Hick accepts the soul-making view of life in this defense of God's ways in the face of evil.

Study Questions

1. Why is the problem of evil a dilemma?
2. Which solutions to the problem does Hick rule out as unacceptable?
3. Does the Hebrew-Christian view of the world judge matter to be evil?
4. What is a *negative* theodicy?
5. What does Hick mean by *moral* versus *non-moral* evil?
6. Why couldn't God create people who were both free and totally good?
7. What does Hick say about non-moral evil? Why is it here and what is its function in human development?
8. According to Hick what is the purpose of our creation?
9. Why does Hick reject a world without suffering and harm?

TO MANY, THE MOST powerful positive objection to belief in God is the fact of evil. Probably for most agnostics it is the appalling depth and extent of human suffering, more than anything else, that makes the idea of a loving Creator seem too implausible and disposes them toward one or another of the various naturalistic theories of religion.

As a challenge to theism, the problem of evil has traditionally been posed in the form of a dilemma: if God is perfectly loving, he must wish to abolish evil; and if he is all-powerful, he must be able to abolish evil. But evil exists; therefore God cannot be both omnipotent and perfectly loving.

Certain solutions, which at once suggest themselves, have to be ruled out so far as the Judaic-Christian faith is concerned.

To say, for example (with contemporary Christian Science), that evil is an illusion of the human mind, is impossible within a religion based upon the stark realism of the Bible. Its pages faithfully reflect the characteristic mixture of good and evil in human experience. They record every kind of sorrow and suffering, every mode of man's inhumanity to man and of his painfully insecure existence in the world. There is no attempt to regard evil as anything but dark, menacingly ugly, heartrending, and crushing. In the Christian scriptures, the climax of this history of evil is the crucifixion of Jesus, which is presented not only as a case of utterly unjust suffering, but as the violent and murderous rejection of God's Messiah. There can be no doubt, then, that for biblical faith, evil is unambiguously evil, and stands in direct opposition to God's will.

Again, to solve the problem of evil by means of the theory (sponsored for example, by the Boston "Personalist" School) of a finite deity

From John Hick, Philosophy of Religion, *3 ed.,* © *1963, pp. 40–46. Reprinted by permission of Prentice-Hall, Inc., Englewood Cliffs, New Jersey.*

who does the best he can with a material, intractable and coeternal with himself, is to have abandoned the basic premise of Hebrew-Christian monotheism; for the theory amounts to rejecting belief in the infinity and sovereignty of God.

Indeed, any theory which would avoid the problem of the origin of evil by depicting it as an ultimate constituent of the universe, coordinate with good, has been repudiated in advance by the classic Christian teaching, first developed by Augustine, that evil represents the going wrong of something which in itself is good. Augustine holds firmly to the Hebrew-Christian conviction that the universe is *good*—that is to say, it is the creation of a good God for a good purpose. He completely rejects the ancient prejudice, widespread in his day, that matter is evil. There are, according to Augustine, higher and lower, greater and lesser goods in immense abundance and variety; but everything which has being is good in its own way and degree, except in so far as it may have become spoiled or corrupted. Evil—whether it be an evil will, an instance of pain, or some disorder or decay in nature—has not been set there by God, but represents the distortion of something that is inherently valuable. Whatever exists is, as such, and in its proper place, good: evil is essentially parasitic upon good, being disorder and perversion in a fundamentally good creation. This understanding of evil as something negative means that it is not willed and created by God; but it does not mean (as some have supposed) that evil is unreal and can be disregarded. On the contrary, the first effect of this doctrine is to accentuate even more the question of the origin of evil.

Theodicy,[1] as many modern Christian thinkers see it, is a modest enterprise, negative rather than positive in its conclusions. It does not claim to explain, nor to explain away, every instance of evil in human experience, but only to point to certain considerations which prevent the fact of evil (largely incomprehensible though it remains) from constituting a final and insuperable bar to rational belief in God.

In indicating these considerations it will be useful to follow the traditional division of the subject. There is the problem of *moral evil* or wickedness: why does an all-good and all-powerful God permit this? And there is the problem of the *non-moral evil* of suffering and pain, both physical and mental: why has an all-good and all-powerful God created a world in which this occurs?

Christian thought has always considered moral evil in its relation to human freedom and responsibility. To be a person is to be a finite center of freedom, a (relatively) free and self-directing agent responsible for one's own decisions. This involves being free to act wrongly as well as to act rightly. The idea of a person who can be infallibly guaranteed always to act rightly is self-contradictory. There can be no guarantee in advance that a genuinely free moral agent will never choose amiss. Consequently, the possibility of wrongdoing or sin is logically inseparable from the creation of finite persons, and to say that God should not have created beings who might sin amounts to saying he should not have created people.

This thesis has been challenged in some recent philosophical discussions of the problem of evil, in which it is claimed that no contradiction is involved in saying that God might have made people who would be genuinely free and who could yet be guaranteed always to act rightly. A quote from one of these discussions follows:

> If there is no logical impossibility in a man's freely choosing the good on one, or on several occasions, there cannot be a logical impossibility in his freely choosing the good on every occasion. God was not, then, faced with a choice between making innocent automata and making beings who, in acting freely, would sometimes go wrong: there was open to him the obviously better possibility of making beings who would act freely but always go right. Clearly, his failure to avail himself of this possibility is inconsistent with his being both omnipotent and wholly good.[2]

A reply to this argument is suggested in another recent contribution to the discussion.[3] If by a free action we mean an action which is not externally compelled but which flows from the nature of the agent as he reacts to the circumstances in which he finds himself, there is, indeed, no contradiction between our being free and our actions being "caused" (by our own nature) and therefore being in principle predictable. There is a contradiction, however, in saying that God is the cause of our acting as we do but that we are free beings in relation to God. There is, in other words, a contradiction in saying that God has made us so that we shall of necessity act in a certain way, and that we are genuinely independent persons in relation to him. If all our thoughts and actions are divinely predestined, however free and morally responsible we may seem to be to ourselves, we cannot be free and morally responsible in the sight of God, but must instead be his helpless puppets. Such "freedom" is like that of a patient acting out a series of post-hypnotic suggestions: he appears, even to himself, to be free, but his volitions have actually been pre-determined by another will, that of the hypnotist, in relation to whom the patient is not a free agent.

A different objector might raise the question of whether or not we deny God's omnipotence if we admit that he is unable to create persons who are free from the risks inherent in personal freedom. The answer that has always been given is that to create such beings is logically impossible. It is no limitation upon God's power that he cannot accomplish the logically impossible, since there is nothing here to accomplish, but only a meaningless conjunction of words—in this case "person who is not a person." God is able to create beings of any and every conceivable kind; but creatures who lack moral freedom, however superior they might be to human beings in other respects, would not be what we mean by persons. They would constitute a different form of life which God might have brought into existence instead of persons. When we ask why God did not create such beings in place of persons, the traditional answer is that only persons could, in any meaningful sense, become "children of God," capable of entering into a personal relationship with their Creator by a free and uncompelled response to his love.

When we turn from the possibility of moral evil as a correlate of man's personal freedom to its actuality, we face something which must remain inexplicable even when it can be seen to be possible. For we can never provide a complete causal explanation of a free act; if we could, it would not be a free act. The origin of moral evil lies forever concealed within the mystery of human freedom.

The necessary connection between moral freedom and the possibility, now actualized, of sin throws light upon a great deal of the suffering which afflicts mankind. For an enormous amount of human pain arises either from the inhumanity or the culpable incompetence of mankind. This includes such major scourges as poverty, oppression and persecution, war, and all the injustice, indignity, and inequity which occur even in the most advanced societies. These evils are manifestations of human sin. Even disease is fostered to an extent, the limits of which have not yet been determined by psychosomatic medicine, by moral and emotional factors seated both in the individual and in his social environment. To the extent that all of these evils stem from human failures and wrong decisions, their possibility is inherent in the creation of free persons inhabiting a world which presents them with real choices which are followed by real consequences.

We may now turn more directly to the problem of suffering. Even though the major bulk of actual human pain is traceable to man's misused freedom as a sole or part cause, there remain other sources of pain which are entirely independent of the human will, for example, earthquake, hurricane, storm, flood, drought, and blight. In practice it is often impossible to trace a boundary between the suffering which results from human wickedness and folly and that which falls upon mankind from without. Both kinds of suffering are inextricably mingled together in human experience. For our present purpose, however, it is important to note that the latter category does exist and that it seems to be built into the very structure of our world. In response to it, theodicy, if it is wisely conducted, follows a negative path. It is not possible to show positively that each item of human pain serves the divine purpose of good; but, on the other hand, it does seem possible to show that the divine purpose as it is understood in Judaism and Christianity could not be forwarded in a world which was designed as a permanent hedonistic paradise.

An essential premise of this argument concerns the divine purpose in creating the world. The skeptic's assumption is that man is to be viewed as a completed creation and that God's purpose in making the world was to provide a suitable dwelling-place for this fully-formed creature. Since God is good and loving, the environment which he has created for human life to inhabit is naturally as pleasant and comfortable as possible. The problem is essentially similar to that of a man who builds a cage for some pet animal. Since our world, in fact, contains sources of hardship, inconvenience, and danger of innumerable kinds, the conclusion follows that this world cannot have been created by a perfectly benevolent and all-powerful deity.

Christianity, however, has never supposed that God's purpose in the creation of the world was to construct a paradise whose inhabitants would experience a maximum of pleasure and a minimum of pain. The world is seen, instead, as a place of "soul-making" in which free beings, grappling with the tasks and challenges of their existence in a common environment, may become "children of God" and "heirs of eternal life." A way of thinking theologically of God's continuing creative purpose for man was suggested by some of the early Hellenistic Fathers of the Christian Church, especially Irenaeus. Following hints from St. Paul, Irenaeus taught that man has been made as a person in the image

of God but has not yet been brought as a free and responsible agent into the finite likeness of God, which is revealed in Christ. Our world, with all its rough edges, is the sphere in which this second and harder stage of the creative process is taking place.

This conception of the world (whether or not set in Irenaeus' theological framework) can be supported by the method of negative theodicy. Suppose, contrary to fact, that this world were a paradise from which all possibility of pain and suffering were excluded. The consequences would be very far-reaching. For example, no one could ever injure anyone else; the murderer's knife would turn to paper or his bullets to thin air; the bank safe, robbed of a million dollars, would miraculously become filled with another million dollars (without this device, on however large a scale, proving inflationary); fraud, deceit, conspiracy, and treason would somehow always leave the fabric of society undamaged. Again, no one would ever be injured by accident: the mountain-climber, steeplejack, or playing child falling from a height would float unharmed to the ground; the reckless driver would never meet with disaster. There would be no need to work, since no harm could result from avoiding work; there would be no call to be concerned for others in time of need or danger, for in such a world there could be no real needs or dangers.

To make possible this continual series of individual adjustments, nature would have to work by "special providences" instead of running according to general laws which men must learn to respect on penalty of pain or death. The laws of nature would have to be extremely flexible: sometimes gravity would operate, sometimes not; sometimes an object would be hard and solid, sometimes soft. There could be no sciences, for there would be no enduring world structure to investigate. In eliminating the problems and hardships of an objective environment, with its own laws, life would become like a dream in which, delightfully but aimlessly, we would float and drift at ease.

One can at least begin to imagine such a world. It is evident that our present ethical concepts would have no meaning in it. If, for example, the notion of harming someone is an essential element in the concept of a wrong action, in our hedonistic paradise there could be no wrong actions—nor any right actions in distinction from wrong. Courage and fortitude would have no point in an environment in which there is, by definition, no danger of difficulty. Generosity, kindness, the *agape* aspect of love, prudence, unselfishness, and all other ethical notions which presuppose life in a stable environment, could not even be formed. Consequently, such a world, however well it might promote pleasure, would be very ill adapted for the development of the moral qualities of human personality. In relation to this purpose it would be the worst of all possible worlds.

It would seem, then, that an environment intended to make possible the growth in free beings of the finest characteristics of personal life, must have a good deal in common with our present world. It must operate according to general and dependable laws; and it must involve real dangers, difficulties, problems, obstacles, and possibilities of pain, failure, sorrow, frustration, and defeat. If it did not contain the particular trials and perils which—subtracting man's own very considerable contribution—our world contains, it would have to contain others instead.

To realize this is not, by any means, to be in possession of a detailed theodicy. It is to understand that this world, with all its "heartaches and the thousand natural shocks that flesh is heir to," an environment so manifestly not designed for the maximization of human pleasure and the minimization of human pain, may be rather well adapted to the quite different purpose of "soul-making."

NOTES

1. The word "theodicy," from the Greek *theos* (God) and *dike* (righteous), means the justification of God's goodness in the face of the fact of evil.

2. J. L. Mackie, "Evil and Omnipotence." *Mind* (April 1955), 209.

3. Flew, in *New Essays in Philosophical Theology*.

For Further Reflection

1. How convincing is Hick's argument? Does it explain natural evil (what Hick calls *non-moral evil*; that is, disease, earthquakes, famines, and floods)?

2. What would Hick say to the problem of animal suffering? How does that work towards soul-making?

3. Some have said that it is not just the existence of evil but the sheer quantity of evil in the world that makes it hard to believe that a good God exists. Why doesn't God intervene at crucial moments to prevent a holocaust or, to take Dostoevski's example, a child from being torn to death by ferocious dogs?

Is Faith Compatible with Reason?

One of the most important areas of philosophy of religion is that of the relationship of faith to reason. Is religious belief rational? Or is faith essentially irrational? If we cannot prove the claims of religious belief, is it nevertheless reasonable to believe these claims? For example, even if we do not have a deductive proof for the existence of God, is it nevertheless reasonable to believe that God exists? In the debate over faith and reason, two opposing positions have dominated the field. The first position asserts that faith and reason are compatible (i.e., it is rational to believe in God). The second position denies this assertion. Those holding to the first position differ among themselves as to the extent of the compatibility between faith and reason; most adherents follow Thomas Aquinas in relegating the compatibility to the "preambles of faith" (e.g., the existence of God and his nature) over against the "articles of faith" (e.g., the doctrine of the incarnation). Few have gone as far as Immanuel Kant, who maintained complete harmony between reason and faith, i.e., a religious belief within the realm of reason alone.

The second position divides into two subpositions: (1) that which asserts that faith is opposed to reason (which includes such unlikely bedfellows as David Hume and Søren Kierkegaard), placing faith in the area of irrationality; and (2) that which asserts that faith is higher than reason, transcends reason. John Calvin and Karl Barth assert that a natural theology is inappropriate because it seeks to meet unbelief on its own ground (ordinary, finite reason). Revelation, however, is "self-authenticating," "carrying with it its own evidence." We may call this position the *transrational* view of faith. Faith is not against reason as above it and beyond its proper domain.

The irrationalist and transrationalist positions are sometimes hard to separate in the incompatibilist's argument. At least, it seems that faith gets such a high value that reason comes off looking not simply inadequate but culpable. To use reason where faith claims the field is not only inappropriate but irreverent and faithless.

In the following readings, each of these positions is represented.

Yes, Faith Is a Logical Bet   II.8

BLAISE PASCAL

Blaise Pascal (1623–1662) was a French scientist, philosopher, and mathematician. He founded probability theory and made important contributions to science through his studies of barometric pressure. His conversion to a radical form of Catholicism in 1653 caused him to turn all his attention to religious matters. In this famous section from his *Pensées* (Thoughts), Pascal argues that if we do a cost-benefit analysis of the matter, it turns out that it is eminently reasonable to get ourselves to believe that God exists, regardless of whether we have good evidence for that belief. The argument goes something like this: Regarding the proposition "God exists," reason is neutral. It can neither prove nor disprove it. But we must make a choice on this matter, for not to choose for God is in effect to choose against him and lose the possible benefits that belief would bring. Since these benefits of faith promise to be infinite and the loss equally infinite, we must take a gamble on faith.

Study Questions

1. What is the relationship between our finitude and infinity? What is the infinite?
2. Why can we not know the existence or nature of God?
3. What does Pascal say regarding those who blame Christians for not producing evidence or proofs for the existence of God? Can God's existence be proved? Why or why not?
4. What is the wager Pascal advocates, and how does he calculate the cost-benefit ratio?

INFINITE—NOTHING .—Our soul is cast into a body, where it finds number, time, dimension. Thereupon it reasons, and calls this nature, necessity, and can believe nothing else.

Unity joined to infinity adds nothing to it, no more than one foot to an infinite measure. The finite is annihilated in the presence of the infinite, and becomes a pure nothing. So our spirit before God, so our justice before divine justice. There is not so great disproportion between our justice and that of God, as between unity and infinity.

The justice of God must be vast like His compassion. Now, justice to the outcast is less vast, and ought less to offend our feelings than mercy towards the elect.

We know that there is an infinite, and are ignorant of its nature. As we know it to be false that numbers are finite, it is therefore true that there is an infinity in number. But we do not know what it is. It is false that it is even, it is false that it is odd; for the addition of a unit can make no change in its nature. Yet it is a number, and every number is odd or even (this is certainly true of every finite number). So we may well know that there is a God without knowing what He is. Is there not one substantial truth, seeing there are so many things which are not the truth itself?

We know then the existence and nature of the finite, because we also are finite and have extension. We know the existence of the infinite, and are ignorant of its nature, because it has extension like us, but not limits like us. But we know neither the existence nor the nature of God, because He has neither extension nor limits.

But by faith we know His existence; in glory we shall know His nature. Now, I have already shown that we may well know the existence of a thing, without knowing its nature.

Let us now speak according to natural lights.

If there is a God, He is infinitely incomprehensible, since, having neither parts nor limits, He has no affinity to us. We are then incapable of knowing either what He is or if He is. This being so, who will dare to undertake the decision of the question? Not we, who have no affinity to Him.

Who then will blame Christians for not being able to give a reason for their belief, since they profess a religion for which they cannot give a reason? They declare, in expounding it to the world, that it is a foolishness, *stultitiam;* and then you complain that they do not prove it! If they proved it, they would not keep their words; it is in lacking proofs, that they are not lacking in sense. "Yes, but although this excuses those who offer it as such, and take away from them the blame of putting it forward without reason, it does not excuse those who receive it." Let us then examine this point, and say, "God is, or He is not." But to which side shall we incline? Reason can decide nothing here. There is an infinite chaos which separates us. A game is being played at the extremity of this infinite distance where heads or tails will turn up. What will you wager?

Reprinted from Blaise Pascal, Thoughts, *translated by W. F. Trotter (New York: Collier & Son, 1910).*

According to reason, you can do neither the one thing nor the other; according to reason, you can defend neither of the propositions.

Do not then reprove for error those who have made a choice; for you know nothing about it. "No, but I blame them for having made, not this choice, but a choice; for again both he who chooses heads and he who chooses tails are equally at fault, they are both in the wrong. The true course is not to wager at all."

—Yes; but you must wager. It is not optional. You are embarked. Which will you choose then; Let us see. Since you must choose, let us see which interests you least. You have two things to lose, the true and the good; and two things to stake, your reason and your will, your knowledge and your happiness; and your nature has two things to shun, error and misery. Your reason is no more shocked in choosing one rather than the other, since you must of necessity choose. This is one point settled. But your happiness? Let us weigh the gain and the loss in wagering that God is. Let us estimate these two chances. If you gain, you gain all; if you lose, you lose nothing. Wager then without hesitation that He is.—"That is very fine. Yes, I must wager; but I may perhaps wager too much."—Let us see. Since there is an equal risk of gain and of loss, if you had only to gain two lives, instead of one, you might still wager. But if there were three lives to gain, you would have to play (since you are under the necessity of playing), and you would be imprudent, when you are forced to play, not to chance your life to gain three at a game where there is an equal risk of loss and gain. But there is an eternity of life and happiness. And this being so, if there were an infinity of chances, of which one only would be for you, you would still be right in wagering one to win two, and you would act stupidly, being obliged to play, by refusing to stake one life against three at a game in which out of an infinity of an infinitely happy life to gain. But there is here an infinity of an infinitely happy life to gain, a chance of gain against a finite number of chances of loss, and what you stake is finite. It is all divided; wherever the infinite is and there is not an infinity of chances of loss against that of gain, there is no time to hesitate, you must give all. And thus, when one is forced to play, he must renounce reason to preserve his life, rather than risk it for infinite gain, as likely to happen as the loss of nothingness.

For it is no use to say it is uncertain if we will gain, and it is certain that we risk, and that the infinite distance between the *certainty* of what is staked and the *uncertainty* of what will be gained, equals the finite good which is certainly staked against the uncertain infinite. It is not so, as every player stakes a certainty to gain an uncertainty, and yet he stakes a finite certainty to gain a finite uncertainty, without transgressing against reason. There is not an infinite distance between the certainty staked and the uncertainty of the gain; that is untrue. In truth, there is an infinity between the certainty of gain and the certainty of loss. But the uncertainty of the gain is proportioned to the certainty of the stake according to the proportion of the chances of gain and loss. Hence it comes that, if there are as many risks on one side as on the other, the course is to play even; and then the certainty of the stake is equal to the uncertainty of the gain, so far is it from the fact that there is an infinite distance between them. And so our proposition is of infinite force, when there is the finite to stake in a game where there are equal risks of gain and of loss, and the infinite to gain. This is demonstrable; and if men are capable of any truths, this is one.

"I confess it, I admit it. But still is there no means of seeing the faces of the cards?"—Yes, Scripture and the rest, &c.—"Yes, but I have my hands tied and my mouth closed; I am forced to wager, and am not free. I am not released, and am so made that I cannot believe. What then would you have me do?"

"True. But at least learn your inability to believe, since reason brings you to this, and yet you cannot believe. Endeavour then to convince yourself, not by increase of proofs of God, but by the abatement of your passions. You would like to attain faith, and do not know the way; you would like to cure yourself of unbelief, and ask the remedy for it. Learn of those who have been bound like you, and who now stake all their possessions. These are people who know the way which you would follow, and who are cured of an ill of which you would be cured. Follow the way by which they began; by acting as if they believe, taking the holy water, having masses said, &c. Even this will naturally make you believe, and deaden your acuteness.—"But this is what I am afraid of."—And why? What have you to lose?

But to show you that this leads you there, it is this which will lessen the passions, which are your stumbling-blocks.

The end of this discourse.—Now what harm will befall you in taking this side? You will be faithful, honest, humble, grateful, generous, a sincere friend, truthful. Certainly you will not have those poisonous pleasures, glory and luxury; but will you not have others? I will tell you that you will thereby gain in this life, and that, at each step you take on this road, you will see so great certainty of gain, so much nothingness in what you risk, that you will at last recognize that you have wagered for something certain and infinite, for which you have given nothing.

"Ah! This discourse transports me, charms me," &c.

If this discourse pleases you and seems impressive, know that it is made by a man who has knelt, both before and after it, in prayer to that Being, infinite and without parts, before whom he lays all he has, for you also to lay before Him all you have for your own good and for His glory, so that strength may be given to lowliness.

For Further Reflection

1. Do you agree with Pascal that by a cost-benefit analysis it is good common sense to wager on God?

2. Is there anything problematic with Pascal's argument? Can other religions make similar or even more striking claims and use Pascal's argument to urge us to give up our religion and join theirs?

3. Could it be that God, if there be one, disdains making faith in him an outcome of a wager and not an honest estimation of the evidence?

II.9   A Debate on the Rationality of Religious Belief

ANTONY FLEW, R. M. HARE, AND BASIL MITCHELL

Antony Flew, for many years professor of philosophy at the University of Reading in England, is presently teaching at Bowling Green University. R. M. Hare and Basil Mitchell were, until their recent retirements, professors of philosophy at Oxford University. All three were educated at Oxford University, where they all began their teaching careers. In this 1948 Oxford University symposium, Flew challenges theists to state the conditions under which they would give up their faith, for, he contends, unless one can state what would falsify one's belief, one does not have a meaningful belief. If nothing could count against the belief, it does not make a serious assertion, for serious truth claims must be ready to undergo rational scrutiny. Hare responds by arguing that this is the wrong way to describe faith, for religious faith consists of a set of profoundly unfalsifiable assumptions, which he calls "bliks," which govern all of a person's other beliefs. There are insane and sane bliks, but we cannot escape having them. Even the scientist has such fundamental assumptions. Hence religion should not be subject to the kind of rational scrutiny Flew urges. Mitchell opts for a compromise position. Rational considerations enter into the debate on faith, but no one can say exactly when a gradual accumulation of evidence is sufficient to overthrow religious belief. Although rational considerations count against faith, the believer will not let them count decisively against it.

Study Questions

1. What is the significance of the parable of the garden? How does Flew interpret it? Do you agree with him?

2. What does Flew mean by his statement that a brash hypothesis can be "killed by inches, the death by a thousand qualifications"?

3. What is Hare's strategy in telling the story of the paranoid student who believes that all dons (viz., teachers) intend to harm him?

4. What is a "blik"? Describe it.

5. How does Hare disagree with Flew?

6. What is the one thing that Mitchell allows to count against his faith in God? How much should it count against one's faith?

7. How does Mitchell illustrate his thesis? How does his story throw light on the relationship of faith to reason?

Antony Flew

LET US BEGIN WITH A PARABLE. It is a parable developed from a tale told by John Wisdom in his haunting and revelatory article "Gods."[1] Once upon a time two explorers came upon a clearing in the jungle. In the clearing were growing many flowers and many weeds. One explorer says, "Some gardener must tend this plot." The other disagrees, "There is no gardener." So they pitch their tents and set a watch. No gardener is ever seen. "But perhaps he is an invisible gardener." So they set up a barbed-wire fence. They electrify it. They patrol with bloodhounds. (For they remember how H. G. Wells's *The Invisible Man* could be both smelt and touched though he could not be seen.) But no shrieks ever suggest that some intruder has received a shock. No movements of the wire ever betray an invisible climber. The bloodhounds never give cry. Yet

From New Essays in Philosophical Theology, *edited by Antony Flew and Alasdair MacIntyre (London: SCM Press, 1955), pp. 96–105. Copyright © 1955 by Antony Flew and Alasdair MacIntyre; renewed © 1963. Reprinted by permission of Macmillan Publishing Company. Footnote edited.*

still the Believer is not convinced. "But there is a gardener, invisible, intangible, insensible to electric shocks, a gardener who has no scent and makes no sound, a gardener who comes secretly to look after the garden which he loves." At last the Sceptic despairs. "But what remains of your original assertion? Just how does what you call an invisible, intangible, eternally elusive gardener differ from an imaginary gardener or even from no gardener at all?"

In this parable we can see how what starts as an assertion, that something exists or that there is some analogy between certain complexes of phenomena, may be reduced step by step to an altogether different status, to an expression perhaps of a "picture preference." The Sceptic says there is no gardener. The Believer says there is a gardener (but invisible, etc.). One man talks about sexual behaviour. Another man prefers to talk of Aphrodite (but knows that there is not really a superhuman person additional to, and somehow responsible for, all sexual phenomena). The process of qualification may be checked at any point before the original assertion is completely withdrawn and something of that first assertion will remain (Tautology). Mr. Wells's invisible man could not, admittedly, be seen, but in all other respects he was a man like the rest of us. But though the process of qualification may be, and of course usually is, checked in time, it is not always judiciously so halted. Someone may dissipate his assertion completely without noticing that he has done so. A fine brash hypothesis may thus be killed by inches, the death by a thousand qualifications.

And in this, it seems to me, lies the peculiar danger, the endemic evil, of theological utterance. Take such utterances as "God has a plan," "God created the world," "God loves us as a father loves his children." They look at first sight very much like assertions, vast cosmological assertions. Of course, this is no sure sign that they either are, or are intended to be, assertions. But let us confine ourselves to the cases where those who utter such sentences intend them to express assertions. (Merely remarking parenthetically that those who intend or interpret such utterances as crypto-commands, expressions of wishes, disguised ejaculations, concealed ethics, or as anything else but assertions, are unlikely to succeed in making them either properly orthodox or practically effective.)

Now to assert that such and such is the case is necessarily equivalent to denying that such and such is not the case. Suppose then that we are in doubt as to what someone who gives vent to an utterance is asserting, or suppose that, more radically, we are sceptical as to whether he is really asserting anything at all, one way of trying to understand (or perhaps it will be to expose) his utterance is to attempt to find what he would regard as counting against, or as being incompatible with, its truth. For if the utterance is indeed an assertion, it will necessarily be equivalent to a denial of the negation of that assertion. And anything which would count against the assertion, or which would induce the speaker to withdraw it and to admit that it had been mistaken, must be part of (or the whole of) the meaning of the negation of that assertion. And to know the meaning of the negation of an assertion, is as near as makes no matter, to know the meaning of that assertion. And if there is nothing which a putative assertion denies then there is nothing which it asserts either: and so it is not really an assertion. When the Sceptic in the parable asked the Believer, "Just how does what you call an invisible, intangible, eternally elusive gardener differ from an imaginary gardener or even from no gardener at all?" he was suggesting that the Believer's earlier statement had been eroded by qualification that it was no longer as assertion at all.

Now it often seems to people who are not religious as if there was no conceivable event or series of events the occurrence of which would be admitted by sophisticated religious people to be a sufficient reason for conceding "There wasn't a

God after all" or "God does not really love us then." Someone tells us that God loves us as a father loves his children. We are reassured. But then we see a child dying of inoperable cancer of the throat. His earthly father is driven frantic in his efforts to help, but his Heavenly Father reveals no obvious sign of concern. Some qualification is made—God's love is "not a merely human love" or it is "an inscrutable love," perhaps—and we realize that such sufferings are quite compatible with the truth of the assertion that "God loves us as a father (but, of course, . . .)." We are reassured again. But then perhaps we ask: what is this assurance of God's (appropriately qualified) love worth, what is this apparent guarantee really a guarantee against? Just what would have to happen not merely (morally and wrongly) to tempt but also (logically and rightly) to entitle us to say "God does not love us" or even "God does not exist"? I therefore put to the succeeding symposiasts the simple central questions, "What would have to occur or to have occurred to constitute for you a disproof of the love of, or of the existence of, God?"

R. M. Hare

I wish to make it clear that I shall not try to defend Christianity in particular, but religion in general—not because I do not believe in Christianity, but because you cannot understand what Christianity is, until you have understood what religion is.

I must begin by confessing that, on the ground marked out by Flew, he seems to me to be completely victorious. I therefore shift my ground by relating another parable. A certain lunatic is convinced that all dons want to murder him. His friends introduce him to all the mildest and most respectable dons that they can find, and after each of them has retired, they say, "You see, he doesn't really want to murder you; he spoke to you in a most cordial manner; surely you are

convinced now?" But the lunatic replies "Yes, but that was only his diabolical cunning; he's really plotting against me the whole time, like the rest of them; I know it I tell you." However many kindly dons are produced, the reaction is still the same.

Now we say that such a person is deluded. But what is he deluded about? About the truth or falsity of an assertion? Let us apply Flew's test to him. There is no behaviour of dons that can be enacted which he will accept as counting against his theory; and therefore his theory, on this test, asserts nothing. But it does not follow that there is no difference between what he thinks about dons and what most of us think about them—otherwise we should not call him a lunatic and ourselves sane, and dons would have no reason to feel uneasy about his presence in Oxford.

Let us call that in which we differ from this lunatic, our respective *bliks*. He has an insane *blik* about dons; we have a sane one. It is important to realize that we have a sane one, not no *blik* at all; for there must be two sides to any argument—if he has a wrong *blik*, then those who are right about dons must have a right one. Flew has shown that a *blik* does not consist in an assertion or system of them; but nevertheless it is very important to have the right *blik*.

Let us try to imagine what it would be like to have different *bliks* about other things than dons. When I am driving my car, it sometimes occurs to me to wonder whether my movements of the steering-wheel will always continue to be followed by corresponding alterations in the direction of the car. I have never had a steering failure, though I have had skids, which must be similar. Moreover, I know enough about how the steering of my car is made, to know the sort of thing that would have to go wrong for the steering to fail—steel joints would have to part, or steel rods break, or something—but how do I know that this won't happen? The truth is, I don't know; I just have a *blik* about steel and its properties, so that normally I trust the steering of my car; but I find it not at all difficult to imagine what it would be like to lose this *blik* and acquire the opposite one. People would say I was silly about steel; but there would be no mistaking the reality of the difference between our respective *bliks*—for example, I should never go in a motor-car. Yet I should hesitate to say that the difference between us was the difference between contradictory assertions. No amount of safe arrivals or bench-tests will remove my *blik* and restore the normal one: for my *blik* is compatible with any finite number of such tests.

It was Hume who taught us that our whole commerce with the world depends upon our *blik* about the world; and that differences between *bliks* about the world cannot be settled by observation of what happens in the world. That was why, having performed the interesting experiment of doubting the ordinary man's *blik* about the world, and showing that no proof could be given to make us adopt one *blik* rather than another, he turned to backgammon to take his mind off the problem. It seems, indeed, to be impossible even to formulate as an assertion the normal *blik* about the world which makes me put my confidence in the future reliability of steel joints, in the continued ability of the road to support my car, and not gape beneath it revealing nothing below; in the general non-homicidal tendencies of dons; in my own continued well-being (in some sense of that word that I may not now fully understand) if I continued to do what is right according to my lights; in the general likelihood of people like Hitler coming to a bad end. But perhaps a formulation less inadequate than most is to be found in the Psalms: "The earth is weak and all the inhabiters thereof: I bear up the pillars of it."

The mistake of the position which Flew selects for attack is to regard this kind of talk as some sort of *explanation*, as scientists are accustomed to use the word. As such, it would obviously be ludicrous. We no longer believe in

God as an Atlas—*nous n'avons pas besoin de cette hypothèse*. But it is nevertheless true to say that, as Hume saw, without a *blik* there can be no explanation; for it is by our *bliks* that we decide what is and what is not an explanation. Suppose we believed that everything that happened, happened by pure chance. This would not of course be an assertion; for it is compatible with anything happening or not happening, and so, incidentally, is its contradictory. But if we had this belief, we should not be able to explain or predict or plan anything. Thus, although we should not be *asserting* anything different from those of a more normal belief, there would be a great difference between us; and this is the sort of difference that there is between those who really believe in God and those who really disbelieve in him.

The word "really" is important, and may excite suspicion. I put it in, because when people have had a good Christian upbringing, as have most of those who now profess not to believe in any sort of religion, it is very hard to discover what they really believe. The reason why they find it so easy to think that they are not religious, is that they have never got into the frame of mind of one who suffers from the doubts to which religion is the answer. Not for them the terrors of the primitive jungle. Having abandoned some of the more picturesque fringes of religion, they think that they have abandoned the whole thing—whereas in fact they still have got, and could not live without, a religion of a comfortably substantial, albeit highly sophisticated, kind, which differs from that of many "religious people" in little more than this, that "religious people" like to sing Psalms about theirs—a very natural and proper thing to do. But nevertheless there may be a big difference lying behind—the difference between two people who, though side by side, are walking in different directions. I do not know in what direction Flew is walking; perhaps he does not know either. But we have had some examples recently of various ways in which one can walk away from Christianity, and there are any number of possibilities. After all, man has not changed biologically since primitive times; it is his religion that has changed, and it can easily change again. And if you do not think that such changes make a difference, get acquainted with some Sikhs and some Mussulmans of the same Punjabi stock; you will find them quite different sorts of people.

There is an important difference between Flew's parable and my own which we have not yet noticed. The explorers do not *mind* about their garden; they discuss it with interest, but not with concern. But my lunatic, poor fellow, minds about dons; and I mind about the steering of my car; it often has people in it that I care for. It is because I mind very much about what goes on in the garden in which I find myself, that I am unable to share the explorers' detachment.

Basil Mitchell

Flew's article is searching and perceptive, but there is, I think, something odd about his conduct of the theologian's case. The theologian surely would not deny that the fact of pain counts against the assertion that God loves men. This very incompatibility generates the most intractable of theological problems—the problem of evil. So the theologian *does* recognize the fact of pain as counting against Christian doctrine. But it is true that he will not allow it—or anything—to count decisively against it; for he is committed by his faith to trust in God. His attitude is not that of the detached observer, but of the believer.

Perhaps this can be brought out by yet another parable. In time of war in an occupied country, a member of the resistance meets one night a stranger who deeply impresses him. They spend that night together in conversation. The Stranger tells the partisan that he himself is on the side of the resistance—indeed that he is in command of it, and urges the partisan to have faith in him no matter what happens. The partisan is utterly convinced at that meeting of the Stranger's sincerity and constancy and undertakes to trust him.

They never meet in conditions of intimacy again. But sometimes the Stranger is seen helping members of the resistance, and the partisan is grateful and says to his friends, "He is on our side."

Sometimes he is seen in the uniform of the police handing over patriots to the occupying power. On these occasions his friends murmur against him: but the partisan still says, "He is on our side." He still believes that, in spite of appearances, the Stranger did not deceive him. Sometimes he asks the Stranger for help and receives it. He is then thankful. Sometimes he asks and does not receive it. Then he says, "The Stranger knows best." Sometimes his friends, in exasperation, say "Well, what *would* he have to do for you to admit that you were wrong and that he is not on our side?" But the partisan refuses to answer. He will not consent to put the Stranger to the test. And sometimes his friends complain, "Well, if *that's* what you mean by his being on our side, the sooner he goes over to the other side the better."

The partisan of the parable does not allow anything to count decisively against the proposition "The Stranger is on our side." This is because he has committed himself to trust the Stranger. But he of course recognizes that the Stranger's ambiguous behaviour *does* count against what he believes about him. It is precisely this situation which constitutes the trial of his faith.

When the partisan asks for help and doesn't get it, what can he do? He can (*a*) conclude that the stranger is not on our side or: (*b*) maintain that he is on our side, but that he has reasons for withholding help.

The first he will refuse to do. How long can he uphold the second position without its becoming just silly?

I don't think one can say in advance. It will

depend on the nature of the impression created by the Stranger in the first place. It will depend, too, on the manner in which he takes the Stranger's behaviour. If he blandly dismisses it as of no consequence, as having no bearing upon his belief, it will be assumed that he is thoughtless or insane. And it quite obviously won't do for him to say easily, "Oh, when used of the Stranger the phrase 'is on our side' *means* ambiguous behavior of this sort." In that case he would like the religious man who says blandly of a terrible disaster "It is God's will." No, he will only be regarded as sane and reasonable in his belief, if he experiences in himself the full force of the conflict.

It is here that my parable differs from Hare's. The partisan admits that many things may and do count against his belief: whereas Hare's lunatic who has a *blik* about dons doesn't admit that anything counts against his *blik*. Nothing *can* count against *bliks*. Also the partisan has a reason for having in the first instance committed himself, viz. the character of the Stranger; whereas the lunatic has no reason for his *blik* about dons—because, of course, you can't have reasons for *bliks*.

This means that I agree with Flew that theological utterances must be assertions. The partisan is making an assertion when he says, "The Stranger is on our side."

Do I want to say that the partisan's belief about the Stranger is, in any sense, an explanation? I think I do. It explains and makes sense of the Stranger's behaviour: it helps to explain also the resistance movement in the context of which he appears. In each case it differs from the interpretation which the others put upon the same facts.

"God loves men" resembles "the Stranger is on our side" (and many other significant statements, e.g. historical ones) in not being conclusively falsifiable. They can both be treated in at least three different ways: (1) As provisional hypotheses to be discarded if experience tells

against them; (2) As significant articles of faith; (3) As vacuous formulae (expressing, perhaps, a desire for reassurance) to which experience makes no difference and which make no difference to life.

The Christian, once he has committed himself, is precluded by his faith from taking up the first attitude: "Thou shalt not tempt the Lord thy God." He is in constant danger, as Flew has observed, of slipping into the third. But he need not; and, if he does, it is a failure in faith as well as in logic.

Antony Flew

It has been a good discussion: and I am glad to have helped to provoke it. But now—at least in *University*—it must come to an end: and the Editors of *University* have asked me to make some concluding remarks. Since it is impossible to deal with all the issues raised or to comment separately upon each contribution, I will concentrate on Mitchell and Hare, as representative of two very different kinds of response to the challenge made in "Theology and Falsification."

The challenge, it will be remembered, ran like this. Some theological utterances seem to, and are intended to, provide explanations or express assertions. Now an assertion, to be an assertion at all, must claim that things stand thus and thus; *and not otherwise*. Similarly an explanation, to be an explanation at all, must explain why this particular thing occurs; *and not something else*. Those last clauses are crucial. And yet sophisticated religious people—or so it seemed to me—are apt to overlook this, and tend to refuse to allow, not merely that anything actually does occur, but that anything conceivably could occur, which would count against their theological assertions and explanations. But in so far as they do this their supposed explanations are actually bogus, and their seeming assertions are really vacuous.

Mitchell's response to this challenge is admirably direct, straightforward, and understanding. He agrees "that theological utterances must be assertions." He agrees that if they are to be assertions, there must be something that would count against their truth. He agrees, too, that believers are in constant danger of transforming their would-be assertions into "vacuous formulae." But he takes me to task for an oddity in my "conduct of the theologian's case. The theologian surely would not deny that the fact of pain counts against the assertion that God loves men. This very incompatibility generates the most intractable of theological problems, the problem of evil." I think he is right. I should have made a distinction between two very different ways of dealing with what looks like evidence against the love of God: the way I stressed was the expedient of qualifying the original assertion; the way the theologian usually takes, at first, is to admit that it looks bad but to insist that there is—there must be—some explanation which will show that, in spite of appearances, there really is a God who loves us. His difficulty, it seems to me, is that he has given God attributes which rule out all possible saving explanations. In Mitchell's parable of the Stranger it is easy for the believer to find plausible excuses for ambiguous behaviour: for the Stranger is a man. But suppose the Stranger is God. We cannot say that he would like to help but cannot: God is omnipotent. We cannot say that he would help if he only knew: God is omniscient. We cannot say that he is not responsible for the wickedness of others: God creates those others. Indeed an omnipotent, omniscient God must be an accessory before (and during) the fact to every human misdeed; as well as being responsible for every non-moral defect in the universe. So, though I entirely concede that Mitchell was absolutely right to insist against me that the theologian's first move is to look for an *explanation,* I still think that in the end, if relentlessly pursued, he will have to resort to the avoiding action of *qualification.* And there lies the danger of that death by a thousand qualifications, which would, I agree, constitute "a failure in faith as well as in logic."

Hare's approach is fresh and bold. He confesses that "on the ground marked out by Flew, he seems to me to be completely victorious." He therefore introduces the concept of *blik.* But while I think that there is room for some such concept in philosophy, and that philosophers should be grateful to Hare for his invention, I nevertheless want to insist that any attempt to analyse Christian religious utterances as expressions or affirmations of a *blik* rather than as (at least would-be) assertions about the cosmos is fundamentally misguided. *First,* because thus interpreted they would be entirely unorthodox. If Hare's religion really is a *blik,* involving no cosmological assertions about the nature and activities of a supposed personal creator, then surely he is not a Christian at all? *Second,* because thus interpreted, they could scarcely do the job they do. If they were not even intended as assertions then many religious activities would become fraudulent, or merely silly. If "You ought *because* it is God's will" asserts no more than "You ought," then the person who prefers the former phraseology is not really giving a reason, but a fraudulent substitute for one, a dialectical dud cheque. If "My soul must be immortal *because* God loves his children, etc." asserts no more than "My soul must be immortal," then the man who reassures himself with theological arguments for immortality is being as silly as the man who tries to clear his overdraft by writing his bank a cheque on the same account. (Of course neither of these utterances would be distinctively Christian: but this discussion never pretended to be so confined.) Religious utterances may indeed express false or even bogus assertions: but I simply do not believe that they are not both intended and interpreted to be or at any rate to presuppose assertions, at least in the context of religious practice; whatever shifts may be demanded, in another context, by the exigencies of theological apologetic.

One final suggestion. The philosophers of religion might well draw upon George Orwell's last appalling nightmare *1984* for the concept of *doublethink*. "*Doublethink* means the power of holding two contradictory beliefs simultaneously, and accepting both of them. The party intellectual knows that he is playing tricks with reality, but by the exercise of *doublethink* he also satisfies himself that reality is not violated" (*1984*, p. 220). Perhaps religious intellectuals too are sometimes driven to doublethink in order to retain their faith in a loving God in face of the reality of a heartless and indifferent world. But of this more another time, perhaps.

NOTE

1. *P.A.S.*, 1944–5, reprinted as Ch. X of *Logic and Language,* Vol. I (Blackwell, 1951), and in his *Philosophy and Psychoanalysis* (Blackwell, 1953).

For Further Study

1. Analyze the different strategies in our three philosophers' statements. Who has made the best case?

2. Should the believer follow Flew's advice and give an account of what would count against his or her faith? Should one's faith be open to revision or rejection on the basis of arguments?

3. Does the believer need to be able to cite evidence before he or she can affirm that it is rational to believe in God?

II.10   Religious Belief Without Evidence

ALVIN PLANTINGA

Alvin Plantinga (1932–) is a professor of philosophy at the University of Notre Dame and has written widely in metaphysics and philosophy of religion, including *The Nature of Necessity* (1974) and *God, Freedom and Evil* (1974). In the following essay, he argues that it is rational to believe in God despite the lack of evidence for such belief. Those (like W. K. Clifford) who insist that we must have evidence for all our beliefs simply fail to make their case, because the evidentialists have not set forth clear criteria that would account for all the clear cases of justified beliefs and that would exclude the belief in God. Plantinga outlines the position of the foundationalist-evidentialist as claiming that all justified beliefs must either (1) be "properly basic" by fulfilling certain criteria, or (2) be based on other beliefs that eventually result in a treelike construction with properly basic beliefs at the bottom, or foundation. Plantinga shows that many beliefs we seem to be justified in holding do not fit into the foundationalist framework; such beliefs as memory beliefs (for example, that I ate breakfast this morning), belief in an external world, and belief in other minds. These beliefs do not depend on other beliefs, yet neither are they self-evident, incorrigible (impossible not to believe), or evident to the senses.

Having shown the looseness of what we can accept as "properly basic," Plantinga next shows that the Protestant reformers saw belief in God as "properly basic." He asks us to consider this belief as a legitimate option, and examines possible objections to it.

Study Questions

1. What is the main objection many philosophers have raised against belief in God?
2. What does W. K. Clifford say about the correct or ethical way to believe?
3. How does Antony Flew think the debate between theism and atheism should begin? Where should the burden of proof lie? Does Plantinga agree with Flew?
4. What are the two premises of the evidentialist's objection to belief in God?
5. Do Reformed thinkers and theologians accept natural theology (the attempt to establish God's existence through human reason)? Why (or why not)?
6. How do Reformed theologians view belief in God?
7. What is the difference between *prima facie* obligations and *all-things-considered* obligations?
8. Plantinga links evidentialism with classical foundationalism. What is classical foundationalism?
9. What does Plantinga say is wrong with classical foundationalism?
10. What is the Great Pumpkin objection?

The Evidentialist Objection to Theistic Belief

MANY PHILOSOPHERS—Clifford, Blanshard, Russell, Scriven, and Flew, to name a few—have argued that belief in God is irrational, or unreasonable, or not rationally acceptable, or intellectually irresponsible, or somehow noetically below par because, as they say, there is *insufficient evidence* for it.[1] Bertrand Russell was once asked what he would say if, after dying, he were brought into the presence of God and asked why he hadn't been a believer. Russell's reply: "I'd say, 'Not enough evidence, God! Not enough evidence!'"[2] I don't know just how such a response would be received; but Russell, like many others, held that theistic belief is unreasonable because there is insufficient evidence for it. We

all remember W. K. Clifford, that delicious *enfant terrible*, as William James called him, and his insistence that it is immoral, wicked, and monstrous, and maybe even impolite to accept a belief for which you don't have sufficient evidence:

> Who so would deserve well of his fellows in this matter will guard the purity of his belief with a very fanaticism of jealous care, lest at any time it should rest on an unworthy object, and catch a stain which can never be wiped away.

He adds that if a

> belief has been accepted on insufficient evidence, the pleasure is a stolen one. Not only does it deceive ourselves by giving us a sense of power which we do not really possess, but it is sinful, because it is stolen in defiance of our duty to mankind. That duty is to guard our-

From Religious Experience and Religious Belief, *ed. Joseph Runzo and Craig Ihara (New York: University Press of America, 1986). Reprinted with permission.*

selves from such beliefs as from a pestilence which may shortly master our body and spread to the rest of the town.

and finally:

To sum up: it is wrong always, everywhere, and for anyone to believe anything upon insufficient evidence.

(It is not hard to detect, in these quotations, the "tone of robustious pathos" with which James credits him.) Clifford, of course, held that one who accepts belief in God *does* accept that belief on insufficient evidence, and has indeed defied his duty to mankind. More recently, Bertrand Russell has endorsed the evidentialist injunction "Give to any hypothesis which is worth your while to consider, just that degree or credence which the evidence warrants."

More recently, Antony Flew[3] has commended what he calls Clifford's "luminous and compulsive essay" (perhaps "compulsive" here is a misprint for "compelling"); and Flew goes on to claim that there is, in his words a "presumption of atheism." What is a presumption of atheism, and why should we think there is one? Flew puts it as follows:

The debate about the existence of God should properly begin from the presumption of atheism . . . the onus of proof must lie upon the theist. The word "atheism," however, has in this contention to be construed unusually. Whereas nowadays the usual meaning of "atheist" in English is "someone who asserts there is no such being as God," I want the word to be understood not positively but negatively. I want the original Greek prefix "a" to be read in the same way in "atheist" as it is customarily read in such other Greco-English words as "amoral," "atypical," and "asymmetrical." In this interpretation an atheist becomes: not someone who positively asserts the non-existence of God; but someone who is simply not a theist.

What the protagonist of my presumption of atheism wants to show is that the debate about the existence of God ought to be conducted in a particular way, and that the issue should be seen in a certain perspective. His thesis about the onus of proof involves that it is up to the theist: first to introduce and to defend his proposed concept of God; and second, to provide sufficient reason for believing that this concept of his does in fact have an application.

How shall we understand this? What does it mean, for example, to say that the debate "should properly begin from the presumption of atheism"? What sorts of things do debates begin from, and what is it for one to begin from such a thing? Perhaps Flew means something like this: to speak of where a debate should begin is to speak of the sorts of premises to which the affirmative and negative sides can properly appeal in arguing their cases. Suppose you and I are debating the question whether, say, the United States has a right to seize Mideast oil fields if the OPEC countries refuse to sell us oil at what we think is a fair price. I take the affirmative, and produce for my conclusion an argument one premise of which is the proposition that the United States has indeed a right to seize these oil fields under those conditions. Doubtless that maneuver would earn me very few points. Similarly, a debate about the existence of God cannot sensibly start from the assumption that God does indeed exist. That is to say, the affirmative can't properly appeal, in its arguments, to such premises as that there is such a person as God; if it could, it'd have much too easy a time of it. So in this sense of "start," Flew is quite right: the debate can't start from the assumption that God exists.

Of course, it is also true that the debate can't start from the assumption that God does *not* exist; using "atheism" in its ordinary sense, there is equally a presumption of aatheism (which, by a familiar principle of logic, reduces to theism). So it looks as if there is in Flew's sense a presumption of atheism, all right, but in that same sense an equal presumption of aatheism. If this is what Flew means, then what he says is entirely correct, if something of a truism.

In another passage, however, Flew seems to

understand the presumption of atheism in quite another different fashion:

> It is by reference to this inescapable demand for grounds that the presumption of atheism is justified. If it is to be established that there is a God, then we have to have good grounds for believing that this is indeed so. Until or unless some such grounds are produced we have literally no reason at all for believing; and in that situation the only reasonable posture must be that of either the negative atheist or the agnostic.

Here we have the much more substantial suggestion that it is unreasonable or irrational to accept theistic belief in the absence of sufficient grounds or reasons. And of course Flew, along with Russell, Clifford, and many others, holds that in fact there aren't sufficient grounds or evidence for belief in God. The evidentialist objection, therefore, appeals to the following two premises:

(A) It is irrational or unreasonable to accept theistic belief in the absence of sufficient evidence or reasons.

and

(B) There is no evidence, or at any rate not sufficient evidence, for the proposition that God exists.

(B), I think, is at best dubious. At present, however, I'm interested in the objector's other premise—the claim that it is irrational or unreasonable to accept theistic belief in the absence of evidence or reasons. Why suppose *that's* true? Why suppose a theist must have evidence or reason to think there *is* evidence for this belief, if he is not to be irrational? This isn't just *obvious*, after all.

Now many Reformed thinkers and theologians[4] have rejected *natural theology* (thought of as the attempt to provide proofs or arguments for the existence of God). They have held not merely that the proffered arguments are unsuccessful, but that the whole enterprise is in some way radically misguided. I have argued (1980) that the Reformed rejection of natural theology

is best construed as an inchoate and unfocused rejection of (A). What these Reformed thinkers really mean to hold, I think, is that belief in God is properly basic: it need not be based on argument or evidence from other propositions at all. They mean to hold that the believer is entirely within his intellectual right in believing as he does, even if he doesn't know of any good theistic argument (deductive or inductive), even if he doesn't believe that there is any such argument, and even if in fact no such argument exists. They hold that it is perfectly rational to accept belief in God without accepting it on the basis of any other beliefs or propositions at all. Why suppose that the believer must have evidence if he is not to be irrational? Why should anyone accept (A)? What is to be said in its favor?

Suppose we begin by asking what the objector means by describing a belief as *irrational*. What is the force of his claim that the theistic belief is irrational and how is it to be understood? The first thing to see is that this claim is rooted in a *normative* contention. It lays down conditions that must be met by anyone whose system of beliefs is *rational*; and here "rational" is to be taken as a normative or evaluative term. According to the objector, there is a right way and a wrong way with respect to belief. People have responsibilities, duties and obligations with respect to their believings just as they do with respect to their actions—or if we think believings are a kind of action, their *other* actions. Professor Brand Blanshard puts this clearly:

> everywhere and always belief has an ethical aspect. There is such a thing as a general ethics of the intellect. The main principle of that ethic I hold to be the same inside and outside religion. This principle is simple and sweeping: Equate your assent to the evidence. (*Reason and Belief,* p. 401)

and according to Michael Scriven:

> Now even belief in something for which there is no evidence, i.e., a belief which goes beyond the evidence, although a lesser sin than a be-

lief in something which is contrary to well-established laws, is plainly irrational in that it simply amounts to attaching belief where it is not justified. So the proper alternative, when there is no evidence, is not mere suspension of belief, e.g., about Santa Claus, it is disbelief. It most certainly is not faith. (*Primary Philosophy*, p. 103)

Perhaps this sort of obligation is really a special case of a more general moral obligation; or perhaps, on the other hand, it is *sui generis*. In any event, says the objector, there are such obligations: to conform to them is to be rational and to go against them is to be irrational.

Now here the objector seems right; there are duties and obligations with respect to beliefs. One's own welfare and that of others sometimes depends on what one believes. If we're descending the Grand Teton and I'm setting the anchor for the 120-foot rappel into the Upper Saddle, I have an obligation to form such beliefs as *this anchor point is solid* only on the basis of careful scrutiny and testing. One commissioned to gather intelligence—the spies Joshua sent into Canaan, for example—has an obligation to get it right. I have an obligation with respect to the belief that Justin Martyr was a Latin apologist—an obligation arising from the fact that I teach medieval philosophy, must make a declaration on this issue, and am obliged not to mislead my students here. The precise *form* of these obligations may be hard to specify: am I obliged to believe that J. M. was a Latin apologist if and only if J. M. *was* a Latin apologist? Or to form a belief on this topic only after the appropriate amount of checking and investigating? Or maybe just to tell the students the truth about it, whatever I myself believe in the privacy of my own study? Or to tell them what's generally thought by those who should know? In the rappel case: Do I have a duty to believe that the anchor point is solid if and only if it is? Or just to check carefully before forming the belief? Or perhaps there's no obligation to believe at all, but only to *act on* a certain belief only after appropriate investiga-

tion. In any event, it seems plausible to hold that there are obligations and norms with respect to belief, and I do not intend to contest this assumption.

The objector begins, therefore, from the plausible contention that there are duties or obligations with respect to belief: call them *intellectual duties*. These duties can be understood in several ways. First, we could construe them teleologically; we could adopt an intellectual utilitarianism. Here the rough idea is that our intellectual obligations arise out of a connection between our beliefs and what is intrinsically good and intrinsically bad; and our intellectual obligations are just a special case of the general obligation so to act to maximize good and minimize evil. Perhaps this is how W. K. Clifford thinks of the matter. If people accepted such propositions as *this DC-10 is airworthy* when the evidence is insufficient, the consequences could be disastrous: so perhaps some of us, at any rate, have an obligation to believe that proposition only in the presence of adequate evidence. The intellectual utilitarian could be an ideal utilitarian; he could hold that certain epistemic states are intrinsically valuable—knowledge, perhaps, or believing the truth, or a skeptical and judicial temper that is not blown about by every wind of doctrine. Among our duties, then, is a duty to try to bring about these valuable states of affairs. Perhaps this is how Professor Roderick Chisholm is to be understood when he says

Let us consider the concept of what might be called an "intellectual requirement." We may assume that every person is subject to a purely intellectual requirement: that of trying his best to bring it about that, for every proposition that he considers, he accepts it if and only if it is true. (*Theory of Knowledge*, 2nd ed., p. 9)

Secondly, we could construe intellectual obligations *aretetically;* we could adopt what Professor Frankena calls a "mixed ethics of virtue" with respect to the intellect. There are valuable noetic or intellectual states (whether intrinsically or extrinsically valuable); there are also the corresponding intellectual virtues, the habits of acting so as to produce or promote or enhance those valuable states. One's intellectual obligations, then, are to try to produce and enhance these intellectual virtues in oneself and others.

Thirdly, we could construe intellectual obligations *deontologically;* we could adopt a *pure* ethics of obligation with respect to the intellect. Perhaps there are intellectual obligations that do not arise from any connection with good or evil, but attach to us just by virtue of our having the sorts of noetic powers human beings do in fact display. The quotation from Chisholm could also be understood along these lines.

Intellectual obligations, therefore, can be understood teleologically or aretetically or deontologically. And perhaps there are purely intellectual obligations of the following sorts. Perhaps I have a duty not to take as basic a proposition whose denial seems self-evident. Perhaps I have a duty to take as basic the proposition *I seem to see a tree* under certain conditions. With respect to certain kinds of propositions, perhaps I have a duty to believe them only if I have evidence for them, and a duty to proportion the strength of my belief to the strength of my evidence.

Of course, these would be *prima facie* obligations. One presumably has an obligation not to take bread from the grocery store without permission and another to tell the truth. Both can be overridden, in specific circumstances, by other obligations—in the first case, perhaps, an obligation to feed my starving children and in the second, an obligation to protect a human life. So we must distinguish *prima facie* duties or obligations from *all-things-considered* or *on-balance (ultima facie?)* obligations. I have a *prima facie* obligation to tell the truth; in a given situation, however, that obligation may be overridden by others, so that my duty, all things considered, is to tell a lie. This is the grain of truth contained in situation ethics and the ill-named "new morality."

And *prima facie* intellectual obligations can

conflict, just as obligations of other sorts. Perhaps I have a *prima facie* obligation to believe what seems to me self-evident, and what seems to me to follow self-evidently from what seems to me self-evident. But what if, as in the Russell paradoxes, something that seems self-evidently false apparently follows, self-evidently, from what seems self-evidently true? Here *prima facie* intellectual obligations conflict, and no matter what I do I will violate a *prima facie* obligation. Another example: in reporting the Grand Teton rappel, I neglected to mention the violent electrical storm coming in from the southwest; to escape it we must get off in a hurry, so that I have a *prima facie* obligation to inspect the anchor point carefully, but anchor to set up the rappel rapidly, which means I can't spend a lot of time inspecting the anchor point.

Thus lightly armed, suppose we return to the evidential objector. Does he mean to hold that the theist without evidence is violating some intellectual obligation? If so, which one? Does he claim, for example, that the theist is violating his *ultima facie* intellectual obligation in thus believing? Perhaps he thinks anyone who believes in God without evidence is violating his all-things-considered intellectual duty. This, however, seems unduly harsh. What about the fourteen-year-old theist brought up to believe in God in a community where everyone believes? This fourteen-year-old theist, we may suppose, doesn't believe on the basis of evidence. He doesn't argue thus: everyone around here says God loves us and cares for us; most of what everyone around here says is true; so probably *that's* true. Instead, he simply believes what he's taught. Is he violating an all-things-considered intellectual duty? Surely not. And what about the mature theist—Thomas Aquinas, let's say—who thinks he *does* have adequate evidence? Let's suppose he's wrong; let's suppose all of his arguments are failures. Nevertheless, he has reflected long, hard, and conscientiously on the matter and thinks he *does* have adequate evidence. Shall we suppose he's violating an all-things-considered intellectual duty here? I should think not. So construed, the objector's contention is totally implausible.

Perhaps, then, he is to be understood as claiming that there is a *prima facie* intellectual duty not to believe in God without evidence. This duty can be overridden by circumstances, of course; but there is a *prima facie* obligation to believe propositions of this sort only on the basis of evidence. But here too there are problems. The suggestion is that I now have the *prima facie* obligation to believe propositions of this sort only on the basis of evidence. I have a *prima facie* duty to comply with the following command: either have evidence or don't believe. But this may be a command I can't comply with. The objector thinks there *isn't* adequate evidence for this belief, so presumably I can't *have* adequate evidence for it, unless we suppose I could create some. And it is also not within my power to refrain from believing this proposition. My beliefs aren't for the most part directly within my control. If you order me now, for example, to cease believing that the earth is very old, there's no way I can comply with your order. But in the same way it isn't within my power to cease believing in God now. So this alleged *prima facie* duty is one it isn't within my power to comply with. But how can I have a *prima facie* duty to do what isn't within my power to do?

Presumably, then, the objector means to be understood in still another fashion. Although it is not within my power now to cease believing now, there may be a series of actions now, such that I can now take the first, and after taking the first, will be able to take the second, and so on; and after taking the whole series of actions, I will no longer believe in God. Perhaps the objector thinks it is my *prima facie* duty to undertake whatever sort of regimen will at some time in the future result in my not believing without evidence. Perhaps I should attend a Universalist Unitarian Church, for example, and consort with members of the Rationalist Society of America. Perhaps I should read a lot of Voltaire and Bertrand Russell. Even if I can't now stop believing without evidence, perhaps there are other ac-

tions I can now take, such that if I do take them, then at some time in the future I won't be in this deplorable condition.

There is still another option available to the objector. He need not hold that the theist without evidence is violating some duty, *prima facie*, *ultima facie* or otherwise. Consider someone who believes that Venus is smaller than Mercury, not because he has evidence, but because he finds it amusing to believe what everyone disbelieves—or consider someone who holds this belief on the basis of an outrageously bad argument. Perhaps there is no obligation he has failed to meet; nevertheless his intellectual condition is defective in some way; or perhaps alternatively there is a commonly achieved excellence he fails to display. Perhaps he is like someone who is easily gulled, or walks with a limp, or has a serious astigmatism, or is unduly clumsy. And perhaps the evidentialist objection is to be understood, not as the claim that the theist without evidence has failed to meet some obligation, but that he suffers from a certain sort of intellectual deficiency. If this is the objector's view, then his proper attitude towards the theist would be one of sympathy rather than censure.

These are some of the ways, then, in which the evidentialist objection could be developed; and of course there are still other possibilities. For ease of exposition, let us take the claim deontologically; what I shall say will apply *mutatis mutandis* if we take it one of the other ways. The evidentialist objector, then, holds that it is irrational to believe in God without evidence. He doesn't typically hold, however, that the same goes for *every* proposition; for given certain plausible conditions on the evidence relation it would follow that if we believe anything, then we are under obligation to believe infinitely many propositions. Let's say that proposition p is *basic* for a person S if S believes p but does not have evidence for p; and let's say that p is *properly basic* for S if S is within his epistemic rights in taking p as basic. The evidentialist objection, therefore, presupposes some view about what sorts of propositions are correctly or rightly or justifiably taken as basic; it presupposes a view about what is properly basic. And the minimally relevant claim for the evidentialist objector is that belief in God is *not* properly basic. Typically this objection has been rooted in some form of *classical foundationalism,* an enormously popular picture or total way of looking at faith, knowledge, justified belief, rationality and allied topics. This picture had been widely accepted ever since the days of Plato and Aristotle; its near relatives, perhaps, remain the dominant ways of thinking about these topics. According to the classical foundationalist, some propositions are *properly* or *rightly* basic for a person and some are not. Those that are not rationally accepted only on the basis of *evidence* where the evidence must trace back, ultimately, to what is properly basic. Now there are two varieties of classical foundationalism. According to the ancient and medieval variety, a proposition is properly basic for a person *S* if and only if it is either self-evident to *S* or "evident to the senses," to use Aquinas' term for *S;* according to the modern variety, a proposition is properly basic for *S* if and only if it is either self-evident to *S* or incorrigible for him. For ease of exposition, let's say that classical foundationalism is the disjunction of ancient and medieval with modern foundationalism; according to the classical foundationalist, then, a proposition is properly basic for a person *S* if and only if it is either self-evident to *S* or incorrigible for *S* or evident to the senses for *S*.

Now I said that the evidentialist objection to theistic belief is typically rooted in classical foundationalism. Insofar as it is so rooted, it is *poorly* rooted. For classical foundationalism is self-referentially incoherent. Consider the main tenet of classical foundationalism:

(C) *p* is properly basic for *S* if and only if *p* is self-evident, incorrigible, or evident to the senses for *S*.

Now of course the classical foundationalist accepts (C) and proposes that we do so as well. And either he takes (C) as basic or he doesn't. If he doesn't, then if he is rational in accepting it,

he must by his own claims have an argument for it from propositions that are properly basic, by argument forms whose corresponding conditionals are properly basic. Classical foundationalists do not, so far as I know, offer such arguments for (C). I suspect the reason is that they don't know of any arguments of that sort for (C). It is certainly hard to see what such an argument would be. Accordingly, classical foundationalists probably take (C) as basic. But then according to (C) itself, if (C) is properly taken as basic, it must be either self-evident, incorrigible, or evident to the senses for the foundationalist, and clearly it isn't any of those. If the foundationalist takes (C) as basic, therefore, he is self-referentially inconsistent. We must conclude, I think, that the classical foundationalist is in self-referential hot water—his own acceptance of the central tenet of his view is irrational by his own standards.

Objections to Taking Belief in God as Basic

Insofar as the evidentialist objection is rooted in classical foundationalism, it is poorly rooted indeed; and so far as I know, no one has developed and articulated any other reason for supporting that belief in God is not properly basic. Of course it doesn't follow that it *is* properly basic; perhaps the class of properly basic propositions is broader than classical foundationalists think, but still not broad enough to admit belief in God. But why think so? What might be the objections to the Reformed view that belief in God is properly basic?

I've heard it argued that if I have no evidence for the existence of God, then if I accept that proposition, my belief will be *groundless,* or *gratuitous,* or *arbitrary.* I think this is an error; let me explain.

Suppose we consider perceptual beliefs, memory beliefs, and beliefs ascribing mental states to other persons: such beliefs as

(1) I see a tree.
(2) I had breakfast this morning.
(3) That person is angry.

Although beliefs of this sort are typically and properly taken as basic, it would be a mistake to describe them as *groundless*. Upon having experience of a certain sort, I believe that I am perceiving a tree. In the typical case I do not hold this belief on the basis of other beliefs; it is nonetheless not groundless. My having that characteristic sort of experience—to use Professor Chisholm's language, my being appeared treely to—plays a crucial role in the formation and justification of that belief. We might say this experience, together, perhaps, with other circumstances, is what *justifies* me in holding it; this is the *ground* of my justification, and, by extension, the ground of the belief itself.

If I see someone displaying typical pain behavior, I take it that he or she is in pain. Again, I don't take the displayed behavior as *evidence* for that belief; I don't infer that belief from others I hold; I don't accept it on the basis of other beliefs. Still, my perceiving the pain behavior plays a unique role in the formation and justification of that belief; as in the previous case, it forms the ground of my justification for the belief in question. The same holds for memory beliefs. I seem to remember having breakfast this morning; that is, I have an inclination to believe the proposition that I had breakfast, along with a certain past-tinged experience that is familiar to all but hard to describe. Perhaps we should say that I am appeared to pastly; but perhaps that insufficiently distinguishes the experience in question from that accompanying beliefs about the past not grounded in my own memory. The phenomenology of memory is a rich and unexplored realm; here I have no time to explore it. In this case as in the others, however, there is a justifying circumstance present, a condition that forms the ground of my justification for accepting the memory belief in question.

In each of these cases, a belief is taken as basic, and in each case properly taken as basic. In each case there is some circumstance or condition that confers justification; there is a circumstance that serves as the *ground* of justification.

So in each case there will be some true proposition of the sort:

(4) In condition C, S is justified in taking p as basic. Of course C will vary with p.

For a perceptual judgment such as

(5) I see a rose-colored wall before me,

C will include my being appeared to in a certain fashion. No doubt C will include more. If I'm appeared to in the familiar fashion but know that I am wearing rose-colored glasses, or that I am suffering from a disease that causes me to be thus appeared to, no matter what the color of the nearby objects, then I am not justified in taking (5) as basic. Similarly for memory. Suppose I know that my memory is unreliable; it often plays me tricks. In particular, when I seem to remember having breakfast, then, more often than not, I *haven't* had breakfast. Under these conditions I am not justified in taking it as basic that I had breakfast, even though I seem to remember that I did.

So being appropriately appeared to, in the perceptual case, is not sufficient for justification; some further condition—a condition hard to state in detail—is clearly necessary. The central point, here, however, is that a belief is properly basic only in certain conditions; these conditions are, we might say, the ground of its justification and, by extension, the ground of the belief itself. In this sense, basic beliefs are not, or are not necessarily, *groundless* beliefs.

Now similar things may be said about belief in God. When the Reformers claim that this belief is properly basic, they do not mean to say, of course, that there are no justifying circumstances for it, or that it is in that sense groundless or gratuitous. Quite the contrary. Calvin holds that God "reveals and daily discloses himself in the whole workmanship of the universe," and the divine art "reveals itself in the innumerable and yet distinct and well-ordered variety of the heavenly host." God has so created us that we have a tendency or disposition to see his hand in the world about us. More precisely, there is in us a disposition to believe propositions of the sort *this flower was created by God* or *this vast and intricate universe was created by God* when we contemplate the flower or behold the starry heavens or think about the vast reaches of the universe.

Calvin recognizes, at least implicitly, that other sorts of conditions may trigger this disposition. Upon reading the Bible, one may be impressed with a deep sense that God is speaking to one. Upon having done what I know is cheap, or wrong, or wicked, I may feel guilty in God's sight and form the belief *God disapproves of what I've done*. Upon confession and repentance, I may feel forgiven, forming the belief *God forgives me for what I've done*. A person in grave danger may turn to God, asking for His protection and help; and of course he or she then forms the belief that God is indeed able to hear and help if He sees fit. When life is sweet and satisfying, a spontaneous sense of gratitude may well up within the soul; someone in this condition may thank and praise the Lord for His goodness, and will of course form the accompanying belief that indeed the Lord is to be thanked and praised.

There are therefore many conditions and circumstances that call forth belief in God: guilt, gratitude, danger, a sense of God's presence, a sense that He speaks, perception of various parts of the universe. A complete job would explore the phenomenology of all these conditions and of more besides. This is a large and important topic; but here I can only point to the existence of these conditions.

Of course, none of the beliefs I mentioned a moment ago is the simple belief that God exists. What we have instead are such beliefs as

(6) God is speaking to me.
(7) God has created all this.
(8) God disapproves of what I have done.
(9) God forgives me.
(10) God is to be thanked and praised.

These propositions are properly basic in the right circumstances. But it is quite consistent with this to suppose that the proposition *there is such a person as God* is neither properly basic nor taken as basic by those who believe in God. Perhaps what they take as basic are such propositions as (6)–(10), believing in the existence of God on the basis of such propositions. From this point of view, it isn't exactly right to say that belief in God is properly basic; more exactly, what are properly basic are such propositions (6)–(10), each of which self-evidently entails that God exists. It isn't the relatively high level and general proposition *God exists* that is properly basic, but instead propositions detailing some of His attributes or actions.

Suppose we return to the analogy between belief in God and belief in the existence of perceptual objects, other persons, and the past. Here too it is relatively specific and concrete propositions rather than their more general and abstract colleagues that are properly basic. Perhaps such items as

(11) There are trees.
(12) There are other persons.
(13) The world has existed for more than 5 minutes

are not properly basic; it is instead such propositions as

(14) I see a tree.
(15) That person is pleased.
(16) I had breakfast more than an hour ago

that deserve the accolade. Of course, propositions of the latter sort immediately and self-evidently entail propositions of the former sort; and perhaps there is thus no harm in speaking of the former as properly basic, even though so to speak is to speak a bit loosely.

The same must be said about belief in God. We may say, speaking loosely, that belief in God is properly basic; strictly speaking, however, it is probably not that proposition but such propositions as (6)–(10) that enjoy that status. But the main point, here, is this: belief in God or (6)–(10) are properly basic; to say so, however, is not to deny that there are justifying conditions for these beliefs, or conditions that confer justification on one who accepts them as basic. They are therefore not groundless or gratuitous.

A second objection I've often heard: If belief in God is properly basic, why can't *just any* belief be properly basic? What about voodoo or astrology? What about the belief that the Great Pumpkin returns every Halloween? Could I properly take *that* as basic? And if I can't, why can I properly take belief in God as basic? Suppose I believe that if I flap my arms with sufficient vigor, I can take off and fly about the room; could I defend myself against the charge of irrationality by claiming this belief is basic? If we say that belief in God is properly basic, won't we be committed to holding that just anything, or nearly anything, can properly be taken as basic, thus throwing wide the gates to irrationalism and superstition?

Certainly not. What might lead one to think the Reformed epistemologist is in this kind of trouble? The fact that he rejects the criteria for proper basicality purveyed by classical foundationalism? But why should *that* be thought to commit him to such tolerance or irrationality? Consider an analogy. In the palmy days of positivism, the positivists went about confidently wielding their verifiability criterion and declaring meaningless much that was obviously meaningful. Now suppose someone rejected a formulation of that criterion—the one to be found in the second edition of A. J. Ayer's *Language, Truth and Logic*, for example. Would that mean she was committed to holding that

(17) 'Twas brillig; and the slithy toves did gyre and gimble in the wabe

contrary to appearances, makes good sense? Of course not. But then the same goes for the Reformed epistemologist; the fact that he rejects the Classical Foundationalist's criterion of proper basicality does not mean that he is committed to supposing just anything is properly basic.

But what then is the problem? Is it that the Reformed epistemologist not only rejects those criteria for proper basicality, but seems in no hurry to produce what he takes to be a better substitute? If he has no such criterion, how can

he fairly reject belief in the Great Pumpkin as properly basic?

This objection betrays an important misconception. How do we rightly arrive at or develop criteria for meaningfulness, or justified belief, or proper basicality? Where do they come from? Must one have such a criterion before one can sensibly make any judgments—positive or negative—about proper basicality? Surely not. Suppose I don't know of a satisfactory substitute for the criteria proposed by Classical Foundationalism; I am nevertheless entirely within my rights in holding that certain propositions are not properly basic in certain conditions. Some propositions seem self-evident when in fact they are not; that is the lesson of some of the Russell paradoxes. Nevertheless it would be irrational to take as basic the denial of a proposition that seems self-evident to you. Similarly, suppose it seems to you that you see a tree; you would then be irrational in taking as basic the proposition that you don't see a tree, or that there aren't any trees. In the same way, even if I don't know of some illuminating criterion of meaning, I can quite properly declare (17) meaningless.

And this raises an important question—one Roderick Chisholm has taught us to ask. What is the status of the criteria for knowledge, or proper basicality, or justified belief? Typically, these are universal statements. The modern foundationalist's criterion for proper basicality, for example, is doubly universal:

(18) For any proposition A and person S, A is properly basic for S if and only if A is incorrigible for S or self-evident to S.

But how could one know a thing like that? What are its credentials? Clearly enough, (18) isn't self-evident or just obviously true. But if it isn't, how does one arrive at it? What sorts of arguments would be appropriate? Of course, a foundationalist might find (18) so appealing, he simply takes it to be true, neither offering argument for it, nor accepting it on the basis of other things he believes. If he does so, however, his noetic structure will be self-referentially incoherent. (18)

itself is neither self-evident nor incorrigible; hence in accepting (18) as basic, the modern foundationalist violates the condition of proper basicality he himself lays down in accepting it. On the other hand, perhaps the foundationalist will try to produce some argument for it from premises that are self-evident or incorrigible: it is exceedingly hard to see, however, what such an argument might be like. And until he has produced such arguments, what shall the rest of us do—we who do not find (18) at all obvious or compelling? How could he use (18) to show us that belief in God, for example, is not properly basic? Why should we believe (18), or pay it any attention?

The fact is, I think, that neither (18) nor any other revealing necessary and sufficient condition for proper basicality follows from clearly self-evident premises by clearly acceptable arguments. And hence the proper way to arrive at such a criterion is, broadly speaking, *inductive*. We must assemble examples of beliefs and conditions such that the former are obviously properly basic in the latter, and examples of beliefs and conditions such that the former are obviously *not* properly basic in the latter. We must then frame hypotheses on the necessary and sufficient conditions of proper basicality and test these hypotheses by reference to those examples. Under the right conditions, for example, it is clearly rational to believe that you see a human person before you: a being who has thoughts and feelings, who knows and believes things, who makes decisions and acts. It is clear, furthermore, that you are under no obligation to reason to this belief from others you hold; under those conditions that belief is properly basic for you. But then (18) must be mistaken; the belief in question, under those circumstances, is properly basic, though neither self-evident nor incorrigible for you. Similarly, you may seem to remember that you had breakfast this morning, and perhaps you know of no reason to suppose your memory is playing you tricks. If so, you are entirely justified in taking that belief as basic. Of course it isn't properly basic on the criteria offered by classical

foundationalists; but that fact counts not against you but against those criteria.

Accordingly, criteria for proper basicality must be reached from below rather than above; they should not be presented as *obiter dicta,* but argued to and tested by a relevant set of examples. But there is no reason to assume, in advance, that everyone will agree on the examples. The Christian will of course suppose that belief in God is entirely proper and rational; if he doesn't accept this belief on the basis of other propositions, he will conclude that it is basic for him and quite properly so. Followers of Bertrand Russell and Madelyn Murray O'Hare may disagree, but how is that relevant? Must my criteria, or those of the Christian community, conform to their examples? Surely not. The Christian community is responsible to *its* set of examples, not to theirs.

Accordingly, the Reformed epistemologist can properly hold that belief in the Great Pumpkin is not properly basic, even though he holds that belief in God *is* properly basic and even if he has no full-fledged criterion of proper basicality. Of course he is committed to supposing that there is a relevant *difference* between belief in God and belief in the Great Pumpkin, if he holds that the former, but not the latter, is properly basic. But this should prove no great embarrassment; there are plenty of candidates. These candidates are to be found in the neighborhood of the conditions I mentioned in the last section that justify and ground belief in God. Thus, for example, the Reformed epistemologist may concur with Calvin in holding that God has implanted in us a natural tendency to see his hand in the world around us; the same cannot be said for the Great Pumpkin, there being no Great Pumpkin and no natural tendency to accept beliefs about the Great Pumpkin.

By way of conclusion, then: being self-evident, or incorrigible, or evident to the senses is not a necessary condition of proper basicality. Furthermore, one who holds that belief in God *is* properly basic is not thereby committed to the idea that belief in God is groundless or gratuitous or without justifying circumstances. And even if he lacks a general criterion of proper basicality, he is not obliged to suppose that just any, or nearly any, belief—belief in the Great Pumpkin, for example—is properly basic. Like everyone should, he begins with examples; and he may take belief in the Great Pumpkin, in certain circumstances, as a paradigm of irrational basic belief.

NOTES

1. See, for example, Blanshard, *Reason and Belief,* pp. 400ff; Clifford, "The Ethics of Belief," pp. 345ff;

Flew, *The Presumption of Atheism,* p. 22; Russell, "Why I Am Not a Christian," pp. 3ff; and Scriven, *Primary Philosophy,* pp. 87ff. In Plantinga, "Is Belief in God Rational?"

2. W. Salmon, "Religion and Science: A New Look at Hume's Dialogues," *Philosophical Studies* 33 (1978), p. 176.

3. A. G. N. Flew, *The Presumption of Atheism* (London: Pemberton Publishing Co., 1976).

4. A Reformed thinker or theologian is one whose intellectual sympathies lie with the Protestant tradition going back to John Calvin (not someone who was formerly a theologian and has since seen the light).

For Further Reflection

1. Has Plantinga successfully defended the view that one has no rational obligation to support one's belief in God with evidence? Explain. Compare Plantinga's view with the argument that anyone who claims that something exists must be able to give good reasons for its existence.

2. Is there a relevant difference between believing in the Great Pumpkin and believing in God? Could a worshiper of a devil use Plantinga's argument to claim that there is a natural human tendency to believe in a Creator Devil?

D. A Contemporary Debate: Does God Exist?

In March 1988 at the University of Mississippi, J. P. Moreland, a theist, and Kai Nielsen, an atheist, debated whether we are justified in believing that God exists. The debates as well as several responses are contained in the book *Does God Exist? The Great Debate* by J. P. Moreland and Kai Nielsen.

II.11   Yes, God Exists

J. P. MORELAND

J. P. Moreland (1948–) teaches philosophy at Talbot School of Theology at Biola University in California. He is the author of *Scaling the Secular City* and *Christianity and the Nature of Science.* In the debate he defends the theist position via versions of the design argument and the cosmological argument.

Study Questions

1. What does Moreland say about the possibility of proving that God exists?
2. Which arguments for the existence of God does Moreland make use of?
3. How does Moreland illustrate the classic argument with contemporary science?
4. What is Hoyle's analogy to the possibility of life arising in the universe? How likely does Hoyle say it is that life would arise?
5. How do Carl Sagan's claims about extraterrestrial intelligence support the design argument?
6. What is the difference between an actual and a potential infinite?
7. What is Moreland's argument against an actual infinite?
8. Why does Moreland think that the universe had an actual beginning?

IS IT REASONABLE in today's world to believe that God exists? My answer is yes, and the thesis I wish to defend is that it is rational to believe that God exists. I do not mean that God's existence can be proved with mathematical certainty, but I do want to argue that there are good reasons for believing in God, and the believer is well within her epistemic rights in believing that God exists.

There are a number of arguments I could offer on behalf of my thesis. Take, for example, the argument for God based on the design in the universe. In spite of David Hume, this argument has received strong support in recent years from astronomy, physics, and biology. Scientists are discovering that the universe is a finely-tuned and delicately-balanced harmony of fundamental constants, or cosmic singularities. These constants are the numerical values assigned to the various facets of the universe, such as the rate of expansion of the Big Bang, the value of the weak and strong nuclear forces, and a host of other constants of nature.

For example, in the formation of the universe, the balance of matter to antimatter had to be accurate to one part in ten billion for the universe to even arise. Had it been larger or greater by one part in ten billion, no universe would have arisen. There would also have been no universe capable of sustaining life if the expansion rate of the Big Bang had been one billionth of a percent larger or smaller.

Furthermore, the chance possibilities of life arising spontaneously through mere chance has been calculated by Cambridge astronomer Fred Hoyle as being 1×10^{40}, which Hoyle likens to the probabilities of a tornado blowing through a junkyard and forming a Boeing 747. Had these values, these cosmic constants which are independent of one another, been infinitesimally greater or smaller than what they are, no life remotely similar to ours—indeed, no life at all—would have been possible. The more we discover, the more it appears, as one scientist put it, "The universe seems to have evolved with life in mind."

The harmony of these features cannot be explained by mere chance. Says Paul Davies, theoretical physicist at Cambridge: "It is hard to resist the impression that the present structure of the universe, apparently so sensitive to minor alterations in the numbers, has been rather carefully thought out . . . the seemingly miraculous concurrence of these numerical values must remain the most compelling evidence for cosmic design."

Reprinted from Does God Exist? The Great Debate *by J. P. Moreland and Kai Nielsen (Thomas Nelson, 1990) by permission of the authors. Notes have been omitted.*

In biology, scientists have discovered that DNA molecules do not merely contain redundant order, but they contain what they call information. They say that DNA can be transcribed into RNA, and RNA can be translated into protein. Now Carl Sagan, and this is one of the few times I agree with him, has made certain claims about the search for extraterrestrial intelligence, called SETI. According to Sagan, in that search all we need to do is find one message with information in it from outer space, and we will be able to recognize the presence of intelligence. We don't even need to be able to translate it; it is the presence of information instead of order that will tip us off to the presence of intelligence. Well, what is sauce for the artificial goose ought to be sauce for the DNA gander, and I argue that the information in DNA molecules is evidence of intelligence behind it.

Or consider the arguments for God from the existence of moral value and meaning in life. If God does not exist, it is hard to see how there could be any such thing as prescriptive, nonnatural morality. It just doesn't seem that the Big Bang could spit out moral values, at least not at the rate it spit out hydrogen atoms.

As one philosopher put it: "In a world without God, mankind could not be more significant than a swarm of mosquitoes or a barnyard of pigs, for the same cosmic process that coughed them both up in the first place will eventually swallow them all up again." Even the late J. L. Mackie, perhaps the greatest atheist of our century, said, "Moral properties constitute so odd a cluster of qualities and relations that they are most unlikely to have arisen in the ordinary course of events without an all-powerful god to create them."

A typical atheist response to all of this is to say there are no irreducible moral truths in the world or irreducible moral properties. What one must do is to "create" values or decide to adopt the moral point of view. But it doesn't seem to me that the choice between Mother Teresa and Hitler can be likened, say, to the choice as to whether I am going to be a baseball player or a tuba player. Such a choice is not a rational one, and according to this response to the theistic argument, neither is the choice of adopting a moral point of view.

Mention could also be made of the arguments from the exciting archaeological confirmations of much of the Bible, the puzzling question of how mind or consciousness could have arisen in a world of only matter, and even if it did, how it could be trusted to give us truth about the world; and the fact that millions of people claim to have direct experiences of a benevolent Creator. . . .

Consider the first premise: *God created the universe from nothing a finite time ago.* This belief is rational in light of the philosophical and scientific support for it.

First the philosophical argument. It is impossible to traverse or cross an actual infinite number of events by successive addition. An actual infinite, what mathematicians call *aleph null,* $\aleph_0$ is a set of distinct things whose number is actually infinite. Infinity, plus or minus any number including infinity, is still infinity. This contrasts with a potential infinite which can increase forever without limit but is always finite.

By contrast, an actual infinite has no room for growth and is nonfinite; that is, one of its subsets can be put into one-to-one correspondence with the set itself. The impossibility of crossing an actual infinite has sometimes been put by saying that one cannot count to infinity no matter how long he counts. For he will always be at some specific number which could be increased by one to generate another specific number; and that is true even if one counted forever.

Now if one cannot cross an actual infinite, then the past must have been finite. If it were infinite, then to come to the present moment, one would have had to have traversed an actual infinite to get here, which is impossible. Without a first event, there could be no second, third, or any specifiable number of events including the present one. To get to the present moment by crossing an actual infinite would be like trying to jump out of a bottomless pit. Not only could one never complete the jump, one could never even get started; for to reach any point in the series, one must already have crossed an infinite number of points to get to that point, as Zeno's puzzles clearly showed.

Put differently, suppose you go back through the events of the past in your mind. You will either come to a beginning, or you will not. If you come to a beginning, then the past is finite and my argument is settled. That would be the first event. If you had never come to a beginning, then the past is actually infinite; and as you go back in your mind, you never in principle could exhaust the events of the past. It would be impossible to traverse the past going backward in your mind.

Since time doesn't go backward but forward, and the number of events traversed is not a function of the direction of movement, this amounts to saying that the present could never be realized. But since it has been realized—after all, here we are—there must have been a first event, and this event must have been spontaneously generated by a situation that was immutable, unchanging, timeless, and free.

Now most of the experiences we have in life where an event is spontaneously generated without sufficient conditions prior to it occur by means of *agent causation,* or what we would call agent causes. That is, you and I act everyday; we raise our arms; we do things. It seems reasonable, based upon agent causation, therefore, to say that the first event was spontaneously caused to be by a personal agent of some kind. The major alternative is that the first event popped into existence out of nothing without a cause, and that doesn't seem reasonable to me.

That there was a beginning to the universe is confirmed by two areas of science as well as philosophy. The first is the Second Law of Thermodynamics, which states that in a closed system the amount of energy available to do work is always decreasing. It can also be put by saying that the amount of disorganization, or randomness,

increases toward a maximum. Applied to the universe as a whole, the Second Law states that everyday the universe becomes more and more disorganized. In other words, it is burning up. It will eventually die a cold death. The main implication of this is, as one physicist put it, "the universe cannot have existed forever. Otherwise it would have already reached its equilibrium end state an infinite time ago. Conclusion: The universe did not always exist." Scientist Richard Slagel says, "In some way the universe must have been wound up."

The Big Bang provides another argument. In 1929 Edwin Hubble discovered a phenomenon known as the red shift, which implies that space is expanding outward and that all bodies in space are growing apart.

These and other observations have led to the Big Bang theory, which has two key features. First, around 15 billion years ago, according to the theory, everything—space, time, energy— was all compacted into a mathematical point with no dimensions, and this exploded to form the present universe. In the words of Cambridge astronomer Fred Hoyle, "The universe was shrunk down to nothing." So the Big Bang implies the universe sprang into existence from a state of affairs that has been described by some as nothingness.

Second, because of the density of the universe, there was only one initial creation, and there will be no contraction or further explosion in the future. There was only one initial creation, or first event. What is the atheist to do here? Oxford's Anthony Kenny has the answer. He says, "A proponent of the Big Bang theory, at least if he is an atheist, must believe that the matter of the universe came from nothing and by nothing."

I would like to conclude by noting an observation by Robert Jastrow, director of NASA's Goddard Institute for Space Studies. Jastrow says, "For the scientist who has lived by his faith in the power of reason, the story ends like a bad dream. He has scaled the mountains of ignorance; he is about to conquer the highest peak; as he pulls himself over the final rock, he is greeted by a band of theologians who have been sitting there for centuries."

Philosophically and scientifically, the belief that God created the universe a finite time ago is eminently reasonable. . . .

In summary, I have argued there are good reasons to believe that a personal God created the world a finite time ago. In addition to the ar-guments I cited at the beginning, I appealed to the philosophical argument against the possibil-ity of traversing an actual infinite and the scien-tific arguments employing the Second Law of Thermodynamics and the uniqueness of the Big Bang, which make this proposition reasonable.

For these and other reasons one is well within his or her epistemic rights in believing that the Christian God exists.

For Further Reflection

1. How strong are Moreland's arguments? Moreland seems to be making a cumulative case for Christian theism, apparently conceding that no one argument is decisive but claiming that altogether they make a strong case. Some have called it the ten leaky buckets argument. If no one bucket holds water because of its leaks, ten leaky buckets together won't either. Of course, if the leaky buckets are pressed close together and if they do not have holes in the same place, they may all together hold water. How can one adjudicate this problem?

II.12   No, There Is No God

KAI NIELSEN

Kai Nielsen (1926–) is professor of philosophy at Calgary University in Canada and is the author of over three hundred articles and twenty-four books, including *Ethics without God* and *Philosophy and Atheism*. In the debate he argues that the idea of a nonembodied God is incoherent. The idea of an anthropomorphic god, like Zeus, where god is said to have a body, emotions, desires, and other human-like limitations, would be *coherent*, but there is no reason to think such a being exists.

Study Questions

1. According to Nielsen, can it be rational for educated people to believe in God?
2. What is the standard view on the matter of proving the existence of God? Does either Moreland or Nielsen accept the standard view?
3. Why does Nielsen think belief in God is irrational for educated people?
4. What does Nielsen say about the anthropomorphic view of God?

5. Why is belief in a nonanthropomorphic, ethereal God incoherent?

6. How does Nielsen put "all his eggs in one basket"? Why is this risky for his purposes? What are its strengths? (See the "married bachelor" example.)

I AM GOING TO ARGUE quite to the contrary to what Professor Moreland has been saying, and this is what will seem offensive to many of you, but I certainly don't intend it to be offensive. I am going to argue that for somebody living in the twentieth century with a good philosophical and a good scientific education, who thinks carefully about the matter, that for such a person it is irrational to believe in God.

Now I don't mean by that that I think I'm more rational than Professor Moreland or the rest of you. Rational people in my view can have irrational beliefs. I'm sure I have some. If I can spot them or they're pointed out to me, I'll reject them. I also mean this in a doubly hypothetical way. By that I mean that *if* my arguments are right—that is the first hypothetical—and *if* people do have a good scientific and philosophical education—you can have one without the other—that then they should come to see that it is irrational to believe in God. What I will do is provide an argument for that in just a moment.

All right. Is the Christian view of our world the true one? The Christian, of course, sees the world in the same way as others, but sees more besides. Part of this "more besides," but not all of it, of course, is that God exists. Does He?

That question, I first want to contend, is not as straightforward as it may seem. The standard view—I mean the standard view at present, among at least philosophers and a large number of theologians, though it is not a view that either Professor Moreland or I myself accept, but it is a very standard view—is that you can't prove that God does exist and you can't prove that He doesn't exist. Indeed, some will say you can't even successfully argue that it is more probable that He does exist or more probable that God

doesn't exist. In debates concerning religion neither side has been able to win the day here.

This being so, the argument goes—this is, let me repeat, the standard view—the believer is not being unreasonable in continuing to believe, and the atheist is not being unreasonable in not believing in God. Reason, a thoughtful attention to our experience or the reflective use of our intelligence, will not settle matters here. Whether we believe or not, so the standard view has had it, is a straight matter of faith. There is no showing that belief or unbelief is the more reasonable, though it can be shown that both atheism and theism are reasonable views. What you can't do is show that one is more reasonable than the other. That is, by now, a very standard view. Philosophical theologians like John Hick or Terence Penelhum believe this—and indeed have given distinguished articulations of such views.

Now the first thing I want to note is that this is a far cry from the grand tradition of natural theology. In the Middle Ages, Thomas Aquinas and Duns Scotus and William of Occam thought they could prove that God exists and that it is irrational to be an atheist or an agnostic. Now, that's a great distance from the standard view. The standard view is a rather modern invention. A Moslem philosopher that I know regards it as a kind of a revisionism of Christianity, or, for that matter, of Islam where it is so influenced. And I take it that Professor Moreland, though he waffled a bit about this, doesn't have that standard view. He thinks that it is more probable that God exists than He does not, and in that sense you can give some kind of a proof of the existence of God. That is brave of him indeed because there are very, very few Christians, at

Reprinted from Does God Exist? The Great Debate *by J. P. Moreland and Kai Nielsen (Thomas Nelson, 1990) by permission of the authors. Notes have been omitted.*

least Christians who are philosophers, people of Thomist persuasions apart, who think you can do that. In my discussion later, I will come to some of his arguments for this.

I reject the standard view as well. I think, as I said to you initially, that belief in God is irrational. That is, it is irrational for someone who has a good scientific and philosophic education. And I point out to you that I don't mean to say by this that I think that I'm more rational than Professor Hick or some religious person, because I remind you that rational people can have irrational beliefs. And what I'm maintaining is that belief in God for people in the twentieth century, not people at all times and at all places, with a good scientific and philosophic education, is irrational.

Now why do I say that? Why, in my view, is belief in God irrational? Take a belief in a Zeus-like, *anthropomorphic* God. Such a belief is just plainly false and superstitious. Such a being is an odd kind of being, and there is no evidence for His reality. Moreover, anything that could be observed, as an anthropomorphic God could or in any way directly be detected, would not be the God of Christianity or at least of advanced Judeo-Christianity. As I think it was Kierkegaard who quipped, "God is not a great green parrot you can possibly see." But the anthropomorphic God, and anthropomorphic conception of God, is not incoherent; it's just superstitious to believe in such a god. But at least since the Middle Ages, and even earlier than that, religious people have long since, at least when they are reflecting about the nature of God, ceased believing in an anthropomorphic Zeus-like God, while continuing to believe in the God of developed Judaism, Christianity, and Islam. And it is this belief, a much far more ethereal conception of God, that I maintain is incoherent.

There are a number of arguments for that. But I am going to stick with just one, developing it in some detail. This is a dangerous strategy because it puts all your eggs in one basket, but it will allow me to develop one argument I take to be of vital importance. I'm going to use the opposite argumentative strategy from Professor Moreland. Professor Moreland gave you a battery of arguments. I'm going to give you one sustained argument principally. And if I have enough time, I'll give you some supplementary ones which will argue to the same conclusion.

Consider the problem about the reference of the word "God" or any alternative word in some other language with the same meaning. What does the word "God" refer to for Christians or for Jews?

Consider the sentence, "God made the heavens and the earth," as distinct from "Louis made pasta and cake." Consider those two sentences. What is "God" in this first sentence supposed to stand for, and how is the referent of that term to be identified? Compare this with "Louis." I can say "Somebody asked, 'Who's Louis?'" and I'll say, "That chap over there." That's what philosophers would call an *ostensive definition,* an extra-linguistic definition. I point out the reference of the term "Louis" by pointing to its referent. There is another way to give meaning to the term. I could say, "Well, the professor, one of the professors of philosophy at the University of Mississippi," or "the professor of philosophy at the University of Mississippi who studied Kierkegaard in Denmark," or "the man sitting on the platform with the dark glasses on." I could give you a number of intra-linguistic definitions, what philosophers call "definite descriptions," which identify who Louis is. So when I say, "Louis made pasta and cake," you can understand what would make that sentence true or false.

Now go back to the religious sentence, "God made the heavens and the earth." How do we know, as we said when we rejected the anthropomorphic conception, that anything that could be pointed to or literally seen or literally observed or literally experienced or literally noted wouldn't be God? It would be some kind of temporal something that you could detect; something limited. So God, unlike Louis [Pojman, the moderator of this debate], can't be identified ostensively, extra-linguistically.

Well, let us try to identify, try to establish what this God is that we speak of and concerning whom we try to use premises to prove His existence. Let us try to identify God by means of definite descriptions, that is, intra-linguistically. Suppose we say, "God is the maker of the heavens and the earth," or "The being transcendent to the world on whom all things depend and who depends on nothing himself," or "the being of infinite love to whom all things are owed," or "the infinite sustainer of the universe," or "the heavenly father of us all."

Now the difficulty with those definite descriptions, unlike the ones I used to identify Louis, is that with them, if you have trouble about knowing what was referred to by the word "God," you are going to be equally puzzled about "A being transcendent to the world." How would you identify that? Or "the being of infinite love to whom all things are owed"? How do you know what it would be like to meet such a being? What is it that you're talking about in talking about a being of infinite love? Or "The maker of the heavens and the earth," rather than "The maker of the pasta and the cake"? How would you know what that refers to?

What I'm trying to say is (and I don't say these expressions are meaningless; or that they are linguistic irregularities) that they are what philosophers would call problematic conceptions. Indeed, they are so problematic and so obscure that it turns out that we don't know what we are talking about when we use them. We have a kind of familiar pictorial sense that we know what we are talking about, but when we think very carefully about what these expressions mean, they are so problematic that we can't use them to make true or false claims.

Suppose someone says, "Look, Nielsen, you should know better than that. God, in Judeo-Christianity and Islamic religions, is the Ultimate Mystery." And that is almost definitional. A non-mysterious god might be the god of some

form of deism, but it wouldn't be the God of Christianity. But, if we say definitionally, "God is the Ultimate Mystery," if we are puzzled about the referent of "God," we are going to be terribly puzzled about what is "the Ultimate Mystery."

What are we talking about there? We need to have some account of who or what we are talking about in speaking of God. Some minimal understanding is necessary even for faith to be possible. If you have no understanding of those terms at all, then you can't take them on faith or take them on trust, because you don't know *what* to take on faith or you don't know *what* to take on trust. Nor would you use such terms in a premise. For something to be a premise in an argument, its terms must not be so problematic that we do not understand them. No matter how tight Moreland's arguments might be, he can't use them in premises if we don't know what they mean. But—or so I shall argue—we don't know what they mean.

Suppose we say, "Look, Nielsen, if you're so bloody empiricist, what you are going to do is rule out molecular biology too." We often explain biological phenomena in physical chemical terms. But the relevant chemical processes are unobservable. There is an important distinction to be made here. They are only contingently unobservable; there is no logical ban on the possibility of their being observed, even if we don't know what it would be like presently to observe them. And the same thing is true about physics. There is no logical ban; they are just contingently unobservable.

In the case of God, however, anything that could be observed would not be the God of Christianity. It would be the anthropomorphic Zeus-like god that it would be superstitious to believe in. One of the responses to this is to say, "Well, God isn't directly observable, but He is indirectly observable. You observe Him through His works and so forth and so on, through the design *in* the world and the like." This, I shall add in passing, is very different than the design *of* the world, if indeed there is design. You observe God, it is said, indirectly in His works. But it makes no sense whatsoever to say something is indirectly observable, if it is not at least in theory or in principle directly observable as well. Suppose I say to you, "There's a glass of water under this podium," or, better still, suppose I say, "There's a still over there." And you say, "How do you know there's a still?" "Well, can't you see the smoke coming up?" I respond. That is, many believe, pretty good indirect evidence for there being a still. Yet, even if it is not in reality terribly good evidence, still it is reasonable indirect evidence to there being a still there. But it is only indirect evidence at all, good or bad, because you know what it would be like to observe the bloody still, and to say, "Ah, yeah, that's what's making the smoke." That is plain enough, isn't it?

But there is no directly observing of God or directly noting His existence or personally encountering God. You can't encounter a transcendent being. (Think here literally of what you are saying.) And if so, then there is a logical ban on the very *possibility* of direct acquaintance with God. Being then parallel with the other cases, there can't be any indirect observation either. It just makes no sense to say you can indirectly observe something you have no idea of what it could even mean to directly observe.

Suppose one says, by way of counter argument, "But look, mathematical objects are unobservable. We need numbers to do mathematics, and we need mathematics to do science." That is, of course, perfectly true. We do need numbers to do mathematics, and we do need mathematics to do science. Still we need not reify numbers into queer Platonic objects. There is one group of mathematicians that does this, but a lot of them don't. There is no need to make such a reification.

But suppose, all the same, we do reify numbers; that is, objectify them as to some sort of queer objects. Let us, for the sake of the argument, allow this to be legitimate—something I wouldn't in fact allow for the moment. Let us,

that is, read numbers Platonically, and talk of numbers being eternal, of their being mathematical objects. If we do so, we cannot now, it will be claimed, say that the concept of God is incoherent. Remember, my principal basis for saying that it is irrational to believe in God is that I believe the concept of God in developed Judeo-Christianity is incoherent. I would also have to say then that to believe that there are numbers is incoherent, and that is absurd.

We can, we are now allowing, think of eternal realities, namely numbers. But God is also said to be an infinite *individual,* an infinite *person* transcendent to the universe. Acknowledging that there are eternal realities, such as numbers, gives us no purchase on this. We have no understanding of what we are talking about when we speak of an infinite person or an infinite individual transcendent to the world. Numbers, after all, are types, and not tokens, not individuals.

Let me explain what I mean by that bit of philosophical jargon. Suppose there were a blackboard here, and I wrote down the number *2* three times. How many numbers are there on the blackboard? Well, normally you would say, "There's one number; that is, one type and three tokens, three physical representations of the word *2*." So that is the difference between the words *types* and *tokens*.

Numbers are, after all, types and not tokens, and they can be eternal objects, if you want to talk in that Platonic way. But we have no understanding of what it is for an individual, a token as distinct from a type, to be eternal, such that it could not *not* exist in any possible world. But God is supposed to be a person—an individual.

We compound the trouble when we speak of infinite individuals. And remember, God has to be an individual, not a type. God is not a "kind" term. "God" does not refer to a kind of reality but supposedly to an utterly unique, infinite individual. My argument is that it doesn't make sense when you think it through. God is an infinite individual who created and sustained the world. And so even if numbers are eternal realities, and so we can give sense to eternal realities, we still haven't given sense to an individual, a token, being an eternal reality, to say nothing of giving sense to there being an infinite individual.

The definite description, "The infinite individual who made the world," is as puzzling as is God. Suppose it is said, "God's reality is *sui generis*. God just has a distinct reality which is different from any other kind of reality. It is not like mathematical reality; it is not like physical reality and so forth." But such talk of being *sui generis* is, I believe, evasive. Suppose I ask you to believe in *poy,* an utterly nonsensical term, a made-up word of mine. But I can't tell you what poy is. You can't in that circumstance, no matter how much you want to, believe in poy or have faith in poy. To do that, you would have to have some understanding of what poy is. Now what I'm trying to argue is when you really think through to what God is supposed to be, you will see that you have no more understanding of God, except as a familiarity in the language, than you have an understanding of poy. There's no way of conceptually identifying God that isn't equally problematic. . . .

Suppose someone says . . . "God by definition is eternal." That's fair enough, but it may have been eternally the case that there are no eternal individuals or persons. In saying that God is eternal, we are not saying that there are any eternal individuals or persons. We are only saying that *if* there is a God, He exists eternally. But of course, there might not be; there might never have been any eternal individuals or persons. Eternally, it might have been the case that there are no eternal individuals.

You need an argument to show that there must be an eternal individual or person. Professor Moreland tried to give one. To do that we must show that the very idea of there not being such a reality is self-contradictory. That seems at least to be either patently false or itself incoherent. To put it minimally, the notion of a logically necessary individual or person is itself at best problematical.

This being so, we cannot give coherent sense to the concept of God by that alleged definite description. It has been said, "Well, why couldn't I offer any of the following: 'God is a being which cannot not exist.' 'God is the being which exists in every possible world'?" But these are just alternative ways of speaking of a logically necessary individual or person, and it is this very notion that is so thoroughly problematic as to appear to be at least incoherent.

Let us go back, and I'm now about to finish, to our question at the beginning: Does God exist? If I am right in claiming that the concept of God in developed Judeo-Christian discourses is incoherent, then there can be no question of proving God's existence or establishing that He exists. Proof requires premises and conclusions. But if the concept of God is incoherent, it cannot be used in a premise purporting to prove that God exists. Moreover, it as well, and for the same reasons, cannot be used in a conclusion purporting to have been established by premises not employing the concept of God or other religious concepts. If the concept of God in developed Judeo-Christianity is incoherent, as I have argued it is, then arguments of the ontological type, cosmological type, or design type cannot possibly get off the ground. This being so, there is no need to consider their details. But these are the standard arguments for the existence of God. Moreover, if the very idea of there being a God of the requisite type for Judeo-Christianity is incoherent, no other argument can fare any better.

To worry this out a little bit, let me argue by analogy. Suppose I say, "All married bachelors are irascible. Jones is a married bachelor. Jones is irascible." Now that's a valid form, but it couldn't be a sound argument. Sound arguments are valid arguments with true premises, but if a premise is incoherent, then there can be no question of its being true. There is no need, if my argument is sound, even to look at the proof. Nothing could prove there is a round square or a married bachelor or that procrastination drinks melancholy. The very idea of such a thing is incoherent.

Before we go to the proofs or the evidence for God's existence, the believer must show that we know what we are talking about when we speak of God. And in closing, just one more thing. We, in some not very clear way, know our way around when we speak of God anthropomorphically, as we of course learned to use God-talk as children. That gives us the *illusion* that we understand what we are talking about when we speak of God. We are told that God is our *heavenly* Father, not a father like our real father, but our *heavenly* Father. And what's that? And eventually we move from anthropomorphic conceptions of God, which we do in some way understand, to nonanthropomorphic ones. When we engage in our devotions (if we do such things), the anthropomorphic ones reassert themselves and we feel comfortable that we understand what we are praying to, worshiping, and the like. But when we reflect, we realize that neither our religious nor our intellectual impulses will sustain the anthropomorphic conceptions. That way makes religion into superstition. So we are driven, when we reflect, to ever less anthropomorphic ones, but in doing so we pass over, unwittingly, in the very effort to gain a religiously adequate conception of God, to an incoherent conception. We do so de-anthropomorphize that we no longer understand what we are saying. Yet an anthropomorphic conception of God of any sort gives us a materially tainted God which is subject to evident empirical disconfirmation in the more obvious anthropomorphic forms, made so pantheistic that religion is naturalized, made into what in reality is a secular belief-system disguised in colorful language.

For Further Reflection

1. Nielsen argues that the concept of God is either anthropomorphic or ethereal. If God is anthropomorphic, we should be able to point him or her out. Since no one has, there's no reason to believe in such a being. If he is ethereal, it is impossible to point him or her out, so the very idea is incoherent. Is this a good argument?

2. Note that Mormons and some versions of Hinduism believe in an embodied deity. Hindus believe that Lord Krishna does manifest himself to devotees. How would Nielsen deal with this sort of claim?

Moreland's Rebuttal

Study Questions

1. Why does Moreland think that Nielsen's thesis is presumptuous?
2. Does Moreland think that it is possible to have ostensive (direct) knowledge of God? Explain.
3. What is the centipede fallacy? What does Moreland say about it in relationship to Nielsen?

MORELAND: Thank you, Dr. Nielsen, for your remarks. I'd like to center my comments on three or four different things.

First of all, consider Professor Nielsen's statement that God cannot be detected. It seems to me a little bit presumptuous and prima facie odd to say that 99.9 percent of the entire human race has literally not known what they were talking about when they used the word "God." As Professor Nielsen knows, a lot of people who have reviewed his books on his theory of the meaning of God-talk have not been particularly favorable; and though I may be wrong on this, I don't think the majority of contemporary sophisticated atheists follow him in this view. J. L. Mackie, for example, was quite willing to grant the intelligibility of God-talk. In a debate I read recently involving Antony Flew, a leading atheist, he agreed that if Jesus of Nazareth did rise from the dead, it would make the existence of God more probable. And it was at least intelligible to hold that such a thing was the case.

Second, I disagree with Professor Nielsen that God cannot be detected. I think that God can be detected in religious experience. I believe that there is a form of perception called numinous perception. People who study these sorts of things are even able to describe laws governing the nature of numinous perception. And I find numinous perception to be very, very similar to sensory perception. I argue this in *Scaling the Secular City,* and I refer you to the last chapter in that book and to a very interesting article by Wainwright on the comparison. These go into more detail than I can attempt right now.

But let me just say that I believe that God could be defined ostensively in religious experience, in awareness of a being who is holy, who is loving, wonderful, kind, and so forth. It is not the case, by the way, that the concept of God is only defined by ostension. I believe that it is possible to give content to the concept of God by inferring God as a theoretical explanation, very much as is done in science, contrary to what Professor Nielsen said.

Scientists do postulate theoretical entities, and they give theoretical terms meaning as they are embedded in theories and used to explain certain effects. The term "electron" gets some of its meaning as such and such an entity to explain such and such an effect. It is interesting to me that

two leading philosophers of science—Stanley Jaki who is a Christian and Bas van Fraasen who, I have been told, was not a Christian at the time that he wrote *The Scientific Image,* though I have heard that he has recently converted to Christianity, but I have not had a chance to check that out and I am not certain that this is true—both of these men believe that scientific realism, that is, the view that you postulate theoretical entities to explain effects in the world, utilizes a method for giving meaning to theoretical terms which is like the way Aquinas and other theists argue from effects to give meaning to the concept of God.

Now Professor Nielsen disagrees with that, but I don't see that he has made his case. It seems to me that the type of argument where you give content to a casual notion which explains a set of effects is analogous in theological and scientific causal explanations. Van Fraasen and Jaki and others in the philosophy of science have agreed.

Further, it is not true that theoretical entities in science are unobservable in practice but they could be in principle. Magnetic fields are not even observable in principle; neither is gravity, especially if you take gravity as a field rather than as an exchange of gravitons. Neither is energy, at least in its relativistic sense before it is frozen into matter. None of these things is observable in principle.

Let me say in addition that I think things like numbers do exist, but that is not the point. Professor Nielsen does not believe that numbers exist. I happen to believe they do, but whether he is or I am right on that, the point is that there have been a number of philosophers who have believed that one can have direct ostensive awareness of Platonic entities called numbers. Further, you can be aware of types, not just the tokens. I have written a book on the problem of universals, and I disagree with Nielsen's view of types and tokens.

Consider the property redness, for example. I take redness to be a Platonic entity called a universal. I can see redness even though redness is timeless. But redness, even though timeless and spaceless itself, can be instanced in a ball in my child's toy box. I can see the timeless, spaceless entity in so far as it is instanced, and I am not merely looking at the token. I am also looking at the type; I am looking at the entity redness itself.

It seems to me then that it's possible to have ostensive knowledge of God. It's also possible to have knowledge of him as you infer a cause to explain a set of effects. I would further say that Jesus of Nazareth has caused the garden to have been visited. C. S. Lewis called earth the visited planet. Perhaps miraculous acts of God could be baptismal events, to use Kripke's phrase, and meanings associated with those events, for example, "God," could be passed on through salvation history in a way similar to a Kripkian ancestral chain view of reference. Suppose that God has appeared to certain people in the past, the reference was fixed, and content given to the term "God." Salvation history could be the path in which fixity of reference was passed on through an ancestral chain very much like the way Kripke has talked about reference.

So I disagree that God cannot be detected. I believe that God-talk makes sense through ostension, through the fact that the garden has been visited by Jesus of Nazareth, through a very similar kind of meaning postulate as is used in science, and through analogy with myself as I reflect upon my own faculties and form a conception of God as a being who has intellect, emotion, and will.

What Nielsen has done is to commit what I call the centipede fallacy. If the centipede took long enough to look at his legs and figure out how in the world he walks, he would probably end up stumbling and falling. And philosophers are guilty of the centipede effect all the time. The centipede knows very well that he can walk, even though he can't give you all the details about how he does so. Most people know very well what "God" means, and they use it to refer, even if they cannot give you a complete theory of reference and meaning to explain this.

There is no philosophical topic of interest wherein philosophers are in universal agreement regarding how we talk about it or what its definition is. No philosopher to my knowledge has given a universally accepted definition of "knowledge." I couldn't for the life of me define "history." I'm not sure I could define "love"; I'm not sure that I could define to everyone's satisfaction what a number is. And I couldn't define to everyone's satisfaction what God is nor how I refer to any of these entities. Nonetheless, it does seem reasonable that I could know something about these things, whether or not I could give an exhaustive treatment of how those terms get meaning. We can know them truly without knowing them exhaustively.

Take design, for example. As I mentioned earlier, there are a number of examples of design. Richard Taylor gives the following illustration: Suppose you were driving on a train and you saw a sign on the hillside that said, "Wales in ten miles." Suppose that you knew that the wind had blown that sign together. If the sign had been put together by a purely nonintelligent random process, says Taylor, there would be no reason to trust the information conveyed by the sign.

Similarly, it seems to me that if our intellectual and sensory faculties were merely the result of the wind blowing, as it were, or a struggle for survival, there would be no reason to trust that they give us accurate information about the world. All that would be needed for survival value would be consistency. If an amoeba saw as small an enemy that was really large, and a thing that was really small was seen as large, as long as it could see things consistently, it could survive, evolutionarily speaking. It would not need to have the truth or see accurately.

As Alvin Plantinga has recently argued, the reliability of our cognitive and sensory capacities is most reasonably explained in light of the fact that they were designed to give us reliable information about the world.

Nielsen's Rebuttal

Study Questions

1. How does Nielsen deal with Moreland's claim that God can be detected, e.g., in the resurrection of Jesus?

2. What does Nielsen say about mystical experiences? Do they cause people to detect God? Why or why not?

3. What is the Platonic fallacy which Nielsen accuses Moreland of committing?

4. What does Nielsen say about the plurality of religions?

NIELSEN: I appreciate Professor Moreland's thoughtful remarks, and what I think I will do before I go to what he said himself in his initial remarks is to respond to some of the comments he has just made.

He wants to argue—it surprises me a bit—that he thinks God can be detected. You can have an ostensive definition of God. Now he says that even Antony Flew, whose views on religion are rather like mine, believes that if Jesus of Nazareth was raised from the dead this would give us an ostensive definition of God, enabling us to give intelligibility to God-talk and would, if true, provide some evidence that God exists. I don't see how. Jesus, let us suppose—I don't know much about such things and to be perfectly frank, I'm not terribly interested in them—but let us just suppose it were the case that Jesus was raised from the dead. Suppose you collected the bones, and they together in some way reconstituted the living Jesus. Suppose something like that really happened. Suppose there were good historical evidence for it. I have no idea if there is or isn't; I suspect for anything like that, there isn't very good evidence, but let us assume there is. This wouldn't show there was an infinite intelligible being. It wouldn't give you any way of being able to detect if there is a God. It would be just that a very strange happening happened, namely, that somebody who died—or certainly appeared to have died—came together again as a living human being. It would not enable you to understand at all what you were talking about

concerning an infinite individual. It would just be a very peculiar fact we hadn't explained and indeed lacked the scientific resources to explain. And the same thing is true of the familiar resurrection story.

When Moreland says that about 99 percent of the philosophers agree that God can be detected, I doubt that very much. But what they do say when they say that God-talk is intelligible, and I grant this, is that *anthropomorphic* God-talk is intelligible. Where the concept is sufficiently anthropomorphic, the concept is perfectly intelligible. Moreover, I've never said that God-talk is meaningless. I simply said that it is so problematic, when you get a completely ethereal God who is supposed to be an infinite individual transcendent to the world, that we literally don't know what we are talking about, though we have the illusion that we do.

Suppose, Moreland remarked, referring to the famous work of a very interesting man, Rudolph Otto, we advert to numinous perceptions. But these were numinous feelings; they weren't perceptions in any ordinary sense. And they weren't the sort of thing that enabled you to observe or detect God. Religious experience doesn't enable you to detect God. It is, of course, perfectly true that people have religious experiences, including mystical experiences. But that is a different matter. That is a matter of having certain feelings. Moreover, Buddhists have such experiences, but Buddhists don't claim to see God but Christians and Sufis do. It depends upon what religious framework you start with. Religious experience is a matter of feelings, and feelings are not a way of cognition. But even if religious experience were a form of cognition, it is so variously interpreted from religious tradition to religious tradition that there is no good reason to believe it yields a direct knowledge of God.

Moreland talked today about scientific realism and potentialities and he referred to Bas van Fraasen. . . . His view is a very instrumentalist view of these things. It is hardly a matter of realism. The point is that when a theoretical entity in physics is an entity that could be real in the world, it is something that, like an electron or a neutron, is judged to be just very very very very very much smaller than some microscopic objects. In some cases, say that of a photon, we have no idea what it would be like to observe it or what we would have to observe to observe. We only see its traces. But still if it is really a minuscule particle in the universe, there can be no logical ban on the possibility of its being observed. If it really is part of the same universe as rocks and trees and grains of sand, it cannot be logically impossible to see it. It is, as the positivists used to say, in principle possible directly to verify that there are photons.

There are other notions, perhaps fields of forces, that may be theoretical *constructions*. They may just be useful devices for talking about the world. They are not meant to point to things in the world that could be detected. Which of the conceptions of physics are which—which are constructs and which are real entities—is not for Moreland and myself to decide, but for physicists to decide, and physicists often disagree about this.

Moreland wants to give analogies to seeing God. He can, he tells us, see redness or types. He can't see redness; what he sees is various red objects which have the characteristic redness. There's no seeing of redness and the like. He says, "Well, look, definitions are hard to give by definite description." But to note problems here,

he said, indicates that I committed the centipede fallacy. Well, I do not know exactly or even inexactly what is involved here or whether it is even a kind of fallacy.

He commits the more familiar *Platonic fallacy*. It is as difficult to define "chair" as it is to define "knowledge," to give necessary and sufficient conditions for all of those things and only those things which are chairs. Nobody has been able to do that. We can identify chairs perfectly well, and what he's referring to is that we do know what knowledge is even though we can't define knowledge. But I'm saying that for an entity as mysterious as God, some people think they understand and believe in its reality and some people don't. There are real doubts, as is not the case, with chairs or with knowledge. Moreover, it is impossible to identify God. If I can't define a chair, at least I can point to one. But by contrast, to point out the God you can't define is impossible.

Moreland made an appeal to arguments for design. As far as I can see, they only point at best to design in the world. They don't point to design *of* the world, nor do they show that a personal infinite creator created it. There could have been a number of creators, some of them long gone. The same thing is true about actual infinities. The most, the very most it could give him would be some *factually* necessary beings or being. It wouldn't give him an infinite eternal God. It wouldn't be able to link up with the Jesus of Nazareth who supposedly is the one true God or at least the son of the one true God.

One thing about the historicity of Jesus. When I bring this out you will see why I'm not much interested in it. What I read in Moreland's book about his account of the historicity of Jesus is that he shows clearly enough that it wasn't a myth that the Christian community tried to purvey, rather they were recording what they actually believed happened. As I read that, it seemed a very plausible thing to say, though I don't know what biblical scholars would say about it. But this shows us nothing at all about Jesus being divine. It only shows us that some people thought he was.

One of the things he does about quoting authorities—he quotes the ones on his side, not the ones on the other side, for the most part. And that is an easy game to play. There are plenty of such authorities.

These matters are much more problematical about actual infinites than he gives to understand. But even if his argument about actual infinites would work, and I'm not sure that it does, again this would not get you to an infinite God. Even more seriously, it wouldn't get you to something that wasn't utterly naturalistic.

Finally, even if there is this historicity side, the point is that there is a historicity side to the other religions too. And if you want to say, "I'm going to accept my Christian faith on the basis of the revelations in the Bible and so forth," then it is natural to ask why the Christian ones rather than Jewish ones or Hindu ones and the like. Putative revelations are plentiful. How do you know that the Christian putative revelations are the genuine ones and not the Hindu ones? If you stick with claims internal to the Christian Bible, you go in a vicious circle. Granting its historicity, Christianity makes a lot of claims that are beyond empirical check. Some of them are incapable of empirical check. So do all the other reli-

gious doctrines. Why the Bible rather than the Koran? Why the Bible rather than the canonical Buddhist texts? Why the Bible rather than the Hindu texts? Why the Bible rather than the religious revelations of other people? If you look at religion anthropologically, you will see that there are thousands of religions all claiming "The truth."

And just because there are more Christians than there are of any other religion doesn't prove anything. Suppose Hitler had won the war. First you would get rid of the Jews, then the Blacks (Christians and non-Christians), and then the Indians. After that cleansing is done, you start getting rid of the Christian whites until there is only a small sect of Christian whites left. Would that prove that the Christian message is any less true? Would it in those circumstances be less true because there weren't very many Christians about? So what I'm trying to say is there are thousands of putative revelations in the world. And as far as I can see, there is no more reason to rely on the Christian revelation than any of those others.

I ask you, why the Bible rather than the Koran? Why the Bible rather than any other historically extensive systems of faith? And do not say that really they are all saying the same thing because they do not. Buddhism is very different indeed from Christianity.

Suggestions for Further Reading

GENERAL

Davies, Brian. *An Introduction to the Philosophy of Religion.* Oxford: Oxford University Press, 1982. Readable, reliable, written from a distinctive theistic framework.
Hick, John. *Arguments for the Existence of God.* London: Macmillan, 1971. A clearly written, insightful examination.
Mackie, J. L. *The Miracle of Theism.* Oxford: Oxford University Press, 1982. A lively discussion of the proofs by one of the ablest atheist philosophers of our time, but uneven.
Matson, Wallace. *The Existence of God.* Ithaca, NY: Cornell University Press, 1965. A cogent attack on the traditional arguments.
Pojman, Louis. *Philosophy of Religion: An Anthology.* Belmont, CA: Wadsworth, 1987.

Rowe, William. *Philosophy of Religion: An Introduction*. Belmont, CA: Dickenson, 1978. A very readable and reliable introduction for beginners.

Swinburne, Richard. *The Existence of God*. Oxford: Clarendon Press, 1979. Perhaps the most sustained, if not the overall best, defense of the traditional arguments since the Middle Ages.

Yandell, Keith. *Christianity and Philosophy*. Grand Rapids, MI: Eerdmans, 1984. A rigorously analytic approach, crammed full of outlines of arguments without as much discussion as one might like.

THE COSMOLOGICAL ARGUMENT

Craig, William. *The Cosmological Argument from Plato to Leibniz*. New York: Barnes & Noble, 1980. A good survey of the history of the argument.

Rowe, William. *The Cosmological Argument*. Princeton, NJ: Princeton University Press, 1975. A very thorough and penetrating study of the classic formulations (especially Aquinas, Scotus, and Clark).

THE TELEOLOGICAL ARGUMENT

McPherson, Thomas. *The Argument from Design*. London: Macmillan, 1972. A good introduction to the various forms of the argument.

Salmon, Wesley. "Religion and Science: A New Look at Hume's Dialogue." *Philosophical Studies* 33 (1978), 145.

Swinburne, Richard. "The Argument from Design—A Defence." *Religious Studies* 8 (1972), 193–205.

Swinburne, Richard. "The Argument from Design." *Philosophy* 43 (1968). A detailed response to Hume.

Tennant, R. R. *Philosophical Theology*. Cambridge, England: Cambridge University Press, 1928–30. A classic post-Humean version of the teleological argument.

THE ONTOLOGICAL ARGUMENT

Barnes, Jonathan. *The Ontological Argument*. London: Macmillan, 1972. A good general discussion of the argument.

Plantinga, Alvin, ed. *The Ontological Argument from St. Anselm to Contemporary Philosophers*. Garden City, NY: Doubleday, 1965.

THE PROBLEM OF EVIL

Lewis, C. S. *The Problem of Pain*. London: Geoffrey Bles, 1940. Clear and cogent.

Mackey, J. L. "Evil and Omnipotence." *Mind* 64 (1955), 200–212. One of the earlier contemporary attacks on the existence of God from the argument from evil, used in many anthologies.

Mackie, J. L. *The Miracle of Theism*. Oxford: Oxford University Press, 1982. Chapter 9 is insightful and well-argued from an atheist's point of view.

McCloskey, H. J. "God and Evil." *The Philosophical Quarterly* 10 (1960). A sharp attack on theism, arguing that given the problem of evil theism is indefensible.

Pike, Nelson. "Hume on Evil." *The Philosophical Review* LXXII (1963), 180–97. A trenchant criticism of Hume's position.

Plantinga, Alvin. *The Nature of Necessity*. Oxford: Clarendon Press, 1974. Chapter 9 is an excellent article developing in detail a version of the free will defense. A more accessible version of his argument is found in Plantinga's *God, Freedom and Evil* (New York: Harper & Row, 1974).

Rowe, William. "The Problem of Evil and Some Varieties of Atheism." *APQ* 16 (1970), 335–41.

Swinburne, Richard. *The Existence of God*. Oxford: Oxford University Press, 1978. Chapter 11 contains a fuller defense than is in the article included in this volume.

Wainwright, William J. "God and the Necessity of Physical Evils." *Sophia* 11 (1972), 16–19.

FAITH AND REASON

Delaney, C. F., ed. *Rationality and Religious Belief*. University of Notre Dame Press, 1978. A good collection of essays on faith and reason.

Flew, Antony. *The Presumption of Atheism*. New York: Harper & Row, 1976. Part I, Chapters 1, 2, and 5 are relevant to the discussion.

Mackie, J. L. *The Miracle of Theism: Arguments for and against the Existence of God*. Oxford: Clarendon Press, 1982. Probably the best defense of atheism in recent years, taking into consideration every major argument in the field.

Mavrodes, George. *Belief in God*. New York: Random House, 1970. A clear presentation of religious epistemology.

Mitchell, Basil. *The Justification of Religious Belief*. London: Macmillan, 1973. A good discussion of the cumulative case for theism.

Phillips, D. Z. *Religion without Explanation*. Oxford: Basil Blackwell, 1976. A valuable study by one of the foremost Wittgensteinian philosophers.

Plantinga, Alvin and Wolterstorff, Nicholas, eds. *Faith and Rationality*. Notre Dame: University of Notre Dame Press, 1983.

Pojman, Louis. *Religious Belief and the Will*. London: Routledge & Kegan Paul, 1986.

Swinburne, Richard. *Faith and Reason*. Oxford: Clarendon Press, 1981. One of the best studies of the subject in recent years.

Part III

Knowledge

I am the wisest man alive, for I know one thing, and that is that I know nothing.

SOCRATES in Plato's *The Apology*

WHAT DO WE REALLY KNOW? How can we be certain that we have the truth?

The theory of knowledge, or epistemology (from the Greek "the science of knowledge"), inquires into the nature of knowledge and justification of our beliefs. Many philosophers believe that it is the central area of philosophy, for if philosophy is the quest for truth, then we need to know how we obtain the truth and justify our beliefs, how we judge propositions as true. The first issue that arises is whether we can possess any truth at all.

To claim to know something is to claim to possess the truth. But can we ever be certain that we do possess the truth? People make knowledge claims everyday which turn out to be false. We often misremember and misperceive. Sometimes we make knowledge claims that are contradicted by those of others. For example, you and your sister each claim to have washed the dishes last night. A Moslem priest and a Roman Catholic theologian each claims that his is the true religion. While hiking in the forest, you feel sure that the campsite is to the right, while your friend is equally convinced that it is to the left. You are absolutely sure that Communism is evil, while your roommate is equally convinced that it is the only hope for a better world.

In these contrary cases both parties cannot be correct, but it could turn out that neither is. It could be that both you and your sister are misremembering that you washed the dishes last night, and that your mother did. It is logically possible that neither Islam nor Catholicism is the truth. Both you and your friend could be wrong about the whereabouts of the campsite, for it could be in front of or behind you. And it could turn out that Communism is neither completely evil nor the only hope for a better world.

What do we really know? And how can we know when indeed we really *do* know something? Could it be that we know nothing at all? Could it be that we do not even know that we know nothing at all? *Skepticism* is the theory that we do not have any knowledge; that we cannot be completely certain of any of our beliefs, not even the belief that we cannot be completely certain of any of our beliefs. For all we know, the universe and everything in it could have doubled in size last night while we were sleeping. We cannot check this by measuring our height with a ruler, because the ruler has also doubled in size. How could we prove that the world didn't double in size or become 27 percent smaller? How can we prove that the world and ourselves were not created seven minutes ago with all our apparent memories of the past built into our minds, fossils built into the stones, and buildings artificially aged? Could the world all be an illusion? How can we prove there are indeed other minds, that the other beings in our classroom are not just cleverly constructed robots programmed to speak and smile and write exams? How do you know that you are not the only person who exists and that everything else is merely part of a long dream you are dreaming? Soon you will awaken and be surprised to discover that what you thought were dreams were really mini-dreams within one grand and glorious maxi-dream. Or perhaps you are simply a brain suspended in a tub full of a chemical solution in a laboratory and wired to a computer which is causing you to have your apparent present experiences? If you are under the control of an ingenious scientist (me, the author of this introduction), you will never discover it, for I have arranged it that you will only be able to compare your beliefs to the experiences I simulate. Your tub is your destiny!

Can you defeat the skeptic? In our first reading, the French philosopher René Descartes (1596–1650), the father of modern philosophy, attempts to use skepticism in order to defeat skepticism. He doubted in such a way that, he hoped, would pave the way for the end of doubt and the beginning of absolute certainty. Like many perceptive young people, Descartes had been disillusioned by the discovery that many of the so-called "truths" which he had been taught in home and school turned out to be false. Having a healthy hatred of deception and an equally healthy love of truth, he endeavored to find a method that would guarantee truth and insure against error.

Descartes was a *rationalist* who believed that all truth can be known by the mind alone by inquiring within itself. He held to the doctrine of innate ideas (that the mind possesses knowledge at birth) which we know *a priori*—i.e., prior to experience, though experience may be necessary to stimulate awareness of this knowledge.

Our next three readings, by John Locke (1632–1704), George Berkeley (1685–1753), and David Hume (1711–1776), represent an opposite tradition, called *empiricism*. This is the school of philosophy which asserts that the source of all knowledge is experience. John Locke stated that our minds were like blank slates (*tabula rasa*) on which experience writes her messages. There are no innate ideas. There is no *a priori* knowledge; all knowledge is known *a posteriori,* on the basis of experience. Berkeley rejects Locke's commonsense notion of a material world which is the object of perception and claims that matter doesn't exist. Only perceivers and perceptions exist. Hume sets forth an empirical version of skepticism.

Immanuel Kant (1724–1804), in our fifth reading, attempts to reconcile rationalism and empiricism. In our sixth reading, John Hospers offers a modern account of knowledge as true, justified belief.

Cartesian Theory of Knowledge III.

RENÉ DESCARTES

René Descartes (1596–1650) was born in France and educated by the Jesuits at the College of La Fleche. After a three-year career as a professional soldier, he travelled through Europe, trying to complete his education by reading the "great book of the world." Finally, he settled in Holland and began to write philosophical treatises. These were radically innovative because instead of starting with the accumulated authority of the medieval tradition, Descartes began with his own experience and philosophized from there. The self becomes the center of authority instead of the tradition. His two major works are *Discourse on Method* (1637) and *Meditations on First Philosophy* (1641), from which our present selection is taken.

Descartes writes philosophy in the first person singular. He desires to know the truth, and he realizes that this will be an arduous enterprise since he has discovered by painful experience that much of what he has been taught and has taken for granted is false. He must destroy his tottering house of "knowledge" and lay a new foundation upon which to construct an indestructible edifice. The method consists of doubting everything that can be doubted, and then, upon the pure remainder of certain truth, beginning the process of constructing an indubitable system of knowledge. The result is a type of rationalism in which the only certainties are discovered by the mind through self-evident insight or reason.

Study Questions

1. What caused Descartes to begin the process of doubting everything?
2. Why does he not examine all of his beliefs separately?
3. Why does he doubt his senses?
4. Why does he posit the idea of an evil genius who always deceives him?
5. What is the first thing that Descartes comes to know with certainty?

Meditation One: Concerning Those Things That Can Be Called into Doubt

SEVERAL YEARS HAVE NOW PASSED since I first realized how many were the false opinions that in my youth I took to be true, and thus how doubtful were all the things that I subsequently built upon these opinions. From the time I became aware of this, I realized that for once I had to raze everything in my life, down to the very bottom, so as to begin again from the first foundations, if I wanted to establish anything firm and lasting in the sciences. But the task seemed so enormous that I waited for a point in my life that was so ripe that no more suitable a time for laying hold of these disciplines would come to pass. For this reason, I have delayed so long that I would be at fault were I to waste on deliberation the time that is left for action. Therefore, now that I have liberated my mind from all cares, and I have secured for myself some leisurely and carefree time, I withdraw in solitude. I will, in short, apply myself earnestly and openly to the general destruction of my former opinions.

Yet to this end it will not be necessary that I show that all my opinions are false, which perhaps I could never accomplish anyway. But because reason now persuades me that I should withhold my assent no less carefully from things which are not plainly certain and indubitable than I would to what is patently false, it will be sufficient justification for rejecting them all, if I find a reason for doubting even the least of them. Nor therefore need one survey each opinion one after the other, a task of endless proportion. Rather—because undermining the foundations will cause whatever has been built upon them to fall down of its own accord—I will at once attack those principles which supported everything that I once believed.

Reprinted from Descartes' Meditations on First Philosophy, *trans. Donald A. Cress (Hackett Publishing Company, 1979) by permission of the publisher. Copyright © 1979.*

Whatever I had admitted until now as most true I took in either from the senses or through the senses; however, I noticed that they sometimes deceived me. And it is a mark of prudence never to trust wholly in those things which have once deceived us.

But perhaps, although the senses sometimes deceive us when it is a question of very small and distant things, still there are many other matters which one certainly cannot doubt, although they are derived from the very same senses: that I am sitting here before the fireplace wearing my dressing gown, that I feel this sheet of paper in my hands, and so on. But how could one deny that these hands and that my whole body exist? Unless perhaps I should compare myself to insane people whose brains are so impaired by a stubborn vapor from a black bile that they continually insist that they are kings when they are in utter poverty, or that they are wearing purple robes when they are naked, or that they have a head made of clay, or that they are gourds, or that they are made of glass. But they are all demented, and I would appear no less demented if I were to take their conduct as a model for myself.

All of this would be well and good, were I not a man who is accustomed to sleeping at night, and to undergoing in my sleep the very same things—or now and then even less likely ones— as do these insane people when they are awake. How often has my evening slumber persuaded me of such customary things as these: that I am here, clothed in my dressing gown, seated at the fireplace, when in fact I am lying undressed between the blankets! But right now I certainly am gazing upon this piece of paper with eyes wide awake. This head which I am moving is not heavy with sleep. I extend this hand consciously and deliberately and I feel it. These things would not be so distinct for one who is asleep. But this all seems as if I do not recall having been deceived by similar thoughts on other occasions in my dreams. As I consider these cases more intently, I see so plainly that there are no defi-

nite signs to distinguish being awake from being asleep that I am quite astonished, and this astonishment almost convinces me that I am sleeping.

Let us say, then, for the sake of argument, that we are sleeping and that such particulars as these are not true: that we open our eyes, move our heads, extend our hands. Perhaps we do not even have these hands, or any such body at all. Nevertheless, it really must be admitted that things seen in sleep are, as it were, like painted images, which could have been produced only in the likeness of true things. Therefore at least these general things (eyes, head, hands, the whole body) are not imaginary things, but are true and exist. For indeed when painters wish to represent sirens and satyrs by means of bizarre and unusual forms, they surely cannot ascribe utterly new natures to these creatures. Rather, they simply intermingle the members of various animals. And even if they concoct something so utterly novel that its likes have never been seen before (being utterly fictitious and false), certainly at the very minimum the colors from which the painters compose the thing ought to be true. And for the same reason, although even these general things (eyes, head, hands, and the like) can be imaginary, still one must necessarily admit that at least other things that are even more simple and universal are true, from which, as from true colors, all these things—be they true or false—which in our thought are images of things, are constructed.

To this class seems to belong corporeal nature in general, together with its extension; likewise the shape of extended things, their quantity or size, their number; as well as the place where they exist, the time of their duration, and other such things.

Hence perhaps we do not conclude improperly that physics, astronomy, medicine, and all the other disciplines that are dependent upon the consideration of composite things are all doubtful. But arithmetic, geometry, and other such disciplines—which treat of nothing but the simplest and most general things and which are indifferent as to whether these composite things do or do not exist—contain something certain and indubitable. For whether I be awake or asleep, two plus three makes five, and a square does not have more than four sides; nor does it seem possible that such obvious truths can fall under the suspicion of falsity.

All the same, a certain opinion of long standing has been fixed in my mind, namely that there exists a God who is able to do anything and by whom I, such as I am, have been created. How do I know that he did not bring it about that there be no earth at all, no heavens, no extended thing, no figure, no size, no place, and yet all these things should seem to me to exist precisely as they appear to do now? Moreover—for I judge that others sometimes make mistakes in matters that they believe they know most perfectly—how do I know that I am not deceived every time I add two and three or count the sides of a square or perform an even simpler operation, if such can be imagined? But perhaps God has not willed that I be thus deceived, for it is said that he is good in the highest degree. Nonetheless, if it were repugnant to his goodness that he should have created me such that I be deceived all the time, it would seem, from this same consideration, to be foreign to him to permit me to be deceived occasionally. But we cannot make this last assertion.

Perhaps there are some who would rather deny such a powerful God, than believe that all other matters are uncertain. Let us not put these people off just yet; rather, let us grant that everything said here about God is fictitious. Now they suppose that I came to be what I am either by fate or by chance or by a continuous series of events or by some other way. But because being deceived and being mistaken seem to be imperfections, the less powerful they take the author of my being to be, the more probable it will be that I would be so imperfect as to be deceived perpetually. I have nothing to say in response to these arguments. At length I am forced to admit that there is nothing, among the things I once believed to be true, which it is not permissible to doubt—not for reasons of frivolity or a lack of forethought, but because of valid and considered arguments. Thus I must carefully withhold assent no less from these things than from the patently false, if I wish to find anything certain.

But it is not enough simply to have made a note of this; I must take care to keep it before my mind. For long-standing opinions keep coming back again and again, almost against my will; they seize upon my credulity, as if it were bound over to them by long use and the claims of intimacy. Nor will I get out of the habit of assenting to them and believing in them, so long as I take them to be exactly what they are, namely, in some respects doubtful as by now is obvious, but nevertheless highly probable, so that it is much more consonant with reason to believe them than to deny them. Hence, it seems to me, I would do well to turn my will in the opposite direction, to deceive myself and pretend for a considerable period that they are wholly false and imaginary, until finally, as if with equal weight of prejudice* on both sides, no bad habit should turn my judgment from the correct perception of things. For indeed I know that no danger or error will follow and that it is impossible for me to indulge in too much distrust, since I now am concentrating only on knowledge, not on action.

Thus I will suppose not a supremely good God, the source of truth, but rather an evil genius, as clever and deceitful as he is powerful, who has directed his entire effort to misleading me. I will regard the heavens, the air, the earth, colors, shapes, sounds, and all external things as nothing but the deceptive games of my dreams, with which he lays snares for my credulity. I will regard myself as having no hands, no eyes, no flesh, no blood, no senses, but as nevertheless falsely believing that I possess all these things.

---

*A "prejudice" is a prejudgment, that is, an adjudication of an issue without having first reviewed the appropriate evidence.

I will remain resolutely fixed in this meditation, and, even if it be out of my power to know anything true, certainly it is within my power to take care resolutely to withhold my assent to what is false, lest this deceiver, powerful and clever as he is, have an effect on me. But this undertaking is arduous, and laziness brings me back to my customary way of living. I am not unlike a prisoner who might enjoy an imaginary freedom in his sleep. When he later begins to suspect that he is sleeping, he fears being awakened and conspires slowly with these pleasant illusions. In just this way, I spontaneously fall back into my old beliefs, and dread being awakened, lest the toilsome wakefulness which follows upon a peaceful rest, have to be spent thenceforward not in the light but among the inextricable shadows of the difficulties now brought forward.

Meditation Two: Concerning the Nature of the Human Mind: That the Mind Is More Known Than the Body

Yesterday's meditation filled my mind with so many doubts that I can no longer forget about them—nor yet do I see how they are to be resolved. But, as if I had suddenly fallen into a deep whirlpool, I am so disturbed that I can neither touch my foot to the bottom, nor swim up to the top. Nevertheless I will work my way up, and I will follow the same path I took yesterday, putting aside everything which admits of the least doubt, as if I had discovered it to be absolutely false. I will go forward until I know something certain—or, if nothing else, until I at least know for certain that nothing is certain. Archimedes sought only a firm and immovable point in order to move the entire earth from one place to another. Surely great things are to be hoped for if I am lucky enough to find at least one thing that is certain and indubitable.

Therefore I will suppose that all I see is false. I will believe that none of those things that my deceitful memory brings before my eyes ever existed. I thus have no senses: body, shape, extension, movement, and place are all figments of my imagination. What then will count as true? Perhaps only this one thing: that nothing is certain.

But on what grounds do I know that there is nothing over and above all those which I have just reviewed, concerning which there is not even the least cause for doubt? Is there not a God (or whatever name I might call him) who instills these thoughts in me? But why should I think that, since perhaps I myself could be the author of these things? Therefore am I not at least something? But I have already denied that I have any senses and any body. Still, I hesitate; for what follows from that? Am I so tied to the body and to the senses that I cannot exist without them? But I have persuaded myself that there is nothing at all in the world: no heaven, no earth, no minds, no bodies. Is it not then true that I do not exist? But certainly I should exist, if I were to persuade myself of something. But there is a deceiver (I know not who he is) powerful and sly in the highest degree, who is always purposely deceiving me. Then there is no doubt that I exist, if he deceives me. And deceive me as he will, he can never bring it about that I am nothing so long as I shall think that I am something. Thus it must be granted that, after weighing carefully and sufficiently everything, one must come to the considered judgment that the statement "I am, I exist" is necessarily true every time it is uttered by me or conceived in my mind.

But I do not yet understand well enough who I am—I, who now necessarily exist. And from this point on, I must take care lest I imprudently substitute something else in place of myself; and thus be mistaken even in that knowledge which I claim to be the most certain and evident of all. To this end, I shall meditate once more on what I once believed myself to be before having embarked upon these deliberations. For this reason, then, I will set aside whatever can be refuted even to a slight degree by the arguments brought forward, so that at length there shall remain precisely nothing but what is certain and unshaken.

What therefore did I formerly think I was? A man, of course. But what is a man? Might I not say a rational animal? No, because then one would have to inquire what an "animal" is and what "rational" means. And then from only one question we slide into many more difficult ones. Nor do I now have enough free time that I want to waste it on subtleties of this sort. But rather here I pay attention to what spontaneously and by my own nature came into my thought beforehand whenever I pondered what I was. Namely, it occurred to me first that I have a face, hands, arms, and this entire mechanism of bodily members, the very same as are discerned in a corpse— which I referred to by the name "body." It also occurred to me that I eat, walk, feel and think; these actions I used to assign to the soul as their cause. But what this soul was I either did not think about or I imagined it was something terribly insubstantial—after the fashion of a wind, fire, or ether—which has been poured into my coarser parts. I truly was not in doubt regarding the body; rather I believed that I distinctly knew its nature, which, were I perhaps tempted to describe it such as I mentally conceived it, I would explain it thus: by "body," I understand all that is suitable for being bounded by some shape, for being enclosed in some place, and thus for filling up space, so that it excludes every other body from that space; for being perceived by touch, sight, hearing, taste, or smell; for being moved in several ways, not surely by itself, but by whatever else that touches it. For I judged that the power of self-motion, and likewise of sensing or of thinking, in no way pertains to the nature of the body. Nonetheless, I used to marvel especially that such faculties were found in certain bodies.

But now what am I, when I suppose that some deceiver—omnipotent and, if I may be allowed to say it, malicious—takes all the pains he can in order to deceive me? Can I not affirm that I possess at least a small measure of all those traits which I already have said pertain to the nature of the body? I pay attention, I think, I deliberate—but nothing happens. I am wearied of repeating this in vain. But which of these am I to ascribe to the soul? How about eating or walking? These are surely nothing but illusions, because I do not have a body. How about sensing? Again, this also does not happen without a body, and I judge that I really did not sense those many things I seemed to have sensed in my dreams. How about thinking? Here I discover that thought is an attribute that really does not belong to me. This alone cannot be detached from me. I am; I exist; this is certain. But for how long? For as long as I think. Because perhaps it could also come to pass that if I should cease from all thinking I would then utterly cease to exist. I now admit nothing that is not necessarily true. I am therefore precisely only a thing that thinks; that is, a mind, or soul, or intellect, or reason—words the meaning of which I was ignorant before. Now, I am a true thing, and truly existing; but what kind of thing? I have said it already: a thing that thinks.

What then? I will set my imagination going to see if I am not something more. I am not that connection of members which is called the human body. Neither am I some subtle air infused into these members, not a wind, not a fire, not a vapor, not a breath—nothing that I imagine to myself, for I have supposed all these to be nothing. The assertion stands: the fact still remains that I am something. But perhaps it is the case that nevertheless, these very things which I take to be nothing (because I am ignorant of them) in reality do not differ from that self which I know. This I do not know. I shall not quarrel about it right now; I can make a judgment only regarding things which are known to me. I know that I exist; I ask now who is this "I" whom I know. Most certainly the knowledge of this matter, thus precisely understood, does not depend upon things that I do not yet know to exist. Therefore, it is not dependent upon any of those things that I feign in my imagination. But this word "feign" warns me of my error. For I would be feigning if I should "imagine" that I am something, because imagining is merely the contemplation of the shape or image of a corporeal thing. But I know now with certainty that I am, and at the same time it could happen that all these images—and, generally, everything that pertains to the nature of the body—are nothing but dreams. When these things are taken into account, I would speak no less foolishly were I to say: "I will imagine so that I might recognize more distinctly who I am," than were I to say: "Now I surely am awake, and I see something true, but because I do not yet see it with suffi-cient evidence, I will take the trouble of going to sleep so that my dreams might show this to me more truly and more evidently." Thus I know that none of what I can comprehend by means of the imagination pertains to this understanding that I have of myself. Moreover, I know that I must be most diligent about withdrawing my mind from these things so that it can perceive its nature as distinctly as possible.

But what then am I? A thing that thinks. What is that? A thing that doubts, understands, affirms, denies, wills, refuses, and which also imagines and knows.

For Further Reflection

1. Are you convinced by Descartes' argument? Is the self the most certain of objects?

2. Is Descartes' argument against trusting the senses a valid one? Why should we always distrust the senses? Discuss this issue and compare it with what Locke says when you get to the next reading. Descartes is a *rationalist,* believing that unaided reason can discover all truth, whereas Locke and Hume are *empiricists,* believing that sense perception is the only way to knowledge. Keep this in mind as you continue in this section.

3. Does Descartes convince you that the mind is more certain than matter?

Empiricist Theory of Knowledge   III.2

JOHN LOCKE

The English philosopher John Locke (1632–1704) was educated at Oxford University, where he became a tutor in Greek rhetoric and philosophy. Later he was a practicing physician and assistant to the Earl of Shaftesbury. His work on representative government and human rights greatly influenced the founding fathers of the United States. His principal works are *Two Treatises on Government* (1689), *The Reasonableness of Christianity* (1695), and *An Essay Concerning Human Understanding* (1689), from which the present reading is taken.

Locke's work in the theory of knowledge is the first systematic assault on Cartesian rationalism, the view that reason alone guarantees knowledge. Locke argued that if our claims to knowledge make any sense, they must be derived from the world. He rejects the rationalist notion that we have innate ideas (actual knowledge of metaphysical truths, such as mathematical truths, universals, and the laws of nature) because (1) there is not good deductive argument establishing the existence of such entities, (2) children and idiots do not seem to possess them, and (3) an empirical way of knowing, which seems far more reasonable, has no place for such entities. Locke does believe that we have intuitive knowledge of our own existence and that the existence of God can be demonstrated by reason (see Book IV, Chapter XI in this selection). Scholars are puzzled at this apparent inconsistency, but Locke would respond that it is no inconsistency. We know that we exist upon immediate reflection because of the nature of consciousness, not because of any prior knowledge hidden within us. Neither have we innate knowledge of God. It is simply that we can reason from empirical truths about the world to the existence of God (using such arguments as the cosmological and teleological arguments we discussed in Part II).

According to Locke, the mind at birth is a *tabula rasa,* a blank slate. It is like white paper, devoid of characteristics until it receives sense perceptions. All knowledge begins with sensory experience upon which the powers of the mind operate, developing complex ideas, abstractions, and the like. In place of the absolute certainty that the rationalists sought to find, Locke says that apart from the knowledge of the self, most of what we know we know in degrees of certainty derived from inductive generalizations. For example, we see the sun rise every morning and infer that it is highly probable that it will rise tomorrow, but we cannot be absolutely certain.

Study Questions

1. Why is it important to inquire into the structure of human understanding?
2. Describe Locke's design of purpose. Which ideas does he plan to treat and which to omit?
3. What is his method?
4. What does he mean by the word "idea"?
5. What are so-called "innate principles" (or "ideas")? What is Locke's view of them?
6. What does Locke argue is the origin of our ideas?
7. What is the difference between primary and secondary qualities?
8. Describe Locke's view of the degrees of knowledge. What are the highest degrees of knowledge and what do we know to lesser degrees?
9. What is Locke's view of probability?

Introduction

1. AN INQUIRY INTO THE UNDERSTANDING *pleasant and useful.*——Since it is the *understanding* that sets man above the rest of sensible beings, and gives him all the advantage and dominion which he has over them; it is certainly a subject, even for its nobleness, worth our labour to inquire into. The understanding, like the eye, whilst it makes us see and perceive all other things, takes no notice of itself; and it requires art and pains to set it at a distance and

From An Essay Concerning Human Understanding *(London: E. Holt, 1689).*

make it its own object. But whatever be the difficulties that lie in the way of this inquiry; whatever it be that keeps us so much in the dark to ourselves; sure I am that all the light we can let in upon our minds, all the acquaintance we can make with our own understandings, will not only be very pleasant, but bring us great advantage, in directing our thoughts in the search of other things.

2. *Design.*——This, therefore, being my purpose—to inquire into the original, certainty, and extent of *human knowledge,* together with the grounds and degrees of *belief, opinion,* and *assent;*—I shall not at present meddle with the physical consideration of the mind; or trouble myself to examine wherein its essence consists; or by what motions of our spirits or alterations of our bodies we come to have any *sensation* by our organs, or any *ideas* in our understandings; and whether those ideas do in their formation, any or all of them, depend on matter or not. These are speculations which, however curious and entertaining, I shall decline, as lying out of my way in the design I am now upon. It shall suffice to my present purpose, to consider the discerning faculties of a man, as they are employed about the objects which they have to do with. And I shall imagine I have not wholly misemployed myself in the thoughts I shall have on this occasion, if, in this historical, plain method, I can give any account of the ways whereby our understandings come to attain those notions of things we have; and can set down any measures of the certainty of our knowledge; or the grounds of those persuasions which are to be found amongst men, so various, different, and wholly contradictory; and yet asserted somewhere or other with such assurance and confidence, that he that shall take a view of the opinions of mankind, observe their opposition, and at the same time consider the fondness and devotion wherewith they are embraced, the resolution and eagerness wherewith they are maintained, may perhaps have reason to suspect, that either there is no such thing as truth at all, or that mankind

hath no sufficient means to attain a certain knowledge of it.

3. *Method.*——It is therefore worth while to search out the bounds between opinion and knowledge; and examine by what measures, in things whereof we have no certain knowledge, we ought to regulate our assent and moderate our persuasion. In order whereunto I shall pursue this following method:—

First, I shall inquire into the original of those *ideas,* notions, or whatever else you please to call them, which a man observes, and is conscious to himself he has in his mind; and the ways whereby the understanding comes to be furnished with them.

Secondly, I shall endeavour to show what *knowledge* the understanding hath by those ideas; and the certainty, evidence, and extent of it.

Thirdly, I shall make some inquiry into the nature and grounds of *faith* or *opinion:* whereby I mean that assent which we give to any proposition as true, of whose truth yet we have no certain knowledge. And here we shall have occasion to examine the reasons and degrees of *assent.*

Book I

CHAPTER I

1. It is an established opinion amongst some men, that there are in the understanding certain *innate principles;* some primary notions, κοιναὶ ἔννοιαι, characters, as it were stamped upon the mind of man; which the soul receives in its very first being, and brings into the world with it. It would be sufficient to convince unprejudiced readers of the falseness of this supposition, if I should only show (as I hope I shall in the following parts of this Discourse) how men, barely by the use of their natural faculties, may attain to all the knowledge they have, without the help of any innate impressions; and may arrive at certainty, without any such original notions or principles. For I imagine any one will easily grant that it would be impertinent to suppose

the ideas of colours innate in a creature to whom god hath given sight, and a power to receive them by the eyes from external objects: and no less unreasonable would it be to attribute several truths to the impressions of nature, and innate characters, when we may observe in ourselves faculties fit to attain as easy and certain knowledge of them as if they were originally imprinted on the mind.

But because a man is not permitted without censure to follow his own thoughts in the search of truth, when they lead him ever so little out of the common road, I shall set down the reasons that made me doubt of the truth of that opinion, as an excuse for my mistake, if I be in one; which I leave to be considered by those who, with me, dispose themselves to embrace truth wherever they find it.

2. There is nothing more commonly taken for granted than that there are certain *principles,* both *speculative* and *practical* (for they speak of both), universally agreed upon by all mankind: which therefore, they argue, must needs be the constant impressions which the souls of men receive in their first beings, and which they bring into the world with them, as necessarily and really as they do any of their inherent faculties.

3. This argument, drawn from universal consent, has this misfortune in it, that if it were true in matter of fact, that there were certain truths wherein all mankind agreed, it would not prove them innate, if there can be any other way shown how men may come to that universal agreement, in the things they do consent in, which I presume may be done.

4. But, which is worse, this argument of universal consent, which is made use of to prove innate principles, seems to me a demonstration that there are none such because there are none to which all mankind give an universal assent. I shall begin with the speculative, and instance in those magnified principles of demonstration, "Whatsoever is, is," and "It is impossible for the same thing to be and not to be;" which, of all others, I think have the most allowed title to innate. These have so settled a reputation of maxims universally received, that it will no doubt be thought strange if any one should seem to question it. But yet I take liberty to say, that these propositions are so far from having an universal assent, that there are a great part of mankind to whom they are not so much as known.

5. For, first, it is evident, that all children and idiots have not the least apprehension or thought of them. And the want of that is enough to destroy that universal assent which must needs be the necessary concomitant of all innate truths: it seeming to me near a contradiction to say, that there are truths imprinted on the soul, which it perceives or understands not: imprinting, if it signify anything, being nothing else but the making certain truths to be perceived. For to imprint anything on the mind without the mind's perceiving it, seems to me hardly intelligible. If therefore children and idiots have souls, have minds, with those impressions upon them, *they* must unavoidably perceive them, and necessarily know and assent to these truths; which since they do not, it is evident that there are no such impressions. For if they are not notions naturally imprinted, how can they be innate? and if they are notions imprinted, how can they be unknown? To say a notion is imprinted on the mind, and yet at the same time to say that the mind is ignorant of it, and never yet took notice of it, is to make this impression nothing. No proposition can be said to be in the mind which it never yet knew, which it was never yet conscious of. For if any one may, then, by the same reason, all propositions that are true, and the mind is capable ever of assenting to, may be said to be in the mind, and to be imprinted: since, if any one can be said to be in the mind, which it never yet knew, it must be only because it is capable of knowing it; and so the mind is of all truths it ever shall know. Nay, thus truths may be imprinted on the mind which it never did, nor ever shall know; for a man may live long, and die

at last in ignorance of many truths which his mind was capable of knowing, and that with certainty. So that if the capacity of knowing be the natural impression contended for, all the truths a man ever comes to know will, by this account, be every one of them innate; and this great point will amount to no more, but only to a very improper way of speaking; which, whilst it pretends to assert the contrary, says nothing different from those who deny innate principles. For nobody, I think, ever denied that the mind was capable of knowing several truths. The capacity, they say, is innate; the knowledge acquired. But then to what end such contest for certain innate maxims? If truths can be imprinted on the understanding without being perceived, I can see no difference there can be between any truths the mind is *capable* of knowing in respect of their original: they must all be innate or all adventitious: in vain shall a man go about to distinguish them. He therefore that talks of innate notions in the understanding, cannot (if he intend thereby any distinct sort of truths) mean such truths to be in the understanding as it never perceived, and is yet wholly ignorant of. For if these words "to be in the understanding" have any propriety, they signify to be understood. So that to be in the understanding, and not to be understood; to be in the mind and never to be perceived, is all one as to say anything is and is not in the mind or understanding. If therefore these two propositions, "Whatsoever is, is," and "It is impossible for the same thing to be and not to be," are by nature imprinted, children cannot be ignorant of them: infants, and all that have souls, must necessarily have them in their understandings, know the truth of them, and assent to it. . . .

Book II

CHAPTER I

1. Every man being conscious to himself that he thinks and that which his mind is applied about whilst thinking being the *ideas* that are there, it is past doubt that men have in their minds several ideas,—such as are those expressed by the words *whiteness, hardness, sweetness, thinking, motion, man, elephant, army, drunkenness,* and others: it is in the first place then to be inquired, *How he comes by them?*

I know it is a received doctrine, that men have native ideas, and original characters, stamped upon their minds in their very first being. This opinion I have at large examined already; and, I suppose what I have said in the foregoing Book will be much more easily admitted, when I have shown whence the understanding may get all the ideas it has; and by what ways and degrees they may come into the mind;—for which I shall appeal to every one's own observation and experience.

2. Let us then suppose the mind to be, as we say, white paper, void of all characters, without any ideas:—How comes it to be furnished? Whence comes it by that vast store which the busy and boundless fancy of man has painted on it with an almost endless variety? Whence has it all the *materials* of reason and knowledge? To this I answer, in one word, from EXPERIENCE. In that all our knowledge is founded; and from that it ultimately derives itself. Our observation employed either, about external sensible objects, or about the internal operations of our minds perceived and reflected on by ourselves, is that which supplies our understandings with all the *materials* of thinking. These two are the fountains of knowledge, from whence all the ideas we have, or can naturally have, do spring.

3. First, our Senses, conversant about particular sensible objects, do convey into the mind several distinct perceptions of things, according to those various ways wherein those objects do affect them. And thus we come by those *ideas* we have of *yellow, white, heat, cold, soft, hard, bitter, sweet,* and all those which we call sensible qualities; which when I say the senses convey into the mind, I mean, they from external objects convey into the mind what produces there those percep-

tions. This great source of most of the ideas we have, depending wholly upon our senses, and derived by them to the understanding, I call SENSATION.

4. Secondly, the other fountain from which experience furnisheth the understanding with ideas is,—the perception of the operations of our own mind within us, as it is employed about the ideas it has got;—which operations, when the soul comes to reflect on and consider, do furnish the understanding with another set of ideas, which could not be had from things without. And such are *perception, thinking, doubting, believing, reasoning, knowing, willing,* and all the different actings of our own minds;—which we being conscious of, and observing in ourselves, do from these receive into our understandings as distinct ideas as we do from bodies affecting our senses. This source of ideas every man has wholly in himself, and though it be not sense, as having nothing to do with external objects, yet it is very like it, and might properly enough be called *internal sense*. But as I call the other Sensation, so I call this REFLECTION, the ideas it affords being such only as the mind gets by reflecting on its own operations within itself. By reflection then, in the following part of this discourse, I would be understood to mean, that notice which the mind takes of its own operations, and the manner of them, by reason whereof there come to be ideas of these operations in the understanding. These two, I say, viz. external material things, as the objects of SENSATION, and the operations of our own minds within, as the objects of REFLECTION, are to me the only originals from whence all our ideas take their beginnings. The term *operations* here I use in a large sense, as comprehending not barely the actions of the mind about its ideas, but some sort of passions arising sometimes from them, such as is the satisfaction or uneasiness arising from any thought.

5. The understanding seems to me not to have the least glimmering of any ideas which it doth not receive from one of these two. *External objects* furnish the mind with the ideas of sensible qualities, which are all those different perceptions they produce in us; and *the mind* furnishes the understanding with ideas of its own operations.

These, when we have taken a full survey of them, and their several modes, combinations, and relations, we shall find to contain all our whole stock of ideas; and that we have nothing in our minds which did not come in one of these two ways. Let any one examine his own thoughts, and thoroughly search into his understanding; and then let him tell me, whether all the original ideas he has there, are any other than of the objects of his senses, or of the operations of his mind, considered as objects of his reflection. And how great a mass of knowledge soever he imagines to be lodged there, he will, upon taking a strict view, see that he has not any idea in his mind but what one of these two have imprinted;—though perhaps, with infinite variety compounded and enlarged by the understanding, as we shall see hereafter.

6. He that attentively considers the state of a child, at his first coming into the world, will have little reason to think him stored with plenty of ideas, that are to be the matter of his future knowledge. It is *by degrees* he comes to be furnished with them. And though the ideas of obvious and familiar qualities imprint themselves before the memory begins to keep a register of time or order, yet it is often so late before some unusual qualities come in the way, that there are few men that cannot recollect the beginning of their acquaintance with them. And if it were worth while, no doubt a child might be so ordered as to have but a very few, even of the ordinary ideas, till he were grown up to a man. But all that are born into the world, being surrounded with bodies that perpetually and diversely affect them, variety of ideas, whether care be taken of it or not, are imprinted on the minds of children. Light and colours are busy at hand everywhere, when the eye is but open; sounds and some tangible qualities fail not to solicit

their proper senses, and force an entrance to the mind;—but yet, I think, it will be granted easily, that if a child were kept in a place where he never saw any other but black and white till he were a man, he would have no more ideas of scarlet or green, than he that from his childhood never tasted an oyster, or a pine-apple, has of those particular relishes. . . .

CHAPTER VIII

8. Whatsoever the mind perceives *in itself*, or is the immediate object of perception, thought, or understanding, that I call *idea;* and the power to produce any idea in our mind, I call *quality* of the subject wherein that power is. Thus a snow-ball having the power to produce in us the ideas of white, cold, and round,—the power to produce those ideas in us, as they are in the snow-ball, I call qualities; and as they are sensations or perceptions in our understandings, I call them ideas; which *ideas,* if I speak of sometimes as in the things themselves, I would be understood to mean those qualities in the objects which produce them in us.

9. Qualities thus considered in bodies are, *First,* such as are utterly inseparable from the body, in what state soever it be; and such as in all the alterations and changes it suffers, all the force can be used upon it, it constantly keeps; and such as sense constantly finds in every particle of matter which has bulk enough to be perceived; and the mind finds inseparable from every particle of matter, though less than to make itself singly be perceived by our senses: v.g. Take a grain of wheat, divide it into two parts; each part has still solidity, extension, figure, and mobility: divide it again, and it retains still the same qualities; and so divide it on, till the parts become insensible; they must retain still each of them all those qualities. For division (which is all that a mill, or pestle, or any other body, does upon another, in reducing it to insensible parts) can never take away either solidity, extension, figure, or mobility from any body, but

only makes two or more distinct separate masses of matter, of that which was but one before; all which distinct masses, reckoned as so many distinct bodies, after division, make a certain number.

These I call *original* or *primary qualities* of body, which I think we may observe to produce simple ideas in us, viz. solidity, extension, figure, motion or rest, and number.

10. *Secondly,* such qualities which in truth are nothing in the objects themselves but powers to produce various sensations in us by their primary qualities, i.e. by the bulk, figure, texture, and motion of their insensible parts, as colours, sounds, tastes, etc. These I call *secondary qualities.* To these might be added a *third* sort, which are allowed to be barely powers; though they are as much real qualities in the subject as those which I, to comply with the common way of speaking, call qualities, but for distinction, secondary qualities. For the power in fire to produce a new colour, or consistency, in *wax* or *clay,*—by its primary qualities, is as much a quality in fire, as the power it has to produce in *me* a new idea or sensation of warmth or burning, which I felt not before,—by the same primary qualities, viz. the bulk, texture, and motion of its insensible parts. . . .

13. . . . let us suppose at present that the different motions and figures, bulk and number, of such particles, affecting the several organs of our senses, produce in us those different sensations which we have from the colours and smells of bodies; v.g. that a violet, by the impulse of such insensible particles of matter, of peculiar figures and bulks, and in different degrees and modifications of their motions, causes the ideas of the blue colour, and sweet scent of that flower to be produced in our minds. It being no more impossible to conceive that God should annex such ideas to such motions, with which they have no similitude, than that he should annex the idea of pain to the motion of a piece of steel dividing our flesh, with which that idea hath no resemblance.

14. What I have said concerning colours and smells may be understood also of tastes and sounds, and other the like sensible qualities; which, whatever reality we by mistake attribute to them, are in truth nothing in the objects themselves, but powers to produce various sensations in us; and depend on those primary qualities, viz. bulk, figure, texture, and motion of parts as I have said.

15. From whence I think it easy to draw this observation,—that the ideas of primary qualities of bodies are resemblances of them, and their patterns do really exist in the bodies themselves, but the ideas produced in us by these secondary qualities have no resemblance of them at all. There is nothing like our ideas, existing in the bodies themselves. They are, in the bodies we denominate from them, only a power to produce those sensations in us: and what is sweet, blue, or warm in idea, is but the certain bulk, figure, and motion of the insensible parts, in the bodies themselves, which we call so.

16. Flame is denominated hot and light; snow, white and cold; and manna, white and sweet, from the ideas they produce in us. Which qualities are commonly thought to be the same in those bodies that those ideas are in us, the one the perfect resemblance of the other, as they are in a mirror, and it would by most men be judged very extravagant if one should say otherwise. And yet he that will consider that the same fire that, at one distance produces in us the sensation of warmth, does, at a nearer approach, produce in us the far different sensation of pain, ought to bethink himself what reason he has to say—that this idea of warmth, which was produced in him by the fire, is *actually in the fire;* and his idea of pain, which the same fire produced in him the same way, is *not* in the fire. Why are whiteness and coldness in snow, and pain not, when it produces the one and the other idea in us; and can do neither, but by the bulk, figure, number, and motion of its solid parts? . . .

21. Ideas being thus distinguished and under-

stood, we may be able to give an account how the same water, at the same time, may produce the idea of cold by one hand and of heat by the other: whereas it is impossible that the same water, if those ideas were really in it, should at the same time be both hot and cold. For, if we imagine *warmth,* as it is in our hands, to be nothing but a certain sort and degree of motion in the minute particles of our nerves or animal spirits, we may understand how it is possible that the same water may, at the same time, produce the sensations of heat in one hand and cold in the other; which yet *figure* never does, that never producing the idea of a square by one hand which has produced the idea of a globe by another. But if the sensation of heat and cold be nothing but the increase or diminution of the motion of the minute parts of our bodies, caused by the corpuscles of any other body, it is easy to be understood, that if that motion be greater in one hand than in the other; if a body be applied to the two hands, which has in its minute particles a greater motion than in those of one of the hands, and a less than in those of the other, it will increase the motion of the one hand and lessen it in the other; and so cause the different sensations of heat and cold that depend thereon. . . .

When children have, by repeated sensations, got ideas fixed in their memories, they begin by degrees to learn the use of signs. And when they have got the skill to apply the organs of speech to the framing of articulate sounds, they begin to make use of words, to signify their ideas to others. These verbal signs they sometimes borrow from others, and sometimes make themselves, as one may observe among the new and unusual names children often give to things in the first use of language.

The use of words then being to stand as outward marks of our internal ideas, and those ideas being taken from particular things, if every particular idea that we take in should have a distinct name, names must be endless. To prevent this, the mind makes the particular ideas received from particular objects to become general; which is done by considering them as they are in the mind such appearances,—separate from all other existences, and the circumstances of real existence, as time, place, or any other concomitant ideas. This is called ABSTRACTION, whereby ideas taken from particular beings become general representatives of all of the same kind; and their names general names, applicable to whatever exists conformable to such abstract ideas. Such precise, naked appearances in the mind, without considering how, whence, or with what others they came there, the understanding lays up (with names commonly annexed to them) as the standards to rank real existences into sorts, as they agree with these patterns, and to denominate them accordingly. Thus the same colour being observed to-day in chalk or snow, which the mind yesterday received from milk, it considers that appearance alone, makes it a representative of all of that kind; and having given it the name *whiteness*, it by that sound signifies the same quality wheresoever to be imagined or met with; and thus universals, whether ideas or terms, are made. . . .

Book IV

CHAPTER II

1. All our knowledge consisting, as I have said, in the view the mind has of its own ideas, which is the utmost light and greatest certainty we, with our faculties, and in our way of knowledge, are capable of, it may not be amiss to consider a little the degrees of its evidence. The different clearness of our knowledge seems to me to lie in the different way of perception the mind has of the agreement or disagreement of any of its ideas. For if we will reflect on our own ways of thinking, we will find, that sometimes the mind perceives the agreement or disagreement of two ideas *immediately by themselves,* without the intervention of any other: and this I think we may call *intuitive knowledge.* For in this the mind is at

no pains of proving or examining, but perceives the truth as the eye doth light, only by being directed towards it. Thus the mind perceives that *white* is not *black,* that a *circle* is not a *triangle,* that *three* are more than *two* and equal to *one and two.* Such kinds of truths the mind perceives at the first sight of the ideas together, by bare intuition; without the intervention of any other idea: and this kind of knowledge is the clearest and most certain that human frailty is capable of. This part of knowledge is irresistible, and, like bright sunshine, forces itself immediately to be perceived, as soon as ever the mind turns its view that way; and leaves no room for hesitation, doubt, or examination, but the mind is presently filled with the clear light of it. *It is on this intuition that depends all the certainty and evidence of all our knowledge;* which certainty every one finds to be so great, that he cannot imagine, and therefore not require a greater: for a man cannot conceive himself capable of a greater certainty than to know that any idea in his mind is such as he perceives it to be; and that two ideas, wherein he perceives a difference, are different and not precisely the same. He that demands a greater certainty than this, demands he knows not what, and shows only that he has a mind to be a sceptic, without being able to be so. Certainty depends so wholly on this intuition, that, in the next degree of knowledge which I call demonstrative, this intuition is necessary in all the connexions of the intermediate ideas, without which we cannot attain knowledge and certainty.

2. The next degree of knowledge is, where the mind perceives the agreement or disagreement of any ideas, but not immediately. Though wherever the mind perceives the agreement or disagreement of any of its ideas, there be certain knowledge; yet it does not always happen, that the mind sees that agreement or disagreement, which there is between them, even where it is discoverable; and in that case remains in ignorance, and at most gets no further than a probable conjecture. The reason why the mind can-

not always perceive presently the agreement or disagreement of two ideas, is, because those ideas, concerning whose agreement or disagreement the inquiry is made, cannot by the mind be so put together as to show it. In this case then, when the mind cannot so bring its ideas together as by their immediate comparison, and as it were juxta-position or application one to another, to perceive their agreement or disagreement, it is fain, *by the intervention of other ideas* (one or more, as it happens) to discover the agreement or disagreement which it searches; and this is that which we call *reasoning*. Thus, the mind being willing to know the agreement or disagreement in bigness between the three angles of a triangle and two right ones, cannot by an immediate view and comparing them do it: because the three angles of a triangle cannot be brought at once, and be compared with any other one, or two, angles; and so of this the mind has no immediate, no intuitive knowledge. In this case the mind is fain to find out some other angles, to which the three angles of a triangle have an equality; and, finding those equal to two right ones, comes to know their equality to two right ones.

3. Those intervening ideas, which serve to show the agreement of any two others, are called *proofs;* and where the agreement and disagreement is by this means plainly and clearly perceived, it is called *demonstration;* it being *shown* to the understanding, and the mind made to see that it is so. A quickness in the mind to find out these intermediate ideas (that shall discover the agreement or disagreement of any other), and to apply them right, is, I suppose, that which is called *sagacity*.

4. This knowledge, by intervening proofs, though it be certain, yet the evidence of it is not altogether so clear and bright, nor the assent so ready, as in intuitive knowledge. For, though in demonstration the mind does at last perceive the agreement or disagreement of the ideas it considers; yet it is not without pains and attention:

there must be more than one transient view to find it. A steady application and pursuit are required to this discovery: and there must be a progression by steps and degrees, before the mind can in this way arrive at certainty, and come to perceive the agreement or repugnancy between two ideas that need proofs and the use of reason to show it.

5. Another difference between intuitive and demonstrative knowledge is, that, though in the latter all doubt be removed when, by the intervention of the intermediate ideas, the agreement or disagreement is perceived, yet before the demonstration there was a doubt; which in intuitive knowledge cannot happen to the mind that has its faculty of perception left to a degree capable of distinct ideas; no more than it can be a doubt to the eye (that can distinctly see white and black), whether this ink and this paper be all of a colour. If there be sight in the eyes, it will, at first glimpse, without hesitation, perceive the words printed on this paper different from the colour of the paper: and so if the mind have the faculty of distinct perception, it will perceive the agreement or disagreement of those ideas that produce intuitive knowledge. If the eyes have lost the faculty of seeing, or the mind of perceiving, we in vain inquire after the quickness of sight in one, or clearness of perception in the other. . . .

14. These two, viz. intuition and demonstration, are the degrees of our *knowledge;* whatever comes short of one of these, with what assurance soever embraced, is but *faith* or *opinion*, but not knowledge, at least in all general truths. There is, indeed, another perception of the mind, employed about *the particular existence of finite beings without us,* which, going beyond bare probability, and yet not reaching perfectly to either of the foregoing degrees of certainty, passes under the name of *knowledge*. There can be nothing more certain than that the idea we receive from an external object is in our minds: this is intuitive knowledge. But whether there be any-

thing more than barely that idea in our minds; whether we can thence certainly infer the existence of anything without us, which corresponds to that idea, is that whereof some men think there may be a question made; because men may have such ideas in their minds, when no such thing exists, no such object affects their senses. But yet here I think we are provided with an evidence that puts us past doubting. For I ask any one, Whether he be not invincibly conscious to himself of a different perception, when he looks on the sun by day, and thinks on it by night; when he actually tastes wormwood, or smells a rose, or only thinks on that savour or odour? We as plainly find the difference there is between any idea revived in our minds by our own memory, and actually coming into our minds by our senses, as we do between any two distinct ideas. If any one say, a dream may do the same thing, and all these ideas may be produced in us without any external objects; he may please to dream that I make him this answer:—1. That it is no great matter, whether I remove his scruple or no: where all is but dream, reasoning and arguments are of no use, truth and knowledge nothing. 2. That I believe he will allow a very manifest difference between dreaming of being in the fire, and being actually in it. But yet if he be resolved to appear so sceptical as to maintain, that what I call being actually in the fire is nothing but a dream; and that we cannot thereby certainly know, that any such thing as fire actually exists without us: I answer, That we certainly finding that pleasure or pain follows upon the application of certain objects to us, whose existence we perceive, or dream that we perceive, by our senses; this certainty is as great as our happiness or misery, beyond which we have no concernment to know or to be. So that, I think, we may add to the two former sorts of knowledge this also, of the existence of particular external objects, by that perception and consciousness we have of the actual entrance of ideas from them, and allow these three degrees of knowledge, viz.

intuitive, demonstrative, and *sensitive:* in each of which there are different degrees and ways of evidence and certainty. . . .

CHAPTER XI　OF OUR KNOWLEDGE OF THE EXISTENCE OF OTHER THINGS

1. The knowledge of our own being we have by intuition. The existence of a God, reason clearly makes known to us, as has been shown.

The knowledge of the existence of *any other thing* we can have only by *sensation:* for there being no necessary connexion of real existence with any *idea* a man hath in his memory; nor of any other existence but that of God with the existence of any particular man: no particular man can know the existence of any other being, but only when, by actual operating upon him, it makes itself perceived by him. For, the having the idea of anything in our mind, no more proves the existence of that thing, than the picture of a man evidences his being in the world, or the visions of a dream make thereby a true history.

2. It is therefore the *actual receiving* of ideas from without that gives us notice of the existence of other things, and makes us know, that something doth exist at that time without us, which causes that idea in us; though perhaps we neither know nor consider how it does it. For it takes not from the certainty of our senses, and the ideas we receive by them, that we know not the manner wherein they are produced: v.g. whilst I write this, I have, by the paper affecting my eyes, that idea produced in my mind, which, whatever object causes, I call *white;* by which I know that that quality or accident (i.e. whose appearance before my eyes always causes that idea) doth really exist, and hath a being without me. And of this, the greatest assurance I can possibly have, and to which my faculties can attain, is the testimony of my eyes, which are the proper and sole judges of this thing; whose testimony I have reason to rely on as so certain, that I can no more doubt, whilst I write this, that I see white

and black, and that something really exists that causes that sensation in me, than that I write or move my hand; which is a certainty as great as human nature is capable of, concerning the existence of anything, but a man's self alone, and of God.

3. The notice we have by our senses of the existing of things without us, though it be not altogether so certain as our intuitive knowledge, or the deductions of our reason employed about the clear abstract ideas of our own minds; yet it is an assurance that deserves the name of *knowledge*. If we persuade ourselves that our faculties act and inform us right concerning the existence of those objects that affect them, it cannot pass for an ill-grounded confidence: for I think nobody can, in earnest, be so sceptical as to be uncertain of the existence of those things which he sees and feels. At least, he that can doubt so far (whatever he may have with his own thoughts), will never have any controversy with me; since he can never be sure I say anything contrary to his own opinion. As to myself, I think God has given me assurance enough of the existence of things without me: since, by their different application, I can produce in myself both pleasure and pain, which is one great concernment of my present state. This is certain: the confidence that our faculties do not herein deceive us, is the greatest assurance we are capable of concerning the existence of material beings. For we cannot act anything but by our faculties; nor talk of knowledge itself, but by the help of those faculties which are fitted to apprehend even what knowledge is.

But besides the assurance we have from our senses themselves, that they do not err in the information they give us of the existence of things without us, when they are affected by them, we are further confirmed in this assurance by other concurrent reasons:—

4. I. It is plain those perceptions are produced in us by exterior causes affecting our senses: because those that want the *organs* of any sense, never can have the ideas belonging to that sense produced in their minds. This is too evident to be doubted: and therefore we cannot but be assured that they come in by the organs of that sense, and no other way. The organs themselves, it is plain, do not produce them: for then the eyes of a man in the dark would produce colours, and his nose smell roses in the winter: but we see nobody gets the relish of a pineapple, till he goes to the Indies, where it is, and tastes it.

5. II. Because sometimes I find that *I cannot avoid the having those ideas produced in my mind.* For though, when my eyes are shut, or windows fast, I can at pleasure recall to my mind the ideas of light, or the sun, which former sensations had lodged in my memory; so I can at pleasure lay by *that* idea, and take into my view that of the smell of a rose, or taste of sugar. But, if I turn my eyes at noon towards the sun, I cannot avoid the ideas which the light or sun then produces in me. So that there is a manifest difference between the ideas laid up in my memory (over which, if they were there only, I should have constantly the same power to dispose of them, and lay them by at pleasure), and those which force themselves upon me, and I cannot avoid having. And therefore it must needs be some exterior cause, and the brisk acting of some objects without me, whose efficacy I cannot resist, that produces those ideas in my mind, whether I will or no. Besides, there is nobody who doth not perceive the difference in himself between contemplating the sun, as he hath the idea of it in his memory, and actually looking upon it: of which two, his perception is so distinct, that few of his ideas are more distinguishable one from another. And therefore he hath certain knowledge that they are not *both* memory, or the actions of his mind, and fancies only within him; but that actual seeing hath a cause without. . . .

CHAPTER XV   OF PROBABILITY

1. As *demonstration* is the showing the agreement or disagreement of two ideas, by the intervention of one or more proofs, which have a

constant, immutable, and visible connexion one with another; so *probability* is nothing but the appearance of such an agreement or disagreement, by the intervention of proofs, whose connexion is not constant and immutable, or at least is not perceived to be so, but is, or appears for the most part to be so, and is enough to induce the mind to judge the proposition to be true or false, rather than the contrary. For example: in the demonstration of it a man perceives the certain, immutable connexion there is of equality between the three angles of a triangle, and those intermediate ones which are made use of to show their equality to two right ones; and so, by an intuitive knowledge of the agreement or disagreement of the intermediate ideas in each step of the progress, the whole series is continued with an evidence, which clearly shows the agreement or disagreement of those three angles in equality to two right ones: and thus he has certain knowledge that it is so. But another man, who never took the pains to observe the demonstration, hearing a mathematician, a man of credit, affirm the three angles of a triangle to be equal to two right ones, assents to it, i.e. receives it for true: in which case the foundation of his assent is the probability of the thing; the proof being such as for the most part carries truth with it: the man on whose testimony he receives it, not being wont to affirm anything contrary to or besides his knowledge, especially in matters of this kind: so that that which causes his assent to this proposition, that the three angles of a triangle are equal to two right ones, that which makes him take these ideas to agree, without knowing them to do so, is the wonted veracity of the speaker in other cases, or his supposed veracity in this.

2. Our knowledge, as has been shown, being very narrow, and we not happy enough to find certain truth in everything which we have occasion to consider; most of the propositions we think, reason, discourse—nay, act upon, are such as we cannot have undoubted knowledge of their truth: yet some of them border so near upon certainty, that we make no doubt at all about them; but assent to them as firmly, and act, according to that assent, as resolutely as if they were infallibly demonstrated, and that our knowledge of them was perfect and certain. But there being degrees herein, from the very neighbourhood of certainty and demonstration, quite down to improbability and unlikeness, even to the confines of impossibility; and also degrees of assent from full assurance and confidence, quite down to conjecture, doubt, and distrust: I shall come now (having, as I think, found out *the bounds of human knowledge and certainty*), in the next place, to consider *the several degrees and grounds of probability, and assent or faith*. . . .

5. Probability wanting that intuitive evidence which infallibly determines the understanding and produces certain knowledge, the mind, if it *will proceed rationally*, ought to examine all the grounds of probability, and see how they make more or less for or against any proposition, before it assents to or dissents from it; and, upon a due balancing the whole, reject or receive it, with a more or less firm assent, proportionably to the preponderancy of the greater grounds of probability on one side or the other.

For Further Reflection

1. Has Locke successfully refuted the theory of innate ideas? How does he account for our intuitive certainty of the laws of logic or the reality of the self, two items which the rationalists consider innate knowledge?

2. Is Lockean empiricism plausible? Are our minds like empty paper until experience writes its message upon them? Note, Locke is not denying that the mind has capabilities and that some humans have greater capabilities to learn than others.

3. How does Locke deal with the problem of skepticism about sensory experience, which is so prominent in Descartes? Is he successful? Hume will disagree with him, as you will see in a later reading.

III.3   An Idealist Theory of Knowledge

GEORGE BERKELEY

George Berkeley (1685–1753), an Irish philosopher and Anglican bishop, was educated at Trinity College, Dublin, where he subsequently taught. A deeply committed Christian, he sought to reconcile science with his faith by proving that although matter does not exist, the laws of physics, being God's laws, govern a universe made up of ideas. To exist is to be perceived, and God is that being who, perceiving all, causes them to exist as ideas in his mind. This position is called *philosophical idealism*. Berkeley's principal works are *A Treatise on the Principles of Knowledge* (1710) and *Three Dialogues between Hylas and Philonous* (1713), from which the present selection is taken.

In this dialogue Berkeley defends his idealism, i.e., his belief that only ideas exist. "To be is to be perceived"—to be is to be an idea in a mind—and hence matter existing apart from the mind does not exist. In this dialogue Hylas (from the Greek word for "matter") debates with Philonous (from the Greek "love of mind"). The unique thing about Berkeley's idealism is that unlike traditional idealism (e.g., Plato's), it is not rationalistic. It does not propose that ideas exist independently, but rather it assumes an empirical foundation. It agrees with Locke that all ideas originate in sense experience, and proceeds to show that all we ever experience is ideas. The only reality that exists to be known is perceivers and perceptions. To hold all of this ideal reality together one must posit a Divine mind who perceives us and hence causes our existence as ideas in his mind.

Study Questions

1. What is the most "extravagant opinion that ever entered into the mind of man"?
2. What is Philonous' response to Hylas' surprise at his views? How does he attempt to rebut the charge of skepticism?
3. What are sensible things according to Hylas and Philonous?
4. How does Philonous convince Hylas that heat and pain are ideas in the mind? Go through the argument step by step.
5. What is the point Philonous makes with the experiment of putting a cold and a warm hand into the same vessel of water?
6. What does Hylas mean by "to exist is one thing and to be perceived is another"?
7. Why does Philonous reject the notion of a material substratum, i.e., matter that exists independently of our perceptions?

From Three Dialogues between Hylas and Philonous, *1713.*

8. What conclusion does Philonous eventually force Hylas to accept regarding perceptions?

9. Why does the world continue to exist when we are not perceiving it, e.g., when we are asleep?

HYL.: YOU WERE REPRESENTED in last night's conversation as one who maintained the most extravagant opinion that ever entered into the mind of man, to wit, that there is no such thing as "material substance" in the world.

Phil.: That there is no such thing as what philosophers call "material substance," I am seriously persuaded; but if I were made to see anything absurd or skeptical in this, I should then have the same reason to renounce this that I imagine I have now to reject the contrary opinion.

Hyl.: What! Can anything be more fantastical, more repugnant to common sense or a more manifest piece of skepticism than to believe there is no such thing as matter?

Phil.: Softly, good Hylas. What if it should prove that you, who hold there is, are, by virtue of that opinion, a greater skeptic and maintain more paradoxes and repugnances to common sense than I who believe no such thing? . . .

How comes it to pass then, Hylas, that you pronounce me a skeptic because I deny what you affirm, to wit, the existence of matter? Since, for aught you can tell, I am as peremptory in my denial as you in your affirmation.

Hyl.: Hold, Philonous, I have been a little out in my definition; but every false step a man makes in discourse is not to be insisted on. I said indeed that a "skeptic" was one who doubted of everything, but I should have added: or who denies the reality and truth of things.

Phil.: What things? Do you mean the principles and theorems of sciences? But these you know are universal intellectual notions, and consequently independent of matter; the denial therefore of this does not imply the denying them.

Hyl.: I grant it. But are there no other things? what think you of distrusting the senses, of denying the real existence of sensible things, or pretending to know nothing of them. Is not this sufficient to denominate a man a skeptic?

Phil.: Shall we therefore examine which of us it is that denies the reality of sensible things or professes the greatest ignorance of them, since, if I take you rightly, he is to be esteemed the greatest skeptic?

Hyl.: That is what I desire.

Phil.: What mean you by "sensible things"?

Hyl.: Those things which are perceived by the senses. Can you imagine that I mean anything else?

Phil.: Pardon me, Hylas, if I am desirous clearly to apprehend your notions, since this may much shorten our inquiry. Suffer me then to ask you this further question. Are those things only perceived by the senses which are perceived immediately? Or may those things properly be said to be "sensible" which are perceived immediately, or not without the intervention of others?

Hyl.: I do not sufficiently understand you.

Phil.: In reading a book, what I immediately perceive are the letters, but mediately, or by means of these, are suggested to my mind the notions of God, virtue, truth, etc. Now, that the letters are truly sensible things, or perceived by sense, there is no doubt; but I would know whether you take the things suggested by them to be so too.

Hyl.: No, certainly; it were absurd to think God or virtue sensible things, though they may be signified and suggested to the mind by sensible marks with which they have an arbitrary connection.

Phil.: It seems, then, that by "sensible things" you mean those only which can be perceived immediately by sense.

Hyl.: Right.

Phil.: Does it not follow from this that, though I see one part of the sky red, and another blue, and that my reason does thence evidently conclude there must be some cause of that diversity of colors, yet that cause cannot be said to be a sensible thing or perceived by the sense of seeing?

Hyl.: It does.

Phil.: In like manner, though I hear variety of sounds, yet I cannot be said to hear the causes of those sounds.

Hyl.: You cannot.

Phil.: And when by my touch I perceive a thing to be hot and heavy, I cannot say, with any truth or propriety, that I feel the cause of its heat or weight.

Hyl.: To prevent any more questions of this kind, I tell you once for all that by "sensible things" I mean those only which are perceived by sense, and that in truth the senses perceive nothing which they do not perceive immediately, for they make no inferences. The deducing therefore of causes or occasions from effects and appearances, which alone are perceived by sense, entirely relates to reason.

Phil.: This point then is agreed between us— that *sensible things are those only which are immediately perceived by sense.* You will further inform me whether we immediately perceive by sight anything besides light and colors and figures; or by hearing, anything but sounds; by the palate, anything besides tastes; by the smell, besides odors; or by the touch, more than tangible qualities.

Hyl.: We do not.

Phil.: It seems, therefore, that if you take away all sensible qualities, there remains nothing sensible?

Hyl.: I grant it.

Phil.: Sensible things therefore are nothing else but so many sensible qualities or combinations of sensible qualities?

Hyl.: Nothing else.

Phil.: Heat is then a sensible thing?

Hyl.: Certainly.

Phil.: Does the reality of sensible things consist in being perceived, or is it something distinct from their being perceived, and that bears no relation to the mind?

Hyl.: To *exist* is one thing, and to be *perceived* is another.

Phil.: I speak with regard to sensible things only; and of these I ask, whether by their real existence you mean a subsistence exterior to the mind and distinct from their being perceived?

Hyl.: I mean a real absolute being, distinct from and without any relation to their being perceived.

Phil.: Heat therefore, if it be allowed a real being, must exist without the mind?

Hyl.: It must.

Phil.: Tell me, Hylas, is this real existence equally compatible to all degrees of heat, which we perceive, or is there any reason why we should attribute it to some and deny it to others? And if there be, pray, let me know that reason.

Hyl.: Whatever degree of heat we perceive by sense, we may be sure the same exists in the object that occasions it.

Phil.: What! the greatest as well as the least?

Hyl.: I tell you, the reason is plainly the same in respect of both: they are both perceived by sense; nay, the greater degree of heat is more sensibly perceived; and consequently, if there is any difference, we are more certain of its real existence than we can be of the reality of a lesser degree.

Phil.: But is not the most vehement and intense degree of heat a very great pain?

Hyl.: No one can deny it.

Phil.: And is any unperceiving thing capable of pain or pleasure?

Hyl.: No, certainly.

Phil.: Is your material substance a senseless being or a being endowed with sense and perception?

Hyl.: It is senseless, without doubt.

Phil.: It cannot, therefore, be the subject of pain?

Hyl.: By no means.

Phil.: Nor, consequently, of the greatest heat perceived by sense, since you acknowledge this to be no small pain?

Hyl.: I grant it.

Phil.: What shall we say then of your external object: is it a material substance, or no?

Hyl.: It is a material substance with the sensible qualities inhering in it.

Phil.: How then can a great heat exist in it, since you own it cannot in a material substance? I desire you would clear this point.

Hyl.: Hold, Philonous, I fear I was out in yielding intense heat to be a pain. It should seem rather that pain is something distinct from heat, and the consequence or effect of it.

Phil.: Upon putting your hand near the fire, do you perceive one simple uniform sensation or two distinct sensations?

Hyl.: But one simple sensation.

Phil.: Is not the heat immediately perceived?

Hyl.: It is.

Phil.: And the pain?

Hyl.: True.

Phil.: Seeing therefore they are both immediately perceived at the same time, and the fire affects you only with one simple or uncompounded idea, it follows that this same simple idea is both the intense heat immediately perceived and the pain; and, consequently, that the intense heat immediately perceived is nothing distinct from a particular sort of pain.

Hyl.: It seems so.

Phil.: Again, try in your thoughts, Hylas, if you can conceive a vehement sensation to be without pain or pleasure.

Hyl.: I cannot.

Phil.: Or can you frame to yourself an idea of sensible pain or pleasure, in general, abstracted from every particular idea of heat, cold, tastes, smells, etc.?

Hyl.: I do not find that I can.

Phil.: Does it not therefore follow that sensible pain is nothing distinct from those sensations or ideas—in an intense degree?

Hyl.: It is undeniable; and, to speak the truth, I begin to suspect a very great heat cannot exist but in a mind perceiving it.

Phil.: What! are you then in that *skeptical* state

of suspense, between affirming and denying?

Hyl.: I think I may be positive in the point. A very violent and painful heat cannot exist without the mind.

Phil.: It has not therefore, according to you, any real being?

Hyl.: I own it.

Phil.: Is it therefore certain that there is no body in nature really hot?

Hyl.: I have not denied there is any real heat in bodies. I only say there is no such thing as an intense real heat.

Phil.: But did you not say before that all degrees of heat were equally real, or, if there was any difference, that the greater were more undoubtedly real than the lesser?

Hyl.: True; but it was because I did not then consider the ground there is for distinguishing between them, which I now plainly see. And it is this: because intense heat is nothing else but a particular kind of painful sensation, and pain cannot exist but in a perceiving being, it follows that no intense heat can really exist in an unperceiving corporeal substance. But this is no reason why we should deny heat in an inferior degree to exist in such a substance.

Phil.: But how shall we be able to discern those degrees of heat which exist only in the mind from those which exist without it?

Hyl.: That is no difficult matter. You know the least pain cannot exist unperceived; whatever, therefore, degree of heat is a pain exists only in the mind. But as for all other degrees of heat nothing obliges us to think the same of them.

Phil.: I think you granted before that no unperceiving being was capable of pleasure any more than of pain.

Hyl.: I did.

Phil.: And is not warmth, or a more gentle degree of heat than what causes uneasiness, a pleasure?

Hyl.: What then?

Phil.: Consequently, it cannot exist without the mind in an unperceiving substance, or body.

Hyl.: So it seems.

Phil.: Since, therefore, as well those degrees of heat that are not painful, as those that are, can exist only in a thinking substance, may we not conclude that external bodies are absolutely incapable of any degree of heat whatsoever?

Hyl.: On second thoughts, I do not think it is so evident that warmth is a pleasure as that a great degree of heat is pain.

Phil.: I do not pretend that warmth is as great a pleasure as heat is a pain. But if you grant it to be even a small pleasure, it serves to make good my conclusion.

Hyl.: I could rather call it an "indolence." It seems to be nothing more than a privation of both pain and pleasure. And that such a quality or state as this may agree to an unthinking substance, I hope you will not deny.

Phil.: If you are resolved to maintain that warmth, or a gentle degree of heat, is no pleasure, I know not how to convince you otherwise than by appealing to your own sense. But what think you of cold?

Hyl.: The same that I do of heat. An intense degree of cold is a pain; for to feel a very great cold is to perceive a great uneasiness; it cannot therefore exist without the mind; but a lesser degree of cold may, as well as a lesser degree of heat.

Phil.: Those bodies, therefore, upon whose application to our own we perceive a moderate degree of heat must be concluded to have a moderate degree of heat or warmth in them; and those upon whose application we feel a like degree of cold must be thought to have cold in them.

Hyl.: They must.

Phil.: Can any doctrine be true that necessarily leads a man into an absurdity?

Hyl.: Without doubt it cannot.

Phil.: Is it not an absurdity to think that the same thing should be at the same time both cold and warm?

Hyl.: It is.

Phil.: Suppose now one of your hands is hot, and the other cold, and that they are both at once put into the same vessel of water, in an intermediate state, will not the water seem cold to one hand, and warm to the other?

Hyl.: It will.

Phil.: Ought we not therefore, by your principles, to conclude it is really both cold and warm at the same time, that is, according to your own concession, to believe an absurdity?

Hyl.: I confess it seems so.

Phil.: Consequently, the principles themselves are false, since you have granted that no true principle leads to an absurdity.

Hyl.: But, after all, can anything be more absurd than to say, *there is no heat in the fire?*

Phil.: To make the point still clearer; tell me whether, in two cases exactly alike, we ought not to make the same judgment?

Hyl.: We ought.

Phil.: When a pin pricks your finger, does it not rend and divide the fibres of your flesh?

Hyl.: It does.

Phil.: And when a coal burns your finger, does it any more?

Hyl.: It does not.

Phil.: Since, therefore, you neither judge the sensation itself occasioned by the pin, nor anything like it to be in the pin, you should not, conformably to what you have now granted, judge the sensation occasioned by the fire, or anything like it, to be in the fire.

Hyl.: Well, since it must be so, I am content to yield this point and acknowledge that heat and cold are only sensations existing in our minds. But there still remain qualities enough to secure the reality of external things.

Phil.: But what will you say, Hylas, if it shall appear that the case is the same with regard to all other sensible qualities, and that they can no more be supposed to exist without the mind than heat and cold?

Hyl.: Then, indeed, you will have done something to the purpose; but this is what I despair of seeing proved.

Phil.: Let us examine them in order. What think you of tastes—do they exist without the mind, or no?

Hyl.: Can any man in his senses doubt whether sugar is sweet or wormwood bitter?

Phil.: Inform me, Hylas. Is a sweet taste a particular kind of pleasure or pleasant sensation, or is it not?

Hyl.: It is.

Phil.: And is not bitterness some kind of uneasiness or pain?

Hyl.: I grant it.

Phil.: If therefore sugar and wormwood are unthinking corporeal substances existing without the mind, how can sweetness and bitterness, that is, pleasure and pain, agree to them? . . .

Hyl.: I see it is to no purpose to hold out, so I give up the cause as to those mentioned qualities, though I profess it sounds oddly to say that sugar is not sweet.

Phil.: But, for your further satisfaction, take this along with you: that which at other times seems sweet shall, to a distempered palate, appear bitter, and nothing can be plainer than that divers persons perceive different tastes in the same food, since that which one man delights in, another abhors. And how could this be if the taste was something really inherent in the food?

Hyl.: I acknowledge I know not how.

Phil.: In the next place, odors are to be considered. And with regard to these I would fain know whether what has been said of tastes does not exactly agree to them? Are they not so many pleasing or displeasing sensations?

Hyl.: They are.

Phil.: Can you then conceive it possible that they should exist in an unperceiving thing?

Hyl.: I cannot.

Phil.: Or can you imagine that filth and ordure affect those brute animals that feed on them out of choice with the same smells which we perceive in them?

Hyl.: By no means.

Phil.: May we not therefore conclude of smells, as of the other forementioned qualities, that they cannot exist in any but a perceiving substance or mind?

Hyl.: I think so.

Phil.: Then as to sounds, what must we think of them, are they accidents really inherent in external bodies or not?

Hyl.: That they inhere not in the sonorous bodies is plain from hence; because a bell struck in the exhausted receiver of an air-pump sends forth no sound. The air, therefore, must be thought the subject of sound.

Phil.: What reason is there for that, Hylas?

Hyl.: Because, when any motion is raised in the air, we perceive a sound greater or less, in proportion to the air's motion; but without some motion in the air we never hear any sound at all.

Phil.: And granting that we never hear a sound but when some motion is produced in the air, yet I do not see how you can infer from thence that the sound itself is in the air.

Hyl.: It is this very motion in the external air that produces in the mind the sensation of sound. For, striking on the drum of the ear, it causes a vibration which by the auditory nerves being communicated to the brain, the soul is thereupon affected with the sensation called "sound."

Phil.: What! is sound then a sensation?

Hyl.: I tell you, as perceived by us it is a particular sensation in the mind.

Phil.: And can any sensation exist without the mind?

Hyl.: No, certainly.

Phil.: How then can sound, being a sensation, exist in the air if by the "air" you mean a senseless substance existing without the mind?

Hyl.: You must distinguish, Philonous, between sound as it is perceived by us, and as it is in itself; or (which is the same thing) between the sound we immediately perceive and that which exists without us. The former, indeed, is a particular kind of sensation, but the latter is merely a vibrative or undulatory motion in the air.

Phil.: I thought I had already obviated that distinction by the answer I gave when you were applying it in a like case before. But, to say no more of that, are you sure then that sound is really nothing but motion?

Hyl.: I am.

Phil.: Whatever, therefore, agrees to real sound may with truth be attributed to motion?

Hyl.: It may.

Phil.: It is then good sense to speak of "motion" as of a thing that is *loud, sweet, acute,* or *grave.*

Hyl.: I see you are resolved not to understand me. Is it not evident those accidents or modes belong only to sensible sound, or sound in the common acceptation of the word, but not to sound in the real and philosophic sense, which, as I just now told you, is nothing but a certain motion of the air?

Phil.: It seems then there are two sorts of sound—the one vulgar, or that which is heard, the other philosophical and real?

Hyl.: Even so.

Phil.: And the latter consists in motion?

Hyl.: I told you so before.

Phil.: Tell me, Hylas, to which of the senses, think you, the idea of motion belongs? To the hearing?

Hyl.: No, certainly; but to the sight and touch.

Phil.: It should follow then that, according to you, real sounds may possibly be *seen* or *felt,* but never *heard.*

Hyl.: Look you, Philonous, you may, if you please, make a jest of my opinion, but that will not alter the truth of things. I own, indeed, the inferences you draw me into sound something oddly, but common language, you know, is framed by, and for the use of, the vulgar. We must not therefore wonder if expressions adapted to exact philosophic notions seem uncouth and out of the way.

Phil.: Is it come to that? I assure you I imagine myself to have gained no small point since you make so light of departing from common phrases and opinions, it being a main part of our inquiry to examine whose notions are widest of the common road and most repugnant to the general sense of the world. But can you think it no more than a philosophical paradox to say that "real sounds are never heard," and that the idea of them is obtained by some other sense? And is there nothing in this contrary to nature and the truth of things?

Hyl.: To deal ingenuously, I do not like it.

And, after the concessions already made, I had as well grant that sounds, too, have no real being without the mind. . . .

I frankly own, Philonous, that it is in vain to stand out any longer. Colors, sounds, tastes, in a word, all those termed "secondary qualities," have certainly no existence without the mind. But by this acknowledgment I must not be supposed to derogate anything from the reality of matter or external objects; seeing it is no more than several philosophers maintain, who nevertheless are the farthest imaginable from denying matter. For the clearer understanding of this you must know sensible qualities are by philosophers divided into "primary" and "secondary." The former are extension, figure, solidity, gravity, motion, and rest. And these they hold exist really in bodies. The latter are those above enumerated, or, briefly, all sensible qualities besides the primary, which they assert are only so many sensations or ideas existing nowhere but in the mind. But all this, I doubt not, you are already apprised of. For my part I have been a long time sensible there was such an opinion current among philosophers, but was never thoroughly convinced of its truth till now.

Phil.: You are still then of opinion that *extension* and *figures* are inherent in external unthinking substances?

Hyl.: I am.

Phil.: But what if the same arguments which are brought against secondary qualities will hold good against these also?

Hyl.: Why then I shall be obliged to think they too exist only in the mind. . . .

I acknowledge, Philonous, that, upon a fair observation of what passes in my mind, I can discover nothing else but that I am a thinking being affected with variety of sensations; neither is it possible to conceive how a sensation should exist in an unperceiving substance. But then, on the other hand, when I look on sensible things in a different view, considering them as so many modes and qualities, I find it necessary to suppose a material *substratum,* without which they cannot be conceived to exist.

Phil.: "Material substratum" call you it? Pray, by which of your senses came you acquainted with that being?

Hyl.: It is not itself sensible; its modes and qualities only being perceived by the senses.

Phil.: I presume then it was by reflection and reason you obtained the idea of it?

Hyl.: I do not pretend to any proper positive idea of it. However, I conclude it exists because qualities cannot be conceived to exist without a support.

Phil.: It seems then you have only a relative notion of it, or that you conceive it not otherwise than by conceiving the relation it bears to sensible qualities? . . .

Hyl.: Right.

Phil.: Be pleased, therefore, to let me know wherein that relation consists.

Hyl.: Is it not sufficiently expressed in the term "substratum" or "substance"?

Phil.: If so, the word "substratum" should import that it is spread under the sensible qualities or accidents?

Hyl.: True.

Phil.: And consequently under extension?

Hyl.: I own it.

Phil.: It is therefore somewhat in its own nature distinct from extension?

Hyl.: I tell you extension is only a mode, and matter is something that supports modes. And is it not evident the thing supported is different from the thing supporting?

Phil.: So that something distinct from, and exclusive of, extension is supposed to be the *substratum* of extension?

Hyl.: Just so.

Phil.: Answer me, Hylas, can a thing be spread without extension, or is not the idea of extension necessarily included in *spreading*?

Hyl.: It is.

Phil.: Whatsoever therefore you suppose spread under anything must have in itself an extension distinct from the extension of that thing under which it is spread?

Hyl.: It must.

Phil.: Consequently, every corporeal substance being the *substratum* of extension must have in itself another extension by which it is qualified to be a *substratum,* and so on to infinity? And I ask whether this be not absurd in itself and repugnant to what you granted just now, to wit, that the *substratum* was something distinct from and exclusive of extension?

Hyl.: Aye, but, Philonous, you take me wrong. I do not mean that matter is *spread* in a gross literal sense under extension. The word "substratum" is used only to express in general the same thing with "substance."

Phil.: Well then, let us examine the relation implied in the term "substance." Is it not that it stands under accidents?

Hyl.: The very same.

Phil.: But that one thing may stand under or support another, must it not be extended?

Hyl.: It must.

Phil.: Is not therefore this supposition liable to the same absurdity with the former?

Hyl.: You still take things in a strict literal sense; that is not fair, Philonous.

Phil.: I am not for imposing any sense on your words; you are at liberty to explain them as you please. Only, I beseech you, make me understand something by them. You tell me matter supports or stands under accidents. How! is it as your legs support your body?

Hyl.: No; that is the literal sense.

Phil.: Pray let me know any sense, literal or not literal, that you understand it in.—How long must I wait for an answer, Hylas?

Hyl.: I declare I know not what to say. I once thought I understood well enough what was meant by matter's supporting accidents. But now, the more I think on it, the less can I comprehend it; in short, I find that I know nothing of it.

Phil.: It seems then you have no idea at all, neither relative nor positive, of matter? you know neither what it is in itself nor what relation it bears to accidents?

Hyl.: I acknowledge it. . . .

Other men may think as they please, but for your part you have nothing to reproach me with.

My comfort is you are as much a skeptic as I am.

Phil.: There, Hylas, I must beg leave to differ from you.

Hyl.: What! have you all along agreed to the premises, and do you now deny the conclusion and leave me to maintain those paradoxes by myself which you led me into? This surely is not fair.

Phil.: I deny that I agreed with you in those notions that led to skepticism. You indeed said the *reality* of sensible things consisted in an *absolute existence* out of the minds of spirits, or distinct from their being perceived. And, pursuant to this notion of reality, you are obliged to deny sensible things any real existence; that is, according to your own definition, you profess yourself a skeptic. But I neither said nor thought the reality of sensible things was to be defined after that manner. To me it is evident, for the reasons you allow of, that sensible things cannot exist otherwise than in a mind or spirit. Whence I conclude, not that they have no real existence, but that, seeing they depend not on my thought and have an existence distinct from being perceived by me, *there must be some other mind wherein they exist.* As sure, therefore, as the sensible world really exists, so sure is there an infinite omnipresent Spirit, who contains and supports it.

Hyl.: What! this is no more than I and all Christians hold; nay, and all others, too, who believe there is a God and that He knows and comprehends all things.

Phil.: Aye, but here lies the difference. Men commonly believe that all things are known or perceived by God, because they believe the being of a God; whereas I, on the other side, immediately and necessarily conclude the being of a God, because all sensible things must be perceived by him.

Hyl.: But so long as we all believe the same thing, what matter is it how we come by that belief?

Phil.: But neither do we agree in the same opinion. For philosophers, though they acknowledge all corporeal beings to be perceived by God, yet they attribute to them an absolute subsistence distinct from their being perceived by any mind whatever, which I do not. Besides, is there no difference between saying, *there is a God, therefore He perceives all things,* and saying, *sensible things do really exist; and if they really exist, they are necessarily perceived by an infinite mind: therefore there is an infinite mind, or God?* This furnishes you with a direct and immediate demonstration, from a most evident principle, of the *being of a God.* Divines and philosophers had proved beyond all controversy, from the beauty and usefulness of the several parts of the creation, that it was the workmanship of God. But that—setting aside all help of astronomy and natural philosophy, all contemplation of the contrivance, order and adjustment of things—an infinite mind should be necessarily inferred from the bare *existence* of the sensible world is an advantage peculiar to them only who have made this easy reflection, that the sensible world is that which we perceive by our several senses; and that nothing is perceived by the senses besides ideas; and that no idea or archetype of an idea can exist otherwise than in a mind.

For Further Reflection

1. Do you agree with Berkeley that only ideas exist? Does it seem to you obvious that matter really does exist? If you disagree with Berkeley, can you show where he has made an error in his argument?

2. According to Berkeley there is no sound independent of our hearing it and no reality but our experiencing it. Does this mean that when we leave our rooms, they disappear? There is an old Oxford limerick on this point:

There was a young man who said, "God
Must think it exceedingly odd
If he finds that this tree
Continues to be,
When there's no one about in the quad."

Dear Sir, your astonishment's odd
I'm always about in the quad,
And that's why the tree
Continues to be,
Since observed by,

      Yours faithfully,

       God

The question is in whose mind does God exist? Does the notion of God fit into Berkeley's system?

Radical Empiricism   III.4

DAVID HUME

In this selection from *An Enquiry Concerning Human Understanding* (1748) we have an extension of the empiricism begun with Locke. Like Locke, Hume locates the foundation of all our ideas in sensory experience. But Hume moves even further away from the possibility of absolute certainty of knowledge towards the view that we can justly only have relative certainty. We can only be certain of analytic truths ("relations of ideas"), viz. mathematics and tautologies. With regard to synthetic truths ("matters of fact") we, at best, can have a high degree of probability. But even the notion of probability is dubious and leads to a certain skepticism, because the notion of cause and effect upon which experiential knowledge is based is itself not an impression but an idea.

(A biographical note on Hume is found on p. 46.)

Study Questions

1. What is the origin of our ideas? How does Hume distinguish ideas from impressions?
2. What does Hume say about the reputed "unbounded liberty" of thought? How free is it?
3. What are Hume's two proofs for his thesis about ideas and impressions?
4. What are the practical implications of Hume's empiricism? What effect would it have on metaphysical speculation?

5. What sort of knowledge is certain? What kind lacks certainty?

6. Why is causal reasoning doubtful? What does Hume mean by saying causal relations can never be discovered by *a priori* argument?

7. What is Hume's solution to the problem of doubt? What is the principle or cause that leads us to rely on experience in spite of the inherent difficulties of justifying the procedure?

Of the Origin of Ideas

EVERY ONE WILL READILY ALLOW, that there is a considerable difference between the perceptions of the mind, when a man feels the pain of excessive heat, or the pleasure of moderate warmth, and when he afterwards recalls to his memory this sensation, or anticipates it by his imagination. These faculties may mimic or copy the perceptions of the senses; but they never can entirely reach the force and vivacity of the original sentiment. The utmost we say of them, even when they operate with greatest vigor, is, that they represent their object in so lively a manner, that we could *almost* say we feel or see it: But, except the mind be disordered by disease or madness, they never can arrive at such a pitch of vivacity, as to render these perceptions altogether undistinguishable. All the colors of poetry, however splendid, can never paint natural objects in such a manner as to make the description be taken for a real landscape. The most lively thought is still inferior to the dullest sensation.

We may observe a like distinction to run through all the other perceptions of the mind. A man in a fit of anger, is actuated in a very different manner from one who only thinks of that emotion. If you tell me, that any person is in love, I easily understand your meaning, and form a just conception of his situation; but never can mistake that conception for the real disorders and agitations of the passion. When we reflect on our past sentiments and affections, our thought is a faithful mirror, and copies its objects truly; but the colors which it employs are faint and dull, in comparison of those in which our original perceptions were clothed. It requires no nice discernment or metaphysical head to mark the distinction between them.

Here therefore we may divide all the perceptions of the mind into two classes or species, which are distinguished by their different degrees of force and vivacity. The less forcible and lively are commonly denominated *Thoughts* or *Ideas*. The other species want a name in our language, and in most others; I suppose, because it was not requisite for any, but philosophical purposes, to rank them under a general term or appellation. Let us, therefore, use a little freedom, and call them *Impressions;* employing that word in a sense somewhat different from the usual. By the term *impression,* then, I mean all our more lively perceptions, when we hear, or see, or feel, or love, or hate, or desire, or will. And impressions are distinguished from ideas, which are the less lively perceptions, of which we are conscious, when we reflect on any of those sensations or movements above mentioned.

Nothing, at first view, may seem more unbounded than the thought of man, which not only escapes all human power and authority, but is not even restrained within the limits of nature and reality. To form monsters, and join incongruous shapes and appearances, costs the imagination no more trouble than to conceive the most natural and familiar objects. And while the body is confined to one planet, along which it creeps with pain and difficulty; the thought can in an instant transport us into the most distant regions of the universe; or even beyond the universe, into the unbounded chaos, where nature is supposed to lie in total confusion. What never

Reprinted from An Enquiry Concerning Human Understanding *(Oxford: Clarendon Press, 1748)*.

was seen, or heard of, may yet be conceived; nor is any thing beyond the power of thought, except what implies an absolute contradiction.

But though our thought seems to possess this unbounded liberty, we shall find, upon a nearer examination, that it is really confined within very narrow limits, and that all this creative power of the mind amounts to no more than the faculty of compounding, transposing, augmenting, or diminishing the materials afforded us by the senses and experience. When we think of a golden mountain, we only join two consistent ideas, *gold,* and *mountain,* with which we were formerly acquainted. A virtuous horse we can conceive; because, from our own feeling, we can conceive virtue; and this we may unite to the figure and shape of a horse, which is an animal familiar to us. In short, all the materials of thinking are derived either from our outward or inward sentiment: the mixture and composition of these belongs alone to the mind and will. Or, to express myself in philosophical language, all our ideas or more feeble perceptions are copies of our impressions or more lively ones.

To prove this, the two following arguments will, I hope, be sufficient. First, when we analyze our thoughts or ideas, however compounded or sublime, we always find that they resolve themselves into such simple ideas as were copied from a precedent feeling or sentiment. Even those ideas, which, at first view, seem the most wide of this origin, are found, upon a nearer scrutiny, to be derived from it. The idea of God, as meaning an infinitely intelligent, wise, and good Being, arises from reflecting on the operations of our own mind, and augmenting, without limit, those qualities of goodness and wisdom. We may prosecute this enquiry to what length we please; where we shall always find, that every idea which we examine is copied from a similar impression. Those who would assert that this position is not universally true nor without exception, have only one, and that an easy method of refuting it; by producing that idea, which, in their opinion, is not derived from this source. It will then be incumbent on us, if we would maintain our doctrine, to produce the impression, or lively perception, which corresponds to it.

Secondly. If it happen, from a defect of the organ, that a man is not susceptible of any species of sensation, we always find that he is as little susceptible of the correspondent ideas. A blind man can form no notion of colors; a deaf man of sounds. Restore either of them that sense in which he is deficient; by opening this new inlet for his sensations, you also open an inlet for the ideas; and he finds no difficulty in conceiving these objects. . . .

Here, therefore, is a proposition, which not only seems, in itself, simple and intelligible; but, if a proper use were made of it, might render every dispute equally intelligible, and banish all that jargon, which has so long taken possession of metaphysical reasonings, and drawn disgrace upon them. All ideas, especially abstract ones, are naturally faint and obscure: the mind has but a slender hold of them: they are apt to be confounded with other resembling ideas; and when we have often employed any term, though without a distinct meaning, we are apt to imagine it has a determinate idea annexed to it. On the contrary, all impressions, that is, all sensations, either outward or inward, are strong and determined: nor is it easy to fall into any error or mistake with regard to them. When we entertain, therefore, any suspicion that a philosophical term is employed without any meaning or idea (as is but too frequent), we need but enquire, *from what impression is that supposed idea derived?* And if it be impossible to assign any, this will serve to confirm our suspicion. By bringing ideas into so clear a light we may reasonably hope to remove all dispute, which may arise, concerning their nature and reality.

Sceptical Doubts Concerning the Operations of the Understanding

PART I

All the objects of human reason or enquiry may naturally be divided into two kinds, to wit, *Relations of Ideas,* and *Matters of Fact.* Of the first kind are the sciences of Geometry, Algebra, and Arithmetic; and in short, every affirmation which is either intuitively or demonstratively certain. *That the square of the hypotenuse is equal to the squares of the two sides,* is a proposition which expresses a relation between these figures. *That three times five is equal to the half of thirty,* expresses a relation between these numbers. Propositions of this kind are discoverable by the mere operation of thought, without dependence on what is anywhere existent in the universe. Though there never were a circle or triangle in nature, the truths demonstrated by Euclid would for ever retain their certainty and evidence.

Matters of fact, which are the second objects of human reason, are not ascertained in the same manner; nor is our evidence of their truth, however great, of a like nature with the foregoing. The contrary of every matter of fact is still possible; because it can never imply a contradiction, and is conceived by the mind with the same facility and distinctness, as if ever so conformable to reality. *That the sun will not rise tomorrow* is no less intelligible a proposition, and implies no more contradiction than the affirmation, *that it will rise*. We should in vain, therefore, attempt to demonstrate its falsehood. Were it demonstratively false, it would imply a contradiction, and could never be distinctly conceived by the mind.

It may, therefore, be a subject worthy of curiosity, to enquire what is the nature of that evidence which assures us of any real existence and matter of fact, beyond the present testimony of our senses, or the records of our memory. This part of philosophy, it is observable, has been little cultivated, either by the ancients or moderns; and therefore our doubts and errors, in the prosecution of so important an enquiry, may be the more excusable; while we march through such difficult paths without any guide or direction. They may even prove useful, by exciting curiosity, and destroying that implicit faith and security, which is the bane of all reasoning and free enquiry. The discovery of defects in the common philosophy, if any such there be, will not, I presume, be a discouragement, but rather an incitement, as is usual, to attempt something more full and satisfactory than has yet been proposed to the public.

All reasonings concerning matter of fact seem to be founded on the relation of *Cause and Effect*. By means of that relation alone we can go beyond the evidence of our memory and senses. If you were to ask a man, why he believes any matter of fact, which is absent; for instance, that his friend is in the country, or in France; he would give you a reason; and this reason would be some other fact; as a letter received from him, or the knowledge of his former resolutions and promises. A man finding a watch or any other machine in a desert island, would conclude that there had once been men in that island. All our reasonings concerning fact are of the same nature. And here it is constantly supposed that there is a connection between the present fact and that which is inferred from it. Were there nothing to bind them together, the inference would be entirely precarious. The hearing of an articulate voice and rational discourse in the dark assures us of the presence of some person: Why? because these are the effects of the human make and fabric, and closely connected with it. If we anatomize all the other reasonings of this nature, we shall find that they are founded on the relation of cause and effect, and that this relation is either near or remote, direct or collateral. Heat and light are collateral effects of fire, and the one effect may justly be inferred from the other.

If we would satisfy ourselves, therefore, concerning the nature of that evidence, which assures us of matters of fact, we must enquire how we arrive at the knowledge of cause and effect. . . .

This proposition, *that causes and effects are discoverable, not by reason but by experience,* will readily be admitted with regard to such objects, as we remember to have once been altogether unknown to us; since we must be conscious of the utter inability, which we then lay under, of foretelling what would arise from them. Present two smooth pieces of marble to a man who has no tincture of natural philosophy; he will never discover that they will adhere together in such a manner as to require great force to separate them in a direct line, while they make so small a resistance to a lateral pressure. Such events, as bear little analogy to the common course of nature, are also readily confessed to be known only by experience; nor does any man imagine that the explosion of gunpowder, or the attraction of a loadstone, could ever be discovered by arguments *a priori*. In like manner, when an effect is supposed to depend upon an intricate machinery or secret structure of parts, we make no difficulty in attributing all our knowledge of it to experience. Who will assert that he can give the ultimate reason, why milk or bread is proper nourishment for a man, not for a lion or a tiger?

But the same truth may not appear, at first sight, to have the same evidence with regard to events, which have become familiar to us from our first appearance in the world, which bear a close analogy to the whole course of nature, and which are supposed to depend on the simple qualities of objects, without any secret structure of parts. We are apt to imagine that we could discover these effects by the mere operation of our reason, without experience. We fancy, that were we brought on a sudden into this world, we could at first have inferred that one Billiard-ball would communicate motion to another upon impulse; and that we needed not to have waited for the event, in order to pronounce with certainty concerning it. Such is the influence of custom, that, where it is strongest, it not only covers our natural ignorance, but even conceals itself, and seems not to take place, merely because it is found in the highest degree.

But to convince us that all the laws of nature, and all the operations of bodies without exception, are known only by experience, the following reflections may, perhaps, suffice. Were any object presented to us, and were we required to pronounce concerning the effect, which will result from it, without consulting past observation; after what manner, I beseech you, must the

mind proceed in this operation? It must invent or imagine some event, which it ascribes to the object as its effect; and it is plain that this invention must be entirely arbitrary. The mind can never possibly find the effect in the supposed cause, by the most accurate scrutiny and examination. For the effect is totally different from the cause, and consequently can never be discovered in it. Motion in the second Billiard-ball is a quite distinct event from motion in the first; nor is there anything in the one to suggest the smallest hint of the other. A stone or piece of metal raised into the air, and left without any support, immediately falls: but to consider the matter *a priori,* is there anything we discover in this situation which can beget the idea of a downward, rather than an upward, or any other motion, in the stone or metal?

And as the first imagination or invention of a particular effect, in all natural operations, is arbitrary, where we consult not experience; so must we also esteem the supposed tie or connection between the cause and effect, which binds them together, and renders it impossible that any other effect could result from the operation of that cause. When I see, for instance, a Billiard-ball moving in a straight line towards another; even suppose motion in the second ball should by accident be suggested to me, as the result of their contact or impulse; may I not conceive, that a hundred different events might as well follow from that cause? May not both these balls remain at absolute rest? May not the first ball return in a straight line, or leap off from the second in any line or direction? All these suppositions are consistent and conceivable. Why then should we give the preference to one, which is no more consistent or conceivable than the rest? All our reasonings *a priori* will never be able to show us any foundation for this preference.

In a word, then, every effect is a distinct event from its cause. It could not, therefore, be discovered in the cause, and the first invention or conception of it, *a priori,* must be entirely arbitrary. And even after it is suggested, the conjunction of it with the cause must appear equally arbitrary; since there are always many other effects, which, to reason, must seem fully as consistent and natural. In vain, therefore, should we pretend to determine any single event, or infer any cause of effect, without the assistance of observation and experience. . . .

PART II

But we have not yet attained any tolerable satisfaction with regard to the question first proposed. Each solution still gives rise to a new question as difficult as the foregoing, and leads us on to farther enquiries. When it is asked, *What is the nature of all our reasonings concerning matter of fact?* the proper answer seems to be, that they are founded on the relation of cause and effect. When again it is asked, *What is the foundation of all our reasonings and conclusions concerning that relation?* it may be replied in one word, Experience. But if we still carry on our sifting humor, and ask, *What is the foundation of all conclusions from experience?* this implies a new question, which may be of more difficult solution and explication. Philosophers, that give themselves airs of superior wisdom and sufficiency, have a hard task when they encounter persons of inquisitive dispositions, who push them from every corner to which they retreat, and who are sure at last to bring them to some dangerous dilemma. The best expedient to prevent this confusion, is to be modest in our pretensions; and even to discover the difficulty ourselves before it is objected to us. By this means, we may make a kind of merit of our very ignorance.

I shall content myself, in this section, with an easy task, and shall pretend only to give a negative answer to the question here proposed. I say then, that, even after we have experience of the operations of cause and effect, our conclusions from that experience are *not* founded on reasoning, or any process of the understanding. This answer we must endeavor both to explain and to defend. . . .

In reality, all arguments from experience are founded on the similarity which we discover among natural objects, and by which we are induced to expect effects similar to those which we have found to follow from such objects. And though none but a fool or madman will ever pretend to dispute the authority of experience, or to reject that great guide of human life, it may surely be allowed a philosopher to have so much curiosity at least as to examine the principle of human nature, which gives this mighty authority to experience, and makes us draw advantage from that similarity which nature has placed among different objects. From causes which appear *similar* we expect similar effects. This is the sum of all our experimental conclusions. Now it seems evident that, if this conclusion were formed by reason, it would be as perfect at first, and upon one instance, as after ever so long a course of experience. But the case is far otherwise. Nothing so like as eggs; yet no one, on account of this appearing similarity, expects the same taste and relish in all of them. It is only after a long course of uniform experiments in any kind, that we attain a firm reliance and security with regard to a particular event. Now where is that process of reasoning which, from one instance, draws a conclusion, so different from that which it infers from a hundred instances that are nowise different from that single one? This question I propose as much for the sake of information, as with an intention of raising difficulties. I cannot find, I cannot imagine any such reasoning. But I keep my mind still open to instruction, if any one will vouchsafe to bestow it on me.

Should it be said that, from a number of uniform experiments, we *infer* a connection between the sensible qualities and the secret powers; this, I must confess, seems the same difficulty, couched in different terms. The question still recurs, on what process of argument this *inference* is founded? Where is the medium, the interposing ideas, which join propositions so very wide of each other? It is confessed that the color, consistence, and other sensible qualities of bread appear not, of themselves, to have any connection with the secret powers of nourishment and support. For otherwise we could infer these secret powers from the first appearance of these sensible qualities, without the aid of experience; contrary to the sentiment of all philosophers, and contrary to plain matter of fact. Here, then, is our natural state of ignorance with regard to the powers and influence of all objects. How is this remedied by experience? It only shows us a number of uniform effects, resulting from certain objects, and teaches us that those particular objects, at that particular time, were endowed with such powers and forces. When a new object, endowed with similar sensible qualities, is produced, we expect similar powers and forces, and look for a like effect. From a body of like color and consistence with bread we expect like nourishment and support. But this surely is a step or progress of the mind, which wants to be explained. When a man says, *I have found, in all past instances, such sensible qualities conjoined with such secret powers:* And when he says, *Similar sensible qualities will always be conjoined with similar secret powers,* he is not guilty of a tautology, nor are these propositions in any respect the same. You say that the one proposition is an inference from the other. But you must confess that the inference is not intuitive; neither is it demonstrative: Of what nature is it, then? To say it is experimental, is begging the question. For all inferences from experience suppose, as their foundation, that the future will resemble the past, and that similar powers will be conjoined with similar sensible qualities. If there be any suspicion that the course of nature may change, and that the past may be no rule for the future, all experience becomes useless, and can give rise to no inference or conclusion. It is impossible, therefore, that any arguments from experience can prove this resemblance of the past to the future; since all these arguments are founded on the supposition of that resemblance. Let the course of things be allowed hitherto ever so regular; that alone, without some new argument

or inference, proves not that, for the future, it will continue so. In vain do you pretend to have learned the nature of bodies from your past experience. Their secret nature, and consequently all their effects and influence, may change, without any change in their sensible qualities. This happens sometimes, and with regard to some objects: Why may it [not] happen always, and with regard to all objects? What logic, what process of argument secures you against this supposition? My practice, you say, refutes my doubts. But you mistake the purport of my question. As an agent, I am quite satisfied in the point; but as a philosopher, who has some share of curiosity, I will not say scepticism, I want to learn the foundation of this inference. No reading, no enquiry has yet been able to remove my difficulty, or give me satisfaction in a matter of such importance. Can I do better than propose the difficulty to the public, even though, perhaps, I have small hopes of obtaining a solution? We shall, at least, by this means, be sensible of our ignorance, if we do not augment our knowledge.

I must confess that a man is guilty of unpardonable arrogance who concludes, because an argument has escaped his own investigation, that therefore it does not really exist. I must also confess that, though all the learned, for several ages, should have employed themselves in fruitless search upon any subject, it may still, perhaps, be rash to conclude positively that the subject must, therefore, pass all human comprehension. Even though we examine all the sources of our knowledge, and conclude them unfit for such a subject, there may still remain a suspicion, that the enumeration is not complete, or the examination not accurate. But with regard to the present subject, there are some considerations which seem to remove all this accusation of arrogance or suspicion of mistake.

It is certain that the most ignorant and stupid peasants—nay infants, nay even brute beasts—improve by experience, and learn the qualities of natural objects, by observing the effects which result from them. When a child has felt the sensation of pain from touching the flame of a candle, he will be careful not to put his hand near any candle; but will expect a similar effect from a cause which is similar in its sensible qualities and appearance. If you assert, therefore, that the understanding of the child is led into this conclusion by any process of argument or ratiocination, I may justly require you to produce that argument; nor have you any pretense to refuse so equitable a demand. You cannot say that the argument is abtruse, and may possibly escape your enquiry; since you confess that it is obvious to the capacity of a mere infant. If you hesitate, therefore, a moment, or if, after reflection, you produce any intricate or profound argument, you, in a manner, give up the question, and confess that it is not reasoning which engages us to suppose the past resembling the future, and to expect similar effects from causes which are, to appearance, similar. This is the proposition which I intended to enforce in the present section. If I be right, I pretend not to have made any mighty discovery. And if I be wrong, I must acknowledge myself to be indeed a very backward scholar; since I cannot now discover an argument which, it seems, was perfectly familiar to me long before I was out of my cradle.

Sceptical Solution of These Doubts

PART I

. . . Nature will always maintain her rights, and prevail in the end over any abstract reasoning whatsoever. Though we should conclude, for instance, as in the foregoing section, that, in all reasonings from experience, there is a step taken by the mind which is not supported by any argument or process of the understanding; there is no danger that these reasonings, on which almost all knowledge depends, will ever be affected by such a discovery. If the mind be not engaged by argument to make this step, it must be induced by some other principle of equal weight and authority; and that principle will preserve its influence as long as human nature remains the

same. What that principle is may well be worth the pains of enquiry.

Suppose a person, though endowed with the strongest faculties of reason and reflection, to be brought on a sudden into this world; he would, indeed, immediately observe a continual succession of objects, and one event following another; but he would not be able to discover anything farther. He would not, at first, by any reasoning, be able to reach the idea of cause and effect; since the particular powers, by which all natural operations are performed, never appear to the senses; nor is it reasonable to conclude, merely because one event, in one instance, precedes another, that therefore the one is the cause, the other the effect. Their conjunction may be arbitrary and casual. There may be no reason to infer the existence of one from the appearance of the other. And in a word, such a person, without more experience, could never employ his conjecture or reasoning concerning any matter of fact, or be assured of anything beyond what was immediately present to his memory and senses.

Suppose, again, that he has acquired more experience, and has lived so long in the world as to have observed familiar objects or events to be constantly conjoined together; what is the consequence of this experience? He immediately infers the existence of one object from the appearance of the other. Yet he has not, by all his experience, acquired any idea or knowledge of the secret power by which the one object produces the other; nor is it, by any process of reasoning, he is engaged to draw this inference. But still he finds himself determined to draw it: And though he should be convinced that his understanding has no part in the operation, he would nevertheless continue in the same course of thinking. There is some other principle which determines him to form such a conclusion.

This principle is Custom or Habit. For wherever the repetition of any particular act or operation produces a propensity to renew the same act or operation, without being impelled by any reasoning or process of the understanding, we always say, that this propensity is the effect of *Cus-*

tom. By employing that word, we pretend not to have given the ultimate reason of such a propensity. We only point out a principle of human nature, which is universally acknowledged, and which is well known by its effects. Perhaps we can push our enquiries no farther, or pretend to give the cause of this cause; but must rest contented with it as the ultimate principle, which we can assign, of all our conclusions from experience. It is sufficient satisfaction, that we can go so far, without repining at the narrowness of our faculties because they will carry us no farther. And it is certain we here advance a very intelligible proposition at least, if not a true one, when we assert that, after the constant conjunction of two objects—heat and flame, for instance, weight and solidity—we are determined by custom alone to expect the one from the appearance of the other. This hypothesis seems even the only one which explains the difficulty, why we draw, from a thousand instances, an inference which we are not able to draw from one instance, that is, in no respect, different from them. Reason is incapable of any such variation. The conclusions which it draws from considering one circle are the same which it would form upon surveying all the circles in the universe. But no man, having seen only one body move after being impelled by another, could infer that every other body will move after a like impulse. All inferences from experience, therefore, are effects of custom, not of reasoning.

Custom, then, is the great guide of human life. It is that principle alone which renders our experience useful to us, and makes us expect, for the future, a similar train of events with those which have appeared in the past. Without the influence of custom, we should be entirely ignorant of every matter of fact beyond what is immediately present to the memory and senses. We should never know how to adjust means to ends, or to employ our natural powers in the production of any effect. There would be an end at once of all action, as well as of the chief part of speculation.

But here it may be proper to remark, that though our conclusions from experience carry us beyond our memory and senses, and assure us of matters of fact which happened in the most distant places and most remote ages, yet some fact must always be present to the senses or memory, from which we may first proceed in drawing these conclusions. A man, who should find in a desert country the remains of pompous buildings, would conclude that the country had, in ancient times, been cultivated by civilized inhabitants; but did nothing of this nature occur to him, he could never form such an inference. We learn the events of former ages from history; but then we must peruse the volumes in which this instruction is contained, and thence carry up our inferences from one testimony to another, till we arrive at the eyewitnesses and spectators of these distant events. In a word, if we proceed not upon some fact, present to the memory or senses, our reasonings would be merely hypothetical; and however the particular links might be connected with each other, the whole chain of inferences would have nothing to support it, nor could we ever, by its means, arrive at the knowledge of any real existence. If I ask why you believe any particular matter of fact, which you relate, you must tell me some reason; and this reason will be some other fact, connected with it. But as you cannot proceed after this manner, *in infinitum,* you must at last terminate in some fact, which is present to your memory or senses; or must allow that your belief is entirely without foundation.

What, then, is the conclusion of the whole matter? A simple one; though, it must be confessed, pretty remote from the common theories of philosophy. All belief of matter of fact or real existence is derived merely from some object, present to the memory or senses, and a customary conjunction between that and some other object. Or in other words; having found in many instances, that any two kinds of objects—flame and heat, snow and cold—have always been conjoined together; if flame or snow be presented anew to the senses, the mind is carried by custom to expect heat or cold, and to *believe* that such a quality does exist, and will discover itself upon a nearer approach. This belief is the necessary result of placing the mind in such circumstances. It is an operation of the soul, when we are so situated, as unavoidable as to feel the passion of love, when we receive benefits; or hatred, when we meet with injuries. All these operations are a species of natural instincts, which no reasoning or process of the thought and understanding is able either to produce or to prevent.

For Further Reflection

1. Hume's empiricism is more radical than Locke's because it leads to skepticism over metaphysical issues which Locke thought safe (e.g., the nature of the self, causality, the existence of God). Hume closes the book from which our selection comes with these words: "By way of conclusion to these reflections on diverse questions: When we run over libraries, persuaded of the principles here expounded, what havoc must we make? If we take in hand any volume, of divinity or metaphysics, for instance, let us ask: Does it contain any reasoning concerning quantity or number? No. Does it contain any experimental (probable) reasoning concerning matter of fact? No. Commit it then to the flames: for it can contain nothing but sophistry and illusion." Are you convinced by Hume's reasoning? If not, how would you go about arguing against him?

2. Do you understand Hume's argument against justifying our belief that the future will resemble the past? Note that (1) the foundation of reasoning regarding matters of fact is the idea of causation, (2) the foundation of reasoning concerning causation is *experience*, and (3) the foundation of all conclusions regarding trust in experience is the principle of the uniformity of nature (e.g., bread will continue to nourish us in the future as it has in the past and the sun will rise tomorrow because it always has in the past). But why should we accept (3) the uniformity of nature? There is no contradiction in supposing its opposite (e.g., that bread will cease to nourish us or that the sun will not rise tomorrow). We cannot reason that it will continue to do so because it has always done so in the past, for that is begging the question. It seems that the foundation of (3) is our trust in causation of which (3) is supposed to be the foundation. Do you see the circularity? Can you find anything wrong in Hume's reasoning?

III.5   The Kantian Compromise

IMMANUEL KANT

Immanuel Kant (1724–1804) was born into a deeply pietistic Lutheran family in Konigsberg, Germany, lived in that town his entire life, and taught at the University of Konigsberg. He lived a duty-bound, methodical life, so regular that citizens were said to have set their clocks by his walks. Kant is one of the premier philosophers in the Western tradition. In his monumental work *The Critique of Pure Reason* (1781), from which this selection is taken, he inaugurated a Copernican-like revolution in the theory of knowledge.

Who is right—the rationalists from Plato to Descartes who argue that reason alone is the ultimate source of knowledge, or the empiricists like Locke and Hume who argue that experience is the only source of knowledge? Are there innate ideas, as the rationalists contend, or are our minds completely blank at birth and need experience to write upon them?

Kant began as a rationalist but on reading Hume was struck with the cogency of his argument. Hume "woke me from my dogmatic slumbers," Kant wrote, and he henceforth accepted the idea that all of our knowledge begins with experience. But Kant thought that Hume had made an invalid inference in concluding that all our knowledge arises from experience. Kant sought to demonstrate that the rationalists had an invaluable insight, which had been lost in their flamboyant speculation, that there is something determinate in the mind that causes us to know what we know.

Kant argued that the mind is so structured and empowered that it imposes interpretive categories on our experience, so that we do not simply experience the world, as the empiricists alleged, but interpret it through the constitutive mechanisms of the mind. This is sometimes called Kant's Copernican revolution, as explained by Kant himself in the reading.

Another word is in order about *a priori* and *a posteriori* knowledge. Remember, *a priori* knowledge is that which we know *prior* to experience. It is opposed to *a posteriori* knowledge, which is based on experience. Recall that for Hume all knowledge of matters of fact was *a posteriori* and only analytic statements (e.g., mathematical truths or statements such as "all mothers are women") were known *a priori*. Kant rejects this formula. For him it is possible to have *a priori* matters of fact. Indeed, he thinks that mathematical truth is not analytic but synthetic (the predicate adds something to the subject) and that there is other synthetic *a priori* knowledge, such as our knowledge of time, space, causality, and the moral law.

Study Questions

1. What is Kant's Copernican revolution in knowledge? Explain.

2. What does Kant mean by saying that although "all our knowledge begins with experience, it by no means follows that all arises out of experience"?

3. What does he mean by *a priori* and *a posteriori* knowledge? What examples does he offer of *a priori* knowledge (or cognition)?

4. What is the distinction between analytic and synthetic judgments?

Preface to the Second Edition

. . . UNTIL NOW WE HAVE ASSUMED that all our knowledge must conform to objects. But every attempt to extend our knowledge of objects by establishing something in regard to them *à priori*, by means of concepts, have, on this assumption, ended in failure. Therefore, we must see whether we may have better success in our metaphysical task if we begin with the assumption that objects must conform to our knowledge. In this way we would have knowledge of

From Kant's Critique of Pure Reason *(1781). The preface selection is my translation. The rest is from J. M. D. Meiklejohn translation (Wiley, 1855).*

objects *à priori*. We should then be proceeding in the same way as Copernicus in his revolutionary hypothesis. After he failed to make progress in explaining the movements of the heavenly bodies on the supposition that they all revolved around the observer, he decided to reverse the relationship and made the observer revolve around the heavenly body, the sun, which was at rest. A similar experiment can be done in metaphysics with regard to the intuition of objects. If our intuition must conform to the constitution of the object, I do not see how we could know anything of the object *à priori*, but if the object of sense must conform to the constitution of our faculty of intuition, then *à priori* knowledge is possible. . . .

Introduction

I.—OF THE DIFFERENCE BETWEEN PURE AND EMPIRICAL KNOWLEDGE

That all our knowledge begins with experience there can be no doubt. For how is it possible that the faculty of cognition should be awakened into exercise otherwise than by means of objects which affect our senses, and partly of themselves produce representations, partly rouse our powers of understanding into activity, to compare, to connect, or to separate these, and so to convert the raw material of our sensuous impressions into a knowledge of objects, which is called experience? In respect of time, therefore, no knowledge of ours is antecedent to experience, but begins with it.

But, though all our knowledge begins with experience, it by no means follows that all arises out of experience. For, on the contrary, it is quite possible that our empirical knowledge is a compound of that which we receive through impressions, and that which the faculty of cognition supplies from itself (sensuous impressions giving merely the *occasion*), an addition which we cannot distinguish from the original element given by sense, till long practice has made us attentive to, and skilful in separating it. It is,

therefore, a question which requires close investigation, and is not to be answered at first sight—whether there exists a knowledge altogether independent of experience, and even of all sensuous impressions? Knowledge of this kind is called *à priori*, in contradistinction to empirical knowledge, which has its sources *à posteriori*, that is, in experience.

But the expression, "*à priori*," is not as yet definite enough adequately to indicate the whole meaning of the question above started. For, in speaking of knowledge which has its sources in experience, we are wont to say, that this or that may be known *à priori*, because we do not derive this knowledge immediately from experience, but from a general rule, which, however, we have itself borrowed from experience. Thus, if a man undermined his house, we say, "he might know *à priori* that it would have fallen"; that is, he needed not to have waited for the experience that it did actually fall. But still, *à priori*, he could not know even this much. For, that bodies are heavy, and, consequently, that they fall when their supports are taken away, must have been known to him previously, by means of experience.

By the term "knowledge *à priori*," therefore, we shall in the sequel understand, not such as is independent of this or that kind of experience, but such as is absolutely so of *all* experience. Opposed to this is empirical knowledge, or that which is possible only *à posteriori*, that is, through experience. Knowledge *à priori* is either pure or impure. Pure knowledge *à priori* is that with which no empirical element is mixed up. For example, the proposition, "Every change has a cause," is a proposition *à priori*, but impure, because change is a conception which can only be derived from experience.

II.—THE HUMAN INTELLECT, EVEN IN AN UNPHILOSOPHICAL STATE, IS IN POSSESSION OF CERTAIN COGNITIONS, *À PRIORI*

The question now is as to a *criterion*, by which we may securely distinguish a pure from an empirical cognition. Experience no doubt teaches us that this or that object is constituted in such and such a manner, but not that it could not possibly exist otherwise. Now, in the first place, if we have a proposition which contains the idea of necessity in its very conception, it is a judgment *à priori;* if, moreover, it is not derived from any other proposition, unless from one equally involving the idea of necessity, it is absolutely *à priori.* Secondly, an empirical judgment never exhibits strict and absolute, but only assumed and comparative universality (by induction); therefore, the most we can say is—so far as we have hitherto observed, there is no exception to this or that rule. If, on the other hand, a judgment carries with it strict and absolute universality, that is, admits of no possible exception, it is not derived from experience, but is valid absolutely *à priori.*

Empirical universality is, therefore, only an arbitrary extension of validity, from that which may be predicated of a proposition valid in most cases, to that which is asserted of a proposition which holds good in all; as, for example, in the affirmation, "all bodies are heavy." When, on the contrary, strict universality characterizes a judgment, it necessarily indicates another peculiar source of knowledge, namely, a faculty of cognition *à priori.* Necessity and strict universality, therefore, are infallible tests for distinguishing pure from empirical knowledge, and are inseparably connected with each other. But as in the use of these criteria the empirical limitation is sometimes more easily detected than the contingency of the judgment, or the unlimited universality which we attach to a judgment is often a more convincing proof than its necessity, it may be advisable to use the criteria separately, each being by itself infallible.

Now, that in the sphere of human cognition, we have judgments which are necessary, and in the strictest sense universal, consequently pure *à priori,* it will be an easy matter to show. If we desire an example from the sciences, we need only take any proposition in mathematics. If we cast our eyes upon the commonest operations of the understanding, the proposition, "every change must have a cause," will amply serve our purpose. In the latter case, indeed, the conception of a cause so plainly involves the conception of a necessity of connection with an effect, and of a strict universality of the law, that the very notion of a cause would entirely disappear, were we to derive it, like Hume, from a frequent association of what happens with that which precedes, and the habit thence originating of connecting representations—the necessity inherent in the judgment being therefore merely subjective. Besides, without seeking for such examples of principles existing *à priori* in cognition, we might easily show that such principles are the indispensable basis of the possibility of experience itself, and consequently prove their existence *à priori.* For whence could our experience itself acquire certainty, if all the rules on which it depends were themselves empirical, and consequently fortuitous? No one, therefore, can admit the validity of the use of such rules as first principles. But, for the present, we may content ourselves with having established the fact, that we do possess and exercise a faculty of pure *à priori* cognition; and, secondly, with having pointed out the proper tests of such cognition, namely, universality and necessity.

Not only in judgments, however, but even in conceptions, is an *à priori* origin manifest. For example, if we take away by degrees from our conceptions of a body all that can be referred to mere sensuous experience—color, hardness or softness, weight, even impenetrability—the body will then vanish; but the space which it occupied still remains, and this it is utterly impossible to annihilate in thought. Again, if we take away, in like manner, from our empirical conception of any object, corporeal or incorporeal, all properties which mere experience has taught us to connect with it, still we cannot think away those through which we cogitate it as substance, or adhering to substance, although our conception of substance is more determined than that of an object. Compelled, therefore, by that necessity with which the conception of substance forces itself upon us, we must confess that it has its seat in our faculty of cognition *à priori*. . . .

IV.—OF THE DIFFERENCE BETWEEN ANALYTICAL AND SYNTHETICAL JUDGMENTS

In all judgments wherein the relation of a subject to the predicate is thought (I mention affirmative judgments only here; the application to negative will be very easy), this relation is possible in two different ways. Either the predicate B belongs to the subject A, as somewhat which is contained (though covertly) in the conception A; or the predicate B lies completely out of the conception A, although it stands in connection with it. In the first instance, I term the judgment analytical, in the second, synthetical. Analytical judgments (affirmative) are therefore those in which the connection of the predicate with the subject is cogitated through identity; those in which this connection is cogitated without identity, are called synthetical judgments. The former may be called *explicative,* the latter *augmentative** judgments; because the former add in the predicate nothing to the conception of the subject, but only analyze it into its constituent conceptions, which were thought already in the subject, although in a confused manner; the latter add to our conceptions of the subject a predicate which was not contained in it, and which no analysis could ever have discovered therein. For example, when I say, "all bodies are extended," this is an analytical judgment. For I need not go beyond the conception of *body* in order to find extension connected with it, but merely analyze the conception, that is, become conscious of the manifold properties which I think in that conception, in order to discover this predicate in it: it is therefore an analytical judgment. On the other hand, when I say, "all bodies are heavy,"

*That is, judgments which really add to, and do not merely analyze or explain the conceptions which make up the sum of our knowledge.

the predicate is something totally different from that which I think in the mere conception of a body. But the addition of such a predicate therefore, it becomes a synthetical judgment.

Judgments of experience, as such, are always synthetical. For it would be absurd to think of grounding an analytical judgment on experience, because in forming such a judgment, I need not go out of the sphere of my conceptions, and therefore recourse to the testimony of experience is quite unnecessary. That "bodies are extended" is not an empirical judgment, but a proposition which stands firm *à priori*. For before addressing myself to experience, I already have in my conception all the requisite conditions for the judgment, and I have only to extract the predicate from the conception, according to the principle of contradiction, and thereby at the same time become conscious of the necessity of the judgment, a necessity which I could never learn from experience. On the other hand, though at first I do not at all include the predicate of weight in my conception of body in general, that conception still indicates an object of experience, a part of the totality of experience, to which I can still add other parts; and this I do when I recognize by observation that bodies are heavy. I can cognize beforehand by analysis the conception of body through the characteristics of extension, impenetrability, shape, etc., all which are cogitated in this conception. But now I extend my knowledge, and looking back on experience from which I had derived this conception of body, I find weight at all times connected with the above characteristics, and therefore I synthetically add to my conceptions this as a predicate, and say, "all bodies are heavy." Thus it is experience upon which rests the possibility of the synthesis of the predicate of weight with the conception of body, because both conceptions, although the one is not contained in the other, still belong to one another (only contingently, however), as parts of a whole, namely, of experience, which is itself a synthesis of intuitions.

But to synthetical judgments *à priori,* such aid is entirely wanting. If I go out of and beyond the conception A, in order to recognize another B as connected with it, what foundation have I to rest one, whereby to render the synthesis possible? I have here no longer the advantage of looking out in the sphere of experience for what I want. Let us take, for example, the proposition, "everything that happens has a cause." In the conception of *something that happens,* I indeed think an existence which a certain time antecedes, and from this I can derive analytical judgments. But the conception of a cause lies quite out of the above conception, and indicates something entirely different from "that which happens," and is consequently not contained in that conception. How then am I able to assert concerning the general conception—"that which happens"—something entirely different from that conception, and to recognize the conception of cause although not contained in it, yet as belonging to it, and even necessarily? what is here the unknown = X, upon which the understanding rests when it believes it has found, out of the conception A a foreign predicate B, which it nevertheless considers to be connected with it? It cannot be experience, because the principle adduced annexes the two representations, cause and effect, to the representation existence, not only with universality, which experience cannot give, but also with the expression of necessity, therefore completely *à priori* and from pure conceptions. Upon such synthetical, that is augmentative propositions, depends the whole aim of our speculative knowledge *à priori;* for although analytical judgments are indeed highly important and necessary, they are so, only to arrive at that clearness of conceptions which is requisite for a sure and extended synthesis, and this alone is a real acquisition.

V.—IN ALL THEORETICAL SCIENCES OF REASON, SYNTHETICAL JUDGMENTS *À PRIORI* ARE CONTAINED AS PRINCIPLES

1. Mathematical judgments are always synthetical. Hitherto this fact, though incontestably true and very important in its consequences, seems to have escaped the analysts of the human mind, nay, to be in complete opposition to all their conjectures. For as it was found that mathematical conclusions all proceed according to the principle of contradiction (which the nature of every apodictic certainty requires), people became persuaded that the fundamental principles of the science also were recognized and admitted in the same way. But the notion is fallacious; for although a synthetical proposition can certainly be discerned by means of the principle of contradiction, this is possible only when another synthetical proposition precedes, from which the latter is deduced, but never of itself.

Before all, be it observed, that proper mathematical propositions are always judgments *à priori,* and not empirical, because they carry along with them the conception of necessity, which cannot be given by experience. If this be demurred to, it matters not; I will then limit my assertion to *pure* mathematics, the very conception of which implies, that it consists of knowledge altogether non-empirical and *à priori.*

We might, indeed, at first suppose that the proposition $7 + 5 = 12$, is a merely analytical proposition, following (according to the principle of contradiction), from the conception of the sum of seven and five. But if we regard it more narrowly, we find that our conception of the sum of seven and five contains nothing more than the uniting of both sums into one, whereby it cannot at all be cogitated what this single number is which embraces both. The conception of twelve is by no means obtained by merely cogitating the union of seven and five; and we may analyze our conception of such a possible sum as long as we will, still we shall never discover in it the notion of twelve. We must go beyond these conceptions, and have recourse to an intuition which corresponds to one of the two— our five fingers, for example, or like Segner in his "Arithmetic," five points, and so by degrees, add the units contained in the five given in the intuition, to the conception of seven. For I first take the number 7, and, for the conception of 5 calling in the aid of the fingers of my hand as objects of intuition, I add the units, which I before took together to make up the number 5, gradually now by means of the material image my hand, to the number 7, and by this process, I at length see the number 12 arise. That 7 should be added to 5, I have certainly cogitated in my conception of a sum = 7 + 5, but not that this sum was equal to 12. Arithmetical propositions are therefore always synthetical, of which we may become more clearly convinced by trying large numbers. For it will thus become quite evident, that, turn and twist our conceptions as we may, it is impossible, without having recourse to intuition, to arrive at the sum total or product by means of the mere analysis of our conceptions. Just as little is any principle of pure geometry analytical. "A straight line between two points is the shortest," is a synthetical proposition. For my conception of *straight*, contains no notion of *quantity*, but is merely *qualitative*. The conception of the *shortest* is therefore wholly an addition, and by no analysis can it be extracted from our conception of a straight line. Intuition must therefore here lend its aid, by means of which and thus only, our synthesis is possible.

Some few principles preposited by geometricians are, indeed, really analytical, and depend on the principle of contradiction. They serve, however, like identical propositions, as links in the chain of method, not as principles—for example, *a* = *a*, the whole is equal to itself, or $(a + b) > a$, the whole is greater than its part. And yet even these principles themselves, though they derive their validity from pure conceptions, are only admitted in mathematics because they can be presented in intuition. What causes us here commonly to believe that the predicate of such apodictic judgments is already contained in our conception, and that the judgment is therefore analytical, is merely the equivocal nature of the expression. We must join in thought a certain predicate to a given conception, and this necessity cleaves already to the conception. But the question is, not what we must join in thought to

the given conception, but what we really think therein, though only obscurely, and then it becomes manifest, that the predicate pertains to these conceptions, necessarily indeed, yet not as thought in the conception itself, but by virtue of an intuition, which must be added to the conception.

2. The science of Natural Philosophy (Physics) contains in itself synthetical judgments *à priori*, as principles. I shall adduce two propositions. For instance, the proposition, "in all changes of the material world, the quantity of matter remains unchanged"; or, that, "in all communication of motion, action and reaction must always be equal." In both of these, not only is the necessity, and therefore their origin, *à priori* clear, but also that they are synthetical propositions. For in the conception of matter, I do not cogitate its permanency, but merely its presence in space, which it fills. I therefore really go out of and beyond the conception of matter, in order to think on to it something *à priori*, which I did not think in it. The proposition is therefore not analytical, but synthetical, and nevertheless conceived *à priori*; and so it is with regard to the other propositions of the pure part of natural philosophy.

3. As to Metaphysics, even if we look upon it merely as an attempted science, yet, from the nature of human reason, an indispensable one, we find that it must contain synthetical propositions *à priori*. It is not merely the duty of metaphysics to dissect, and thereby analytically to illustrate the conceptions which we form *à priori* of things; but we seek to widen the range of our *à priori* knowledge. For this purpose, we must avail ourselves of such principles as add something to the original conception—something not identical with, nor contained in it, and by means of synthetical judgments *à priori*, leave far behind us the limits of experience; for example, in the proposition, "the world must have a beginning," and such like. Thus metaphysics, according to the proper aim of the science, consists merely of synthetical *à priori* propositions.

For Further Reflection

What do you think of this revolutionary system of combining empiricist with rationalist aspects? Is it a successful compromise or synthesis? Or is something lost? For example, Kant affirms that we can never know reality in itself, the *ding an sich*, but only the appearances of reality filtered through the categories of the mind. But if causality is one of the categories of the mind and not in reality, how do we know the appearances have anything to do with reality?

A Contemporary Analysis of Knowledge   III.6

JOHN HOSPERS

John Hospers is professor of philosophy at the University of Southern California and editor of the *Pacific Journal of Philosophy*. He is the founder of the Libertarian party and was that party's candidate for president of the United States in 1972. He is the author of several textbooks as well as *Libertarianism: A Political Philosophy for Tomorrow* (1971).

In this essay Hospers first analyzes the different uses of the word "know" and then sets forth the conditions of descriptive knowledge. After that he distinguishes a weak sense of knowledge from a strong sense and uses this distinction to argue against the claims of skepticism.

Study Questions

1. What are the three senses of "know" that Hospers describes? Which is the most important philosophically?
2. What are the three conditions for propositional knowledge?
3. Why is it important to have good evidence before one can rightly be said to know?
4. What are the weak and strong senses of knowledge?
5. How does this distinction bear on the claims of skepticism?

I. Requirements for Knowing

THE WORD "KNOW" IS SLIPPERY. It is not always used in the same way. Here are some of its principal uses:

[*Senses of "know"*] 1. Sometimes when we talk about knowing, we are referring to *acquaintance* of some kind. For example, "Do you know Richard Smith?" means approximately the same as "Are you acquainted with Richard Smith? (have you met him? etc.) . . ."

2. Sometimes we speak of knowing *how*: Do you know how to ride a horse, do you know how to use a soldering iron? We even use a colloquial noun, "know-how," in talking about this. Knowing how is an *ability*—we know how to

From John Hospers, An Introduction to Philosophical Analysis, *2/E © 1967, pp. 143–145, 148–155. Reprinted by permission of Prentice-Hall, Inc., Englewood Cliffs, NJ.*

ride a horse if we have the ability to ride a horse, and the test of whether we have the ability is whether in the appropriate situation we can perform the activity in question. . . .

3. But by far the most frequent use of the word "know"—and the one with which we shall be primarily concerned—is the *propositional* sense: "I know that . . ." where the word "that" is followed by a proposition: "I know that I am now reading a book," "I know that I am an American citizen," and so on. There is some relation between this last sense of "know" and the earlier ones. We cannot be acquainted with Smith without knowing some things about him (without knowing *that* certain propositions about him are true), and it is difficult to see how one can know *how* to swim without knowing some true propositions about swimming, concerning what you must do with your arms and legs when in the water. (But the dog knows how to swim, though presumably he knows no propositions about swimming.) . . .

[*Conditions for knowing that*] Now, what is required for us to know in this third and most important sense? Taking the letter *p* to stand for any proposition, what requirements must be met in order for one to assert truly that he knows *p*? There are, after all, many people who claim to know something when they don't; so how can one separate the rightful claims to know from the mistaken ones?

a. *p must be true.* The moment you have some reason to believe that a proposition is not true, this immediately negates a person's claim to know it: You can't know *p* if *p* isn't true. If I say, "I know *p*, but *p* is not true," my statement is self-contradictory, for part of what is involved in knowing *p* is that *p* is true. Similarly, if I say, "He knows *p*, but *p* is not true," this too is self-contradictory. It may be that I *thought* I knew *p*; but if *p* is false, I didn't really know it. I only thought I did. If I nevertheless claim to know *p*, while admitting that *p* is false, my hearers may rightly conclude that I have not yet learned how to use the word "know." This is already implicit in our previous discussion, for what is it that you know about *p* when you know *p*? You know *that p is true,* of course; the very formulation gives away the case: Knowing *p* is knowing that *p* is true. . . .

But the truth-requirement, though necessary, is not sufficient. There are plenty of true propositions, for example in nuclear physics, that you and I do not know to be true unless we happen to be specialists in that area. But the fact that they are true does not imply that we know them to be true. . . .

b. *Not only must p be true: We must believe that p is true.* This may be called the "subjective requirement": We must have a certain attitude toward *p*—not merely that of wondering or speculating about *p,* but positively *believing* that *p* is true. "I know that *p* is true, but I don't believe that it is" would not only be a very peculiar thing to say, it would entitle our hearers to conclude that we had not learned in what circumstances to use the word "know." There may be numerous statements that you believe but do not know to be true, but there can be none which you know to be true but don't believe, since believing is a part (a defining characteristic) of knowing.

"I know *p*" implies "I believe *p*," and "He knows *p*" implies "He believes *p*," for believing is a defining characteristic of knowing. But believing *p* is *not* a defining characteristic of *p*'s *being true*: *p* can be true even though neither he nor I nor anyone else believes it. (The earth was round even before anyone believed that it was.) There is no contradiction whatever in saying, "He believed *p* (that is, believed it to be true), but *p* is not true." Indeed, we say things of this kind all the time: "He believes that people are persecuting him, but of course it isn't true." . . .

We have now discussed two requirements for knowing, an "objective" one (*p* must be true) and a "subjective" one (one must believe *p*). Are these sufficient? Can you be said to know something if you believe it and if what you believe is true? If so, we can simply define knowledge as true belief, and that will be the end of the matter.

Unfortunately, however, the situation is not so simple. True belief is not yet knowledge. A proposition may be true, and you may believe it to be true, and yet you may not *know* it to be true. Suppose you believe that there are sentient beings on Mars, and suppose that in the course of time, after space-travelers from the earth have landed there, your belief turns out to be true. The statement was true at the time you uttered it, and you also believed it at the time you uttered it—but did you *know* it to be true at the time you uttered it? Certainly not, we would be inclined to say; you were not in a position to know. It was a lucky guess. Even if you had *some* evidence that it was true, you didn't *know* that it was true at the time you said it. Some further condition, therefore, is required to prevent a lucky guess from passing as knowledge. . . .

c. *You must have evidence for p (reason to believe p)*. When you guessed which tosses of the coin would be heads, you had no reason to believe that your guesses would be correct, so you did not *know*. But after you watched all the tosses and carefully observed which way the coin tossed each time, then you knew. You had the evidence of your senses—as well as of people around you, and photographs if you wished to take them—that this throw was heads, that one tails, and so on. Similarly, when you predict on the basis of tonight's red sunset that tomorrow's weather will be fair, you don't yet *know* that your prediction will be borne out by the facts; you have some reason (perhaps) to believe it, but you cannot be sure. But tomorrow when you go outdoors and see for yourself what the weather is like, you do know for sure; when tomorrow comes you have the full evidence before you, which you do not yet have tonight. Tomorrow "the evidence is in"; tonight, it is not knowledge but only an "educated guess."

[*Problem*] This, then, is our third requirement—evidence. But at this point our troubles begin. How much evidence must there be?

"Some evidence" won't suffice as an answer: there may be *some* evidence that tomorrow will be sunny, but you don't yet know it. How about "all the evidence that is available"? But this won't do either; all the evidence that is now available may not be enough. All the evidence that is now available is far from sufficient to enable us to know whether there are conscious beings on other planets. We just don't know, even after we have examined all the evidence at our disposal.

How about "enough evidence to give us *good reason* to believe it"? But how much evidence is this? I may have known someone for years and found him to be scrupulously honest during all that time; by virtually any criterion, this would constitute good evidence that he will be honest the next time—and yet he may not be; suppose that the next time he steals someone's wallet. I had good reason to believe that he would remain honest, but nevertheless I didn't *know* that he would remain honest, for it was not true. We are all familiar with cases in which someone had good reason to believe a proposition that nevertheless turned out to be false.

What then *is* sufficient? We are now tempted to say, "Complete evidence—all the evidence there could ever be—the works, everything." But if we say this, let us notice at once that there are very few propositions whose truth we can claim to know. Most of those propositions that in daily life we claim to know without the slightest hesitation we would *not* know according to this criterion. For example, we say, "I know that if I were to let go of this pencil, it would fall," and we don't have the slightest hesitation about it; but although we may have excellent evidence (pencils and other objects have always fallen when let go), we don't have *complete* evidence, for we have not yet observed the outcome of letting go of it *this* time. To take an even more obvious case, we say, "I know that there is a book before me now," but we have not engaged in every possible observation that would be relevant to determining the truth of this statement: We have not examined the object (the one we take to be a book) from *all* angles (and since there are an infinite number of angles, who could?), and even if we have looked at it steadily for half an hour, we have not done so for a hundred hours, or a million; and yet it would *seem* (though some have disputed this, as we shall see) that if one observation provides evidence, a thousand observations should provide more evidence—and when could the accumulation of evidence end? . . .

We might, nevertheless, stick to our definition and say that we really do *not* know most of the propositions that in daily life we claim to know: Perhaps I don't *know* that this is a book before me, that I am now indoors and not outdoors, that I am now reading sentences written in the English language, or that there are any other people in the world. But this is a rather astounding claim and needs to be justified. We are all convinced that we know these things: We act on them every day of our lives, and if we were asked outside a philosophy classroom whether we knew them, we would say "yes" without hesitation. Surely we cannot accept a definition of "know" that would practically define knowledge out of existence? But if not, what alternative have we?

"Perhaps we don't have to go so far as to say '*all* the evidence,' '*complete* evidence,' and so on. All we have to say is that we must have *adequate* evidence." But when is the evidence adequate? Is anything less than "all the evidence there could ever be" adequate? "Well, adequate for enabling us to know." But this little addition to our definition lands us in a circle. We are trying to define "know," and we cannot in doing so employ the convenient phrase "enough to enable us to know"—for the last word in this definition is the very one we are trying to define. But once we have dropped the phrase "to know," we are left with our problem once more: How much evidence is adequate evidence? Is it adequate when anything less than *all* the evidence is in? If not all the evidence is in, but only 99.99 percent of it, couldn't that .01 percent go contrary to the rest

of it and require us to conclude that the proposition might not be true after all, and that therefore we didn't know it? Surely it has happened often enough that a statement that we thought we knew, perhaps even would have staked our lives on, turned out in the end to be false, or just doubtful. But in that case we didn't really *know* it after all: The evidence was good, even overwhelming, but yet not good enough, not really adequate, for it was not enough to guarantee the truth of the proposition. Can we know *p* with anything less than *all* the evidence there ever could be for *p*?

II. Strong and Weak Senses of "Know"

[*Disputes About Knowing*] In daily life we say we know—not just believe or surmise, but *know*—that heavier-than-air objects fall, that snow is white, that we can read and write, and countless other things. If someone denies this, and no fact cited by the one disputant suffices to convince the other, we may well suspect that there is a verbal issue involved: in this case, that they are operating on two different meanings of "know," because they construe the third requirement—the evidence requirement—differently.

[*Case 1*] Suppose I say, "There is a bookcase in my office," and someone challenges this assertion. I reply, "I *know* that there is a bookcase in my office. I put it there myself, and I've seen it there for years. In fact, I saw it there just two minutes ago when I took a book out of it and left the office to go into the classroom." Now suppose we both go to my office, take a look, and there is the bookcase, exactly as before. "See, I *knew* it was here," I say. "Oh no," he replies, "you *believed with good reason* that it was still there, because you had seen it there often before and you didn't see or hear anyone removing it. But you didn't *know* it was there when you said it, for at that moment you were in the classroom and not in your office."

At this point, I may reply, "But I did know it

was there, even when I said it. I knew it because *(1) I believed it, (2) I had good grounds on which to base the belief, and (3) the belief was true.* And I would call it knowledge whenever these three conditions are fulfilled. This is the way we use the word 'know' every day of our lives. One knows those true propositions that one believes with good reason. And when I said the bookcase was still in my office, I was uttering one of those propositions."

But now my opponent may reply, "But you still didn't know it. You had good reason to say it, I admit, for you had not seen or heard anyone removing it. You had good reason, but not *sufficient* reason. The evidence you gave was still compatible with your statement being false—and if it was false, you of course did not *know* that it was true. [*Case 2*] Suppose that you had made your claim to knowledge, and I had denied your claim, and we had both gone into your office, and to your great surprise (and mine too) the bookcase was no longer there. Could you *then* have claimed to know that it was still there?"

"Of course not. The falsity of a statement always invalidates the claim to know it. If the bookcase had not been there, I would not have been entitled to say that I knew it was there; my claim would have been mistaken."

"Right—it would have been mistaken. But now please note that the only difference between the two cases is that in the first case the bookcase was there and in the second case it wasn't. *The evidence in the two cases was exactly the same.* You had exactly the same reason for saying that the bookcase was still there in the *second* case (when we found it missing) that you did in the *first* case (when we found it still there). And since you—as you yourself admit—didn't know it in the second case, you couldn't have known it in the first case either. You believed it with good reason, but you didn't *know* it."

[*Solution*] Here my opponent may have scored an important point; he may have convinced me that since I admittedly didn't know in the second

case I couldn't have known in the first case either. But here I may make an important point in return: "My belief was the same in the two cases; the evidence was the same in the two cases (I had seen the bookcase two minutes before, had heard or seen no one removing it). The only difference was that in the first case the bookcase was there and in the second case it wasn't (*p* was true in the first case, false in the second). But *this doesn't show that I didn't know* in the first case. What it does show is that *although I might have been mistaken, I wasn't mistaken.* Had the bookcase not been there, I couldn't have claimed to know that it was; but since the bookcase in fact *was* still there, I *did* know, although (on the basis of the evidence I had) I *might* have been mistaken."

"Yes, it turned out to be true—you were lucky. But as we both agree, a lucky guess isn't the same as knowledge."

"But this wasn't just a lucky guess. I had excellent reasons for believing that the bookcase was still there. So the evidence requirement was fulfilled."

"No, it wasn't. You had good reason, excellent reason, but not *sufficient* reason—both times—for believing that the bookcase was still there. But in the second case it wasn't there, so you didn't know; therefore, in the first case where your evidence was *exactly the same*, you didn't know either; you just believed it with good reason, but that wasn't enough: your reason wasn't sufficient, and so you didn't *know*."

Now the difference in the criterion of knowing between the two disputants begins to emerge. According to me, I did know *p* in the first case because my belief was based on excellent evidence and was also true. According to my opponent, I did not know *p* in the first case because my evidence was still less than complete—I wasn't in the room seeing or touching the bookcase when I made the statement. It seems, then, that I am operating with a less demanding definition of "know" than he is. I am using "know" in the *weak* sense, in which I know a proposition when I believe it, have good reason for believing it, and it is true. But he is using "know" in a more demanding sense: He is using it in the *strong* sense, which requires that in order to know a proposition, it must be true, I must believe it, and I must have absolutely *conclusive* evidence in favor of it.

[*Examples*] Let us contrast these two cases:

Suppose that after a routine medical examination the excited doctor reports to me that the X-ray photographs show that I have no heart. I should tell him to get a new machine. I should be inclined to say that the fact that I have a heart is one of the few things that I can count on as absolutely certain. I can feel it beat. I know it's there. Furthermore, how could my blood circulate if I didn't have one? Suppose that later on I suffer a chest injury and undergo a surgical operation. Afterwards the astonished surgeons solemnly declare that they searched my chest cavity and found no heart, and that they made incisions and looked about in other likely places but found it not. They are convinced that I am without a heart. They are unable to understand how circulation can occur or what accounts for the thumping in my chest. But they are in agreement and obviously sincere, and they have clear photographs of my interior spaces. What would be my attitude? Would it be to insist that they were all mistaken? I think not. I believe that I should eventually accept their testimony and the evidence of the photographs. I should consider to be false what I now regard as an absolute certainty. [When I say I know I have a heart, I know it in the weak sense.]

Suppose that as I write this paper someone in the next room were to call out to me, "I can't find an ink-bottle; is there one in the house?" I should reply, "Here is an ink-bottle." If he said in a doubtful tone, "Are you sure? I looked there before," I should reply, "Yes, I know there is; come and get it."

Now could it turn out to be false that there is an ink-bottle directly in front of me on this desk? Many philosophers have thought so. They would say that many things could happen

of such a nature that if they did happen it would be proved that I am deceived. I agree that many extraordinary things could happen, in the sense that there is no logical absurdity in the supposition. It could happen that when I next reach for this ink-bottle my hand should seem to pass *through* it and I should not feel the contact of any object. It could happen that in the next moment the ink-bottle will suddenly vanish from sight; or that I should find myself under a tree in the garden with no ink-bottle about; or that one or more persons should enter this room and declare with apparent sincerity that they see no ink-bottle on this desk; or that a photograph taken now of the top of the desk should clearly show all of the objects on it except the ink-bottle. Having admitted that these things *could happen*, am I compelled to admit that if they did happen, then it would be proved that there is no ink-bottle here *now*? Not at all. I could say that when my hand seemed to pass through the ink-bottle I should *then* be suffering from hallucination; that if the ink-bottle suddenly vanished, it would have miraculously ceased to exist; that the other persons were conspiring to drive me mad, or were themselves victims of remarkable concurrent hallucinations; that the camera possessed some strange flaw or that there was trickery in developing the negative: . . . Not only do I not *have* to admit that those extraordinary occurrences would be evidence that there is no ink-bottle here; the fact is that I *do not* admit it. There is nothing whatever that could happen in the next moment or the next year that would by me be called *evidence* that there is not an ink-bottle here now. No future experience or investigation could prove to me that I am mistaken. Therefore, if I were to say, "I know that there is an ink-bottle here," I should be using "know" in the strong sense.[1]

It is in the weak sense that we use the word "know" in daily life, as when I say I know that I have a heart, that if I let go of this piece of chalk it will fall, that the sun will rise tomorrow, and so on. I have excellent reason (evidence) to believe all these things, evidence so strong that (so we say) it amounts to certainty. And yet there are events that could conceivably occur which, if they did occur, would cast doubt on the beliefs or even show them to be false. . . .

III. Argument Against Skepticism

[*Skepticism*] But the philosopher is apt to be more concerned with "know" in the strong sense. He wants to inquire whether there are any propositions that we can know without the shadow of a doubt will never be proved false, or even rendered dubious to the smallest degree. "You can say," he will argue, "and I admit that it would be good English usage to say, that you know that you have a heart and that the sun is more than 90 million miles from the earth. But you don't know it until you have absolutely conclusive evidence, and you must admit that the evidence you have, while very strong, is not conclusive. So I shall say, using 'know' in the strong sense, that you do not know these propositions. I want then to ask what propositions can be known in the strong sense, the sense that puts the proposition forever past the possibility of doubt."

And on this point many philosophers have been quite skeptical; they have granted few if any propositions whose truth we could know in the strong sense. . . . Such a person is a *skeptic*. We claim (he says) to know many things about the world, but in fact none of these propositions can be known for certain. What are we to say of the skeptic's position?

[*Criticism*] Let us first note that in the phrase "know for certain" the "for certain" is redundant—how can we know except for certain? If it is less than certain, how can it be knowledge? We do, however, use the word "certain" ambiguously: (1) Sometimes we say "I am certain," which just means that I have a feeling of certainty about it—"I feel certain that I locked the

door of the apartment"—and of course the feeling of certainty is no guarantee that the statement is true. People have very strong feelings of certainty about many propositions that they have no evidence for at all, particularly if they want to believe them or are consoled by believing them. The phrase "feeling certain," then, refers simply to a psychological state, whose existence in no way guarantees that what the person feels certain about is true. But (2) sometimes when we say "I am certain" we mean that it *is* certain—in other words, that we *do* know the proposition in question to be true. This, of course, is the sense of "certain" that is of interest to philosophers (the first sense is of more interest to psychiatrists in dealing with patients). Thus we could reformulate our question, "Is anything certain?" or "Are any propositions certain?"

"I can well understand," one might argue, "how you could question some statements, even most statements. But if you carry on this merry game until you have covered *all* statements, you are simply mistaken, and I think I can show you why. You may see someone in a fog or in a bad light and not know (not be certain) whether he has a right hand. But don't you know that *you* have a right hand? There it is! Suppose I now raise my hand and say, 'Here is a hand.' Now you say to me, 'I doubt that there's a hand.' But what evidence do you want? What does your doubt consist of? You don't believe your eyes, perhaps? Very well, then come up and touch the hand. You still aren't satisfied? Then keep on looking at it steadily and touching it, photograph it, call in other people for testimony if you like. If after all this you still say it isn't certain, what more do you want? Under what conditions would you admit that it *is* certain, that you *do* know it? I can understand your doubt when there is some condition left unfulfilled, some test left uncompleted. At the beginning, perhaps you doubted that *if* you tried to touch my hand you would find anything there to touch; but then you did touch, and so you resolved *that* doubt. You resolved further doubts by calling in other people and so on. You performed all the relevant tests, and they turned out favorably. So now, at the end of the process, what is it that you doubt? Oh, I know what you *say:* 'I still doubt that that's a hand.' But isn't this saying 'I doubt' now an empty formula? I can no longer attach any content to that so-called doubt, for there is nothing left to doubt; you yourself *cannot specify any further test that, if performed, would resolve your doubt.* 'Doubt' now becomes an empty word. You're not doubting now that *if* you raised your hand to touch mine, you would touch it, or that *if* Smith and others were brought in, they would also testify that this is a hand—we've already gone through all that. So what is it specifically that you doubt? What possible test is there the negative result of which you fear? I submit that there isn't any. You are confusing a situation in which doubt is understandable (*before* you made the tests) with the later situation in which it isn't, for it has all been dispelled. . . .

"But your so-called doubt becomes meaningless when there is nothing left to doubt—when the tests have been carried out and their results are all favorable. Suppose a physician examines a patient and says, 'It's probable that you have an inflamed appendix.' Here one can still doubt, for the signs may be misleading. So the physician operates on the patient, finds an inflamed appendix and removes it, and the patient recovers. *Now* what would be the sense of the physician's saying, 'It's *probable* that he had an inflamed appendix'? If seeing it and removing it made it only *probable,* what would make it certain? Or you are driving along and you hear a rapid regular thumping sound and you say, 'It's probable that I have a flat tire.' So far you're right; it's only probable—the thumping might be caused by something else. So you go out and have a look, and there is the tire, flat. You find a nail embedded in it, change the tire, and then resume your ride with no more thumping. Are you *now* going to say, 'It's merely *probable* that the car had

a flat tire'? But if given all those conditions it would be merely probable, what in the world would make it certain? Can you describe to me the circumstances in which you would say it's certain? If you can't, then the phrase 'being certain' has no meaning as you are using it. You are simply using it in such a special way that it has no application at all, and there is no reason at all why anyone else should follow your usage. In daily life we have a very convenient and useful distinction between the application of the words 'probable' and 'certain.' We say appendicitis is probable *before* the operation, but when the physician has the patient's appendix visible before him on the operating table, now it's certain—that's just the kind of situation in which we apply the word 'certain,' as opposed to 'probable'. Now you, for some reason, are so fond of the word 'probable' that you want to use it for everything—you use it to describe *both* the preoperative and postoperative situations, and the word 'certain' is left without any application at all. But this is nothing but a *verbal manipulation* on your part. You have changed nothing; you have only taken, as it were, two bottles with different contents, and instead of labeling them differently ('probable' and 'certain'), as the rest of us do, you put the same label ('probable') on both of them! What possible advantage is there in this? It's just verbal contrariness. And since you have pre-empted the word 'probable' to cover *both* the situations, we now have to devise a *different* pair of words to mark the perfectly obvious distinction between the situation *before* the surgery and the situation *during* the surgery—the same difference we previously marked by the words 'probable' and 'certain' until you used the word 'probable' to apply to both of them. What gain is there in this *verbal manipulation* of yours?" . . .

NOTE

1. Norman Malcolm, "Knowledge and Belief," in *Knowledge and Certainty,* pp. 66–68.

For Further Reflection

1. Do you think that Hospers' conditions for knowing are adequate? Do you see how they differ from Descartes, who would only allow absolute certainty to count as knowledge? Who is right?

2. Is Hospers correct in saying that the skeptic holds up an unrealistic standard (too strong a sense) of knowledge?

3. In Hospers' sense of knowledge can we ever "know that we know"? Or can we be justified only in believing that we know? If this is so, then should the focus of discussion be on the adequacy of justified belief?

Suggestions for Further Reading

Audi, Robert. *Belief, Justification and Knowledge*. Belmont, CA: Wadsworth, 1988. The best short introduction to the subject.

Blanshard, Brand. *The Nature of Thought*. 2 vols. George Allen & Unwin, 1940.

Chisholm, R. M. *Theory of Knowledge,* 3rd ed. Englewood Cliffs, NJ: Prentice-Hall, 1989. A rich outline of a foundational approach to epistemology.

Dancy, Jonathan. *Introduction to Contemporary Epistemology*. Blackwell, 1985. A penetrating analysis of contemporary problems, though not always clear.

Moser, Paul and Arnold Vander Nat, eds. *Human Knowledge*. Oxford: Oxford University Press, 1987. A recent comprehensive anthology.

Pollock, John. *Knowledge and Justification*. Rowman and Littlefield, 1986. Innovative and well argued.

Quine, W. V. and Joseph Ullian. *The Web of Belief,* 2nd ed. New York: Random House, 1978. A very useful book for beginners.

Russell, Bertrand. *The Problems of Philosophy*. Oxford: Oxford University Press, 1912.

Woozley, A. D. *Theory of Knowledge*. George Allen & Unwin, 1949.

Part IV

The Mind/Body Problem

The curiosity of Man, and the cunning of his Reason, have revealed much of what Nature held hidden. The structure of spacetime, the constitution of matter, the many forms of energy, the nature of life itself; all of these mysteries have become open books to us. To be sure, deep questions remain unanswered and revolutions await us still, but it is difficult to exaggerate the explosion in scientific understanding we humans have fashioned over the past 500 years.

Despite this general advance, a central mystery remains largely a mystery: the nature of conscious intelligence.

PAUL CHURCHLAND, *Matter and Consciousness*

F OR MILLENNIA, from biblical times until very recently, human beings thought of themselves as standing midway between the ape and the angel. The Psalmist praised God for our essential dignity:

> When I consider Thy heavens, the work of Thy fingers, the moon and the stars, which Thou hast ordained; What is man, that thou art mindful of him? and the son of man, that Thou hast visitest him? For Thou hast made him a little lower than the angels, and hast crowned him with glory and honor. Thou madest him to have dominion over the works of Thy hands; Thou hast put all things under his feet. (Ps. 8 : 3–6)

Today there is a tendency to see humans as standing somewhere between the ape and the computer. It was never seriously denied that we were animals or had an animal aspect in behaving like animals in eating, excreting, procreating, breathing, sleeping, and dying. But there was something more. We were esteemed as rational, spiritual, deliberative beings, made in the image of God, a little lower than the angels. The biblical image of humanity is noble and inspiring. The contemporary model of homo-computer is less inspiring. Being mechanistic, we are seen as lacking a free will, hence as lacking responsibility and intrinsic value altogether. Indeed, all that marks us off from a moderately reliable computer is the animal in us, the nonrational elements of sensation, emotions, and consciousness. If the latter model is closer to the truth, we will have to make the best of it. But the question of our essential nature is worth asking and pursuing: Is there something special about us, a soul or mind which perdures through change and survives our death, something which constitutes our true identity and is the locus of eternal value? Or is the mind simply a function of the body, in particular, of the brain? The theory that there is a mind (or soul) separate from the body is called *dualism*. The theory that the mind (or soul) is really an aspect or function of the brain is called *materialism* (or *physicalism*). In this part of our book we will examine arguments for and against these two theses.

What Am I? A Mind or a Body?

Intuitively, there seem to be two different types of reality: mind and body, that is, mental and physical (material).

Bodies are solid, material entities, extended in three-dimensional space, publicly observable, measurable, capable of causing things to happen in accordance with invariant laws of mechanics.

A mind, on the other hand, has none of these properties. Consciousness is not solid or material, is not extended in three-dimensional space, does not occupy space at all, is directly observable only by the person who owns it, cannot be measured, and seems incapable of causing things to happen in accordance with invariant laws of mechanics. Only the person him- or herself can think his thoughts, feel his emotions, and suffer his pain. Although neurologists can open your skull and observe your brain, they cannot observe your mind or your beliefs, sensations, emotions, or desires.

Unlike physical bodies, mental entities have no shape, weight, length, width, height, color, mass, velocity, or temperature. It would sound odd, indeed, to speak of a belief weighing 16 ounces like a cut of beef, or a feeling of love measuring $4'' \times 4'' \times 10'$ like a piece of lumber, or a pain being as heavy as a cement bag, or a desire that was green and had a temperature of 102.

Yet common sense tells us that these two entities somehow interact. We step on a nail, and it pierces our skin, sending a message through our nervous system which results in something altogether different from the shape or size of the nail or skin, something that does not possess size or shape and which cannot be seen, smelt, tasted, or heard—a feeling of distress or pain. Whereas the nail is public, the pain is private.

On the other hand, our mind informs us that it would be a good thing to get a bandage to put over the cut which has resulted (maybe a tetanus shot, too)—so the mind causes us to move our body. Our legs carry us to the medicine cabinet, where we stop, raise our arms, and with our hands take hold of the cabinet, open it, and take the bandage out and then apply it dexterously to the wound.

Here we have an instance where the body affects the mind and the mind, in turn, affects the body. So common sense shows that there is an interaction between the two radically different entitites. But how exactly does this transaction occur? and where does it occur? Or could it be that the mind is really simply a function of the body, not a separate substance at all? Or that the body is really an illusion and that there is only one substance, the mind alone? The following schema may help you through the readings in this part of the work. Berkeley's idealism was already considered in the last part (III.3).

Theory	Dualist interactionism	Ideal monism	Material monism
Nature of Substance	Mental and physical	Mental	Physical
Philosophers	Plato	Berkeley	Hume
	Descartes		Russell
	Locke		Taylor
	Moreland		

Dualistic Interactionism   IV.1

RENÉ DESCARTES

According to René Descartes there are three kinds of objects or substances in the universe: (1) the eternal substance, God; (2) his creation in terms of mind; (3) his creation in terms of matter: "We may thus easily have two clear and distinct notions or ideas, the one of created substance which thinks, and the other of corporeal substances, provided we carefully separate all the attributes of thought from those of extension."

We are thinking substances or embodied minds, "for I am not only lodged in my body as a pilot in a ship, but I am very closely united to it, and so to speak so intermingle with it that I seem to compose with it one whole. For if that were not the case, when my body hurt, I, who am merely a thinking thing, should perceive this wound by the understanding only, just as the sailor perceives by sight when something is damaged in his vessel."

The two kinds of substances which make us each a person intermingle in such a way that they causally act upon each other. Although it might be that a mind interacts with each part of its body separately, Descartes' view is that mind interacts only with the brain. The material event that causally stimulates one of our five senses (light hitting the retina of the eye) results in a chain of physical causation which leads to a certain brain process from which a certain sensation results. Then, in turn, being affected by the brain, the mind through mental events acts on the brain, which in turn affects the body. Descartes thought he could pinpoint the place in the brain where the interaction between mind and brain took place. "The part of the body in which the soul exercises its function immediately is in nowise the heart, nor the whole of the brain, but merely the most inward of all its parts, to wit, a certain very small gland which is situated in the middle of its substance."

Descartes identified this seat of consciousness with the pineal gland. It functions, pace Descartes, as the intermediary that transmits the effects of the mind to the brain and the effects of the brain to the mind. Modern neurophysiology has shown Descartes was wrong about this, but that doesn't affect the central thesis of Descartes' theory. Even if he was wrong about the precise details of the interaction, dualist interactionism could still be the correct account of mental activity.

With this introduction we turn to our reading. We pick up the discussion where we left off toward the end of the second meditation (reading III.1), where Descartes has discovered his self as the only indubitable piece of knowledge and begins to realize that all knowledge is a mental experience.

(A biographical sketch of Descartes is found on p. 113.)

Study Questions

1. How does Descartes characterize the self? What characteristics does it have? Can you recall the argument that led him to his conclusion about the nature of the self?

2. Why is Descartes tempted to regard the material as more certain than the mental? What is his explanation of this phenomenon?

3. How does the illustration of the piece of wax illustrate his thesis about the priority of the mental over the material?

4. What reason does Descartes give for believing that he has a body?

5. Why does he believe that there are other bodies besides his own?

6. What is the difference between the body and the mind?

7. What is the relationship of the body to the mind?

8. Where do the body and mind interact?

I SHALL EXERCISE MY IMAGINATION [in order to see if I am not something more]. I am not a collection of members which we call the human body: I am not a subtle air distributed through these members, I am not a wind, a fire, a vapour, a breath, nor anything at all which I can imagine or conceive; because I have assumed that all these were nothing. Without changing that supposition I find that I only leave myself certain of the fact that I am somewhat. But perhaps it is true that these same things which I supposed were non-existent because they are unknown to me, are really not different from the self which I know. I am not sure about this, I shall not dispute about it now; I can only give judgment on things that are known to me. I know that I exist, and I inquire what I am, I whom I know to exist. But it is very certain that the knowledge of my existence taken in its precise significance does not depend on things whose existence is not yet known to me; consequently it does not depend on those which I can feign in imagination. And indeed the very term *feign* in imagination proves to me my error, for I really do this if I image myself a something, since to imagine is nothing else than to contemplate the figure or image of a corporeal thing. But I already know for certain that I am, and that it may be that all these images, and, speaking generally, all things that relate to the nature of body are nothing but dreams [and chimeras]. For this reason I see clearly that I have as little reason to say, 'I shall stimulate my imagination in order to know more distinctly what I am,' than if I were to say, 'I am now awake, and I perceive somewhat that is real and true: but because I do not yet perceive it distinctly enough, I shall go to sleep of express purpose, so that my dreams may represent the perception with greatest truth and evidence.' And, thus, I know for certain that nothing of all that I can understand by means of my imagination belongs to this knowledge which

I have of myself, and that it is necessary to recall the mind from this mode of thought with the utmost diligence in order that it may be able to know its own nature with perfect distinctness.

But what then am I? A thing which thinks. What is a thing which thinks? It is a thing which doubts, understands, [conceives], affirms, denies, wills, refuses, which also imagines and feels.

Certainly it is no small matter if all these things pertain to my nature. But why should they not so pertain? Am I not that being who now doubts nearly everything, who nevertheless understands certain things, who affirms that one only is true, who denies all the others, who desires to know more, is averse from being deceived, who imagines many things, sometimes indeed despite his will, and who perceives many likewise, as by the intervention of the bodily organs? Is there nothing in all this which is as true as it is certain that I exist, even though I should always sleep and though he who has given me being employed all his ingenuity in deceiving me? Is there likewise any one of these attributes which can be distinguished from my thought, or which might be said to be separated from myself? For it is so evident of itself that it is I who doubts, who understands, and who desires, that there is no reason here to add anything to explain it. And I have certainly the power of imagining likewise; for although it may happen (as I formerly supposed) that none of the things which I imagine are true, nevertheless this power of imagining does not cease to be really in use, and it forms part of my thought. Finally, I am the same who feels, that is to say, who perceives certain things, as by the organs of sense, since in truth I see light, I hear noise, I feel heat. But it will be said that these phenomena are false and that I am dreaming. Let it be so; still it is at least quite certain that it seems to me that I see light, that I hear noise and that I feel

Reprinted from the Philosophical Works of Descartes, *trans. Elizabeth Haldane and G. Ross, vol. I (Cambridge University Press, 1931).*

heat. That cannot be false; properly speaking it is what is in me called feeling; and used in this precise sense that is no other thing than thinking.

From this time I begin to know what I am with a little more clearness and distinction than before; but nevertheless it still seems to me, and I cannot prevent myself from thinking, that corporeal things, whose images are framed by thought, which are tested by the senses, are much more distinctly known than that obscure part of me which does not come under the imagination. Although really it is very strange to say that I know and understand more distinctly these things whose existence seems to me dubious, which are unknown to me, and which do not belong to me, than others of the truth of which I am convinced, which are known to me and which pertain to my real nature, in a word, than myself. But I see clearly how the case stands: my mind loves to wander, and cannot yet suffer itself to be retained within the just limits of truth. Very good, let us once more give it the freest rein, so that, when afterwards we seize the proper occasion for pulling up, it may the more easily be regulated and controlled.

Let us begin by considering the commonest matters, those which we believe to be the most distinctly comprehended, to wit, the bodies which we touch and see; not indeed bodies in general, for these general ideas are usually a little more confused, but let us consider one body in particular. Let us take, for example, this piece of wax: it has been taken quite freshly from the hive, and it has not yet lost the sweetness of the honey which it contains; it still retains somewhat of the odour of the flowers from which it has been culled; its colour, its figure, its size are apparent; it is hard, cold, easily handled, and if you strike it with the finger, it will emit a sound. Finally all the things which are requisite to cause us distinctly to recognise a body, are met with in it. But notice that while I speak and approach the fire what remained of the taste is exhaled, the smell evaporates, the colour alters, the figure is destroyed, the size increases, it becomes liquid, it

heats, scarcely can one handle it, and when one strikes it, no sound is emitted. Does the same wax remain after this change? We must confess that it remains; none would judge otherwise. What then did I know so distinctly in this piece of wax? It could certainly be nothing of all that the senses brought to my notice, since all these things which fall under taste, smell, sight, touch, and hearing, are found to be changed, and yet the same wax remains.

Perhaps it was what I now think, viz. that this wax was not that sweetness of honey, nor that agreeable scent of flowers, nor that particular whiteness, nor that figure, nor that sound, but simply a body which a little while before appeared to me as perceptible under these forms, and which is now perceptible under others. But what, precisely, is it that I imagine when I form such conceptions? Let us attentively consider this, and, abstracting from all that does not belong to the wax, let us see what remains. Certainly nothing remains excepting a certain extended thing which is flexible and movable. But what is the meaning of flexible and movable? Is it not that I imagine that this piece of wax being round is capable of becoming square and of passing from a square to a triangular figure? No, certainly it is not that, since I imagine it admits of an infinitude of similar changes, and I nevertheless do not know how to compass the infinitude by my imagination, and consequently this conception which I have of the wax is not brought about by the faculty of imagination. What now is this extension? Is it not also unknown? For it becomes greater when the wax is melted, greater when it is boiled, and greater still when the heat increases; and I should not conceive [clearly] according to truth what wax is, if I did not think that even this piece that we are considering is capable of receiving more variations in extension than I have ever imagined. We must then grant that I could not even understand through the imagination what this piece of wax is, and that it is my mind alone which perceives it. I say this piece of wax in particular, for as to wax in general it is yet clearer. But what is this piece of wax which cannot be understood excepting by the [understanding or] mind? It is certainly the same that I see, touch, imagine, and finally it is the same which I have always believed it to be from the beginning. But what must particularly be observed is that its perception is neither an act of vision, nor of touch, nor of imagination, and has never been such although it may have appeared formerly to be so, but only an intuition of the mind, which may be imperfect and confused as it was formerly, or clear and distinct as it is at present, according as my attention is more or less directed to the elements which are found in it, and of which it is composed.

Yet in the meantime I am greatly astonished when I consider [the great feebleness of mind] and its proneness to fall [insensibly] into error; for although without giving expression to my thoughts I consider all this in my own mind, words often impede me and I am almost deceived by the terms of ordinary language. For we say that we see the same wax, if it is present, and not that we simply judge that it is the same from its having the same colour and figure. From this I should conclude that I knew the wax by means of vision and not simply by the intuition of the mind; unless by chance I remember that, when looking from a window and saying I see men who pass in the street, I really do not see them, but infer that what I see is men, just as I say that I see wax. And yet what do I see from the window but hats and coats which may cover automatic machines? Yet I judge these to be men. And similarly solely by the faculty of judgment which rests in my mind, I comprehend that which I believed I saw with my eyes.

A man who makes it his aim to raise his knowledge above the common should be ashamed to derive the occasion for doubting from the forms of speech invented by the vulgar; I prefer to pass on and consider whether I had a more evident and perfect conception of what the wax was when I first perceived it, and when I believed I knew it by means of the external senses or at least by the common sense as it is called, that is to say by the imaginative faculty, or whether my present conception is clearer now that I have most carefully examined what it is, and in what way it can be known. It would certainly be absurd to doubt as to this. For what was there in this first perception which was distinct? What was there which might not as well have been perceived by any of the animals? But when I distinguish the wax from its external forms, and when, just as if I had taken from it its vestments, I consider it quite naked, it is certain that although some error may still be found in my judgment, I can nevertheless not perceive it thus without a human mind.

But finally what shall I say of this mind, that is, of myself, for up to this point I do not admit in myself anything but mind? What then, I who seem to perceive this piece of wax so distinctly, do I not know myself, not only with much more truth and certainty, but also with much more distinctness and clearness? For if I judge that the wax is or exists from the fact that I see it, it certainly follows much more clearly that I am or that I exist myself from the fact that I see it. For it may be that what I see is not really wax, it may also be that I do not possess eyes with which to see anything; but it cannot be that when I see, or (for I no longer take account of the distinction) when I think I see, that I myself who think am nought. So if I judge that the wax exists from the fact that I touch it, the same thing will follow, to wit, that I am; and if I judge that my imagination, or some other cause, whatever it is, persuades me that the wax exists, I shall still conclude the same. And what I have here remarked of wax may be applied to all other things which are external to me [and which are met with outside of me]. And further, if the [notion or] perception of wax has seemed to me clearer and more distinct, not only after the sight or the touch, but also after many other causes have rendered it quite manifest to me, with how much more [evidence] and distinctness must it be said that I now know myself, since all the reasons which contribute to the knowledge of wax, or any other body whatever, are yet better proofs of the nature of my mind! And there are so many other things in the mind itself which may contribute to the elucidation of its nature, that those which depend on body such as these just mentioned, hardly merit being taken into account.

But finally here I am, having insensibly reverted to the point I desired, for, since it is now manifest to me that even bodies are not properly speaking known by the senses or by the faculty of imagination, but by the understanding only, and since they are not known from the fact that they are seen or touched, but only because they are understood, I see clearly that there is nothing which is easier for me to know than my mind. But because it is difficult to rid oneself so promptly of an opinion to which one was accustomed for so long, it will be well that I should halt a little at this point, so that by the length of my meditation I may more deeply imprint on my memory this new knowledge.

Meditation III: Of God: That He Exists

I shall now close my eyes, I shall stop my ears, I shall call away all my senses, I shall efface even from my thoughts all the images of corporeal things, or at least (for that is hardly possible) I shall esteem them as vain and false; and thus holding converse only with myself and considering my own nature, I shall try little by little to reach a better knowledge of and a more familiar acquaintanceship with myself. I am a thing that thinks, that is to say, that doubts, affirms, denies, that knows a few things, that is ignorant of many [that loves, that hates], that wills, that desires, that also imagines and perceives; for as I remarked before, although the things which I perceive and imagine are perhaps nothing at all apart from me and in themselves, I am nevertheless assured that these modes of thought that I call perceptions and imaginations, inasmuch only as they are modes of thought, certainly reside [and are met with] in me. . . .

On the Separation of the Mind from the Body

But now that I begin to know myself better, and to discover more clearly the author of my being, I do not in truth think that I should rashly admit all the matters which the senses seem to teach us, but, on the other hand, I do not think that I should doubt them all universally.

And first of all, because I know that all things which I apprehend clearly and distinctly can be created by God as I apprehend them, it suffices that I am able to apprehend one thing apart from another clearly and distinctly in order to be certain that the one is different from the other, since they may be made to exist in separation at least by the omnipotence of God; and it does not signify by what power this separation is made in order to compel me to judge them to be different: and, therefore, just because I know certainly that I exist, and that meanwhile I do not notice that any other thing necessarily pertains to my nature or essence, excepting that I am a thinking thing, I rightly conclude that my essence consists solely in the fact that I am a thinking thing [or a substance whose whole essence or nature is to think]. And although possibly (or rather certainly, as I shall say in a moment) I possess a body with which I am very intimately conjoined, yet because, on the one side, I have a clear and distinct idea of myself inasmuch as I am only a thinking and unextended thing, and as, on the other, I possess a distinct idea of body, inasmuch as it is only an extended and unthinking thing, it is certain that this I [that is to say, my soul by which I am what I am], is entirely and absolutely distinct from my body, and can exist without it.

I further find in myself faculties employing modes of thinking peculiar to themselves, to wit, the faculties of imagination and feeling, without which I can easily conceive myself clearly and distinctly as a complete being; while, on the other hand, they cannot be so conceived apart from me, that is without an intelligent substance in which they reside, for [in the notion we have of these faculties, or, to use the language of the Schools] in their formal concept, some kind of intellection is comprised, from which I infer that they are distinct from me as its modes are from a thing. I observe also in me some other faculties such as that of change of position, the assumption of different figures and such like, which cannot be conceived, any more than can the preceding, apart from some substance to which they are attached, and consequently cannot exist without it; but it is very clear that these faculties, if it be true that they exist, must be attached to some corporeal or extended substance, and not to an intelligent substance, since in the clear and distinct conception of these there is some sort of extension found to be present, but no intellection at all. There is certainly further in me a certain passive faculty of perception, that is, of receiving and recognising the ideas of sensible things, but this would be useless to me [and I could in no way avail myself of it], if there were not either in me or in some other thing another active faculty capable of forming and producing these ideas. But this active faculty cannot exist in me [inasmuch as I am a thing that thinks] seeing that it does not presuppose thought, and also that those ideas are often produced in me without my contributing in any way to the same, and often even against my will; it is thus necessarily the case that the faculty resides in some substance different from me in which all the reality which is objectively in the ideas that are produced by this faculty is formally or eminently contained, as I remarked before. And this substance is either a body, that is, a corporeal nature in which there is contained formally [and really] all that which is objectively [and by representation] in those ideas, or it is God Himself, or some other creature more noble than body in which that same is contained eminently. But, since God is no deceiver, it is very manifest that He does not communicate to me these ideas immediately and by Himself, nor yet by the intervention of some creature in which their reality is not formally, but only eminently, contained. For

since He has given me no faculty to recognise that this is the case, but, on the other hand, a very great inclination to believe [that they are sent to me or] that they are conveyed to me by corporeal objects, I do not see how He could be defended from the accusation of deceit if these ideas were produced by causes other than corporeal objects. Hence we must allow that corporeal things exist. However, they are perhaps not exactly what we perceive by the senses, since this comprehension by the senses is in many instances very obscure and confused; but we must at least admit that all things which I conceive in them clearly and distinctly, that is to say, all things which, speaking generally, are comprehended in the object of pure mathematics, are truly to be recognised as external objects.

As to other things, however, which are either particular only, as, for example, that the sun is of such and such a figure, etc., or which are less clearly and distinctly conceived, such as light, sound, pain and the like, it is certain that although they are very dubious and uncertain, yet on the sole ground that God is not a deceiver, and that consequently He has not permitted any falsity to exist in my opinion which He has not likewise given me the faculty of correcting, I may assuredly hope to conclude that I have within me the means of arriving at the truth even here. And first of all there is no doubt that in all things which nature teaches me there is some truth contained; for by nature, considered in general, I now understand no other thing than either God Himself or else the order and disposition which God has established in created things; and by my nature in particular I understand no other thing than the complexus of all the things which God has given me.

But there is nothing which this nature teaches me more expressly [nor more sensibly] than that I have a body which is adversely affected when I feel pain, which has need of food or drink when I experience the feelings of hunger and thirst, and so on; nor can I doubt there being some truth in all this.

Nature also teaches me by these sensations of pain, hunger, thirst, etc., that I am not only lodged in my body as a pilot in a vessel, but that I am very closely united to it, and so to speak so intermingled with it that I seem to compose with it one whole. For if that were not the case, when my body is hurt, I, who am merely a thinking thing, should not feel pain, for I should perceive this wound by the understanding only, just as the sailor perceives by sight when something is damaged in his vessel; and when my body has need of drink or food, I should clearly understand the fact without being warned of it by confused feelings of hunger and thirst. For all these sensations of hunger, thirst, pain, etc. are in truth none other than certain confused modes of thought which are produced by the union and apparent intermingling of mind and body. . . .

. . . It still remains to inquire how the goodness of God does not prevent the nature of man so regarded from being fallacious.

In order to begin this examination, then, I here say, in the first place, that there is a great difference between mind and body, inasmuch as body is by nature always divisible, and the mind is entirely indivisible. For, as a matter of fact, when I consider the mind, that is to say, myself inasmuch as I am only a thinking thing, I cannot distinguish in myself any parts, but apprehend myself to be clearly one and entire; and although the whole mind seems to be united to the whole body, yet if a foot, or an arm, or some other part, is separated from my body, I am aware that nothing has been taken away from my mind. And the faculties of willing, feeling, conceiving, etc. cannot be properly speaking said to be its parts, for it is one and the same mind which employs itself in willing and in feeling and under-

standing. But it is quite otherwise with corporeal or extended objects, for there is not one of these imaginable by me which my mind cannot easily divide into parts, and which consequently I do not recognise as being divisible; this would be sufficient to teach me that the mind or soul of man is entirely different from the body, if I had not already learned it from other sources.

I further notice that the mind does not receive the impressions from all parts of the body immediately, but only from the brain, or perhaps even from one of its smallest parts, to wit, from that in which the common sense is said to reside, which, whenever it is disposed in the same particular way, conveys the same thing to the mind, although meanwhile the other portions of the body may be differently disposed, as is testified by innumerable experiments which it is unnecessary here to recount. . . .

[From *The Passions of the Souls*]

The small gland which is the main seat of the souls is so suspended between the cavities which contain the spirits that it can be moved by them in as many ways as there are sensible diversities in the object, but that it may also be moved in diverse ways by the soul, whose nature is such that it receives in itself as many diverse impressions, that is to say, that it possesses as many diverse perceptions, as there are diverse movements in this gland. Reciprocally, likewise, the machine of the body is so formed that from the simple fact that this gland is diversely moved by the soul, or by such other cause, whatever it is, it thrusts the spirits which surround it towards the pores of the brain, which conducts them by the nerves into the muscles, by which means it causes them to move the limbs.

For Further Reflection

Here is a summary of Descartes' argument. Examine it and see whether you agree with his premises and his reasoning.

1. We can know the mind better than anything else (except possibly God's existence).

2. We can know the mind as distinct from the body (waking up in the morning, I do not need to open my eyes to see that I exist in order to know that I do).

3. It makes more sense to suppose that the mind and the body interact and face the difficulties of interactionist dualism than to say that they are one and struggle to explain the phenomena of consciousness.

4. The mind is in the pineal gland within the brain. At least it is clear that consciousness must reside in the brain since (a) sleep and disease which affect only the brain interrupt the operations of the senses; (b) if the nerves between external sense organs and the brain are cut, no sensations occur; and (c) it is possible to have sensations when the apparent place of sensation no longer exists (e.g., the phantom limb syndrome wherein an amputee imagines pain in his arm—even though he has none).

Exorcising Descartes' "Ghost in the Machine"   IV.2

GILBERT RYLE

Gilbert Ryle (1900–1976), an English philosopher, was educated at Oxford University, where he taught and greatly influenced a generation of students until his death in 1976. He was the editor of *Mind*, one of the most important philosophy journals, from 1948–1971. His principal works are *The Concept of Mind*, from which the present selection is taken, and *Dilemmas* (1954).

In this selection Ryle criticizes Cartesian dualism, which he labels "the Ghost in the Machine," as involving a category mistake. A category mistake is a confusion one slips into when something that belongs to one category or context is mistakenly taken to belong to another. Jokes intentionally thrive on this. For example, "The average woman in the United States has 2.5 children" would be an example of such a mistake if one went looking for the .5 child, treating a functional term "average woman" as a proper noun.

Ryle attempts to show that Descartes' dualism commits a similar category confusion. That is, just because we speak of bodily functions and mental functions as different in no way entails that they are two entirely separate entities. Ryle believes that this functional language can be reduced to observation language.

Study Questions

1. What is the official doctrine? Describe it.
2. What are the person's private and public histories? What does Ryle say about them?
3. What is Ryle's estimation of the official doctrine?
4. What is a category mistake? How does Ryle illustrate this concept?
5. What is the origin of the Cartesian category mistake?

The Absurdity of the Official Doctrine of "the Ghost in the Machine"

THE OFFICIAL DOCTRINE

THERE IS A DOCTRINE about the nature and place of minds which is so prevalent among theorists and even among laymen that it deserves to be described as the official theory. Most philosophers, psychologists and religious teachers subscribe, with minor reservations, to its main articles and, although they admit certain theoretical difficulties in it, they tend to assume that these can be overcome without serious modifications being made to the architecture of the theory. It will be argued here that the central principles of the doctrine are unsound and conflict with the whole body of what we know about minds when we are not speculating about them.

The official doctrine, which hails chiefly from Descartes, is something like this. With the doubtful exceptions of idiots and infants in arms every human being has both a body and a mind. Some would prefer to say that every human being is both a body and a mind. His body and his mind are ordinarily harnessed together, but after the death of the body his mind may continue to exist and function.

Human bodies are in space and are subject to the mechanical laws which govern all other bodies in space. Bodily processes and states can be inspected by external observers. So a man's bodily life is as much a public affair as are the lives of animals and reptiles and even as the careers of trees, crystals and planets.

But minds are not in space, nor are their operations subject to mechanical laws. The workings of one mind are not witnessable by other observers; its career is private. Only I can take direct cognisance of the states and processes of my own mind. A person therefore lives through two collateral histories, one consisting of what happens in and to his body, the other consisting of what happens in and to his mind. The first is public, the second private. The events in the first history are events in the physical world, those in the second are events in the mental world.

It has been disputed whether a person does or can directly monitor all or only some of the episodes of his own private history; but, according to the official doctrine, of at least some of these episodes he has direct and unchallengeable cognisance. In consciousness, self-consciousness and introspection he is directly and authentically apprised of the present states and operations of his mind. He may have great or small uncertainties about concurrent and adjacent episodes in the physical world, but he can have none about at least part of what is momentarily occupying his mind.

It is customary to express this bifurcation of his two lives and of his two worlds by saying that the things and events which belong to the physical world, including his own body, are external, while the workings of his own mind are internal. This antithesis of outer and inner is of course meant to be construed as a metaphor, since minds, not being in space, could not be described as being spatially inside anything else, or as having things going on spatially inside themselves. But relapses from this good intention are common and theorists are found speculating how stimuli, the physical sources of which are yards or miles outside a person's skin, can generate mental responses inside his skull, or how decisions framed inside his cranium can set going movements of his extremities.

Even when "inner" and "outer" are construed as metaphors, the problem of how a person's mind and body influence one another is notoriously charged with theoretical difficulties. What the mind wills, the legs, arms and the tongue execute; what affects the ear and the eye has something to do with what the mind perceives;

grimaces and smiles betray the mind's moods and bodily castigations lead, it is hoped, to moral improvement. But the actual transactions between the episodes of the private history and those of the public history remain mysterious, since by definition they can belong to neither series. They could not be reported among the happenings described in a person's autobiography of his inner life, but nor could they be reported among those described in some one else's biography of that person's overt career. They can be inspected neither by introspection nor by laboratory experiment. They are theoretical shuttlecocks which are forever being bandied from the physiologist back to the psychologist and from the psychologist back to the physiologist.

Underlying this partly metaphorical representation of the bifurcation of a person's two lives there is a seemingly more profound and philosophical assumption. It is assumed that there are two different kinds of existence or status. What exists or happens may have the status of physical existence, or it may have the status of mental existence. Somewhat as the faces of coins are either heads or tails, or somewhat as living creatures are either male or female, so, it is supposed, some existing is physical existing, other existing is mental existing. It is a necessary feature of what has physical existence that it is in space and time; it is a necessary feature of what has mental existence that it is in time but not in space. What has physical existence is composed of matter, or else is a function of matter; what has mental existence consists of consciousness, or else is a function of consciousness.

There is thus a polar opposition between mind and matter, an opposition which is often brought out as follows. Material objects are situated in a common field, known as "space," and what happens to one body in one part of space is mechanically connected with what happens to other bodies in other parts of space. But mental happenings occur in insulated fields, known as "minds," and there is, apart maybe from telepathy, no direct causal connection between what

happens in one mind and what happens in another. Only through the medium of the public physical world can the mind of one person make a difference to the mind of another. The mind is its own place and in his inner life each of us lives the life of a ghostly Robinson Crusoe. People can see, hear and jolt one another's bodies, but they are irremediably blind and deaf to the workings of one another's minds and inoperative upon them.

What sort of knowledge can be secured of the workings of a mind? On the one side, according to the official theory, a person has direct knowledge of the best imaginable kind of the workings of his own mind. Mental states and processes are (or are normally) conscious states and processes, and the consciousness which irradiates them can engender no illusions and leaves the door open for no doubts. A person's present thinkings, feelings and willings, his perceivings, rememberings and imaginings are intrinsically "phosphorescent"; their existence and their nature are inevitably betrayed to their owner. The inner life is a stream of consciousness of such a sort that it would be absurd to suggest that the mind whose life is that stream might be unaware of what is passing down it.

True, the evidence adduced recently by Freud seems to show that there exist channels tributary to this stream, which run hidden from their owner. People are actuated by impulses the existence of which they vigorously disavow; some of their thoughts differ from the thoughts which they acknowledge; and some of the actions which they think they will to perform they do not really will. They are thoroughly gulled by some of their own hypocrisies, and they successfully ignore facts about their mental lives, which, on the official theory, ought to be patent to them. Holders of the official theory tend, however, to maintain that anyhow in normal circumstances a person must be directly and authentically seized of the present state and workings of his own mind.

Besides being currently supplied with these alleged immediate data of consciousness, a person is also generally supposed to be able to exercise from time to time a special kind of perception, namely inner perception, or introspection. He can take a (non-optical) "look" at what is passing in his mind. Not only can he view and scrutinize a flower through his sense of sight and listen to and discriminate the notes of a bell through his sense of hearing; he can also reflectively or introspectively watch, without any bodily organ of sense, the current episodes of his inner life. This self-observation is also commonly supposed to be immune from illusion, confusion or doubt. A mind's reports of its own affairs have a certainty superior to the best that is possessed by its reports of matters in the physical world. Sense-perceptions can, but consciousness and introspection cannot, be mistaken or confused.

On the other side, one person has no direct access of any sort to the events of the inner life of another. He cannot do better than make problematic inferences from the observed behaviour of the other person's body to the states of mind which, by analogy from his own conduct, he supposes to be signalised by that behaviour. Direct access to the workings of a mind is the privilege of that mind itself; in default of such privileged access, the workings of one mind are inevitably occult to everyone else. For the supposed arguments from bodily movements similar to their own, to mental workings similar to their own, would lack any possibility of observational corroboration. Not unnaturally, therefore, an adherent of the official theory finds it difficult to resist this consequence of his premises, that he has no good reason to believe that there do exist minds other than his own. Even if he prefers to believe that to other human bodies there are harnessed minds not unlike his own, he cannot claim to be able to discover their individual characteristics, or the particular things that they undergo and do. Absolute solitude is on this showing the ineluctable destiny of the soul. Only our bodies can meet.

As a necessary corollary of this general scheme there is implicitly prescribed a special way of construing our ordinary concepts of mental powers and operations. The verbs, nouns and adjectives, with which in ordinary life we describe the wits, characters and higher-grade performances of the people with whom we have to do, are required to be construed as signifying special episodes in their secret histories, or else as signifying tendencies for such episodes to occur. When someone is described as knowing, believing or guessing something, as hoping, dreading, intending or shirking something, as designing this or being amused at that, these verbs are supposed to denote the occurrence of specific modifications in his (to us) occult stream of consciousness. Only his own privileged access to this stream in direct awareness and introspection could provide authentic testimony that these mental-conduct verbs were correctly or incorrectly applied. The onlooker, be he teacher, critic, biographer or friend, can never assure himself that his comments have any vestige of truth. Yet it was just because we do in fact all know how to make such comments, make them with general correctness and correct them when they turn out to be confused or mistaken, that philosophers found it necessary to construct their theories of the nature and place of minds. Finding mental-conduct concepts being regularly and effectively used, they properly sought to fix their logical geography. But the logical geography officially recommended would entail that there could be no regular or effective use of these mental-conduct concepts in our descriptions of, and prescriptions for, other people's minds.

THE ABSURDITY OF THE OFFICIAL DOCTRINE

Such in outline is the official theory. I shall often speak of it, with deliberate abusiveness, as "the dogma of the Ghost in the Machine." I hope to prove that it is entirely false, and false not in detail but in principle. It is not merely an assemblage of particular mistakes. It is one big mistake and a mistake of a special kind. It is, namely, a category-mistake. It represents the facts of mental life as if they belonged to one logical type or category (or range of types or categories), when they actually belong to another. The dogma is therefore a philosopher's myth. In attempting to explode the myth I shall probably be taken to be denying well-known facts about the mental life of human beings, and my plea that I aim at doing nothing more than rectify the logic of mental-conduct concepts will probably be disallowed as mere subterfuge.

I must first indicate what is meant by the phrase "Category-mistake." This I do in a series of illustrations.

A foreigner visiting Oxford or Cambridge for the first time is shown a number of colleges, libraries, playing fields, museums, scientific departments and administrative offices. He then asks "But where is the University? I have seen where the members of the Colleges live, where the Registrar works, where the scientists experiment and the rest. But I have not yet seen the University in which reside and work the members of your University." It has then to be explained to him that the University is not another collateral institution, some ulterior counterpart to the colleges, laboratories and offices which he has seen. The university is just the way in which all that he has already seen is organized. When they are seen and when their co-ordination is understood, the University has been seen. His mistake lay in his innocent assumption that it was correct to speak of Christ Church, the Bodleian Library, the Ashmolean Museum *and* the University, to speak, that is, as if "the University" stood for an extra member of the class of which these other units are members. He was mistakenly allocating the University to the same category as that to which the other institutions belong.

The same mistake would be made by a child witnessing the march-past of a division who, having had pointed out to him such and such battalions, batteries, squadrons, etc., asked when the division was going to appear. He would be supposing that a division was a counterpart to the units already seen, partly similar to them and partly unlike them. He would be shown his mistake by being told that in watching the battalions, batteries and squadrons marching past he had been watching the division marching past. The march-past was not a parade of battalions, batteries, squadrons *and* a division; it was a parade of the battalions, batteries and squadrons *of* a division.

One more illustration. A foreigner watching his first game of cricket learns what are the functions of the bowlers, the batsmen, the fielders, the umpires and the scorers. He then says, "But there is no one left on the field to contribute the famous element of team-spirit. I see who does the bowling, the batting and the wicket-keeping; but I do not see whose role it is to exercise *esprit de corps*." Once more, it would have to be explained that he was looking for the wrong type of thing. Team-spirit is not another cricketing-operation supplementary to all of the other special tasks. It is, roughly, the keenness with which each of the special tasks is performed, and performing a task keenly is not performing two tasks. Certainly exhibiting team-spirit is not the same thing as bowling or catching, but nor is it a third thing such that we can say that the bowler first bowls *and* then exhibits team-spirit or that a fielder is at a given moment *either* catching *or* displaying *esprit de corps*.

These illustrations of category-mistakes have a common feature which must be noticed. The mistakes were made by people who did not know how to wield the concepts *University, division* and *team-spirit*. Their puzzles arose from inability to use certain items in the English vocabulary.

The theoretically interesting category-mistakes are those made by people who are perfectly competent to apply concepts, at least in the situations with which they are familiar, but are still liable in their abstract thinking to allocate those concepts to logical types to which they do not belong. An instance of a mistake of this sort would be the following story. A student of politics has learned the main differences between the British, the French and the American Constitutions, and has learned also the differences and connections between the Cabinet, Parliament, the various Ministries, the Judicature and the Church of England. But he still becomes embarrassed when asked questions about the connections between the Church of England, the Home Office and the British Constitution. For while the Church and the Home Office are institutions, the British Constitution is not another institution in the same sense of that noun. So inter-institutional relations which can be asserted or denied to hold between the Church and the Home Office cannot be asserted or denied to hold between either of them and the British Constitution. "The British Constitution" is not a term of the same logical type as "the Home Office" and "the Church of England." In a partially similar way, John Doe may be a relative, a friend, an enemy or a stranger to Richard Roe; but he cannot be any of these things to the Average Taxpayer. He knows how to talk sense in certain sorts of discussions about the Average Taxpayer, but he is baffled to say why he could not come across him in the street as he can come across Richard Roe.

It is pertinent to our main subject to notice that, so long as the student of politics continues to think of the British Constitution as a counterpart to the other institutions, he will tend to describe it as a mysteriously occult institution; and so long as John Doe continues to think of the Average Taxpayer as a fellow-citizen, he will tend to think of him as an elusive insubstantial man, a ghost who is everywhere yet nowhere.

My destructive purpose is to show that a family of radical category-mistakes is the source of the double-life theory. The representation of a person as a ghost mysteriously ensconced in a machine derives from this argument. Because, as is true, a person's thinking, feeling and purposive doing cannot be described solely in the idioms of physics, chemistry and physiology, therefore they must be described in counterpart idioms. As the human body is a complex organised unit, so the human mind must be another complex organised unit, though one made of a different sort of stuff and with a different sort of structure. Or, again, as the human body, like any other parcel of matter, is a field of causes and effects, so the mind must be another field of causes and effects, though not (Heaven be praised) mechanical causes and effects.

THE ORIGIN OF THE CATEGORY-MISTAKE

One of the chief intellectual origins of what I have yet to prove to be the Cartesian category-mistake seems to be this. When Galileo showed that his methods of scientific discovery were competent to provide a mechanical theory which should cover every occupant of space, Descartes found in himself two conflicting motives. As a man of scientific genius he could not but endorse the claims of mechanics, yet as a religious and moral man he could not accept, as Hobbes accepted, the discouraging rider to those claims, namely that human nature differs only in degree of complexity from clockwork. The mental could not be just a variety of the mechanical.

He and subsequent philosophers naturally but erroneously availed themselves of the following escape-route. Since mental-conduct words are not to be construed as signifying the occurrence of mechanical processes, they must be construed as signifying the occurrence of non-mechanical processes; since mechanical laws explain movements in space as the effects of other movements in space, other laws must explain some of the non-spatial workings of minds as the effects of other non-spatial workings of minds. The difference between the human behaviours which we describe as intelligent and those which we describe as unintelligent must be a difference in their causation; so, while some movements of human tongues and limbs are the effects of mechanical causes, others must be the effects of non-mechanical causes, i.e. some issue from movements of particles of matter, others from workings of the mind.

The differences between the physical and the mental were thus represented as differences inside the common framework of the categories of "thing," "stuff," "attribute," "state," "process," "change," "cause" and "effect." Minds are things, but different sorts of things from bodies; mental processes are causes and effects, but different sorts of causes and effects from bodily movements. And so on. Somewhat as the foreigner expected the University to be an extra edifice, rather like a college but also considerably different, so the repudiators of mechanism represented minds as extra centres of causal processes, rather like machines but also considerably dif-

ferent from them. Their theory was a paramechanical hypothesis. . . .

If my argument is successful, there will follow some interesting consequences. First, the hallowed contrast between mind and matter will be dissipated, but dissipated not by either of the equally hallowed absorptions of mind by matter or of matter by mind, but in quite a different way. For the seeming contrast of the two will be shown to be as illegitimate as would be the contrast of "she came home in a flood of tears" and "she came home in a sedan-chair." The belief that there is a polar opposition between mind and matter is the belief that they are terms of the same logical type.

For Further Reflection

1. What is the value of Ryle's essay? Does it severely undermine Cartesian dualism? Does it argue directly against dualism or does it try to suggest another way of looking at the problem?

2. Do you think that Descartes has committed a category mistake as Ryle charges? Is there something missing, unaccounted for, in Ryle's portrayal of dualism? Can a functional monism successfully escape the problems of the mind-body controversy?

A Contemporary Defense of Dualism   IV.3

J. P. MORELAND

In this selection Moreland defends dualist interactionism, arguing that the mind is distinct from the brain. He compares physicalism, the view that the only thing that exists in the universe is matter, with substance dualism, the view that mind is separate from dualism. He gives several reasons for rejecting physicalism and accepting dualism. Moreland claims that the idea of dualism is best understood from within a wider metaphysic, such as theism.

(A biographical sketch of Moreland is found on page 92.)

Study Questions

1. What are the two primary issues involved in the mind/body dispute?
2. What is the name for the view that holds that matter is the only thing that exists?
3. Identify the two varieties of dualism. Which has been the historic Christian view?
4. What are some problems with physicalism?
5. Moreland contends that the physicalist must show that mental and brain phenomena are not only inseparable (like the redness and roundness of an apple) but also that they are ———.
6. What are examples of mental events?
7. What are some of Moreland's reasons for believing in the distinction between physical and mental events?
8. How does Moreland describe *intentionality*? How does it support a dualist view?
9. How do dualists and physicalists differ regarding personal identity?
10. What is Quine's view on personal identity?
11. What is the emergent property view (EPV)?
12. Why does Moreland reject the EPV?

Arguments for Dualism: Dualism Defined

THE MIND/BODY PROBLEM focuses on two main issues. First, is a human being composed of just one ultimate component or two? Second, if the answer is two, how do these two relate to one another? Physicalism is one solution to the problem. As a general worldview, physicalism holds that the only thing which exists is matter (where matter is defined by an ideal, completed form of physics). Applied to the mind/body problem, physicalism asserts that a human being is just a physical system. There is no mind or soul, just a brain and central nervous system. Dualism is the opponent of physicalism and it asserts that in addition to the body, a human being also has a nonphysical component called a soul, mind, or self (words which will be used interchangeably for our purposes).

There are two main varieties of dualism—property dualism and substance dualism. In order to understand the difference, we must first spell out the distinction between a property and a substance. A property is an entity: redness, hardness, wisdom, triangularity, or painfulness. A property has at least four characteristics which distinguish it from a substance. First, a property is a universal, not a particular. It can be in more than one thing or at more than one place at the same time. Redness can be in my coat and your flag at the same time. Second, a property is immutable and does not contain opposites (hot and cold, red and green) within it. When a leaf goes from green to red, the *leaf* changes. Greenness does not become redness. Greenness leaves the leaf and redness replaces it. Greenness and redness remain the same. Third, properties can be had by something else. They can be in another thing which has them. Redness is in the apple. The apple *has* the redness. Fourth, properties do not have causal powers. They do not act as efficient causes. Properties are not agents which act on other agents in the world.

A substance is an entity like an apple, my dog Fido, a carbon atom, a leaf, or an angel. Substances contrast with properties in the four characteristics listed. First, substances are particulars.

From J. P. Moreland, Scaling the Secular City (Baker Books, 1987). Reprinted by permission of the author and the publisher.

For example, my dog Fido cannot be in more than one place at the same time. Second, a substance can change and have opposites. A leaf can go from green to red or hot to cold by gaining or losing properties. During the process of change, the substance gains and loses properties, but it is still the same substance. The same leaf which was green is now red. Third, substances are basic, fundamental existents. They are not *in* other things or *had by* other things. Fido is not a property of some more basic entity. Rather, Fido *has* properties. Fido is a unity of properties (dogness, brownness, shape), parts (paws, teeth, ears), and dispositions or capacities (law-like tendencies to realize certain properties in the process of growth if certain conditions obtain; for instance, the capacity to grow teeth if the fetus is nourished). They are all united into the substance Fido and possessed by him. Finally, a substance has causal powers. It can act as a causal agent in the world. A carbon atom can act on another atom. A dog can bark or pick up a bone. A leaf can hit the ground.

Property dualists hold that the mind is a property of the body. As Richard Taylor puts it, "A person is a living physical body having mind, the mind consisting, however, of nothing but a more or less continuous series of conscious or unconscious states and events . . . which are the effects but never the causes of bodily activity." This view is called *epiphenomenalism*. The mind is to the body as smoke is to fire. Smoke is different from fire, but smoke does not cause anything. Smoke is a byproduct of fire. Similarly, mind is a byproduct of the body which does not cause anything. It just "rides" on top of the events in the body. Body events cause mind as a byproduct. The mind is a property of the body which ceases to exist when the body ceases to function.

Though some theists have denied it recently, the historic Christian view has been substance dualism. The mind, distinct from the body, is a real substance which can cause things to happen by acting and which can exist when the body ceases to function.

Dualism Defended

PROBLEMS WITH PHYSICALISM AS A GENERAL WORLDVIEW

Physicalism as a worldview holds that everything that exists is nothing but a single spatio-temporal system which can be completely described in terms of some ideal form of physics. Matter/energy is all that exists. God, souls, and nonphysical abstract entities do not exist. If physicalism is true at the worldview level, then obviously, mind/body physicalism would follow. But is physicalism adequate as a worldview? Several factors indicate that it is not.

First, if theism is true, then physicalism as a worldview is false. God is not a physical being. Second, a number of people have argued that numbers exist and that they are abstract, nonphysical entities (e.g., sets, substances, or properties). Several arguments can be offered for the existence of numbers, but two appear frequently. For one thing, mathematics claims to give us knowledge. But if this is so, there must be something that mathematics is about. Just as the biologist *discovers* biological truths about biological objects (organisms), so the mathematician often *discovers* mathematical truths (he does not invent them all the time) and these truths are about mathematical objects. If one denies the existence of numbers, then it is hard to rescue mathematics as a field which conveys knowledge about something. Without numbers, mathematics becomes merely an internally consistent game which is invented.

A second argument is often given for holding to the existence of numbers. Scientific laws and theories seem to assert their existence. For example, a calcium ion has a positive charge of two which is expressed in the formula Ca^{+2}. The number two here seems to be more than a mere formula for calculating relative amounts of compounds in laboratory reactions. Two expresses a property of the calcium ion itself. The property of twoness is just as much a real property of the charge of the calcium as the property of positiveness. If one denies that numbers exist, it is hard to continue to maintain that science gives us a real description of the world rather than a set of operations that work in the laboratory. In sum, without numbers, mathematical and scientific knowledge is hard to maintain. But if numbers exit, physicalism as a worldview is false because numbers are not physical entities.

Some have argued that values, in addition to God and numbers, exist and are not physical. Certain objects (persons, animals) and certain events (helping a stranger, for example) have a nonphysical property of worth or goodness. Furthermore, moral laws are often held to be absolute, objective realities (e.g., one should not torture babies). But if certain objects possess goodness, and if certain moral laws are objective realities, then physicalism must be false, because the property of goodness and the nature of moral laws are not physical. For example, it makes no sense to ask how much goodness weighs, or to ask where a moral law exists. Such realities are not physical.

Fourth, if physicalism is true, it is hard to see what one should make of the existence and nature of theories, meanings, concepts, propositions, the laws of logic, and truth itself. It would seem that theories themselves exist and can be discovered. The laws of logic seem to be real laws that govern the relationships between propositions. Propositions seem to exist and be the content of thoughts which become associated with the physical scratchings of a given language called sentences. Sentences may be made of black ink, be on a page, and be four inches long. But it is hard to see how the *content* of the sentence (i.e., the proposition or thought expressed by the sentence) could be on the page. Such entities seem to be nonphysical entities which can be in the mind. Truth appears to be a relation of correspondence between a thought and the world. If a thought really describes the world accurately, it is true. It stands to the world in a relation of correspondence. But whatever else one wants to say about the relation of correspondence, it does not seem to be a physical relation like cause and effect.

Finally, universals seem to exist and they are not material. A universal is an entity that can be in more than one place at the same time. Some universals are properties (redness, hardness, triangularity); others are relations (larger than, to the left of). Whatever else one may use to characterize the nature of matter, it is clear that a clump of matter is a particular. A piece of matter cannot be in more than one place at the same time. Physicalists deny the existence of universals at the level of general worldview, because universals are not physical entities.

The entities listed have caused a lot of difficulty for physicalists. They have spent a good deal of time trying to do away with numbers, values, propositions, laws of logic, and universals by reducing them to notions compatible with physicalism. But these reductionist attempts have failed and physicalism as a worldview cannot adequately handle the existence of these entities. Theism can embrace them, however, by holding that God created these nonphysical entities and sustains them in existence. The falsity of physicalism as a worldview does not refute mind/body physicalism. One could hold to the existence of numbers and values but deny the existence of the soul. But much of the motivation for mind/body physicalism has been the desire to argue for physicalism at the worldview level. If physicalism at that level is false, then part of the reason for holding to mind/body physicalism is removed. For example, just because one cannot see the soul, weigh it, or say where it is, it does not follow that the soul does not exist. One cannot see, weigh, or locate numbers or values, but they still exist.

PROBLEMS WITH MIND/BODY PHYSICALISM

In order to facilitate an understanding of some of the arguments against mind/body physicalism, we must first examine the nature of identity. Suppose you know that someone named J. P. Moreland exists and that the author of this book exists. Assume further that you do not know that J. P. Moreland wrote this book. If someone asked you whether J. P. Moreland is identical to the author of this book, how would you decide? How would you determine that the "two" individuals are identical instead of being two different people? If you could find something true of J. P. Moreland which is not true of the author of this book or vice versa, then they would be different people. They could not be identical. For example, if J. P. Moreland is married to Hope Moreland but the author of this book is not, they would be different people. On the other hand, if everything true of one is true of the other, "they" would be one person.

In general, if "two" things are identical, then whatever is true of the one is true of the other, since in reality only one thing is being discussed. However, if something is true of the one which is not true of the other, then they are two things and not one. This is sometimes called the indiscernibility of identicals and is expressed as follows:

$$(x)(y)[(x = y) \rightarrow (P)(Px \leftrightarrow Py)]$$

For any entities *x* and *y,* if *x* and *y* are really the same thing, then for any property *P, P* is true of *x* if and only if *P* is true of *y.*[1] If *x* is the mind or one of its states and *y* is a body or part or state of the body (e.g., the brain), then if physicalism is true, *x* must be identical to *y.* On the other hand, if something is true of the mind which is not true of the body, then the mind is not identical to the body and physicalism is false. This would be true even if the mind and body are inseparable. The roundness of an apple cannot be separated from its redness. One does not find redness sitting on a table by itself and roundness sitting next to it. But the redness of an apple is not identical to the roundness of the apple. One is a color and one is a shape.

Every time something happens in the mind (someone has a thought of an ice cream cone), some event may be going on in the brain which could be described by a neurophysiologist. In general, brain events may always have mental events that correlate with them and vice versa.

They may be inseparable in that one does not occur without the other in an embodied person. But this does not mean that the mental thought is identical to the brain event. The redness and roundness of an apple, though inseparable, are not identical. The property of having three sides (trilaterality) and the property of having three angles (triangularity) always go together. They are inseparable. But they are not identical. Physicalists must not only show that mental and brain phenomena are inseparable to make their case. They must also show that they are identical. With this in mind let us turn to some arguments for dualism.

The Distinctiveness of Mental and Physical Properties   Mental events include episodes of thoughts, feelings of pain, the experience of being a person, or episodes of having sensory experience, e.g., a picture of a ball in my mind. Physical events are events in the brain or central nervous system which can be described exhaustively using terms of chemistry, physics, and (for now) biology. The difficulty for physicalism is that mental events do not seem to have properties that hold for physical events. My thought of Kansas City is not ten centimeters long, it does not weigh anything, it is not located anywhere (it is not two inches from my left ear). Nor is it identical to any behavior or tendency to behave in a certain way (shouting "Kansas City" when I hear the name *George Brett*). But the brain event associated with having this thought may be located inside my head, it may have a certain chemical composition and electrical current, and so forth. My afterimage of a ball (the impression of the ball present to my consciousness when I close my eyes after seeing the ball) may be pink, but nothing in my brain is pink.[2] Mental events and properties have different attributes and therefore they are not identical.[3]

Private Access and Incorrigibility   Mental events are self-presenting. I seem to be in a position to know my own thoughts and mental processes in a way not available to anyone else. I am in a privileged position with regard to my own mental life. I have private access to my own thoughts in a way not open to anyone else. Furthermore, my mental states seem to be incorrigible, at least some of the time. That is, I cannot be mistaken about them. Suppose I am experiencing what I take to be a green rug. It is possible that the rug is not there or that the light is poor and the rug is really gray. I could be mistaken about the rug itself. But it does not seem to be possible for me to be mistaken that I am experiencing what I take to be a green rug right now. That is, my mental state is directly present to me and I know my own mental states immediately.

It would be possible for a brain surgeon to know more about my brain than I do. He may be looking into my brain, seeing it better than I, and knowing its operations better than I. But he does not—indeed, he cannot—know my mental life as well as I. I have private, privileged access to that. Further, it seems that one could always be wrong about his knowledge of some physical state of affairs in the world. The brain surgeon could be wrong about what is happening in my brain. But I cannot be wrong about what is currently happening in my mind. It would seem then that I have privileged, private access to my mental states which is sometimes incorrigible. But neither I nor anyone else has private access to my brain states, and whatever access someone has is irreducibly third-person access (described from a standpoint outside of me) and is not incorrigible.[4]

The Experience of First-Person Subjectivity The subjective character of experience is hard to capture in physicalist terms. The simple fact of consciousness is a serious difficulty for physicalism. To see this consider the following. Suppose a deaf scientist became the world's leading expert on the neurology of hearing. It would be possible for him to know and describe everything there is to the physical processes involved in hearing. However, something would still be left out of such a description—the experience of what it is like to be a human who hears. As Howard Robinson puts it:

> The notion of *having something as an object of experience* is not, *prima facie*, a physical notion; it does not figure in any physical science. *Having something as an object of experience* is the same as the subjective feel or the *what it is like* of experience (*Matter and Sense*, p. 7).

Subjective states of experiences exist. My experience of what it is like to be me, to hear a bird or see a tree, exists, and I have a first-person awareness of it. Such first-person experiences of my own self or "I" which has experiences cannot be reduced to a third-person "he" or "it," because the latter do not describe the experience itself or its first-person standpoint. A physicalist, scientific description of the world leaves out this character of subjective awareness. Such a description characterizes the world in impersonal, third-person terms (e.g., "there exists an object with such and such properties and states") and leaves out the first-person, subjective experience itself (e.g., "I feel sad and food tastes sour to me").

Speaking of the character of subjective awareness, Thomas Nagel has this to say:

> If physicalism is to be defended, the phenomenological features [the sounds, colors, smells, tastes of experience that make the experience what it is] must themselves be given a physical account. But when we examine their subjective character it seems that such a result is impossible. The reason is that every subjective phenomenon is essentially connected with a single point of view, and it seems inevitable that an objective, physical theory will abandon that point of view (*Mortal Questions*, p. 167).

Secondary Qualities Secondary qualities are qualities such as colors, tastes, sounds, smells, and textures. Physicalism seems to imply that such qualities do not exist in the external world. But we do sense such qualities, so where are they, if they are not in the external world? They must exist as sense data (mental objects or images) in the mind. Frank Jackson has put the point this way:

> It is a commonplace that there is an apparent clash between the picture Science gives of the world around us and the picture our senses give us. We *sense* the world as made up of coloured, materially continuous, macroscopic, stable objects; Science and, in particular, Physics, tells us that the material world is constituted of clouds of minute, colourless, highly-mobile particles. . . . Science forces us to acknowledge that physical or material things are not coloured. . . . This will enable us to conclude that sense-data are all mental, for they are coloured (*Perception*, p. 121).

In other words, science does away with secondary qualities, but since we know they do exist—we see them—they must exist in our minds as sense data. This shows that there must be minds, and sense data must be little images or pictures which exist as mental objects in minds.

I do not accept this understanding of secondary qualities, because it implies that I do not see the world when I use my senses. Rather, it implies that I see my sense images of the world. But if this view is correct, then it would seem that some form of dualism is correct. If, on the other hand, one holds (as I do) that secondary qualities are real properties of objects in the world, physicalism as a worldview may still be in trouble. If macroscopic objects (regular-sized tables, apples, dogs) do have properties of color, odor, stability, continuous surfaces, and the like, then there must be more to them than what physics tells us. Physics tends to reduce objects to mere heaps of colorless, odorless, rapid-moving packets of matter/energy. But if objects have macro-properties which escape description in these terms, then these properties, call them metaphysical properties, are not physical. That does not mean that they are mental. But it does show that a full treatment of objects must appeal to metaphysical properties which deal with the objects as wholes. If physicalism reduces objects to the mere heaps of microphysics, then physical-ism is incomplete as a worldview. On the other hand, if secondary qualities are in fact mental sense data, then physicalism is inadequate as a mind/body theory. Either way, physicalism as a general theory is in trouble.

Intentionality   Some have argued that the mark of the mental is intentionality. Intentionality is the mind's aboutness or ofness. Mental states point beyond themselves to other objects even if those objects do not exist. I have a thought *about* my wife, I hope *for* a new car, I dream *of* a unicorn. The mind has the ability to transcend itself and be of or about something else. This aboutness is not a property of anything physical. Some physicalists have tried to reduce intentionality to the mere ability to receive input, give output, and advance to some other internal state. A computer receives input from a keyboard, gives output on a printer, and advances to a new internal state where it is ready to receive new input. But the computer still has no awareness of or about anything. It seems, then, that physical states do not have intentionality and thus the fact of intentionality is evidence that the self is not physical but mental.

Personal Identity   Imagine a wooden table which had all its parts removed one by one and replaced by metal parts. When the top and all the legs were replaced would it still be the same table? The answer would seem to be no. In fact, it would be possible to take all the original wooden parts and rearrange them into the original table. Even when the table had just one leg replaced, it would not literally be the same table. It would be a table similar to the original.

Losing old parts and gaining new ones changes the identity of the object in question. But now a question arises regarding persons. Am I literally the same self that I was a moment ago? Are my baby pictures really pictures of *me* or are they pictures of an ancestor of me who resembles me? I am constantly losing physical parts. I lose hair and fingernails; atoms are constantly being replaced, and every seven years my cells are almost entirely replaced. Do I maintain literal, absolute identity through change or not?

Substance dualists argue that persons do maintain absolute identity through change, because they have, in addition to their bodies, a soul that remains constant through change, and personal identity is constituted by sameness of soul, not sameness of body.

Physicalists have no alternative but to hold that personal identity is not absolute. Usually they argue that persons are really ancestral chains of successive "selves" which are connected with one another in some way. At each moment a new self exists (since the self or physical organism is constantly in flux, losing and gaining parts) and this self resembles the self prior to and after it. The relation of resemblance between selves plus the fact that later selves have the same memories as earlier selves and the body of each self traces a continuous path through space when the whole chain of selves is put together, constitute a relative sense of personal identity.

So substance dualists hold to a literal, absolute sense of personal identity and physicalists hold to a loose, relative sense of personal identity which amounts to a stream of successive selves held together into "one" person by resemblance between each self (also called a person stage), similarity of memory, and spatial continuity. For the physicalist, a person becomes a space-time worm (i.e., a path traced through space and time). The person is the entire path marked off at the time and place of his birth and death. At any given moment and location where "I" happen to be, "I" am not a person, just a person stage. The person is the whole path. So there is no literal sameness through change.

But now certain problems arise for physicalism. First, why should "I" ever fear the future? When it gets here, "I" will not be present; rather, another self who looks like me will be there but "I" will have ceased to exist. Second, why should anyone be punished? The self who did the crime in the past is not literally the same self who is present at the time of punishment.

Physicalism seems to require a radical readjustment of our common-sense notions of future expectations and past actions because both presuppose a literal identity of the same self present in past, present, and future.

Third, physicalists not only have difficulty handling the unity of the self through time, but also cannot explain the unity of the self at a given time. As Harvard philosopher W. V. O. Quine puts it, according to physicalism the self becomes a sum or heap of scattered physical parts. The unity of the self is like the unity of an assembly of building blocks. If I have a pain in my foot while I am thinking about baseball, each is a distinct experience involving different physical parts. There is no self which *has* each experience. The self is merely a bundle or heap of parts and experiences. It has no real unity. The dualist says that the soul is diffused throughout the body and it is present before each experience. The soul has each experience. The unity of consciousness is due to the fact that the same soul is the possessor of each and every experience of consciousness. But the physicalist must say that each experience is possessed by different parts of the body and there is no real unity. However, my own experience of the unity of my consciousness shows this unity to be genuine and not arbitrary. *I* have my experiences. They are all *mine*. Physicalism does not adequately explain this fact.

The Origin of Mind: The Emergent Property View

We have seen that there are good reasons for holding that strict physicalism is false. But most physicalists are recalcitrant. If they embrace dualism at all, they embrace epiphenomenalism because, as I will show later, it is more compatible with physicalism than is substance dualism. Mind is not matter, but it comes from matter through evolution when matter reaches a suitable structural arrangement for mind to emerge. . . .

There are serious difficulties with epiphenomenalism. To see these we must first clarify what epiphenomenalism involves. The view is also called holism, and when mind is seen to emerge through the coming together of matter in a certain way (for instance, through the evolution of the central nervous system and brain) the position is called the emergent property view (EPV). Here are four main features of the EPV.

Wholes and Parts   In nature, wholes are often greater than the sum of their parts. Nature exhibits a hierarchy of systems—subatomic particles, atoms, molecules, cells, organs, whole organisms. Each level has properties of the wholes at that level which are not properties of their constituent parts. For example, water has the property of being wet, but this property is not true of either hydrogen or oxygen. Similarly, the mind is a property of the brain.

Levels of Explanation and Complementarity   Each level in a hierarchy can be explained by using concepts appropriate at that level. Further, all the levels are complementary. For example, an explanation of a person's behavior could be given at a psychological level which used the concepts *beliefs, desires,* or *fears.* The same behavior could be given an explanation at the neurophysiological level using the concepts *neurons, synapses,* and so forth. These two levels of explanation are not in competition; they complement one another by offering descriptions of the same behavior at different levels.

Causation Between Levels   Lower levels in the hierarchy cause things to happen at higher levels but not vice versa. When it comes to persons, events at the physical level can be characterized in terms of physical laws which make no reference to the causal efficaciousness of future events (e.g., the purposes of the agent) or higher levels of organization. The events at the physical level obey deterministic physical laws and mental events are mere byproducts.

Resultant View of the Self   The self is not some mental substance added to the brain from the "outside" when the brain reaches a certain level

of complexity. It is an emergent property which supervenes upon the brain. The self becomes a discontinuous series of mental events when mental properties are instanced in different brain events. The self is a series of events which "ride" on top of the brain. Consider the following diagram:

$$M_1 \quad M_2 \quad M_3 \quad M_4$$
$$\nearrow \quad \nearrow \quad \nearrow \quad \nearrow$$
$$B_1 \rightarrow B_2 \rightarrow B_3 \rightarrow B_4$$

Suppose M_1 is the mental state of seeing an apple from a distance of five feet. It is a *mental* state since it involves the conscious awareness of seeing the apple, and conscious awareness is something true of minds and not matter. Now suppose M_2 is the mental state of seeing the apple from one foot, M_3 the state of feeling a pain on the toe, and M_4 the state of hearing a plane fly overhead. B_1 through B_4 are brain states which are associated with each mental state.

Three things stand out immediately. First, B_1 through B_4 stand in rigid physical, causal relations with one another. B_1 causes B_2 and so on. There is no room for a rational agent to intervene in this causal sequence. Mental agents do not act here. The physical level determines all the action. Mental states are mere byproducts of their physical states as smoke is a byproduct of fire.

Second, there is no unified, enduring self at the mental level. According to substance dualism, the self is not identical to its states; it *has* its states. The mind *has* its thoughts and experiences and the same mind can have two experiences at the same time (hearing a plane and seeing an apple) or it can have one experience followed by another. The *self* is present at both experiences and underlies the change of experiences.

When a leaf goes from green to red, green does not become red. Rather, green leaves and is replaced by red *in* the leaf. The leaf is the same substance present at both ends of the process. When a substance gains or loses properties, *it* remains the same while the properties come and go. They are replaced. Red replaces green. The EPV says that M_1 through M_4 are properties of the body. There is no enduring mental substance which has them. There is just one mental property at one time which leaves and is replaced by another mental property at another time. The "self" is a series of mental events where mental properties are had by physical states.

Third, it is hard to see what sense can be given to intentionality. How is it that M_1 is of or about an apple? M_1 is just a dummy, a free rider on B_1. At best, B_1 would just be a state caused by light waves from the apple but it is hard to see how this would cause M_1 to be really a state *about* that apple. Even if it were, what difference would it make? Any further body states (the act of touching the apple or eating it) would be caused totally by brain states and make no reference to mental states at all.

It should now be clear why epiphenomenalism was ruled out as an inadequate account of the necessary features of rationality. It cannot account for the existence of intentionality, it leaves no room for genuine rational agency to freely choose mental beliefs, and there is no enduring "I" to be present through the process of thought.

But let us waive these problems for the moment. Where would the mind as an emergent property come from? How can mind, the capacity to know truth, and so forth, emerge from mindless, nonrational matter? Remember, mind here is not identical to the brain's structure. If it were, then the view would be some form of crude materialism or, perhaps, some unclear intermediate view between dualism and physicalism. But in either case, the position would be worse than epiphenomenalism, for it would suffer from the same deficiencies as the latter, as well as those raised earlier against physicalism in its pure form.

The EPV holds that mind is a genuine mental property (or series of properties) which supervenes on top of matter. Consider water again. Wetness emerges when hydrogen and oxygen come together into a structure known as H_2O.

Wetness is not identical to that structure. Wetness is a simple quality; the structure is a set of relationships which can be quantified (spatial relations, relations of force, which can be given numerical values). So the structure is not the same thing as the wetness. Similarly, the mind is not the same thing as the brain's structure; it supervenes over that structure in the EPV view. So it is a genuinely new entity which must come into being somehow or other.

It does not seem that it could come into being from nothing. For one thing, that would violate a generally accepted principle that something does not come from nothing. Some have disputed this principle, but it still seems reasonable, especially at the macroscopic level and not the level of the microparticles of physics (though I believe it to hold at that level as well). And it is the macroscopic level that is involved when mind emerges, since it emerges over an object the size of a structured brain.

One could respond that the mind is not itself a macroscopic entity—perhaps by saying that the macro/micro distinction does not hold for minds. But if the EPV view means that mind emerges over a structured brain out of nothing and that this fact is not anchored to the nature of that brain, then it is hard to see why mind emerges time and again over just this type of structured matter and not over a nickel or a bowling pin. The defender of the EPV cannot appeal to the causal efficacy of the mind itself and argue that the mind of a child comes from the mind of its parents, for this allows minds to cause something, and this is not allowed according to the EPV.

At the level of normal-sized macroscopic objects (objects visible to normal sight) things just do not pop in and out of existence. Even if mind is not such an object, its emergence seems to be tied to the brain. And the brain is such an object. So it is not very promising to account for the emergence of mind by saying it comes from nothing.

There is, however, a more promising view.

Aristotle taught us long ago that when something new emerges, it does not come from nothing but from potentiality. When a leaf turns from green to red, the red does not simply come into existence; it was already in the leaf potentially. When an apple seed produces apples, the apples were in the seed potentially. In general, when a property emerges in a substance, it comes to actuality from potentiality, not from pure nonbeing. The property was in the substance potentially and when it emerges, it becomes actual.

Mind must somehow be in matter potentially such that when matter reaches a certain stage of development, mind becomes actual. This is a more plausible version of the EPV, but it still has serious difficulties.

First, it is hard to see how this is compatible with the doctrines and motives of physicalism. Physicalism is embraced in part out of a desire to promote science as the ultimate, perhaps only, kind of knowledge. So physicalists often assert that the world is a network of physical causes wherein only physical causality does anything. Further, the world for a physicalist is in principle describable in strictly physical laws. But if mind is potential in matter, then physicalism seems to become some form of panpsychism, the view that mind is ultimate. Matter no longer is describable in terms of familiar physical properties and laws alone. Now it contains elusive mental potentialities.

After wrestling with this problem, Nobel Prize–winning scientist Max Delbruck argued that "our ideas about the objective character of the physical world, and hence of the nature of truth have been revised. In other words, mind looks less psychic and matter looks less materialistic. . . ." So if one admits that mind is potential in matter, then one can no longer hold that reality is exhausted by the spatio-temporal physical universe.

Second, this emergent property view could not rule out the future existence of God. If mind can emerge from matter when a high-level system reaches a certain point of complexity, why is it not possible for a large-scale Mind to emerge at a later period in evolutionary development? In other words, the EPV cannot rule out Hegelianism, the view that mind emerges from matter all the way up to the emergence of God himself. This may sound far-fetched. But the point is that the EPV cannot rule it out, for the emergence of mind over brains is a startling fact which could hardly have been predicted from the properties of matter alone. So why should one think the process of emergence should stop with finite, human minds? Why could not some form of deity emerge, since mind is in some sense a basic constituent of the universe? Christian philosopher Richard Purtill has called this the God-not-yet view. And it should come as no comfort to an atheist, who is trying to save some form of minimal physicalism, to be told that his view seems to imply some form of emergent theism. At the very least, emergent theism cannot be ruled out.

Finally, Clark points out that it is hard to specify just what these potential mental properties are. Are these potential properties conscious? If so, then why do we have no memory from them when they emerge to form our own minds? Does it really make sense to say that my mind is composed of several particles of mind dust (i.e., little selves which came together to form my own mental life)? If these potential properties are not conscious, how are they still mental? These questions may have an answer, but they are certainly puzzling and the EPV seems to commit one to the existence of rather odd potential mental properties, odd at least from the standpoint of one who wants to maintain some form of respectable physicalism.

The simple fact is that the existence of mind has always been a problem for the physicalist. As physicalist Paul M. Churchland argues,

> The important point about the standard evolutionary story is that the human species and all of its features are the wholly physical outcome

of a purely physical process. . . . If this is the correct account of our origins, then there seems neither need, nor room, to fit any nonphysical substances or properties into our theoretical account of ourselves. We are creatures of matter (*Matter and Consciousness*, p. 21).

Physicalism is false because it fails to adequately handle several general arguments raised against it. And it is self-refuting, for it undercuts the very prerequisites of rational thought itself. Once one grants the existence of mind, then the question arises as to where it came from. The emergent property view is one answer to this question. But it fails as an adequate theory of mind itself, and it postulates either the origin of mind from nothing or its emergence from potentiality in matter. Both options are problematic. Mind appears to be a basic feature of the cosmos and its origin at a finite level of persons is best explained by postulating a fundamental Mind who gave finite minds being and design.

As Calvin put it, the endowments which we possess cannot possibly be from ourselves. They point to the ultimate Mind and ground of rationality himself.

NOTES

1. The identity relation is necessary. That is, for all x and all y, if x is identical to y, then, *necessarily*, x is identical to y. There is no possible world where one obtains without the other.

2. Again, pains are natural kinds whose essential nature is a conscious feeling, but a conscious feeling is not an essential part of anything physical.

3. An individual pain or type of pain could exist without the presence of any individual physical state existing. Indeed, it is logically possible for a person to exist and have a pain in a completely disembodied state. Thus, persons and their states are not identical to bodies and their states, given that the identity relation is necessary.

4. Private access and incorrigibility are two pieces of evidence for the claim that mental entities are self-presenting. But no physical entity is self presenting.

For Further Reflection

1. Do you accept Moreland's analysis of the mind/body problem? Can you find weaknesses in his rejection of physicalism or acceptance of dualism? Can you think of other alternatives? What do you make of the *panpsychism* hinted at by the view of the physicist Max Delbruck, mentioned in the article? Could matter itself already contain mind?

2. He lists two issues. (1) "Is a human being composed of just one ultimate component or two?" and (2) "If the answer is two how do these two relate to one another?" Has Moreland given a clear explanation of how dualism solves the second problem? Is physicalism more plausible on this problem?

3. Is Moreland's argument for mathematical entities relevant to the mind/body problem? Explain.

IV.4   Burying the Mind-Body Problem

RICHARD TAYLOR

Richard Taylor (1919–) until his recent retirement was professor of philosophy at the University of Rochester. He is one of America's most prolific philosophers, having written important work on almost every major topic. His principal works are *Good and Evil* (1970) and *Ethics, Faith and Reason* (1985).

Taylor argues that the mind-body problem is a pseudo-problem, "a philosophical fabrication, resting on no genuine data at all." There is only one reality, and it is material. "A person or self and his body are one and same thing." Taylor tries to explain the causes for dualism and meet objections to his position.

Study Questions

1. Why does Taylor think that the mind-body problem is a fabrication?
2. Why, according to Taylor, can't philosophical argument prove that something does or does not exist?
3. What is the grand presupposition of the dualists?
4. How does Taylor contrast the two theses: mentalism and materialism?
5. What are the four arguments of dualism and how does Taylor handle them?
6. What is Taylor's reply in his conclusion to those who object that it sounds fantastic to say that matter thinks, as his thesis entails?

THE MIND-BODY PROBLEM, in all its variants, is a philosophical fabrication resting on no genuine data at all. It has arisen from certain presuppositions about matter and human nature familiar to philosophy from the time of the Pythagoreans, presuppositions which have persisted just to the extent that they have been left unexamined. And they have not been questioned very much simply because they are so familiar.

There are vexing, unsolved problems of psychology and problems of mental health, but there are no mind-body problems. And there are problems of "philosophical psychology," as they are sometimes called today—problems of perception, sensation, the analysis of deliberation, of purposeful behavior, and so on—but there are no mind-body problems.

The reason why there are no mind-body problems is the most straightforward imaginable: It is because there are no such things as *minds* in the first place. There being no minds, there are in strictness no mental states or events; there are only certain familiar states, capacities, and abilities which are conventionally but misleadingly called "mental." They are so-called, partly in def-

erence to certain philosophical presuppositions, and partly as a reflection of our lack of understanding of them, that is of our ignorance.

Men and women are not minds, nor do they "have" minds. It is not merely that they do not "have" minds the way they have arms and legs; they do not have minds in any proper sense at all. And just as no man or woman has or ever has had any mind, so also are cats, dogs, frogs, vegetables, and the rest of living creation without minds—though philosophers of the highest rank, such as Aristotle, have felt driven to say that all living things, vegetables included, must have souls (else how could they be *living* things?) just as others of similar eminence, like Descartes, have thought that men must have minds, else how could they be *thinking* things? Today, when philosophers talk about mind-body problems, and advance various claims concerning the possible relationships between "mental" and "physical" states and events, they are, of course, talking about men. But they might as well be talking about frogs, because the presuppositions that give rise to these theories apply to other animals as well as to men.

From Richard Taylor, "How to Bury the Mind-Body Problem," American Philosophical Quarterly 6 *(April 1969): 136–43. Reprinted by permission of the author and the publisher.*

I. Philosophical Arguments for the Existence or Nonexistence of Things

There cannot be any philosophical argument proving that something does or does not exist, so long as the description or definition of it is self-consistent. Thus there cannot be a philosophical argument proving that men do or do not, as some medieval thinkers believed, have an indestructible bone in their bodies. One can only say that such a bone has never been found (which is not a philosophical argument) and then exhibit the groundlessness or falsity of the presuppositions that gave rise to the belief in the first place. (In this case it was certain presuppositions concerning the requirements of the resurrection of the body.) Similarly, there can be no philosophical argument proving that men do or do not have souls, spirits, or minds, or that there are not *sui generis* mental states or events, assuming that these can be described in a self-consistent way. One can only note that such things have never been found in any man, living or dead, and then exhibit the arbitrariness and apparent falsity of the presuppositions that give rise to these opinions in the first place. Now of course, as far as *finding* them goes, many philosophers claim to find them all the time, *within themselves*. They are alleged to be *private* things, deeply hidden, discernible only by their possessors. All they really "find," however, are the most commonplace facts about themselves that are perfectly well known to anyone who knows anything at all—but of this, more later.

II. The Grand Presupposition of the Mind-Body Problem

What I must do now, then, is consider the presupposition that has given birth to the so-called "mind-body" problem, and show that there is nothing in it at all that anyone needs to believe; that, on the contrary, we have good evidence that it is false.

The presupposition can be tersely expressed by saying: *Matter cannot think*. That is the way a Cartesian would put it, but philosophers now spell it out a little better. Thus, we are apt to be told that thinking, choosing, deliberating, reasoning, perceiving, and even feeling, are not concepts of physics and chemistry, so that these terms have no application to bodies. Since, however, men do think, choose, deliberate, reason, perceive and feel, it follows that men are not "mere bodies." They are instead minds or souls or, as it is more common to say today "selves" or "persons," and such terms as "is thinking," "is choosing," "is perceiving," etc., are not physical or bodily but *personal* predications. A man may be in one clear sense a physical object, having arms and legs and so on, but a person is not just that visible and palpable object; there is more to a self or person than this. For it is the self or person that thinks, chooses, deliberates, feels, and so on, and not his body or some part of it.

Again—and this is really only another way of expressing the same presupposition—we are apt to be told that thoughts, choices, reasons, feelings, etc., are not physical things. It makes no sense to ask how large a thought is, whether it is soluble in alcohol, and so on. Yet these things do exist—any man can be aware of them, "within himself." Hence, that "self" within which such things occur must be something more than or other than the body. It might be just the totality of all those nonphysical ("mental") things, but in any case it is mental in nature, so a self or person is not the same thing as his body.

Or again, in case one boggles at calling thoughts, feelings, and the like, "things," at least (it is said) no one can deny that they are events or states. But they are not events or states that occur or obtain in the laboratories of physicists and chemists—except in the sense that they sometimes occur in physicists and chemists themselves, who sometimes happen to be in laboratories. No one could ever truly represent whatever might be happening in a test tube or vacuum tube as the transpiring of a thought or feeling. These things just do not—indeed, obviously could not—happen in test tubes or vacuum tubes, because they are not the *kind* of event involving changes of matter. They are a kind of "mental" event. And since these things do, obviously, happen in men, then things happen in men which are nonphysical, "mental," in nature. . . .

III. *"Selves" or "Persons" as Minds and Bodies*

The word "self" and the plural "selves" are fairly common items of contemporary philosophical vocabulary. These words never occur outside of philosophy, except as suffixes to personal pronouns, but in philosophical contexts they are sometimes taken to denote rather extraordinary things. Selves are, indeed, about the strangest inhabitants of nature that one can imagine—except that, as sometimes described in philosophy, they are not even imaginable in the first place, being quite nonphysical. You cannot poke a self with a stick; the nearest you can come to that is to poke his body. The self that has that body is not supposed to be quite the same thing as his body—that is a (mere) physical object, a possible subject matter for physics and chemistry. *That* is not what thinks, reasons, deliberates, and so on; it is the self that does things like this.

At the same time, selves are never doubted to be the same things as *persons,* and persons are thought to be the same things as people, as men. And there is no doubt at all that men are visible, palpable objects, having arms and legs and so on: That they are in short, physical objects. So the thing becomes highly ambiguous. We do not, in contexts in which it would seem silly or embarrassing to do so, have to say that selves (men) are spirit beings (minds) which in some sense or other happen to "have" bodies. Clearly men are visible and palpable things, that is, are bodies. We can say that all right. But at the same time we need not say—indeed, *must* not say—that men are just (mere) bodies. There is, after all, a difference between a man's body, and that

which thinks, perceives, feels, deliberates, and so on; and those are things that men (selves) do, not things that bodies do. Or again, there is, after all, a difference between bodily predicates (weighs 160 pounds, falls, is warm, etc.) and personal predicates (chooses, believes, loves his country, etc.). The former can be predicated of a man's body, just like any other body, but it would "make no sense" to predicate the latter of any (mere) body, and hence of any man's body. They are only predicated of persons. So even though selves are persons and persons are men and men are visible, palpable beings, we must not think that they are just nothing but physical beings. They are physical bodies with minds, or, as some would prefer, minds with physical bodies or, as most writers on this subject want to say, they are somehow *both.*

So the "mental" is discriminated from the (merely) "physical," and the mind-body problem emerges at once: What is the *connection* between them? What is the relationship between men's minds and their bodies? Or between mental and physical events? Or between personal and physical predicates? Anyone who raises this question—for these all amount to one and the same question—can see at once that it is going to be extremely difficult to answer. And this means that it is capable of nourishing a vast amount of philosophy. It has, in fact, kept philosophers on scattered continents busy for hundreds of years, and even today claims much of the time of philosophical faculties and their proteges. It seems a conceit to undertake to put an end to all this, but that is what I propose now to do.

IV. *Mentalism and Materialism*

Consider the following two theses:

(I) A person is not something that has, possesses, utilizes, or contains a mind. That is, a person is not one thing and his mind another thing. A person or self and his mind are one and the same thing.

(II) A person is not something that has, possesses, utilizes, or occupies a body. That is, a person is not one thing and his body another thing. A person or self and his body are one and the same thing.

We can call these two theses "mentalism" and "materialism" respectively, since the first asserts that men are minds and not bodies, and the second that they are bodies and not minds.

Now the first thing to note about these two rather crudely stated theses is that both of them cannot be true, since each asserts what the other denies. They could, of course, both be false, since a person might be identical neither with his body nor with his mind (though it is hard to think of any other candidate for the title of "person"), or a person might somehow be identical with the two of them at once. These two simple theses are, nevertheless, a good starting point for discussion, and I am going to maintain that (II), the materialist thesis, is absolutely true.

Philosophers have tended to regard (I), or some more sophisticated version of it, as correct, and to dismiss (II) as unworthy of consideration. In fact, however—and it is hard to see how this could have been so generally overlooked—*any* philosophical argument in favor of (I) against (II) is just as good an argument for (II) against (I). This I shall illustrate shortly.

In the meantime, let us give what is due to the humble fact that there are considerations drawn from common sense, indeed from the common knowledge of mankind, which favor, without proving, (II). It is common knowledge that there are such things as human bodies, that there are men and women in the world. There is also one such body which everyone customarily, and without the least suggestion of absurdity, refers to as himself; he sees himself in the mirror, dresses himself, scratches himself, and so on. This is known, absolutely as well as anything can be known, and if any man were to profess doubt about it—if he doubted, for example, that there are such physical objects in the world as men and women, and therefore doubted the reality of his own body—then that man would have to be considered *totally* ignorant. For there is nothing more obvious than this. A man would be ignorant indeed if he did not know that there are such things as the sun, moon, earth, rivers, and lakes. I have never met anyone so ignorant as that. But a man who did not even know that there are men and women in the world, and that he—his body—was one of them, would be totally ignorant.

Now there is no such common knowledge of the existence of minds or souls. No one has ever found such a thing anywhere. Belief in such things rests either on religious persuasion or on philosophical arguments, sometimes on nothing but the connotations of familiar words. Such beliefs are opinions, easily doubted, and nothing that anyone knows. If a man denies that such things exist, as many have, then he exhibits no ignorance; he expresses only scepticism or doubt concerning certain religious or philosophical presuppositions or arguments.

If, accordingly, we are seeking some sort of thing with which to identify persons, then this is a *prima facie* consideration in favor of identifying them with their bodies, with things we know to be real, rather than with things postulated to suit the requirements of philosophical arguments or religious faith. This does not prove that men are nothing but bodies, of course, but it is enough to show that, since we know there are such things as persons, and we know there are such things as men (living human bodies), we had better regard these as the very same things *unless* there are some facts which would prohibit our doing so. And I shall maintain that there are no such facts. There are only philosophical arguments, not one of which proves anything.

THE ARGUMENTS FOR MENTALISM

I shall now consider the arguments I know, already adumbrated, in favor of what I have called mentalism. Of course not all philosophers who take seriously the mind-body problem subscribe to this simple thesis as I have formulated it, but the more sophisticated versions can be considered as we go along, and it will be seen that the arguments for these are equally inconclusive.

The First Argument.   There are certain predicates that undoubtedly apply to persons, but not to their bodies. Persons and their bodies cannot, therefore, be the same. One can sometimes truly say of a person, for example, that he is intelligent, sentimental, that he loves his country, believes in God, holds strange theories on the doctrine of universals, and so on. But it would sound very odd—indeed, not even make sense—to assert any such things of any physical object whatever and hence of any man's body. It would at best be a confusion of categories to say that a certain man's *body* loves its country, for example.

Reply.   If the foregoing is considered a good argument for the nonidentity of persons and bodies, then the following is obviously just as good an argument for not identifying them with their minds: There are certain predicates that undoubtedly apply to persons, but not to their minds. A person and his mind cannot, therefore, be the same. One can sometimes truly say of a person, for example, that he is walking, ran into a post, is feverish, or that he fell down. But it would sound very odd—indeed not even make sense—to assert such things of any mind whatever. It would at best be a confusion of categories to say, for instance, that a certain man's *mind* ran into a post.

Considerations such as these have led many philosophers to affirm that a person or the "true self" is neither a mind, nor a body. Hence, a person must be either (*a*) something else altogether or, as some would prefer to say, the term "person" must express a "primitive" concept or (*b*) both mind and body; i.e., a person must be something having both mental and physical properties.

The former of these alternatives is simply evasive. Persons are real beings, so there must be existing things which are persons. If when we bump into a man we are not bumping into a person, and if at the same time we are not referring to a person when we say of someone that he is thinking, then it is quite impossible to see what is left to fill the role of a person. The word "person" may indeed be a primitive one, but this, I think, only means that such arguments as the two just cited are equally good and equally bad.

The second alternative that persons are beings having both mental and physical properties, is obviously only as good as the claim that there are such things as "mental properties" to begin with. Indeed, it is not even that good, for just as a physical property can be nothing but a property of a physical thing, i.e., a body, so also a mental property can be nothing but the property of a mental thing, i.e., a mind. For something to count as a physical property of something it is sufficient, and necessary, that the thing in question is a physical object. By the same token, for something to count as a mental property it is sufficient, and necessary, that it be the property that some mind possesses. Any property whatsoever that can be truly claimed to be the property of some body, animate or inanimate, is a physical property; the assertion that some body possesses a nonphysical property is simply a contradiction. This second alternative, that persons are beings possessing both physical and mental properties, therefore amounts to saying that a person is at one and the same time *two* utterly different things—a body with its physical properties and a mind with its mental properties. These are not supposed to be two things in the same sense that a family, for instance, is a plurality of beings consisting of husband, wife, and perhaps one or more children, but two wholly disparate kinds of beings having, as Descartes put it, nothing in common. Now this is no resolution of the antithesis between what I have called mentalism and materialism. It is only a reformulation of that issue. For now we can surely ask: Which of these two is the person, the true self? The body which has a mind, or the mind which has a body? And we are then back where we started.

The Second Argument. This argument consists of pointing out the rather remarkable things that a person can do but which, it is alleged, no physical object, of whatever complexity, can do, from which it of course follows that a person is not a physical object and hence not identical with his own body. A person, for example, can reason, deliberate about ends and means, plan for the future, draw inferences from evidence, speculate, and so on. No physical objects do such things, and even complicated machines can at best only simulate these activities. Indeed, it would not even make sense to say that a man's body was, for example, speculating on the outcome of an election, though this would not be an absurd description of some person. A person, therefore, is not the same thing as his body, and can only be described in terms of certain concepts of mind.

Reply. This argument is not very different from the first; it only substitutes activities for properties which are baptized "mental." And one reply to it is the same as to the first argument; namely, that since persons often do things that no mind could do—for instance, they run races, go fishing, raise families, and so on—then it follows that persons are not minds.

A far better reply, however, and one that is not so question-begging as it looks, is to note that since men do reason, deliberate, plan, speculate, draw inferences, run races, go fishing, raise families, and so on, and since the men that do all such things are the visible, palpable beings that we see around us all the time, then it follows that *some* physical objects—namely, men—do all these things. All are, accordingly, the activities of physical objects; they are not activities divided between a physical object, the visible man, on the one hand, and some invisible thing, his mind, on the other.

Consider the statement: "I saw George yesterday; he was trying to figure out the best way to get from Albany to Montpelier." Now this statement obviously refers, in a normal context, to a person, and it is perfectly clear that the name "George" and the pronoun "he" refer to *one and the same* being, that person. And what they both refer to is something that was seen, a certain man's body; they do not refer to some unseen thing, of which that body is some sort of visible manifestation. If that were so, then the statement would not really be true. And in any case, it would be embarrassingly silly to suppose that a more accurate rendition of the thought expressed in this statement might be: "I saw George's body yesterday. His mind was trying to figure out how to get (how to get what?) from Albany to Montpelier." It is, accordingly, one and the same thing which (*a*) is seen, and (*b*) figures and plans, and that thing is undoubtedly the physical object George. Now if conventions incline to describe figuring out something as a "mental" activity, then we shall have to say that some purely physical objects—namely, living men—engage in mental activities. But this is simply misleading, if not contradictory, for it suggests that we are ascribing to a physical object an activity of something that is not physical, but mental. It would, therefore, be far better to say that some physical objects, namely, men or persons, sometimes perform physical activities such as figuring and planning which are quite unlike those we are accustomed to finding in certain other physical objects such as machines and the like.

The Third Argument. This argument, the commonest of all, is to the effect that while there may or may not be such things as "minds" (whatever that might mean), there are indisputably certain nonphysical things which are quite properly called "mental," as anyone can verify within himself. Indeed, it is sometimes claimed that nothing, not even the reality of our own bodies, is as certain as the existence of these mental things, which are perceived "directly."

Reply. What are here referred to as mental entities are, of course, such things as thoughts, mental images, after-images, sensations, feelings, and so on. Pains are frequently mentioned in this context, being, presumably, things whose existence no one would question. Having got to this point then the next step, of course, is to speculate on the connection between these mental things and certain "physical" states of the body. They evidently are not the same, and yet it is hard to see what the connection could be. Speculation also extends to such questions as whether two or more men might have "the same" pain, or why it is impossible that they should, in view of the fact that they can hold common possession of ordinary "physical" things like clocks and books. Again, curiosity is aroused by the fact that a mental image, for instance, seems to have color, and yet it somehow can be perceived only by one person, its owner. Again, images sometimes seem to have shape—enough so that a perceiver can distinguish one from another, for instance—and yet no assignable size. Here, really, is a gold mine for philosophical speculation, and such speculations have filled, as they still fill, volumes.

Now surely there is a *better* way to express all that is known to be true in all this, and it is a way that does not even permit these odd theories to get started. What we know is true, and all we know is true, is that men think, sense, imagine, feel, etc. It is sheer redundancy to say that men think things called "thoughts," sense things called "sensations," imagine "images," and feel "feelings." There are no such things. And to say there are no such things is *not* to deny that men think, sense, imagine, and feel.

What, for instance, does it mean to say a man feels a pain in his foot? Absolutely nothing, except that his foot hurts. But this hurting, what sort of thing is it? It is not a thing at all; not a thing felt, and certainly not a mental thing that is felt *in his foot*. It is a state, and in no sense a state of his mind, but a straightforward state of his foot. But can that be a *physical* state? Well, it is assuredly a state of his foot, and that is a physical object; there is nothing else—no spirit foot, no spirit being, no spirit mind—that it can be a state of. Why, then, cannot other people have that same state? Why cannot other people feel the same pain I feel in my foot? And if it is a

physical state, why cannot we open the foot and *see* it there? Or make some straightforward test of its presence in another man's foot?

To ask questions like these is just not to understand what is meant by describing an object as being in a certain state. Consider a piece of molten lead. Now this molten state, what sort of thing is it? The answer is that it is not a thing at all; it is a state or condition of a thing. Is it a physical state? Well, it is a state of the lead, and that is a physical object; there is nothing else for it to be a state of. Why, then, cannot another piece of lead have that same state? Why cannot something else have the molten state of this piece of lead? Of course something else can, in the only meaningful sense that can be attached to such a question; that is, another piece of lead, or some things which are not lead can melt the same way this piece of lead melted. To ask why another piece of lead cannot have the molten state of this piece of lead is, of course, unintelligible, unless it is interpreted the way just suggested, in which case the answer is that it can. But similarly, to ask why another man cannot have the pain that this man is feeling is also unintelligible, unless construed as the question why other men cannot suffer pain, in which case its presupposition is wrong—they can. And if the piece of lead's being melted is a "physical" state, why can we not separate the lead into drops and see that state? Simply because it is a state of the lead, and not some other thing contained in the lead. Indeed, to separate it into drops *is* to see, not its meltedness (there is no such thing), but that it is melted—that is just the test. We do not have to *ask* the lead whether it is melted, and rely upon its testimony; we can tell by its behavior. And in the same way we can sometimes—admittedly not always—see that a man is suffering, without having to ask him. That we sometimes go wrong here does not result from the fact that his suffering is something quite hidden within him, which he alone can find and then report; there is nothing hidden, and nothing for him to find. Still, there is a straightforward way of testing whether a piece of lead is melted, and there is no similarly straightforward way of testing whether a man's foot hurts—he may only be pretending it is. Does this indicate that there might be a pain, which he has found in his foot but might conceal, as he might conceal the contents of his wallet? Surely not; it shows only that men, unlike pieces of lead, are capable of dissimulating. No philosophy was needed to unearth that commonplace fact. It is easier to test for the presence of some states of properties than others, and this is true not only of the states of men's bodies, but of everything under the sun. But things that are hard to establish do not, just by virtue of that, warrant the title of "mental."

Similar remarks can be made about images, which are frequent candidates for the role of mental entities. When queried about their mental imagery, people often will describe it in colorful detail and even with pride, not unlike the regard one might have for a precious gem accessible only to himself. It turns out, though, that all one thereby describes is his power of imagination, which is, of course, sometimes quite great. To say that one has a lively imagination, even great powers of imagination, does not mean that he can create within his mind . . . things called "images" and composed of some mental, nonphysical, spiritual material. There is no material that is nonmaterial, and there are no images composed of this or anything else—except, of course, those physical objects (pictures, etc.) visible to anyone who can see, which are rightly called images of things. When someone *sees* something, there is (*i*) the man who sees, and (*ii*) the thing seen; for instance, some building or scene. There is not, between these, a third thing called the appearance of what is seen; philosophers are pretty much agreed on this. But similarly, when someone *imagines* something or, as it is misleadingly put, "forms an image" of it, there is (*i*) the man who imagines, and (*ii*) sometimes, but not always, something that he imagines; for instance, some building or scene, which might or might not be real. There is not, between these, a third thing called the image of what is imagined. There is just the imagining of the thing in question. And to say that a man is imagining something is to say what he is doing, or perhaps to refer to some state he is in; it is not to refer to some inner thing that he creates and, while it lasts, exclusively possesses.

It is enough, it seems to me, to point this out; that is, to point out that we can say all we want to say about men's powers of imagination without ever introducing the substantive "an image." Philosophy is robbed of nothing by the disposal of these, and there is absolutely no fact about human nature which requires us to affirm their existence. But if one does insist upon the reality of mental images, and professes, for instance, to find them right in his own mind by introspecting—and it is astonishing how eager students of philosophy seem to be to make this claim—then we can ask some very embarrassing questions. Suppose, for instance, one professes to be able to form a very clear image of, say, the campus library—he can bring it before his mind, hold it there, perhaps even turn it bottom side up, and banish it at will. We ask him, then, to hold it before his mind and count the number of steps in the image, the number of windows, the number and disposition of pigeons on the roof, and so on. He could do these things if he had a photograph of the thing before him. But he cannot do them with the image, in spite of the fact that it is supposed to be right there "before his mind," easily and "directly" inspectable. He can tell how many steps there are only if he has sometime counted the steps on the building itself (or in a photograph of it) and now *remembers*—but that is not counting the steps in the image. Or he can *imagine* that it has, say, 30 steps, and then *say* "30"—but that is not counting anything either; it is only a performance. The image he professes to "have" there, so clearly and with such detail, does not even exist. He claims to have produced in his mind an image of the library; but all he has actually done is imagine the library.

What, then, is imagining something? Is it an

activity, a state, or what? It does not really matter here how we answer that; it is only *not* the producing of an entity called a "mental image." Let us suppose for this context, then, that to be imagining something is to be in a certain *state*. Is it, then, a *physical* state? Well, it is a state of a man, just as drunkenness, sleep, perspiration, obesity, etc., are sometimes states of this man or that. What is meant by asking whether these are "physical" states, other than asking whether they are states of a physical object? What shall we say of being in a state of sleep, for instance? It is the state of a man, and a man is a physical—that is, a visible and palpable—being. You cannot poke a man's state of imagining something with a stick; all you can do is poke him. That is true. But you cannot poke his somnolence with a stick either. There is nothing to poke; there is only the man sleeping, or the man imagining, or the man becoming drunk, or whatever.

How then can a man, if he is nothing but a (mere) physical object, be in such a state as this, that is, of imagining something? If he is only a body and can do this, why cannot sticks and stones be in such a state, for are they not bodies too? The answer is: For just the same reason that sticks and stones cannot be drunken, asleep, perspiring, obese, or hungry; namely, that they are sticks and stones and not men. The reason is not that they lack minds. Even if they had them, they still could not be drunken, asleep, perspiring, obese or hungry, for they would still be sticks and stones and not men.

The Fourth (and last) Argument.   It is fairly common for people, including philosophers, to say that they can perfectly well imagine surviving the death of their bodies, which would be quite impossible for anyone who supposed that he and his body were one and the same thing. Admittedly no one knows whether there is any survival of death, but it is at least not necessarily false. The doctrine of metempsychosis,* for example, though there may be no reason for be-

lieving it, cannot be shown to be impossible just on philosophical grounds. It would be impossible, however, if a person and his body were identical, and so would any other form of survival. We know the fate of the body: dust. If I am the same as my body, then it is logically impossible that I should not share that fate.

Reply.   All this argument shows is that not everyone, perhaps even no one, *knows* that he and his body are one and the same thing. It does not in the least show that, in fact, they are not. Some things, like the Evening Star and the Morning Star, which some are accustomed to thinking of and describing as different things, nevertheless do turn out to be the same.

Suppose a god were to promise me a life after death—promising, perhaps, to have me (the very person that I am) reborn elsewhere with a different body. Now such a promise might quicken a real hope in me, provided I am capable (as everyone is) of thinking of myself as being something different from my body. But the fact that I can think such a distinction does not show that there is one, and in case there is not—in case I happen to be identical with my body— then of course no god could fulfill such a promise. Consider this analogy: If an enemy of our country did not know that Albany is (the same thing as) the capital of New York, then he might be very interested in a proposal to bomb the one but to spare the other. It would nevertheless be a proposal that no one could carry out. The fact that someone who is ignorant of this identity can entertain the possibility of its being carried out does not show that it is possible; it shows only that he does not know that it is not.

V. The Soul as Life and the Soul as Thought

It is useful in concluding, I think, to compare the philosophical conception of the mind with what was once the philosophical conception of life. It was once pretty much taken for granted that men and other animals *possess* something

---

*The passing of the soul at death into another body. [ED.]

which inanimate things lack, namely, life, and that it is *because* they possess this that they can do all sorts of things that inanimate things cannot do, such as move themselves, assimilate nourishment, reproduce their kind, and so on. Aristotle classified the souls of living things according to the abilities they imparted to their owners, and thought that even vegetables had souls. Indeed, an animal's *life* and *soul* were generally thought to be one and the same thing. The very word "animal" has its origin in this belief. Socrates, according to Plato, was even able to convince himself of his own immortality on the basis of this notion for, he thought, if it is only because he has a life or soul to begin with that he is a living man, then it is idle to fear the death of that very soul. Life seemed to him identical with his soul, but accidental to his body, indeed even foreign to such a thing of clay. A similar model was at work in Descartes' philosophy when he declared that the soul could never stop thinking. Thought seemed to him identical with his soul, but positively foreign to his body.

Now of course we still talk of life that way, but we no longer take such common modes of speech as descriptive of any reality. We speak of a man "losing" his life, of a man "taking" another's life, of the "gift" of life, and even of the "breath" of life which God is supposed to infuse into an otherwise *lifeless* body. But these are plainly metaphors. No one supposes that a man or animal moves, assimilates nourishment, reproduces, and so on *because* it is possessed of life. We no longer think of life as something added to an animal body, some separable thing that quickens matter. To distinguish something as a living animal is only to call attention to the very complicated way the matter of its body is organized and to a large class of capacities which result from such organization. A living body is simply one in which certain processes, some of them frightfully complex and ill understood, take place. A living body, in short, differs from a nonliving one, not in what it possesses, but in what it does, and these are facts about it that can be verified in a straightforward way.

I have been urging a similar way of speaking of the mind; not as something mysteriously *embodied* here and there, and something that is supposed to *account* for the more or less intelligent behavior of certain beings. A being capable of more or less intelligent thought and action differs from one lacking such capacities, not in something it possesses, but precisely in what it does. And this, incidentally, explains why a man tends to regard it as a deep insult to be told that he has no mind. It is not because he is thus divested in our eyes of some possession dearly prized, but rather, because such a remark is quite rightly taken to mean that he lacks certain important and distinctively human abilities and capacities. If a man is assured that his possession of certain more or less intellectual abilities is in no way in question, he feels divested of nothing upon learning that among his parts or possessions there is none that is properly denoted "a mind."

VI. Does Matter Think?

Probably every philosopher has felt more or less acutely at one time or another a profound puzzlement in the idea of (mere) matter doing those various things rightly ascribable only to persons. How, it is wondered, can a body think, deliberate, imagine things, figure and plan, and so on?

This is really no proper source of bafflement, however. No one can say, *a priori*, what the highly organized material systems of one's body are or are not capable of. It was once thought incredible that matter, unquickened by any soul, could be alive, for matter seemed to inquirers to be inert or lifeless by its very nature. Yet we see around us all the time specimens of living matter—in the merest insects, for instance—so philosophical prejudice has had to yield to the fact. Similarly, I submit, we see around us all the time specimens of thinking matter; that is, material beings which deliberate, imagine, plan, and so on. For men do in fact do these things, and when we see a man, we are seeing a material being—a dreadfully complex and highly organized one, to be sure, but no less a visible and palpable object for that. In any case, the seeming mystery or incredibility that may attach to the idea of matter exercising intellectual capacities is hardly dissolved by postulating something *else* to exercise those capacities. If there is a difficulty in comprehending how a body can do such things, there is surely no less difficulty in seeing how something which is not a body can do them any better.

For Further Reflection

1. Does Taylor do justice to the mind-body problem? Do you agree with his account of why philosophers have fabricated the issue? After reading his essay and the other essays in this section, does he convince you that it is a pseudo-problem?

2. Has Taylor given positive reasons for believing in materialism? Or is his argument mainly that materialism is defensible?

Who Am I? The Problem of Personal Identity

Suppose you wake up tomorrow in a strange room. There are pictures of unfamiliar people on the light blue walls. The furniture in the room is very odd. You wonder how you got here. You remember being in the hospital where you were dying of cancer. Your body was wasting away and your death was thought to be a few days away. Dr. Thomas had kindly given you an extra dose of morphine to kill the pain. That's all you can remember. You notice a calendar on the wall in front of you. The date is April 1, 1992. "This can't be," you think, "for yesterday was December 2nd, 1991." "Where have I been all this time?" Suddenly, you see a mirror. In horror you reel back, for it's not your body that you spy in the glass, but a large woman's body. You have more than doubled your previous weight and look 20 years older. You feel tired and confused and frightened and start to cry. Soon a strange man, about 45 years of age, comes into your room. "I was wondering when you would waken, Maria. The doctor said that I should let you sleep as long as possible, but I didn't think that you would be asleep two whole days. Anyway, the operation was a success. We had feared that the accident had ended your life. The children and I are so grateful. Juanita and Caesar will be home in an hour and will be so happy to see you awake. How do you feel?"

"Can this be a bad joke?" you wonder. "Who is this strange man and who am I?" Unbeknownst to you, your doctor, Dr. Thomas, needed a living brain to implant in the head of Mrs. Maria Garcia, mother of four children. She had been in a car accident and arrived at the hospital on a ventilator but brain dead. Your brain was in excellent shape but lacked a healthy body. Maria Garcia's body was intact but needed a brain. Being an enterprising brain surgeon, Dr. Thomas saw his chance of performing the first successful brain transplant. Frightened and confused, you wonder if this fate is worse than death. The fact that the operation was a success was of little comfort to you, for you're not sure whether you are *you!*

The problem of personal identity is one of the most fascinating in the history of philosophy. It is especially complicated since it involves not one but three, and possibly four, philosophical questions: (1) What is it to be a person? (2) What is identity? (3) What is personal identity? and (4) How is survival possible given the problems of personal identity? Let us look briefly at the first three questions with reference to the readings in this section of our book. We will discuss the fourth question in the next section of this part.

1. What is it to be a person?

In our first reading, John Locke (1632–1704) says that a person is defined by having a soul, and the criterion of having a soul is the ability to reflect and reason. That is, our ability to introspect and survey our memories and intentions sets us apart from the animals as being of greater value. The view may be challenged by the materialist who says that it is really our brain (or our brain and our body) which defines our personhood, that it is the fact that we have a more developed brain that sets us apart from other animals. Of course, we are conscious beings. Although we do not understand how consciousness works, the physicalist believes that consciousness is a function of the brain. In our second reading, David Hume (1711–1776) argues that the notion of a self or soul is very likely a fiction. "I" am merely a bundle of perceptions. There is consciousness of a continuing succession of experiences, but not of a continuing experiencer. This view is compatible with the physicalist view of personhood.

2. What is identity?

This sounds like an absurdly simple question. Identity is the fact that everything is itself and not another. In logic, the Law of Identity (A = A) formally states the definition of identity. But we are not interested in a formal definition of mere identity but identity *over time,* or *reidentification* (sometimes this is referred to as "numerical identity"). What is it to be the *same* thing over time? Suppose that you go to an automobile dealership to buy a new car. You see several blue Fords parked side by side. They resemble each other so much that you cannot tell them apart. They are the same type of car and are exactly similar to each other. Suppose you pick one out at random and buy it. Your car is a different car than the other blue Fords even though you couldn't tell the difference between them. A year passes and your blue Ford now has 20,000 miles on it and a few scratches. Is it the same car that you originally bought? Most of us would probably agree that it is. The changes have altered it but not destroyed its identity as the blue car that you bought and have driven 20,000 miles.

What does your blue Ford have that causes it to be the same car over the period of one year? A common history, continuity over time. The car is linked together by a succession of spatial-temporal events from its origins in Detroit to its present place in your parking lot. This distinguishes it from all the other Fords that were ever built, no matter how similar they appear. So we might conclude that *continuity over time* is the criterion of identity.

But immediately we find problems with this criterion. The Rio Grande dries up in places in New Mexico every summer, only to reappear as a running river in the early spring. Is the Rio Grande the same river this year as it was the last? There isn't any continuity over time of water flowing over the riverbed. Perhaps we can escape the problem by saying that by "river" we really mean the riverbed, which must hold running water sometimes but need not always convey it. Does this solve the problem?

Consider another counter-example: The Chicago White Sox are playing the New York Yankees in Yankee Stadium in late April. The game is called in the fifth inning with the Yankees leading 3–2. Shortly afterwards there is a baseball strike and all the players take to the picket lines while a new set of players come up from the minor leagues to fill their positions. The "game" is continued in Chicago in August with a whole new set of players on both sides. The White Sox win, and the game decides who wins the division. Suppose a Yankee player who has had some philosophy argues that this latter game was not part of the original game played in April. There was no *continuity* between them. He demands that a new game be played from the start since it is impossible to play the same game as was played four months ago or even four days ago. Would he have a point? Should the commissioner of baseball call for a make-up game?

The most perplexing problem with regard to the notion of "sameness" or identity over time is illustrated by the ancient tale of Theseus' ship. Suppose you have a small ship that is in need of some repairs. You begin (at time t_1) to replace the old planks and material with new planks and material until after one year (time t_2) the ship is completely made up of different material. Do you have the same ship at t_2 as you had at t_1? If so, at what point did it (call it *Theseus 2*) become a different ship?

People disagree as to whether Theseus' ship has changed its identity. Suppose that you argue that it has not changed its identity, for it had a continuous history over time and therefore is the same ship. But now suppose that your friend takes the material discarded from the original *Theseus* and reconstructs "that" ship (call it *Theseus 3*). Which ship is now Theseus' ship? There is continuity of the ship between *Theseus 1* and *2* but continuity of material between *Theseus 1* and *3*. If it worries you that there was a time when the material of *Theseus 1* was not functioning as a ship, we could alter the example and suppose that as the planks were taken from *Theseus 1* they were transformed to another ship, *Argos*, where they replaced the *Argos'* planks, ending up with a ship that contained every board and nail from the original *Theseus* (call this transformed *Argos, Theseus 4*). Which is now the original *Theseus*?

Does there seem something peculiar about the notion of identity?

3. What is personal identity?

What is it to be the same person over time? Are you the same person that you were when you were one year old or even sixteen years old? We recall Locke's idea of personhood. It was the mental characteristics (ability to reflect or introspect) that constituted personhood. Personal identity was indicated by the successive memories that the person had, the continuity over time of a set of experiences which were remembered. We may call this the *psychological states criterion of personal identity*. The main competitor of this view is the *brain criterion*, though some philosophers hold to a *body criterion*. Let us examine each of these briefly.

The psychological states criterion holds that our memories constitute our identity over time. You are the same person you were at ten years of age because you have a continuous set of memories which contains all those that you had at ten plus others that continued after that year. There are several problems with this view. In the first place, our memories are not continuous in our consciousness. When we sleep, we cease to have memories at all. In partial amnesia do we cease to be who we were? Thomas Reid suggests a problem of transitivity in memories. Suppose there is a gallant officer who at age twenty-five is a hero in a battle and who remembers getting a flogging in his childhood. Later, at age sixty-five, he recalls the heroic deed done at twenty-five but cannot recall the flogging. Since he cannot remember the earlier deed, is he the same person he was when he did remember it? Can Locke answer Reid?

What about the phenomenon of split personalities and multiple personalities, the most famous of which is Sybil, who allegedly expressed sixteen different personalities with sixteen different sets of memories? On a psychological states account, would we have to say that one body contains sixteen persons? Are there different persons inside each of us, expressed by different "sides" of our personalities?

Sometimes a person expresses apparent memories of events that occurred in distant times and to different "persons." Is the body of the contemporary being possessed by another person? If your friend suddenly starts reminiscing about the Battle of Waterloo and the beautiful Empress Josephine, has Napoleon suddenly come alive in your friend's body? This would truly be a case of reincarnation. But what if two of your friends came to you with the same "foreign" memories? And what is to prohibit complete soul flow, a different person inside you each day? How do you know that the soul that is remembering today is the same soul that remembered yesterday? You might object that this couldn't be the case because you have the same body, but that objection won't work since the body has nothing to do with the psychological states criterion. If you think that the body is important, this might be an indication that the memory criterion is inadequate on its own and depends on a physical body for continuity.

The body criterion has difficulties, one of which is the fact that the body can undergo radical changes and we would still want to call the person the same person. Almost all of the cells of our body change every seven years. Do we become a new person every seven years? Or think of the story at the beginning of this section in which Dr. Thomas transplants your brain into Maria Garcia's body. Wouldn't you still be you?

This suggests the third criterion, the brain criterion of personal identity. Our memories are contained within our brains, so we might want to say that having the same brain constitutes the same person. But this has difficulties, as are brought out in our third reading by Derek Parfit. It is well known that if the corpus callosum, the great band of fibers which unites the two hemispheres of the brain, is cut, two different centers of consciousness can be created. When either side of the cerebral cortex brain is destroyed, the person can live on as a conscious being. It is also possible in principle to transplant brains. Suppose that your body is destroyed and neurologists transplant each half of your brain into a different body. Dr. Thomas transplants one half of your brain into Maria Garcia and the other half into the head of Kareem Abdul Jabbar's look-alike. "You" wake up with two personalities. Do you survive the operation? There seems to be just three possible answers: (1) you do not survive; (2) you survive as one of the two; and (3) you survive as two people.

All of these options seem unsatisfactory. It seems absurd to say (1) that you don't survive, for there is continuity of consciousness (in the Lockean sense) as though you had gone to sleep and awakened. If you had experienced the destruction of one half of your brain, we would still say you survived with half a brain, so why not say so now when each half is autonomous? The logic of this thesis would seem to say that double life equals death.

But (2) seems arbitrary. Why say that you only survive as one of the two, and which one is it? And (3) that you survive as both is not satisfactory either since it gives up the notion of identity. You cannot be numerically one with two centers of consciousness and two spatial-temporal bodies. Otherwise we might say when we wreck our new Ford that the other one left in the automobile dealer's parking lot (the blue Ford which was exactly like yours) was indeed yours.

If this is an accurate analysis of the personal identity problem, what sense can we make of the concept? Not much, according to Parfit. We should speak of survival of the person, not the identity of the person. Persons, as psychological states, survive and gradually merge (like Theseus' rebuilt ship) into descendent persons. Your memories and personality gradually emerged from the sixteen-year-old who gradually developed from the ten-year-old who bore your name. These were your ancestor selves. But you too will merge with future or descendent selves as you have different experiences, take on new memories, and forget old ones. Suppose every year neurologists could transplant half of your brain into another body, in which a new half would duplicate the present state of the transferred half. In this way a tree-like operation would continue to spread successors of yourself as though by psychological parthenogenesis. You would survive in a sense, but it would make no sense to speak of personal identity, a concept which Parfit wants to get rid of. We could also imagine a neurological game of musical hemispheres as half of your brain was merged with half of someone else's brain in a third person's head. You could continue the hemisphere moving game every six months so that you might even get re-merged with your own other half at some future time—kind of like meeting your spouse again after other adventures. You'd have a lot to talk about through the medium of the corpus callosum!

Of course, Parfit's point is that we are going through significant changes all the time, so that as we have new experiences, we take on new selfhood. Something in us survives but with a difference. If Parfit is right about the relativity of identity in survival, then we might be less interested in our future than our immediate future. After all, that person ten years down the line is less like us than the person we'll be tomorrow. This might encourage a sort of general utilitarianism, for since our distant interests really are not as pressing, we would be free to work for the total greater good. On the other hand, it could have the opposite effect of making us indifferent to the future of society. This notion of proximate identity also raises the question of whether we should be concerned about our distant death fifty years down the line which one of our successor selves will have to face. This view might also cause us to prohibit long-term prison sentences for criminal actions, for why punish a descendent for what one of his or her ancestors did? Finally, it could be used to argue against exorbitant awards in malpractice litigation. Often a jury is asked to award a sum of money (as high as $12 million) to a severely retarded child whose damage has been incurred through medical malpractice. The justification for the large sum is the expectation that the child could have become, for example, a physician or lawyer and made an enormous sum of money in his or her lifetime. But if we were to take the notion of proximate identity seriously, we could only sue the physician for the damages done to the immediate person, not to his or her descendent selves.

What is the truth about personal identity? Are you the same person that you were at sixteen? And will you be still the same person at sixty?

IV.5   Our Psychological Properties Define the Self

JOHN LOCKE

In this selection Locke sets forth his psychological state theory of personal identity, locating the criterion of personal identity in terms of consciousness, especially memory. The soul or essence of the person, defined as a reflective being, could take on different bodily forms and still preserve the same identity.

(A biographical sketch of Locke is found on p. 119.)

Study Questions

1. What is Locke's definition of a person?
2. In what does personal identity consist?
3. Is it necessary that consciousness be the same identical substance?
4. Can we be the same persons though we have different bodies?
5. How is Locke's view relevant to the question of life after death?
6. What is the lesson of the story of the prince and the cobbler?

. . . IF THE IDENTITY OF *soul alone* makes the same *man,* and there be nothing in the nature of matter why the same individual spirit may not be united to different bodies, it will be possible that those men, living in distant ages, and of different tempers, may have been the same man: which way of speaking must be from a very strange use of the word man, applied to an idea out of which body and shape are excluded. . . .

An animal is a living organized body; and consequently the same animal, as we have observed, is the same continued *life* communicated to different particles of matter, as they happen successively to be united to that organized living

From John Locke, An Essay Concerning Human Understanding, *Book II, Chapter 27, "Of Ideas of Identity and Diversity." First published in 1690.*

body. And whatever is talked of other definitions, ingenious observation puts it past doubt, that the idea in our minds, of which the sound "man" in our mouths is the sign, is nothing else but of an animal of such a certain form. . . .

I presume it is not the idea of a thinking or rational being alone that makes the *idea of a man* in most people's sense: but of a body, so and so shaped, joined to it; and if that be the idea of a man, the same successive body not shifted all at once, must, as well as the same immaterial spirit, go to the making of the same man.

This being premised, to find wherein personal identity consists, we must consider what *person* stands for;—which, I think, is a thinking intelligent being, that has reason and reflection, and can consider itself as itself, the same thinking thing, in different times and places; which it does only by that consciousness which is inseparable from thinking, and, as it seems to me, essential to it: it being impossible for any one to perceive without *perceiving* that he does perceive. When we see, hear, smell, taste, feel, meditate, or will anything, we know that we do so. Thus it is always as to our present sensations and perceptions: and by this every one is to himself that which he calls self:—it not being considered, in this case, whether the same self be continued in the same or divers substances. For, since consciousness always accompanies thinking, and it is that which makes every one to be what he calls self, and thereby distinguishes himself from all other thinking things, in this alone consists personal identity, i.e. the sameness of a rational being: and as far as this consciousness can be extended backwards to any past action or thought, so far reaches the identity of that person; it is the same self now it was then; and it is by the same self with this present one that now reflects on it, that that action was done.

But it is further inquired, whether it be the same identical substance. This few would think they had reason to doubt of, if these perceptions, with their consciousness, always remained present in the mind, whereby the same thinking thing would be always consciously present, and, as would be thought, evidently the same to itself. But that which seems to make the difficulty is this, that this consciousness being interrupted always by forgetfulness, there being no moment of our lives wherein we have the whole train of all our past actions before our eyes in one view, but even the best memories losing the sight of one part whilst they are viewing another; and we sometimes, and that the greatest part of our lives, not reflecting on our past selves, being intent on our present thoughts, and in sound sleep having no thoughts at all, or at least none with that consciousness which remarks our waking thoughts,—I say, in all these cases, our consciousness being interrupted, and we losing the sight of our past selves, doubts are raised whether we are the same thinking thing, i.e. the same *substance* or no. Which, however reasonable or unreasonable, concerns not *personal* identity at all. The question being what makes the same person; and not whether it be the same identical substance, which always thinks in the same person, which, in this case, matters not at all: different substances, by the same consciousness (where they do partake in it) being united into one person, as well as different bodies by the same life are united into one animal, whose identity is perceived in that change of substances by the unity of one continued life. For, it being the same consciousness that makes a man be himself to himself, personal identity depends on that only, whether it be annexed solely to one individual substance, or can be continued in a succession of several substances. For as far as any intelligent being *can* repeat the idea of any past action with the same consciousness it had of it at first, and with the same consciousness it has of any present action; so far it is the same personal self. For it is by the consciousness it has of its present thoughts and actions, that it is *self to itself* now, and so will be the same self, as far as the same consciousness can extend to actions past or to come; and would be by distance of time, or change of substance, no more two persons, than a man be two men by wearing other clothes to-day than he did yesterday, with a long or a short sleep between: the same consciousness uniting those distant actions in the same person, whatever substances contributed to their production.

That this is so, we have some kind of evidence in our very bodies, all whose particles, whilst vitally united to this same thinking conscious self, so that *we feel* when they are touched, and are affected by, and conscious of good or harm that happens to them, are a part of ourselves; i.e. of our thinking conscious self. Thus, the limbs of his body are to every one a part of himself; he sympathizes and is concerned for them. Cut off a hand, and thereby separate it from that consciousness he had of its heat, cold, and other affections, and it is then no longer a part of that which is himself, any more than the remotest part of matter. Thus, we see the *substance* whereof personal self consisted at one time may be varied at another, without the change of personal identity; there being no question about the same person, though the limbs which but now were a part of it, be cut off. . . .

And thus may we be able, without any difficulty, to conceive the same person at the resurrection, though in a body not exactly in make or parts the same which he had here,—the same consciousness going along with the soul that inhabits it. But yet the soul alone, in the change of bodies, would scarce to any one but to him that makes the soul the man, be enough to make the same man. For should the soul of a prince, carrying with it the consciousness of the prince's past life, enter and inform the body of a cobbler, as soon as deserted by his own soul, every one sees he would be the same *person* with the prince, accountable only for the prince's actions: but who would say it was the same *man*? The body too goes to the making the man, and would, I guess, to everybody determine the man in this case, wherein the soul, with all its princely thoughts about it, would not make another man: but he would be the same cobbler to every one besides himself. I know that, in the ordinary way of speaking, the same person, and the same man,

stand for one and the same thing. And indeed every one will always have a liberty to speak as he pleases, and to apply what articulate sounds to what ideas he thinks fit, and change them as often as he pleases. But yet, when we will inquire what makes the same *spirit, man,* or *person,* we must fix the ideas of spirit, man, or person in our minds; and having resolved with ourselves what we mean by them, it will not be hard to determine in either of them, or the like, when it is the same, and when not.

But though the immaterial substance or soul does not alone, wherever it be, and in whatsoever state, make the same *man;* yet it is plain, consciousness, as far as ever it can be extended—should it be to ages past—unites existences and actions very remote in time into the same *person,* as well as it does the existences and actions of the immediately preceding moment: so that whatever has the consciousness of present and past actions, is the same person to whom they both belong. Had I the same consciousness that I saw the ark and Noah's flood, as that I saw an overflowing of the Thames last winter, or as that I write now, I could no more doubt that I who write this now, that saw the Thames overflowed last winter, and that viewed the flood at the general deluge, was the same *self,*—place that self in what *substance* you please—than that I who write this am the same *myself* now whilst I write (whether I consist of all the same substance, material or immaterial, or no) that I was yesterday. For as to this point of being the same self, it matters not whether this present self be made up of the same or other substances—I being as much concerned, and as justly accountable for any action that was done a thousand years since, appropriated to me now by this self-consciousness, as I am for what I did the last moment. . . .

But yet possibly it will still be objected,—Suppose I wholly lose the memory of some parts of my life, beyond a possibility of retrieving them, so that perhaps I shall never be conscious of them again; yet am I not the same person that did those actions, had those thoughts that I once was conscious of, though I have now forgot them? To which I answer, that we must here take notice what the word *I* is applied to; which, in this case, is the *man* only. And the same man being presumed to be the same person, I is easily here supposed to stand also for the same person. But if it be possible for the same man to have distinct incommunicable consciousness at different times, it is past doubt the same man would at different times make different persons; which, we see, is the sense of mankind in the solemnest declaration of their opinions, human laws not punishing the mad man for the sober man's actions, nor the sober man for what the mad man did,—thereby making them two persons: which is somewhat explained by our way of speaking in English when we say such an one is "not himself," or is "beside himself"; in which phrases it is insinuated, as if those who now, or at least first used them, thought that self was changed; the selfsame person was no longer in that man.

But yet it is hard to conceive that Socrates, the same individual man, should be two persons. To help us a little in this, we must consider what is meant by Socrates, or the same individual *man*.

First, it must be either the same individual, immaterial, thinking substance; in short, the same numerical soul, and nothing else.

Secondly, or the same animal, without any regard to the immaterial soul.

Thirdly, or the same immaterial spirit united to the same animal.

Now, take which of these suppositions you please, it is impossible to make personal identity to consist in anything but consciousness; or reach any further than that does.

For Further Reflection

1. How would Locke respond to the objection that memories are not continuous in our consciousness? When we sleep, we cease to have memories at all. In partial amnesia do we cease to be who we were? Recall Thomas Reid's suggestion of the problem of transitivity in memories. Suppose there is a gallant officer who at age twenty-five is a hero in a battle and who remembers getting a flogging in his childhood. Later, at age sixty-five, he recalls the heroic deed done at twenty-five but cannot recall the flogging. Since he cannot remember the earlier deed, is he the same person he was when he did remember it? Can Locke answer Reid?

2. What about the phenomenon of split personalities and multiple personalities, also discussed in the introduction to this section, the most famous of which is Sybil, who allegedly expressed sixteen different personalities with sixteen different sets of memories? On a psychological states account, would we have to say that one body contains sixteen persons? Are there different persons inside each of us, expressed by different "sides" of our personalities?

We Have No Substantial Self with Which We Are Identical

IV.6

DAVID HUME

Hume does not believe that we have a self. For Hume, you may recall from reading III.4, all learning comes from sensory impressions. Since there does not seem to be a separate impression of the self which we experience, there is no reason to believe that we have a self. The most we can identify ourselves with is our consciousness, and that constantly changes. There is no separate, permanent self which endures over time. Hence, personal identity is a fiction.

(A biographical sketch of Hume is found on p. 46.)

Study Questions

1. What does Hume mean by saying that the self is not any one impression, and what significance does this have for him?
2. What does Hume say of people who differ with him?
3. What is the "self"?
4. What does Hume say about the problem of identity?

THERE ARE SOME PHILOSOPHERS, who imagine we are every moment intimately conscious of what we call our Self; that we feel its existence and its continuance in existence; and are certain, beyond the evidence of a demonstration, both of its perfect identity and simplicity. . . .

Unluckily all these positive assertions are contrary to that very experience, which is pleaded for them, nor have we any idea of *self*, after the manner it is here explained. For from what impression could this idea be derived? This question 'tis impossible to answer without a manifest contradiction and absurdity; and yet 'tis a question, which must necessarily be answered, if we would have the idea of self pass for clear and intelligible. It must be some one impression, that gives rise to every real idea. But self or person is not any one impression, but that to which our several impressions and ideas are supposed to have a reference. If any impression gives rise to the idea of self, that impression must continue invariably the same, through the whole course of our lives; since self is supposed to exist after that manner. But there is no impression constant and invariable. Pain and pleasure, grief and joy, passions and sensations succeed each other, and never all exist at the same time. It cannot, therefore, be from any of these impressions, or from any other, that the idea of self is derived; and consequently there is no such idea.

But farther, what must become of all our particular perceptions upon this hypothesis? All these are different, and distinguishable, and separable from each other, and may be separately considered, and may exist separately, and have no need of any thing to support their existence. After what manner, therefore, do they belong to self; and how are they connected with it? For my part, when I enter most intimately into what I call *myself*, I always stumble on some particular perception or other, of heat or cold, light or shade, love or hatred, pain or pleasure. I never can catch *myself* at any time without a perception, and never can observe any thing but the perception. When my perceptions are removed for any time, as by sound sleep; so long am I insensible of *myself*, and may truly be said not to exist. And were all my perceptions removed by death, and could I neither think, nor feel, nor see, nor love, nor hate after the dissolution of my body, I should be entirely annihilated, nor do I conceive what is farther requisite to make me a perfect nonentity. If any one upon serious and unprejudiced reflection, thinks he has a different notion of *himself*, I must confess I can reason no longer with him. All I can allow him is, that he may be in the right as well as I, and that we are essentially different in this particular. He may, perhaps, perceive something simple and continued, which he calls *himself*; though I am certain there is no such principle in me.

But setting aside some metaphysicians of this kind, I may venture to affirm of the rest of mankind, that they are nothing but a bundle or col-

From David Hume, A Treatise of Human Nature. *First published in England in 1738.*

lection of different perceptions, which succeed each other with an inconceivable rapidity, and are in a perpetual flux and movement. Our eyes cannot turn in their sockets without varying our perceptions. Our thought is still more variable than our sight; and all our other senses and faculties contribute to this change; nor is there any single power of the soul, which remains unalterably the same, perhaps for one moment. The mind is a kind of theatre, where several perceptions successively make their appearance; pass, re-pass, glide away, and mingle in an infinite variety of postures and situations. There is properly no *simplicity* in it at one time, nor *identity* in different; whatever natural propension we may have to imagine that simplicity and identity. The comparison of the theatre must not mislead us. They are the successive perceptions only, that constitute the mind; nor have we the most distant notion of the place, where these scenes are represented, or of the materials, of which it is composed.

What then gives us so great a propension to ascribe an identity to these successive perceptions, and to suppose ourselves possessed of an invariable and uninterrupted existence through the whole course of our lives? . . .

We have a distinct idea of an object, that remains invariable and uninterrupted through a supposed variation of time; and this idea we call that of *identity* or *sameness*. We have also a distinct idea of several different objects existing in succession, and connected together by a close relation; and this to an accurate view affords as perfect a notion of *diversity*, as if there was no manner of relation among the objects. But though these two ideas of identity, and a succession of related objects be in themselves perfectly distinct, and even contrary, yet 'tis certain, that in our common way of thinking they are generally confounded with each other. That action of the imagination, by which we consider the uninterrupted and invariable object, and that by which we reflect on the succession of related objects, are almost the same to the feeling, nor is there much more effort of thought required in the

latter case than in the former. The relation facilitates the transition of the mind from one object to another, and renders its passage as smooth as if it contemplated one continued object. This resemblance is the cause of the confusion and mistake, and makes us substitute the notion of identity, instead of that of related objects. . . .

Thus we feign the continued existence of the perceptions of our senses, to remove the interruption; and run into the notion of a *soul*, and *self*, and *substance*, to disguise the variation. But we may farther observe, that where we do not give rise to such a fiction, our propension to confound identity with relation is so great, that we are apt to imagine something unknown and mysterious, connecting the parts, beside their relation; and this I take to be the case with regard to the identity we ascribe to plants and vegetables. And even when this does not take place, we still feel a propensity to confound these ideas, though we are not able fully to satisfy ourselves in that particular, nor find any thing invariable and uninterrupted to justify our notion of identity.

Thus the controversy concerning identity is not merely a dispute of words. For when we attribute identity, in an improper sense, to variable or interrupted objects, our mistake is not confined to the expression, but is commonly attended with a fiction, either of something invariable and uninterrupted, or of something mysterious and inexplicable, or at least with a propensity to such fictions. What will suffice to prove this hypothesis to the satisfaction of every fair enquirer, is to show from daily experience and observation, that the objects, which are variable or interrupted, and yet are supposed to continue the same, are such only as consist of a succession of parts, connected together by resemblance, contiguity, or causation. . . .

A ship, of which a considerable part has been changed by frequent reparations, is still considered as the same; nor does the difference of the materials hinder us from ascribing an identity to it. The common end, in which the parts conspire, is the same under all their variations, and affords an easy transition of the imagination from one situation of the body to another. . . .

Though every one must allow, that in a very few years both vegetables and animals endure a *total* change, yet we still attribute identity to them, while their form, size, and substance are entirely altered. An oak, that grows from a small plant to a large tree, is still the same oak; though there be not one particle of matter, or figure of its parts the same. An infant becomes a man, and is sometimes fat, sometimes lean, without any change in his identity. . . . A man, who hears a noise, that is frequently interrupted and renewed, says, it is still the same noise; though 'tis evident the sounds have only a specific identity or resemblance, and there is nothing numerically the same, but the cause, which produced them. In like manner it may be said without breach of the propriety of language, that such a church, which was formerly of brick, fell to ruin, and that the parish rebuilt the same church of freestone, and according to modern architecture. Here neither the form nor materials are the same, nor is there any thing common to the two ob-

jects, but their relation to the inhabitants of the parish; and yet this alone is sufficient to make us denominate them the same. . . .

From thence it evidently follows, that identity is nothing really belonging to these different perceptions, and uniting them together; but is merely a quality, which we attribute to them, because of the union of their ideas in the imagination, when we reflect upon them. . . .

The only question, therefore, which remains, is, by what relations this uninterrupted progress of our thought is produced, when we consider the successive existence of a mind or thinking person. And here 'tis evident we must confine ourselves to resemblance and causation. . . . Also, as memory alone acquaints us with the continuance and extent of this succession of perceptions, 'tis to be considered, upon that account chiefly, as the source of personal identity. Had we no memory, we never should have any notion of causation, nor consequently of that chain of causes and effects, which constitute our self or person.

For Further Reflection

Kant criticized Hume for reducing the mind to a stream of consciousness. The fact to be explained, says Kant, is not the succession of awarenesses, but an awareness of succession. If that which is aware passed with the awareness, there would be no awareness of succession, but it *doesn't* pass with it. This suggests that there is a transcendent self beyond the stream of consciousness of which Hume speaks. What do you make of this as an objection to Hume?

IV.7   Brain Transplants and Personal Identity: A Dialogue

DEREK PARFIT AND GODFREY VESEY

Derek Parfit is an English philosopher who was educated and now teaches at Oxford University. He has made outstanding contributions to the subjects of ethical theory and the problem of personal identity. His major work is *Reasons and Persons* (1984). Godfrey Vesey was educated at Cambridge University and is a professor of philosophy at the Open University. His principal works are *Perception* (1971) and *Personal Identity* (1974).

In this dialogue Vesey introduces the problem of split-brain transplants. That is, a brain is divided in two, and half is put into each of two other people's brainless heads. What do we say about this situation? Does the original person survive? Parfit then responds by developing his ideas of personal identity as psychological identity.

Study Questions

1. Describe the imaginary situation of Mr. Brown and Mr. Robinson's brain transplant.
2. What is a "*q*-memory"?
3. What does Parfit think of the "all-or-nothing" view of personal identity? Why does he hold to his position?
4. What are the three possible answers to the question "What's going to happen to me?" in the split-brain case and how does Parfit treat them?
5. What is Parfit's solution to the problem?

Brain Transplants

IN 1973 IN THE *Sunday Times* there was a report of how a team from the Metropolitan Hospital in Cleveland under Dr. R. J. White had successfully transplanted a monkey's head on to another monkey's body.[1] Dr. White was reported as having said, 'Technically a human head transplant is possible', and as hoping that 'it may be possible eventually to transplant *parts* of the brain or other organs inside the head.'

The possibility of brain transplants gives rise to a fascinating philosophical problem. Imagine the following situation:

Two men, a Mr Brown and a Mr Robinson, had been operated on for brain tumours and brain extractions had been performed on both of them. At the end of the operations, however, the assistant inadvertently put Brown's brain in Robinson's head, and Robinson's brain in Brown's head. One of these men immediately dies, but the other, the one with Robinson's body and Brown's brain, eventually regains consciousness. Let us call the latter 'Brownson'. Upon regaining consciousness Brownson exhibits great shock and surprise at the appearance of his body. Then, upon seeing Brown's body, he exclaims incredulously 'That's me

lying there!' Pointing to himself he says 'This isn't my body; the one over there is!' When asked his name he automatically replies 'Brown'. He recognizes Brown's wife and family (whom Robinson had never met), and is able to describe in detail events in Brown's life, always describing them as events in his own life. Of Robinson's past life he evinces no knowledge at all. Over a period of time he is observed to display all of the personality traits, mannerisms, interests, likes and dislikes, and so on, that had previously characterized Brown, and to act and talk in ways completely alien to the old Robinson.[2]

The next step is to suppose that Brown's brain is not simply transplanted whole into someone else's brainless head, but is divided in two and half put into each of *two* other people's brainless heads. The same memory having been coded in many parts of the cortex, they *both* then say they are Brown, are able to describe events in Brown's life as if they are events in their own lives, etc. What should we say now?

The implications of this case for what we should say about personal identity are considered by Derek Parfit in a paper entitled 'Personal Identity'. Parfit's own view is expressed in terms of a relationship he calls 'psychological continuity'. He analyses this relationship partly in terms of what he calls 'q-memory' ('q' stands for 'quasi'). He sketches a definition of 'q-memory' as follows:

> I am q-remembering an experience if (1) I have a belief about a past experience which seems in itself like a memory belief, (2) someone did have such an experience, and (3) my belief is dependent upon this experience in the same way (whatever that is) in which a memory of an experience is dependent upon it.[3]

The significance of this definition of q-memory is that *two* people can, in theory, q-remember doing what only one person did. So two people can, in theory, be psychologically continuous with one person.

Parfit's thesis is that there is nothing more to personal identity than this 'psychological continuity'. This is *not* to say that whenever there is a sufficient degree of psychological continuity there is personal identity, for psychological continuity could be a one-two, or 'branching', relationship, and we are able to speak of 'identity' only when there is a one-one relationship. It *is* to say that a common belief—in the special nature of personal identity—is mistaken.

In the discussion that follows I began by asking Parfit what he thinks of this common belief.

Personal Identity

Vesey: Derek, can we begin with the belief that you claim most of us have about personal identity? It's this: whatever happens between now and some future time either I shall still exist or I shan't. And any future experience will either be my experience or it won't. In other words, personal identity is an all or nothing matter: either I survive or I don't. Now what do you want to say about that?

Parfit: It seems to me just false. I think the true view is that we can easily describe and imagine large numbers of cases in which the question, 'Will that future person be me—or someone else?', is both a question which doesn't have any answer at all, and there's no puzzle that there's no answer.

Vesey: Will you describe one such case.

Parfit: One of them is the case discussed in the correspondence material, the case of division in which we suppose that each half of my brain is to be transplanted into a new body and the two resulting people will both seem to remember the whole of my life, have my character and be psychologically continuous with me in every way. Now in this case of division there were only three possible answers to the question, 'What's going to happen to *me?*' And all three of them seem to me open to very serious objections. So the conclusion to be drawn from the case is that the question of what's going to happen to me, just doesn't have an answer. I think the case also shows that that's not mysterious at all.

Vesey: Right, let's deal with these three possibilities in turn.

Parfit: Well, the first is that I'm going to be both of the resulting people. What's wrong with that answer is that it leads very quickly to a contradiction.

Vesey: How?

Parfit: The two resulting people are going to be different people from each other. They're going to live completely different lives. They're going to be as different as any two people are. But if they're different people from each other it can't be the case that I'm going to be both of them. Because if I'm both of them, then one of the resulting people is going to be the same person as the other.

Vesey: Yes. They can't be different people and be the same person, namely me.

Parfit: Exactly. So the first answer leads to a contradiction.

Vesey: Yes. And the second?

Parfit: Well, the second possible answer is that I'm not going to be both of them but just one of them. This doesn't lead to a contradiction, it's just wildly implausible. It's implausible because my relation to each of the resulting people is exactly similar.

Vesey: Yes, so there's no reason to say that I'm one rather than the other?

Parfit: It just seems absurd to suppose that, when you've got exactly the same relation, one of them is identity and the other is nothing at all.

Vesey: It does seem absurd, but there are philosophers who would say that sort of thing. Let's go on to the third.

Parfit: Well, the only remaining answer, if I'm not going to be both of them or only one of them, is that I'm going to be neither of them. What's wrong with this answer is that it's grossly misleading.

Vesey: Why?

Parfit: If I'm going to be neither of them, then there's not going to be anyone in the world after the operation who's going to be me. And that implies, given the way we now think, that the operation is as bad as death. Because if there's going to be no one who's going to be me, then I cease to exist. But it's obvious on reflection that the operation isn't as bad as death. It isn't bad in any way at all. That this is obvious can be shown by supposing that when they do the operation only one of the transplants succeeds and only one of the resulting people ever comes to consciousness again.

Vesey: Then I think we would say that this person is me. I mean we'd have no reason to say that he wasn't.

Parfit: On reflection I'm sure we would all think that I would survive as that one person.

Vesey: Yes.

Parfit: Yes. Well, if we now go back to the case where both operations succeed . . .

Vesey: Where there's a double success . . .

Parfit: It's clearly absurd to suppose that a double success is a failure.

Vesey: Yes.

Parfit: So the conclusion that I would draw from this case is firstly, that to the question, 'What's going to happen to me?', there's no true answer.

Vesey: Yes.

Parfit: Secondly, that if we decide to say one of the three possible answers, what we say is

going to obscure the true nature of the case.

Vesey: Yes.

Parfit: And, thirdly, the case isn't in any way puzzling. And the reason for that is this. My relation to each of the resulting people is the relation of full psychological continuity. When I'm psychologically continuous with only one person, we call it identity. But if I'm psychologically continuous with two future people, we can't call it identity. It's not puzzling because we know exactly what's going to happen.

Vesey: Yes, could I see if I've got this straight? Where there is psychological continuity in a one-one case, this is the sort of case which we'd ordinarily talk of in terms of a person having survived the operation, or something like that.

Parfit: Yes.

Vesey: Now what about when there is what you call psychological continuity—that's to say, where the people seem to remember having been me and so on—in a one-two case? Is this survival or not?

Parfit: Well, I think it's just as good as survival, but the block we have to get over is that we can't say that anyone in the world after the operation is going to be me.

Vesey: No.

Parfit: Well, we can say it but it's very implausible. And we're inclined to think that if there's not going to be anyone who is me tomorrow, then I don't survive. What we need to realize is that my relation to each of those two people is just as good as survival. Nothing is missing at all in my relation to both of them, as compared with my relation to myself tomorrow.

Vesey: Yes.

Parfit: So here we've got survival without identity. And that only seems puzzling if we think that identity is a further fact over and above psychological continuity.

Vesey: It is very hard not to think of identity being a further fact, isn't it?

Parfit: Yes, I think it is. I think that the only way to get rid of our temptation to believe this is to consider many more cases than this one case of division. Perhaps I should give you another one. Suppose that the following is going to happen to me. When I die in a normal way, scientists are going to map the states of all the cells in my brain and body and after a few months they will have constructed a perfect duplicate of me out of organic matter. And this duplicate will wake up fully psychologically continuous with me, seeming to remember my life with my character, etc.

Vesey: Yes.

Parfit: Now in this case, which is a secular version of the Resurrection, we're very inclined to think that the following question arises and is very real and very important. The question is, 'Will that person who wakes up in three months be me or will he be some quite other person who's merely artificially made to be exactly like me?'

Vesey: It does seem to be a real question. I mean in the one case, if it is going to be me, then I have expectations and so on, and in the other case, where it isn't me, I don't.

Parfit: I agree, it seems as if there couldn't be a bigger difference between it being me and it being someone else.

Vesey: But you want to say that the two possibilities are in fact the same?

Parfit: I want to say that those two descriptions, 'It's going to be me' and 'It's going to be someone who is merely exactly like me', don't describe different outcomes, different courses of events, only one of which can happen. They are two ways of describing one and the same course of events. What I mean by that perhaps could be shown if we take an exactly comparable case involving not a person but something about which I think we're not inclined to have a false view.

Vesey: Yes.

Parfit: Something like a club. Suppose there's some club in the nineteenth century . . .

Vesey: The Sherlock Holmes Club or something like that?

Parfit: Yes, perhaps. And after several years of meeting it ceases to meet. The club dies.

Vesey: Right.

Parfit: And then two of its members, let's say,

have emigrated to America, and after about fifteen years they get together and they start up a club. It has exactly the same rules, completely new membership except for the first two people, and they give it the same name. Now suppose someone came along and said: 'There's a real mystery here, because the following question is one that must have an answer. But how can we answer it?' The question is, 'Have they started up the very same club—is it the same club as the one they belonged to in England—or is it a completely new club that's just exactly similar?'

Vesey: Yes.

Parfit: Well, in that case we all think that this man's remark is absurd; there's no difference at all. Now that's my model for the true view about the case where they make a duplicate of me. It seems that there's all the difference in the world between its being me and its being this other person who's exactly like me. But if we think there's no difference at all in the case of the clubs, why do we think there's a difference in the case of personal identity, and how can we defend the view that there's a difference?

Vesey: I can see how some people would defend it. I mean, a dualist would defend it in terms of a soul being a simple thing, but . . .

Parfit: Let me try another case which I think helps to ease us out of this belief we're very strongly inclined to hold.

Vesey: Go on.

Parfit: Well, this isn't a single case, this is a whole range of cases. A whole smooth spectrum of different cases which are all very similar to the next one in the range. At the start of this range of cases you suppose that the scientists are going to replace one per cent of the cells in your brain and body with exact duplicates.

Vesey: Yes.

Parfit: Now if that were to be done, no one has any doubt that you'd survive. I think that's obvious because after all you can *lose* one per cent of the cells and survive. As we get further along the range they replace a larger and larger percentage of cells with exact duplicates, and of course at the far end of this range, where they replace a hundred per cent, then we've got my case where they just make a duplicate out of wholly fresh matter.

Vesey: Yes.

Parfit: Now on the view that there's all the difference in the world between its being me and its being this other person who is exactly like me, we ought in consistency to think that in some case in the middle of that range, where, say, they're going to replace fifty per cent, the same question arises: is it going to be me or this completely different character? I think that even the most convinced dualist who believes in the soul is going to find this range of cases very embarrassing, because he seems committed to the view that there's some crucial percentage up to which it's going to be him and after which it suddenly ceases to be him. But I find that wholly unbelievable.

Vesey: Yes. He's going to have to invent some sort of theory about the relation of mind and body to get round this one. I'm not quite sure how he would do it. Derek, could we go on to a related question? Suppose that I accepted what you said, that is, that there isn't anything more to identity than what you call psychological continuity in a one-one case. Suppose I accept that, then I would want to go on and ask you, well, what's the philosophical importance of this?

Parfit: The philosophical importance is, I think, that psychological continuity is obviously, when we think about it, a matter of degree. So long as we think that identity is a further fact, one of the things we're inclined to think is that it's all or nothing, as you said earlier. Well, if we give up that belief and if we realize that what matters in my continued existence is a matter of degree, then this does make a difference in actual cases. All the cases that I've considered so far are of course bizarre science fiction cases. But I think that in actual life it's obvious on reflection that, to give an example, the relations between me now and me next year are much closer in every way than the relations between me now

and me in twenty years. And the sorts of relations that I'm thinking of are relations of memory, character, ambition, intention—all of those. Next year I shall remember much more of this year than I will in twenty years. I shall have a much more similar character. I shall be carrying out more of the same plans, ambitions and, if that is so, I think there are various plausible implications for our moral beliefs and various possible effects on our emotions.

Vesey: For our moral beliefs? What have you in mind?

Parfit: Let's take one very simple example. On the view which I'm sketching it seems to me much more plausible to claim that people deserve much less punishment, or even perhaps no punishment, for what they did many years ago as compared with what they did very recently. Plausible because the relations between them now and them many years ago when they committed the crime are so much weaker.

Vesey: But they are still the people who are responsible for the crime.

Parfit: I think you say that because even if they've changed in many ways, after all it was just as much they who committed the crime. I think that's true, but on the view for which I'm arguing, we would come to think that it's a completely trivial truth. It's like the following truth: it's like the truth that all of my relatives are just as much my relatives. Suppose I in my will left more money to my close relatives and less to my distant relatives; a mere pittance to my second cousin twenty-nine times removed. If you said, 'But that's clearly unreasonable because all of your relatives are just as much your relatives', there's a sense in which that's true but it's obviously too trivial to make my will an unreasonable will. And that's because what's involved in kinship is a matter of degree.

Vesey: Yes.

Parfit: Now, if we think that what's involved in its being the same person now as the person who committed the crime is a matter of degree, then the truth that it was just as much him who committed the crime, will seem to us trivial in the way in which the truth that all my relatives are equally my relatives is trivial.

Vesey: Yes. So you think that I should regard myself in twenty years' time as like a fairly distant relative of myself?

Parfit: Well, I don't want to exaggerate; I think the connections are much closer.

Vesey: Suppose I said that this point about psychological continuity being a matter of degree—suppose I said that this isn't anything that anybody denies?

Parfit: I don't think anybody does on reflection deny that psychological continuity is a matter of degree. But I think what they may deny, and I think what may make a difference to their view, if they come over to the view for which I'm arguing—what they may deny is that psychological continuity is all there is to identity. Be-

cause what I'm arguing against is this further belief which I think we're all inclined to hold even if we don't realize it. The belief that however much we change, there's a profound sense in which the changed us is going to be just as much us. That even if some magic wand turned me into a completely different sort of person—a prince with totally different character, mental powers—it would be just as much me. That's what I'm denying.

Vesey: Yes. This is the belief which I began by stating, and I think that if we did lose that belief that would be a change indeed.

NOTES

1. *Sunday Times*, 9 December, 1973, p. 13.
2. Shoemaker (1963) pp. 23–4.
3. Parfit (1971) p. 15.

For Further Reflection

1. Is Parfit's analysis of the problem of the split-brain case plausible? Do you think that he correctly construes the issue or does he already presuppose controversial premises?

2. Do you think that there is another solution to the problem of personal identity?

Is There Life After Death? Am I Immortal?

Suppose the ingenious neurologist Dr. Thomas were to design a brain just like yours in his laboratory, and suppose he were to design a body like yours but virtually indestructible (well, a nuclear bomb could destroy it, but failing that it would be impervious to alteration). The brain is now dormant, but at your death, Dr. Thomas will activate it and bring it to life within the prosthetic body. Now Thomas tells you that he needs to kill you to allow your alter ego to exist. You complain, but Thomas assures you that one exactly similar to you will live again with all your memories (or copies of them, but Alter Ego won't know the difference). Would you be comforted by that news? Would you take comfort in the fact that you will live again?

Where does all of this leave us with regard to survival after death? If there is no continuity of consciousness, is it the same person who would be resurrected or reconstituted by God at some future time? Or is the reconstituted person like Thomas' replica of you? A different token of the same generic type? Could God make several tokens of your type—say, five of you—which could be reconstituted and go on to live a new and eternal life? Quintuple resurrection!

Are the disembodied memories of a person enough to constitute survival? The question is perplexing. On the one hand, it seems that our identity is somehow tied to our psychological states (e.g., memories and personality traits), which don't seem to depend on a body. But, then, if this is so, would our survival occur if a computer stored much of the information about our personalities and memory states?

We seem to need a body and brain to instantiate our consciousness and personalities. It is hard to imagine any learning or experiencing or communication with others without a recognizable body. And the brain seems to be the locus of conscious experience. But our bodies and brains die and disintegrate. What happens to our consciousness and our personal identity? Is the gap between the present conscious life and the next simply like a long sleep during which God prepares a new and glorified body for our personality? Or does the fact that there will have to be a new creation rule out the possibility of personal survival altogether? Or can it be that there is an intrinsically spiritual character to our selves which both survives the death of the body and perdures in a life beyond this one?

The issue is as difficult as it is important to us. In this section our first reading from Plato's *Phaedo* sets forth a view of the soul that is separate and of infinitely higher value than the body. The soul is good and the body evil. The body is really an encumbrance of the soul, which longs to be liberated from it. Death releases the soul from the body so that it can attain a wholly spiritual existence devoid of evil. In our second reading, John Perry uses a dialogue to highlight the problems involved in our notion of personal identity and immortality. In our third reading, Bertrand Russell challenges the notion of survival after death and argues that it is essentially incoherent. In our fourth reading John Hick responds to those who say that personal immortality is impossible. He sets forth conditions for justifying our belief in survival and shows that those conditions could be met. According to Hick, there is nothing incoherent about the notion of immortality.

Arguments for the Immortality of the Soul   IV.8

PLATO

Plato (427–347 B.C.) believed that human beings were composed of two substances, a body and a soul. Of these, the true self is the soul, which lives on after the death of the body. All of Plato's writings are in the form of dialogues. In the first dialogue (from *Alcibiades I*) Socrates argues with Alcibiades about the true self. The second dialogue (from the *Phaedo*) takes place in prison, where Socrates has been condemned to die. He is offered a way of escape but rejects it, arguing that it would be immoral to flee such a fate at this time and that he is certain of a better life after death.

Study Questions

1. How does Socrates argue in *Alcibiades I* for the reality of the soul?
2. In the *Phaedo,* what is the role of the body with regard to attaining knowledge? What should the philosopher do about the body?
3. What is the significance in the argument of ideas such as absolute justice and beauty?
4. What is the attitude of the true philosopher towards death, and why?
5. How does Plato describe the process that leads to the attainment of wisdom?
6. How does the soul resemble the divine?

From Alcibiades I

SOC.: AND IS SELF-KNOWLEDGE an easy thing, and was he to be lightly esteemed who inscribed the text on the temple at Delphi? Or is self-knowledge a difficult thing, which few are able to attain?

Al.: At times, I fancy, Socrates, that anybody can know him self; at other times, the task appears to be very difficult.

Soc.: But whether easy or difficult, Alcibiades, still there is no other way; knowing what we are, we shall know how to take care of ourselves, and if we are ignorant we shall not know.

Al.: That is true.

Soc.: Well, then, let us see in what way the self-existent can be discovered by us; that will give us a chance to discovering our own existence, which without that we can never know.

Al.: You say truly.

Soc.: Come, now, I beseech you, tell me with whom you are conversing?—with whom but with me?

Al.: Yes.

Soc.: As I am with you?

Al.: Yes.

Soc.: That is to say, I, Socrates, am talking?

Al.: Yes.

Soc.: And I in talking use words?

Al.: Certainly.

Soc.: And talking and using words are, as you would say, the same?

Al.: Very true.

Soc.: And the user is not the same as the thing which he uses?

Al.: What do you mean?

Soc.: I will explain: the shoemaker, for example, uses a square tool, and a circular tool, and other tools for cutting?

Al.: Yes.

Soc.: But the tool is not the same as the cutter and user of the tool?

Al.: Of course not.

Soc.: And in the same way the instrument of the harper is to be distinguished from the harper himself?

Al.: He is.

Soc.: Now the question which I asked was whether you conceive the user to be always different from that which he uses?

Al.: I do.

Soc.: Then what shall we say of the shoemaker? Does he cut with his tools only or with his hands?

Al.: With his hands as well.

Soc.: He uses his hands too?

Al.: Yes.

Soc.: And does he use his eyes in cutting leather?

Al.: He does.

Soc.: And we admit that the user is not the same with the things which he uses?

Al.: Yes.

Soc.: Then the shoemaker and the harper are to be distinguished from the hands and feet which they use?

Al.: That is clear.

Soc.: And does not a man use the whole body?

Al.: Certainly.

Reprinted from Alcibiades I *and the* Phaedo, *translated by William Jowett (New York: Charles Scribner's Sons, 1889).*

Soc.: And that which uses is different from that which is used?

Al.: True.

Soc.: Then a man is not the same as his own body?

Al.: That is the inference.

Soc.: What is he, then?

Al.: I cannot say.

Soc.: Nay, you can say that he is the user of the body.

Al.: Yes.

Soc.: And the user of the body is the soul?

Al.: Yes, the soul.

Soc.: And the soul rules?

Al.: Yes.

Soc.: Let me make an assertion which will, I think, be universally admitted.

Al.: What is that?

Soc.: That man is one of three things.

Al.: What are they?

Soc.: Soul, body, or the union of the two.

Al.: Certainly.

Soc.: But did we not say that the actual ruling principle of the body is man?

Al.: Yes, we did.

Soc.: And does the body rule over itself?

Al.: Certainly not.

Soc.: It is subject, as we were saying?

Al.: Yes.

Soc.: Then that is not what we are seeking?

Al.: It would seem not.

Soc.: But may we say that the union or the two rules over the body, and consequently that this is man?

Al.: Very likely.

Soc.: The most unlikely of all things: for if one of the members is subject, the two united cannot possibly rule.

Al.: True.

Soc.: But since neither the body, nor the union of the two, is man, either man has no real existence, or the soul is man?

Al.: Just so.

Soc.: Would you have a more precise proof that the soul is man?

Al.: No; I think that the proof is sufficient.

Soc.: If the proof, although not quite precise, is fair, that is enough for us; more precise proof will be supplied when we have discovered that which we were led to omit, from a fear that the inquiry would be too much protracted.

Al.: What was that?

Soc.: What I meant, when I said that absolute existence must be first considered; but now, instead of absolute existence, we have been considering the nature of individual existence, and that may be sufficient; for surely there is nothing belonging to us which has more absolute existence than the soul?

Al.: There is nothing.

Soc.: Then we may truly conceive that you and I are conversing with one another, soul to soul?

Al.: Very true.

Soc.: And that is just what I was saying—that I, Socrates, am not arguing or talking with the face of Alcibiades, but with the real Alcibiades; and that is with his soul.

Al.: True. . . .

From the Phaedo

Socrates: What again shall we say of the actual acquirement of knowledge?—is the body, if invited to share in the inquiry, a hinderer or a helper? I mean to say, have sight and hearing any truth in them? Are they not, as the poets are always telling us, inaccurate witnesses? and yet, if even they are inaccurate and indistinct, what is to be said of the other senses?—for you will allow that they are the best of them?

Certainly, he replied.

Then when does the soul attain truth?—for in attempting to consider anything in company with the body she is obviously deceived.

Yes, that is true.

Then must not existence be revealed to her in thought, if at all?

Yes.

And thought is best when the mind is gathered into herself and none of these things trouble her—neither sounds nor sights nor pain nor any pleasure,—when she has as little as possible to do with the body, and has no bodily sense of feeling, but is aspiring after being?

That is true.

And in this the philosopher dishonors the body; his soul runs away from the body and desires to be alone and by herself?

That is true.

Well, but there is another thing, Simmias: Is there or is there not an absolute justice?

Assuredly there is.

And an absolute beauty and absolute good?

Of course.

But did you ever behold any of them with your eyes?

Certainly not.

Or did you ever reach them with any other bodily sense? (and I speak not of these alone, but of absolute greatness, and health, and strength, and of the essence of true nature of everything). Has the reality of them ever been perceived by you through the bodily organs? or rather, is not the nearest approach to the knowledge of their several natures made by him who so orders his intellectual vision as to have the most exact conception of the essence of that which he considers?

Certainly.

And he attains to the knowledge of them in their highest purity who goes to each of them with the mind alone, not allowing when in the act of thought the intrusion or introduction of sight or any other sense in the company of reason, but with the very light of the mind in her clearness penetrates into the very light of truth in each; he has got rid, as far as he can, of eyes and ears and of the whole body, which he conceives of only as a disturbing element, hindering the soul from the acquisition of knowledge when in company with her—is not this the sort of man who, if ever man did, is likely to attain the knowledge of existence?

There is admirable truth in that, Socrates, replied Simmias.

And when they consider all this, must not true philosophers make a reflection, of which

they will speak to one another in such words as these: We have found, they will say, a path of speculation which seems to bring us and the argument to the conclusion, that while we are in the body, and while the soul is mingled with this mass of evil, our desire will not be satisfied, and our desire is of the truth. For the body is a source of endless trouble to us by reason of the mere requirement of food; and also is liable to diseases which overtake and impede us in the search after truth: and by filling us so full of loves, and lusts, and fears, and fancies, and idols, and every sort of folly, prevents our ever having, as people say, so much as a thought. From whence come wars, and fightings, and factions? whence but from the body and the lusts of the body? For wars are occasioned by the love of money, and money has to be acquired for the sake and in the service of the body; and in consequence of all these things the time which ought to be given to philosophy is lost. Moreover, if there is time and an inclination toward philosophy, yet the body introduces a turmoil and confusion and fear into the course of speculation, and hinders us from seeing the truth, and all experience shows that if we would have pure knowledge of anything we must be quit of the body, and the soul in herself must behold all things in themselves: then I suppose that we shall attain that which we desire, and of which we say that we are lovers, and that is wisdom; not while we live, but after death, as the argument shows; for if while in company with the body, the soul cannot have pure knowledge, one of two things seems to follow—either knowledge is not to be attained at all, or, if at all, after death. For then, and not till then, the soul will be in herself alone and without the body. In this present life, I reckon that we make the nearest approach to knowledge when we have the least possible concern or interest in the body, and are not saturated with the bodily nature, but remain pure until the hour when God himself is pleased to release us. And then the foolishness of the body will be cleared away and we shall be pure and hold converse with other pure souls, and know of ourselves the clear light everywhere; and this is surely the light of truth. For no impure thing is allowed to approach the pure. These are the sort of words, Simmias, which the true lovers of wisdom cannot help saying to one another, and thinking. You will agree with me in that?

Certainly, Socrates.

But if this is true, O my friend, then there is great hope that, going whither I go, I shall there be satisfied with that which has been the chief concern of you and me in our past lives. And now that the hour of departure is appointed to me, this is the hope with which I depart, and not I only, but every man who believes that he has his mind purified.

Certainly, replied Simmias.

And what is purification but the separation of the soul from the body, as I was saying before; the habit of the soul gathering and collecting herself into herself, out of all the courses of the body; the dwelling in her own place alone, as in another life, so also in this, as far as she can; the release of the soul from the chains of the body?

Very true, he said.

And what is that which is termed death, but this very separation and release of the soul from the body?

To be sure, he said.

And the true philosophers, and they only, study and are eager to release the soul. Is not the separation and release of the soul from the body their especial study?

That is true.

And as I was saying at first, there would be a ridiculous contradiction in men studying to live as nearly as they can in a state of death, and yet repining when death comes.

Certainly.

Then Simmias, as the true philosophers are ever studying death, to them, of all men, death is the least terrible. Look at the matter in this way: how inconsistent of them to have been always enemies of the body, and wanting to have the soul alone, and when this is granted to them, to be trembling and repining; instead of rejoicing at their departing to that place where, when they arrive, they hope to gain that which in life they loved (and this was wisdom), and at the same time to be rid of the company of their enemy. Many a man has been willing to go to the world below in the hope of seeing there an earthly love, or wife, or son, and conversing with them. And will he who is a true lover of wisdom, and is persuaded in like manner that only in the world below he can worthily enjoy her, still repine at death? Will he not depart with joy? Surely, he will, my friend, if he be a true philosopher. For he will have a firm conviction that there only, and nowhere else, he can find wisdom in her purity. And if this be true, he would be very absurd, as I was saying, if he were to fear death. . . .

Socrates: And were we not saying long ago that the soul when using the body as an instrument of perception, that is to say, when using the sense of sight or hearing or some other sense (for the meaning of perceiving through the body is perceiving through the senses),—were we not saying that the soul too is then dragged by the body into the region of the changeable, and wanders and is confused; the world spins round her, and she is like a drunkard when under their influence?

Very true.

But when returning into herself she reflects; then she passes into the realm of purity, and eternity, and immortality, and unchangeableness, which are her kindred, and with them she ever lives, when she is by herself and is not let or hindered; then she ceases from her erring ways, and being in communion with the unchanging is unchanging. And this state of the soul is called wisdom?

That is well and truly said, Socrates, he replied.

And to which class is the soul more nearly alike and akin, as far as may be inferred from this argument, as well as from the preceding one?

I think, Socrates, that, in the opinion of every one who follows the argument, the soul will be infinitely more like the unchangeable,—even the most stupid person will not deny that.

And the body is more like the changing?

Yes.

Yet once more consider the matter in this light: When the soul and the body are united, then nature orders the soul to rule and govern, and the body to obey and serve. Now which of these two functions is akin to the divine? and which to the mortal? Does not the divine appear to you to be that which naturally orders and rules, and the mortal that which is subject and servant?

True.

And which does the soul resemble?

The soul resembles the divine, and the body the mortal—there can be no doubt of that, Socrates.

Then reflect, Cebes: is not the conclusion of the whole matter this,—that the soul is in the very likeness of the divine, and immortal, and intelligible, and uniform, and indissoluble, and unchangeable; and the body is in the very likeness of the human, and mortal, and unintelligible, and multiform, and dissoluble, and changeable. Can this, my dear Cebes, be denied?

No indeed.

But if this is true, then is not the body liable to speedy dissolution? and is not the soul almost or altogether indissoluble?

Certainly.

And do you further observe, that after a man is dead, the body, which is the visible part of man, and has a visible framework, which is called a corpse, and which would naturally be dissolved and decomposed and dissipated, is not dissolved or decomposed at once, but may remain for a good while, if the constitution be sound at the time of death, and the season of the year favorable? For the body when shrunk and embalmed, as is the custom in Egypt, may remain almost entire through infinite ages; and even in decay, still there are some portions, such as the bones and ligaments, which are practically indestructible. You allow that?

Yes.

And are we to suppose that the soul, which is invisible, in passing to the true Hades, which like her is invisible, and pure, and noble, and on her way to the good and wise God, whither, if God will, my soul is also soon to go,—that the soul, I repeat, if this be her nature and origin, is blown away and perishes immediately on quitting the body, as the many say? That can never be, my dear Simmias and Cebes. The truth rather is, that the soul which is pure at departing draws after her no bodily taint, having never voluntarily had connection with the body, which she is ever avoiding, herself gathered into herself (for such abstraction has been the study of her life). And what does this mean but that she has been a true disciple of philosophy, and has practiced how to die easily? And is not philosophy the practice of death?

Certainly.

That soul, I say, herself invisible, departs to the invisible world,—to the divine and immortal and rational: thither arriving, she lives in bliss and is released from the error and folly of men, their fears and wild passions and all other human ills, and forever dwells, as they say of the initiated, in company with the gods? Is not this true, Cebes?

Yes, said Cebes, beyond a doubt.

For Further Reflection

1. Are Plato's arguments in these two dialogues persuasive? Do the arguments depend overly much on his theory of the forms, which gives ideas separate existence?

2. Is Plato correct in thinking that the body always hinders pure thought? How might a contemporary materialist respond to Plato?

A Dialogue on Personal Identity and Immortality   IV.9

JOHN PERRY

John Perry is a professor of philosophy at Stanford University and has written extensively on the mind-body problem, and especially on personal identity.

In this fictional dialogue Sam Miller, a Christian chaplain, tries to convince Gretchen Weirob, a philosopher in a small midwestern college who is dying of injuries sustained in an accident, that there are good reasons to believe in life after death. The arguments are similar to those of John Locke (reading IV.5). Weirob counters that there are too many difficulties with the notion of personal identity to allow that thesis any credence. David Cohen is a former student of hers. The conversation takes place in Weirob's hospital room.

Study Questions

1. What does Weirob ask Miller to do in his argument? What sort of results would satisfy her and why?

2. How does Weirob define survival?

3. What does the example of the Kleenex box illustrate?

4. What is the difference between the concepts "identical" and "exactly similar," and how does it function in the argument?

5. What does Miller believe about personal identity? What are the problems with Miller's position, according to Weirob?

COHEN: I CAN HARDLY BELIEVE what you say, Gretchen. You are lucid and do not appear to be in great pain. And yet you say things are hopeless?

Weirob: These devices can keep me alive for another day or two at most. Some of my vital organs have been injured beyond anything the doctors know how to repair, apart from certain rather radical measures I have rejected. I am not in much pain. But as I understand it that is not a particularly good sign. My brain was uninjured and I guess that's why I am as lucid as I ever am. The whole situation is a bit depressing, I fear.

But here's Sam Miller. Perhaps he will know how to cheer me up.

Miller: Good evening, Gretchen. Hello, Dave. I guess there's not much point in beating around the bush, Gretchen; the medics tell me you're a goner. Is there anything I can do to help?

Weirob: Crimenetley, Sam! You deal with the dying every day. Don't you have anything more comforting to say than "Sorry to hear you're a goner"?

Miller: Well, to tell you the truth, I'm a little at a loss for what to say to you. Most people I deal with are believers like I am. We talk of the prospects for survival. I give assurance that God, who is just and merciful, would not permit such a travesty as that our short life on this earth should be the end of things. But you and I have talked about religious and philosophical issues for years. I have never been able to find in you the least inclination to believe in God; indeed, it's a rare day when you are sure that your friends have minds, or that you can see your own hand in front of your face, or that there is any reason to believe that the sun will rise tomorrow. How can I hope to comfort you with the prospect of life after death, when I know you will regard it as having no probability whatsoever?

Weirob: I would not require so much to be comforted, Sam. Even the possibility of something quite improbable can be comforting, in certain situations. When we used to play tennis, I beat you no more than one time in twenty. But this was enough to establish the possibility of beating you on any given occasion, and by focusing merely on the possibility I remained eager to play. Entombed in a secure prison, thinking our situation quite hopeless, we may find unutterable joy in the information that there is, after all, the slimmest possibility of escape. Hope provides comfort, and hope does not always require probability. But we must believe that what we hope for is at least possible. So I will set an easier task for you. Simply persuade me that my survival after the death of this body, is *possible,* and I promise to be comforted. Whether you succeed or not, your attempts will be a diversion, for you know I like to talk philosophy more than anything else.

Miller: But what is possibility, if not reasonable probability?

Weirob: I do not mean possible in the sense of likely, or even in the sense of conforming to the known laws of physics or biology. I mean possible only in the weakest sense—of being conceivable, given the unavoidable facts. Within the next couple of days, this body will die. It will be buried and it will rot away. I ask that, given these facts, you explain to me how it even makes *sense* to talk of me continuing to exist. Just ex-

plain to me what it is I am to *imagine,* when I imagine surviving, that is consistent with these facts, and I shall be comforted.

Miller: But then what is there to do? There are many conceptions of immortality, of survival past the grave, which all seem to make good sense. Surely not the possibility, but only the probability, can be doubted. Take your choice! Christians believe in life, with a body, in some Hereafter—the details vary, of course, from sect to sect. There is the Greek idea of the body as a prison, from which we escape at death—so that we have continued life without a body. Then there are conceptions in which, so to speak, we merge with the flow of being—

Weirob: I must cut short your lesson in comparative religion. Survival means surviving, no more, no less. I have no doubts that I shall merge with being; plants will take root in my remains, and the chemicals that I am will continue to make their contribution to life. I am enough of an ecologist to be comforted. But survival, if it is anything, must offer comforts of a different sort, the comforts of *anticipation.* Survival means that tomorrow, or sometime in the future, there will be someone who will experience, who will see and touch and smell—or at the very least, think and reason and remember. And this person will be *me.* This person will be related to me in such a way that it is correct for me to anticipate, to look forward to, those future experiences. And I am related to her in such a way that it will be right for her to remember what I have thought and done, to feel remorse for what I have done wrong, and pride in what I have done right. And the only relation that supports anticipation and memory in this way, is simply *identity.* For it is never correct to anticipate, as happening to oneself, what will happen to someone else, is it? Or to remember, as one's own thoughts and deeds, what someone else did? So don't give me merger with being, or some such nonsense. Give me identity, or let's talk about baseball or fishing— but I'm sorry to get so emotional. I react strongly when words which mean one thing are used for another—when one talks about survival, but does not mean to say that the same person will continue to exist. It's such a sham!

Miller: I'm sorry. I was just trying to stay in touch with the times, if you want to know the truth, for when I read modern theology or talk to my students who have studied Eastern religions, the notion of survival simply as continued existence of the same person seems out of date. Merger with Being! Merger with Being! That's all I hear. My own beliefs are quite simple, if somewhat vague. I think you will live again—with or without a body, I don't know—*I* draw comfort from my belief that you and I will be together again, after I also die. We will communicate, somehow. We will continue to grow spiritually. That's what I believe, as surely as I believe that I am sitting here. For I don't know how God could be excused, if this small sample of life is all that we are allotted; I don't know why He should have created us, if these few years of toil and torment are the end of it—

Weirob: Remember our deal, Sam. You don't have to convince me that survival is probable, for we both agree you would not get to first base. You have only to convince me that it is possible. The only condition is that it be real survival we are talking about, not some up-to-date ersatz survival, which simply amounts to what any ordinary person would call totally ceasing to exist.

Miller: I guess I just miss the problem, then. Of course, it's possible. You just continue to exist, after your body dies. What's to be defended or explained? You want details? Okay. Two people meet a thousand years from now, in a place that may or may not be part of this physical universe. I am one and you are the other. So you must have survived. Surely you can imagine that. What else is there to say?

Weirob: But in a few days *I* will quit breathing, *I* will be put into a coffin, *I* will be buried. And in a few months or in a few years *I* will be reduced to so much humus. That, I take it, is obvious, is given. How then can you say that I am one of these persons a thousand years from now?

Suppose I took this box of Kleenex and lit fire to it. It is reduced to ashes and I smash the ashes and flush them down the john. Then I say to you, go home and on the shelf will be *that very box of Kleenex*. It has survived! Wouldn't that be absurd? What sense could you make of it? And yet that is just what you say to me. I will rot away. And then, a thousand years later, there I will be. What sense does that make?

Miller: There could be an *identical* box of Kleenex at your home, one just like it in every respect. And, in this sense, there is no difficulty in there being someone identical to you in the Hereafter, though your body has rotted away.

Weirob: You are playing with words again. There could be an *exactly similar* box of Kleenex on my shelf. We sometimes use "identical" to mean "exactly similar," as when we speak of "identical twins." But I am using "identical" in a way in which *identity* is the condition of memory and correct anticipation. If I am told that tomorrow, though I will be dead, someone else that looks and sounds and thinks just like me will be alive—would that be comforting? Could I correctly *anticipate* having her experiences? Would it make sense for me to fear her pains and look forward to her pleasures? Would it be right for her to feel remorse at the harsh way I am treating you? Of course not. Similarity, however exact, is not identity. I use identity to mean there is but one thing. If I am to survive, there must be one person who lies in this bed now, and who talks to someone in your Hereafter ten or a thousand years from now. After all, what comfort could there be in the notion of a heavenly imposter, walking around getting credit for the few good things I have done?

Miller: I'm sorry. I see that I was simply confused. Here is what I should have said. If you were merely a live human body—as the Kleenex box is merely cardboard and glue in a certain arrangement—then the death of your body would be the end of you. But surely you are more than that, fundamentally more than that. What is fundamentally you is not your body, but your soul or self or mind.

Weirob: Do you mean these words, "soul," "self," or "mind" to come to the same thing?

Miller: Perhaps distinctions could be made, but I shall not pursue them now. I mean the nonphysical and nonmaterial aspects of you, your consciousness. It is this that I get at with these words, and I don't think any further distinction is relevant.

Weirob: Consciousness? I am conscious, for a while yet. I see, I hear, I think, I remember. But "to be conscious"—that is a verb. What is the subject of the verb, the thing which is conscious? Isn't it just this body, the same object that is overweight, injured, and lying in bed?—and which will be buried and not be conscious in a day or a week at the most?

Miller: As you are a philosopher, I would expect you to be less muddled about these issues. Did Descartes not draw a clear distinction between the body and the mind, between that which is overweight, and that which is conscious? Your mind or soul is immaterial, lodged in your body while you are on earth. The two are intimately related but not identical. Now clearly, what concerns us in survival is your mind or soul. It is this which must be identical to the person before me now, and to the one I expect to see in a thousand years in heaven.

Weirob: So I am not really this body, but a soul or mind or spirit? And this soul cannot be seen or felt or touched or smelt? That is implied, I take it, by the fact that it is immaterial?

Miller: That's right. Your soul sees and smells, but cannot be seen or smelt.

Weirob: Let me see if I understand you. You would admit that I am the very same person with whom you had lunch last week at Dorsey's?

Miller: Of course you are.

Weirob: Now when you say I am the same person, if I understand you, that is not a remark about this body you see and could touch and I fear can smell. Rather it is a remark about a soul, which you cannot see or touch or smell. The fact that the same body that now lies in front of you on the bed was across the table from you at Dorsey's—that would not mean that the same *person* was present on both occasions, if the same soul

were not. And if, through some strange turn of events, the same soul were present on both occasions, but lodged in different bodies, then it *would* be the same person. Is that right?

Miller: You have understood me perfectly. But surely, you understood all of this before!

Weirob: But wait. I can repeat it, but I'm not sure I understand it. If you cannot see or touch or in any way perceive my soul, what makes you think the one you are confronted with now *is* the very same soul you were confronted with at Dorsey's?

Miller: But I just explained. To say it is the same soul and to say it is the same person, are the same. And, of course, you are the same person you were before. Who else would you be if not yourself? You *were* Gretchen Weirob, and you *are* Gretchen Weirob.

Weirob: But how do you know you are talking to Gretchen Weirob at all, and not someone else, say Barbara Walters or even Mark Spitz!

Miller: Well, it's just obvious. I can see who I am talking to.

Weirob: But all you can see is my body. You can see, perhaps, that the same body is before you now that was before you last week at Dorsey's. But you have just said that Gretchen Weirob is not a body but a soul. In judging that the same person is before you now as was before you then, you must be making a judgment about souls—which, you said, cannot be seen or touched or smelt or tasted. And so, I repeat, how do you know?

Miller: Well, I *can* see that it is the same body before me now that was across the table at Dorsey's. And I know that the same soul is connected with the body now that was connected with it before. That's how I know it's you. I see no difficulty in the matter.

Weirob: You reason on the principle, "Same body, same self."

Miller: Yes.

Weirob: And would you reason conversely also? If there were in this bed Barbara Walters' body—that is, the body you see every night on the news—would you infer that it was not me, Gretchen Weirob, in the bed?

Miller: Of course I would. How would you have come by Barbara Walters' body?

Weirob: But then merely extend this principle to Heaven, and you will see that your conception of survival is without sense. Surely this very body, which will be buried and as I must so often repeat, *rot away,* will not be in your Hereafter. Different body, different person. Or do you claim that a body can rot away on earth, and then still wind up somewhere else? Must I bring up the Kleenex box again?

Miller: No, I do not claim that. But I also do not extend a principle, found reliable on earth, to such a different situation as is represented by the Hereafter. That a correlation between bodies and souls has been found on earth does not make it inconceivable or impossible that they should separate. Principles found to work in one circumstance may not be assumed to work in vastly altered circumstances. January and snow go together here, and one would be a fool to expect otherwise. But the principle does not apply in southern California.

Weirob: So the principle, "same body, same soul," is a well-confirmed regularity, not something you know "a priori."

Miller: By "a priori" you philosophers mean something which can be known without observing what actually goes on in the world—as I can know that two plus two equals four just by thinking about numbers, and that no bachelors are married, just by thinking about the meaning of "bachelor"?

Weirob: Yes.

Miller: Then you are right. If it was part of the meaning of "same body" that wherever we have the same body we have the same soul, it would have to obtain universally, in Heaven as well as on earth. But I just claim it is a generalization we know by observation on earth, and it need not automatically extend to Heaven.

Weirob: But where do you get this principle? It simply amounts to a correlation between be-

ing confronted with the same body and being confronted with the same soul. To establish such a correlation in the first place, surely one must have some *other* means of judging sameness of soul. You do not have such a means; your principle is without foundation; either you really do not know the person before you now is Gretchen Weirob, the very same person you lunched with at Dorsey's, or what you do know has nothing to do with sameness of some immaterial soul.

Miller: Hold on, hold on. You know I can't follow you when you start spitting out arguments like that. Now what is this terrible fallacy I'm supposed to have committed?

Weirob: I'm sorry. I get carried away. Here— by way of a peace offering—have one of the chocolates Dave brought.

Miller: Very tasty. Thank you.

Weirob: Now why did you choose that one?

Miller: Because it had a certain swirl on the top which shows that it is a caramel.

Weirob: That is, a certain sort of swirl is correlated with a certain type of filling—the swirls with caramel, the rosettes with orange, and so forth.

Miller: Yes. When you put it that way, I see an analogy. Just as I judged that the filling would be the same in this piece as in the last piece that I ate with such a swirl, so I judge that the soul with which I am conversing is the same as the last soul with which I conversed when sitting across from that body. We *see* the outer wrapping and infer what is inside.

Weirob: But how did you come to realize that swirls of that sort and caramel insides were so associated?

Miller: Why, from eating a great many of them over the years. Whenever I bit into a candy with that sort of swirl, it was filled with caramel.

Weirob: Could you have established the correlation had you never been allowed to bite into a candy and never seen what happened when someone else bit into one? You could have formed the hypothesis, "same swirl, same filling." But could you have ever established it?

Miller: It seems not.

Weirob: So your inference, in a particular case, to the identity of filling from the identity of swirl would be groundless?

Miller: Yes, it would. I think I see what is coming.

Weirob: I'm sure you do. Since you can never, so to speak, bite into my soul, can never see or touch it, you have no way of testing your hypothesis that sameness of body means sameness of self.

Miller: I daresay you are right. But now I'm a bit lost. What is supposed to follow from all of this?

Weirob: If, as you claim, identity of persons consisted in identity of immaterial unobservable souls, then judgments of personal identity of the sort we make every day whenever we greet a friend or avoid a pest are really judgments about such souls.

Miller: Right.

Weirob: But if such judgments were really about souls, they would all be groundless and without foundation. For we have no direct method of observing sameness of soul, and so— and this is the point made by the candy example—we can have no indirect method either.

Miller: That seems fair.

Weirob: But our judgments about persons are not all simply groundless and silly, so we must not be judging of immaterial souls after all.

Miller: Your reasoning has some force. But I suspect the problem lies in my defense of my position, and not the position itself. Look here— there *is* a way to test the hypothesis of a correlation after all. When I entered the room, I expected you to react just as you did—argumentatively and skeptically. Had the person with this body reacted completely differently perhaps I would have been forced to conclude it was not you. For example, had she complained about not being able to appear on the six o'clock news, and missing Harry Reasoner, and so forth, I might eventually have been persuaded it *was* Barbara

Walters and not you. Similarity of psychological characteristics—a person's attitudes, beliefs, memories, prejudices, and the like—is observable. These are correlated with identity of body on the one side, and of course with sameness of soul on the other. So the correlation between body and soul can be established after all by this intermediate link.

Weirob: And how do you know that?

Miller: Know what?

Weirob: That where we have sameness of psychological characteristics, we have sameness of soul.

Miller: Well, now you are really being just silly. The soul or mind is just that which is responsible for one's character, memory, belief. These are aspects of the mind, just as one's height, weight, and appearance are aspects of the body.

Weirob: Let me grant for the sake of argument that belief, character, memory, and so forth are states of mind. That is, I suppose, I grant that what one thinks and feels is due to the states one's mind is in at that time. And I shall even grant that a mind is an immaterial thing—though I harbor the gravest doubts that this is so. I do not see how it follows that similarity of such traits requires, or is evidence to the slightest degree, for identity of the mind or soul.

Let me explain my point with an analogy. If we were to walk out of this room, down past the mill and out towards Wilbur, what would we see?

Miller: We would come to the Blue River, among other things.

Weirob: And how would you recognize the Blue River? I mean, of course if you left from here, you would scarcely expect to hit the Platte or Niobrara. But suppose you were actually lost, and came across the Blue River in your wandering, just at that point where an old dam partly blocks the flow. Couldn't you recognize it?

Miller: Yes, I'm sure as soon as I saw that part of the river I would again know where I was.

Weirob: And how would you recognize it?

Miller: Well, the turgid brownness of the

water, the sluggish flow, the filth washed up on the banks, and such.

Weirob: In a word, the states of the water which makes up the river at the time you see it.

Miller: Right.

Weirob: If you saw blue clean water, with bass jumping, you would know it wasn't the Blue River.

Miller: Of course.

Weirob: So you expect, each time you see the Blue, to see the water, which makes it up, in similar states—not always exactly the same, for sometimes it's a little dirtier, but by and large similar.

Miller: Yes, but what do you intend to make of this?

Weirob: Each time you see the Blue, it consists of *different* water. The water that was in it a month ago may be in Tuttle Creek Reservoir or in the Mississippi or in the Gulf of Mexico by now. So the *similarity* of states of water, by which you judge the sameness of river, does not require *identity* of the water which is in those states at these various times.

Miller: And?

Weirob: And so just because you judge as to personal identity by reference to similarity of states of mind, it does not follow that the mind, or soul, is the same in each case. My point is this. For all you know, the immaterial soul which you think is lodged in my body might change from day to day, from hour to hour, from minute to minute, replaced each time by another soul psychologically similar. You cannot see it or touch it, so how would you know?

Miller: Are you saying I don't really know who you are?

Weirob: Not at all. *You* are the one who say personal identity consists in sameness of this immaterial, unobservable, invisible, untouchable soul. I merely point out that *if* it did consist in that, you *would* have no idea who I am. Sameness of body would not necessarily mean sameness of person. Sameness of psychological char-

acteristics would not necessarily mean sameness of person. I am saying that if you do know who I am then you are wrong that personal identity consists in sameness of immaterial soul.

Miller: I see. But wait. I believe my problem is that I simply forgot a main tenet of my theory. The correlation can be established in my own case. I know that *my* soul and my body are intimately and consistently found together. From this one case I can generalize, at least as concerns life in this world, that sameness of body is a reliable sign of sameness of soul. This leaves me free to regard it as intelligible, in the case of death, that the link between the particular soul and the particular body it has been joined with is broken.

Weirob: This would be quite an extrapolation, wouldn't it, from one case directly observed, to a couple of billion in which only the body is observed? For I take it that we are in the habit of assuming, for every person now on earth, as well as those who have already come and gone, that the principle "one body, one soul" is in effect.

Miller: This does not seem an insurmountable obstacle. Since there is nothing special about my case, I assume the arrangement I find in it applies universally until given some reason to believe otherwise. And I never have been.

Weirob: Let's let that pass. I have another problem that is more serious. How is it that you know in your own case that there is a single soul which has been so consistently connected with your body?

Miller: Now you really cannot be serious, Gretchen. How can I doubt that I am the same person I was? Is there anything more clear and distinct, less susceptible to doubt? How do you expect me to prove anything to you, when you are capable of denying my own continued existence from second to second? Without knowledge of our own identity, everything we think and do would be senseless. How could I think if I did not suppose that the person who begins my thought is the one who completes it? When I act, do I not assume that the person who forms the intention is the very one who performs the action?

Weirob: But I grant you that a single *person* has been associated with your body since you were born. The question is whether one immaterial soul has been so associated—or more precisely, whether you are in a position to know it. You believe that a judgment that one and the same person has had your body all these many years is a judgment that one and the same immaterial soul has been lodged in it. I say that such judgments concerning the soul are totally mysterious, and that if our knowledge of sameness of persons consisted in knowledge of sameness of immaterial soul, it too would be totally mysterious. To point out, as you do, that it is not mysterious, but perhaps the most secure knowledge we have, the foundation of all reason and action, is simply to make the point that it cannot consist of knowledge of identity of an immaterial soul.

Miller: You have simply asserted, and not established, that my judgment that a single soul has been lodged in my body these many years is mysterious.

Weirob: Well, consider these possibilities. One is that a single soul, one and the same, has been with this body I call mine since it was born. The other is that one soul was associated with it until five years ago and then another, psychologically similar, inheriting all the old memories and beliefs, took over. A third hypothesis is that every five years a new soul takes over. A fourth is that every five minutes a new soul takes over. The most radical is that there is a constant flow of souls through this body, each psychologically similar to the preceding, as there is a constant flow of water molecules down the Blue. What evidence do I have that the first hypothesis, the "single soul hypothesis" is true, and not one of the others? Because I am the same person I was five minutes or five years ago? But the issue in question is simply whether from sameness of person, which isn't in doubt, we can infer sameness of soul. Sameness of body? But how do I establish a stable relationship between soul and body? Sameness of thoughts and sensations? But they are in constant flux. By the nature of the case, if the soul cannot be observed, it cannot be observed to be the same. Indeed, no sense has ever been assigned to the phrase "same soul." Nor could any sense be attached to it! One would have to say what a single soul looked like or felt like, how an encounter with a single soul at different times differed from encounters with different souls. But this can hardly be done, since a soul according to your conception doesn't look or feel like *anything* at all. And so of course "souls" can afford no principle of identity. And so they cannot be used to bridge the gulf between my existence now and my existence in the hereafter.

Miller: Do you doubt the existence of your own soul?

Weirob: I haven't based my argument on there being no immaterial souls of the sort you describe, but merely on their total irrelevance to questions of personal identity, and so to questions of personal survival. I do indeed harbor grave doubts whether there are any immaterial souls of the sort to which you appeal. Can we have a notion of a soul unless we have a notion of the *same* soul? But I hope you do not think that means I doubt my own existence. I think I lie here, overweight and conscious. I think you can see me, not just some outer wrapping, for I think I am just a live human body. But that is not the basis of my argument. I give you these souls. I merely observe that they can by their nature provide no principle of personal identity.

Miller: I admit I have no answer.

I'm afraid I do not comfort you, though I have perhaps provided you with some entertainment. Emerson said that a little philosophy turns one away from religion, but that deeper understanding brings one back. I know no one who has thought so long and hard about philosophy as you have. Will it never lead you back to a religious frame of mind?

Weirob: My former husband used to say that a little philosophy turns one away from religion, and more philosophy makes one a pain in the neck. Perhaps he was closer to the truth than Emerson.

Miller: Perhaps he was. But perhaps by tomorrow night I will have come up with a better argument.

Weirob: I hope I live to hear it.

For Further Reflection

Has Weirob been fair to Miller's argument? Has Miller succeeded in fulfilling her condition that survival be shown to be possible? Or is Weirob correct to say that the problems connected with personal identity prevent us even from hoping for survival after death?

The Finality of Death   IV.10

BERTRAND RUSSELL

In this brief essay the eminent British philosopher Bertrand Russell (1872–1970) outlines some of the major objections to the idea of life after death. He argues that it is not reasonable to believe that our personality and memories will survive the destruction of our bodies. He claims that the inclination to believe in immortality comes from emotional factors, notably the fear of death.

Study Questions

1. What does Russell think about the notion of the soul as a separate substance?
2. What is Russell's notion of personal identity?
3. If survival is to occur what will continue to exist? Why does Russell think this unlikely to happen?
4. What does Russell think causes people to believe in a future life?
5. What does Russell say about the likely cause of the world?

BEFORE WE CAN PROFITABLY discuss whether we shall continue to exist after death, it is well to be clear as to the sense in which a man is the same person as he was yesterday. Philosophers used to think that there were definite substances, the soul and the body, that each lasted on from

From Bertrand Russell, Why I Am Not a Christian *(London: George Allen & Unwin, 1957), pp. 88–93. Copyright © 1957, 1985 by Allen & Unwin. Reprinted by permission of Simon & Schuster and Allen & Unwin.*

day to day, that a soul, once created, continued to exist throughout all future time, whereas a body ceased temporarily from death till the resurrection of the body.

The part of this doctrine which concerns the present life is pretty certainly false. The matter of the body is continually changing by processes of nutriment and wastage. Even if it were not, atoms in physics are no longer supposed to have continuous existence; there is no sense in saying: this is the same atom as the one that existed a few minutes ago. The continuity of a human body is a matter of appearance and behavior, not of substance.

The same thing applies to the mind. We think and feel and act, but there is not, in addition to thoughts and feelings and actions, a bare entity, the mind or the soul, which does or suffers these occurrences. The mental continuity of a person is a continuity of habit and memory: there was yesterday one person whose feelings I can remember, and that person I regard as myself of yesterday; but, in fact, myself of yesterday was only certain mental occurrences which are now remembered and are regarded as part of the person who now recollects them. All that constitutes a person is a series of experiences connected by memory and by certain similarities of the sort we call habit.

If, therefore, we are to believe that a person survives death, we must believe that the memories and habits which constitute the person will continue to be exhibited in a new set of occurrences.

No one can prove that this will not happen. But it is easy to see that it is very unlikely. Our memories and habits are bound up with the structure of the brain, in much the same way in which a river is connected with the riverbed. The water in the river is always changing, but it keeps to the same course because previous rains have worn a channel. In like manner, previous events have worn a channel in the brain, and our thoughts flow along this channel. This is the cause of memory and mental habits. But the brain, as a structure, is dissolved at death, and memory therefore may be expected to be also dissolved. There is no more reason to think otherwise than to expect a river to persist in its old course after an earthquake has raised a mountain where a valley used to be.

All memory, and therefore (one may say) all minds, depend upon a property which is very noticeable in certain kinds of material structures but exists little if at all in other kinds. This is the property of forming habits as a result of frequent similar occurrences. For example: a bright light makes the pupils of the eyes contract; and if you repeatedly flash a light in a man's eyes and beat a gong at the same time, the gong alone will, in the end, cause his pupils to contract. This is a fact about the brain and nervous system—that is to say, about a certain material structure. It will be found that exactly similar facts explain our response to language and our use of it, our memories and the emotions they arouse, our moral or immoral habits of behavior, and indeed everything that constitutes our mental personality, except the part determined by heredity. The part determined by heredity is handed on to our posterity but cannot, in the individual, survive the disintegration of the body. Thus both the hereditary and the acquired parts of a personality are, so far as our experience goes, bound up with the characteristics of certain bodily structures. We all know that memory may be obliterated by an injury to the brain, that a virtuous person may be rendered vicious by encephalitis lethargica, and, that a clever child can be turned into an idiot by lack of iodine. In view of such familiar facts, it seems scarcely probable that the mind survives the total destruction of brain structure which occurs at death.

It is not rational arguments but emotions that cause belief in a future life.

The most important of these emotions is fear of death, which is instinctive and biologically useful. If we genuinely and wholeheartedly believed in the future life, we should cease completely to fear death. The effects would be curious, and probably such as most of us would deplore. But our human and subhuman ancestors have fought and exterminated their enemies throughout many geological ages and have profited by courage; it is therefore an advantage to the victors in the struggle for life to be able, on occasion, to overcome the natural fear of death. Among animals and savages, instinctive pugnacity suffices for this purpose; but at a certain stage of development, as the Mohammedans first proved, belief in Paradise has considerable military value as reinforcing natural pugnacity. We should therefore admit that militarists are wise in encouraging the belief in immortality, always supposing that this belief does not become so profound as to produce indifference to the affairs of the world.

Another emotion which encourages the belief in survival is admiration of the excellence of man. As the Bishop of Birmingham says, "His mind is a far finer instrument than anything that had appeared earlier—he knows right and wrong. He can build Westminster Abbey. He can make an airplane. He can calculate the distance of the sun. . . . Shall, then, man at death perish utterly? Does that incomparable instrument, his mind, vanish when life ceases?"

The Bishop proceeds to argue that "the universe has been shaped and is governed by an intelligent purpose," and that it would have been unintelligent, having made man, to let him perish.

To this argument there are many answers. In the first place, it has been found, in the scientific investigation of nature, that the intrusion of moral or aesthetic values has always been an obstacle to discovery. It used to be thought that the heavenly bodies must move in circles because the circle is the most perfect curve, that species must be immutable because God would only create what was perfect and what therefore stood in no need of improvement, that it was useless to combat epidemics except by repentance because they were sent as a punishment for sin, and so on. It has been found, however, that, so far as we can

discover, nature is indifferent to our values and can only be understood by ignoring our notions of good and bad. The Universe may have a purpose, but nothing that we know suggests that, if so, this purpose has any similarity to ours.

Nor is there in this anything surprising. Dr. Barnes tells us that man "knows right and wrong." But, in fact, as anthropology shows, men's views of right and wrong have varied to such an extent that no single item has been permanent. We cannot say, therefore, that man knows right and wrong, but only that some men do. Which men? Nietzsche argued in favor of an ethic profoundly different from Christ's, and some powerful governments have accepted his teaching. If knowledge of right and wrong is to be an argument for immortality, we must first settle whether to believe Christ or Nietzsche, and then argue that Christians are immortal, but Hitler and Mussolini are not, or vice versa. The decision will obviously be made on the battlefield, not in the study. Those who have the best poison gas will have the ethic of the future and will therefore be the immortal ones.

Our feelings and beliefs on the subject of good and evil are, like everything else about us, natural facts, developed in the struggle for existence and not having any divine or supernatural origin. In one of Aesop's fables, a lion is shown pictures of huntsmen catching lions and remarks that, if he had painted them, they would have shown lions catching huntsmen. Man, says Dr. Barnes, is a fine fellow because he can make airplanes. A little while ago there was a popular song about the cleverness of flies in walking upside down on the ceiling, with the chorus: "Could Lloyd George do it? Could Mr. Baldwin do it? Could Ramsay Mac do it? Why, NO." On this basis a very telling argument could be constructed by a theologically-minded fly, which no doubt the other flies would find most convincing.

Moreover, it is only when we think abstractly that we have such a high opinion of man. Of men in the concrete, most of us think the vast majority very bad. Civilized states spend more than half their revenue on killing each other's citizens. Consider the long history of the activities inspired by moral fervor: human sacrifices, persecutions of heretics, witch-hunts, pogroms leading up to wholesale extermination by poison gases, which one at least of Dr. Barnes's episcopal colleagues must be supposed to favor, since he holds pacifism to be un-Christian. Are these abominations, and the ethical doctrines by which they are prompted, really evidence of an intelligent Creator? And can we really wish that the men who practice them should live forever? The world in which we live can be understood as a result of muddle and accident; but if it is the outcome of deliberate purpose, the purpose must have been that of a fiend. For my part, I find accident a less painful and more plausible hypothesis.

For Further Reflection

1. How strong is Russell's argument against survival? Does his notion of personal identity lead to his conclusion, and is that the place to look more carefully?

2. What would Russell say about the following "near-death experience" described by Raymond Moody?

> "A man is dying and, as he reaches the point of greatest physical distress, he hears himself pronounced dead by his doctor. He begins to hear an uncomfortable noise, a loud ringing or buzzing, and at the same time feels himself moving very rapidly through a long dark tunnel. After this, he suddenly finds himself outside of his own physical body, but still in the immediate physical environment, and he sees his own body from a distance, as though he is a spectator. He watches the resuscitation attempt from this unusual vantage point and is in a state of emotional upheaval.
>
> "After a while, he collects himself and becomes more accustomed to his odd condition. He notices that he still has a 'body,' but one of a very different nature and with very different powers from the physical body he has left behind. Soon other things begin to happen. Others come to meet and to help him. He glimpses the spirits of relatives and friends who have already died, and a loving, warm spirit of a kind he has never encountered before—a being of light—appears before him. This being asks him a question, nonverbally, to make him evaluate his life and helps him along by showing him a panoramic, instantaneous playback of the major events of his life. At some point he finds himself approaching some sort of barrier or border, apparently representing the limit between earthly life and the next life. Yet, he finds that he must go back to the earth, that the time for his death has not yet come. At this point he resists, for by now he is taken up with his experiences in the afterlife and does not want to return. He is overwhelmed by intense feelings of joy, love, and peace. Despite his attitude, though, he somehow reunites with his physical body and lives" (*Life After Life* [New York: Bantam Books, 1976], pp. 21f).

Do such experiences lend any credibility to the idea of life after death?

In Defense of Immortality

JOHN HICK

John Hick, a British philosopher who now teaches at Claremont Graduate School, examines the Platonic notion of the immortality of the soul and argues that it is filled with problems. In its place he argues for the New Testament view of the recreation of the psychophysical person, a holistic person who is body-soul in one. He then offers a thought experiment of "John Smith" reappearances to show that recreation is conceivable and worthy of rational belief. In the last part of this essay Hick considers whether parapsychology can provide evidence for our survival of death.

Study Questions

1. How old is the idea of a soul separate from the body?
2. How, according to Hick, is the biblical view of human nature different from the Greek view?
3. What is the significance of the story of John Smith?
4. What does Hick take to be the significance of data obtained through parapsychology?

The Immortality of the Soul

SOME KIND OF DISTINCTION between physical body and immaterial or semimaterial soul seems to be as old as human culture; the existence of such a distinction has been indicated by the manner of burial of the earliest human skeletons yet discovered. Anthropologists offer various conjectures about the origin of the distinction: perhaps it was first suggested by memories of dead persons; by dreams of them; by the sight of reflections of oneself in water and on other bright surfaces; or by meditation upon the significance of religious rites which grew up spontaneously in face of the fact of death.

It was Plato (428/7–348/7 B.C.), the philosopher who has most deeply and lastingly influenced Western culture, who systematically developed the body-mind dichotomy and first attempted to prove the immortality of the soul.[1]

Plato argues that although the body belongs to the sensible world,[2] and shares its changing and impermanent nature, the intellect is related to the unchanging realities of which we are aware when we think not of particular good things but of Goodness itself, not of specific just acts but of Justice itself, and of the other "universals" or eternal Ideas in virtue of which physical things and events have their own specific characteristics. Being related to this higher and abiding realm, rather than to the evanescent world of sense, reason or the soul is immortal. Hence, one who devotes his life to the contemplation of eternal realities rather than to the gratification of the fleeting desires of the body will find at death that whereas his body turns to dust, his soul gravitates to the realm of the unchanging, there to live forever. Plato painted an awe-inspiring picture, of haunting beauty and persuasiveness, which has moved and elevated the minds of men

John H. Hick, Philosophy of Religion, 3d ed., copyright © 1983, pp. 122–32. Reprinted by permission of Prentice-Hall, Englewood Cliffs, N.J. Footnotes edited.

in many different centuries and lands. Nevertheless, it is not today (as it was during the first centuries of the Christian era) the common philosophy of the West; and a demonstration of immortality which presupposes Plato's metaphysical system cannot claim to constitute a proof for the twentieth-century disbeliever.

Plato used the further argument that the only things that can suffer destruction are those that are composite, since to destroy something means to disintegrate it into its constituent parts. All material bodies are composite; the soul, however, is simple and therefore imperishable. This argument was adopted by Aquinas and has become standard in Roman Catholic theology, as in the following passage from the modern Catholic philosopher, Jacques Maritain:

> A spiritual soul cannot be corrupted, since it possesses no matter; it cannot be disintegrated, since it has no substantial parts; it cannot lose its individual unity, since it is self-subsisting, nor its internal energy, since it contains within itself all the sources of its energies. The human soul cannot die. Once it exists, it cannot disappear; it will necessarily exist for ever, endure without end. Thus, philosophic reason, put to work by a great metaphysician like Thomas Aquinas, is able to prove the immortality of the human soul in a demonstrative manner.[3]

This type of reasoning has been criticized on several grounds. Kant pointed out that although it is true that a simple substance cannot disintegrate, consciousness may nevertheless cease to exist through the diminution of its intensity to zero.[4] Modern psychology has also questioned the basic premise that the mind is a simple entity. It seems instead to be a structure of only relative unity, normally fairly stable and tightly integrated but capable under stress of various degrees of division and dissolution. This comment from psychology makes it clear that the assumption that the soul is a simple substance is not an empirical observation but a metaphysical theory. As such, it cannot provide the basis for a general proof of immortality.

The body-soul distinction, first formulated as a philosophical doctrine in ancient Greece, was baptized into Christianity, ran through the medieval period, and entered the modern world with the public status of a self-evident truth when it was redefined in the seventeenth century by Descartes. Since World War II, however, the Cartesian mind-matter dualism, having been taken for granted for many centuries, has been strongly criticized by philosophers of the contemporary analytical school.[5] It is argued that the words that describe mental characteristics and operations—such as "intelligent," "thoughtful," "carefree," "happy," "calculating" and the like—apply in practice to types of human behavior and to behavioral dispositions. They refer to the empirical individual, the observable human being who is born and grows and acts and feels and dies, and not to the shadowy proceedings of a mysterious "ghost in the machine." Man is thus very much what he appears to be—a creature of flesh and blood, who behaves and is capable of behaving in a characteristic range of ways—rather than a nonphysical soul incomprehensibly interacting with a physical body.

As a result of this development much mid-twentieth-century philosophy has come to see man in the way he is seen in the biblical writings, not as an eternal soul temporarily attached to a mortal body, but as a form of finite, mortal, psychophysical life. Thus, the Old Testament scholar, J. Pedersen, says of the Hebrews that for them " . . . the body is the soul in its outward form."[6] This way of thinking has led to quite a different conception of death from that found in Plato and the neo-Platonic strand of European thought.

The Re-Creation of the Psychophysical Person

Only toward the end of the Old Testament period did after-life beliefs come to have any real importance in Judaism. Previously, Hebrew religious insight had focused so fully upon God's covenant with the nation, as an organism that continued through the centuries while successive generations lived and died, that the thought of a divine purpose for the individual, a purpose that transcended this present life, developed only when the breakdown of the nation as a political entity threw into prominence the individual and the problem of his personal destiny.

When a positive conviction arose of God's purpose holding the individual in being beyond the crisis of death, this conviction took the non-Platonic form of belief in the resurrection of the body. By the turn of the eras, this had become an article of faith for one Jewish sect, the Pharisees, although it was still rejected as an innovation by the more conservative Sadducees.

The religious difference between the Platonic belief in the immortality of the soul, and the Judaic-Christian belief in the resurrection of the body is that the latter postulates a special divine act of re-creation. This produces a sense of utter dependence upon God in the hour of death, a feeling that is in accordance with the biblical understanding of man as having been formed out of "the dust of the earth,"[7] a product (as we say today) of the slow evolution of life from its lowly beginnings in the primeval slime. Hence, in the Jewish and Christian conception, death is something real and fearful. It is not thought to be like walking from one room to another, or taking off an old coat and putting on a new one. It means sheer unqualified extinction—passing out from the lighted circle of life into "death's dateless night." Only through the sovereign creative love of God can there be a new existence beyond the grave.

What does "the resurrection of the dead" mean? Saint Paul's discussion provides the basic Christian answer to this question.[8] His conception of the general resurrection (distinguished from the unique resurrection of Jesus) has nothing to do with the resuscitation of corpses in a cemetery. It concerns God's re-creation or re-constitution of the human psychophysical individual, not as the organism that has died but as a *soma pneumatikon*, a "spiritual body," inhabiting a spiritual world as the physical body inhabits our present physical world.

A major problem confronting any such doctrine is that of providing criteria of personal identity to link the earthly life and the resurrection life. Paul does not specifically consider this question, but one may, perhaps, develop his thought along lines such as the following.[9]

Suppose, first, that someone—John Smith—living in the USA were suddenly and inexplicably to disappear from before the eyes of his friends, and that at the same moment an exact replica of him were inexplicably to appear in India. The person who appears in India is exactly similar in both physical and mental characteristics to the person who disappeared in America. There is continuity of memory, complete similarity of bodily features including fingerprints, hair and eye coloration, and stomach contents, and also of beliefs, habits, emotions, and mental dispositions. Further, the "John Smith" replica thinks of himself as being the John Smith who disappeared in the USA. After all possible tests have been made and have proved positive, the factors leading his friends to accept "John Smith" as John Smith would surely prevail and would cause them to overlook even his mysterious transference from one continent to another, rather than treat "John Smith," with all John Smith's memories and other characteristics, as someone other than John Smith.

Suppose, second, that our John Smith, instead of inexplicably disappearing, dies, but that at the moment of his death a "John Smith" replica, again complete with memories and all other characteristics, appears in India. Even with the corpse on our hands we would, I think, still have to accept this "John Smith" as the John Smith who died. We would have to say that he had been miraculously re-created in another place.

Now suppose, third, that on John Smith's death the "John Smith" replica appears, not in India, but as a resurrection replica in a different world altogether, a resurrection world inhabited only by resurrected persons. This world occupies its own space distinct from that with which we are now familiar. That is to say, an object in the resurrection world is not situated at any distance or in any direction from the objects in our present world, although each object in either world is spatially related to every other object in the same world.

This supposition provides a model by which one may conceive of the divine re-creation of the embodied human personality. In this model, the element of the strange and the mysterious has been reduced to a minimum by following the view of some of the early Church Fathers that the resurrection body has the same shape as the physical body,[10] and ignoring Paul's own hint that it may be as unlike the physical body as a full grain of wheat differs from the wheat seed.[11]

What is the basis for this Judaic-Christian belief in the divine recreation or reconstitution of the human personality after death? There is, of course, an argument from authority, in that life after death is taught throughout the New Testament (although very rarely in the Old Testament). But, more basically, belief in the resurrection arises as a corollary of faith in the sovereign purpose of God, which is not restricted by death and which holds man in being beyond his natural mortality. In the words of Martin Luther, "Anyone with whom God speaks, whether in wrath or in mercy, the same is certainly immortal. The Person of God who speaks, and the Word, show that we are creatures with whom God wills to speak, right into eternity, and in an immortal manner."[12] In a similar vein it is argued that if it be God's plan to create finite persons to exist in fellowship with himself, then it contradicts both his own intention and his love for the creatures made in his image if he allows men to pass out of existence when his purpose for them remains largely unfulfilled.

It is this promised fulfillment of God's purpose for man, in which the full possibilities of human nature will be realized, that constitutes the "heaven" symbolized in the New Testament as a joyous banquet in which all and sundry rejoice together. As we saw when discussing the problem of evil, no theodicy can succeed without drawing into itself this eschatological[13] faith in an eternal, and therefore infinite, good which thus outweighs all the pains and sorrows that have been endured on the way to it.

Balancing the idea of heaven in Christian tradition is the idea of *hell*. This, too, is relevant to the problem of theodicy. For just as the reconciling of God's goodness and power with the fact of evil requires that out of the travail of history there shall come in the end an eternal good for man, so likewise it would seem to preclude man's eternal misery. The only kind of evil that is finally incompatible with God's unlimited power and love would be utterly pointless and wasted suffering, pain which is never redeemed and worked into the fulfilling of God's good purpose. Unending torment would constitute precisely such suffering; for being eternal, it could never lead to a good end beyond itself. Thus, hell as conceived by its enthusiasts, such as Augustine or Calvin, is a major part of the problem of evil! If hell is construed as eternal torment, the theological motive behind the idea is directly at variance with the urge to seek a theodicy. However, it is by no means clear that the doctrine of eternal punishment can claim a secure New Testament basis.[14] If, on the other hand, "hell" means a continuation of the purgatorial suffering often experienced in this life, and leading eventually to the high good of heaven, it no longer stands in conflict with the needs of theodicy. Again, the idea of hell may be deliteralized and valued as a *mythos,* as a powerful and pregnant symbol of the grave responsibility inherent in man's freedom in relation to his Maker.

Does Parapsychology Help?

The spiritualist movement claims that life after death has been proved by well-attested cases of communication between the living and the "dead." During the closing quarter of the nineteenth century and the decades of the present century this claim has been made the subject of careful and prolonged study by a number of responsible and competent persons.[15] This work, which may be approximately dated from the founding in London of the Society for Psychical Research in 1882, is known either by the name adopted by that society or in the United States by the name parapsychology.

Approaching the subject from the standpoint of our interest in this chapter, we may initially divide the phenomena studied by the parapsychologist into two groups. There are those phenomena that involve no reference to the idea of a life after death, chief among these being psychokinesis and extrasensory perception (ESP) in its various forms (such as telepathy, clairvoyance, and precognition). And there are those phenomena that raise the question of personal survival after death, such as the apparitions and other sensory manifestations of dead persons and the "spirit messages' received through mediums. This division is, however, only of preliminary use, for ESP has emerged as a clue to the understanding of much that occurs in the second group. We shall begin with a brief outline of the reasons that have induced the majority of workers in this field to be willing to postulate so strange an occurrence as telepathy.

Telepathy is a name for the mysterious fact that sometimes a thought in the mind of one person apparently causes a similar thought to occur to someone else when there are no normal means of communication between them, and under circumstances such that mere coincidence seems to be excluded.

For example, one person may draw a series of pictures or diagrams on paper and somehow transmit an impression of these to someone else in another room who then draws recognizable reproductions of them. This might well be a coincidence in the case of a single successful reproduction; but can a series consist entirely of coincidences?

Experiments have been devised to measure the probability of chance coincidence in supposed cases of telepathy. In the simplest of these, cards printed in turn with five different symbols are used. A pack of fifty, consisting of ten bearing each symbol, is then thoroughly shuffled, and the sender concentrates on the cards one at a time while the receiver (who of course can see neither sender nor cards) tries to write down the correct order of symbols. This procedure is repeated, with constant reshuffling, hundreds or thousands of times. Since there are only five different symbols, a random guess would stand one chance in five of being correct. Consequently, on the assumption that only "chance" is operating, the receiver should be right in about 20 per cent of his tries, and wrong in about 80 per cent; and the longer the series, the closer should be the approach to this proportion. However, good telepathic subjects are right in a far larger number of cases than can be reconciled with random guessing. The deviation from chance expectation can be converted mathematically into "odds against chance" (increasing as the proportion of hits is maintained over a longer and longer series of tries). In this way, odds of over a million to one have been recorded. J. B. Rhine (Duke University) has reported results showing "antichance" values ranging from seven (which equals odds against chance of 100,000 to one) to eighty-two (which converts the odds against chance to billions).[16] S. G. Soal (London University) has reported positive results for precognitive telepathy with odds against chance of $10^{35} \times 5$, or of billions to one.[17] Other researchers have also recorded confirming results. In the light of these reports, it is difficult to deny that some positive factor, and not merely "chance," is operating. "Telepathy" is simply a name for this unknown positive factor.

How does telepathy operate? Only negative conclusions seem to be justified to date. It can, for example, be said with reasonable certainty that telepathy does not consist in any kind of physical radiation, analogous to radio waves. For, first, telepathy is not delayed or weakened in proportion to distance, as are all known forms of radiation; and, second, there is no organ in the brain or elsewhere that can plausibly be regarded as its sending or receiving center. Telepathy appears to be a purely mental occurrence.

It is not, however, a matter of transferring or transporting a thought out of one mind into another—if, indeed, such an idea makes sense at all. The telepathized thought does not leave the sender's consciousness in order to enter that of the receiver. What happens would be better described by saying that the sender's thought gives rise to a mental "echo" in the mind of the receiver. This "echo" occurs at the unconscious level, and consequently the version of it that rises into the receiver's consciousness may be only fragmentary and may be distorted or symbolized in various ways, as in dreams.

According to one theory that has been tentatively suggested to explain telepathy, our minds are separate and mutually insulated only at the conscious (and preconscious) level. But at the deepest level of the unconscious, we are constantly influencing one another, and it is at this level that telepathy takes place.

How is a telepathized thought directed to one particular receiver among so many? Apparently the thoughts are directed by some link of emotion or common interest. For example, two friends are sometimes telepathically aware of any grave crisis or shock experienced by the other, even though they are at opposite ends of the earth.

We shall turn now to the other branch of parapsychology, which has more obvious bearing upon our subject. The *Proceedings of the Society for Psychical Research* contains a large number of carefully recorded and satisfactorily attested cases of the appearance of the figure of someone who has recently died to living people (in rare instances to more than one at a time) who were, in many cases, at a distance and unaware of the death. The S.P.R. reports also establish beyond reasonable doubt that the minds that operate in the mediumistic trance, purporting to be spirits of the departed, sometimes give personal information the medium could not have acquired by normal means and at time even give informa-

tion, later verified, which had not been known to any living person.

On the other hand, physical happenings, such as the "materializations" of spirit forms in a visible and tangible form, are much more doubtful. But even if we discount the entire range of physical phenomena, it remains true that the best cases of trance utterance are impressive and puzzling, and taken at face value are indicative of survival and communication after death. If, through a medium, one talks with an intelligence that gives a coherent impression of being an intimately known friend who has died and establishes identity by a wealth of private information and indefinable personal characteristics—as has occasionally happened—then we cannot dismiss without careful trial the theory that what is taking place is the return of a consciousness from the spirit world.

However, the advance of knowledge in the other branch of parapsychology, centering upon the study of extrasensory perception, has thrown unexpected light upon this apparent commerce with the departed. For it suggests that unconscious telepathic contact between the medium and his or her client is an important and possibly a sufficient explanatory factor. This was vividly illustrated by the experience of two women who decided to test the spirits by taking into their minds, over a period of weeks, the personality and atmosphere of an entirely imaginary character in an unpublished novel written by one of the women. After thus filling their minds with the characteristics of this fictitious person, they went to a reputable medium, who proceeded to describe accurately their imaginary friend as a visitant from beyond the grave and to deliver appropriate messages from him.

An even more striking case is that of the "direct voice" medium (i.e., a medium in whose seances the voice of the communicating "spirit" is heard apparently speaking out of the air) who produced the spirit of one "Gordon Davis" who spoke in his own recognizable voice, displayed considerable knowledge about Gordon Davis, and remembered this death. This was extremely impressive until it was discovered that Gordon Davis was still alive; he was, of all ghostly occupations, a real-estate agent, and had been trying to sell a house at the time when the séance took place!

Such cases suggest that genuine mediums are simply persons of exceptional telepathic sensitiveness who unconsciously derive the "spirits" from their clients' minds.

In connection with "ghosts," in the sense of apparitions of the dead, it has been established that there can be "meaningful hallucinations," the source of which is almost certainly telepathic. To quote a classic and somewhat dramatic example: a woman sitting by a lake sees the figure of a man running toward the lake and throwing himself in. A few days later a man commits suicide by throwing himself into this same lake. Presumably, the explanation of the vision is that the man's thought while he was contemplating suicide had been telepathically projected onto the scene via the woman's mind.

In many of the cases recorded there is delayed action. The telepathically projected thought lingers in the recipient's unconscious mind until a suitable state of inattention to the outside world enables it to appear to his conscious mind in a dramatized form—for example, by a hallucinatory voice or vision—by means of the same mechanism that operates in dreams.

If phantoms of the living can be created by previously experienced thoughts and emotions of the person whom they represent, the parallel possibility arises that phantoms of the dead are caused by thoughts and emotions that were experienced by the person represented when he was alive. In other words, ghosts may be "psychic footprints," a kind of mental trace left behind by the dead, but not involving the presence or even the continued existence of those whom they represent.

These considerations tend away from the hopeful view that parapsychology will open a window onto another world. However, it is too early for a final verdict; and in the meantime one should be careful not to confuse absence of knowledge with knowledge of absence.

NOTES

1. *Phaedo.*
2. The world known to us through our physical senses.
3. Jacques Maritain, *The Range of Reason* (London: Geoffrey Bles Ltd. and New York: Charles Scribner's Sons, 1953), p. 60.
4. Kant, *Critique of Pure Reason, Transcendental Dialectic,* "Refutation of Mendelessohn's Proof of the Permanence of the Soul."
5. Gilbert Ryle's *The Concept of Mind* (London: Hutchinson & Co., Ltd., 1949) is a classic statement of this critique.
6. *Israel* (London: Oxford University Press, 1926), I, 170.
7. Genesis, 2:7; Psalm 103:14.
8. I Corinthians 15.
9. The following paragraphs are adapted, with permission, from a section of my article, "Theology and Verification," published in *Theology Today* (April, 1960) and reprinted in *The Existence of God* (New York: The Macmillan Company, 1964).
10. For example, Irenaeus, *Against Heresies,* Book II, Chap. 34, para. 1.
11. I Corinthians. 15:37.
12. Quoted by Emil Brunner, *Dogmatics,* II, 69.
13. From the Greek *eschaton,* end.
14. The Greek word *aionios,* which is used in the New Testament and which is usually translated as "eternal" or "everlasting," can bear either this meaning or the more limited meaning of "for the aeon, or age."
15. The list of past presidents of the Society for Psychical Research includes the philosophers Henri Bergson, William James, Hans Driesch, Henry Sidgwick, F. C. S. Schiller, C. D. Broad, and H. H. Price; the psychologists William McDougall, Gardner Murphy, Franklin Prince, and R. H. Thouless; the physicists Sir William Crookes, Sir Oliver Lodge, Sir William Barrett, and Lord Rayleigh; and the classicist Gilbert Murray.
16. J. B. Rhine, *Extrasensory Perception* (Boston: Society for Psychical Research, 1935), Table XLIII, p. 162. See also Rhine, *New Frontiers of the Mind* (New York: Farrar and Rinehart, Inc., 1937), pp. 69f.
17. S. G. Soal, *Proceedings of the Society for Psychical Research,* XLVI, 152–98 and XLVII, 21–150. See also S. G. Soal's *The Experimental Situation in Psychical Research* (London: The Society for Psychical Research, 1947).

For Further Reflection

1. Has Hick successfully shown the plausibility of survival after death? Has he made the Judeo-Christian view intelligible in the light of modern psychology?

2. How would Hick respond to Weirob's charge that this sort of argument only establishes that someone "exactly similar" to you or me might be recreated, but does not show that you or I may survive?

Suggestions for Further Reading

Borst, C. V., ed. *The Mind/Brain Identity Theory.* St. Martin's, 1970. Contains the best overall collection on the identity theory.

Campbell, Keith. *Body and Mind.* Doubleday, 1970.

Churchland, Paul. *Matter and Consciousness.* MIT, 1984.

Cornman, James and Kieth Lehrer. *Philosophical Problems and Arguments.* New York: Macmillan, 1982. Chapter 4, "The Mind-Body Problem," is excellent and accessible to lower-division college students.

Dennett, Daniel. *Brainstorms.* MIT, 1978.

Ducasse, Curt J. *A Critical Examination of the Belief in Life after Death.* Thomas, 1961.

Flew, Antony, ed. *Body, Mind and Death.* New York: Macmillan, 1974. Contains the classic readings.

Hofstadter, Douglas and Daniel Dennett, eds. *The Mind's I.* Bantam, 1982. A scintillating set of articles on the idea of the self.

McGinn, Colin. *The Character of Mind.* Oxford, 1982. A good, concise introduction to the subject.

Perry, John. *Personal Identity.* University of California, 1975. A very fine set of articles.

Penelhum, Terrence. *Survival and Disembodied Existence.* London: Routledge & Kegan Paul, 1970.

Quinton, Anthony. "The Soul." *Journal of Philosophy,* 1962.

Ryle, Gilbert. *The Concept of Mind.* Barnes and Noble, 1949. A classic in logical behaviorism.

Shaffer, Jerome. *Philosophy of Mind.* Englewood Cliffs, NJ: Prentice-Hall, 1963. Almost a classic summary of the problems.

Swinburne, Richard. *The Evolution of the Soul.* Oxford: Clarendon Press, 1986. This contains Swinburne's 1983–84 Gifford's Lectures. It treats the subject from a theistic perspective.

Part V

Freedom of the Will and Determinism

If I were capable of correct reasoning, and if, at the same time, I had a complete knowledge both of his disposition and of all the events by which he was surrounded, I should be able to foresee the line of conduct which, in consequence of those events, he would adopt.

H. T. BUCKLE in his *History of Civilization in England* (1857)

T HE PROBLEM OF FREEDOM OF THE WILL and determinism is one of the most intriguing and difficult in the whole of philosophy. It constitutes a paradox. If we look at ourselves, at our ability to deliberate and make choices, it seems obvious that we are free. On the other hand, if we look at what we believe about causality (i.e., that every event and thing must have a cause), then it appears that we do not have free wills but are determined. So we seem to have inconsistent beliefs.

Let us look closer at the two theses involved in order to see how they work and what support there is for each of them.

1. *Determinism:* The theory that everything in the universe (or at least the macroscopic universe) is entirely determined by causal laws, so that whatever happens at any given moment is the effect of some antecedent cause.

2. *Libertarianism:* The theory that there are some actions which are exempt from the causal laws, in which the individual is the sole (or decisive) cause of the act, the act originating *ex nihilo,* cut off from all other causes but the self's origination.

There is a third position which tries to combine the best of the two positions. Called *compatibilism* or *soft determinism,* it admits that while everything is determined, we can still be free insofar as we can still act voluntarily.

Determinism (Sometimes Called "Hard Determinism")

Determinism is the theory that everything in the universe is governed by causal laws. That is, everything in the universe is entirely determined so that whatever happens at any given moment is the effect of some antecedent cause. If we were omniscient, we could predict exactly everything that would happen for the rest of this hour, for the rest of our life time, for the rest of time itself, simply because we know how everything hitherto is causally related. This theory, which, it is claimed, is the basic presupposition of science, implies that there is no such thing as an uncaused event (sometimes this is modified to include only the macrocosmic world, leaving the microcosmic world in doubt). Hence, since all human actions are events, human actions are not undetermined, are not *free* in a radical sense but are the product of a causal process. Hence, while we may self-importantly imagine that we are autonomous and possess free will, in reality we are totally conditioned by heredity and environment.

The outline of the argument for determinism goes something like this:

1. Every event (or state of affairs) must have a cause.
2. Human actions (as well as the agent who gives rise to those actions) are events (or state of affairs).

250

3. Therefore, every human action (including the agent himself) is caused.

4. Hence determinism is true.

While the hypothesis of universal causality cannot be proved, it is something we all assume—either because of considerable inductive evidence or as an *a priori* truth which seems to make sense of the world. We cannot easily imagine an uncaused event taking place in ordinary life. For example, imagine how you would feel if, on visiting your dentist for relief of a toothache, he were to conclude his oral examination with the remark, "I certainly can see that you are in great pain because of your toothache, but I'm afraid that I can't help you, for there is no cause of this toothache." Perhaps he calls his partner over to confirm his judgment. "Sure enough," she says, "this is one of those interesting noncausal cases. Sorry, there's nothing we can do for you. Even medicine and pain-relievers won't help these noncausal types."

Why do we believe that everything has a cause? Most philosophers have echoed John Stuart Mill's answer that the doctrine of universal causality is a conclusion of inductive reasoning. We have had an enormous range of experience wherein we have found causal explanations to individual events, which in turn seem to participate in a further causal chain. The problem with this answer, however, is that we have only experienced a very small part of the universe, not enough of it to warrant the conclusion that every event must have a cause.

It was David Hume (cf. reading III.4) who pointed out that the idea of causality was not a logical truth (like the notion that all triangles have three sides). The hypothesis that every event has a cause arises from the observation of regular conjunctions. "When many uniform instances appear, and the same object is always followed by the same event; we then begin to entertain the notion of cause and connexion" (*Enquiry*, p. 78). So after a number of successful tries at putting water over a fire and seeing it disappear, we conclude that heat (or fire) causes water to disappear (or vaporize). But we cannot prove causality. We never see it. All we see are two events in constant spatio-temporal order and infer from this constant conjunction a binding relation between them. For example, we see one billiard ball (a) hit another (b), and we see (b) move away from (a), and we conclude that (a's) hitting (b) at a certain velocity is the cause of (b's) moving away as it did. However, we cannot prove that it is the sufficient cause of the movement.

It was Immanuel Kant (reading III.5) who first suggested that the principle of universal causality is a synthetic *a priori*—i.e., an assumption that we cannot prove by experience but simply cannot conceive not to be the case. Our mental construction demands that we read all experience in the light of universal causation. We have no knowledge of what the world is in itself, or whether there really is universal causation, but we cannot understand experience except by means of causal explanation. The necessary idea of causality is part and parcel of our noetic structure. We are programmed to read our experience in the causal script.

Kant saw that there was a powerful incentive to believe in determinism, but he also thought that the notion of morality provided a powerful incentive to believe in freedom of the will. Hence, Kant's dilemma.

The man who used the idea of determinism more effectively for practical purposes than any one before him was the great American criminal lawyer Clarence Darrow. In the 1920s two teenage geniuses from the University of Chicago, Leopold and Loeb, committed what they regarded as the perfect murder. They grotesquely dismembered a child and buried the parts in a prairie. Caught, they faced an outraged public who demanded the death penalty. The defense attorney was Clarence Darrow, champion of lost causes. He conceded that the boys committed the deed, but argued that they were, nevertheless, "innocent." His argument was based on the theory of determinism. It is worth reading part of the plea.

> We are all helpless. . . . This weary world goes on, begetting, with birth and with living and with death; and all of it is blind from the beginning to the end. I do not know what it was that made these boys do this mad act, but I do know there is a reason for it. I know they did not beget themselves. I know that anyone of an infinite number of causes reaching back to the beginning might be working out in these boys' minds, whom you are asked to hang in malice and in hatred and injustice. . . .
>
> Nature is strong and she is pitiless. She works in her own mysterious way, and we are her victims. We have not much to do with it ourselves. Nature takes this job in hand, and we play our part. In the words of old Omar Khayam, we are:
>
> *But helpless pieces in the game He plays*
> *Upon the chess board of nights and days;*
> *Hither and thither moves, and checks and slays,*
> *And one by one back in the closet lays.*
>
> What had this boy to do with it? He was not his own father, he was not his own mother; he was not his own grandparents. All of this was handed to him. He did not surround himself with governesses and wealth. He did not make himself. And yet he is to be compelled to pay. (Clarence Darrow, *Attorney for the Damned*. New York: Simon and Schuster, 1957.)

This was sufficient to convince the jury to go against public opinion and recommend a life sentence in lieu of the death penalty. If Leopold and Loeb were determined by antecedent causes to do the deed, we cannot blame them for what they did, any more than we can blame a cow for not being able to fly.

Determinism has received new attention and respect due to modern neurological studies which suggest the hypothesis that there is a one-to-one correlation between mental states and brain states, so that every conscious action can be traced back to a causally sufficient brain state. In other words, the laws of physics deterministically produce mental states.

Libertarianism

Libertarianism is the theory that we do have free wills. It contends that given the same antecedent conditions at time t_1, an agent S could do either act A1 or A2. That is, it is up to S what the world will look like after t_1, and that his act is causally underdetermined, the self making the unexplained difference. Libertarians do not contend that all our actions are free, only some of them. Neither do they offer an explanatory theory of free will. Their arguments are indirect. They offer two main arguments for their position: the argument from deliberation and the argument from moral responsibility.

The Argument from Deliberation

The position is nicely summed up in the words of Corliss Lamont: "[There] is the unmistakable intuition of virtually every human being that he is free to make the choices he does and that the deliberations leading to those choices are also free flowing. The normal man feels too, after he has made a decision, that he could have decided differently. That is why regret or remorse for a past choice can be so disturbing."

There is a difference between a knee jerk and purposefully kicking a football. In the first case, the behavior is involuntary, a reflex action. In the second case, we deliberate, notice that we have an alternative (viz. not kicking the ball), consciously choose to kick the ball, and, if successful, we find our body moving in the requisite manner, so that the ball is kicked.

Deliberation may take a short or long time, be foolish or wise, but the process is a conscious one wherein we believe that we really can do either of the actions (or any of many possible actions). That is, in deliberating we assume we are free to choose between alternatives and that we are not determined to do simply one action. Otherwise, why deliberate?

Furthermore, there seems to be something psychologically lethal about accepting determinism in human relations; it tends to curtail deliberation and paralyze actions. If people really believe themselves totally determined, the tendency is for them to excuse their behavior. Human effort seems pointless. As Arthur Eddington put it, "What significance is there to my mental struggle tonight whether I shall or shall not give up smoking, if the laws which govern the matter of the physical universe already preordain for the morrow a configuration of matter consisting of pipe, tobacco, and smoke connected to my lips?" The determinist has an objection to this argument, which you will encounter in D'Holbach's and Hospers' essays. And the libertarian has a counter-response in agent causation, a version of which will be found in Susan Anderson's article.

The Argument from Moral Responsibility

Determinism seems to conflict with the thesis that we have moral responsibilities, for responsibility implies that we could have done otherwise than we did. We do not hold a dog responsible for chewing up our philosophy book or a one-month-old baby responsible for crying, because they could not help it, but we do hold a twenty-year-old student responsible for her cheating because (we believe) she could have done otherwise. Blackbacked sea gulls will tear apart a stray baby herring gull without the slightest suspicion that their act may be immoral, but if humans lack this sense, we judge them as pathological, as substandard.

Moral responsibility is something that we take very seriously. We believe that we do have duties, oughts, over which we feel rational guilt at failure to perform. But there can be no such things as duties, oughts, praise, blame or rational guilt, if we are not essentially free. The argument form is the following.

1. If determinism is true, and our actions are merely the product of the laws of nature and antecedent states of affairs, then it is not up to us to choose what we do.

2. But if it is not up to us to choose what we do, we cannot be said to be responsible for what we do.

3. So if determinism is true, we are not responsible for what we do.

4. But our belief in moral responsibility is self-evident, at least as strong as our belief in universal causality.

5. So if we believe that we have moral responsibilities, determinism cannot be accepted.

We must reject the notion of determinism even if we cannot give a full explanatory account of how agents choose.

Here the determinist usually bites the bullet and admits that we do not have moral responsibilities, and that it is just an illusion that we do. But we are determined to have such an illusion, so there is nothing we can do about it. We cannot consciously live as determinists, but why should we think that we can? We are finite and fallible creatures, driven by causal laws, but with self-consciousness that makes us aware of part (but only a part) of the process that governs our behavior.

Compatibilism (How to Have Your Cake and Eat It Too)

However there is another response to the problem of free will and determinism, one similar to Kant but perhaps more subtle. It may be called reconciling determinism or soft-determinism or compatibilism. It argues that although we are determined, we still have moral responsibilities, that the distinction is between *voluntary* and *involuntary* behavior.

The language of freedom and the language of determinism are but two different ways of talking about certain human or rational events, both necessary for mankind (one is necessary for science and the other is necessary for morality and personal relationships). The compatibilist argues that the fact that we are determined does not affect our interpersonal relations. We will still have feelings which we must deal with, using internalist insights. We will still feel resentment when someone hurts us "on purpose." We will still feel grateful for services rendered and hold people responsible for their actions. Only we will still acknowledge that from the external perspective the determinist's account of all of this is valid.

Along these lines, Walter T. Stace in our third reading argues that the problem of freedom and determinism is really only a semantic one, a dispute about the meanings of words. Freedom has to do with acts done voluntarily and determinism with the causal processes that underlie all behavior and events. These need not be incompatible. Gandhi's fasting because he wanted to free India was a voluntary or free act, whereas a man starving in the desert is not doing so voluntarily or as a free act. A thief purposefully and voluntarily steals, whereas a kleptomaniac cannot help stealing. In both cases each act or event has causal antecedents, but the former in each set are free, whereas the latter are unfree. According to Stace, "Acts freely done are those whose immediate causes are psychological states in the agent. Acts not freely done are those whose immediate causes are states of affairs external to the agent." Compatibilism is attacked from both sides in our readings, by James, Hospers, and Anderson. James calls it a "quagmire of evasion."

We Are Completely Determined   V.1

BARON D'HOLBACH

Baron Paul Henri D'Holbach (1723–1789), born in Edesheim, Germany, and growing up in France, was one of the leading philosophers of the French Enlightenment. He was a materialist who believed that nature is one grand machine, and humans are particular machines within this grand machine—a machine which needs no machinist. He was a significant contributor to the *Encyclopedie* and a friend of Diderot, Hume, and Rousseau. His principal writings are *Christianity Unveiled* (1767), *The System of Nature* (1770), from which the present selection is taken, and *Common Sense, or Natural Ideas Opposed to Supernatural Ideas* (1772).

D'Holbach is one of the first philosophers to provide a sustained systematic critique of the doctrine of free will. According to him, if we accept science, which he equates with a system of material particles operating according to fixed laws of motion, then we will see that free will is an illusion. There is no such entity as a soul, but we are simply material objects in motion, having very complicated brains which lead the unreflective to believe that they are free.

Study Questions

1. What is the result of dualism, which separates soul from body?
2. What does D'Holbach believe has been proved about the relation of the soul to body?
3. How does he characterize human life?
4. What is the role that the doctrine of free will plays in religion and our system of punishment?
5. Deliberation between alternative courses of action has often been used by libertarians as evidence of free will. What does D'Holbach say about this psychological activity?
6. What are the causes of our belief in free will?

THOSE WHO HAVE AFFIRMED that the *soul* is distinguished from the body, is immaterial, draws its ideas from its own peculiar source, acts by its own energies, without the aid of any exterior object, have, by a consequence of their own system, enfranchised [liberated] it from those

From Chapter XI, "Of the System of Man's Free Agency," of The System of Nature *(1770). The translation is by* H. D. Robinson.

physical laws according to which all beings of which we have a knowledge are obliged to act. They have believed that the soul is mistress of its own conduct, is able to regulate its own peculiar operations, has the faculty to determine its will by its own natural energy; in a word, they have pretended that man is a *free agent*.

It has been already sufficiently proved that the soul is nothing more than the body considered relatively to some of its functions more concealed than others: it has been shown that this soul, even when it shall be supposed immaterial, is continually modified conjointly with the body, is submitted to all its motion, and that without this it would remain inert and dead; that, consequently, it is subjected to the influence of those material and physical causes which give impulse to the body; of which the mode of existence, whether habitual or transitory, depends upon the material elements by which it is surrounded, that form its texture, constitute its temperament, enter into it by means of the aliments, and penetrate it by their subtility. The faculties which are called *intellectual,* and those qualities which are styled *moral,* have been explained in a manner purely physical and natural. In the last place it has been demonstrated that all the ideas, all the systems, all the affections, all the opinions, whether true or false, which man forms to himself, are to be attributed to his physical and material senses. Thus man is a being purely physical; in whatever manner he is considered, he is connected to universal nature, and submitted to the necessary and immutable laws that she imposes on all the beings she contains, according to their peculiar essences or to the respective properties with which, without consulting them, she endows each particular species. Man's life is a line that nature commands him to describe upon the surface of the earth, without his ever being able to swerve from it, even for an instant. He is born without his own consent; his organization does in nowise depend upon himself; his ideas come to him involuntarily; his habits are in the power of those who cause him to contract them; he is unceasingly modified by causes, whether visible or concealed, over which he has no control, which necessarily regulate his mode of existence, give the hue to his way of thinking, and determine his manner of acting. He is good or bad, happy or miserable, wise or foolish, reasonable or irrational, without his will being for any thing in these various states. Nevertheless, in despite of the shackles by which he is bound, it is pretended he is a free agent, or that independent of the causes by which he is moved, he determines his own will, and regulates his own condition.

However slender the foundation of this opinion, of which every thing ought to point out to him the error, it is current at this day and passes for an incontestable truth with a great number of people, otherwise extremely enlightened; it is the basis of religion, which, supposing relations between man and the unknown being she has placed above nature, has been incapable of imagining how man could either merit reward or deserve punishment from this being, if he was not a free agent. Society has been believed interested in this system; because an idea has gone abroad, that if all the actions of man were to be contemplated as necessary, the right of punishing those who injure their associates would no longer exist. At length human vanity accommodated itself to a hypothesis which, unquestionably, appears to distinguish man from all other physical beings, by assigning to him the special privilege of a total independence of all other causes, but of which a very little reflection would have shown him the impossibility. . . .

The will . . . is a modification of the brain, by which it is disposed to action, or prepared to give play to the organs. This will is necessarily determined by the qualities, good or bad, agreeable or painful, of the object or the motive that acts upon his senses, or of which the idea remains with him, and is resuscitated by his memory. In consequence, he acts necessarily, his action is the result of the impulse he receives either from the motive, from the object, or from the idea which has modified his brain, or disposed his will. When he does not act according to this impulse, it is because there comes some new cause, some new motive, some new idea, which modifies his brain in a different manner, gives him a new impulse, determines his will in another way, by which the action of the former impulse is suspended: thus, the sight of an agreeable object, or its idea, determines his will to set him in action to procure it; but if a new object or a new idea more powerfully attracts him, it gives a new direction to his will, annihilates the effect of the former, and prevents the action by which it was to be procured. This is the mode in which reflection, experience, reason, necessarily arrests or suspends the action of man's will: without this he would of necessity have followed the anterior impulse which carried him towards a then desirable object. In all this he always acts according to necessary laws, from which he has no means of emancipating himself.

If when tormented with violent thirst, he figures to himself in idea, or really perceives a fountain, whose limpid streams might cool his feverish want, is he sufficient master of himself to desire or not to desire the object competent to satisfy so lively a want? It will no doubt be conceded, that it is impossible he should not be desirous to satisfy it; but it will be said—if at this moment it is announced to him that the water he so ardently desires is poisoned, he will, notwithstanding his vehement thirst, abstain from drinking it: and it has, therefore, been falsely concluded that he is a free agent. The fact, however, is, that the motive in either case is exactly the same: his own conservation. The same necessity that determined him to drink before he knew the water was deleterious, upon this new discovery equally determines him not to drink; the desire of conserving himself either annihilates or suspends the former impulse; the second motive becomes stronger than the preceding, that is, the fear of death, or the desire of preserving himself,

necessarily prevails over the painful sensation caused by his eagerness to drink; but, it will be said, if the thirst is very parching, an inconsiderate man without regarding the danger will risk swallowing the water. Nothing is gained by this remark: in this case the anterior impulse only regains the ascendency; he is persuaded that life may possibly be longer preserved, or that he shall derive a greater good by drinking the poisoned water than by enduring the torment, which, to his mind, threatens instant dissolution: thus the first becomes the strongest and necessarily urges him on to action. Nevertheless, in either case, whether he partakes of the water, or whether he does not, the two actions will be equally necessary; they will be the effect of that motive which finds itself most puissant; which consequently acts in the most coercive manner upon his will.

This example will serve to explain the whole phenomena of the human will. This will, or rather the brain, finds itself in the same situation as a bowl, which, although it has received an impulse that drives it forward in a straight line, is deranged in its course whenever a force superior to the first obliges it to change its direction. The man who drinks the poisoned water appears a madman; but the actions of fools are as necessary as those of the most prudent individuals. The motives that determine the voluptuary and the debauchee to risk their health, are as powerful, and their actions are as necessary, as those which decide the wise man to manage his. But, it will be insisted, the debauchee may be prevailed on to change his conduct: this does not imply that he is a free agent; but that motives may be found sufficiently powerful to annihilate the effect of those that previously acted upon him; then these new motives determine his will to the new mode of conduct he may adopt as necessarily as the former did to the old mode.

Man is said to *deliberate,* when the action of the will is suspended; this happens when two opposite motives act alternately upon him. *To deliberate,* is to hate and to love in succession; it is to be alternately attracted and repelled; it is to be moved, sometimes by one motive, sometimes by another. Man only deliberates when he does not distinctly understand the quality of the objects from which he receives impulse, or when experience has not sufficiently apprised him of the effects, more or less remote, which his actions will produce. He would take the air, but the weather is uncertain; he deliberates in consequence; he weighs the various motives that urge his will to go out or to stay at home; he is at length determined by that motive which is most probable; this removes his indecision, which necessarily settles his will, either to remain within or to go abroad: his motive is always either the immediate or ultimate advantage he finds, or thinks he finds, in the action to which he is persuaded.

Man's will frequently fluctuates between two objects, of which either the presence or the ideas move him alternately: he waits until he has contemplated the objects, or the ideas they have left in his brain which solicit him to different actions; he then compares these objects or ideas; but even in the time of deliberation, during the comparison, pending these alternatives of love and hatred which succeed each other, sometimes with the utmost rapidity, he is not a free agent for a single instant; the good or the evil which he believes he finds successively in the objects, are the necessary motives of these momentary wills; of the rapid motion of desire or fear, that he experiences as long as his uncertainty continues. From this it will be obvious that deliberation is necessary; that uncertainty is necessary; that whatever part he takes, in consequence of this deliberation, it will always necessarily be that which he has judged, whether well or ill, is most probable to turn to his advantage.

When the soul is assailed by two motives that act alternately upon it, or modify it successively, it deliberates; the brain is in a sort of equilibrium, accompanied with perpetual oscillations, sometimes towards one object, sometimes to-

wards the other, until the most forcible carries the point, and thereby extricates it from this state of suspense, in which consists the indecision of his will. But when the brain is simultaneously assailed by causes equally strong that move it in opposite directions, agreeable to the general law of all bodies when they are struck equally by contrary powers, it stops . . . it is neither capable to will nor to act; it waits until one of the two causes has obtained sufficient force to overpower the other; to determine its will; to attract it in such a manner that it may prevail over the efforts of the other cause.

This mechanism, so simple, so natural, suffices to demonstrate why uncertainty is painful, and why suspense is always a violent state for man. The brain, an organ so delicate and so mobile, experiences such rapid modifications that it is fatigued; or when it is urged in contrary directions, by causes equally powerful, it suffers a kind of compression, that prevents the activity which is suitable to the preservation of the whole, and which is necessary to procure what is advantageous to its existence. This mechanism will also explain the irregularity, the indecision, the inconstancy of man, and account for that conduct which frequently appears an inexplicable mystery, and which is, indeed, the effect of the received systems. In consulting experience, it will be found that the soul is submitted to precisely the same physical laws as the material body. If the will of each individual, during a given time, was only moved by a single cause or passion, nothing would be more easy than to foresee his actions; but his heart is frequently assailed by contrary powers, by adverse motives, which either act on him simultaneously or in succession; then his brain, attracted in opposite directions, is either fatigued, or else tormented by a state of compression, which deprives it of activity. Sometimes it is in a state of incommodious inaction; sometimes it is the sport of the alternate shocks it undergoes. Such, no doubt, is the state in which man finds himself when a lively passion solicits him to the commission of crime, whilst fear points out to him the danger by which it is attended; such, also, is the condition of him whom remorse, by the continued labour of his distracted soul, prevents from enjoying the objects he has criminally obtained.

Choice by no means proves the free agency of man: he only deliberates when he does not yet know which to choose of the many objects that move him, he is then in an embarrassment, which does not terminate until his will is decided by the greater advantage he believes he shall find in the object he chooses, or the action he undertakes. From whence it may be seen, that choice is necessary, because he would not determine for an object, or for an action, if he did not believe that he should find in it some direct advantage. That man should have free agency it were needful that he should be able to will or choose without motive, or that he could prevent motives coercing his will. Action always being the effect of his will once determined, and as his will cannot be determined but by a motive which is not in his own power, it follows that he is never the master of the determination of his own peculiar will; that consequently he never acts as a free agent. It has been believed that man was a free agent because he had a will with the power of choosing; but attention has not been paid to the fact that even his will is moved by causes independent of himself; is owing to that which is inherent in his own organization, or which belongs to the nature of the beings acting on him. Is he the master of willing not to withdraw his hand from the fire when he fears it will be burnt? Or has he the power to take away from fire the property which makes him fear it? Is he the master of not choosing a dish of meat, which he knows to be agreeable or analogous to his palate; of not preferring it to that which he knows to be disagreeable or dangerous? It is always according to his sensations, to his own peculiar experience, or to his suppositions, that he judges of things, either well or ill; but whatever may be his judgment, it depends necessarily on his mode of feeling, whether habitual or accidental, and the qualities he finds in the causes that move him, which exist in despite of himself. . . .

When it is said, that man is not a free agent, it is not pretended to compare him to a body moved by a simple impulsive cause: he contains within himself causes inherent to his existence; he is moved by an interior organ, which has its own peculiar laws, and is itself necessarily determined in consequence of ideas formed from perceptions resulting from sensations which it receives from exterior objects. As the mechanism of these sensations, of these perceptions, and the manner they engrave ideas on the brain of man, are not known to him; because he is unable to unravel all these motions; because he cannot perceive the chain of operations in his soul, or the motive principle that acts within him, he supposes himself a free agent; which, literally translated, signifies, that he moves himself by himself; that he determines himself without cause: when he rather ought to say, that he is ignorant how or for why he acts in the manner he does. It is true the soul enjoys an activity peculiar to itself; but it is equally certain that this activity would never be displayed, if some motive or some cause did not put it in a condition to exercise itself: at least it will not be pretended that the soul is able either to love or to hate without being moved, without knowing the objects, without having some idea of their qualities. Gunpowder has unquestionably a particular activity, but this activity will never display itself, unless fire be applied to it; this, however, immediately sets it in motion.

It is the great complication of motion in man, it is the variety of his action, it is the multiplicity of causes that move him, whether simultaneously or in continual succession, that persuades him he is a free agent: if all his motions were simple, if the causes that move him did not confound themselves with each other, if they were distinct, if his machine were less complicated, he would perceive that all his actions were necessary, because he would be enabled to recur instantly to the cause that made him act. A man who should be always obliged to go towards the west, would always go on that side; but he would feel that, in so going, he was not a free agent: if he had another sense, as his actions or his motion, augmented by a sixth, would be still more varied and much more complicated, he would believe himself still more a free agent than he does with his five senses.

It is, then, for want of recurring to the causes that move him; for want of being able to analyze, from not being competent to decompose the complicated motion of his machine, that man believes himself a free agent; it is only upon his own ignorance that he founds the profound yet deceitful notion he has of his free agency; that he builds those opinions which he brings forward as a striking proof of his pretended freedom of action. If, for a short time, each man was willing to examine his own peculiar actions, search out their true motives to discover their concatenation, he would remain convinced that the sentiment he has of his natural free agency, is a chimera that must speedily be destroyed by experience.

Nevertheless it must be acknowledged that the multiplicity and diversity of the causes which continually act upon man, frequently without even his knowledge, render it impossible, or at least extremely difficult for him to recur to the true principles of his own peculiar actions, much less the actions of others: they frequently depend upon causes so fugitive, so remote from their effects, and which, superficially examined, appear to have so little analogy, so slender a relation with them, that it requires singular sagacity to bring them into light. This is what renders the study of the moral man a task of such difficulty; this is the reason why his heart is an abyss, of which it is frequently impossible for him to fathom the depth. He is then obliged to content himself with a knowledge of the general and necessary laws by which the human heart is regulated: for the individuals of his own species these laws are pretty nearly the same; they vary only in consequence of the organization that is peculiar to each, and of the modification it undergoes: this, however, cannot be rigorously the same in any two. It suffices to know, that by his essence, man tends to conserve himself, and to render his existence happy: this granted, whatever may be his actions, if he recur back to this first principle, to this general, this necessary tendency of his will, he never can be deceived with regard to his motives.

For Further Reflection

1. Has D'Holbach proved that we do not have free will? Is his argument that science precludes such a notion convincing?

2. D'Holbach points out that without the doctrine of free will, the notion of just punishment crumbles: that religion could not justify God's sending people to hell for their sins, and the Law could not justify its system of punishments without the doctrine. Do you agree with D'Holbach?

3. Could we go even farther and say that we would not have any place for moral praise or blame without a notion of free will? What would D'Holbach make of moral responsibility?

4. J.B.S. Haldane has written, "If my mental processes are determined wholly by the motion of atoms in my brain, I have no reason to suppose that my beliefs are true . . . and hence I have no reason for supposing my brain to be composed of atoms." Does this show that determinism is self-refuting?

The Dilemma of Determinism V.2

WILLIAM JAMES

William James (1842–1910), an American philosopher and psychologist, was born in New York City and educated at Harvard. He was the brother of Henry James the novelist. James struggled through much of his life with ill health. He was assailed by doubts over freedom of the will and the existence of God, and he developed the philosophy of pragmatism in part as a response to these difficulties. Pragmatism originated with James' friend Charles Peirce but underwent crucial changes and popularization in the hands of James. His principal works are *The Principles of Psychology* (1890), *The Will to Believe* (1897), *The Varieties of Religious Experience* (1902), and *Pragmatism, A New Name for Some Old Ways of Thinking* (1907).

In this essay, James argues that while neither the doctrine of freedom of the will nor the doctrine of determinism can be proved, there are good reasons to choose the doctrine of free will. First of all, it makes better sense of the universe in terms of satisfying our deepest intellectual and emotional needs. Secondly, it makes sense of the notions of regret, especially moral regret that things are not better. Essentially, the choice between the two doctrines is not intellectual but is based on different personality types: "possibility men" and "anti-possibility men."

Study Questions

1. What is James' purpose in this essay?
2. What are the two suppositions set forth at the outset?
3. How does James characterize the principle of causality?
4. What are the two types of determinism and why is one type a "quagmire of evasion"?
5. How is determinism described with regard to the idea of possibilities?
6. How is indeterminism described with regard to the notion of possibilities?
7. How does James think that people choose between these two ways of looking at the world?
8. How is the notion of chance described?
9. What are the limits put on the idea of free will?
10. Formulate James' argument that the notion of regret involves the determinist in a dilemma.
11. What is James' conclusion to the problem of free will versus determinism?

Rationality and the Free-Will Controversy

A COMMON OPINION PREVAILS that the juice has ages ago been pressed out of the free-will controversy, and that no new champion can do more than warm up stale arguments which everyone has heard. This is a radical mistake. I know of no subject less worn out, or in which

This selection is reprinted, with omissions, from "The Dilemma of Determinism," an essay which first appeared in 1884.

inventive genius has a better chance of breaking open new ground—not, perhaps, of forcing a conclusion or of coercing assent, but of deepening our sense of what the issue between the two parties really is, and of what the ideas of fate and of free will imply. At our very side almost, in the past few years, we have seen falling in rapid succession from the press works that present the alternative in entirely novel lights. Not to speak of the English disciples of Hegel, such as Green and Bradley; not to speak of Hinton and Hodgson, nor of Hazard here—we see in the writings of Renouvier, Fouillée, and Delboeuf how completely changed and refreshed is the form of the old disputes. I cannot pretend to vie in originality with any of the masters I have named, and my ambition limits itself to just one little point. If I can make two of the necessarily implied corollaries of determinism clearer to you than they have been made before, I shall have made it possible for you to decide before or against that doctrine with a better understanding of what you are about. And if you prefer not to decide at all, but to remain doubters, you will at least see more plainly what the subject of your hesitation is. I thus declaim openly on the threshold all pretension to prove to you that the freedom of the will is true. The most I hope is to induce some of you to follow my own example in assuming it true, and acting as if it were true. If it be true, it seems to me that this is involved in the strict logic of the case. Its truth ought not to be forced willy-nilly down our indifferent throats. It ought to be freely espoused by men who can equally well turn their backs upon it. In other words, our first act of freedom, if we are free, ought in all inward propriety to be to affirm that we are free. This should exclude, it seems to me, from the free-will side of the question all hope of a coercive demonstration—a demonstration which I, for one, am perfectly contented to go without.

With thus much understood at the outset, we can advance. But, not without one more point understood as well. The arguments I am about to urge all proceed on two suppositions: first, when we make theories about the world and discuss them with one another, we do so in order to attain a conception of things which shall give us subjective satisfaction; and, second, if there be two conceptions, and the one seems to us, on the whole, more rational than the other, we are entitled to suppose that the more rational one is truer of the two. I hope that you are all willing to make these suppositions with me; for I am afraid that if there be any of you here who are not, they will find little edification in the rest of what I have to say. I cannot stop to argue the point; but I myself believe that all the magnificent achievements of mathematical and physical science—our doctrines of evolution, of uniformity of law, and the rest—proceed from our indomitable desire to cast the world into a more rational shape in our minds than the shape into which it is thrown there by the crude order of our experience. The world has shown itself, to a great extent, plastic to this demand of ours for rationality. How much farther it will show itself plastic no one can say. Our only means of finding out is to try; and I, for one, feel as free to try conceptions of moral as of mechanical or of logical rationality. If a certain formula for expressing the nature of the world violates my moral demand, I shall feel free to throw it overboard, or at least to doubt it, as if it disappointed my demand for uniformity of sequence, for example; the one demand being, so far as I can see, quite as subjective and emotional as the other is. The principle of causality, for example—what is it but a postulate, an empty name covering simply a demand that the sequence of events shall some day manifest a deeper kind of belonging of one thing with another than the mere juxtaposition which now phenomenally appears? It is as much an altar to an unknown god as the one that Saint Paul found at Athens. All our scientific and philosophic ideals are altars to unknown gods. Uniformity is as much so as is free will. If this be admitted, we can debate on even terms. But if any one pretends that while freedom and variety are, in the first instance, subjective demands, necessity and uniformity are something altogether different, I do not see how we can debate at all.

To begin, then, I must suppose you acquainted with all the usual arguments on the subject. I cannot stop to take up the old proofs from causation, from statistics, from the certainty with which we can foretell one another's conduct, from the fixity of character, and all the rest. But there are two *words* which usually encumber these classical arguments, and which we must immediately dispose of if we are to make any progress. One is the eulogistic word *freedom,* and the other is the opprobrious word *chance.* The word "chance" I wish to keep, but I wish to get rid of the word "freedom." Its eulogistic associations have so far overshadowed all the rest of its meaning that both parties claim the sole right to use it, and determinists today insist that they alone are freedom's champions. Old-fashioned determinism was what we may call *hard* determinism. It did not shrink from such words as fatality, bondage of the will, necessitation, and the like. Nowadays, we have a *soft* determinism which abhors harsh words, and, repudiating fatality, necessity, and even predetermination, says that its real name is freedom; for freedom is only necessity understood, and bondage to the highest is identical with true freedom. Even a writer as little used to making capital out of soft words as Mr. Hodgson hesitates not to call himself a "free-will determinist."

Now, all this is a quagmire of evasion under which the real issue of fact has been entirely smothered. Freedom in all these senses presents simply no problem at all. No matter what the soft determinist mean by it—whether he mean the acting without external constraint; whether he mean the acting rightly, or whether he mean the acquiescing in the law of the whole—who cannot answer him that sometimes we are free and sometimes we are not? But there *is* a problem, an issue of fact and not of words, an issue of the most momentous importance, which is often

decided without discussion in one sentence—nay, in one clause of a sentence—by those very writers who spin out whole chapters in their efforts to show what "true" freedom is; and that is the question of determinism, about which we are to talk tonight.

Possibilities and Actualities

Fortunately, no ambiguities hang about this word or about its opposite, indeterminism. Both designate an outward way in which things may happen, and their cold and mathematical sound has no sentimental associations that can bribe our partiality either way in advance. Now, evidence of an external kind to decide between determinism and indeterminism is, as I intimated a while back, strictly impossible to find. Let us look at the difference between them and see for ourselves. What does determinism profess?

It professes that those parts of the universe already laid down absolutely appoint and decree what the other parts shall be. The future has no ambiguous possibilities hidden in its womb: the part we call the present is compatible with only one totality. Any other future complement than the one fixed from eternity is impossible. The whole is in each and every part, and welds it with the rest into an absolute unity, an iron block, in which there can be no equivocation or shadow of turning.

> With earth's first clay they did the last man knead,
> And there of the last harvest sowed the seed.
> And the first morning of creation wrote
> What the last dawn of reckoning shall read.

Indeterminism, on the contrary, says that the parts have a certain amount of loose play on one another, so that the laying down of one of them does not necessarily determine what the others shall be. It admits that possibilities may be in excess of actualities, and that things not yet revealed to our knowledge may really in themselves be ambiguous. Of two alternative futures which we conceive, both may now be really possible; and the one become impossible only at the very moment when the other excludes it by becoming real itself. Indeterminism thus denies the world to be one unbending unit of fact. It says there is a certain ultimate pluralism in it; and, so saying, it corroborates our ordinary unsophisticated view of things. To that view, actualities seem to float in a wider sea of possibilities from out of which they are chosen; and, somewhere, indeterminism says, such possibilities exist, and form a part of truth.

Determinism, on the contrary, says they exist *nowhere,* and that necessity on the one hand and impossibility on the other are the sole categories of the real. Possibilities that fail to get realized are, for determinism, pure illusions: they never were possibilities at all. There is nothing inchoate, it says, about this universe of ours, all that was or is or shall be actual in it having been from eternity virtually there. The cloud of alternatives our minds escort this mass of actuality withal is a cloud of sheer deceptions, to which "impossibilities" is the only name which rightfully belongs.

The issue, it will be seen, is a perfectly sharp one, which no eulogistic terminology can smear over or wipe out. The truth *must* lie with one side or the other, and its lying with one side makes the other false.

The question relates solely to the existence of possibilities, in the strict sense of the term, as things that may, but need not, be. Both sides admit that a volition, for instance, has occurred. The indeterminists say another volition might have occurred in its place: the determinists swear that nothing could possibly have occurred in its place. Now, can science be called in to tell us which of these two point-blank contradicters of each other is right? Science professes to draw no conclusions but such as are based on matters of fact, things that have actually happened; but how can any amount of assurance that something actually happened give us the least grain of information as to whether another thing might or might not have happened in its place? Only facts can be proved by other facts. With things

that are possibilities and not facts, facts have no concern. If we have no other evidence than the evidence of existing facts, the possibility-question must remain a mystery never to be cleared up.

And the truth is that facts practically have hardly anything to do with making us either determinists or indeterminists. Sure enough, we make a flourish of quoting facts this way or that; and if we are determinists, we talk about the infallibility with which we can predict one another's conduct; while if we are indeterminists, we lay great stress on the fact that it is just because we cannot foretell one another's conduct, either in war or statecraft or in any of the great and small intrigues and businesses of men, that life is so intensely anxious and hazardous a game. But who does not see the wretched insufficiency of this so-called objective testimony on both sides? What fills up the gaps in our minds is something not objective, not external. What divides us into *possibility* men and *anti-possibility* men is different faiths or postulates—postulates of rationality. To this man the world seems more rational with possibilities in it—to that man more rational with possibilities excluded; and talk as we will about having to yield to evidence, what makes us monists or pluralists, determinists or indeterminists, is at bottom always some sentiment like this.

The Idea of Chance

The stronghold of the deterministic sentiment is the antipathy to the idea of chance. As soon as we begin to talk indeterminism to our friends, we find a number of them shaking their heads. This notion of alternative possibility, they say, this admission that any one of several things may come to pass, is, after all, only a round-about name for chance; and chance is something the notion of which no sane mind can for an instant tolerate in the world. What is it, they ask, but barefaced crazy unreason, the negation of intelligibility and law? And if the slightest particle of it exists anywhere, what is to prevent the whole fabric from falling together, the stars from going out, and chaos from recommencing her topsy-turvy reign?

Remarks of this sort about chance will put an end to discussion as quickly as anything one can find. I have already told you that "chance" was a word I wished to keep and use. Let us then examine exactly what it means, and see whether it ought to be such a terrible bugbear to us. I fancy that squeezing the thistle boldly will rob it of its sting.

The sting of the word "chance" seems to lie in the assumption that it means something positive, and that if anything happens by chance, it must needs be something of an intrinsically irrational and preposterous sort. Now, chance means nothing of the kind. It is a purely negative and relative term, giving us no information about that of which it is predicated, except that it happens to be disconnected with something else—not controlled, secured, or necessitated by other things in advance of its own actual presence. As this point is the most subtle one of the whole lecture, and at the same time the point on which all the rest hinges, I beg you to pay particular attention to it. What I say is that it tells us nothing about what a thing may be in itself to call it "chance." It may be a bad thing, it may be a good thing. It may be lucidity, transparency, fitness incarnate, matching the whole system of other things, when it has once befallen, in an unimaginably perfect way. All you mean by calling it "chance" is that this is not guaranteed, that it may also fall out otherwise. For the system of other things has no positive hold on the chance-thing. Its origin is in a certain fashion negative: it escapes, and says, "Hands off!" coming, when it comes, as a free gift, or not at all.

This negativeness, however, and this opacity of the chance-thing when thus considered *ab extra*, or from the point of view of previous things or distant things, do not preclude its having any amount of positiveness and luminosity from within, and at its own place and moment. All that its chance-character asserts about it is that there is something in it really of its own,

something that is not the unconditional property of the whole. If the whole wants this property, the whole must wait till it can get it, if it be a matter of chance. That the universe may actually be a sort of joint-stock society of this sort, in which the sharers have both limited liabilities and limited powers, is of course a simple and conceivable notion.

Nevertheless, many persons talk as if the minutest dose of disconnectedness of one part with another, the smallest modicum of independence, the faintest tremor of ambiguity about the future, for example, would ruin everything, and turn this goodly universe into a sort of insane sand-heap or nulliverse—no universe at all. Since future human volitions are, as a matter of fact, the only ambiguous things we are tempted to believe in, let us stop for a moment to make ourselves sure whether their independent and accidental character need be fraught with such direful consequences to the universe as these.

What is meant by saying that my choice of which way to walk home after the lecture is ambiguous and matter of chance as far as the present moment is concerned? It means that both Divinity Avenue and Oxford Street are called; but that only one, and that one *either* one shall be chosen. Now, I ask you seriously to suppose that this ambiguity of my choice is real; and then to make the impossible hypothesis that the choice is made twice over, and each time falls on a different street. In other words, imagine that I first walk through Divinity Avenue, and then imagine that the powers governing the universe annihilate ten minutes of time with all that it contained, and set me back at the door of this hall just as I was before the choice was made. Imagine then that, everything else being the same, I now make a different choice and traverse Oxford Street. You, as passive spectators, look on and see the two alternative universes—one of them with me walking through Divinity Avenue in it, the other with the same me walking through Oxford Street. Now, if you are determinists you believe one of these universes to have been from eternity impossible: you believe it to have been impossible because of the intrinsic irrationality or accidentality somewhere involved in it. But looking outwardly at these universes, can you say which is the impossible and accidental one, and which the rational and necessary one? I doubt if the most iron-clad determinist among you could have the slightest glimmer of light at this point. In other words, either universe *after the fact* and once there would, to our means of observation and understanding, appear just as rational as the other. There would be absolutely no criterion by which we might judge one necessary and the other matter of chance. Suppose now we relieve the gods of their hypothetical task and assume my choice, once made, to be made forever. I go through Divinity Avenue for good and all. If, as good determinists, you now begin to affirm, what all good determinists punctually do affirm, that in the nature of things I couldn't have gone through Oxford Street—had I done so it would have been chance, irrationality, insanity, a horrid gap in nature—I simply call your attention to this, that your affirmation is what the Germans call a *Machtspruch,* a mere conception fulminated as a dogma and based on no insight into details. Before my choice, either street seemed as natural to you as to me. Had I happened to take Oxford Street, Divinity Avenue would have figured in your philosophy as the gap in nature; and you would have so proclaimed it with the best deterministic conscience in the world.

But what a hollow outcry, then, is this against a chance which, if it were present to us, we could by no character whatever distinguish from a rational necessity! I have taken the most trivial of examples, but no possible example could lead to any different result. For what are the alternatives which, in point of fact, offer themselves to human volition? What are those futures that now seem matters of chance? Are they not one and all like the Divinity Avenue and Oxford Street of our example? Are they not all of them *kinds* of things already here and based in the existing frame of nature? Is any one ever tempted to produce an *absolute* accident, something utterly

irrelevant to the rest of the world? Do not all the motives that assail us, all the futures that offer themselves to our choice, spring equally from the soil of the past; and would not either one of them, whether realized through chance or through necessity, the moment it was realized, seem to us to fit that past, and in the completest and most continuous manner to interdigitate with the phenomena already there?

A favorite argument against free will is that if it be true, a man's murderer may as probably be his best friend as his worst enemy, a mother be as likely to strangle as to suckle her first-born, and all of us be as ready to jump from fourth-story windows as to go out of front doors, etc. Users of this argument should probably be excluded from debate till they learn what the real question is. "Free-will" does not say that everything that is physically conceivable is also morally possible. It merely says that of alternatives that really *tempt* our will more than one is really possible. Of course, the alternatives that do thus tempt our will are vastly fewer than the physical possibilities we can coldly fancy. Persons really tempted often do murder their best friends, mothers do strangle their first-born, people do jump out of fourth stories, etc.

The more one thinks of the matter, the more one wonders that so empty and gratuitous a hubbub as this outcry against chance should have found so great an echo in the hearts of men. It is a word which tells us absolutely nothing about what chances, or about the *modus operandi* of the chancing; and the use of it as a war-cry shows only a temper of intellectual absolutism, a demand that the world shall be a solid block, subject to one control—which temper, which demand, the world may not be bound to gratify at all. In every outwardly verifiable and practical respect, a world in which the alternatives that now actually distract *your* choice were decided by pure chance would be by *me* absolutely undistinguished from the world in which I now live. I am, therefore, entirely willing to call it, so far as your choices go, a world of chance for me. To *yourselves,* it is true, those very acts of choice, which to me are so blind, opaque, and external, are the opposites of this, for you are within them and effect them. To you they appear as decisions; and decisions, for him who makes them, are altogether peculiar psychic facts. Self-luminous and self-justifying at the living moment in which they occur, they appeal to no outside moment to put its stamp upon them or make them continuous with the rest of nature. Themselves it is rather who seem to make nature continuous; and in their strange and intense function of granting consent to one possibility and withholding it from another, to transform an equivocal and double future into an inalterable and simple past.

But with the psychology of the matter we have no concern this evening. The quarrel which determinism has with chance fortunately has nothing to do with this or that psychological detail. It is a quarrel altogether metaphysical. Determinism denies the ambiguity of future volitions, because it affirms that nothing future can be ambiguous. But we have said enough to meet the issue. Indeterminate future volitions *do* mean chance. Let us not fear to shout it from the house-tops if need be; for we now know that the idea of chance is, at bottom, exactly the same thing as the idea of gift—the one simply being a disparaging, and the other a eulogistic, name for anything on which we have no effective *claim*. And whether the world be the better or the worse for having either chances or gifts in it will depend altogether on *what* these uncertain and unclaimable things turn out to be.

The Moral Implications of Determinism

And this at last brings us within sight of our subject. We have seen what determinism means: we have seen that indeterminism is rightly described as meaning chance; and we have seen that chance, the very name of which we are urged to shrink from as from a metaphysical pestilence, means only the negative fact that no part of the world, however big, can claim to control absolutely the destinies of the whole. But although, in discussing the word "chance," I may at moments have seemed to be arguing for its real existence, I have not meant to do so yet. We have not yet ascertained whether this be a world of chance or no; at most, we have agreed that it seems so. And I now repeat what I said at the outset, that, from any strict theoretical point of view, the question is insoluble. To deepen our theoretic sense of the *difference* between a world with chances in it and a deterministic world is the most I can hope to do; and this I may now at last begin upon, after all our tedious clearing of the way.

I wish first of all to show you just what the notion that this is a deterministic world implies. The implications I call your attention to are all bound up with the fact that it is a world in which we constantly have to make what I shall, with your permission, call judgments of regret. Hardly an hour passes in which we do not wish that something might be otherwise; and happy indeed are those of us whose hearts have never echoed the wish of Omar Khayyam—

> That we might clasp, ere closed, the book of fate,
> And make the writer on a fairer leaf
> Inscribe our names, or quite obliterate.

> Ah! Love, could you and I with fate conspire
> To mend this sorry scheme of things entire,
> Would we not shatter it to bits, and then
> Remould it nearer to the heart's desire?

Now, it is undeniable that most of these regrets are foolish, and quite on a par in point of philosophic value with the criticisms on the universe of that friend of our infancy, the hero of the fable, "The Atheist and the Acorn"—

> Fool! had that bough a pumpkin bore,
> Thy whimsies would have worked no more,
> etc.

Even from the point of view of our own ends, we should probably make a botch of remodelling the universe. How much more then from the point of view of ends we cannot see! Wise men therefore regret as little as they can. But still some regrets are pretty obstinate and hard to stifle—regrets for acts of wanton cruelty or treachery, for example, whether performed by others or by ourselves. Hardly any one can remain *entirely* optimistic after reading the confession of the murderer at Brockton the other day: how, to get rid of the wife whose continued existence bored him, he inveigled her into a deserted spot, shot her four times, and then, as she lay on the ground and said to him, "You didn't do it on purpose, did you, dear?" replied, "No, I didn't do it on purpose," as he raised a rock and smashed her skull. Such an occurrence, with the mild sentence and self-satisfaction of the prisoner, is a field for a crop of regrets, which one need not take up in detail. We feel that, although a perfect mechanical fit to the rest of the universe, it is a bad moral fit, and that something else would really have been better in its place.

But for the deterministic philosophy the murder, the sentence, and the prisoner's optimism were all necessary from eternity; and nothing else for a moment had a ghost of a chance of being put in their place. To admit such a chance, the determinists tell us, would be to make a suicide of reason; so we must steel our hearts against the thought. And here our plot thickens, for we see the first of those difficult implications of determinism and monism which it is my purpose to make you feel. If this Brockton murder was called for by the rest of the universe, if it had come at its preappointed hour, and if nothing else would have been consistent with the sense of the whole, what are we to think of the universe? Are we stubbornly to stick to our judgment of regret, and say, though it *couldn't* be, yet it *would* have been a better universe with something different from this Brockton murder in it? That, of course, seems the natural and spontaneous thing for us to do; and yet it is nothing short of deliberately espousing a kind of pessimism. The judgment of regret calls the murder bad. Calling a thing bad means, if it means anything at all, that the thing ought not be, that something else ought to be in its stead. Determinism, in denying that anything else can be in

its stead, virtually defines the universe as a place in which what ought to be is impossible—in other words, as an organism whose constitution is afflicted with an incurable taint, and irremediable flaw. The pessimism of a Schopenhauer says no more than this—that the murder is a symptom; and that it is a vicious symptom because it belongs to a vicious whole, which can express its nature no otherwise than by bringing forth just such a symptom as that at this particular spot. Regret for the murder must transform itself, if we are determinists and wise, into a larger regret. It is absurd to regret the murder alone. Other things being what they are, *it* could not be different. What we should regret is that whole frame of things of which the murder is one member. I see no escape whatever from this pessimistic conclusion if, being determinists, our judgment of regret is to be allowed to stand at all.

The only deterministic escape from pessimism is everywhere to abandon the judgment of regret. That this can be done, history shows to be not impossible. The devil, *quoad existentiam,* may be good. That is, although he be a *principle* of evil, yet the universe, with such a principle in it, may practically be a better universe than it could have been without. On every hand, in a small way, we find that a certain amount of evil is a condition by which a higher form of good is brought. There is nothing to prevent anybody from generalizing this view, and trusting that if we could but see things in the largest of all ways, even such matters as this Brockton murder would appear to be paid for by the uses which follow in their train. An optimism *quand même,* a systematic and infatuated optimism like that ridiculed by Voltaire in his *Candide,* is one of the possible ideal ways in which a man may train himself to look upon life. Bereft of dogmatic hardness and lit up with the expression of a tender and pathetic hope, such an optimism has been the grace of some of the most religious characters that ever lived.

Throb thine with Nature's throbbing breast,
And all is clear from east to west.

Even cruelty and treachery may be among the absolutely blessed fruits of time, and to quarrel with any of their details may be blasphemy. The only real blasphemy, in short, may be that pessimistic temper of the soul which lets it give way to such things as regrets, remorse, and grief.

Thus, our deterministic pessimism may become a deterministic optimism at the price of extinguishing our judgments of regret.

But does not this immediately bring us into a curious logical predicament? Our determinism leads us to call our judgments of regret wrong, because they are pessimistic in implying that what is impossible yet ought to be. But how then about the judgments of regret themselves? If they are wrong, other judgments, judgments of approval presumably, ought to be in their place. But as they are necessitated, nothing else *can* be in their place; and the universe is just what it was before—namely, a place in which what ought to be appears impossible. We have got one foot out of the pessimistic bog, but the other one sinks all the deeper. We have rescued our actions from the bonds of evil, but our judgments are now held fast. When murders and treacheries cease to be sins, regrets are theoretic absurdities and errors. The theoretic and the active life thus play a kind of see-saw with each other on the ground of evil. The rise of either sends the other down. Murder and treachery cannot be good without regret being bad: regret cannot be good without treachery and murder being bad. Both, however, are supposed to have been foredoomed; so something must be fatally unreasonable, absurd, and wrong in the world. It must be a place of which either sin or error forms a necessary part. From this dilemma there seems at first sight no escape. Are we then so soon to fall back into the pessimism from which we thought we had emerged? And is there no possible way by which we may, with good intellectual consciences, call the cruelties and the treacheries, the reluctances and the regrets, *all* good together?

Certainly there is such a way, and you are probably most of you ready to formulate it your-

selves. But, before doing so, remark how inevitably the question of determinism and indeterminism slides us into the question of optimism and pessimism, or, as our fathers called it, "The question of evil." The theological form of all these disputes is simplest and the deepest, the form from which there is the least escape—not because, as some have sarcastically said, remorse and regret are clung to with a morbid fondness by the theologians as spiritual luxuries, but because they are existing facts in the world, and as such must be taken into account in the deterministic interpretation of all that is fated to be. If they are fated to be error, does not the bat's wing of irrationality cast its shadow over the world? . . .

Morality and Indeterminism

The only consistent way of representing a pluralism and a world whose parts may affect one another through their conduct being either good or bad is the indeterministic way. What interest, zest, or excitement can there be in achieving the right way, unless we are enabled to feel that the wrong way is also a possible and a natural way— nay, more, a menacing and an imminent way? And what sense can there be in condemning ourselves for taking the wrong way, unless we need have done nothing of the sort, unless the right way was open to us as well? I cannot understand the willingness to act, no matter how we feel, without the belief that acts are really good and bad. I cannot understand the belief that an act is bad, without regret at its happening. I cannot understand regret without the admission of real, genuine possibilities in the world. Only then is it other than a mockery to feel, after we have failed to do our best, that an irreparable opportunity is gone from the universe, the loss of which it must forever after mourn.

If you insist that this is all superstition, that possibility is in the eye of science and reason impossibility, and that if I act badly 'tis that the universe was foredoomed to suffer this defect, you fall right back into the dilemma, the labyrinth, of pessimism and subjectivism, from out of whose toils we have just wound our way.

Now, we are of course free to fall back, if we please. For my own part, though, whatever difficulties may beset the philosophy of objective right and wrong, and the indeterminism it seems to imply, determinism, with its alternative pessimism or romanticism, contains difficulties that are greater still. But you will remember that I expressly repudiated awhile ago the pretension to offer any arguments which could be coercive in a so-called scientific fashion in this matter. And I consequently find myself, at the end of this long talk, obliged to state my conclusions in an altogether personal way. This personal method of appeal seems to be among the very conditions of the problem; and the most any one can do is to confess as candidly as he can the grounds for the faith that is in him, and leave his example to work on others as it may.

Let me, then, without circumlocution say just this. The world is enigmatical enough in all conscience, whatever theory we may take up toward it. The indeterminism I defend, the free-will theory of popular sense based on the judgment of regret, represents that world as vulnerable, and liable to be injured by certain of its parts if they act wrong. And it represents their acting wrong as a matter of possibility or accident, neither inevitable nor yet to be infallibly warded off. In all this, it is a theory devoid either of transparency or of stability. It gives us a pluralistic, restless universe, in which no single point of view can ever take in the whole scene; and to a mind possessed of the love of unity at any cost, it will, no doubt, remain forever inacceptable. A friend with such a mind once told me that the thought of my universe made him sick, like the sight of the horrible motion of a mass of maggots in their carrion bed.

But while I freely admit that the pluralism and the restlessness are repugnant and irrational in a certain way, I find that every alternative to them is irrational in a deeper way. The indeterminism with its maggots, if you please to speak so about it, offends only the native absolutism of my intellect—an absolutism which, after all, perhaps, deserves to be snubbed and kept in check. But the determinism with its necessary carrion, to continue the figure of speech, and with no possible maggots to eat the latter up, violates my sense of moral reality through and through. When, for example, I imagine such carrion as the Brockton murder, I cannot conceive it as an act by which the universe, as a whole, logically and necessarily expresses its nature without shrinking from complicity with such a whole. And I deliberately refuse to keep on terms of loyalty with the universe by saying blankly that the murder, since it does flow from the nature of the whole, is not carrion. There are *some* instinctive reactions which I, for one, will not tamper with. The only remaining alternative, the attitude of gnostical romanticism, wrenches my personal instincts in quite as violent a way. It falsifies the simple objectivity of their deliverance. It makes the goose-flesh the murder excites in me a sufficient reason for the perpetration of the crime. It transforms life from a tragic reality into an insincere melodramatic exhibition, as foul or as tawdry as any one's diseased curiosity pleases to carry it out. And with its consecration of the *roman naturaliste* state of mind, and its enthronement of the baser crew of Parisian *littérateurs* among the eternally indispensable organs by which the infinite spirit of things attains to that subjective illumination which is the task of its life, it leaves me in presence of a sort of subjective carrion considerably more noisome than the objective carrion I called it in to take away.

No! better a thousand times, than such systematic corruption of our moral sanity, the plainest pessimism, so that it be straightforward; but better far than that, the world of chance. Make as great an uproar about chance as you please, I know that chance means pluralism and nothing more. If some of the members of the pluralism are bad, the philosophy of pluralism, whatever broad views it may deny me, permits me, at least, to turn to the other members with a clean breast of affection and an unsophisticated moral sense. And if I still wish to think of the world as a totality, it lets me feel that a world with a chance in it of being altogether good, even if the chance never come to pass, is better than a world with no such chance at all. That "chance" whose very notion I am exhorted and conjured to banish from my view of the future as the suicide of reason concerning it, that "chance" is—what? Just this—the chance that in moral respects the future may be other and better than the past has been. This is the only chance we have any motive for supposing to exist. Shame, rather, on its repudiation and its denial! For its presence is the vital air which lets the world live, the salt which keeps it sweet. . . .

For Further Reflection

1. Do you agree with James that the question of free will versus determinism is unprovable and largely a matter of sentiment based on personality type? In that case, are we determined to choose one view or the other?

2. Is James correct to reject the high status of the principle of causality (the idea that every event or state of affairs must have an antecedent cause), characterizing it as an "altar to an unknown god"?

Compatibilism   V.3

W. T. STACE

W. T. Stace (1886–1967) was born in Britain and educated at Trinity College, Dublin, and he served in the British Civil Service in Ceylon. In 1932 he came to the United States to teach at Princeton University. One of his chief goals was to reconcile empiricism with mysticism. Among his works are *The Concept of Morals* (1952), *Time and Eternity* (1952), and *Mysticism and Philosophy* (1960).

Stace attempts to reconcile free will with causal determinism. He takes the position which James labelled "soft determinism," what is sometimes called compatibilism. It is necessary that we have free will in order to be held morally responsible, and yet it seems plausible that all of our actions are caused. How can these two apparently inconsistent ideas be brought together? Stace argues that the problem is merely a verbal dispute, and that, rightly understood, there is no inconsistency in holding to both doctrines. Free actions are those we do voluntarily, whereas unfree actions are those that we do involuntarily.

Study Questions

1. Why is it important to discover whether we have free will? Explain Stace's argument.
2. In practice by what doctrine do even determinists live?

3. How does Stace characterize the dispute between free will and determinism?

4. What is Stace's strategy in consulting common language usage to show that free will is compatible with determinism?

5. What is the difference between a free and an unfree act?

6. What is Stace's general conclusion?

7. How does moral responsibility actually require determinism, according to Stace?

I SHALL FIRST DISCUSS the problem of free will, for it is certain that if there is no free will there can be no morality. Morality is concerned with what men ought and ought not to do. But if a man has no freedom to choose what he will do, if whatever he does is done under compulsion, then it does not make sense to tell him that he ought not to have done what he did and that he ought to do something different. All moral precepts would in such case be meaningless. Also if he acts always under compulsion, how can he be held morally responsible for his actions? How can he, for example, be punished for what he could not help doing?

It is to be observed that those learned professors of philosophy or psychology who deny the existence of free will do so only in their professional moments and in their studies and lecture rooms. For when it comes to doing anything practical, even of the most trivial kind, they invariably behave as if they and others were free. They inquire from you at dinner whether you will choose this dish or that dish. They will ask a child why he told a lie, and will punish him for not having chosen the way of truthfulness. All of which is inconsistent with a disbelief in free will. This should cause us to suspect that the problem is not a real one; and this, I believe, is the case. The dispute is merely verbal, and is due to nothing but a confusion about the meanings of words. It is what is now fashionably called a semantic problem.

How does a verbal dispute arise? Let us consider a case which, although it is absurd in the sense that no one would ever make the mistake

which is involved in it, yet illustrates the principle which we shall have to use in the solution of the problem. Suppose that someone believed that the word "man" means a certain sort of five-legged animal; in short that "five-legged animal" is the correct *definition* of man. He might then look around the world, and rightly observing that there are no five-legged animals in it, he might proceed to deny the existence of men. This preposterous conclusion would have been reached because he was using an incorrect definition of "man." All you would have to do to show him his mistake would be to give him the correct definition; or at least show him that his definition was wrong. Both the problem and its solution would, of course, be entirely verbal. The problem of free will, and its solution, I shall maintain, is verbal in exactly the same way. The problem has been created by the fact that learned men, especially philosophers, have assumed an incorrect definition of free will, and then finding that there is nothing in the world which answers to their definition, have denied its existence. As far as logic is concerned, their conclusion is just as absurd as that of the man who denies the existence of men. The only difference is that the mistake in the latter case is obvious and crude, while the mistake which the deniers of free will have made is rather subtle and difficult to detect.

Throughout the modern period, until quite recently, it was assumed, both by the philosophers who denied free will and by those who defended it, that *determinism is inconsistent with free will*. If a man's actions were wholly determined by chains of causes stretching back into the re-

Specified excerpts (pp. 248–258) from Religion and the Modern Mind *by W. T. Stace (J. B. Lippincott Company). Copyright 1952 by W. T. Stace. Reprinted by permission of HarperCollins Publishers.*

mote past, so that they could be predicted beforehand by a mind which knew all the causes, it was assumed that they could not in that case be free. This implies that a certain definition of actions done from free will was assumed, namely that they are actions *not* wholly determined by causes or predictable beforehand. Let us shorten this by saying that free will was defined as meaning indeterminism. This is the incorrect definition which has led to the denial of free will. As soon as we see what the true definition is we shall find that the question whether the world is deterministic, as Newtonian science implied, or in a measure indeterministic, as current physics teaches, is wholly irrelevant to the problem.

Of course there is a sense in which one can define a word arbitrarily in any way one pleases. But a definition may nevertheless be called correct or incorrect. It is correct if it accords with a *common usage* of the word defined. It is incorrect if it does not. And if you give an incorrect definition, absurd and untrue results are likely to follow. For instance, there is nothing to prevent you from arbitrarily defining a man as a five-legged animal, but this is incorrect in the sense that it does not accord with the ordinary meaning of the word. Also it has the absurd result of leading to a denial of the existence of men. This shows that *common usage is the criterion for deciding whether a definition is correct or not*. And this is the principle which I shall apply to free will. I shall show that indeterminism is not what is meant by the phrase "free will" *as it is commonly used*. And I shall attempt to discover the correct definition by inquiring how the phrase is used in ordinary conversation.

Here are a few samples of how the phrase might be used in ordinary conversation. It will be noticed that they include cases in which the question whether a man acted with free will is asked in order to determine whether he was morally and legally responsible for his acts.

Jones: I once went without food for a week.
Smith: Did you do that of your own free will?

Jones: No. I did it because I was lost in a desert and could find no food.

But suppose that the man who had fasted was Mahatma Gandhi. The conversation might then have gone:

Gandhi: I once fasted for a week.
Smith: Did you do that of your own free will?
Gandhi: Yes. I did it because I wanted to compel the British Government to give India its independence.

Take another case. Suppose that I had stolen some bread, but that I was as truthful as George Washington. Then, if I were charged with the crime in court, some exchange of the following sort might take place:

Judge: Did you steal the bread of your own free will?
Stace: Yes. I stole it because I was hungry.

Or in different circumstances the conversation might run:

Judge: Did you steal of your own free will?
Stace: No. I stole because my employer threatened to beat me if I did not.

At a recent murder trial in Trenton some of the accused had signed confessions, but afterwards asserted that they had done so under police duress. The following exchange might have occurred:

Judge: Did you sign the confession of your own free will?
Prisoner: No. I signed it because the police beat me up.

Now suppose that a philosopher had been a member of the jury. We could imagine this conversation taking place in the jury room.

Foreman of the Jury: The prisoner says he signed the confession because he was beaten, and not of his own free will.
Philosopher: This is quite irrelevant to the case. There is no such thing as free will.

Foreman: Do you mean to say that it makes no difference whether he signed because his conscience made him want to tell the truth or because he was beaten?

Philosopher: None at all. Whether he was caused to sign by a beating or by some desire of his own—the desire to tell the truth, for example—in either case his signing was causally determined, and therefore in neither case did he act of his own free will. Since there is no such thing as free will, the question whether he signed of his own free will ought not to be discussed by us.

The foreman and the rest of the jury would rightly conclude that the philosopher must be making some mistake. What sort of a mistake could it be? There is only one possible answer. The philosopher must be using the phrase "free will" in some peculiar way of his own which is not the way in which men usually use it when they wish to determine a question of moral responsibility. That is, he must be using an incorrect definition of it as implying action not determined by causes.

Suppose a man left his office at noon, and were questioned about it. Then we might hear this:

Jones: Did you go out of your own free will?
Smith: Yes. I went out to get my lunch.

But we might hear:

Jones: Did you leave your office of your own free will?
Smith: No. I was forcibly removed by the police.

We have now collected a number of cases of actions which, in the ordinary usage of the English language, would be called cases in which people have acted of their own free will. We should also say in all these cases that they *chose* to act as they did. We should also say that they could have acted otherwise, if they had chosen. For instance, Mahatma Gandhi was not com-pelled to fast; he chose to do so. He could have eaten if he had wanted to. When Smith went out to get his lunch, he chose to do so. He could have stayed and done some work, if he had wanted to. We have also collected a number of cases of the opposite kind. They are cases in which men were not able to exercise their free will. They had no choice. They were compelled to do as they did. The man in the desert did not fast of his own free will. He had no choice in the matter. He was compelled to fast because there was nothing for him to eat. And so with the other cases. It ought to be quite easy, by an inspection of these cases, to tell what we ordinarily mean when we say that a man did or did not exercise free will. We ought therefore to be able to extract from them the proper definition of the term. Let us put the cases in a table:

FREE ACTS	UNFREE ACTS
Gandhi fasting because he wanted to free India.	The man fasting in the desert because there was no food.
Stealing bread because one is hungry.	Stealing because one's employer threatened to beat one.
Signing a confession because one wanted to tell the truth.	Signing because the police beat one.
Leaving the office because one wanted one's lunch.	Leaving because forcibly removed.

It is obvious that to find the correct definition of free acts we must discover what characteristic is common to all the acts in the left-hand column, and is, at the same time, absent from all the acts in the right-hand column. This characteristic which all free acts have, and which no unfree acts have, will be the defining characteristic of free will.

Is being uncaused, or not being determined by causes, the characteristic of which we are in search? It cannot be, because although it is true that all the acts in the right-hand column have causes, such as the beating by the police or the absence of food in the desert, so also do the acts in the left-hand column. Mr. Gandhi's fasting was caused by his desire to free India, the man leaving his office by his hunger, and so on. Moreover there is no reason to doubt that these causes of the free acts were in turn caused by prior conditions, and that these were again the results of causes, and so on back indefinitely into the past. Any physiologist can tell us the causes of hunger. What caused Mr. Gandhi's tremendously powerful desire to free India is no doubt more difficult to discover. But it must have had causes. Some of them may have lain in peculiarities of his glands or brain, others in his past experiences, others in his heredity, others in his education. Defenders of free will have usually tended to deny such facts. But to do so is plainly a case of special pleading, which is unsupported by any scrap of evidence. The only reasonable view is that all human actions, both those which are freely done and those which are not, are either wholly determined by causes, or at least as much determined as other events in nature. It may be true, as the physicists tell us, that nature is not as deterministic as was once thought. But whatever degree of determinism prevails in the world, human actions appear to be as much determined as anything else. And if this is so, it cannot be the case that what distinguishes actions freely chosen from those which are not free is that the latter are determined by causes while the former are not. Therefore, being uncaused or being undetermined by causes, must be an incorrect definition of free will.

What, then, is the difference between acts which are freely done and those which are not? What is the characteristic which is present to all the acts in the left-hand column and absent from all those in the right-hand column? Is it not obvious that, although both sets of actions have causes, the causes of those in the left-hand column are *of a different kind* from the causes of those in the right-hand column? The free acts are all caused by desires, or motives, or by some sort of internal psychological states of the agent's

mind. The unfree acts, on the other hand, are all caused by physical forces or physical conditions, outside the agent. Police arrest means physical force exerted from the outside; the absence of food in the desert is a physical condition of the outside world. We may therefore frame the following rough definitions. *Acts freely done are those whose immediate causes are psychological states in the agent. Acts not freely done are those whose immediate causes are states of affairs external to the agent.*

It is plain that if we define free will in this way, then free will certainly exists, and the philosopher's denial of its existence is seen to be what it is—nonsense. For it is obvious that all those actions of men which we should ordinarily attribute to the exercise of their free will, or of which we should say that they freely chose to do them, are in fact actions which have been caused by their own desire, wishes, thoughts, emotions, impulses, or other psychological states.

In applying our definition we shall find that it usually works well, but that there are some puzzling cases which it does not seem exactly to fit. These puzzles can always be solved by paying careful attention to the ways in which words are used, and remembering that they are not always used consistently. I have space for only one example. Suppose that a thug threatens to shoot you unless you give him your wallet, and suppose that you do so. Do you, in giving him your wallet, do so of your own free will or not? If we apply our definition, we find that you acted freely, since the immediate cause of the action was not an actual outside force but the fear of death, which is a psychological cause. Most people, however, would say that you did not act of your own free will but under compulsion. Does this show that our definition is wrong? I do not think so. Aristotle, who gave a solution of the problem of free will substantially the same as ours (though he did not use the term "free will") admitted that there are what he called "mixed" or borderline cases in which it is difficult to know whether we ought to call the acts free or compelled. In the case under discussion, though no actual force was used, the gun at your forehead so nearly approximated to actual force that we tend to say the case was one of compulsion. It is a borderline case.

Here is what may seem like another kind of puzzle. According to our view an action may be free though it could have been predicted beforehand with certainty. But suppose you told a lie, and it was certain beforehand that you would tell it. How could one then say, "You could have told the truth"? The answer is that it is perfectly true that you could have told the truth *if* you had wanted to. In fact you would have done so, for in that case the causes producing your action, namely your desires, would have been different, and would therefore have produced different effects. It is a delusion that predictability and free will are incompatible. This agrees with common sense. For if, knowing your character, I predict that you will act honorably, no one would say when you do act honorably, that this shows you did not do so of your own free will.

Since free will is a condition of moral responsibility, we must be sure that our theory of free will gives a sufficient basis for it. To be held morally responsible for one's actions means that one may be justly punished or rewarded, blamed or praised, for them. But it is not just to punish a man for what he cannot help doing. How can it be just to punish him for an action which it was certain beforehand that he would do? We have not attempted to decide whether, as a matter of fact, all events, including human actions, are completely determined. For that question is irrelevant to the problem of free will. But if we assume for the purposes of argument that complete determinism is true, but that we are nevertheless free, it may then be asked whether such a deterministic free will is compatible with moral responsibility. For it may seem unjust to punish a man for an action which it could have been predicted with certainty beforehand that he would do.

But that determinism is incompatible with moral responsibility is as much a delusion as

that it is incompatible with free will. You do not excuse a man for doing a wrong act because, knowing his character, you felt certain beforehand that he would do it. Nor do you deprive a man of a reward or prize because, knowing his goodness or his capabilities, you felt certain beforehand that he would win it.

Volumes have been written on the justification of punishment. But so far as it affects the question of free will, the essential principles involved are quite simple. The punishment of a man for doing a wrong act is justified, either on the ground that it will correct his own character, or that it will deter other people from doing similar acts. The instrument of punishment has been in the past, and no doubt still is, often unwisely used; so that it may often have done more harm than good. But that is not relevant to our present problem. Punishment, if and when it is justified, is justified only on one or both of the grounds just mentioned. The question then is how, if we assume determinism, punishment can correct character or deter people from evil actions.

Suppose that your child develops a habit of telling lies. You give him a mild beating. Why? Because you believe that his personality is such that the usual motives for telling the truth do not cause him to do so. You therefore supply the missing cause, or motive, in the shape of pain and the fear of future pain if he repeats his untrustful behavior. And you hope that a few treatments of this kind will condition him to the habit of truth-telling, so that he will come to tell the truth without the infliction of pain. You assume that his actions are determined by causes, but that the usual causes of truth-telling do not in him produce their usual effects. You therefore supply him with an artificially injected motive, pain and fear, which you think will in the future cause him to speak truthfully.

The principle is exactly the same where you hope, by punishing one man, to deter others from wrong actions. You believe that the fear of punishment will cause those who might otherwise do evil to do well.

We act on the same principle with non-human, and even with inanimate, things, if they do not behave in the way we think they ought to behave. The rose bushes in the garden produce only small and poor blooms, whereas we want large and rich ones. We supply a cause which will produce large blooms, namely fertilizer. Our automobile does not go properly. We supply a cause which will make it go better, namely oil in the works. The punishment for the man, the fertilizer for the plant, and the oil for the car, are all justified by the same principle and in the same way. The only difference is that different kinds of things require different kinds of causes to make them do what they should. Pain may be the appropriate remedy to apply, in certain cases, to human beings, and oil to the machine. It is, of course, of no use to inject motor oil into the boy or to beat the machine.

Thus we see that moral responsibility is not only consistent with determinism, but requires it. The assumption on which punishment is based is that human behavior is causally determined. If pain could not be a cause of truth-telling there would be no justification at all for punishing lies. If human actions and volitions were uncaused, it would be useless either to punish or reward, or indeed to do anything else to correct people's bad behavior. For nothing that you could do would in any way influence them. Thus moral responsibility would entirely disappear. If there were no determinism of human beings at all, their actions would be completely unpredictable and capricious, and therefore irresponsible. And this is in itself a strong argument against the common view of philosophers that free will means being undetermined by causes.

For Further Reflection

1. Has Stace successfully reconciled free will with determinism? Does his analysis of ordinary language settle the matter? In our next reading, we shall examine John Hospers' evaluation of that claim. You may want to turn to that article before you decide on the matter.

A Psychoanalytic Defense of Hard Determinism V.4

JOHN HOSPERS

Hospers rejects the compatibilist's attempt to reconcile free will and determinism, arguing that compatibilism is founded on a superficial view of being *compelled*. The compatibilist proceeds as though all compulsion were external, but in fact, argues Hospers, psychoanalysis shows that there is deep inward compulsion, and this factor counts against the distinction which the compatibilist makes. Hospers argues that psychoanalytic research destroys the compatibilist's case and leads us to accept hard determinism.

(A biographical sketch of Hospers appears on p. 157.)

Study Questions

1. Why does Hospers focus on the idea of unconscious motivation in his discussion?
2. What are the main features of the psychoanalytic doctrine?
3. What are Hospers' four illustrations of unconscious motivation?
4. How does Hospers apply his analysis to normal people?
5. Do we have moral responsibility?
6. How does a determinist justify punishing people?
7. What is the point of Hospers' quotation from Butler's *Erehwon* ("nowhere" spelled backwards)?
8. Is there any room at all for freedom of the will?

[Hospers makes reference to a philosopher named Schlick. Schlick's position and argument were the same as Stace's compatibilist position and argument.]

I. [A Critique of Compatibilism]

... SCHLICK'S ANALYSIS IS INDEED clarifying and helpful to those who have fallen victim to the confusions he exposes—and this probably includes most persons in their philosophical growing-pains. But *is* this the end of the matter? Is it true that all acts, though caused, are free as long as they are not compelled in the sense which he specifies? May it not be that, while the identification of "free" with "uncompelled" is acceptable, the area of compelled acts is vastly greater than he or most other philosophers have ever suspected? (Moore is more cautious in this respect than Schlick; while for Moore an act is free if it is voluntary in the sense specified above, he thinks there may be another sense in which human beings, and human acts, are not free at all.[1]) We remember statements about human beings being pawns of their early environment, victims of conditions beyond their control, the result of causal influences stemming from their parents, and the like, and we ponder and ask, "Still, are we really free?" Is there not something in what generations of sages have said

about man being fettered? Is there not perhaps something too facile, too sleight-of-hand, in Schlick's cutting of the Gordian knot? For example, when a metropolitan newspaper headlines an article with the words "Boy Killer Is Doomed Long before He Is Born," and then goes on to describe how a twelve-year-old boy has been sentenced to prison for the murder of a girl, and how his parental background includes records of drunkenness, divorce, social maladjustment, and paresis, are we still to say that his act, though voluntary and assuredly not done at the point of a gun, is free? The boy has early displayed a tendency toward sadistic activity to hide an underlying masochism and "prove that he's a man"; being coddled by his mother only worsens this tendency, until, spurned by a girl in his attempt on her, he kills her—not simply in a fit of anger, but calculatingly, deliberately. Is he free in respect of his criminal act, or for that matter in most of the acts of his life? Surely to ask this question is to answer it in the negative. Perhaps I have taken an extreme case; but it is only to show the superficiality of the Schlick analysis the more clearly. Though not everyone has criminotic tendencies, everyone has been molded by influences which in large measure at least determine his present behavior; he is literally the product of these influences, stemming from periods prior to his "years of discretion," giving

Reprinted from Philosophy and Phenomenological Research, *1950, by permission of the publisher.*

him a host of character traits that he cannot change now even if he would. So obviously does what a man is depend upon how a man comes to be, that it is small wonder that philosophers and sages have considered man far indeed from being the master of his fate. It is not as if man's will were standing high and serene above the flux of events that have molded him; it is itself caught up in this flux, itself carried along on the current. An act is free when it is determined by the man's character, say moralists; but what if the most decisive aspects of his character were already irrevocably acquired before he could do anything to mold them? What if even the degree of will power available to him in shaping his habits and disciplining himself now to overcome the influence of his early environment is a factor over which he has no control? What are we to say of this kind of "freedom"? Is it not rather like the freedom of the machine to stamp labels on cans when it has been devised for just that purpose? Some machines can do so more efficiently than others, but only because they have been better constructed.

II. [The Argument from Psychoanalysis]

It is not my purpose here to establish this thesis in general, but only in one specific respect which has received comparatively little attention, namely, the field referred to by psychiatrists as that of unconscious motivation. In what follows I shall restrict my attention to it because it illustrates as clearly as anything the points I wish to make.

Let me try to summarize very briefly the psychoanalytic doctrine on this point. The conscious life of the human being, including the conscious decisions and volitions, is merely a mouthpiece for the unconscious—not directly for the enactment of unconscious drives, but of the compromise between unconscious drives and unconscious reproaches. There is a Big Three behind the scenes which the automaton called the conscious personality carries out: the id, an

"eternal gimme," presents its wish and demands its immediate satisfaction; the super-ego says no to the wish immediately upon presentation, and the unconscious ego, the mediator between the two, tries to keep peace by means of compromise.

To go into examples of the functioning of these three "bosses" would be endless; psychoanalytic case books supply hundreds of them. The important point for us to see in the present context is that *it is the unconscious that determines what the conscious impulse and the conscious action shall be.* Hamlet, for example, had a strong Oedipus wish, which was violently counteracted by super-ego reproaches; these early wishes were vividly revived in an unusual adult situation in which his uncle usurped the coveted position from Hamlet's father and won his mother besides. This situation evoked strong strictures on the part of Hamlet's super-ego, and it was this that was responsible for his notorious delay in killing his uncle. A dozen times Hamlet could have killed Claudius easily; but every time Hamlet "decided" not to: a free choice, moralists would say—but no, listen to the super-ego: "What you feel such hatred toward your uncle for, what you are plotting to kill him for, is precisely the crime which you yourself desire to commit: to kill your father and replace him in the affections of your mother. Your fate and your uncle's are bound up together." This paralyzes Hamlet into inaction. Consciously all he knows is that he is unable to act; this conscious inability he rationalizes, giving a different excuse each time.

We have always been conscious of the fact that we are not masters of our fate in every respect—that there are many things which we cannot do, that nature is more powerful than we are, that we cannot disobey laws without danger of reprisals, etc. We have become "officially" conscious, too, though in our private lives we must long have been aware of it, that we are not free with respect to the emotions that we feel—whom we love or hate, what types we admire, and the like. More lately still we have been reminded that there are unconscious motivations for our basic attractions and repulsions, our compulsive actions or inabilities to act. But what is not welcome news is that our very acts of volition, and the entire train of deliberations leading up to them, are but façades for the expression of unconscious wishes, or rather, unconscious compromises and defenses.

A man is faced by a choice: shall he kill another person or not? Moralists would say, here is a free choice—the result of deliberation, an action consciously entered into. And yet, though the agent himself does not know it, and has no awareness of the forces that are at work within him, his choice is already determined for him: his conscious will is only an instrument, a slave, in the hands of a deep unconscious motivation which determines his action. If he has a great deal of what the analyst calls "free-floating guilt," he will not; but if the guilt is such as to demand immediate absorption in the form of self-damaging behavior, this accumulated guilt will have to be discharged in some criminal action. The man himself does not know what the inner clockwork is; he is like the hands on the clock, thinking they move freely over the face of the clock.

A woman has married and divorced several husbands. Now she is faced with a choice for the next marriage: shall she marry Mr. A, or Mr. B, or nobody at all? She may take considerable time to "decide" this question, and her decision may appear as a final triumph of her free will. Let us assume that A is a normal, well-adjusted, kind, and generous man, while B is a leech, an impostor, one who will become entangled constantly in quarrels with her. If she belongs to a certain classifiable psychological type, she will inevitably choose B, and she will do so even if her previous husbands have resembled B, so that one would think that she "had learned from experience." Consciously, she will of course "give the matter due consideration," etc., etc. To the psychoanalyst all this is irrelevant chaff in the wind—only a camouflage for the inner workings

about which she knows nothing consciously. If she is of a certain kind of masochistic strain, as exhibited in her previous set of symptoms, she *must* choose B: her super-ego, always out to maximize the torment in the situation, seeing what dazzling possibilities for self-damaging behavior are promised by the choice of B, compels her to make the choice she does, and even to conceal the real basis of the choice behind an elaborate façade of rationalizations.

. . . A man has wash-compulsion. He must be constantly washing his hands—he uses up perhaps 400 towels a day. Asked why he does this, he says, "I need to, my hands are dirty"; and if it is pointed out to him that they are not really dirty, he says, "They feel dirty anyway, I feel better when I wash them." So once again he washes them. He "freely decides" every time; he feels that he must wash them, he deliberates for a moment perhaps, but always ends by washing them. What he does not see, of course, are the invisible wires inside him pulling him inevitably to do the thing he does: the infantile id-wish concerns preoccupation with dirt, the super-ego charges him with this, and the terrified ego must respond, "No, I don't like dirt, see how clean I like to be, look how I wash my hands!"

Let us see what further "free acts" the same patient engages in (this is an actual case history): he is taken to a concentration camp, and given the worst of treatment by the Nazi guards. In the camp he no longer chooses to be clean, does not even try to be—on the contrary, his choice is now to wallow in filth as much as he can. All he is aware of now is a disinclination to be clean, and every time he must choose he chooses not to be. Behind the scenes, however, another drama is being enacted: the super-ego, perceiving that enough torment is being administered from the outside, can afford to cease pressing its charges in this quarter—the outside world is doing the torturing now, so the super-ego is relieved of the responsibility. Thus the ego is relieved of the agony of constantly making terrified replies in the form of washing to prove that the super-ego is wrong. The defense no longer being needed, the person slides back into what is his natural predilection anyway, for filth. This becomes too much even for the Nazi guards: they take hold of him one day, saying, "We'll teach you how to be clean!" drag him into the snow, and pour bucket after bucket of icy water over him until he freezes to death. . . .

Let us take a less colorful, more everyday example. A student at a university, possessing wealth, charm, and all that is usually considered essential to popularity, begins to develop the following personality pattern: although well taught in the graces of social conversation, he always makes a *faux pas* somewhere, and always in the worst possible situation; to his friends he makes cutting remarks which hurt deeply—and always apparently aimed in such a way as to hurt the most: a remark that would not hurt A but would hurt B he invariably makes to B rather than to A, and so on. None of this is conscious. Ordinarily he is considerate of people, but he contrives always (unconsciously) to impose on just those friends who would resent it most, and at just the times when he should know that he should not impose: at 3 o'clock in the morning, without forewarning, he phones a friend in a near-by city demanding to stay at his apartment for the weekend; naturally the friend is offended, but the person himself is not aware that he has provoked the grievance ("common sense" suffers a temporary eclipse when the neurotic pattern sets in, and one's intelligence, far from being of help in such a situation, is used in the interest of the neurosis), and when the friend is cool to him the next time they meet, he wonders why and feels unjustly treated. Aggressive behavior on his part invites resentment and aggression in turn, but all that he consciously sees is others' behavior towards him—and he considers himself the innocent victim of an unjustified "persecution."

Each of these acts is, from the moralist's point of view, free: he chose to phone his friend at 3 A.M.; he chose to make the cutting remark that

he did, etc. What he does not know is that an ineradicable masochistic pattern has set in. His unconscious is far more shrewd and clever than is his conscious intellect; it sees with uncanny accuracy just what kind of behavior will damage him most, and unerringly forces him into that behavior. Consciously, the student "doesn't know why he did it"—he gives different "reasons" at different times, but they are all, once again, rationalizations cloaking the unconscious mechanism which propels him willy-nilly into actions that his "common sense" eschews.

The more of this sort of thing one observes, the more he can see what the psychoanalyst means when he talks about *the illusion of freedom*. And the more of a psychiatrist one becomes, the more he is overcome with a sense of what an illusion this free will can be. In some kinds of cases most of us can see it already: it takes no psychiatrist to look at the epileptic and sigh with sadness at the thought that soon this person before you will be as one possessed, not the same thoughtful intelligent person you knew. But people are not aware of this in other contexts, for example when they express surprise at how a person to whom they have been so good could treat them so badly. Let us suppose that you help a person financially or morally or in some other way, so that he is in your debt; suppose further that he is one of the many neurotics who unconsciously identify kindness with weakness and aggression with strength, then he will unconsciously take your kindness to him as weakness and use it as the occasion for enacting some aggression against you. He can't help it, he may regret it himself later; still, he will be driven to do it. If we gain a little knowledge of psychiatry, we can look at him with pity, that a person otherwise so worthy should be so unreliable—but we will exercise realism too, and be aware that there are some types of people that you cannot be good to; in "free" acts of their conscious volition, they will use your own goodness against you.

Sometimes the persons themselves will become dimly aware that "something behind the scenes" is determining their behavior. The divorcee will sometimes view herself with detachment, as if she were some machine (and indeed the psychoanalyst does call her a "repeating-machine"): "I know I'm caught in a net, that I'll fall in love with this guy and marry him and the whole ridiculous merry-go-round will start all over again."

We talk about free will, and we say, for example, the person is free to do so-and-so if he can do so *if* he wants to—and we forget that his wanting to is itself caught up in the stream of determinism, that unconscious forces drive him into the wanting or not wanting to do the thing in question. The analogy of the puppet whose motions are manipulated from behind by invisible wires, or better still, by springs inside, is a telling one at almost every point.

And the glaring fact is that it all started so early, before we knew what was happening. The personality structure is inelastic after the age of five, and comparatively so in most cases after the age of three. Whether one acquires a neurosis or not is determined by that age—and just as involuntarily as if it had been a curse of God . . . only the psychiatrist knows what puppets people really are; and it is no wonder that the protestations of philosophers that "the act which is the result of a volition, a deliberation, a conscious decision, is free" leaves these persons, to speak mildly, somewhat cold.

III. [Do We Have Moral Responsibility?]

. . . Now, what of the notion of responsibility? What happens to it in our analysis?

Let us begin with an example, not a fictitious one. A woman and her two-year-old baby are riding on a train to Montreal in midwinter. The child is ill. The woman wants badly to get to her destination. She is, unknown to herself, the victim of a neurotic conflict whose nature is irrelevant here except for the fact that it forces her to behave aggressively toward the child, partly to spite her husband whom she despises and who

loves the child, but chiefly to ward off super-ego charges of masochistic attachment. Consciously she loves the child, and when she says this she says it sincerely, but she must behave aggressively toward it nevertheless, just as many children love their mothers but are nasty to them most of the time in neurotic pseudo-aggression. The child becomes more ill as the train approaches Montreal; the heating system of the train is not working, and the conductor pleads with the woman to get off the train at the next town and get the child to a hospital at once. The woman refuses. Soon after, the child's condition worsens, and the mother does all she can to keep it alive, without, however, leaving the train, for she declares that it is absolutely necessary that she reach her destination. But before she gets there the child is dead. After that, of course, the mother grieves, blames herself, weeps hysterically, and joins the church to gain surcease from the guilt that constantly overwhelms her when she thinks of how her aggressive behavior has killed her child.

Was she responsible for her deed? In ordinary life, after making a mistake, we say, "Chalk it up to experience." Here we should say, "Chalk it up to the neurosis." *She* could not help it if her neurosis forced her to act this way—she didn't even know what was going on behind the scenes, her conscious self merely acted out its assigned part. This is far more true than is generally realized: criminal actions in general are not actions for which their agents are responsible; the agents are passive, not active—they are victims of a neurotic conflict. Their very hyperactivity is unconsciously determined.

To say this is, of course, not to say that we should not punish criminals. Clearly, for our own protection, we must remove them from our midst so that they can no longer molest and endanger organized society. And, of course, if we use the word "responsible" in such a way that justly to hold someone responsible for a deed is by definition identical with being justified in punishing him, then we can and do hold people responsible. But this is like the sense of "free" in which free acts are voluntary ones. It does not go deep enough. In a deeper sense we cannot hold the person responsible: we can hold his neurosis responsible, but *he is not responsible for his neurosis,* particularly since the age at which its onset was inevitable was an age before he could even speak.

The neurosis is responsible—but isn't the neurosis a part of *him?* We have been speaking all the time as if the person and his unconscious were two separate beings; but isn't he one personality, including conscious and unconscious departments together?

I do not wish to deny this. But it hardly helps us here; for what people want when they talk about freedom, and what they hold to when they champion it, is the idea that the *conscious* will is the master of their destiny. "I am the master of my fate, I am the captain of my soul"—and they surely mean their conscious selves, the self that they can recognize and search and introspect. Between an unconscious that willy-nilly determines your actions, and an external force which pushes you, there is little if anything to choose. The unconscious is just *as if* it were an outside force; and indeed, psychiatrists will assert that the inner Hitler (your super-ego) can torment you far more than any external Hitler can. Thus the kind of freedom that people want, the only kind they will settle for, is precisely the kind that psychiatry says that they cannot have.

Heretofore it was pretty generally thought that, while we could not rightly blame a person for the color of his eyes or the morality of his parents, or even for what he did at the age of three, or to a large extent what impulses he had and whom he fell in love with, one *could* do so for other of his adult activities, particularly the acts he performed voluntarily and with premeditation. Later this attitude was shaken. Many voluntary acts came to be recognized, at least in some circles, as compelled by the unconscious. Some philosophers recognized this too—Ayer talks about the kleptomaniac being unfree, and

about a person being unfree when another person exerts a habitual ascendancy over his personality. But this is as far as he goes. The usual examples, such as the kleptomaniac and the schizophrenic, apparently satisfy most philosophers, and with these exceptions removed, the rest of mankind is permitted to wander in the vast and alluring fields of freedom and responsibility. So far the inroads upon freedom left the vast majority of humanity untouched; they began to hit home when psychiatrists began to realize, though philosophers did not, that the domination of the conscious by the unconscious extended, not merely to a few exceptional individuals, but to all human beings, that the "big three behind the scenes" are not respecters of persons, and dominate us all, even including that *sanctum sanctorum* of freedom, our conscious will. To be sure, the domination by the unconscious in the case of "normal" individuals is somewhat more benevolent than the tyranny and despotism exercised in neurotic cases, and therefore the former have evoked less comment; but the principle remains in all cases the same: the unconscious is the master of every fate and the captain of every soul.

We speak of a machine turning out good products most of the time but every once in a while it turns out a "lemon." We do not, of course, hold the product responsible for this, but the machine, and via the machine, its maker. Is it silly to extend to inanimate objects the idea of responsibility? Of course. But is it any less so to employ the notion in speaking of human creatures? Are not the two kinds of cases analogous in countless important ways? Occasionally a child turns out badly too, even when his environment and training are the same as that of his brothers and sisters who turn out "all right." He is the "bad penny." His acts of rebellion against parental discipline in adult life are traceable to early experiences of real or fancied denial of infantile wishes. Sometimes the denial has been real, though many denials are absolutely necessary if the child is to grow up to observe the common decencies of civilized life; sometimes, if the child has an unusual quantity of narcissism, every event that occurs is interpreted by him as a denial of his wishes, and nothing a parent could do, even granting every humanly possible wish, would help. In any event, the later neurosis can be attributed to this. Can the person himself be held responsible? Hardly. If he engages in activities which are a menace to society, he must be put into prison, of course, but responsibility is another matter. The time when the events occurred which rendered his neurotic behavior inevitable was a time long before he was capable of thought and decision. As an adult, he is a victim of a world he never made—only this world is inside him.

What about the children who turn out "all right"? All we can say is that "it's just lucky for them" that what happened to their unfortunate brother didn't happen to them; *through no virtue of their own* they are not doomed to the life of unconscious guilt, expiation, conscious depression, terrified ego-gestures for the appeasement of a tyrannical super-ego, that he is. The machine turned them out with a minimum of damage. But if the brother cannot be blamed for his evils, neither can they be praised for their good; unless, of course, we should blame people for what is not their fault, and praise them for lucky accidents.

We all agree that machines turn out "lemons," we all agree that nature turns out misfits in the realm of biology—the blind, the crippled, the diseased; but we hesitate to include the realm of the personality, for here, it seems, is the last retreat of our dignity as human beings. Our ego can endure anything but this; this island at least must remain above the encroaching flood. But may not precisely the same analysis be made here also? Nature turns out psychological "lemons" too, in far greater quantities than any other kind; and indeed all of us are "lemons" in some respect or other, the difference being one of degree. Some of us are lucky enough not to have criminotic tendencies or masochistic mother-attachment or

overdimensional repetition-compulsion to make our lives miserable, but most of our actions, those usually considered the most important, are unconsciously dominated just the same. And, if a neurosis may be likened to a curse of God, let those of us, the elect, who are enabled to enjoy a measure of life's happiness without the hell-fire of neurotic guilt, take this, not as our own achievement, but simply for what it is—a gift of God.

Let us, however, quit metaphysics and put the situation schematically in the form of a deductive argument.

1. An occurrence over which we had no control is something we cannot be held responsible for.
2. Events E, occurring during our babyhood, were events over which we had no control.
3. Therefore events E were events which we cannot be held responsible for.
4. But if there is something we cannot be held responsible for, neither can we be held responsible for something that inevitably results from it.
5. Events E have as inevitable consequence Neurosis N, which in turn has as inevitable consequence Behavior B.
6. Since N is the inevitable consequence of E and B is the inevitable consequence of N, B is the inevitable consequence of E.
7. Hence, not being responsible for E, we cannot be responsible for B.

In Samuel Butler's utopian satire *Erewhon* there occurs the following passage, in which a judge is passing sentence on a prisoner:

> It is all very well for you to say that you came of unhealthy parents, and had a severe accident in your childhood which permanently undermined your constitution; excuses such as these are the ordinary refuge of the criminal; but they cannot for one moment be listened to by the ear of justice. I am not here to enter upon curious metaphysical questions as to the origin of this or that—questions to which there would be no end were their introduction once tolerated, and

which would result in throwing the only guilt on the tissues of the primordial cell, or on the elementary gases. There is no question of how you came to be wicked, but only this—namely, are you wicked or not? This has been decided in the affirmative, neither can I hesitate for a single moment to say that it has been decided justly. You are a bad and dangerous person, and stand branded in the eyes of your fellow countrymen with one of the most heinous known offences.[2]

As moralists read this passage, they may perhaps nod with approval. But the joke is on them. The sting comes when we realize what the crime is for which the prisoner is being sentenced: namely, consumption. The defendant is reminded that during the previous year he was sentenced for aggravated bronchitis, and is warned that he should profit from experience in the future. Butler is employing here his familiar method of presenting some human tendency (in this case, holding people responsible for what isn't their fault) to a ridiculous extreme and thereby reducing it to absurdity.

IV. [Do We Have Free Will?]

Assuming the main conclusions of this paper to be true, is there any room left for freedom?

This, of course, all depends on what we mean by "freedom." . . . When "free" means "uncompelled," and only external compulsion is admitted, there are countless free acts. But now we have extended the notion of compulsion to include determination by unconscious forces. With this sense in mind, our question is, "With the concept of compulsion thus extended, and in the light of present psychoanalytic knowledge, is there any freedom left in human behavior?"

If practicing psychoanalysts were asked this question, there is little doubt that their answer would be along the following lines: they would say that they were not accustomed to using the term "free" at all, but that if they had to suggest a criterion for distinguishing the free from the unfree, they would say that a person's freedom is present in *inverse proportion to his neuroticism;* in other words, the more his acts are determined by a *malevolent* unconscious, the less free he is. Thus they would speak of *degrees* of freedom. They would say that as a person is cured of his neurosis, he becomes more free—free to realize capabilities that were blocked by the neurotic affliction. The psychologically well-adjusted individual is in this sense comparatively the most free. Indeed, those who are cured of mental disorders are sometimes said to have *regained their freedom:* they are freed from the tyranny of a malevolent unconscious which formerly exerted as much of a domination over them as if they had been the abject slaves of a cruel dictator.

But suppose one says that a person is free only to the extent that his acts are *not unconsciously determined at all,* be they unconscious benevolent *or* malevolent? If this is the criterion, psychoanalysts would say, most human behavior cannot be called free at all: our impulses and volitions having to do with our basic attitudes toward life, whether we are optimists or pessimists, tough-minded or tender-minded, whether our tempers are quick or slow, whether we are "naturally self-seeking" or "naturally benevolent" (and *all the acts consequent upon these things*), what things annoy us, whether we take to blondes or brunettes, old or young, whether we become philosophers or artists or businessmen—all this has its basis in the unconscious. If people generally call most acts free, it is not because they believe that compelled acts should be called free, it is rather through not knowing how large a proportion of our acts actually are compelled. Only the comparatively "vanilla-flavored" aspects of our lives—such as our behavior toward people who don't really matter to us—are exempted from this rule.

These, I think, are the two principal criteria for distinguishing freedom from the lack of it which we might set up on the basis of psychoanalytic knowledge. Conceivably we might set up others. In every case, of course, it remains trivially true that "it all depends on how we choose to use the word." The facts are what they are, regardless of what words we choose for labeling them. But if we choose to label them in a way which is not in accord with what human beings, however vaguely, have long had in mind in applying these labels, as we would be doing if we labeled as "free" many acts which we know as much about as we now do through modern psychoanalytic methods, then we shall only be manipulating words to mislead our fellow creatures.

NOTES

1. *Ethics,* Chapter 6, pp. 217 ff.
2. Samuel Butler, *Erewhon* (Modern Library edition), p. 107.

For Further Reflection

1. Hospers bases his argument on the doctrine of psychoanalysis. What is the evidence that psychoanalysis is true or completely true? Examine the content mentioned by Hospers to see whether you can detect any debatable premises.

2. Compare Hospers' argument with Stace's argument (reading V.3). Do you think that Hospers has successfully refuted compatibilism? Has he been as successful in refuting libertarianism?

V. 5   A Contemporary Defense of Libertarianism

SUSAN LEIGH ANDERSON

Susan Leigh Anderson (1944–) was educated at Vassar College and the University of California–Los Angeles and is an associate professor of philosophy at the University of Connecticut. Her specialty is philosophy of mind, on which she has written widely.

Anderson first distinguishes between two types of freedom: voluntary action and action in which the agent is the sole cause. The first is the type of freedom defended by the compatibilists, the second by the libertarians. She will defend the second type and does so by answering five objections to it.

Study Questions

1. What are the two distinct concepts of freedom?
2. What are the conditions which must obtain for libertarian freedom to exist?
3. What are the four initial arguments against the libertarian notion and in favor of soft determinism which Anderson mentions and rebuts?

4. What is the crucial fifth argument and how does Anderson deal with it?

5. What is the center-theory of the mind? How does it support libertarianism?

6. What are the two essential things libertarians must do in order to defend their position against attack?

THERE SEEM TO BE (at least) two distinct conceptions of freedom in the literature on the Free Will/Determinism issue, yet this point is seldom made clear in introductions to the topic. According to the first conception, a person is said to be free if he is not acting under compulsion, if he is able to translate his desires into action. In the words of David Hume,

> By liberty . . . we can only mean *a power of acting or not acting according to the determinations of the will;* that is, if we choose to remain at rest, we may; if we choose to move, we also may.[1]

This is the sense of freedom the "Soft" Determinist has in mind when he maintains that although Determinism[2] is the case, most of our actions are free.

The other conception of freedom is that which is associated with the position called Libertarianism. According to this conception, freedom can exist only if Determinism does not. To quote Henri Bergson:

> The argument of the [Determinists] implies that there is only one possible act corresponding to given antecedents; the believers in free will assume, on the other hand, that the same series could issue in several different acts, equally possible.[3]

Being able to perform alternative actions at a given moment in time, all antecedent conditions remaining the same, is not however a *sufficient* condition for saying that the act performed is free. It is also necessary that the agent be the *cause*—the *sole* cause—of the act. Thus C. A. Campbell, the primary spokesman for Liber-

tarianism, states that "an act is 'free' act . . . only if the agent (a) is the sole cause of the act; and (b) could exert his causality in alternative ways."[4] The Libertarian maintains that only if we are free in *this* sense, should we be held morally responsible for our actions. Thus Roderick M. Chisholm, who has recently tried to revive the libertarian notion of freedom, states:

> Let us consider some deed, or misdeed, that may be attributed to a responsible agent: one man, say, shot another. If the man *was* responsible for what he did, then, I would urge, what was to happen at the time of the shooting was something that was entirely up to the man himself. There was a moment at which it was true, both that he could have fired the shot and also that he could have refrained from firing it.[5]

It is this second conception of freedom that I am interested in examining. It is, I am convinced, the type of freedom the "common man" believes one must enjoy before one can rightfully be held responsible for one's actions;[6] yet most contemporary philosophers have found little difficulty in dismissing this notion of freedom. Why? In the first section of this paper, I would like to look at the case against Libertarianism which culminates in the charge that the position is unintelligible. In the second section, I would like to see if it is possible to defend Libertarianism against this ultimate attack. In the third, and final, section, I would like to consider a still further question: Assuming that the libertarian position can be made intelligible, how often are persons able to perform actions that are free in this second (libertarian) sense?

From *"The Libertarian Conception of Freedom,"* International Philosophical Quarterly, *volume 21, number 4 (1981). By permission of* International Philosophical Quarterly.

The Case Against Libertarianism

Most philosophers today accept the position of Determinism and, therefore, of necessity have had to hold that there can be no instances of actions which are free in the second (libertarian) sense. But this is not being fair to the Soft Determinist's position. From his basic conviction, the belief in Determinism, there have arisen a number of classic arguments to show that it must be the *first* conception of freedom, not the second, which we have in mind when we worry about the kind of freedom which is necessary in order to hold people responsible for their actions. Four of these arguments can be, and have been, easily attacked by the Libertarian:

(1) Moral appraisal does not impute freedom to the agent in the second sense; quite the contrary,

> When I pass a moral judgment on another, far from implying his free-will, I tacitly assume that my judgment of him, in so far as he takes cognizance of it, operates as a determining influence on his conduct. Thus moral criticism when interpreted naturalistically harmonizes with the theory of moral determinism.[7]

[The Libertarian replies: It may, indeed, be *effective* to pass a moral judgment on, punish, or reward a person under the theory of Determinism; but he doesn't *deserve* the judgment, punishment, or reward.]

(2) To hold a person morally responsible for an action it is necessary only that "he could have done otherwise if he had chosen to," which amounts to his having freedom in the *first* sense and is compatible with Determinism. [The Libertarian replies: But could he have *chosen* otherwise than he did? Only if he could have *chosen* otherwise—which implies that he has freedom in the *second* sense—should he be held morally responsible for his action.]

(3) If persons had the *second* kind of freedom, there would be no continuity of character, no basis for prediction of people's behavior. But it does seem that we are able to make such predictions. If we could not, social life would be reduced to complete chaos. [One Libertarian, Campbell, replies:

> The Libertarian view is perfectly compatible with prediction within certain limits. . . . (1) There is no question, on our view, of a free will that can will just anything at all. The range of possible choices is limited by the agent's character in every case . . . (2) There is *one* experiential situation, and *one only,* on our view, in which there is any possibility of the act of will not being in accordance with character . . . the situation of moral temptation. Now this is a situation of comparative rarity. . . . (3) Even within that one situation which is relevant to free will, our view can still recognize a certain basis for prediction. . . .[8]]

(4) There is also the argument, which is related to the third, that if persons were free in the Libertarian sense, then we would not be able to causally influence each other's behavior. But obviously we can affect others in this way, so Libertarianism must be false. [Chisholm's reply is that although certain actions are free, other people may exert a causal influence on these actions by *restricting* the agent's options or by *enabling* him to do what he otherwise could not have done.

> Thus if you provide me with the necessary *means* for getting to Boston, means without which I wouldn't have been able to get there, then, if I do go there, you can be said to have contributed causally to what I do even though my undertaking the trip had no sufficient causal conditions.[9]]

There is, however, a fifth argment which is generally thought to clinch the Soft Determinist's case. This argument appears to successfully reduce the libertarian position to absurdity.

> It is constantly objected against the Libertarian doctrine that it is fundamentally *unintelligible.* Libertarianism holds that [a free act] is the self's act, and yet insists at the same time that it is not influenced by any of those determinate features in the self's nature which go to consti-

tute its "character." But, it is asked, do not these two propositions contradict one another? . . . If you really wish to maintain, it is urged, that the act of decision is not determined by the self's character, you ought to admit frankly that it is not determined by the *self* at all. But in that case, of course, you will not be advocating a freedom which lends any kind of support to moral responsibility; indeed very much the reverse.[10]

Can the Libertarian refute this argument? Surely he must be able to make his position intelligible or else he should give up his notion of freedom altogether.

Let us look first at Campbell's "official" reply to the objection that Libertarianism is unintelligible. He says that the objection is the product of

the error of confining one's self to the categories of the external observer in dealing with the actions of human agents. . . .

It is perfectly true that the standpoint of the external observer . . . does not furnish us with even a glimmering of a notion of what can be meant by an entity which acts causally and yet not through any of the determinate features of its character. . . . But then we are *not* obliged to confine ourselves to external observation in dealing with the human agent. . . . if we do adopt [an] inner standpoint . . . we find that we not merely can, but constantly do, attach meaning to a causation which is the self-causation but is yet not exercised by the self's character.[11]

This reply is not very satisfying. We are told that the idea of an act ensuing from the self, but not from the self's character, will be intelligible if we only look at it from an "inner" standpoint. But what if we try this perspective and still don't find the act intelligible? Or, even if we think we do, is it not possible that we are just deluding ourselves? We want some sort of explanation as to *how* this type of act is possible. Yet with this request Campbell becomes defensive. He suspects that what we mean by an "intelligible" act is "one whose occurrence is in principle capable of being inferred." But, of course, the Liber-

tarian's free act will be unintelligible in this sense. This follows from the *definition* of a free act.

I think Campbell has a much better reply to give to the charge that the Libertarian's free act is unintelligible than the one he has given above.[12] It is suggested by many things he says, but it is never explicitly stated. Consider the following passages in which Campbell describes a free act:

The agent distinguishes sharply between the self which makes the decision, and the self which, as formed character, determines not the decision but the situation within which the decision takes place.[13]

The self which makes the decision must be something "beyond" its formed character.[14] Self-consciousness leads to the recognition of a . . . distinction within selfhood, the distinction of the self as it is from the self as it is capable of becoming.[15]

Campbell accepts a certain metaphysical view of the self which he is clearly employing in his descriptions of a free act. He is, of course, a dualist; but this is not what is important to the issue at hand. What is important is his view of the mind which is for him, as for all dualists, where the self is to be located. According to C. D. Broad, one may adopt either a Center-Theory or Non-Center Theory to account for the unity of the mind (and, as a result, the unity of the self). To quote his explanation of the difference between the two:

By a centre-theory I mean a theory which ascribes the unity of the mind to the fact that there is a certain particular existent—a centre—which stands in a common asymmetrical relation to all the mental events which would be said to be states of a certain mind, and does not stand in this relation to any mental events which would not be said to be states of this mind. By a non-centre theory I mean one which denies the existence of any such particular centre and ascribes the unity of the mind to the fact that certain mental events are directly interrelated in certain characteristic ways and that other mental events are not related to these in the particular way in which these are related to each other.[16]

According to the Center-Theory, the self is not a logical construction out of mental experiences while the Non-Center Theory, usually known as the Bundle Theory, holds that it is.

There are, furthermore, two subdivisions within the Center-Theory according to what the center is thought to be. It might be:

1. a particular *substance* which owns, or has, mental experiences but is not itself a mental experience. This is the view which I shall call the *Substantive Center Theory*. It has been defended, historically, by such philosophers as Plato, Descartes, Locke, Reid, Kant and, more recently, by C. A. Campbell, H. J. Paton, H. D. Lewis and Roderick M. Chisholm.

or

2. an *event*. Only William James seems to have espoused such a view.

How does Campbell's Substance Center Theory view of the mind help him to account for the intelligibility of the notion of an act which is caused by the self but which is not the result of the self's character being what it is? We may think of the self's character as having been formed by its past experiences. According to the Non-Center or Bundle Theory, the self at any given moment in time is simply the collection of mental experiences (related in a certain way) which the mind has had up to, and including, that moment. Philosophers holding this view of the self will tend to think of the self, then, as essentially its formed character. If, however, one thinks of the mind as containing, *in addition to* mental experiences (formed character), another entity (the substantive center) which properly speaking is the *self*, it does seem possible that *this* entity could initiate an action which is not in keeping with the self's formed character. The self which performs the free act is an entity which *has* mental experiences but is not to be identified with any particular set of such experiences.

This notion of a substantive center need not, Campbell insists, be assimilated to either Locke's "unknowable substratum" or Kant's noumenal ego, both of which he thinks are too characterless and have been exposed over the years to many objections. Besides the possibility of using it to account for the intelligiblity of the Libertarian's notion of a free act, are there any good reasons for supposing that there *is* a substantive center to the mind? I think there are,[17] but to discuss them here would take us too far from the topic at hand.

Perhaps, even now, the Libertarian should not feel assured that he is on the right road yet. There may still be a major obstacle to his giving a plausible description of a free act.

> How often . . . do we find the Determinist critic saying, in effect, "*Either* the act follows necessarily upon precedent states, *or* it is a mere matter of chance, and accordingly of no moral significance."[18]

Campbell and Chisholm believe that a false dilemma has been created. Let us refer to the denial of Determinism as Indeterminism. Indeterminism, then, is the view that for some events that occur (at least one) there is not some condition or set of conditions sufficient to bring them about. There is, in other words, a break in the causal chain of events. Indeterminism, Campbell and Chisholm would want to maintain, should be thought of as taking two possible forms:

INDETERMINISM
(There is a break in the causal chain of events)

(1) There is at least one action which is caused by the self but is not caused by any earlier event(s)/state(s) of affairs (the Libertarian's free act)

(2) There is at least one action for which there is no cause—"pure chance" operates

Most philosophers think that Libertarianism must eventually boil down to the second form— and the only intelligible one in their eyes—of

Indeterminism, where supposed free acts are due to nothing but pure chance. The Libertarian, however, as we have seen, wants to maintain that it is possible that a decision to act *not* follow necessarily from antecedent events/states of affairs according to causal laws but still be *caused by something,* namely the *self.*

Many philosophers find it difficult to comprehend a notion of causation—*agent* or, as Chisholm calls it, *immanent* causation—which cannot be reduced to causation by earlier events/states of affairs—*event* or *transeunt* causation. Either they claim that there is no such thing as *agent* causation or, like Alvin I. Goldman, they claim that it exists but can always be reduced to event causation:

> Whenever we say that an *object,* O, [and an agent is just a special type of object] is a cause of *x,* this presupposes that there is a *state of O* or an *event involving O* that caused, or was a partial cause of, *x.*[19]

It would seem that the Libertarian, in order to satisfy both sorts of opponents, must show two things: (1) that there *is* such a thing as *agent* causation and (2) that it cannot be reduced to *event* causation. Concerning the first point, both Chisholm[20] and Richard Taylor[21] believe it is simply *obvious* that *agent* causation exists. "[A] perfectly natural way of expressing [the] notion of my activity is to say that, in acting, I make something happen, I cause it, or bring it about."[22] As a matter of fact, they both see this type of causation as more fundamental, as far as our understanding of causation is concerned, than *event* causation.

> The notion of immanent causation, or causation by an agent, is in fact more clear than that of transeunt causation, or causation by an event, . . . it is only by understanding our own causal efficacy, as agents, that we can grasp the concept of *cause* at all.[23]

Let us assume that there is such a thing as *agent* causation. It certainly seems natural to

do so. The *real* issue appears to be: Can *agent* causation be reduced to *event* causation? Chisholm and Taylor both say "no" and essentially for the same reason. They believe that *agent* causation must be analyzed in terms of *intention* or *purpose*—the agent *undertaking x in order to bring about y*—and they don't think that this can be reduced to a relation between events or states of affairs.

Jean-Paul Sartre, another Libertarian, characterizes voluntary actions in the following way: When a person acts he either continues to behave as he has in the past, presently *choosing* to maintain the *status quo,* which indicates that he approves of his present situation, or else he attempts to change his situation because he finds it unpleasant. In either case, the motivating factor is a *value judgment*[24] which the agent alone must, *at that moment,* make. The situation by itself is neither pleasant nor unpleasant and so cannot motivate the action ("No factual state whatever it may be is capable by itself of motivating any act whatsoever."[25]). Even my past value judgements cannot determine my present and future actions because these value judgements are constantly open to reassessment. In a similar vein, Chisholm states that "no set of statements about a man's desires, beliefs, and stimulus situation at any time implies any statement, telling us what the man will try, set out, or undertake to do at that time."

Still, Determinists maintain that there must be a reason why a person acts as he does; the action must be the result of antecedent conditions such as the person's desires, particular circumstances, etc. If correct, this would effectively reduce all cases of *agent* causation to instances of *event* causation. But it can only be done if one assumes the theory of Determinism to be true.

There is another reason why philosophers are generally reluctant to admit that there could be an action which is not caused by earlier events/states of affairs but is caused by the agent. Goldman wonders how, allowing such actions to exist, one could distinguish reflex actions from agent

292 PART FIVE: FREEDOM OF THE WILL AND DETERMINISM

caused non-reflex actions and, more generally, uncaused actions from agent-caused actions.

Chisholm considers how he would answer the question, "What is the difference between A's just happening and the agent's *causing* A to happen?" His reply is simple:

> The only answer, I think, can be this: that the difference between the man's causing A, on the one hand, and the event A just happening, on the other, lies in the fact that, in the first case but not the second, the event *A was* caused and was caused by the man.[26]

He admits that his answer may not seem entirely satisfactory. Someone way wonder what saying, "the man *caused* A" amounts to, but Chisholm challenges the defender of *event* causation to spell out what "event B *caused* event A" amounts to. I think that Chisholm is right in maintaining that "the nature of transeunt causation is no more clear than is that of immanent causation."

After eliminating this objection, it would seem that the belief that the Libertarian notion of freedom is unintelligible—that *agent* causation which cannot be reduced to *event* causation is unintelligible—just boils down to a firm conviction that Determinism must be the case. In the absence of any conclusive evidence for Determinism (and what kind of evidence would be conclusive?), however, this is just not a very good reason for dismissing the libertarian position as being unintelligible.

Conclusion

To conclude, I do not think that the libertarian notion of free will has been shown to be absolutely unintelligible. If one holds a view of the self like the Substantive Center Theory, one has a framework within which it is possible to claim that a free action can be the self's act yet not be the inevitable result of formed character. I do not believe, furthermore, that such actions have to be viewed as chance occurrences.

How often might an individual be free in the libertarian sense? I think it will vary from person to person. The important thing is that the agent sees that he/she has alternative courses of action open to him/her. Others will see to it that a person views himself/herself as having a choice *at least* in genuine moral temptation situations. There is a good reason, then, for Campbell's having focused on such situations. I believe, however, that these situations are even rarer than Campbell supposes because, once "desire" has been extended to include the urge one feels to do what one recognizes to be one's duty, there will be fewer occasions on which one desires to do the "wrong" action at least as much as the "right" one. Furthermore, I think (at least I hope) that this is not the *only* situation in which a person can be free in the libertarian sense, because otherwise two rather strange, related consequences result: *Naturally* good people (as opposed to people who repeatedly perform right actions even though it is difficult for them) will be less free than others; and to the extent that persons who begin asserting their freedom by doing morally correct actions in moral temptation situations start acquiring a *natural inclination* to do these actions, this will diminish the number of occasions in the future when they will be free.

I think it is likely that some people are capable of performing free actions in other situations as well. Those who have become accustomed, in some other specific situations or in general, to consider alternative ways of acting rather than simply following strongest desire will be free more often in the libertarian sense. The ability to envision different courses of action can, I think, be cultivated—remember that it is not necessary that the agent *invent* any of the choices. The behavior of individuals who have developed this ability will be less predictable than others, but that only makes them all the more interesting.

NOTES

1. David Hume, *An Enquiry Concerning Human Understanding,* edited by L. A. Selby-Bigge (Oxford: Clarendon Press, 1894), Section 8, Part I, p. 95.
2. By "Determinism," I shall mean the view which

holds that for every event that occurs there is some condition or set of conditions sufficient to bring about that event.

3. Henri Bergson, *Time and Free Will* (London: Allen & Unwin, 1910), pp. 174–75.

4. C. A. Campbell, "In Defence of Free Will," in *In Defence of Free Will, with Other Philosophical Essays* (London: Allen & Unwin, 1967), p. 37.

5. Roderick M. Chisholm, "Freedom and Action," in *Freedom and Determinism*, edited by Keith Lehrer (Atlantic Highlands, N.J.: Humanities Press, 1976), p. 12.

6. Those who believe in the existence of God, for instance, must believe that we enjoy this type of freedom in order to absolve God from responsibility for our sins. Campbell agrees. See *On Selfhood and Godhood* (London: Allen & Unwin, 1957), pp. 171–72.

7. Ledger Wood, "The Free-Will Controversy," *Philosophy*, 16 (1941), 392–93.

8. Campbell, "In Defence of Free Will," pp. 46–47.

9. Chisholm, "The Agent as Cause," in *Action Theory*, edited by M. Brand and D. Walton (Dordrecht: Reidel, 1976), p. 204.

10. Campbell, "In Defence of Free Will," pp. 47–48.

11. Ibid., p. 48.

12. The reply seems to be related to Kant's position that when a person is viewed as an *object* in the phenomenal world, his actions appear to be determined; but when a person views himself as an *agent*— an object in the noumenal world—he sees that he must be free. It also seems to be related to Sartre's view that human relationships are necessarily unhappy because each person attempts to reduce the other to an object—to define the other as a "fixed" entity—yet neither one believes *himself* to be a "fixed" entity.

13. Campbell, "In Defence of Free Will," p. 43.

14. *On Selfhood and Godhood*, p. 152.

15. "Moral and Non-Moral Values," in *In Defence of Free Will, with Other Philosophical Essays*, p. 91.

16. C. D. Broad, *The Mind and Its Place in Nature* (Paterson, N.J.: Littlefield, Adams, 1960), p. 558.

17. See, for example, Campbell, *On Selfhood and Godhood*, p. 71 and pp. 75–76.

18. Campbell, *On Selfhood and Godhood*, p. 177.

19. Alvin I. Goldman, *A Theory of Human Action* (Englewood Cliffs, N.J.: Prentice-Hall, 1970), p. 81.

20. See Chisholm, "The Agent as Cause," p. 199.

21. See Richard Taylor, *Action and Purpose* (Englewood Cliffs, N.J.: Prentice-Hall, 1966), pp. 111–12, 261–64.

22. Ibid., p. 111.

23. Chisholm, "Freedom and Action," p. 22.

24. How are these value judgments made? According to Sartre, the self must first imagine some ideal state of affairs and then either appreciate his own situation when he compares it favorably to this ideal or find his present situation intolerable when he compares it unfavorably to the ideal. The judgment the self makes about his present situation, the last step prior to action, then, presupposes two previous steps: (1) the imagining of some ideal state of affairs, and then (2) the comparing of one's present situation with the ideal.

25. Jean-Paul Sartre, *Being and Nothingness*, trans. by Hazel Barnes (New York: Philosophical Library, 1956), p. 435.

26. Chisholm, "Freedom and Action," p. 21.

For Further Reflection

1. Compare Anderson's essay with Hospers' article. How would they argue with one another?

2. How successful has Anderson been in rebutting objections to Libertarianism?

3. Is the center-theory of the mind a clear and cogent theory? How crucial is it to Anderson's case?

Suggestions for Further Reading

Dennett, Daniel. *Elbow Room: Varieties of Free Will Worth Wanting.* Cambridge, MA: MIT Press, 1985. The best defense of compatibilism.

Feinberg, Joel, ed. *Reason and Responsibility.* Belmont, CA: Wadsworth, 1985. Part 4 contains a very good selection of readings, including four readings on the implications for justifying punishment.

Honderich, Ted, ed. *Essays on Freedom of Action*. London: Routledge & Kegan Paul, 1973. A good collection of recent essays.

Lehrer, Keith and Cornman, James. *Philosophical Problems and Arguments,* 3rd ed. New York: Macmillan, 1982. Lehrer's essay (Chapter 3) is excellent.

MacKay, Donald M. *Freedom of Action in a Mechanistic Universe*. Cambridge: Cambridge University Press, 1967.

Morgenbesser, Sidney and Walsh, James, eds. *Free Will*. Englewood Cliffs, NJ: Prentice-Hall, 1962. This contains many of the classic readings.

Stace, Walter. *Religion and the Modern Mind*. New York: Lippincott, 1952.

Trusted, Jennifer. *Free Will and Responsibility*. Oxford: Oxford University Press, 1984. One of the clearest introductions to the subject. Accessible to beginners and reliable.

van Inwagen, Peter. *An Essay on Free Will*. Oxford: Oxford University Press, 1983. This is the best critique of compatibilism available.

Watson, Gary. *Free Will*. Oxford: Oxford University Press, 1982. This volume contains the best collections of recent articles on the subject, especially those of Frankfurt, van Inwagen, and Watson. It also contains two clear discussions of the problem of mechanism and freedom of the will: Norman Malcolm's "The Conceivability of Mechanism" and Daniel Dennett's "Mechanism and Responsibility."

Part VI

Ethics

We are discussing no small matter, but how we ought to live.

SOCRATES in Plato's *Republic*

IN 1964 THE NATION WAS STUNNED by a report from Kew Gardens, Queens, in New York City. A young woman, Kitty Genovese, was brutally stabbed in her neighborhood while thirty-eight respectable, law-abiding citizens watched a killer stalk and stab her in three separate attacks. Her neighbors looked on from their bedroom windows for some thirty-five minutes as the assailant beat her, stabbed her, left her, and returned to repeat the process two more times until she died. No one lifted a phone to call the police, no one shouted at the criminal, let alone went to the aid of Kitty. Finally, a 70-year-old woman called the police. It took them two minutes to arrive, but by that time Kitty was dead. Only one other woman came out to testify until the ambulance came an hour later. Then the whole neighborhood poured out. Asked why they didn't do anything, the responses ranged from "I don't know" and "I was tired" to "Frankly, we were afraid."

Who is my neighbor? What should these respectable citizens have done? What would you have done? What kinds of generalizations can we make from this episode about contemporary culture in America? Is it an anomaly or quite indicative of something deeply disturbing?

What is it to be a moral person in contemporary North America? What is the nature of morality? Why should I be moral? What is the good and how shall I know it? Are moral principles absolute or simply relative to social group or culture? Is morality, like beauty, in the eye of the beholder? Is it in my interest to be moral or to be moral when it calls for personal sacrifice? How does one justify one's moral beliefs? What is the relationship between morality and religion? What is the basis of morality? Why do we need morality anyway?

These are some of the questions that we shall be looking at in this part of our work. We want to know how we should live.

What Is Ethics?

The terms "moral" and "ethics" come from Latin and Greek respectively (*mores* and *ethos*), deriving their meaning from the idea of custom. I shall follow the custom of using "morality" and "ethics" synonymously to refer to actual or ideal moralities. Sometimes, however, we use the term *ethics* to refer to the philosophical analysis of morality, the systematic endeavor to understand moral concepts and justify moral principles and theories. It undertakes to analyze such concepts as "right," "wrong," "permissible," "ought," "good," and "evil" in their moral contexts. Moral philosophy seeks to establish principles of right behavior which may serve as action guides for individuals and groups. It investigates which values and virtues are paramount to the worthwhile life or society. It builds and scrutinizes arguments in ethical theories, and it seeks to discover valid principles (e.g., "Never kill innocent human beings") and the relationship between those principles (e.g., Does saving a life in some situations constitute a valid reason for breaking a promise?).

Ethics is concerned with values—not with what is, but what ought to be. How should I live my life? What is the right thing to do in this situation? Should I always tell the truth? Do I have a duty to report a coworker whom I have seen cheating our company? Should I tell my friend that his spouse is having an affair? Is premarital sex morally permissible? Ought a woman ever to have an abortion? Ethics has a distinct action guiding aspect and, as such, belongs to the group of practical institutions which include religion, law, and etiquette.

Ethics may be closely allied to religion, but it need not be. There are both religious and secular ethical systems. Secular or purely philosophical ethics is grounded in reason and common human experience. To use a spatial metaphor, secular ethics are horizontal, lacking a vertical or transcendental dimension. Religious ethics has a vertical dimension, being grounded in revelation or divine authority. These two differing orientations will often generate different moral principles and standards of evaluation, but they need not. Some versions of religious ethics, which posit God's revelation of the moral law in nature or conscience, hold that reason can discover what is right or wrong even apart from divine revelation.

Ethics is also closely related to law, and in some societies (such as that depicted in the Hebrew Old Testament) the two are seen as the same—as a single reality. Many laws are instituted in order to promote well-being, resolve conflicts of interest and/or social harmony, just as morality does, but ethics may judge that some laws are immoral without denying that they are valid laws: for example, laws permitting slavery or irrelevant discrimination against people on the basis of race or sex. A Catholic or antiabortion advocate may believe that the laws permitting abortion are immoral.

In a 1989 PBS television series, *Ethics in America,* James Neal, a trial lawyer, was asked what he would do if he discovered that his client, some years back, had committed a murder for which another man had been convicted and was going to die for in a few days. Mr. Neal said that he had a legal obligation to keep this information confidential, and that if he divulged it he would be disbarred. Some would argue that he has a moral obligation which overrides his legal obligation and which demands that he take action to protect the innocent man from being executed.

Furthermore, there are some aspects of morality that are not covered by law. For example, while it is generally agreed that lying is usually immoral, there is no law against it. College newspapers publish advertisements for phony research papers, which students use in lieu of their own work. Publication of such ads is legal, but it is not moral. Likewise, Kitty Genovese's neighbors were not guilty of any legal wrongdoing, but they were very likely morally culpable for not calling the police or shouting at the assailant.

There is one other major difference between law and morality. In 1351 King Edward the Third of England promulgated a law against treason that made it a crime merely to think homicidal thoughts about the king. But, alas, the law could not be enforced, for no tribunal can search the heart and fathom the intentions of the mind. But there are other problems. If malicious intentions (called in law mens rea) were criminally illegal, would we not all deserve imprisonment? Even if it were possible to detect intentions, when should the punishment be administered? As soon as the subject has the intention? But how do we know that he will not change his mind? Furthermore, is there not a continuum between imagining some harm to X, wishing a harm to X, desiring a harm to X, and intending a harm to X?

While it is impractical to have laws against bad intentions, these intentions are still bad, still morally wrong. Suppose I buy a gun with the intention of killing Uncle Charlie in order to inherit his wealth, but never get a chance to fire it (for example, Uncle Charlie moves to Australia). While I have not committed a crime, I have committed a moral wrong.

Finally, law differs from morality in that there are physical sanctions enforcing the law but only the sanctions of conscience and reputation enforcing morality.

Etiquette also differs from morality in that it concerns form and style rather than the essence of social existence. Etiquette determines what is polite behavior rather than what is *right* behavior in a deeper sense. It represents society's decision as to how we are to dress, greet one another, eat, celebrate festivals, dispose of the dead, and carry out social transactions. Whether we greet each other with a handshake, a bow, a hug, or a kiss on the cheek will differ in different social systems, but none of these rituals has any moral superiority.

People in England hold their fork in their left hand when they eat (and sometimes look at Americans with wonder when they see us holding the fork in our right hand), whereas people in other countries hold it in their right hand or in whichever hand they feel like holding it, and people in India typically eat without a fork at all, using the fingers of the right hand to convey food from plate to mouth.

Although Americans pride themselves on tolerance and awareness of other cultures, custom and etiquette can be a bone of contention. A friend of mine relates an incident that took place early in his marriage. John and his wife were hosting their first Thanksgiving meal. He had been used to small celebrations with his immediate family, whereas his wife had been used to grand celebrations. He writes, "I had been asked to carve, something I had never done before, but I was willing. I put on an apron, entered the kitchen, attacked the bird with as much artistry as I could muster. And what reward did I get? [My wife] burst into tears. In *her* family the turkey is brought to the *table,* laid before [the father], grace is said, and *then* he carves! 'So I fail patriarchy,' I hollered later. 'What do you expect?'"

Etiquette is a spice of life. Polite manners grace our social existence but they are not what social existence is about. They help social transactions to flow smoothly, but are not the substance of those transactions.

At the same time, it can be immoral to disregard or flout etiquette. A cultural crisis recently developed in India when Americans went to the beaches clad in bikini bathing suits. This was highly offensive to the Indians and an uproar erupted.

There is nothing intrinsically wrong with wearing skimpy bathing suits, or with wearing nothing at all, for that matter, but people get used to certain behavioral patterns and it's terribly insensitive to flout those customs—especially when you are a guest in someone else's home or country. Not the bathing suits themselves; it is the *insensitivity* that is morally offensive.

Law, etiquette, and religion are all important institutions, but each has limitations. The limitation of the law is that you can't have a law against every social malady nor can you enforce every desirable rule. The limitation of etiquette is that it doesn't get to the heart of what is of vital importance for personal and social existence. Whether or not one eats with one's fingers pales in significance compared with being honest or trustworthy or just. Etiquette is a cultural invention, but morality claims to be a discovery.

The limitation of the religious injunction is that it rests on authority, and we are not always sure of or in agreement about the credentials of the authority, nor on how the authority would rule in ambiguous or new cases. Since religion is founded not on reason but on revelation, there is no way to convince someone who does not share your religious views that your view is the right one.

Ethics, as the analysis of morality, distinguishes itself from law and etiquette by going deeper into the essence of rational existence. It distinguishes itself from religion in that it seeks reasons, rather than authority, to justify its principles. Its central purpose is to secure valid principles of conduct and values which can be instrumental in guiding human actions and producing good character. As such it is the most important activity known to humans, for it has to do with how we are to live.

We begin with a selection on the death of Socrates from Plato's *Crito,* the earliest recorded discussion of moral philosophy.

The Death of Socrates and the Question of Civil Disobedience

VI.1

PLATO

The introductory reading, Plato's dialogue the *Crito,* is a classic example of ethical thinking. Written in the fourth century B.C., it is one of the earliest sustained treatises on philosophical ethics. That is, it represents an acutely self-conscious attempt to use reasoning to decide what the right course of action in a particular situation is.

The year is 399 B.C., the place, an Athenian jail. Socrates, a seventy-year-old philosopher, has been condemned to death by an Athenian court for not believing in the Athenian gods and for corrupting the youth. In fact, he has been unjustly condemned, but his refusal to compromise with the political powers of his day has provoked extreme behavior.

Now his friends, led by Crito, have planned his escape and have arranged passage to Thessaly, where Socrates has been assured of a tranquil retirement among admirers. The moral issue is: Should Socrates escape? Should he avail himself of Crito's help and attempt to free himself from prison? In other words, should he engage in civil disobedience?

Crito and Socrates engage in a moral argument. As you read this dialogue, identify Crito's arguments and Socrates' counter-arguments. Try to identify the major principles that each holds and decide how valid the arguments are. Note especially the relation between law and morality. In the *Apology*, Socrates seems to put one principle above the law. He says that if the law commands him to refrain from teaching, he will not obey it. In fact, some years before this event, he refused to obey the leaders of Athens when they commanded him to arrest an admiral whom he considered innocent of any crime. Do these actions affect his argument in the *Crito*?

(Biographical sketches of Socrates and Plato appear on p. 6.)

Study Questions

1. What are Crito's reasons in favor of Socrates' escape? Evaluate them.
2. How does Socrates answer Crito's arguments?
3. Does Socrates care about public opinion or what others can do to him? Why or why not?
4. What kind of life is worth living and what kind not worth living according to Socrates?
5. What does Socrates think about retaliation?
6. Explain Socrates' reasons (given through the voice of the Laws) for not escaping. Evaluate them. Try to formulate them into arguments.
7. How does Socrates view the prospects of life in exile in Thessaly?

CRITO: I BRING BAD NEWS, Socrates, not for you, apparently, but for me and all your friends the news is bad and hard to bear. Indeed, I would count it among the hardest.

Socrates: What is it? Or has the ship arrived from Delos, at the arrival of which I must die?

Cr.: It has not arrived yet, but it will, I believe, arrive today, according to a message brought by some men from Sunium, where they left it. This makes it obvious that it will come today, and that your life must end tomorrow.

Socr.: May it be for the best. If it so please the gods, so be it. However, I do not think it will arrive today.

Cr.: What indication have you of this?

Socr.: I will tell you. I must die the day after the ship arrives.

Cr.: That is what those in authority say.

Socr.: Then I do not think it will arrive on this coming day, but on the next. I take to witness of this a dream I had a little earlier during this night. It looks as if it was the right time for you not to wake me.

Cr.: What was your dream?

Socr.: I thought that a beautiful and comely woman dressed in white approached me. She called me and said: "Socrates, may you arrive at fertile Phthia on the third day."

Cr.: A strange dream, Socrates.

Socr.: But it seems clear enough to me, Crito.

Cr.: Too clear it seems, my dear Socrates, but listen to me even now and be saved. If you die, it will not be a single misfortune for me. Not only will I be deprived of a friend, the like of whom I shall never find again, but many people who do not know you or me very well will think that I

Reprinted from The Trial and Death of Socrates, *translated by G. M. A. Grube with extensive help from Richard Hogan and Donald J. Zeyl (Hackett Publishing Company, 2nd ed., 1984) by permission of the publisher.*

could have saved you if I were willing to spend money, but that I did not care to do so. Surely there can be no worse reputation than to be thought to value money more highly than one's friends, for the majority will not believe that you yourself were not willing to leave prison while we were eager for you to do so.

Socr.: My good Crito, why should we care so much for what the majority think? The most reasonable people, to whom one should pay more attention, will believe that things were done as they were done.

Cr.: You see, Socrates, that one must also pay attention to the opinion of the majority. Your present situation makes clear that the majority can inflict not the least but pretty well the greatest evils if one is slandered among them.

Socr.: Would that the majority could inflict the greatest evils, for they would then be capable of the greatest good, and that would be fine, but now they cannot do either. They cannot make a man either wise or foolish, but they inflict things haphazardly.

Cr.: That may be so. But tell me this, Socrates, are you anticipating that I and your other friends would have trouble with the informers if you escape from here, as having stolen you away, and that we should be compelled to lose all our property or pay heavy fines and suffer other punishment besides? If you have any such fear, forget it. We would be justified in running this risk to save you, and worse, if necessary. Do follow my advice, and do not act differently.

Socr.: I do have these things in mind, Crito, and also many others.

Cr.: Have no such fear. It is not much money that some people require to save you and get you out of here. Further, do you not see that those informers are cheap, and that not much money would be needed to deal with them? My money is available and is, I think, sufficient. If, because of your affection for me, you feel you should not spend any of mine, there are those strangers here ready to spend money. One of them, Simmias the Theban, has brought enough for this very

purpose. Cebes, too, and a good many others. So, as I say, do not let this fear make you hesitate to save yourself, nor let what you said in court trouble you, that you would not know what to do with yourself if you left Athens, for you would be welcomed in many places to which you might go. If you want to go to Thessaly, I have friends there who will greatly appreciate you and keep you safe, so that no one in Thessaly will harm you.

Besides, Socrates, I do not think that what you are doing is right, to give up your life when you can save it, and to hasten your fate as your enemies would hasten it, and indeed have hastened it in their wish to destroy you. Moreover, I think you are betraying your sons by going away and leaving them, when you could bring them up and educate them. You thus show no concern for what their fate may be. They will probably have the usual fate of orphans. Either one should not have children, or one should share with them to the end the toil of upbringing and education. You seem to me to choose the easiest path, whereas one should choose the path a good and courageous man would choose, particularly when one claims throughout one's life to care for virtue.

I feel ashamed on your behalf and on behalf of us, your friends, lest all that has happened to you be thought due to cowardice on our part: the fact that your trial came to court when it need not have done so, the handling of the trial itself, and now this absurd ending which will be thought to have got beyond our control through some cowardice and unmanliness on our part, since we did not save you, or you save yourself, when it was possible and could be done if we had been of the slightest use. Consider, Socrates, whether this is not only evil, but shameful, both for you and for us. Take counsel with yourself, or rather the time for counsel is past and the decision should have been taken, and there is no further opportunity, for this whole business must be ended tonight. If we delay now, then it will no longer be possible, it will be too late. Let me persuade you on every count, Socrates, and do not act otherwise.

Socr.: My dear Crito, your eagerness is worth much if it should have some right aim; if not, then the greater your keenness the more difficult it is to deal with. We must therefore examine whether we should act in this way or not, as not only now but at all times I am the kind of man who listens only to the argument that on reflection seems best to me. I cannot, now that this fate has come upon me, discard the arguments I used; they seem to me much the same. I value and respect the same principles as before, and if we have no better arguments to bring up at this moment, be sure that I shall not agree with you, not even if the power of the majority were to frighten us with more bogeys, as if we were children, with threats of incarcerations and executions and confiscation of property. How should we examine this matter most reasonably? Would it be by taking up first your argument about the opinions of men, whether it is sound in every case that one should pay attention to some opinions, but not to others? Or was that well-spoken before the necessity to die came upon me, but now it is clear that this was said in vain for the sake of argument, that it was in truth play and nonsense? I am eager to examine together with you, Crito, whether this argument will appear in any way different to me in my present circumstances, or whether it remains the same, whether we are to abandon it or believe it. It was said on every occasion by those who thought they were speaking sensibly, as I have just now been speaking, that one should greatly value some people's opinions, but not others. Does that seem to you a sound statement?

You, as far as a human being can tell, are exempt from the likelihood of dying tomorrow, so the present misfortune is not likely to lead you astray. Consider then, do you not think it a sound statement that one must not value all the opinions of men, but some and not others? What do you say? Is this not well said?

Cr.: It is.

Socr.: One should value the good opinions, and not the bad ones?

Cr.: Yes.

Socr.: The good opinions are those of wise men, the bad ones those of foolish men?

Cr.: Of course.

Socr.: Come then, what of statements such as this: Should a man professionally engaged in physical training pay attention to the praise and blame and opinion of any man, or to those of one man only, namely a doctor or trainer?

Cr.: To those of one only.

Socr.: He should therefore fear the blame and welcome the praise of that one man, and not those of the many?

Cr.: Obviously.

Socr.: He must then act and exercise, eat and drink in the way the one, the trainer and the one who knows, thinks right, not all the others?

Cr.: That is so.

Socr.: Very well. And if he disobeys the one, disregards his opinion and his praises while valuing those of the many who have no knowledge, will he not suffer harm?

Cr.: Of course.

Socr.: What is the harm, where does it tend, and what part of the man who disobeys does it affect?

Cr.: Obviously the harm is to his body, which it ruins.

Socr.: Well said. So with other matters, not to enumerate them all, and certainly with actions just and unjust, shameful and beautiful, good and bad, about which we are now deliberating, should we follow the opinion of the many and fear it, or that of the one, if there is one who has knowledge of these things and before whom we feel fear and shame more than before all the others. If we do not follow his directions, we shall harm and corrupt that part of ourselves that is improved by just actions and destroyed by unjust actions. Or is there nothing in this?

Cr.: I think there certainly is, Socrates.

Socr.: Come now, if we ruin that which is improved by health and corrupted by disease by not following the opinions of those who know, is life worth living for us when that is ruined? And that is the body, is it not?

Cr.: Yes.

Socr.: And is life worth living with a body that is corrupted and in bad condition?

Cr.: In no way.

Socr.: And is life worth living for us with that part of us corrupted that unjust action harms and just action benefits? Or do we think that part of us, whatever it is, that is concerned with justice and injustice, is inferior to the body?

Cr.: Not at all.

Socr.: It is more valuable?

Cr.: Much more.

Socr.: We should not then think so much of what the majority will say about us, but what he will say who understands justice and injustice, the one, that is, and the truth itself. So that, in the first place, you were wrong to believe that we should care for the opinion of the many about what is just, beautiful, good, and their opposites. "But," someone might say "the many are able to put us to death."

Cr.: That too is obvious, Socrates, and someone might well say so.

Socr.: And, my admirable friend, that argument that we have gone through remains, I think, as before. Examine the following statement in turn as to whether it stays the same or not, that the most important thing is not life, but the good life.

Cr.: It stays the same.

Socr.: And that the good life, the beautiful life, and the just life are the same; does that still hold, or not?

Cr.: It does hold.

Socr.: As we have agreed so far, we must examine next whether it is right for me to try to get out of here when the Athenians have not acquitted me. If it is seen to be right, we will try to do so; if it is not, we will abandon the idea. As for those questions you raise about money, reputation, the upbringing of children, Crito, those considerations in truth belong to those people who easily put men to death and would bring them to life again if they could, without thinking; I mean the majority of men. For us, however, since our argument leads to this, the only valid consideration, as we were saying just now, is whether we should be acting rightly in giving money and gratitude to those who will lead me out of here, and ourselves helping with the escape, or whether in truth we shall do wrong in doing all this. If it appears that we shall be acting unjustly, then we have no need at all to take into account whether we shall have to die if we stay here and keep quiet, or suffer in another way, rather than do wrong.

Cr.: I think you put that beautifully, Socrates, but see what we should do.

Socr.: Let us examine the question together, my dear friend, and if you can make any objection while I am speaking, make it and I will listen to you, but if you have no objection to make, my dear Crito, then stop now from saying the same thing so often, that I must leave here against the will of the Athenians. I think it important to persuade you before I act, and not to act against your wishes. See whether the start of our enquiry is adequately stated, and try to answer what I ask you in the way you think best.

Cr.: I shall try.

Socr.: Do we say that one must never in any way do wrong willingly, or must one do wrong in one way and not in another? Is to do wrong never good or admirable, as we have agreed in the past, or have all these former agreements been washed out during the last few days? Have we at our age failed to notice for some time that in our serious discussions we were no different from children? Above all, is the truth such as we used to say it was, whether the majority agree or not, and whether we must still suffer worse things than we do now, or will be treated more gently, that nonetheless, wrongdoing is in every way harmful and shameful to the wrongdoer? Do we say so or not?

Cr.: We do.

Socr.: So one must never do wrong.

Cr.: Certainly not.

Socr.: Nor must one, when wronged, inflict wrong in return, as the majority believe, since one must never do wrong.

Cr.: That seems to be the case.

Socr.: Come now, should one injure anyone or not, Crito?

Cr.: One must never do so.

Socr.: Well then, if one is oneself injured, is it right, as the majority say, to inflict an injury in return, or is it not?

Cr.: It is never right.

Socr.: Injuring people is no different from wrongdoing.

Cr.: That is true.

Socr.: One should never do wrong in return, nor injure any man, whatever injury one has suffered at his hands. And Crito, see that you do not agree to this, contrary to your belief. For I know that only a few people hold this view or will hold it, and there is no common ground between those who hold this view and those who do not, but they inevitably despise each other's views. So then consider very carefully whether we have this view in common, and whether you agree, and let this be the basis of our deliberation, that neither to do wrong or to return a wrong is ever right, not even to injure in return for an injury received. Or do you disagree and do not share this view as a basis for discussion? I have held it for a long time and still hold it now, but if you think otherwise, tell me now. If, however, you stick to our former opinion, then listen to the next point.

Cr.: I stick to it and agree with you. So say on.

Socr.: Then I state the next point, or rather I ask you: when one has come to an agreement that is just with someone, should one fulfill it or cheat on it?

Cr.: One should fulfill it.

Socr.: See what follows from this: if we leave here without the city's permission, are we injuring people whom we should least injure? And are we sticking to a just agreement, or not?

Cr.: I cannot answer your question, Socrates. I do not know.

Socr.: Look at it this way. If, as we were planning to run away from here, or whatever one should call it, the laws and the state came and confronted us and asked: "Tell me, Socrates, what are you intending to do? Do you not by this action you are attempting intend to destroy us, the laws, and indeed the whole city, as far as you are concerned? Or do you think it possible for a city not to be destroyed if the verdicts of its courts have no force but are nullified and set at naught by private individuals?" What shall we answer to this and other such arguments? For many things could be said, especially by an orator on behalf of this law we are destroying, which orders that the judgments of the courts shall be carried out. Shall we say in answer, "The city wronged me, and its decision was not right." Shall we say that, or what?

Cr.: Yes, by Zeus, Socrates, that is our answer.

Socr.: Then what if the laws said: "Was that the agreement between us, Socrates, or was it to respect the judgments that the city came to?" And if we wondered at their words, they would perhaps add: "Socrates, do not wonder at what we say but answer, since you are accustomed to proceed by question and answer. Come now, what accusation do you bring against us and the city, that you should try to destroy us? Did we not, first, bring you to birth, and was it not through us that your father married your mother and begat you? Tell us, do you find anything to criticize in those of us who are concerned with marriage?" And I would say that I do not criticize them. "Or in those of us concerned with the nurture of babies and the education that you too received? Were those assigned to that subject not right to instruct your father to educate you in the arts and in physical culture?" And I would say that they were right. "Very well," they would continue, "and after you were born and nurtured and educated, could you, in the first place, deny that you are our offspring and servant, both you and your forefathers? If that is so, do you think that we are on an equal footing as regards the right, and that whatever we do to you it is right for you to do to us? You were not on an equal footing with your father as regards the right, nor with your master if you had one, so as to retaliate for anything they did to you, to revile them if they reviled you, to beat them if they beat you, and so with many other things. Do you think you have this right to retaliation against your country and its laws? That if we undertake to destroy you and think it right to do so, you can undertake to destroy us, as far as you can, in return? And will you say that you are right to do so, you who truly care for virtue? Is your wisdom such as not to realize that your country is to be honoured more than your mother, your father and all your ancestors, that it is more to be revered and more sacred, and that it counts for more among the gods and sensible men, that you must worship it, yield to it and placate its anger more than your father's? You must either persuade it or obey its orders, and endure in silence whatever it instructs you to endure, whether blows or bonds, and if it leads you into war to be wounded or killed, you must obey. To do so is right, and one must not give way or retreat or leave one's post, but both in war and in courts and everywhere else, one must obey the commands of one's city and country, or persuade it as to the nature of justice. It is impious to bring violence to bear against your mother or father, it is much more so to use it against your country." What shall we say in reply, Crito, that the laws speak the truth, or not?

Cr.: I think they do.

Socr.: "Reflect now, Socrates," the laws might say "that if what we say is true, you are not treating us rightly by planning to do what you are planning. We have given you birth, nurtured you, educated you, we have given you and all other citizens a share of all the good things we could. Even so, by giving every Athenian the opportunity, after he has reached manhood and observed the affairs of the city and us the laws, we proclaim that if we do not please him, he can take his possessions and go wherever he pleases. Not one of our laws raises any obstacle or forbids him, if he is not satisfied with us or the city, if one of you wants to go and live in a colony or

wants to go anywhere else, and keep his property. We say, however, that whoever of you remains, when he sees how we conduct our trials and manage the city in other ways, has in fact come to an agreement with us to obey our instructions. We say that the one who disobeys does wrong in three ways, first because in us he disobeys his parents, also those who brought him up, and because, in spite of his agreement, he neither obeys us nor, if we do something wrong, does he try to persuade us to do better. Yet we only propose things, we do not issue savage commands to do whatever we order; we give two alternatives, either to persuade us or to do what we say. He does neither. We do say that you too, Socrates, are open to those charges if you do what you have in mind; you would be among, not the least, but the most guilty of the Athenians." And if I should say "Why so?" they might well be right to upbraid me and say that I am among the Athenians who most definitely came to that agreement with them. They might well say: "Socrates, we have convincing proofs that we and the city were congenial to you. You would not have dwelt here most consistently of all the Athenians if the city had not been exceedingly pleasing to you. You have never left the city, even to see a festival, nor for any other reason except military service; you have never gone to stay in any other city, as people do; you have had no desire to know another city or other laws; we and our city satisfied you.

"So decisively did you choose us and agree to be a citizen under us. Also, you have had children in this city, thus showing that it was congenial to you. Then at your trial you could have assessed your penalty at exile if you wished, and you are now attempting to do against the city's wishes what you could then have done with her consent. Then you prided yourself that you did not resent death, but you chose, as you said, death in preference to exile. Now, however, those words do not make you ashamed, and you pay no heed to us, the laws, as you plan to destroy us, and you act like the meanest type of slave by trying to run away, contrary to your undertakings and your agreement to live as a citizen under us. First then, answer us on this very point, whether we speak the truth when we say that you agreed, not only in words but by your deeds, to live in accordance with us." What are we to say to that, Crito? Must we not agree?

Cr.: We must, Socrates.

Socr.: "Surely," they might say, "you are breaking the undertakings and agreements that you made with us without compulsion or deceit, and under no pressure of time for deliberation. You have had seventy years during which you could have gone away if you did not like us, and if you thought our agreements unjust. You did not choose to go to Sparta or to Crete, which you are always saying are well governed, nor to any other city, Greek or foreign. You have been away from Athens less than the lame or the blind or other handicapped people. It is clear that the city has been outstandingly more congenial to you than to other Athenians, and so have we, the laws, for what city can please without laws? Will you then not now stick to our agreements? You will, Socrates, if we can persuade you, and not make yourself a laughingstock by leaving the city.

"For consider what good you will do yourself or your friends by breaking our agreements and committing such a wrong? It is pretty obvious that your friends will themselves be in danger of exile, disfranchisement and loss of property. As for yourself, if you go to one of the nearby cities—Thebes or Megara, both are well governed—you will arrive as an enemy to their government; all who care for their city will look on you with suspicion, as a destroyer of the laws. You will also strengthen the conviction of the jury that they passed the right sentence on you, for anyone who destroys the laws could easily be thought to corrupt the young and the ignorant. Or will you avoid cities that are well governed and men who are civilized? If you do this, will your life be worth living? Will you have social intercourse with them and not be ashamed to talk to them? And what will you say? The same as you did here, that virtue and justice are man's

most precious possession, along with lawful behaviour and the laws? Do you not think that Socrates would appear to be an unseemly kind of person? One must think so. Or will you leave those places and go to Crito's friends in Thessaly? There you will find the greatest license and disorder, and they may enjoy hearing from you how absurdly you escaped from prison in some disguise, in a leather jerkin or some other things in which escapees wrap themselves, thus altering your appearance. Will there be no one to say that you, likely to live but a short time more, were so greedy for life that you transgressed the most important laws? Possibly, Socrates, if you do not annoy anyone, but if you do, many disgraceful things will be said about you.

"You will spend your time ingratiating yourself with all men, and be at their beck and call. What will you do in Thessaly but feast, as if you had gone to a banquet in Thessaly? As for those conversations of yours about justice and the rest of virtue, where will they be? You say you want to live for the sake of your children, that you may bring them up and educate them. How so? Will you bring them up and educate them by taking them to Thessaly and making strangers of them, that they may enjoy that too? Or not so, but they will be better brought up and educated here, while you are alive, though absent? Yes, your friends will look after them. Will they look after them if you go and live in Thessaly, but not if you go away to the underworld? If those who profess themselves your friends are any good at all, one must assume that they will.

"Be persuaded by us who have brought you up, Socrates. Do not value either your children or your life or anything else more than goodness, in order that when you arrive in Hades you may have all this as your defence before the rulers there. If you do this deed, you will not think it better or more just or more pious here, nor will any one of your friends, nor will it be better for you when you arrive yonder. As it is, you depart, if you depart, after being wronged not by us, the laws, but by men; but if you depart after shamefully returning wrong for wrong and injury for injury, after breaking your agreement and contract with us, after injuring those you should injure least—yourself, your friends, your country and us—we shall be angry with you while you are still alive, and our brothers, the laws of the underworld, will not receive you kindly, knowing that you tried to destroy us as far as you could. Do not let Crito persuade you, rather than us, to do what he says."

Crito, my dear friend, be assured that these are the words I seem to hear, as the Corybants seem to hear the music of their flutes, and the echo of these words resounds in me, and makes it impossible for me to hear anything else. As far as my present beliefs go, if you speak in opposition to them, you will speak in vain. However, if you think you can accomplish anything, speak.

Cr.: I have nothing to say, Socrates.

Socr.: Let it be then, Crito, and let us act in this way, since this is the way the god is leading us.

For Further Reflection

1. Was Socrates right to accept his death in the way that he did? Should he have availed himself of the opportunity to escape? What would you have done and why?

2. Is there a note of cultural relativity in this dialogue? Is the respect for and obedience to parents excessive? Do we today have a right to disobey our parents that Socrates denies?

3. What do you think of Socrates' view that some types of life are not worth living?

4. Can you think of other cases where civil disobedience is a moral issue? How do they compare with Socrates' situation?

Are There Any Moral Absolutes or Is Morality Completely Relative?

Ethical relativism is the notion that there are no universally valid moral principles, but that all moral principles are valid relative to cultural or individual choice. It is to be distinguished from *moral skepticism,* the view that there are no valid moral principles at all (or at least none that we can be confident about). There are two forms of ethical relativism: (1) *subjectivism,* which views morality as a personal decision ("Morality is in the eye of the beholder"), and (2) *conventionalism,* which views moral validity in terms of social acceptance. Opposed to ethical relativism are various theories of *ethical objectivism.* All forms of objectivism affirm the universal validity of some moral principles. The strongest form, *moral absolutism,* holds that there is exactly one right answer to every "What should I do in situation *X?*" question, whatever that situation be, and that a moral principle can never be overridden—even by another moral principle. A weaker form of objectivism sees moral principles as universally valid but not always applicable. That is, moral principle A could be overridden by moral principle B in a given situation, and in other situations, there might be no right answer. We turn to our readings. First we have a defense of moral relativism, and after that an attack on moral relativism which defends moral objectivism.

VI.2   In Defense of Moral Relativism

RUTH BENEDICT

Ruth Benedict (1887–1948) was a foremost American anthropologist who taught at Columbia University and is best known for her book *Patterns of Culture* (1934). Benedict views social systems as communities with common beliefs and practices which have become more or less well-integrated patterns of ideas and practices. Like a work of art, the social system chooses which theme of its repertoire of basic tendencies to emphasize and then goes about to produce a holistic grand design favoring those tendencies. The final systems differ from one another in striking ways, but there is no reason to say that one system is better than another. What is considered normal or abnormal behavior will depend on the choices of these social systems, or what Benedict calls the "idea-practice pattern of the culture."

Benedict views morality as dependent on the varying histories and environments of different cultures. In this essay she assembles an impressive amount of data from her anthropological research of tribal behavior on an island in northwest Melanesia from which she draws her conclusion that moral relativism is the correct view of moral principles.

Study Questions

1. What does Benedict see as the purpose of modern social anthropology?
2. What is her thesis about normalcy and abnormalcy?
3. How does Benedict illustrate her thesis? Are the examples sufficient to make her case?
4. What is the point of her illustration of homosexual behavior? Do you find her point plausible?
5. How does Benedict characterize morality? With what phrase is the sentence "It is morally good" synonymous?
6. What is the significance of her final comments on the range of human behavioral tendencies? What does she mean by the phrase "the proportion in which behavior types stand to one another in different societies is not universal"?

MODERN SOCIAL ANTHROPOLOGY has become more and more a study of the varieties and common elements of cultural environment and the consequences of these in human behavior. For such a study of diverse social orders primitive peoples fortunately provide a laboratory not yet entirely vitiated by the spread of a standardized worldwide civilization. Dyaks and Hopis, Fijians and Yakuts are significant for psychological and sociological study because only among

From "Anthropology and the Abnormal," by Ruth Benedict, in The Journal of General Psychology *10 (1934): 59–82, a publication of the Helen Dwight Reid Educational Foundation. Reprinted by permission of Heldref Publications.*

these simpler peoples has there been sufficient isolation to give opportunity for the development of localized social forms. In the higher cultures the standardization of custom and belief over a couple of continents has given a false sense of the inevitability of the particular forms that have gained currency, and we need to turn to a wider survey in order to check the conclusions we hastily base upon this near-universality of familiar customs. Most of the simpler cultures did not gain the wide currency of the one which, out of our experience, we identify with human nature, but this was for various historical reasons, and certainly not for any that gives us as its carriers a monopoly of social good or of social sanity. Modern civilization, from this point of view, becomes not a necessary pinnacle of human achievement but one entry in a long series of possible adjustments.

These adjustments, whether they are in mannerisms like the ways of showing anger, or joy, or grief in any society, or in major human drives like those of sex, prove to be far more variable than experience in any one culture would suggest. In certain fields, such as that of religion or of formal marriage arrangements, these wide limits of variability are well known and can be fairly described. In others it is not yet possible to give a generalized account, but that does not absolve us of the task of indicating the significance of the work that has been done and of the problems that have arisen.

One of these problems relates to the customary modern normal-abnormal categories and our conclusions regarding them. In how far are such categories culturally determined, or in how far can we with assurance regard them as absolute? In how far can we regard inability to function socially as diagnostic of abnormality, or in how far is it necessary to regard this as a function of the culture?

As a matter of fact, one of the most striking facts that emerge from a study of widely varying cultures is the ease with which our abnormals function in other cultures. It does not matter what kind of "abnormality" we choose for illustration, those which indicate extreme instability, or those which are more in the nature of character traits like sadism or delusions of grandeur or of persecution, there are well-described cultures in which these abnormals function at ease and with honor, and apparently without danger or difficulty to the society. . . .

The most notorious of these is trance and catalepsy. Even a very mild mystic is aberrant in our culture. But most peoples have regarded even extreme psychic manifestations not only as normal and desirable, but even as characteristic of highly valued and gifted individuals. This was true even in our own cultural background in that period when Catholicism made the ecstatic experience the mark of sainthood. It is hard for us, born and brought up in a culture that makes no use of the experience, to realize how important a role it may play and how many individuals are capable of it, once it has been given an honorable place in any society. . . .

Cataleptic and trance phenomena are, of course, only one illustration of the fact that those whom we regard as abnormals may function adequately in other cultures. Many of our culturally discarded traits are selected for elaboration in different societies. Homosexuality is an excellent example, for in this case our attention is not constantly diverted, as in the consideration of trance, to the interruption of routine activity which it implies. Homosexuality poses the problem very simply. A tendency toward this trait in our culture exposes an individual to all the conflicts to which all aberrants are always exposed, and we tend to identify the consequences of this conflict with homosexuality. But these consequences are obviously local and cultural. Homosexuals in many societies are not incompetent, but they may be such if the culture asks adjustments of them that would strain any man's vitality. Wherever homosexuality has been given an honorable place in any society, those to whom it is congenial have filled adequately the honorable roles society assigns to them. Plato's *Republic* is, of course, the most convincing statement of such a reading of homosexuality. It is presented as one of the major means to the good life, and it was generally so regarded in Greece at that time.

The cultural attitude toward homosexuals has not always been on such a high ethical plane, but it has been very varied. Among many American Indian tribes there exists the institution of the berdache, as the French called them. These menwomen were men who at puberty or thereafter took the dress and the occupations of women. Sometimes they married other men and lived with them. Sometimes they were men with no inversion, persons of weak sexual endowment who chose this role to avoid the jeers of the women. The berdaches were never regarded as of first-rate supernatural power, as similar menwomen were in Siberia, but rather as leaders in women's occupations, good healers in certain diseases, or, among certain tribes, as the genial organizers of social affairs. In any case, they were socially placed. They were not left exposed to the conflicts that visit the deviant who is excluded from participation in the recognized patterns of his society.

The most spectacular illustrations of the extent to which normality may be culturally defined are those cultures where an abnormality of our culture is the cornerstone of their social structure. It is not possible to do justice to these possibilities in a short discussion. A recent study of an island of northwest Melanesia by Fortune describes a society built upon traits which we regard as beyond the border of paranoia. In this tribe the exogamic groups look upon each other as prime manipulators of black magic, so that one marries always into an enemy group which remains for life one's deadly and unappeasable foes. They look upon a good garden crop as a confession of theft, for everyone is engaged in making magic to induce into his garden the productiveness of his neighbors'; therefore no se-

crecy in the island is so rigidly insisted upon as the secrecy of a man's harvesting of his yams. Their polite phrase at the acceptance of a gift is, "And if you now poison me, how shall I repay you this present?" Their preoccupation with poisoning is constant; no woman ever leaves her cooking pot for a moment untended. Even the great affinal economic exchanges that are characteristic of this Melanesian culture area are quite altered in Dobu since they are incompatible with this fear and distrust that pervades the culture. They go farther and people the whole world outside their own quarters with such malignant spirits that all-night feasts and ceremonials simply do not occur here. They have even rigorous religiously enforced customs that forbid the sharing of seed even in one family group. Anyone else's food is deadly poison to you, so that communality of stores is out of the question. For some months before harvest the whole society is on the verge of starvation, but if one falls to the temptation and eats up one's seed yams, one is an outcast and a beachcomber for life. There is no coming back. It involves, as a matter of course, divorce and the breaking of all social ties.

Now in this society where no one may work with another and no one may share with another, Fortune describes the individual who was regarded by all his fellows as crazy. He was not one of those who periodically ran amok and, beside himself and frothing at the mouth, fell with a knife upon anyone he could reach. Such behavior they did not regard as putting anyone outside the pale. They did not even put the individuals who were known to be liable to these attacks under any kind of control. They merely fled when they saw the attack coming on and kept out of the way. "He would be all right tomorrow." But there was one man of sunny, kindly disposition who liked work and liked to be helpful. The compulsion was too strong for him to repress it in favor of the opposite tendencies of his culture. Men and women never spoke of him without laughing; he was silly and simple and definitely crazy. Nevertheless, to the ethnologist used to a culture that has, in Christianity, made his type the model of all virtue, he seemed a pleasant fellow. . . .

. . . Among the Kwakiutl it did not matter whether a relative had died in bed of disease, or by the hand of an enemy, in either case death was an affront to be wiped out by the death of another person. The fact that one had been caused to mourn was proof that one had been put upon. A chief's sister and her daughter had gone up to Victoria, and either because they drank bad whiskey or because their boat capsized they never came back. The chief called together his warriors, "Now I ask you, tribes, who shall wail? Shall I do it or shall another?" The spokesman answered, of course, "Not you, Chief. Let some other of the tribes." Immediately they set up the war pole to announce their intention of wiping out the injury, and gathered a war party. They set out, and found seven men and two children asleep and killed them. "Then they felt good when they arrived at Sebaa in the evening."

The point which is of interest to us is that in our society those who on that occasion would feel good when they arrived at Sebaa that evening would be the definitely abnormal. There would be some, even in our society, but it is not a recognized and approved mood under the circumstances. On the Northwest Coast those are favored and fortunate to whom that mood under those circumstances is congenial, and those to whom it is repugnant are unlucky. This latter minority can register in their own culture only by doing violence to their congenial responses and acquiring others that are difficult for them. The person, for instance, who, like a Plains Indian whose wife has been taken from him, is too proud to fight, can deal with the Northwest Coast civilization only by ignoring its strongest bents. If he cannot achieve it, he is the deviant in that culture, their instance of abnormality.

This head-hunting that takes place on the Northwest Coast after a death is no matter of blood revenge or of organized vengeance. There is no effort to tie up the subsequent killing with any responsibility on the part of the victim for the death of the person who is being mourned. A chief whose son has died goes visiting wherever his fancy dictates, and he says to his host, "My prince has died today, and you go with him." Then he kills him. In this, according to their interpretation, he acts nobly because he has not been downed. He has thrust back in return. The whole procedure is meaningless without the fundamental paranoid reading of bereavement. Death, like all the other untoward accidents of existence, confounds man's pride and can only be handled in the category of insults.

Behavior honored upon the Northwest Coast is one which is recognized as abnormal in our civilization, and yet it is sufficiently close to the attitudes of our own culture to be intelligible to us and to have a definite vocabulary with which we may discuss it. The megalomaniac paranoid trend is a definite danger in our society. It is encouraged by some of our major preoccupations, and it confronts us with a choice of two possible attitudes. One is to brand it as abnormal and reprehensible, and is the attitude we have chosen in our civilization. The other is to make it an essential attribute of ideal man, and this is the solution in the culture of the Northwest Coast.

These illustrations, which it has been possible to indicate only in the briefest manner, force upon us the fact that normality is culturally defined. An adult shaped to the drives and standards of either of these cultures, if he were transported into our civilization, would fall into our categories of abnormality. He would be faced with the psychic dilemmas of the socially unavailable. In his own culture, however, he is the pillar of society, the end result of socially inculcated mores, and the problem of personal instability in his case simply does not arise.

No one civilization can possibly utilize in its mores the whole potential range of human behavior. Just as there are great numbers of possible phonetic articulations, and the possibility of language depends on a selection and standardization of a few of these in order that speech communication may be possible at all, so the possibility of organized behavior of every sort, from the fashions of local dress and houses to the dicta of a people's ethics and religion, depends upon a similar selection among the possible behavior traits. In the field of recognized economic obligations or sex tabus this selection is as nonrational and subconscious a process as it is in the field of phonetics. It is a process which goes on in the group for long periods of time and is historically conditioned by innumerable accidents of isolation or of contact of peoples. In any comprehensive study of psychology, the selection that different cultures have made in the course of history within the great circumference of potential behavior is of great significance.

Every society, beginning with some slight inclination in one direction or another, carries its preference farther and farther, integrating itself more and more completely upon its chosen basis, and discarding those types of behavior that are uncongenial. Most of those organizations of personality that seem to us most uncontrovertibly abnormal have been used by different civilizations in the very foundations of their institutional life. Conversely the most valued traits of our normal individuals have been looked on in differently organized cultures as aberrant. Normality, in short, within a very wide range, is culturally defined. It is primarily a term for the socially elaborated segment of human behavior in any culture; and abnormality, a term for the segment that that particular civilization does not use. The very eyes with which we see the problem are conditioned by the long traditional habits of our own society.

It is a point that has been made more often in relation to ethics than in relation to psychiatry. We do not any longer make the mistake of deriving the morality of our locality and decade directly from the inevitable constitution of human nature. We do not elevate it to the dignity of a first principle. We recognize that morality differs in every society, and is a convenient term for socially approved habits. Mankind has always preferred to say, "It is a morally good," rather than "It is habitual," and the fact of this preference is matter enough for a critical science of ethics. But historically the two phrases are synonymous.

The concept of the normal is properly a variant of the concept of the good. It is that which society has approved. A normal action is one which falls well within the limits of expected behavior for a particular society. Its variability among different peoples is essentially a function of the variability of the behavior patterns that different societies have created for themselves, and can never be wholly divorced from a consideration of culturally institutionalized types of behavior.

Each culture is a more or less elaborate working-out of the potentialities of the segment it has chosen. In so far as a civilization is well integrated and consistent within itself, it will tend to carry farther and farther, according to its nature, its initial impulse toward a particular type of action, and from the point of view of any other culture those elaborations will include more and more extreme and aberrant traits.

Each of these traits, in proportion as it reinforces the chosen behavior patterns of that culture, is for that culture normal. Those individuals to whom it is congenial either congenitally, or as the result of childhood sets, are accorded prestige in that culture, and are not visited with the social contempt or disapproval which their traits would call down upon them in a society that was differently organized. On the other hand, those individuals whose characteristics are not congenial to the selected type of human behavior in that community are the deviants, no matter how valued their personality traits may be in a contrasted civilization.

The Dobuan who is not easily susceptible to fear of treachery, who enjoys work and likes to be helpful, is their neurotic and regarded as silly.

On the Northwest Coast the person who finds it difficult to read life in terms of an insult contest will be the person upon whom fall all the difficulties of the culturally unprovided for. The person who does not find it easy to humiliate a neighbor, nor to see humiliation in his own experience, who is genial and loving, may, of course, find some unstandardized way of achieving satisfactions in his society, but not in the major patterned responses that his culture requires of him. If he is born to play an important role in a family with many hereditary privileges, he can succeed only by doing violence to his whole personality. If he does not succeed, he has betrayed his culture; that is, he is abnormal.

I have spoken of individuals as having sets toward certain types of behavior, and of these sets as running sometimes counter to the types of behavior which are institutionalized in the culture to which they belong. From all that we know of contrasting cultures it seems clear that differences of temperament occur in every society. The matter has never been made the subject of investigation, but from the available material it would appear that these temperament types are very likely of universal recurrence. That is, there is an ascertainable range of human behavior that is found wherever a sufficiently large series of individuals is observed. But the proportion in which behavior types stand to one another in different societies is not universal. The vast majority of individuals in any group are shaped to the fashion of that culture. In other words, most individuals are plastic to the moulding force of the society into which they are born. In a society that values trance, as in India, they will have supernormal experience. In a society that institutionalizes homosexuality, they will be homosexual. In a society that sets the gathering of possessions as the chief human objective, they will amass property. The deviants, whatever the type of behavior the culture has institutionalized, will remain few in number, and there seems no more difficulty in moulding the vast malleable majority to the "normality" of what we consider an aberrant trait, such as delusions of reference, than to the normality of such accepted behavior patterns as acquisitiveness. The small proportion of the number of the deviants in any culture is not a function of the sure instinct with which that society has built itself upon the fundamental sanities, but of the universal fact that, happily, the majority of mankind quite readily take any shape that is presented to them. . . .

For Further Reflection

1. Is Benedict correct in saying that our culture is "but one entry in a long series of possible adjustments"? What are the implications of this statement?

2. Can we separate the descriptive (or fact-stating) aspect of anthropological study from the prescriptive (evaluative) aspect of evaluating cultures? Are there some independent criteria by which we can say that some cultures are better than others? Can you think how this project might be begun?

3. What are the implications of Benedict's claim that morality is simply whatever a culture deems normal behavior? Is this a satisfactory equation? Can you apply it to the institution of slavery or the Nazi policy of antisemitism?

4. What is the significance of Benedict's statement "The very eyes with which we see the problem are conditioned by the long traditional habits of our own society"? Can we apply the conceptual relativism embodied in this statement to her own position?

VI.3   A Critique of Moral Relativism

LOUIS POJMAN

Louis Pojman is a professor of philosophy at the University of Mississippi and editor of this work. He has written books and articles in the areas of philosophy of religion and ethics, including *Ethics: Discovering Right and Wrong*.

In this article he first analyzes the structure of ethical relativism as constituted by two theses: the diversity thesis and the dependency thesis. He then goes on to examine two types of ethical relativism: subjectivism and conventionalism. Both types, he argues, have serious problems. He indicates a way of taking into account the insights of relativism while maintaining an objectivist position, and ends by offering suggestions as to why people have been misled by relativist arguments.

Study Questions

1. Distinguish carefully between the diversity thesis and the dependency thesis. What roles does each play in the relativist's argument?

2. What is the difference between *cultural relativism* and *ethical relativism*, and why does the author think that cultural relativism is a "neutral fact"?

3. What is the essential difference between subjectivism and conventionalism? Is the author correct in accusing subjectivism of being solipsistic? Is he correct in arguing that conventionalism leads to the same result?

4. Why does the author believe that the ethical relativist is unable to offer moral criticism of cruel behavior in another culture?

5. What is the significance of the difficulty in defining a culture and recognizing that many of us belong to more than one culture?

6. What is the argument for an objective morality?

7. What does the author think is the point or purpose of morality? Do you agree or is he defining objectivism into existence?

8. Why does the author think that there is a modern tendency to accept relativism?

"Who's to judge what's right or wrong?" [A common question asked by students]

IN THE NINETEENTH CENTURY Christian missionaries sometimes used coercion to change the customs of pagan tribal people in parts of Africa and the Pacific Islands. Appalled by the customs of public nakedness, polygamy, work-ing on the Sabbath, and infanticide, they paternalistically went about reforming the "poor pagans." They clothed them, separated wives from their husbands in order to create monogamous households, made the Sabbath a day of rest, and ended infanticide. In the process they sometimes created social malaise, causing the estranged women to despair and their children to be orphaned. The natives often did not understand the new religion, but accepted it in deference to the white man's power. The white people had guns and medicine.

Since the nineteenth century we have made progress in understanding cultural diversity and realize that the social dissonance caused by do-gooders was a bad thing. In the last century or so, anthropology has exposed our penchant for ethnocentrism, the prejudicial view that interprets all of reality through the eyes of our cultural beliefs and values. We have come to see enormous variety in social practices throughout the world.

Eskimos allow their elderly to die by starvation; we believe that this is morally wrong. The Spartans of ancient Greece and the Dobu of New Guinea believe that stealing is morally right; we believe it is wrong. Many cultures, past and present, have practiced or still practice infanticide (a tribe in East Africa once threw deformed infants to hippopotamuses); our society condemns such acts. Sexual practices vary over time and clime. Some cultures permit, while others condemn, homosexual behavior. Some cultures, including Moslem societies, practice polygamy, while most Christian cultures view it as immoral. Ruth Benedict describes a tribe in Melanesia which views cooperation and kindness as vices, and Colin Turnbull has documented that the Ik in Northern Uganda have no sense of duty towards their children or parents. There are societies which make it a duty for children to kill (sometimes strangle) their aging parents.

The ancient Greek historian, Herodotus (485–430 B.C.) tells the story of how Darius, the king of Persia, once brought together some Callatians (Asian tribal people) and some Greeks. He asked the Callatians how they disposed of their deceased parents. They told how they ate the bodies of their dead parents. The Greeks, who cremated their parents, were horrified at such barbarous behavior. No amount of money could tempt them to do such an irreverent thing. Then Darius asked the Callatians what he should give them

"to burn the bodies of their fathers at their decease." The Callatians were utterly horrified at such barbarous behavior and begged Darius to cease from such irreverent discourse. Herodotus concludes, "Custom is the king o'er all."[1]

Today we condemn ethnocentrism, the uncritical belief in the inherent superiority of one's own culture, as tantamount to racism and sexism. What is right in one culture may be wrong in another; what is good east of the river may be bad west of the river; what is a virtue in one nation may be a vice in another—so it behooves us not to judge others but to tolerate diversity.

This rejection of ethnocentrism in the West has contributed to a shift in public opinion about morality, and for a growing number of Westerners, consciousness-raising about the validity of other ways of life has led to an erosion of belief in moral *objectivism*, the view that there are universal moral principles, valid for all people at all times and in all climes. In polls taken in my ethics and introduction to philosophy classes over the past several years (in universities in three different areas of the country) students affirmed by a two to one ratio a version of *moral relativism* over *moral absolutism*, with hardly three percent seeing something between these two opposites. I am not suggesting that all these students had a clear understanding of what is entailed by relativism, for many of those who said that they were ethical relativists also stated, on the same questionnaire, that "abortion except to save the mother's life is always wrong," that "capital punishment is always morally wrong," or that "suicide is never morally permissible." The (apparent) contradictions signal an (apparent) confusion on the matter.

I want to argue that ethical relativism is a mistaken theory and that the cultural differences do not demonstrate that all ways of life are equally valid from a moral perspective. Indeed, ethical relativism, were it true, would spell the death of ethics. In spite of cultural divergences there is a *universally* valid core morality. I call this core morality "moral objectivism," to distinguish it from both "moral absolutism" and "moral relativism."

An Analysis of Relativism

Ethical relativism is the theory that there are no universally valid moral principles; that all moral principles are valid relative to *culture* or *individual choice*. That is, there are two types of relativism: *conventionalism*, which holds that moral principles are relative to the culture or society, and *subjectivism*, which holds that it is the individual choice that determines the validity of a moral principle. We'll start with conventionalism. Philosopher John Ladd, of Brown University, defines *conventional ethical relativism* this way:

> Ethical relativism is the doctrine that the moral rightness and wrongness of actions varies from society to society and that there are no absolute universal moral standards binding on all men at all times. Accordingly, it holds that whether or not it is right for an individual to act in a certain way depends on or is relative to the society to which he belongs (John Ladd, *Ethical Relativism*, Wadsworth, 1973).

According to Ladd, ethical relativism consists of two theses: a *Diversity Thesis*, which specifies that what is considered morally right and wrong varies from society to society, so that there are no moral principles accepted by all societies, and a *Dependency Thesis*, which specifies that all moral principles derive their validity from cultural acceptance. From these two ideas he concludes that there are no universally valid moral principles, objective standards which apply to all people everywhere and at all times.

The first thesis, the *Diversity Thesis*, or what may simply be called *cultural relativism*, is an anthropological thesis, which registers the fact that moral rules differ from society to society. As we noted at the beginning of this essay, there is enormous variety in what may count as a moral principle in a given society. The human condition is malleable in the extreme, allowing any

number of folkways or moral codes. Ruth Benedict has written:

> The cultural pattern of any civilization makes use of a certain segment of the great arc of potential human purposes and motivations . . . that any culture makes use of certain selected material techniques or cultural traits. The great arc along which all the possible human behaviors are distributed is far too immense and too full of contradictions for any one culture to utilize even any considerable portion of it. Selection is the first requirement. [*Patterns of Culture*, New York, 1934, p. 219]

The second thesis, the *Dependency Thesis*, asserts that individual acts are right or wrong depending on the nature of the society from which they emanate. What is considered morally right or wrong must be seen in a context, depending on the goals, wants, beliefs, history, and environment of the society in question. As William Graham Sumner says, "We learn the [morals] as unconsciously as we learn to walk and hear and breathe, and we never know any reason why the [morals] are what they are. The justification of them is that when we wake to consciousness of life we find them facts which already hold us in the bonds of tradition, custom, and habit."[2] Trying to see things from an independent, noncultural point of view would be like taking out our eyes in order to examine their contours and qualities. We are simply culturally determined beings.

In a sense, we all live in radically different worlds. Each person has a different set of beliefs and experiences, a particular perspective that colors all of his or her perceptions. Do the farmer, the real estate dealer, and the artist, looking at the same spatio-temporal field, see the same field? Not likely. Their different orientations, values, and expectations govern their perceptions, so that different aspects of the field are highlighted and some features are missed. Even as our individual values arise from personal experience, so social values are grounded in the peculiar history of the community. Morality, then, is just the set of common rules, habits, and customs which have won social approval over time, so that they seem part of the nature of things, as facts. There is nothing mysterious or transcendent about these codes of behavior. They are the outcomes of our social history.

The conclusion that there are no absolute or objective moral standards binding on all people follows from the first two propositions. Cultural relativism (the Diversity Thesis) plus the Dependency Thesis yields ethical relativism in its classic form. If there are different moral principles from culture to culture and if all morality is rooted in culture, it follows that there are no universal moral principles valid for all cultures and people at all times.

Subjective Ethical Relativism (Subjectivism)

Some people think that even this conclusion is too tame and maintain that morality is not dependent on the society but on the individual. As students sometimes maintain, "Morality is in the eye of the beholder." Ernest Hemingway wrote, "So far, about morals, I know only that what is moral is what you feel good after and what is immoral is what you feel bad after and judged by these moral standards, which I do not defend, the bullfight is very moral to me because I feel very fine while it is going on and have a feeling of life and death and mortality and immortality, and after it is over I feel very sad but very fine."[3]

This form of moral subjectivism has the sorry consequence that it makes morality a useless concept, for, on its premises, little or no interpersonal criticism or judgment is logically possible. Hemingway may feel good about the killing of bulls in a bullfight, while Albert Schweitzer or Mother Teresa may feel the opposite. No argument about the matter is possible. The only basis for judging Hemingway or anyone else wrong would be if he failed to live up to his own principles, but, of course, one of Hemingway's principles could be that hypocrisy is morally per-

missible (he feels good about it), so that it would be impossible for him to do wrong. For Hemingway, hypocrisy and nonhypocrisy could both be morally permissible. On the basis of Subjectivism it could very easily turn out that Adolf Hitler is as moral as Gandhi, so long as each believes he is living by his chosen principles. Notions of moral good and bad, right or wrong cease to have interpersonal evaluative meaning.

Once, Columbia University Professor Sidney Morgenbesser taught a philosophy class in which the students argued vehemently for subjectivism. When a test was taken, Morgenbesser returned all the tests marked "F"—even though his comments showed that most of the tests were of a very high quality. When the students expressed outrage at this injustice, Morgenbesser answered that he had accepted the notion of Subjectivism for purposes of marking the exams in which case the principle of justice had no objective validity.

Absurd consequences follow from subjective ethical relativism. If it is correct, then morality is reduced to aesthetic tastes over which there can be no argument or interpersonal judgment. Although many people say that they hold this position, there seems to be a conflict between it and other of their moral views (e.g., that Hitler is really morally bad or that capital punishment is always wrong). There seems to be a contradiction between subjectivism and the very concept of morality, which it is supposed to characterize, for morality has to do with 'proper' resolution of interpersonal conflict and the amelioration of the human predicament. As Thomas Hobbes pointed out, whatever else it does, morality aims at preventing a state of chaos where life is "solitary, poor, nasty, brutish, and short." But if so, Subjectivism is no help at all in doing this, for it doesn't rest on social *agreement* of principle (as the conventionalist maintains) or on an objectively independent set of norms that bind all people for the common good.

Subjectivism treats individuals as billiard balls on a societal pool table where they meet only in radical collisions, each aiming for its own goal and striving to do in the other fellow before he does it to you. This atomistic view of personality is belied by the fact that we develop in families and mutually dependent communities, in which we share a common language, common institutions, and habits, and that we often feel each other's joys and sorrows. As John Donne said, "No man is an island, entire of itself; every man is a piece of the continent."

Radical individualistic relativism seems incoherent. If so, it follows that the only plausible view of ethical relativism must be one that grounds morality in the group or culture. This form of relativism is called conventionalism, which we looked at earlier and to which we now return.

Conventional Ethical Relativism (Conventionalism)

Conventional ethical relativism, the view that there are no objective moral principles but that all valid moral principles are justified by virtue of their cultural acceptance, recognizes the social nature of morality. That is precisely its power and virtue. It does not seem subject to the same absurd consequences that plague Subjectivism. Recognizing the importance of our social environment in generating customs and beliefs, many people suppose that ethical relativism is the correct ethical theory. They are further drawn to it for its liberal philosophical stance. It seems to be an enlightened response to the "sin of ethnocentricity," and it seems to entail or strongly imply an attitude of tolerance towards other cultures. As Benedict says, in recognizing ethical relativity "we shall arrive at a more realistic social faith, accepting as grounds of hope and as new bases for tolerance the coexisting and equally valid patterns of life which mankind has created for itself from the raw materials of existence."[4] The most famous of those holding this position is the anthropologist Melville Herskovits, who argues even more explicitly than Benedict that ethical relativism entails intercultural tolerance.[5]

The view contains a contradiction. If no moral principles are universally valid, how can tolerance be universally valid? Whence comes its validity? If morality is simply relative to each culture and if the culture does not have a principle of tolerance, its members have no obligation to be tolerant. Herskovits seems to be treating the *principle of tolerance* as the one exception to his relativism—as an absolute moral principle. But from a relativistic point of view, there is no more reason to be tolerant than to be intolerant and neither stance is objectively morally better than the other.

Not only do relativists fail to offer a basis for criticizing those who are intolerant, but they cannot rationally *criticize* anyone who espouses what they might regard as a heinous principle. If, as seems to be the case, valid criticism supposes an objective or impartial standard, relativists cannot morally criticize anyone outside their own culture. Adolf Hitler's genocidal actions, so long as they are culturally accepted, are as morally legitimate as Mother Teresa's works of mercy. If conventional relativism is accepted, racism, genocide, oppression of the poor, slavery, and even the advocacy of war for its own sake are as moral as their opposites. And if a subculture within our own culture decided that starting a nuclear war was somehow morally acceptable, we could not morally criticize the members of that subculture.

Any moral system, whatever its content, is as valid as every other, as well as more valid than ideal moralities, since the latter aren't adhered to by any culture.

There are other disturbing consequences of ethical relativism. It seems to entail that reformers are always (morally) wrong since they go against the tide of cultural standards. William Wilberforce was wrong in the eighteenth century to oppose slavery, the British were immoral in opposing suttee (the burning of widows) in India. The early Christians were wrong in refusing to serve in the Roman army or to bow down to Caesar, acts which the majority in the Roman Empire believed to be moral duties. And Jesus was immoral in breaking the law of his day by healing on the Sabbath and by preaching the Sermon on the Mount, since few in his time (as in ours) accepted its principles.

Yet most of us normally feel just the opposite: that the reformer is the courageous innovator who is right, who has the truth—and that the mindless majority is wrong. Sometimes the individual must stand alone with the truth, risking social censure and persecution. As Dr. Stockman says in Ibsen's *Enemy of the People,* after he loses the battle to declare his town's profitable polluted tourist spa unsanitary, "The most dangerous enemy of the truth and freedom among us—is the compact majority. Yes, the damned, compact and liberal majority. The majority has *might*—unfortunately—but *right* it is not. Right—are I and a few others." Yet if relativism is correct, the opposite is necessarily the case. Truth is with the crowd and error with the individual.

An even more basic problem with the conventionalist view that morality is dependent on cultural acceptance for its validity is that the concept of a culture or society is notoriously difficult to define. This is especially so in a pluralistic society like our own, where the notion seems to be vague, to have unclear boundary lines. One person may belong to several subcultures, each with different value emphases and arrangements of principles. A person may belong to the nation as a single society, with its values of patriotism, honor, and courage, and its laws (including some that are controversial but have majority acceptance, such as the law on abortion). But he or she may also belong to a church that opposes some of the laws of the State. He may also be a member of a socially mixed community where different principles hold sway, and he may belong to clubs and a family with still other rules. Relativism seems to tell us that where he is a member of societies with conflicting moralities he must be judged both wrong and not-wrong,

whatever he does. For example, if Mary is a citizen of the United States and a member of the Roman Catholic Church, she is wrong (qua Catholic) if she chooses to have an abortion and not-wrong (qua citizen of the United States) if she acts against the teaching of her church on abortion. As a member of a racist organization (say the Ku Klux Klan) John has no obligation to treat his fellow black citizens as equals, but as a member of the university community itself (where the principle of equal rights is accepted) he does have the obligation; but as a member of the surrounding community (which may reject the principle of equal rights) he again has no such obligation; but then again as a member of the nation at large (which accepts the principle) he is obligated to treat his fellow with respect. What is the morally right thing for John to do? The question no longer makes much sense in this moral Babel. It has lost its action-guiding function.

Perhaps the relativist would say that in such cases the individual may choose which group to belong to as primary. If Mary chooses to have an abortion, she is choosing to belong to the larger society relative to that issue. If John acts as a racist, he is choosing against belonging to the university and the nation on that issue. The trouble with this option is that it seems to lead back to counterintuitive results. If Gangland Gus of Murder, Incorporated, feels like killing bank president Ortcutt and wants to feel good about it, he identifies with the Murder, Incorporated, society rather than with the general public morality. Does this justify the killing? In fact, couldn't one justify anything simply by forming a small subculture that approved of it? Charles Manson would be moral in killing innocents simply by virtue of forming a coterie. How large must the group be to be a legitimate subculture or society? Does it need ten people or fifteen? How about just three? Come to think about it, why can't my partner in burglary and I found our own society with a morality of its own? Of course, if my partner dies, I could still claim that I was acting from an originally social set of norms. Finally, why can't I dispense with interpersonal agreements altogether and invent my own morality—since morality, on this view, is only an invention anyway? Conventionalist relativism seems to reduce to subjectivism. And subjectivism leads, as we have seen, to the demise of morality altogether.

The Case for Ethical Objectivism

Where does the relativist go wrong? I think the relativist makes an unwarranted slide from the observation that different cultures have different rules to the conclusion that no culture's set of rules is better than any other culture's set of rules, or even an ideal set of rules. Some sets of rules are better than other sets relative to the purposes of morality. As I have argued elsewhere, the purposes of moral rules are the survival of the society, the alleviation of suffering, human flourishing, and the just resolution of conflicts of interest.[6] These purposes will yield a set of common principles that may actually underlie some of the cultural differences reported by anthropologists. In the eighteenth century, David Hume noted that human nature was fundamentally similar throughout time and clime; more recently, the sociobiologist E. O. Wilson has identified over a score of universal features. The anthropologist Clyde Kluckhohn sums up his findings on common cultural features:

> Every culture has a concept of murder, distinguishing this from execution, killing in war, and other "justifiable homicides." The notions of incest and other regulations upon sexual behavior, the prohibitions upon untruth under defined circumstances, of restitution and reciprocity, of mutual obligations between parents and children—these and many other moral concepts are altogether universal ["Ethical Relativity: Sic et Non," *Journal of Philosophy*, LII (1955)].

Colin Turnbull, whose description of the sadistic, semidisplaced Ik in Northern Uganda was cited as evidence of a people without principles of kindness and cooperation, has produced evidence that, underneath the surface of this dying society, there is a deeper moral code from a time when the tribe flourished, and that this occasionally surfaces and shows its nobler face.

The nonrelativist can accept a certain relativity in the way moral principles are *applied* in different cultures, depending on each culture's beliefs, history, and environment. For example, a raw environment with scarce natural resources may justify the Eskimos' brand of euthanasia to the objectivist, who in another environment would consistently reject that practice. The Greeks and the Callatians disposed of their parents differently, but that does not prove that conventionalism is correct. Both groups seem to adhere to a common principle of showing respect to one's elders. Why can't there be latitude in how that respect is shown?

The members of a tribe in East Africa throw their deformed children into the river because of their belief that such infants *belong* to the hippopotamus, the god of the river. We believe that they have a false belief about this, but the same principles—of respect for property and respect for human life—operate in both societies. They differ with us only in belief, not in substantive moral principle. This is an illustration of how nonmoral beliefs (e.g., deformed children belong to the hippopotamus) when applied to common moral principles (e.g., give to each his due) generate different actions in different cultures. In our culture the difference in belief about the status of a fetus (is it a person or only a potential person?) generates opposite moral prescriptions. Both the pro-choice movement and the antiabortionists agree that it is wrong to kill innocent persons, but they disagree as to a fact (not the principle) of whether a fetus is a *person* (a being with a right to life). Roman Catholics believe that the fetus is a person because—they say—it has a soul; most liberal Protestants and secularists deny this. Abortion is a serious moral issue, but what divides many of us is not a moral principle but how that principle should be applied. Antiabortionists believe that the principle of not killing innocent persons applies to fetuses whereas pro-choicers do not. But the two sides do not disagree on the fundamental principle.

The relativist, responding to this point may argue that even if we do *often* share deep principles, we don't *always* share them. Some people may not value life at all. How can we prove them wrong?—"Who's to say which culture is right and which is wrong?" This response is of dubious merit. We can reason and perform thought experiments in order to make a case for one system over another. We may not be able to *know* with certainty that our moral beliefs are closer to the truth than those of another culture (or those of others within our own culture), but we may be *justified* in believing that they are. If we can be closer to the truth regarding factual or scientific matters, why can't we be closer to the truth on moral matters? Why can't a culture simply be confused or wrong about its moral perceptions? Why can't we say that a society like the Ik, which sees nothing wrong with enjoying watching its children fall into fires, is less moral in that regard than the culture that cherishes children and grants them protection and equal rights? To take such a stand is not to commit the fallacy of ethnocentricism, for we are seeking to derive principles through critical reason, not simply uncritical acceptance of one's own mores.

The Positive Case for a Core Morality

The discussion heretofore has been largely negative, against relativism. Now I want to make a case for a core set of moral principles that are necessary to the good society and the good life.

First, I must make it clear that I am distinguishing moral *absolutism* from moral *objectivism*. The absolutist believes that there are non-overridable moral principles which ought never to be violated. Kant's system is a good example of this. One ought never break a promise or tell a lie, no matter what. An objectivist need not

posit any non-overridable principles, at least not in unqualified general form, and so need not be an absolutist. As Renford Bambrough put it,

> To suggest that there is a *right* answer to a moral problem is at once to be accused of or credited with a belief in moral absolutes. But it is no more necessary to believe in moral absolutes in order to believe in moral objectivity than it is to believe in the existence of absolute space or absolute time in order to believe in the objectivity of temporal and spatial relations and of judgements about them. [*Moral Skepticism and Moral Knowledge*, RKP, p. 33]

In the objectivist's account, moral principles are what the Oxford University philosopher William Ross (1877–1971) refers to as prima facie principles—valid rules of action that should generally be adhered to, but that may be overridden by another moral principle in cases of moral conflict.[7] For example, while a principle of justice may generally outweigh a principle of benevolence, there are times when enormous good could be done by sacrificing a small amount of justice, so that an objectivist would be inclined to act according to the principle of benevolence. There may be some absolute or non-overridable principles (indeed the next principle I mention is probably one), but there need not be any or many for objectivism to be true.

If we can establish or show that it is reasonable to believe that there is at least one objective moral principle which is binding on all people everywhere in some ideal sense, we shall have shown that relativism is probably false and that a limited objectivism is true. Actually, I believe that there are many qualified general ethical principles which are binding on all rational beings, but one will suffice to refute relativism. I will call the principle I've chosen "A":

A: It is morally wrong to torture people for the fun of it.

I claim that this principle is binding on all rational agents, so that if agent S rejects A, we should not let that affect our intuition that A is a true principle but rather try to explain S's behavior as perverse, ignorant, or irrational. Suppose Adolf Hitler doesn't accept A, should that affect our confidence in the truth of A? Is it not more reasonable to infer that Hitler is morally deficient, morally blind, ignorant, or irrational than to suppose that his noncompliance is evidence against the truth of A?

Suppose further that there is a tribe of Hitlerites somewhere who enjoy torturing people. The whole culture accepts torturing others for the fun of it. Suppose that Mother Teresa or Gandhi tries unsuccessfully to convince them that they should stop torturing people altogether, and they respond by torturing *them*. Should this affect our confidence in A? Would it not be more reasonable to look for some explanation of Hitlerite behavior? For example, we might hypothesize that this tribe lacked a developed sense of the sympathetic imagination necessary for the moral life. Or we might theorize that this tribe was on a lower evolutionary level than most *Homo sapiens*. Or we might simply conclude that the tribe was closer to a Hobbesian state of nature than most societies, and as such probably would not survive. But we need not know the correct answer as to why the tribe was in such bad shape in order to maintain our confidence in A as a moral principle. If A is a basic or core belief for us, we will be more likely to doubt the Hitlerites' sanity or ability to think morally than to doubt the validity of A.

We can perhaps produce other candidates for membership in our basic objective moral set. For example:

1. Do not kill innocent people.
2. Do not cause unnecessary pain or suffering.
3. Do not commit rape.
4. Keep your promises and contracts.
5. Do not deprive another person of his or her freedom.
6. Do justice, treating equals equally and unequals unequally.
7. Do not commit adultery.
8. Tell the truth.
9. Help other people.
10. Obey just laws.

These ten principles are examples of the core morality—principles necessary for the good life. Fortunately, the ten principles are not arbitrary, for we can give reasons why we believe that these rules will be necessary to any satisfactory social order. Principles like those formulated in the Ten Commandments and the Golden Rule, and the principle of justice—treat equals equally, tell the truth, keep promises, and the like—are central to the fluid progression of social interaction and the resolution of conflicts. These are what ethics is about (at least minimal morality is, even though there may be more to morality than simply these kinds of concerns). For example, language itself depends on a general and implicit commitment to the principle of truth-telling. Accuracy of expression is a primitive form of truthfulness. Hence, every time we use words correctly we are implicitly telling the truth. Without accurate speech, language wouldn't be possible. Likewise, without the recognition of a rule of promise-keeping, contracts are of no avail and cooperation is less likely to occur; without the recognition of rules to protect life and liberty, we could not secure other goals.

A morality would be adequate if it contained the principles of the core morality, but different (adequate) moralities would apply these principles differently. That is, there may be a certain relativity as to secondary principles (whether to opt for monogamy rather than polygamy, whether to include a principle of high altruism in the set of moral duties, whether to allocate more resources to medical care than to environmental concerns, whether to institute a law to drive on the left side of the road or the right side of the road), but in every morality a certain core will remain. The applications would differ because of differences in environment, belief, tradition, and the like.

The core moral rules are analogous to the set of vitamins necessary for a healthy diet. We need an adequate amount of each vitamin—some people needing more of one, some more of another—but in prescribing a nutritious diet we don't have to set forth recipes, specific foods, place settings, or culinary habits. Gourmets will meet the requirements in one way, ascetics and vegetarians in another, but all will receive the basic nutrients.

Imagine that you have been miraculously transported to the dark kingdom of hell, and there you get a glimpse of the sufferings of the damned. What is their punishment? Well, they have eternal back itches, which ebb and flow constantly, but they cannot scratch their backs, for their arms are paralyzed in front of their bodies. And so they writhe with itchiness through eternity. Just as you begin to feel the itch in your own back, you are transported to heaven. What do you see in the kingdom of the blessed? You see people with eternal back itches who cannot scratch their own backs—but they are all smiling instead of writhing. Why? Because everyone has his or her arms stretched out to scratch someone else's back, and, with people so arranged in one big circle, a hell of suffering is turned into a heaven of ecstasy.

If we can imagine some states of affairs or cultures that are better than others in a way that depends on human action, we can ask what are those characteristics that make them so. In our story, people in heaven, but not those in hell, cooperate for the amelioration of suffering and the production of pleasure. These are very primitive goods, not sufficient for a full-blown moral system, but they give us a hint as to the objectivity of morality. Moral goodness has something to do with the amelioration of suffering, the resolution of conflict, and the promotion of human flourishing. If cooperative heaven is really better than itchy hell, then whatever makes it so is constitutively related to moral rightness.

An Explanation of the Attraction of Ethical Relativism

Why, then, is there such a strong inclination toward ethical relativism? The reasons—there are three—have not, I think, been sufficiently talked about. One is that the options are usually presented as though absolutism and relativism were the only alternatives, so conventionalism wins out against an implausible competitor. My student questionnaire reads as follows: "Are there any ethical absolutes, moral duties binding on all persons at all times, or are moral duties relative to culture? Is there any alternative to these two positions?" Hardly three percent suggest a third position and very few of them identify objectivism. Granted it takes a little philosophical sophistication to make the crucial distinctions, and it is precisely for lack of this sophistication or reflection that relativism has procured its enormous prestige. But, as I have argued, one can have an objective morality without being absolutist.

The second reason is that our recent sensitivity to cultural relativism and the evils of ethnocentrism, which have plagued the relations of Europeans and Americans with people of other cultures, has made us conscious of the frailty of many aspects of our moral repertoire, so that there is a tendency to wonder "Who's to judge what's really right or wrong?" However, the move from a reasonable cultural relativism, which rightly causes us to rethink our moral systems, to an ethical relativism, which causes us to give up the heart of morality altogether, is an instance of the fallacy of confusing factual or descriptive statements with normative ones. Cultural relativism doesn't entail ethical relativism. The very reason that we are *against* ethnocentrism constitutes the basis for our being *for* an objective moral system: impartial reason draws us to both conclusions.

We may well agree that cultures differ and that we ought to be cautious in condemning what we don't understand, but this in no way implies that there are not better and worse ways of living. We can understand and excuse, to some degree at least, those who differ from our best notions of morality, without abdicating the notion that cultures without principles of justice, or of promise-keeping, or of protection of the innocent, are morally poorer for these omissions.

The third reason, which has driven some to moral nihilism and others to relativism, is the decline of religion in Western society. As one of Dostoevsky's characters said, "If God is dead, all things are permitted." The person who has lost religious faith feels a deep vacuum and understandably may confuse it with living in a *moral* vacuum, or he or she finally resigns him- or herself to a form of secular conventionalism. Such people reason that if there is no God to guarantee the validity of the moral order, there must not be a universal moral order: There is just radical cultural diversity and death at the end. But even if there turns out to be no God and no immortality, we still will want to live happy, meaningful lives during our fourscore years on earth. If this is true, then it matters by which principles we live, and those principles that win out in the test of time will be objectively valid.

To sum up, there *are* moral truths, principles belonging to the core morality, without which society will not long survive and individuals will not flourish. Reason can discover these principles and it is in our interest to promote them.

So "Who's to judge what's right or wrong?" *We* are. We are to do so on the basis of the best reasoning we can bring forth and with sympathy and understanding.

NOTES

1. *History of Herodotus*, book 3, ch. 38, translated by George Rawlinson (D. Appleton, 1859).
2. *Folkways*, New York, 1906, section 80. And Ruth Benedict indicates the depth of our cultural conditioning this way: "The very eyes with which we see the problem are conditioned by the long traditional habits of our own society." ["Anthropology and the Abnormal," in *The Journal of General Psychology* (1934), reprinted above as "In Defense of Moral Relativism," VI.2]
3. Ernest Hemingway, *Death in the Afternoon* (Scribner's, 1932), p. 4.
4. *Patterns of Culture*, p. 257.
5. Melville Herskovits, *Cultural Relativism* (Random House, 1972).
6. *Ethics: Discovering Right and Wrong* (Wadsworth, 1990), ch. 1.
7. W. D. Ross, *The Right and the Good* (Oxford, 1931).

For Further Reflection

1. On balance, which position is the stronger, some form of ethical relativism or some version of ethical objectivism? Could both theories be partly true? Explain.
2. Could Benedict respond to the objectivist that "the very eyes with which we see the problem are conditioned by the long traditional habits of our own society"? What are the implications of that view and does it rule out objectivism?
3. How would you go about building a suitable morality? What consideration should be brought into consideration? Do you think that morality has a purpose? If so, what is it?

Ethics and Egoism: Why Should We Be Moral?

Why should we be moral? That is, why should we do what morality requires even when it may not be in our best interest? Is it really in our best interest after all, even if we don't realize it? Or is morality only generally in our best interest, so that we should consider breaking its rules whenever they become too burdensome? Or is there some other answer?

In this section we look at various responses to this question. We begin with Glaucon's question to Socrates: Whether justice (what we would call morality) was really only a compromise relationship between the better but unattainable state of exploiting others with impunity (like the shepherd Gyges, who can become invisible) and the worst situation of being exploited by others. Socrates rejects this way of looking at the problem and argues that justice is intrinsically valuable and brings about a healthy soul, so that it is never in our interest to be immoral.

But many reject Socrates' way of viewing the matter. They accuse Socrates of supposing an objective world of values or a divine law which ensures that those who act selfishly will be punished. But take away the notion of a God or a transcendent moral order which affects us and the Socratic picture breaks down. Self-interest may involve exploiting others; treating them "unjustly."

In our second reading, Ayn Rand's "In Defense of Ethical Egoism" (VI.5), morality is made to coincide with prudence or self-interest. Rand sets forth a version of Universal Ethical Egoism which states that everyone ought always to serve his or her own self-interest. That is, everyone ought to do what will maximize one's own expected utility or bring about one's own happiness, even when it means harming others. In our final reading, James Rachels offers three arguments against ethical egoism and concludes that one of these invalidates the theory.

Why Should I Be Moral?
Gyges' Ring and Socrates' Dilemma   VI.4

PLATO

Plato (427–347 B.C.) lived in Athens and is the earliest philosopher for whom extensive works still remain today. In a series of dialogues he immortalized his teacher, Socrates. Perhaps his greatest dialogue is the *Republic,* from which this present reading is taken. The *Republic* is a classic treatise on political philosophy, centering on the concept of justice or moral rightness. In this work, Plato through his idealization of Socrates argues there will only be justice when reason rules and the people are obedient to its commands. This Utopia is only possible in an aristocracy in which the rulers are philosophers—philosopher-kings. In our selection, Glaucon, who is Plato's older brother, asks Socrates whether justice is good in itself or only a necessary evil. Playing the devil's advocate, he puts forth the hypothesis that egotistic power-seeking in which we have complete freedom to indulge ourselves might be the ideal state of existence. However, the hypothesis continues, reason quickly shows us that others might seek to have the same power, which would interfere with our freedom and cause a state of chaos in which no one was likely to have any of one's desires fulfilled. So we compromise and limit our acquisitive instincts. Justice or a system of morality is simply the result of that compromise. It has no intrinsic value but is better than chaos but worse than undisturbed power. It is better to compromise and limit our acquisitive instincts.

To illustrate his point he tells the story of a shepherd named Gyges who comes upon a ring, which at his behest makes him invisible. He uses it to escape the external sanctions of society—its laws and censure—and to serve his greed to the fullest. Glaucon asks whether it is not plausible to suppose that we all would do likewise? Then he offers a thought experiment that compares the life of the seemingly just (but unjust) man who is incredibly successful with the life of the seemingly unjust (but just) man who is incredibly unsuccessful. Which would we choose?

We enter the dialogue in the second book of the *Republic*. Socrates has just shown that the type of egoism advocated by Thrasymachus is contradictory. It is Socrates who is speaking.

Study Questions

1. Note the distinction between different kinds of goods: (1) things desirable in themselves; (2) things not desirable in themselves but instrumental to other goods; and (3) things both intrinsically and instrumentally good. Which kind of good is justice, according to Socrates, and why?

2. What is the popular view of justice, according to Glaucon?

3. What is the lesson to be drawn from the story of Gyges' ring? Do you agree with Glaucon's conclusion about human nature?

4. What is Glaucon's point in comparing the completely just-but-seemingly-unjust man with the completely unjust-but-seemingly-just man? Which would you choose?

Gyges' Ring

WITH THESE WORDS I was thinking that I had made an end of the discussion; but the end, in truth, proved to be only a beginning. For Glaucon, who is always the most pugnacious of men, was dissatisfied at Thrasymachus' retirement; he wanted to have the battle out. So he said to me: Socrates, do you wish really to persuade us, or only to seem to have persuaded us, that to be just is always better than to be unjust?

I should wish really to persuade you, I replied, if I could.

Then you certainly have not succeeded. Let me ask you now:—How would you arrange goods—are there not some which we welcome for their own sakes, and independently of their consequences, as, for example, harmless pleasures and enjoyments, which delight us at the time, although nothing follows from them?

I agree in thinking that there is such a class, I replied.

Is there not also a second class of goods, such as knowledge, sight, health, which are desirable not only in themselves, but also for their results?

Certainly, I said.

And would you not recognize a third class, such as gymnastic, and the care of the sick, and the physician's art; also the various ways of money-making—these do us good but we regard them as disagreeable; and no one would choose them for their own sakes, but only for the sake of some reward or result which flows from them?

There is, I said, this third class also. But why do you ask?

Reprinted from The Dialogues of Plato, *translated by Benjamin Jowett (Charles Scribner's, 1889)*.

Because I want to know in which of the three classes you would place justice?

In the highest class, I replied, among those goods which he who would be happy desires both for their own sake and for the sake of their results.

Then the many are of another mind; they think that justice is to be reckoned in the troublesome class, among goods which are to be pursued for the sake of rewards and of reputation, but in themselves are disagreeable and rather to be avoided.

I know, I said, that this is their manner of thinking, and that this was the thesis which Thrasymachus was maintaining just now, when he censured justice and praised injustice. But I am too stupid to be convinced by him.

I wish, he said, that you would hear me as well as him, and then I shall see whether you and I agree. For Thrasymachus seems to me, like a snake, to have been charmed by your voice sooner than he ought to have been; but to my mind the nature of justice and injustice have not yet been made clear. Setting aside their rewards and results, I want to know what they are in themselves, and how they inwardly work in the soul. If you please, then, I will revive the argument of Thrasymachus. And first I will speak of the nature and origin of justice according to the common view of them. Secondly, I will show that all men who practice justice do so against their will, of necessity, but not as a good. And thirdly, I will argue that there is reason in this view, for the life of the unjust is after all better far than the life of the just—if what they say is true, Socrates, since I myself am not of their opinion. But still I acknowledge that I am perplexed when I hear the voices of Thrasymachus and myriads of others dinning in my ears; and, on the other hand, I have never yet heard the superiority of justice to injustice maintained by any one in a satisfactory way. I want to hear justice praised in respect of itself; then I shall be satisfied, and you are the person from whom I think that I am most likely to hear this; and therefore I will praise the unjust life to the utmost

of my power, and my manner of speaking will indicate the manner in which I desire to hear you too praising justice and censuring injustice. Will you say whether you approve of my proposal?

Indeed I do; nor can I imagine any theme about which a man of sense would oftener wish to converse.

I am delighted, he replied, to hear you say so, and shall begin by speaking, as I proposed, of the nature and origin of justice.

They say that to do injustice is, by nature, good; to suffer injustice, evil; but that the evil is greater than the good. And so when men have both done and suffered injustice and have had experience of both, not being able to avoid the one and obtain the other, they think that they had better agree among themselves to have neither; hence there arise laws and mutual covenants; and that which is ordained by law is termed by them lawful and just. This they affirm to be the origin and nature of justice:—it is a mean or compromise, between the best of all, which is to do injustice and not be punished, and the worst of all, which is to suffer injustice without the power of retaliation; and justice, being at a middle point between the two, is tolerated not as a good, but as the lesser evil, and honoured by reason of the inability of men to do injustice. For no man who is worthy to be called a man would ever submit to such an agreement if he were able to resist; he would be mad if he did. Such is the received account, Socrates, of the nature and origin of justice.

Now that those who practice justice do so involuntarily and because they have not the power to be unjust will best appear if we imagine something of this kind: having given both to the just and the unjust power to do what they will, let us watch and see whither desire will lead them; then we shall discover in the very act the just and unjust man to be proceeding along the same road, following their interest, which all natures deem to be their good, and are only diverted into the path of justice by the force of law. The liberty which we are supposing may be most completely given to them in the form of such a power as is said to have been possessed by Gyges the ancestor of Croesus the Lydian. According to the tradition, Gyges was a shepherd in the service of the king of Lydia; there was a great storm, and an earthquake made an opening in the earth at the place where he was feeding his flock. Amazed at the sight, he descended into the opening, where, among other marvels, he beheld a hollow brazen horse, having doors, at which he stooping and looking in saw a dead body of stature, as appeared to him, more than human, and having nothing on but a gold ring; this he took from the finger of the dead and re-ascended. Now the shepherds met together, according to custom, that they might send their monthly report about the flocks to the king; into their assembly he came having the ring on his finger, and as he was sitting among them he chanced to turn the collet of the ring inside his hand, when instantly he became invisible to the rest of the company and they began to speak of him as if he were no longer present. He was astonished at this, and again touching the ring he turned the collet outwards and reappeared; he made several trials of the ring, and always with the same result—when he turned the collet inwards he became invisible, when outwards he reappeared. Whereupon he contrived to be chosen one of the messengers who were sent to the court; where as soon as he arrived he seduced the queen, and with her help conspired against the king and slew him, and took the kingdom. Suppose now that there were two such magic rings, and the just put on one of them and the unjust the other; no man can be imagined to be of such an iron nature that he would stand fast in justice. No man would keep his hands off what was not his own when he could safely take what he liked out of the market, or go into houses and lie with any one at his pleasure, or kill or release from prison whom he would, and in all respects be like a God among men. Then the actions of the just would be as the actions of the unjust; they would both come at last to the same point. And this we may truly affirm to be a great proof

that a man is just, not willingly or because he thinks that justice is any good to him individually, but of necessity, for wherever any one thinks that he can safely be unjust, there he is unjust. For all men believe in their hearts that injustice is far more profitable to the individual than justice, and he who argues as I have been supposing, will say that they are right. If you could imagine any one obtaining this power of becoming invisible, and never doing any wrong or touching what was another's, he would be thought by the lookers-on to be a most wretched idiot, although they would praise him to one another's faces, and keep up appearances with one another from a fear that they too might suffer injustice. Enough of this.

Now, if we are to form a real judgment of the life of the just and unjust, we must isolate them; there is no other way; and how is the isolation to be effected? I answer: Let the unjust man be entirely unjust, and the just man entirely just; nothing is to be taken away from either of them, and both are to be perfectly furnished for the work of their respective lives. First, let the unjust be like other distinguished masters of craft; like the skillful pilot or physician, who knows intuitively his own powers and keeps within their limits, and who, if he fails at any point, is able to recover himself. So let the unjust make his unjust attempts in the right way, and lie hidden if he means to be great in his injustice (he who is found out is nobody): for the highest reach of injustice is: to be deemed just when you are not. Therefore I say that in the perfectly unjust man we must assume the most perfect injustice; there is to be no deduction, but we must allow him, while doing the most unjust acts, to have acquired the greatest reputation for justice. If he have taken a false step he must be able to recover himself; he must be one who can speak with effect, if any of his deeds come to light, and who can force his way where force is required by his courage and strength, and command of money and friends. And at his side let us place the just man in his nobleness and simplicity, wishing, as

Aeschylus says, to be and not to seem good. There must be no seeming, for if he seem to be just he will be honoured and rewarded, and then we shall not know whether he is just for the sake of justice or for the sake of honours and rewards; therefore, let him be clothed in justice only, and have no other covering; and he must be imagined in a state of life the opposite of the former. Let him be the best of men, and let him be thought the worst; then he will have been put to the proof; and we shall see whether he will be affected by the fear of infamy and its consequences. And let him continue thus to the hour of death; being just and seeming to be unjust. When both have reached the uttermost extreme, the one of justice and the other of injustice, let judgment be given which of them is the happier of the two.

Heavens! my dear Glaucon, I said, how energetically you polish them up for the decision, first one and then the other, as if they were two statues.

I do my best, he said. And now that we know what they are like there is no difficulty in tracing out the sort of life which awaits either of them. This I will proceed to describe; but as you may think the description a little too coarse, I ask you to suppose, Socrates, that the words which follow are not mine.—Let me put them into the mouths of the eulogists of injustice: they will tell you that the just man who is thought unjust will be scourged, racked, bound—will have his eyes burnt out; and, at last, after suffering every kind of evil, he will be impaled: Then he will understand that he ought to seem only, and not to be, just; the words of Aeschylus may be more truly spoken of the unjust than of the just. For the unjust is pursuing a reality; he does not live with a view to appearances—he wants to be really unjust and not to seem only:—

His mind has a soil deep and fertile.
Out of which spring his prudent counsels.

In the first place, he is thought just, and therefore bears rule in the city; he can marry whom he will, and give in marriage to whom he will; also he can trade and deal where he likes, and always to his own advantage, because he has no misgivings about injustice; and at every contest, whether in public or private, he gets the better of his antagonists, and gains at their expense, and is rich, and out of his gains he can benefit his friends, and harm his enemies; moreover, he can offer sacrifices, and dedicate gifts to the gods abundantly and magnificently, and can honour the gods or any man whom he wants to honour in a far better style than the just, and therefore he is likely to be dearer than they are to the gods. And thus, Socrates, gods and men are said to unite in making the life of the unjust better than the life of the just. . . .

[We pick up the discussion in Book 9.]

Book 9

"Now that we've gotten this far," I said, "let's go back to that statement made at the beginning, which brought us here: that it pays for a man to be perfectly unjust if he appears to be just. Isn't that what someone said?"

"Yes."

"Then since we've agreed what power justice and injustice each have, let's have a discussion with him."

"How?"

"By molding in words an image of the soul, so that the one who said that will realize what he was saying."

"What kind of image?"

"Oh, something like those natures the myths tell us were born in ancient times—the Chimaera, Scylla, Cerberus, and others in which many different shapes were supposed to have grown into one."

"So they tell us," he said.

"Then mold one figure of a colorful, many-headed beast with heads of wild and tame animals growing in a circle all around it; one that can change and grow all of them out of itself."

"That's a job for a skilled artist. Still, words mold easier than wax or clay, so consider it done."

"And another of a lion, and one of a man. Make the first by far the biggest, the second second largest."

"That's easier, and already done."

"Now join the three together so that they somehow grow."

"All right."

"Next mold the image of one, the man, around them all, so that to someone who can't see what's inside but looks only at the container it appears to be a single animal, man."

"I have."

"Then shall we inform the gentleman that when he says it pays for this man to be unjust, he's saying that it profits him to feast his multifarious beast and his lion and make them grow strong, but to starve and enfeeble the man in him so that he gets dragged wherever the animals lead him, and instead of making them friends and used to each other, to let them bite and fight and eat each other?"

"That's just what he's saying by praising injustice."

"The one who says justice pays, however, would be saying that he should practice and say whatever will give the most mastery to his inner man, who should care for the many-headed beast like a farmer, raising and domesticating its tame heads and preventing the wild ones from growing, making the lion's nature his partner and ally, and so raise them both to be friends to each other and to him."

"That's exactly what he means by praising justice."

"So in every way the commender of justice is telling the truth, the other a lie. Whether we examine pleasure, reputation, or profit, we find that the man who praises justice speaks truly, the one who disparages it disparages sickly and knows nothing of what he disparages."

"I don't think he does at all."

"Then let's gently persuade him—his error wasn't intended—by asking him a question:

'Shouldn't we say that the traditions of the beautiful and the ugly have come about like this: Beautiful things are those that make our bestial parts subservient to the human—or rather, perhaps, to the divine—part of our nature, while ugly ones are those that enslave the tame to the wild?' Won't he agree?"

"If he takes my advice."

"On this argument then, can it pay for a man to take money unjustly if that means making his best part a slave to the worst? If it wouldn't profit a man to sell his son or his daughter into slavery—to wild and evil men at that—even if he got a fortune for it, then if he has no pity on himself and enslaves the most godlike thing in him to the most godless and polluted, isn't he a wretch who gets bribed for gold into a destruction more horrible than Euriphyle's, who sold her husband's life for a necklace?"

"Much more horrible," said Glaucon.

". . . everyone is better off being ruled by the godlike and intelligent; preferably if he has it inside, but if not, it should be imposed on him from without so that we may all be friends and as nearly alike as possible, all steered by the same thing."

"Yes, and we're right." he said.

"Law, the ally of everyone in the city, clearly intends the same thing, as does the rule of children, which forbids us to let them be free until we've instituted a regime in them as in a city. We serve their best part with a similar part in us, install a like guardian and ruler in them, and only then set them free."

"Clearly."

"Then how, by what argument, Glaucon, can we say that it pays for a man to be unjust or self-indulgent or to do something shameful to get more money or power if by doing so he makes himself worse?"

"We can't," he said.

"And how can it pay to commit injustice without getting caught and being punished? Doesn't getting away with it make a man even worse? Whereas if a man gets caught and punished, his beastlike part is taken in and tamed, his tame part is set free, and his whole soul acquires justice and temperance and knowledge. Therefore his soul recovers its best nature and attains a state more honorable than the state the body attains when it acquires health and strength and beauty, by as much as the soul is more honorable than the body."

"Absolutely."

"Then won't a sensible man spend his life directing all his efforts to this end?"

For Further Reflection

1. Which would you choose to be Glaucon's good but suffering person or his bad but successful person? Is there a third alternative?

2. Socrates' answer to Glaucon and Adeimantus is that, in spite of appearances, we should choose the life of the "unsuccessful" just person because it's to our advantage to be moral. Socrates' answer depends on a notion of mental health. He contends that immorality corrupts the inner person, so that one is happy or unhappy in exact proportion to one's moral integrity. Is this a plausible reply?

3. Is the good always good for you?

In Defense of Ethical Egoism   VI.5

AYN RAND

Ayn Rand (1908–1982) wrote several philosophical novels, including *We the Living* (1936), *The Fountainhead* (1943), and *Atlas Shrugged* (1959), from which the present selection is taken. Her works set forth a form of ethical egoism which was called *objectivism,* the philosophy that the proper life for rational beings is the pursuit of their happiness and that altruism and self-sacrifice are incompatible with rational morality. In this passage she criticizes conventional altruistic morality ("the morality of sacrifice") and praises the morality of selfishness.

Study Questions

1. What is on trial in this age of moral crisis?

2. What has conventional morality taught us about the way to live? What, according to it, is evil and immoral?

3. What is the only fundamental alternative in the universe?

4. What is the difference between animals and human beings?

5. What does Rand call a "metaphysical monstrosity"?

6. What is properly our highest moral purpose?

7. What is the "most *selfish* of all things"?

8. What are the twin ideals of the morality of sacrifice?

9. What does Rand say about the duty to serve others? Is it proper to help others? Why or why not?

Value Yourself

". . . YES, THIS *IS* AN AGE OF moral crisis. Yes, you *are* bearing punishment for your evil. But it is not man who is now on trial and it is not human nature that will take the blame. It is your moral code that's through, this time. Your moral code has reached its climax, the blind alley at the end of its course. And if you wish to go on living, what you now need is not to *return* to morality—you who have never known any—but to *discover* it.

"You have heard no concepts of morality but the mystical or the social. You have been taught that morality is a code of behavior imposed on you by whim, the whim of a supernatural power or the whim of society, to serve God's purpose or your neighbor's welfare, to please an authority beyond the grave or else next door—but not to serve *your* life or pleasure. Your pleasure, you have been taught, is to be found in immorality, your interests would best be served by evil, and any moral code must be designed not *for* you, but *against* you, not to further your life, but to drain it.

"For centuries, the battle of morality was fought between those who claimed that your life belongs to God and those who claimed that it belongs to your neighbors—between those who preached that the good is self-sacrifice for the sake of ghosts in heaven and those who preached that the good is self-sacrifice for the sake of incompetents on earth. And no one came to say that your life belongs to you and that the good is to live it.

"Both sides agreed that morality demands the surrender of your self-interest and of your mind, that the moral and the practical are opposites, that morality is not the province of reason, but the province of faith and force. Both sides agreed that no rational morality is possible, that there is no right or wrong in reason—that in reason there's no reason to be moral.

"Whatever else they fought about, it was against man's mind that all your moralists have stood united. It was man's mind that all their schemes and systems were intended to despoil and destroy. Now choose to perish or to learn that the anti-mind is the anti-life.

"Man's mind is his basic tool of survival. Life is given to him, survival is not. His body is given to him, its sustenance is not. His mind is given to him, its content is not. To remain alive, he must act, and before he can act he must know the nature and purpose of his action. He cannot obtain his food without a knowledge of food and of the way to obtain it. He cannot dig a ditch—or build a cylotron—without a knowledge of his aim and of the means to achieve it. To remain alive, he must think.

"But to think is an act of choice. The key to what you so recklessly call 'human nature,' the open secret you live with, yet dread to name, is the fact that *man is a being of volitional consciousness.* Reason does not work automatically; thinking is not a mechanical process; the connections of logic are not made by instinct. The function of your stomach, lungs, or heart is automatic; the function of your mind is not. In any hour and issue of your life, you are free to think or to evade that effort. But you are not free to escape from your nature, from the fact that *reason* is your means of survival—so that for *you*, who are a human being, the question 'to be or not to be' is the question 'to think or not to think.'

"A being of volitional consciousness has no

automatic course of behavior. He needs a code of values to guide his actions. 'Value' is that which one acts to gain and keep, 'virtue' is the action by which one gains and keeps it. 'Value' presupposes an answer to the question: of value to whom and for what? 'Value' presupposes a standard, a purpose and the necessity of action in the face of an alternative. Where there are no alternatives, no values are possible.

"There is only one fundamental alternative in the universe: existence or non-existence—and it pertains to a single class of entities: to living organisms. The existence of inanimate matter is unconditional, the existence of life is not: it depends on a specific course of action. Matter is indestructible, it changes its forms, but it cannot cease to exist. It is only a living organism that faces a constant alternative: the issue of life or death. Life is a process of self-sustaining and self-generated action. If an organism fails in that action, it dies; its chemical elements remain, but its life goes out of existence. It is only the concept of 'Life' that makes the concept of 'Value' possible. It is only to a living entity that things can be good or evil.

"A plant must feed itself in order to live; the sunlight, the water, the chemicals it needs are the values its nature has set it to pursue; its life is the standard of value directing its actions. But a plant has no choice of action; there are alternatives in the conditions it encounters, but there is no alternative in its function: it acts automatically to further its life, it cannot act for its own destruction.

"An animal is equipped for sustaining its life; its senses provide it with an automatic code of action, an automatic knowledge of what is good for it or evil. It has no power to extend its knowledge or to evade it. In conditions where its knowledge proves inadequate, it dies. But so long as it lives, it acts on its knowledge, with automatic safety and no power of choice, it is unable to ignore its own good, unable to decide to choose the evil and act as its own destroyer.

"Man has no automatic code of survival. His particular distinction from all other living species is the necessity to act in the face of alternatives by means of *volitional choice*. He has no automatic knowledge of what is good for him or evil, what values his life depends on, what course of action it requires. Are you prattling about an instinct of self-preservation? An *instinct* of self-preservation is precisely what man does not possess. An 'instinct' is an unerring and automatic form of knowledge. A desire is not an instinct. A desire to live does not give you the knowledge required for living. And even man's desire to live is not automatic: your secret evil today is that *that* is the desire you do not hold. Your fear of death is not a love for life and will not give you the knowledge needed to keep it. Man must obtain his knowledge and choose his actions by a process of thinking, which nature will not force him to perform. Man has the power to act as his own destroyer—and that is the way he has acted through most of his history.

"A living entity that regarded its means of survival as evil, would not survive. A plant that struggled to mangle its roots, a bird that fought to break its wings would not remain for long in the existence they affronted. But the history of man has been a struggle to deny and to destroy his mind.

"Man has been called a rational being, but rationality is a matter of choice—and the alternative his nature offers him is: rational being or suicidal animal. Man has to be man—by choice; he has to hold his life as a value—by choice; he has to learn to sustain it—by choice; he has to discover the values it requires and practice his virtues—by choice.

"A code of values accepted by choice is a code of morality.

"Whoever you are, you who are hearing me now, I am speaking to whatever living remnant is left uncorrupted within you, to the remnant of the human, to your *mind*, and I say: There *is* a morality of reason, a morality proper to man, and *Man's Life* is its standard of value.

"All that which is proper to the life of a rational being is the good; all that which destroys it is the evil.

"Man's life, as required by his nature, is not the life of a mindless brute, of a looting thug or a mooching mystic, but the life of a thinking being—not life by means of force or fraud, but life by means of achievement—not survival at any price, since there's only one price that pays for man's survival: reason.

"Man's life is the *standard* of morality, but your own life is its *purpose*. If existence on earth is your goal, you must choose your actions and values by the standard of that which is proper to man—for the purpose of preserving, fulfilling and enjoying the irreplaceable value which is your life.

"Since life requires a specific course of action, any other course will destroy it. A being who does not hold his own life as the motive and goal of his actions, is acting on the motive and standard of *death*. Such a being is a metaphysical monstrosity, struggling to oppose, negate and contradict the fact of his own existence, running blindly amuck on a trail of destruction, capable of nothing but pain.

"Happiness is the successful state of life, pain is an agent of death. Happiness is that state of unconsciousness which proceeds from the achievement of one's values. A morality that dares to tell you to find happiness in the renunciation of your happiness—to value the failure of your values—is an insolent negation of morality. A doctrine that gives you, as an ideal, the role of a sacrificial animal seeking slaughter on the altars of others, is giving you *death* as your standard. By the grace of reality and the nature of life, man—every man—is an end in himself, he exists for his own sake, and the achievement of his own happiness is his highest moral purpose.

"But neither life nor happiness can be achieved by the pursuit of irrational whims. Just as man is free to attempt to survive in any random manner, but will perish unless he lives as his nature requires, so he is free to seek his happiness in any mindless fraud, but the torture of frustration is

all he will find, unless he seeks the happiness proper to man. The purpose of morality is to teach you, not to suffer and die, but to enjoy yourself and live.

"Sweep aside those parasites of subsidized classrooms, who live on the profits of the mind of others and proclaim that man needs no morality, no values, no code of behavior. They, who pose as scientists and claim that man is only an animal, do not grant him inclusion in the law of existence they have granted to the lowest of insects. They recognize that every living species has a way of survival demanded by its nature, they do not claim that a fish can live out of water or that a dog can live without its sense of smell—but man, they claim, the most complex of beings, man can survive in any way whatever, man has no identity, no nature, and there's no practical reason why he cannot live with his means of survival destroyed, with his mind throttled and placed at the disposal of any orders *they* might care to issue.

"Sweep aside those hatred-eaten mystics, who pose as friends of humanity and preach that the highest virtue man can practice is to hold his own life as of no value. Do they tell you that the purpose of morality is to curb man's instinct of self-preservation? It is for the purpose of self-preservation that man needs a code of morality. The only man who desires to be moral is the man who desires to live.

"No, you do not have to live; it is your basic act of choice; but if you choose to live, you must live as a man—by the work and the judgment of your mind.

"No, you do not have to live as a man: it is an act of moral choice. But you cannot live as anything else—and the alternative is that state of living death which you now see within you and around you, the state of a thing unfit for existence, no longer human and less than animal, a thing that knows nothing but pain and drags itself through its span of years in the agony of unthinking self-destruction.

"No, you do not have to think; it is an act of

moral choice. But someone had to think to keep you alive; if you choose to default, you default on existence and you pass the deficit to some moral man, expecting him to sacrifice his good for the sake of letting you survive by your evil. . . .

"This much is true: the most *selfish* of all things is the independent mind that recognizes no authority higher than its own and no value higher than its judgment of truth. You are asked to sacrifice your intellectual integrity, your logic, your reason, your standard of truth—in favor of becoming a prostitute whose standard is the greatest good for the greatest number.

"If you search your code for guidance, for an answer to the question: 'What *is* the good?'—the only answer you will find is '*The good of others.*' The good is whatever others wish, whatever you feel they feel they wish, or whatever you feel they ought to feel. 'The good of others' is a magic formula that transforms anything into gold, a formula to be recited as a guarantee of moral glory and as a fumigator for any action, even the slaughter of a continent. Your standard of virtue is not an object, not an act, nor a principle, but an *intention*. You need no proof, no reasons, no success, you need not achieve *in fact* the good of others—all you need to know is that your motive was the good of others, *not* your own. Your only definition of the good is a negation: the good is the 'non-good for me.'

"Your code—which boasts that it upholds eternal, absolute, objective moral values and scorns the conditional, the relative and the subjective—your code hands out, as its version of the absolute, the following rule of moral conduct: If *you* wish it, it's evil; if others wish it, it's good; if the motive of your action is *your* welfare, don't do it; if the motive is the welfare of others, then anything goes.

"As this double-jointed, double-standard morality splits you in half, so it splits mankind into two enemy camps: one is *you,* the other is all the rest of humanity. *You* are the only outcast who has no right to wish or live. *You* are the only servant, the rest are the masters, *you* are the only

giver, the rest are the takers, *you* are the eternal debtor, the rest are the creditors never to be paid off. You must not question their right to your sacrifice, or the nature of their wishes and their needs: their right is conferred upon them by a negative, by the fact that they are 'non-you.'

"For those of you who might ask questions, your code provides a consolation prize and booby-trap: it is for your own happiness, it says, that you must serve the happiness of others, the only way to achieve your joy is to give it up to others, the only way to achieve your prosperity is to surrender your wealth to others, the only way to protect your life is to protect all men except yourself—and if you find no joy in this procedure, it is your own fault and the proof of your evil; if you were good, you would find your happiness in providing a banquet for others, and your dignity in existing on such crumbs as *they* might care to toss you.

"You who have no standard of self-esteem, accept the guilt and dare not ask the questions. But you know the unadmitted answer, refusing to acknowledge what you see, what hidden premise moves your world. You know it, not in honest statement, but as a dark uneasiness within you, while you flounder between guiltily cheating and grudgingly practicing a principle too vicious to name.

"I, who do not accept the unearned, neither in values nor in *guilt,* am here to ask the questions you evaded. Why is it moral to serve the happiness of others, but not your own? If enjoyment is a value, why is it moral when experienced by others, but immoral when experienced by you? If the sensation of eating a cake is a value, why is it an immoral indulgence in your stomach, but a moral goal for you to achieve in the stomach of others? Why is it immoral for you to desire, but moral for others to do so? Why is it immoral to produce a value and keep it, but moral to give it away? And if it is not moral for you to keep a value, why is it moral for others to accept it? If you are selfless and virtuous when you give it, are they not selfish and vicious when they take it? Does virtue consist of serving vice? Is the moral purpose of those who are good, self-immolation for the sake of those who are evil? . . .

"Under a morality of sacrifice, the first value you sacrifice is morality; the next is self-esteem. When need is the standard, every man is both victim and parasite. As a victim, he must labor to fill the needs of others, leaving himself in the position of a parasite whose needs must be filled by others. He cannot approach his fellow men except in one of two disgraceful roles: he is both a beggar and a sucker.

"You fear the man who has a dollar less than you, that dollar is rightfully his, he makes you feel like a moral defrauder. You hate the man who has a dollar more than you, that dollar is rightfully yours, he makes you feel that you are morally defrauded. The man below is a source of your guilt, the man above is a source of your frustration. You do not know what to surrender or demand, when to give and when to grab, what pleasure in life is rightfully yours and what debt is still unpaid to others—you struggle to evade, as 'theory,' the knowledge that by the moral standard you've accepted you are guilty every moment of your life, there is no mouthful of food you swallow that is not *needed* by someone somewhere on earth—and you give up the problem in blind resentment, you conclude that moral perfection is not to be achieved *or desired,* that you will muddle through by snatching as snatch can and by avoiding the eyes of the young, of those who look at you as if self-esteem were possible and they expected you to have it. Guilt is all that you retain within your soul—and so does every other man, as he goes past, avoiding *your* eyes. Do you wonder why your morality has not achieved brotherhood on earth or the good will of man to man?

"The justification of sacrifice, that your morality propounds, is more corrupt than the corruption it purports to justify. The motive of your sacrifice, it tells you, should be *love*—the love you ought to feel for every man. A morality that professes the belief that the values of the spirit are more precious than matter, a morality that teaches you to scorn a whore who gives her body indiscriminately to all men—this same morality demands that you surrender your soul to promiscuous love for all comers.

"As there can be no causeless wealth, so there can be no causeless love or any sort of causeless emotion. An emotion is a response to a fact of reality, an estimate dictated by your standards. To love is to *value*. The man who tells you that it is possible to value without values, to love those whom you appraise as worthless, is the man who tells you that it is possible to grow rich by consuming without producing and that paper money is as valuable as gold.

"Observe that he does not expect you to feel a causeless fear. When his kind get into power, they are expert at contriving means of terror, at giving you ample cause to feel the fear by which they desire to rule you. But when it comes to love, the highest of emotions, you permit them to shriek at you accusingly that you are a moral delinquent if you're incapable of feeling causeless love. When a man feels fear without reason, you call him to the attention of a psychiatrist; you are not so careful to protect the meaning, the nature and the dignity of love.

"Love is the expression of one's values, the greatest reward you can earn for the moral qualities you have achieved in your character and person, the emotional price paid by one man for the joy he receives from the virtues of another. Your morality demands that you divorce your love from values and hand it down to any vagrant, not as response to his worth, but as response to his *need,* not as reward, but as alms, not as a payment for virtues, but as a blank check on vices. Your morality tells you that the purpose of love is to set you free of the bonds of morality, that love is superior to moral judgment, that true love transcends, forgives and survives every manner of evil in its object, and the greater the love the greater the depravity it permits to the loved. To love a man for his virtues is paltry and human, it tells you; to love him for his flaws is divine. To love those who are worthy of it is self-interest; to love the unworthy is sacrifice. You owe your love to those who don't deserve it, and the less they deserve it, the more love you owe them—the more loathsome the object, the nobler your love—the more unfastidious your love, the greater your virtue—and if you can bring your soul to the state of a dump heap that welcomes anything on equal terms, if you can cease to value moral values, you have achieved the state of moral perfection.

"Such is your morality of sacrifice and such are the twin ideals it offers: to refashion the life of your body in the image of a human stock-yards, and the life of your spirit in the image of a dump. . . .

"Since childhood, you have been hiding the guilty secret that you feel no desire to be moral, no desire to seek self-immolation, that you dread and hate your code, but dare not say it even to yourself, that you're devoid of those moral 'instincts' which others profess to feel. The less you felt, the louder you proclaimed your selfless love and servitude to others, in dread of ever letting them discover your own self, the self that you betrayed, the self that you kept in concealment, like a skeleton in the closet of your body. And they, who were at once your dupes and your deceivers, they listened and voiced their loud approval, in dread of ever letting you discover that they were harboring the same unspoken secret. Existence among you is a giant pretense, an act you all perform for one another, each feeling that he is the only guilty freak, each placing his moral authority in the unknowable known only to others, each faking the reality he feels they expect him to fake, none having the courage to break the vicious circle.

"No matter what dishonorable compromise you've made with your impracticable creed, no matter what miserable balance, half-cynicism, half-superstition, you now manage to maintain, you still preserve the root, the lethal tenet: the belief that the moral and the practical are opposites. Since childhood, you have been running

from the terror of a choice you have never dared fully to identify: If the *practical,* whatever you must practice to exist, whatever works, succeeds, achieves your purpose, whatever brings you food and joy, whatever profits you is evil—and if the good, the moral is the *impractical,* whatever fails, destroys, frustrates, whatever injures you and brings you loss or pain—then your choice is to be moral or to live.

"The sole result of that murderous doctrine was to remove morality from life. You grew up to believe that moral laws bear no relation to the job of living, except as an impediment and threat, that man's existence is an amoral jungle where anything goes and anything works. And in that fog of switching definitions which descends upon a frozen mind, you have forgotten that the evils damned by your creed were the virtues required for living, and you have come to believe that actual evils are the *practical* means of existence. Forgetting that the impractical 'good' was self-sacrifice, you believe that self-esteem is impractical; forgetting that the practical 'evil' was production, you believe that robbery is practical. . . .

"Accept the fact that the achievement of your happiness is the only *moral* purpose of your life, and that *happiness*—not pain or mindless self-indulgence—is the proof of your moral integrity, since it is the proof and the result of your loyalty to the achievement of your values. Happiness was the responsibility you dreaded, it required the kind of rational discipline you did not value yourself enough to assume—and the anxious staleness of your days is the monument to your evasion of the knowledge that there is no moral substitute for happiness, that there is no more despicable coward than the man who deserted the battle for his joy, fearing to assert his right to existence, lacking the courage and the loyalty to life of a bird or a flower reaching for the sun. Discard the protective rags of that vice which you called a virtue: humility—learn to value yourself, which means: to fight for your happiness—and when you learn that *pride* is the sum of all virtues, you will learn to live like a man.

"As a basic step of self-esteem, learn to treat as the mark of a cannibal any man's *demand* for your help. To demand it is to claim that your life is *his* property—and loathsome as such claim might be, there's something still more loathsome: your agreement. Do you ask if it's ever proper to help another man? No—if he claims it as his right or as a moral duty that you owe him. Yes—if such is your own desire based on your own selfish pleasure in the value of his person and his struggle.

For Further Reflection

1. Has Rand successfully defended her theory of ethical egoism? How does it relate to Socrates' idea that one ought never to harm anyone else? Could one reconcile Socrates' idea with Rand's theory? Socrates believes that one should never harm anyone else because doing so is never in one's own interest. What would be needed to get Rand's theory to agree with that conclusion?

2. Can the ethical egoist make his or her views public? If you follow Rand, should you let others know where you stand? Should you persuade them to be egoists? If the egoist cannot make his theory public, does this disqualify it as a genuine ethical theory?

3. Can the ethical egoist be a consistent egoist and have friends? If friendship entails loving another in such a way as to sacrifice one's own interest for the friend's, does this give the egoist difficulty?

VI.6   A Critique of Ethical Egoism

JAMES RACHELS

James Rachels (1941–) is professor of philosophy at the University of Alabama at Birmingham and is the author of several articles on moral philosophy. He is the author of *The End of Life: Euthanasia and Morality* (1986) and *The Elements of Moral Philosophy* (1986). In this essay Rachels first distinguished ethical egoism from psychological egoism, the doctrine that people always act out of their own perceived self-interest. Ethical egoism is the doctrine that it is always our duty to act exclusively in our self-interest. He examines three arguments in favor of ethical egoism, showing that they each fail to support their conclusion, and then examines three arguments against the doctrine, concluding that although only one of these is sound, it is enough to invalidate ethical egoism.

Study Questions

1. According to Rachels, why don't we do more to help starving people?
2. What does "common-sense morality" instruct us to do regarding the starving and why?

3. What is the difference between psychological egoism and ethical egoism?

4. What are the three arguments in favor of ethical egoism? Outline each of them and describe their weaknesses.

5. How does the third argument lead to the Golden Rule? Why is it the "best try"?

6. Identify the three arguments against ethical egoism. Which of them, if any, refutes ethical egoism?

Is There a Duty to Contribute for Famine Relief?

EACH YEAR MILLIONS OF PEOPLE die of malnutrition and related health problems. A common pattern among children in poor countries is death from dehydration caused by diarrhea brought on by malnutrition. James Grant, executive director of the United Nations Children's Fund (UNICEF), estimates that about 15,000 children die in this way *every day*. That comes to 5,475,000 children annually. Even if his estimate is too high, the number that die is staggering.

For those of us in the affluent countries, this poses an acute moral problem. We spend money on ourselves, not only for the necessities of life but for innumerable luxuries—for fine automobiles, fancy clothes, stereos, sports, movies, and so on. In our country, even people with modest incomes enjoy such things. The problem is that we *could* forgo our luxuries and give the money for famine relief instead. The fact that we don't suggests that we regard our luxuries as more important than feeding the hungry.

Why do we allow people to starve to death when we could save them? Very few of us actually believe our luxuries are that important. Most of us, if asked the question directly, would probably be a bit embarrassed, and we would say that we probably should do more for famine relief. The explanation of why we do not is, at least in part, that we hardly ever think of the problem. Living our own comfortable lives, we are effectively insulated from it. The starving people are dying at some distance from us; we do not see them, and we can avoid even thinking of them.

When we do think of them, it is only abstractly, as bloodless statistics. Unfortunately for the starving, statistics do not have much power to motivate action.

But leaving aside the question of *why* we behave as we do, what is our *duty*? What *should* we do? We might think of this as the "common-sense" view of the matter: morality requires that we balance our own interests against the interests of others. It is understandable, of course, that we look out for our own interests, and no one can be faulted for attending to his own basic needs. But at the same time the needs of others are also important, and when we can help others—especially at little cost to ourselves—we should do so. Suppose you are thinking of spending ten dollars on a trip to the movies, when you are reminded that ten dollars could buy food for a starving child. Thus you could do a great service for the child at little cost to yourself. Common-sense morality would say, then, that you should give the money for famine relief rather than spending it on the movies.

This way of thinking involves a general assumption about our moral duties: it is assumed that we have moral duties *to other people*—and not merely duties that we create, such as by making a promise or incurring a debt. We have "natural" duties to others *simply because they are people who could be helped or harmed by our actions*. If a certain action would benefit (or harm) other people, then that is a reason why we should (or should not) do that action. The common-sense assumption is that other people's interests *count*, for their own sakes, from a moral point of view.

But one person's common sense is another

From James Rachels, The Elements of Moral Philosophy *(New York: Random House, 1986). Copyright © 1986 by McGraw-Hill, Inc. Reprinted by permission of the publisher.*

person's naive platitude. Some thinkers have maintained that, in fact, we have no "natural" duties to other people. *Ethical Egoism* is the idea that each person ought to pursue his or her own self-interest exclusively. It is different from Psychological Egoism, which is a theory of human nature concerned with how people *do* behave— Psychological Egoism says that people do in fact always pursue their own interests. Ethical Egoism, by contrast, is a normative theory—that is, a theory about how we *ought* to behave. Regardless of how we do behave, Ethical Egoism says we have no moral duty except to do what is best for ourselves.

It is a challenging theory. It contradicts some of our deepest moral beliefs—beliefs held by most of us, at any rate—but it is not easy to refute. We will examine the most important arguments for and against it. If it turns out to be true, then of course that is immensely important. But even if it turns out to be false, there is still much to be learned from examining it—we may, for example, gain some insight into the reasons why we *do* have obligations to other people.

But before looking at the arguments, we should be a little clearer about exactly what this theory says and what it does not say. In the first place, Ethical Egoism does not say that one should promote one's own interests *as well as* the interests of others. That would be an ordinary, unexceptional view. Ethical Egoism is the radical view that one's *only* duty is to promote one's own interests. According to Ethical Egoism, there is only one ultimate principle of conduct, the principle of self-interest, and this principle sums up *all* of one's natural duties and obligations.

However, Ethical Egoism does not say that you should *avoid* actions that help others, either. It may very well be that in many instances your interests coincide with the interests of others, so that in helping yourself you will be aiding others willy-nilly. Or it may happen that aiding others is an effective *means* for creating some benefit for yourself. Ethical Egoism does not forbid such actions; in fact, it may demand them. The theory insists only that in such cases the benefit to

others is not what makes the act right. What makes the act right is, rather, the fact that it is to one's own advantage.

Finally, Ethical Egoism does not imply that in pursuing one's interests one ought always to do what one wants to do, or what gives one the most pleasure in the short run. Someone may want to do something that is not good for himself or that will eventually cause himself more grief than pleasure—he may want to drink a lot or smoke cigarettes or take drugs or waste his best years at the race track. Ethical Egoism would frown on all this, regardless of the momentary pleasure it affords. It says that a person ought to do what *really is* to his or her own best advantage, *over the long run*. It endorses selfishness, but it doesn't endorse foolishness.

Three Arguments in Favor of Ethical Egoism

What reasons can be advanced to support this doctrine? Why should anyone think it is true? Unfortunately, the theory is asserted more often than it is argued for. Many of its supporters apparently think its truth is self-evident, so that arguments are not needed. When it *is* argued for, three lines of reasoning are most commonly used.

1. The first argument has several variations, each suggesting the same general point:

a. Each of us is intimately familiar with our own individual wants and needs. Moreover, each of us is uniquely placed to pursue those wants and needs effectively. At the same time, we know the desires and needs of other people only imperfectly, and we are not well situated to pursue them. Therefore, it is reasonable to believe that if we set out to be "our brother's keeper," we would often bungle the job and end up doing more mischief than good.

b. At the same time, the policy of "looking out for others" is an offensive intrusion into other people's privacy; it is essentially a policy of minding other people's business.

c. Making other people the object of one's

"charity" is degrading to them; it robs them of their individual dignity and self-respect. The offer of charity says, in effect, that they are not competent to care for themselves; and the statement is self-fulfilling—they cease to be self-reliant and become passively dependent on others. That is why the recipients of "charity" are so often resentful rather than appreciative.

What this adds up to is that the policy of "looking out for others" is self-defeating. If we want to promote the best interests of everyone alike, we should *not* adopt so-called altruistic policies of behavior. On the contrary, if each person looks after his or her *own* interests, it is more likely that everyone will be better off, in terms of both physical and emotional well-being. Thus Robert G. Olson says in his book *The Morality of Self-Interest* (1965), "The individual is most likely to contribute to social betterment by rationally pursuing his own best long-range interests." Or as Alexander Pope said more poetically,

> Thus God and nature formed the general frame
> And bade self-love and social be the same.

It is possible to quarrel with this argument on a number of grounds. Of course no one favors bungling, butting in, or depriving people of their self-respect. But is this really what we are doing when we feed hungry children? Is the starving child in Ethiopia really harmed when we "intrude" into "her business" by supplying food? It hardly seems likely. Yet we can set this point aside, for considered as an argument for Ethical Egoism, this way of thinking has an even more serious defect.

The trouble is that it isn't really an argument *for Ethical Egoism* at all. The argument concludes that we should adopt certain policies of action; and on the surface they appear to be egoistic policies. However, the *reason* it is said we should adopt those policies is decidedly *un*egoistic. The reason is one that to an egoist shouldn't matter. It is said that we should adopt those policies because doing so will promote the "betterment of society"—but according to Ethical Egoism, that is something we should not be concerned about.

Spelled out fully, with everything laid on the table, the argument says:

1. We ought to do whatever will promote the best interests of everyone alike.
2. The interests of everyone will best be promoted if each of us adopts the policy of pursuing our own interests exclusively.
3. Therefore, each of us should adopt the policy of pursuing our own interests exclusively.

If we accept this reasoning, then we are not ethical egoists at all. Even though we might end up *behaving* like egoists, our ultimate principle is one of beneficence—we are doing what we think will help everyone, not merely what we think will benefit ourselves. Rather than being egoists, we turn out to be altruists with a peculiar view of what in fact promotes the general welfare.

2. The second argument was put forward with some force by Ayn Rand, a writer little heeded by professional philosophers but who nevertheless was enormously popular on college campuses during the 1960s and 1970s. Ethical Egoism, in her view, is the only ethical philosophy that respects the integrity of the individual human life. She regarded the ethics of "altruism" as a totally destructive idea, both in society as a whole and in the lives of individuals taken in by it. Altruism, to her way of thinking, leads to a denial of the value of the individual. It says to a person: *your* life is merely something that may be sacrificed. "If a man accepts the ethics of altruism," she writes, "his first concern is not how to live his life, but how to sacrifice it." Moreover, those who would *promote* this idea are beneath contempt—they are parasites who, rather than working to build and sustain their own lives, leech off those who do. Again, she writes:

> Parasites, moochers, looters, brutes and thugs can be of no value to a human being—nor can he gain any benefit from living in a society geared to *their* needs, demands and protections, a society that treats him as a sacrificial animal and penalizes him for his virtues in order to reward *them* for their vices, which means: a society based on the ethics of altruism.

By "sacrificing one's life" Rand does not necessarily mean anything so dramatic as dying. A person's life consists (in part) of projects undertaken and goods earned and created. To demand that a person abandon his projects or give up his goods is also a clear effort to "sacrifice his life." Furthermore, throughout her writings Rand also suggests that there is a *metaphysical* basis for egoistic ethics. Somehow, it is the only ethics that takes seriously the *reality* of the individual person. She bemoans "the enormity of the extent to which altruism erodes men's capacity to grasp . . . the value of an individual life; it reveals a mind from which the reality of a human being has been wiped out."

What, then, of the starving people? It might be argued, in response, that Ethical Egoism "reveals a mind from which the reality of a human being has been wiped out"—namely, the human being who is starving. Rand quotes with approval the evasive answer given by one of her followers: "Once, when Barbara Brandon was asked by a student: 'What will happen to the poor . . . ?'— she answered: 'If *you* want to help them, you will not be stopped.'"

All these remarks are, I think, part of one continuous argument that can be summarized like this:

1. A person has only one life to live. If we place any value on the individual—that is, if the individual has any moral worth—then we must agree that this life is of supreme importance. After all, it is all one has, and all one is.

2. The ethics of altruism regards the life of the individual as something one must be ready to sacrifice for the good of others.

3. Therefore, the ethics of altruism does not take seriously the value of the human individual.

4. Ethical Egoism, which allows each person to view his or her own life as being of ultimate value, *does* take the human individual seriously—in fact, it is the only philosophy that does so.

5. Thus, Ethical Egoism is the philosophy that ought to be accepted.

The problem with this argument, as you may already have noticed, is that it relies on picturing the alternatives in such an extreme way. "The ethics of altruism" is taken to be such an extreme philosophy that *nobody,* with the possible exception of certain monks, would find it congenial. As Ayn Rand presents it, altruism implies that one's own interests have *no* value, and that *any* demand by others calls for sacrificing them. If that is the alternative, then any other view, including Ethical Egoism, will look good by comparison. But this is hardly a fair picture of the choices. What we called the common-sense view stands somewhere between the two extremes. It says that one's own interests and the interests of others are both important and must be balanced against one another. Sometimes, when the balancing is done, it will turn out that one should act in the interests of others; other times, it will turn out that one should take care of oneself. So even if the Randian argument refutes the extreme "ethics of altruism," it does not follow that one must accept the other extreme of Ethical Egoism.

3. The third line of reasoning takes a somewhat different approach. Ethical Egoism is usually presented as a *revisionist* moral philosophy, that is, as a philosophy that says our common-sense moral views are mistaken and need to be changed. It is possible, however, to interpret Ethical Egoism in a much less radical way, as a theory that *accepts* common-sense morality and offers a surprising account of its basis.

The less radical interpretation goes as follows. In everyday life, we assume that we are obliged to obey certain rules. We must avoid doing harm to others, speak the truth, keep our promises, and so on. At first glance, these duties appear to be very different from one another. They appear to have little in common. Yet from a theoretical point of view, we may wonder whether there is not some hidden *unity* underlying the hodgepodge of separate duties. Perhaps there is some small number of fundamental principles that explain all the rest, just as in physics there are basic principles that bring together and explain diverse phenomena. From a theoretical point of view, the smaller the number of basic principles, the better. Best of all would be *one* fundamental principle, from which all the rest could be derived. Ethical Egoism, then, would be the theory that all our duties are ultimately derived from the one fundamental principle of self-interest.

Taken in this way, Ethical Egoism is not such a radical doctrine. It does not challenge common-sense morality; it only tries to explain and systematize it. And it does a surprisingly successful job. It can provide plausible explanations of the duties mentioned above, and more:

a. If we make a habit of doing things that are harmful to other people, people will not be reluctant to do things that will harm *us*. We will be shunned and despised; others will not have us as friends and will not do us favors when we need them. If our offenses against others are serious enough, we may even end up in jail. Thus it is to our own advantage to avoid harming others.

b. If we lie to other people, we will suffer all the ill effects of a bad reputation. People will distrust us and avoid doing business with us. We will often need for people to be honest with us, but we can hardly expect them to feel much of an obligation to be honest with us if they know we have not been honest with them. Thus it is to our own advantage to be truthful.

c. It is to our own advantage to be able to enter into mutually beneficial arrangements with other people. To benefit from those arrangements, we need to be able to rely on others to keep their parts of the bargains we make with them—we need to be able to rely on them to keep their promises to us. But we can hardly expect others to keep their promises to us if we are not willing to keep our promises to them. Therefore, from the point of view of self-interest, we should keep our promises.

Pursuing this line of reasoning, Thomas Hobbes suggested that the principle of Ethical Egoism leads to nothing less than the Golden Rule: we should "do unto others" *because* if we do, others will be more likely to "do unto us."

Does this argument succeed in establishing Ethical Egoism as a viable theory of morality? It is, in my opinion at least, the best try. But there are two serious objections to it. In the first place, the argument does not prove quite as much as it needs to prove. At best, it shows only that *as a general rule* it is to one's own advantage to avoid harming others. It does not show that this is *always* so. And it could not show that, for even though it may usually be to one's advantage to avoid harming others, sometimes it is not. Sometimes one might even *gain* from treating another person badly. In that case, the obligation not to harm the other person could *not* be derived from the principle of Ethical Egoism. Thus it appears that not all our moral obligations can be explained as derivable from self-interest.

But set that point aside. There is still a more fundamental question to be asked about the proposed theory. Suppose it is true that, say, contributing money for famine relief is somehow to one's own advantage. It does not follow that this is the only reason, or even the most basic reason, why doing so is a morally good thing. (For example, the most basic reason might be *in order to help the starving people*. The fact that doing so is also to one's own advantage might be only a secondary, less important, consideration.) A demonstration that one could *derive* this duty from self-interest does not prove that self-interest is the *only reason* one has this duty. Only if you accept an additional proposition—namely, the proposition that there is no reason for giving *other than* self-interest—will you find Ethical Egoism a plausible theory.

Three Arguments against Ethical Egoism

Ethical Egoism has haunted twentieth-century moral philosophy. It has not been a popular doctrine; the most important philosophers have rejected it outright. But it has never been very far from their minds. Although no thinker of consequence has defended it, almost everyone has felt it necessary to explain why he was rejecting it—

as though the very possibility that it might be correct was hanging in the air, threatening to smother their other ideas. As the merits of the various "refutations" have been debated, philosophers have returned to it again and again.

The following three arguments are typical of the refutations proposed by contemporary philosophers.

1. In his book *The Moral Point of View* (1958), Kurt Baier argues that Ethical Egoism cannot be correct because it cannot provide solutions for conflicts of interest. We need moral rules, he says, only because our interests sometimes come into conflict. (If they never conflicted, then there would be no problems to solve and hence no need for the kind of guidance that morality provides.) But Ethical Egoism does not help to resolve conflicts of interest; it only exacerbates them. Baier argues for this by introducing a fanciful example:

> Let B and K be candidates for the presidency of a certain country and let it be granted that it is in the interest of either to be elected, but that only one can succeed. It would then be in the interest of B but against the interest of K if B were elected, and vice versa, and therefore in the interest of B but against the interest of K if K were liquidated, and vice versa. But from this it would follow that B ought to liquidate K, that it is wrong for B not to do so, that B has not "done his duty" until he has liquidated K; and vice versa. Similarly K, knowing that his own liquidation is in the interest of B and therefore, anticipating B's attempts to secure it, ought to take steps to foil B's endeavors. It would be wrong for him not to do so. He would "not have done his duty" until he had made sure of stopping B. . . .
>
> This is obviously absurd. For morality is designed to apply in just such cases, namely, those where interests conflict. But if the point of view of morality were that of self-interest, then there could never be moral solutions of conflicts of interest.

Does this argument prove that Ethical Egoism is unacceptable? It does, *if* the conception of morality to which it appeals is accepted. The argument assumes that an adequate morality must provide solutions for conflicts of interest in such a way that everyone concerned can live together harmoniously. The conflict between B and K, for example, should be resolved so that they would no longer be at odds with one another. (One would not then have a duty to do something that the other has a duty to prevent.) Ethical Egoism does not do that, and if you think an ethical theory should, then you will not find Ethical Egoism acceptable.

But a defender of Ethical Egoism might reply that *he* does not accept this conception of morality. For him, life is essentially a long series of conflicts in which each person is struggling to come out on top; and the principle he accepts—the principle of Ethical Egoism—simply urges each one to do his or her best to win. On his view, the moralist is not like a courtroom judge, who resolves disputes. Instead, he is like the Commissioner of Boxing, who urges each fighter to do his best. So the conflict between B and K will be "resolved" not by the application of an ethical theory but by one or the other of them winning the struggle. The egoist will not be embarrassed by this—on the contrary, he will think it no more than a realistic view of the nature of things.

2. Some philosophers, including Baier, have leveled an even more serious charge against Ethical Egoism. They have argued that it is a *logically inconsistent* doctrine—that is, they say it leads to logical contradictions. If this is true, then Ethical Egoism is indeed a mistaken theory, for no theory can be true if it is self-contradictory.

Consider B and K again. As Baier explains their predicament, it is in B's interest to kill K, and obviously it is in K's interest to prevent it. But, Baier says,

> if K prevents B from liquidating him, his act must be said to be both wrong and not wrong—wrong because it is the prevention of what B ought to do, his duty, and wrong for B not to do it; not wrong because it is what K

ought to do, his duty, and wrong for K not to do it. But one and the same act (logically) cannot be both morally wrong and not morally wrong.

Now, does *this* argument prove that Ethical Egoism is unacceptable? At first glance it seems persuasive. However, it is a complicated argument, so we need to set it out with each step individually identified. Then we will be in a better position to evaluate it. Spelled out fully, it looks like this:

1. Suppose it is each person's duty to do what is in his own best interests.
2. It is in B's best interest to liquidate K.
3. It is in K's best interest to prevent B from liquidating him.
4. Therefore B's duty is to liquidate K, and K's duty is to prevent B from doing it.
5. But it is wrong to prevent someone from doing his duty.
6. Therefore it is wrong for K to prevent B from liquidating him.
7. Therefore it is both wrong and not wrong for K to prevent B from liquidating him.
8. But no act can be both wrong and not wrong—that is a self-contradiction.
9. Therefore the assumption with which we started—that it is each person's duty to do what is in his own best interests—cannot be true.

When the argument is set out in this way, we can see its hidden flaw. The logical contradiction—that it is both wrong and not wrong for K to prevent B from liquidating him—does *not* follow simply from the principle of Ethical Egoism. It follows from that principle, *and* the additional premise expressed in step (5)—namely, that "it is wrong to prevent someone from doing his duty." Thus we are not compelled by the logic of the argument to reject Ethical Egoism. Instead, we could simply reject this additional premise, and the contradiction would be avoided. That is surely what the ethical egoist would want to do, for the ethical egoist would never say,

without qualification, that it is always wrong to prevent someone from doing his duty. He would say, instead, that *whether one ought to prevent someone from doing his duty depends entirely on whether it would be to one's own advantage to do so.* Regardless of whether we think this is a correct view, it is, at the very least, a *consistent* view, and so this attempt to convict the egoist of self-contradiction fails.

3. Finally, we come to the argument that I think comes closest to an outright refutation of Ethical Egoism. It is also the most interesting of the arguments, because at the same time it provides the most insight into why the interests of other people *should* matter to a moral agent.

Before this argument is presented, we need to look briefly at a general point about moral values. So let us set Ethical Egoism aside for a moment and consider this related matter.

There is a whole family of moral views that have this in common: they all involve dividing people into groups and saying that the interests of some groups count for more than the interests of other groups. Racism is the most conspicuous example; it involves dividing people into groups according to race and assigning greater importance to the interests of one race than to others. The practical result is that members of the preferred race are to be *treated better* than the others. Anti-Semitism works the same way, and so can nationalism. People in the grip of such views will think, in effect: "*My* race counts for more," or "Those who believe in *my* religion count for more," or "*My* country counts for more," and so on.

Can such views be defended? Those who accept them are usually not much interested in argument—racists, for example, rarely try to offer rational grounds for their position. But suppose they did. What could they say?

There is a general principle that stands in the way of any such defense, namely: *We can justify treating people differently only if we can show that there is some factual difference between them that is relevant to justifying the difference in treatment.*

For example, if one person is admitted to law school while another is rejected, this can be justified by pointing out that the first graduated from college with honors and scored well on the admissions test, while the second dropped out of college and never took the test. However, if *both* graduated with honors and did well on the entrance examination—in other words, if they are in all relevant respects equally well qualified—then it is merely arbitrary to admit one but not the other.

Can a racist point to any differences between, say, white people and black people that would justify treating them differently? In the past, racists have sometimes attempted to do this by picturing blacks as stupid, lacking in ambition, and the like. *If* this were true, then it might justify treating them differently, in at least some circumstances. (This is the deep purpose of racist stereotypes—to provide the "relevant differences" needed to justify differences in treatment.) But of course it is not true, and in fact there are no such general differences between the races. Thus racism is an *arbitrary* doctrine, in that it advocates treating some people differently even though there are no differences between them to justify it.

Ethical Egoism is a moral theory of the same type. It advocates that each of us divide the world into two categories of people—ourselves and all the rest—and that we regard the interests of those in the first group as more important than the interests of those in the second group. But each of us can ask, what is the difference between myself and others that justifies placing myself in this special category? Am I more intelligent? Do I enjoy my life more? Are my accomplishments greater? Do I have needs or abilities that are so different from the needs or abilities of others? *What is it that makes me so special?* Failing

an answer, it turns out that Ethical Egoism is an arbitrary doctrine, in the same way that racism is arbitrary.

The argument, then, is this:

1. Any moral doctrine that assigns greater importance to the interests of one group than to those of another is unacceptably arbitrary unless there is some difference between the members of the groups that justifies treating them differently.
2. Ethical Egoism would have each person assign greater importance to his or her own interests than to the interests of others. *But there is no general difference between oneself and others, to which each person can appeal, that justifies this difference in treatment.*
3. Therefore, Ethical Egoism is unacceptably arbitrary.

And this, in addition to arguing against Ethical Egoism, also sheds some light on the question of why we should care about others.

We should care about the interests of other people *for the very same reason we care about our own interests;* for their needs and desires are comparable to our own. Consider, one last time, the starving people we could feed by giving up some of our luxuries. Why should we care about them? We care about ourselves, of course—if *we* were starving, we would go to almost any lengths to get food. But what is the difference between us and them? Does hunger affect them any less? Are they somehow less deserving than we? If we can find no relevant difference between us and them, then we must admit that if *our* needs should be met, so should *theirs*. It is this realization, that we are on a par with one another, that is the deepest reason why our morality must include some recognition of the needs of others, and why, then, Ethical Egoism fails as a moral theory.

For Further Reflection

1. Go over the three arguments for ethical egoism. Do you agree with Rachels' assessment that they all fail to establish the theory? Could a slight modification in any of them save the theory from Rachels' attack? Explain.

2. Examine the three arguments against ethical egoism. Do you agree with Rachels that only the third one "comes closest" to refuting ethical egoism? Why doesn't Rachels think that this argument actually does refute the doctrine? Does he give us a reason for thinking ethical egoism is still possibly true? Explain.

3. What sort of response might the ethical egoist make to Rachels' final critique? What if the egoist responded thus: "It is not arbitrary to love oneself more than others. It is natural, for I have never experienced any other consciousness but my own, never felt the pain of any one else's toothache but my own, never dreamed or longed for any goal but my own. I am ultimately responsible for myself—and no one else is. Sure we need others to accomplish our goals, so we must cooperate with them. My duty to myself often includes helping or not harming them, but I have no direct duties to them. But we really don't know them. It's simply absurd to call on humanity "to love your neighbor as yourself." There is simply no way that I can be preoccupied with whether my neighbor will fulfill his dreams or is suffering or will come to terms with his death in the way I am preoccupied with my dreams and my suffering and my death." How would one criticize this argument?

Which Is the Correct Moral Theory?

There are three major types of moral theories in Western philosophy:

1. *Virtue ethics,* which state that the emphasis in ethics should be put not on rules, but on character—on the virtues and vices people exhibit in their lives. Ethical goodness is primarily a state of being, and only secondarily a doing.

2. *Deontological ethics,* which views moral value as inherent in certain acts or types of acts [e.g., "killing innocents is just wrong (period)."]. The main form of deontological ethics holds that we ought to follow principles of action, for these principles of action have inherent value. In every moral act we are acting in accordance with an appropriate principle. A second type of deontological ethics [set forth by Bishop Joseph Butler (1692–1752)] holds that the criterion of right and wrong is the voice of conscience.

3. *Teleological ethics,* which assert that the rightness or wrongness of an act is determined by some nonmoral value. Teleological ethical systems may be subdivided into two major forms. *Ethical egoism* is the view that each person ought to do what will promote his or her own greatest good, and *utilitarianism* is the view that persons ought to do the act which will produce the greatest total (or average) good (e.g., "The greatest happiness for the greatest number"—Francis Hutcheson).

Our first three readings in this section represent each of these three types of theories. We begin with Aristotle's virtue theory, one of the oldest accounts of ethics in the history of philosophy. Next we examine the most famous deontological theory, Kantian ethics, followed by a section from John Stuart Mill's classic *Utilitarianism.* Our selection from William Frankena's *Ethics* attempts to reconcile deontological and teleological ethics. This is followed by a type of ethics which defies system and yet is not in the virtue tradition, existentialist ethics, which leaves each decision to the individual in the moment. Jean-Paul Sartre's "Existentialist Ethics" represents this position. We close with a radical critique of traditional ethics by Friedrich Nietzsche, who argues for an ethics of nobility wherein the higher natures have a right to develop themselves at the expense of the lower natures.

VI.7   The Ethics of Virtue

ARISTOTLE

Aristotle (384–322 B.C.), Greek physician, Plato's prize pupil, tutor to Alexander the Great, and one of the most important philosophers who ever lived, wrote importantly on every major subject in philosophy: metaphysics, philosophy of science, philosophical psychology, aesthetics, ethics, and politics. He is the father of formal logic. Although deeply indebted to his teacher, Plato, Aristotle broke with him over the idea of Forms (Plato thought that the Forms had independent existence whereas Aristotle thought that they were in things). Aristotle tended to be more empirical than Plato. The break with the master led to the formation to the second major school of philosophy in Athens, Aristotle's Lyceum.

In this selection from the *Nicomachean Ethics,* Aristotle discusses the nature of ethics and its relationship to human existence. He next turns to the nature of virtue, which he characterizes as traits that enable individuals to live well in communities. To achieve a state of well being (*eudaimonia,* happiness), proper social institutions are necessary. Thus the moral person cannot really exist apart from a flourishing political setting which enables the individual to develop the requisite virtues for the good life. For this reason Aristotle considers ethics to be a branch of politics.

After locating ethics as a part of politics, Aristotle explains that the moral virtues are different from the intellectual ones. While the intellectual virtues may be taught directly, the moral ones must be lived in order to be learned. By living well we acquire the right habits. These habits are in fact the virtues. The virtues are to be sought as the best guarantee to the happy life. But, again, happiness requires that one be lucky enough to live in a flourishing state. The morally virtuous life consists in living in moderation, according to the "Golden Mean."

Study Questions

1. How does Aristotle define politics and ethics? What is the relationship between them?
2. What is the good at which political science and ethics aim?
3. What are the characteristics of the good?
4. What is the function of human beings? How does Aristotle build his case for our having a function and how does this relate to ethics?

5. What is the relationship between habit and ethics? What does Aristotle mean by the statement, "A just man becomes just by doing what is just"? How can one do just things if one isn't already just? How does Aristotle solve this problem?

6. Does every action and emotion have a proper mean (Book II.6)?

Book I

ALL HUMAN ACTIVITIES AIM AT SOME GOOD

Chapter 1. EVERY ART AND EVERY scientific inquiry, and similarly every action and purpose, may be said to aim at some good. Hence the good has been well defined as that at which all things aim. But it is clear that there is a difference in ends; for the ends are sometimes activities, and sometimes results beyond the mere activities. Where there are ends beyond the action, the results are naturally superior to the action.

As there are various actions, arts, and sciences, it follows that the ends are also various. Thus health is the end of the medical art, a ship of shipbuilding, victory of strategy, and wealth of economics. It often happens that a number of such arts or sciences combine for a single enterprise, as the art of making bridles and all such other arts as furnish the implements of horsemanship combine for horsemanship, and horsemanship and every military action for strategy; and in the same way, other arts or sciences combine for others. In all these cases, the ends of the master arts or sciences, whatever they may be, are more desirable than those of the subordinate arts or sciences, as it is for the sake of the former that the latter are pursued. It makes no difference to the argument whether the activities themselves are the ends of the action, or something beyond the activities, as in the above-mentioned sciences.

If it is true that in the sphere of action there is some end which we wish for its own sake, and for the sake of which we wish everything else, and if we do not desire everything for the sake of something else (for, if that is so, the process will go on *ad infinitum,* and our desire will be idle and futile), clearly this end will be good and the supreme good. Does it not follow then that the knowledge of this good is of great importance for the conduct of life? Like archers who have a mark at which to aim, shall we not have a better chance of attaining what we want? If this is so, we must endeavor to comprehend, at least in outline, what this good is, and what science or faculty makes it its object.

It would seem that this is the most authoritative science. Such a kind is evidently the political, for it is that which determines what sciences are necessary in states, and what kinds should be studied, and how far they should be studied by each class of inhabitant. We see too that even the faculties held in highest esteem, such as strategy, economics, and rhetoric, are subordinate to it. Then since politics makes use of the other sciences and also rules what people may do and what they may not do, it follows that its end will comprehend the ends of the other sciences, and will therefore be the good of mankind. For even if the good of an individual is identical with the good of a state, yet the good of the state is evidently greater and more perfect to attain or to preserve. For though the good of an individual by himself is something worth working for, to ensure the good of a nation or a state is nobler and more divine.

These then are the objects at which the present inquiry aims, and it is in a sense a political inquiry. . . .

THE SCIENCE OF THE GOOD FOR MAN IS POLITICS

Chapter 2. As every science and undertaking aims at some good, what is in our view the good

Reprinted from Aristotle's Nichomachean Ethics, *translated by James E. C. Weldon (Macmillan, 1897).*

at which political science aims, and what is the highest of all practical goods? As to its name there is, I may say, a general agreement. The masses and the cultured classes agree in calling it happiness, and conceive that "to live well" or "to do well" is the same thing as "to be happy." But as to what happiness is they do not agree, nor do the masses give the same account of it as the philosophers. The former take it to be something visible and palpable, such as pleasure, wealth, or honor; different people, however, give different definitions of it, and often even the same man gives different definitions at different times. When he is ill, it is health, when he is poor, it is wealth; if he is conscious of his own ignorance, he envies people who use grand language above his own comprehension. Some philosophers, on the other hand, have held that, besides these various goods, there is an absolute good which is the cause of goodness in them all.* It would perhaps be a waste of time to examine all these opinions; it will be enough to examine such as are most popular or as seem to be more or less reasonable.

Chapter 3. Men's conception of the good or of happiness may be read in the lives they lead. Ordinary or vulgar people conceive it to be a pleasure, and accordingly choose a life of enjoyment. For there are, we may say, three conspicuous types of life, the sensual, the political, and, thirdly, the life of thought. Now the mass of men present an absolutely slavish appearance, choosing the life of brute beasts, but they have ground for so doing because so many persons in authority share the tastes of Sardanapalus.† Cultivated and energetic people, on the other hand, identify happiness with honor, as honor is the general end of political life. But this seems too superficial an idea for our present purpose; for honor depends more upon the people who pay it than upon the person to whom it is paid, and the good we feel is something which is proper to a man himself and cannot be easily taken away

from him. Men too appear to seek honor in order to be assured of their own goodness. Accordingly, they seek it at the hands of the sage and of those who know them well, and they seek it on the ground of their virtue; clearly then, in their judgment at any rate, virtue is better than honor. Perhaps then we might look on virtue rather than honor as the end of political life. Yet even this idea appears not quite complete; for a man may possess virtue and yet be asleep or inactive throughout life, and not only so, but he may experience the greatest calamities and misfortunes. Yet no one would call such a life a life of happiness, unless he were maintaining a paradox. But we need not dwell further on this subject, since it is sufficiently discussed in popular philosophical treatises. The third life is the life of thought, which we will discuss later.

The life of money making is a life of constraint; and wealth is obviously not the good of which we are in quest; for it is useful merely as a means to something else. It would be more reasonable to take the things mentioned before—sensual pleasure, honor, and virtue—as ends than wealth, since they are things desired on their own account. Yet these too are evidently not ends, although much argument has been employed to show that they are. . . .

CHARACTERISTICS OF THE GOOD

Chapter 5. But leaving this subject for the present, let us revert to the good of which we are in quest and consider what it may be. For it seems different in different activities or arts; it is one thing in medicine, another in strategy, and so on. What is the good in each of these instances? It is presumably that for the sake of which all else is done. In medicine this is health, in strategy victory, in architecture a house, and so on. In every activity and undertaking it is the end, since it is for the sake of the end that all people do whatever else they do. If then there is an end for all our activity, this will be the good to be accomplished; and if there are several such ends, it will be these.

*Plato
†A half-legendary ruler whose name to the Greeks stood for extreme mental luxury and extravagance.

Our argument has arrived by a different path at the same point as before; but we must endeavor to make it still plainer. Since there are more ends than one, and some of these ends—for example, wealth, flutes, and instruments generally—we desire as means to something else, it is evident that not all are final ends. But the highest good is clearly something final. Hence if there is only one final end, this will be the object of which we are in search; and if there are more than one, it will be the most final. We call that which is sought after for its own sake more final than that which is sought after as a means to something else; we call that which is never desired as a means to something else more final than things that are desired both for themselves and as means to something else. Therefore, we call absolutely final that which is always desired for itself and never as a means to something else. Now happiness more than anything else answers to this description. For happiness we always desire for its own sake and never as a means to something else, whereas honor, pleasure, intelligence, and every virtue we desire partly for their own sakes (for we should desire them independently of what might result from them), but partly also as means to happiness, because we suppose they will prove instruments of happiness. Happiness, on the other hand, nobody desires for the sake of these things, nor indeed as a means to anything else at all.

If we start from the point of view of self-sufficiency, we reach the same conclusion; for we assume that the final good is self-sufficient. By self-sufficiency we do not mean that a person leads a solitary life all by himself, but that he has parents, children, wife and friends and fellow citizens in general, as man is naturally a social being. Yet here it is necessary to set some limit; for if the circle must be extended to include ancestors, descendants, and friends' friends, it will go on indefinitely. Leaving this point, however, for future investigation, we call the self-sufficient that which, taken even by itself, makes life desirable and wanting nothing at all; and this is what we mean by happiness.

Again, we think happiness the most desirable of all things, and that not merely as one good thing among others. If it were only that, the addition of the smallest more good would increase its desirableness; for the addition would make an increase of goods, and the greater of two goods is always the more desirable. Happiness is something final and self-sufficient and the end of all action.

Chapter 6. Perhaps, however, it seems a commonplace to say that happiness is the supreme good; what is wanted is to define its nature a little more clearly. The best way of arriving at such a definition will probably be to ascertain the function of man. For, as with a flute player, a sculptor, or any artist, or in fact anybody who has a special function or activity, his goodness and excellence seem to lie in his function, so it would seem to be with man, if indeed he has a special function. Can it be said that, while a carpenter and a cobbler have special functions and activities, man, unlike them, is naturally functionless? Or, as the eye, the hand, the foot, and similarly each part of the body has a special function, so may man be regarded as having a special function apart from all these? What, then, can this function be? It is not life; for life is apparently something that man shares with plants; and we are looking for something peculiar to him. We must exclude therefore the life of nutrition and growth. There is next what may be called the life of sensation. But this too, apparently, is shared by man with horses, cattle, and all other animals. There remains what I may call the active life of the rational part of man's being. Now this rational part is twofold; one part is rational in the sense of being obedient to reason, and the other in the sense of possessing and exercising reason and intelligence. The active life too may be conceived of in two ways, either as a state of character, or as an activity; but we mean by it the life of activity, as this seems to be the truer form of the conception.

The function of man then is activity of soul in accordance with reason, or not apart from reason. Now, the function of a man of a certain kind, and of a man who is good of that kind—for example, of a harpist and a good harpist—are in our view the same in kind. This is true of all people of all kinds without exception, the superior excellence being only an addition to the function; for it is the function of a harpist to play the harp, and of a good harpist to play the harp well. This being so, if we define the function of man as a kind of life, and this life as an activity of the soul or a course of action in accordance with reason, and if the function of a good man is such activity of a good and noble kind, and if everything is well done when it is done in accordance with its proper excellence, it follows that the good of man is activity of soul in accordance with virtue, or, if there are more virtues than one, in accordance with the best and most complete virtue. But we must add the words "in a complete life." For as one swallow or one day does not make a spring, so one day or a short time does not make a man blessed or happy. . . .

Inasmuch as happiness is an activity of soul in accordance with perfect virtue, we must now consider virtue, as this will perhaps be the best way of studying happiness. . . . Clearly it is human virtue we have to consider; for the good of which we are in search is, as we said, human good, and the happiness, human happiness. By human virtue or excellence we mean not that of the body, but that of the soul, and by happiness we mean an activity of the soul. . . .

Book II

Moral virtues can best be acquired by practice and habit. They imply a right attitude toward pleasures and pains. A good man deliberately chooses to do what is noble and right for its own sake. What is right in matters of moral conduct is usually a mean between two extremes.

Chapter 1. Virtue then is twofold, partly intellectual and partly moral, and intellectual virtue is originated and fostered mainly by teaching; it demands therefore experience and time. Moral virtue on the other hand is the outcome of habit, and accordingly its name, *ethike,* is derived by a slight variation from *ethos,* habit. From this fact it is clear that moral virtue is not implanted in us by nature; for nothing that exists by nature can be transformed by habit. Thus a stone, that naturally tends to fall downwards, cannot be habituated or trained to rise upwards, even if we tried to train it by throwing it up ten thousand times. Nor again can fire be trained to sink downwards, nor anything else that follows one natural law be habituated or trained to follow another. It is neither by nature then nor in defiance of nature that virtues grow in us. Nature gives us the capacity to receive them, and that capacity is perfected by habit.

Again, if we take the various natural powers which belong to us, we first possess the proper faculties and afterwards display the activities. It is obviously so with the senses. Not by seeing frequently or hearing frequently do we acquire the sense of seeing or hearing; on the contrary, because we have the senses we make use of them; we do not get them by making use of them. But the virtues we get by first practicing them, as we do in the arts. For it is by doing what we ought to do when we study the arts that we learn the arts themselves; we become builders by building and harpists by playing the harp. Similarly, it is by doing just acts that we become just, by doing temperate acts that we become temperate, by doing brave acts that we become brave. The experience of states confirms this statement, for it is by training in good habits that lawmakers make the citizens good. This is the object all lawmakers have at heart; if they do not succeed in it, they fail of their purpose; and it makes the distinction between a good constitution and a bad one.

Again, the causes and means by which any virtue is produced and destroyed are the same; and equally so in any part. For it is by playing the harp that both good and bad harpists are produced; and the case of builders and others is similar, for it is by building well that they become good builders and by building badly that they become bad builders. If it were not so, there would be no need of anybody to teach them; they would all be born good or bad in their several crafts. The case of the virtues is the same. It is by our actions in dealings between man and man that we become either just or unjust. It is by our actions in the face of danger and by our training ourselves to fear or to courage that we become either cowardly or courageous. It is much the same with our appetites and angry passions. People become temperate and gentle, others licentious and passionate, by behaving in one or the other way in particular circumstances. In a word, moral states are the results of activities like the states themselves. It is our duty therefore to keep a certain character in our activities, since our moral states depend on the differences in our activities. So the difference between one and another training in habits in our childhood is not a light matter, but important, or rather, all-important.

Chapter 2. Our present study is not, like other studies, purely theoretical in intention; for the object of our inquiry is not to know what virtue is but how to become good, and that is the sole benefit of it. We must, therefore, consider the right way of performing actions, for it is acts, as we have said, that determine the character of the resulting moral states.

That we should act in accordance with right reason is a common general principle, which may here be taken for granted. The nature of right reason, and its relation to the virtues generally, will be discussed later. But first of all it must be admitted that all reasoning on matters of conduct must be like a sketch in outline; it cannot be scientifically exact. We began by laying down the principle that the kind of reasoning demanded in any subject must be such as the subject matter itself allows; and questions of conduct and expediency no more admit of hard and fast rules than questions of health.

If this is true of general reasoning on ethics, still more true is it that scientific exactitude is impossible in treating of particular ethical cases. They do not fall under any art or law, but the actors themselves have always to take account of

circumstances, as much as in medicine or navigation. Still, although such is the nature of our present argument, we must try to make the best of it.

The first point to be observed is that in the matters we are now considering deficiency and excess are both fatal. It is so, we see, in questions of health and strength. (We must judge of what we cannot see by the evidence of what we do see.) Too much or too little gymnastic exercise is fatal to strength. Similarly, too much or too little meat and drink is fatal to health, whereas a suitable amount produces, increases, and sustains it. It is the same with temperance, courage, and other moral virtues. A person who avoids and is afraid of everything and faces nothing becomes a coward; a person who is not afraid of anything but is ready to face everything becomes foolhardy. Similarly, he who enjoys every pleasure and abstains from none is licentious; he who refuses all pleasures, like a boor, is an insensible sort of person. For temperance and courage are destroyed by excess and deficiency but preserved by the mean.

Again, not only are the causes and agencies of production, increase, and destruction in moral states the same, but the field of their activity is the same also. It is so in other more obvious instances, as, for example, strength; for strength is produced by taking a great deal of food and undergoing a great deal of exertion, and it is the strong man who is able to take most food and undergo most exertion. So too with the virtues. By abstaining from pleasures we become temperate, and, when we have become temperate, we are best able to abstain from them. So again with courage; it is by training ourselves to despise and face terrifying things that we become brave, and when we have become brave, we shall be best able to face them.

The pleasure or pain which accompanies actions may be regarded as a test of a person's moral state. He who abstains from physical pleasures and feels pleasure in so doing is temperate; but he who feels pain at so doing is licentious. He who faces dangers with pleasure, or at least without pain, is brave; but he who feels pain at facing them is a coward. For moral virtue is concerned with pleasures and pains. It is pleasure which makes us do what is base, and pain which makes us abstain from doing what is noble. Hence the importance of having a certain training from very early days, as Plato says, so that we may feel pleasure and pain at the right objects; for this is true education. . . .

Chapter 3. But we may be asked what we mean by saying that people must become just by doing what is just and temperate by doing what is temperate. For, it will be said, if they do what is just and temperate they are already just and temperate themselves, in the same way as, if they practice grammar and music, they are grammarians and musicians.

But is this true even in the case of the arts? For a person may speak grammatically either by chance or at the suggestion of somebody else; hence he will not be a grammarian unless he not only speaks grammatically but does so in a grammatical manner, that is, because of the grammatical knowledge which he possesses.

There is a point of difference too between the arts and the virtues. The productions of art have their excellence in themselves. It is enough then that, when they are produced, they themselves should possess a certain character. But acts in accordance with virtue are not justly or temperately performed simply because they are in themselves just or temperate. The doer at the time of performing them must satisfy certain conditions; in the first place, he must know what he is doing; secondly, he must deliberately choose to do it and do it for his own sake; and thirdly, he must do it as part of his own firm and immutable character. If it be a question of art, these conditions, except only the condition of knowledge, are not raised; but if it be a question of virtue, mere knowledge is of little or no avail; it is the other conditions, which are the results of frequently performing just and temperate acts, that are not slightly but all-important. Accordingly, deeds are called just and temperate when they are such as a just and temperate person would

do; and a just and temperate person is not merely one who does these deeds but one who does them in the spirit of the just and the temperate.

It may fairly be said that a just man becomes just by doing what is just, and a temperate man becomes temperate by doing what is temperate, and if a man did not so act, he would not have much chance of becoming good. But most people, instead of acting, take refuge in theorizing; they imagine that they are philosophers and that philosophy will make them virtuous; in fact, they behave like people who listen attentively to their doctors but never do anything that their doctors tell them. But a healthy state of the soul will no more be produced by this kind of philosophizing than a healthy state of the body by this kind of medical treatment.

Chapter 4. We have next to consider the nature of virtue. Now, as the properties of the soul are three, namely, emotions, faculties, and moral states, it follows that virtue must be one of the three. By emotions I mean desire, anger, fear, pride, envy, joy, love, hatred, regret, ambition, pity—in a word, whatever feeling is attended by pleasure or pain. I call those faculties through which we are said to be capable of experiencing these emotions, for instance, capable of getting angry or being pained or feeling pity. And I call those moral states through which we are well or ill disposed in our emotions, ill disposed, for instance, in anger, if our anger be too violent or too feeble, and well disposed, if it be rightly moderate; and similarly in our other emotions.

Now neither the virtues nor the vices are emotions; for we are not called good or bad for our emotions but for our virtues or vices. We are not praised or blamed simply for being angry, but only for being angry in a certain way; but we are praised or blamed for our virtues or vices. Again, whereas we are angry or afraid without deliberate purpose, the virtues are matters of deliberate purpose, or require deliberate purpose. Moreover, we are said to be moved by our emotions, but by our virtues or vices we are not said to be moved but to have a certain disposition.

For these reasons the virtues are not faculties.

For we are not called either good or bad, nor are we praised or blamed for having simple capacity for emotion. Also while Nature gives us our faculties, it is not Nature that makes us good or bad; but this point we have already discussed. If then the virtues are neither emotions nor faculties, all that remains is that they must be moral states.

Chapter 5. The nature of virtue has been now described in kind. But it is not enough to say merely that virtue is a moral state; we must also describe the character of that moral state.

We may assert then that every virtue or excellence puts into good condition that of which it is a virtue or excellence, and enables it to perform its work well. Thus excellence in the eye makes the eye good and its function good, for by excellence in the eye we see well. Similarly, excellence of the horse makes a horse excellent himself and good at racing, at carrying its rider and at facing the enemy. If then this rule is universally true, the virtue or excellence of a man will be such a moral state as makes a man good and able to perform his proper function well. How this will be the case we have already explained, but another way of making it clear will be to study the nature or character of virtue.

Now of everything, whether it be continuous or divisible, it is possible to take a greater, a smaller, or an equal amount, and this either in terms of the thing itself or in relation to ourselves, the equal being a mean between too much and too little. By the mean in terms of the thing itself, I understand that which is equally distinct from both its extremes, which is one and the same for every man. By the mean relatively to ourselves, I understand that which is neither too much nor too little for us; but this is not one nor the same for everybody. Thus if 10 be too much and 2 too little, we take 6 as a mean in terms of the thing itself; for 6 is as much greater than 2 as it is less than 10, and this is a mean in arithmetical proportion. But the mean considered relatively to ourselves may not be ascertained in that way. It does not follow that if 10 pounds of meat is too much and 2 too little for a man to eat, the trainer will order him 6 pounds, since this also may be too much or too little for him who is to take it; it will be too little, for example, for Milo but too much for a beginner in gymnastics. The same with running and wrestling; the right amount will vary with the individual. This being so, the skillful in any art avoids alike excess and deficiency; he seeks and chooses the mean, not the absolute mean, but the mean considered relatively to himself.

Every art then does its work well, if it regards the mean and judges the works it produces by the mean. For this reason we often say of successful works of art that it is impossible to take anything from them or to add anything to them, which implies that excess or deficiency is fatal to excellence but that the mean state ensures it. Good artists too, as we say, have an eye to the mean in their works. Now virtue, like Nature herself, is more accurate and better than any art; virtue, therefore, will aim at the mean. I speak of moral virtue, since it is moral virtue which is concerned with emotions and actions, and it is in these we have excess and deficiency and the mean. Thus it is possible to go too far, or not far enough in fear, pride, desire, anger, pity, and pleasure and pain generally, and the excess and the deficiency are alike wrong; but to feel these emotions at the right times, for the right objects, towards the right persons, for the right motives, and in the right manner, is the mean or the best good, which signifies virtue. Similarly, there may be excess, deficiency, or the mean, in acts. Virtue is concerned with both emotions and actions, wherein excess is an error and deficiency a fault, while the mean is successful and praised, and success and praise are both characteristics of virtue.

It appears then that virtue is a kind of mean because it aims at the mean.

On the other hand, there are many different ways of going wrong; for evil is in its nature infinite, to use the Pythagorean phrase, but good is finite and there is only one possible way of going right. So the former is easy and the latter is difficult; it is easy to miss the mark but difficult to hit it. And so by our reasoning excess and deficiency are characteristics of vice and the mean is a characteristic of virtue.

"For good is simple, evil manifold."

Chapter 6. Virtue then is a state of deliberate moral purpose, consisting in a mean relative to ourselves, the mean being determined by reason, or as a prudent man would determine it. It is a mean, firstly, as lying between two vices, the vice of excess on the one hand, the vice of deficiency on the other, and, secondly, because, whereas the vices either fall short of or go beyond what is right in emotion and action, virtue discovers and chooses the mean. Accordingly, virtue, if regarded in its essence or theoretical definition, is a mean, though, if regarded from the point of view of what is best and most excellent, it is an extreme.

But not every action or every emotion admits of a mean. There are some whose very name implies wickedness, as, for example, malice, shamelessness, and envy among the emotions, and adultery, theft, and murder among the actions. All these and others like them are marked as intrinsically wicked, not merely the excesses or deficiencies of them. It is never possible then to be right in them; they are always sinful. Right or wrong in such acts as adultery does not depend on our committing it with the right woman, at the right time, or in the right manner; on the contrary, it is wrong to do it at all. It would be equally false to suppose that there can be a mean or an excess or deficiency in unjust, cowardly or licentious conduct; for, if that were so, it would be a mean of excess and deficiency, an excess of excess and a deficiency of deficiency. But as in temperance and courage there can be no excess or deficiency, because the mean there is in a sense an extreme, so too in these other cases there cannot be a mean or an excess or a deficiency, but however the acts are done, they are wrong. For in general an excess or deficiency does not have a mean, nor a mean an excess or deficiency. . . .

Chapter 8. There are then three dispositions, two being vices, namely, excess and deficiency, and one virtue, which is the mean between them; and they are all in a sense mutually opposed. The extremes are opposed both to the mean and to each other, and the mean is opposed to the extremes. For as the equal if compared with the less is greater, but if compared with the greater is less, so the mean state, whether in emotion or action, if compared with deficiency is excessive, but if compared with excess is deficient. Thus the brave man appears foolhardy compared with the coward, but cowardly compared with the foolhardy. Similarly, the temperate man appears licentious compared with the insensible man but insensible compared with the licentious; and the liberal man appears extravagant compared with the stingy man but stingy compared with the spendthrift. The result is that the extremes each denounce the mean as belonging to the other extreme; the coward calls the brave man foolhardy, and the foolhardy man calls him cowardly; and so on in other cases.

But while there is mutual opposition between the extremes and the mean, there is greater opposition between the two extremes than between extreme and the mean; for they are further removed from each other than from the mean, as the great is further from the small and the small from the great than either from the equal. Again, while some extremes show some likeness to the mean, as foolhardiness to courage and extravagance to liberality, there is the greatest possible dissimilarity between extremes. But things furthest removed from each other are called opposites; hence the further things are removed, the greater is the opposition between them.

In some cases it is deficiency and in others excess which is more opposed to the mean. Thus it is not foolhardiness, an excess, but cowardice, a deficiency, which is more opposed to courage, nor is it insensibility, a deficiency, but licentiousness, an excess, which is more opposed to temperance. There are two reasons why this should be so. One lies in the nature of the matter itself; for when one of two extremes is nearer and more like the mean, it is not this extreme but its opposite that we chiefly contrast with the mean. For instance, as foolhardiness seems more like and nearer to courage than cowardice, it is cowardice that we chiefly contrast with courage; for things further removed from the mean seem to be more opposite to it. This reason lies in the nature of the matter itself; there is a second which lies in our own nature. The things to which we ourselves are naturally more inclined we think more opposed to the mean. Thus we are ourselves naturally more inclined to pleasures than to their opposites, and are more prone therefore to self-indulgence than to moderation. Accordingly we speak of those things in which we are more likely to run to great lengths as more opposed to the mean. Hence licentiousness, which is an excess, seems more opposed to temperance than insensibility.

Chapter 9. We have now sufficiently shown that moral virtue is a mean, and in what sense it is so; that it is a mean as lying between two vices, a vice of excess on the one side and a vice of deficiency on the other, and as aiming at the mean in emotion and action.

That is why it is so hard to be good; for it is always hard to find the mean in anything; it is not everyone but only a man of science who can find the mean or center of a circle. So too anybody can get angry—that is easy—and anybody can give or spend money, but to give it to the right person, to give the right amount of it, at the right time, for the right cause and in the right way, this is not what anybody can do, nor is it easy. That is why goodness is rare and praise worthy and noble. One then who aims at a mean must begin by departing from the extreme that is more contrary to the mean; he must act in the spirit of Calypso's advice,

"Far from this spray and swell hold thou thy ship,"

for of the two extremes one is more wrong than the other. As it is difficult to hit the mean exactly, we should take the second best course, as the saying is, and choose the lesser of two evils. This we shall best do in the way described, that is, steering clear of the evil which is further from the mean. We must also note the weaknesses to which we are ourselves particularly prone, since different natures tend in different ways; and we may ascertain what our tendency is by observing our feelings of pleasure and pain. Then we must drag ourselves away towards the opposite extreme; for by pulling ourselves as far as possible from what is wrong we shall arrive at the mean, as we do when we pull a crooked stick straight.

In all cases we must especially be on our guard against the pleasant, or pleasure, for we are not impartial judges of pleasure. Hence our attitude towards pleasure must be like that of the elders of the people in the *Iliad* towards Helen, and we must constantly apply the words they use; for if we dismiss pleasure as they dismissed Helen, we shall be less likely to go wrong. By action of this kind, to put it summarily, we shall best succeed in hitting the mean.

Undoubtedly this is a difficult task, especially in individual cases. It is not easy to determine the right manner, objects, occasion and duration of anger. Sometimes we praise people who are deficient in anger, and call them gentle, and at other times we praise people who exhibit a fierce temper as high spirited. It is not however a man who deviates a little from goodness, but one who deviates a great deal, whether on the side of excess or of deficiency, that is blamed; for he is sure to call attention to himself. It is not easy to decide in theory how far and to what extent a man may go before he becomes blameworthy, but neither is it easy to define in theory anything else in the region of the senses; such things depend on circumstances, and our judgment of them depends on our perception.

So much then is plain, that the mean is everywhere praiseworthy, but that we ought to aim at one time towards an excess and at another towards a deficiency; for thus we shall most easily hit the mean, or in other words reach excellence.

For Further Reflection

1. Is Aristotle's concept of happiness clear? Is it a subjective or objective notion? That is, is it subjective, in the mind of the beholder, so one is just as happy as one feels oneself to be; or is it objective, defined by a state of being, and having certain characteristics regardless of how one feels? According to Aristotle, could a criminal be happy?

2. Is Aristotle's ethics sufficiently action guiding? Does it help us make decisions? If I ask what should I do in situation *X*, Aristotle would seem to say, "Do what the virtuous person would do." But if I ask how I am to recognize the virtuous person, he would seem to say, "He is one who acts justly." Is there something circular about this reasoning? Does virtue ethics need supplementation from other ethical systems or can it solve this problem?

VI.8   The Moral Law

IMMANUEL KANT

Our reading is from Kant's classic work *The Foundations of the Metaphysic of Morals,* written in 1785, in which he outlines his ethical system. Kant rejects those ethical theories, such as the theory of moral sentiments set forth by the Scottish moralists Francis Hutcheson (1694) and David Hume (1711–1776), in which morality is contingent and hypothetical. The moral sentiment view is contingent in that it is based on human nature and, in particular, on our feelings or sentiments. Had we been created differently, we would have a different nature and, hence, different moral duties. Moral duties or imperatives are hypothetical in that they depend on our desires for their realization. For example, we should obey the law because we want a peaceful, orderly society.

Kant rejects this naturalistic account of ethics. Ethics is not contingent but absolute, he argues, and its duties or imperatives are not hypothetical but categorical (nonconditional). Ethics is based not on feeling but on reason. It is because we are rational beings that we are valuable and capable of discovering moral laws binding on all persons at all times. As such, our moral duties are not dependent on feelings but on reason. They are unconditional, universally valid, and necessary, regardless of the possible consequences or opposition to our inclinations.

Kant's first formulation of his *categorical imperative* is, "Act only on that maxim whereby thou canst at the same time will that it would become a universal law." This imperative is given as the criterion (or second-order principle) by which to judge all other principles. If we could consistently will that everyone would do some type of action, then there is an application of the categorical imperative enjoining that type of action. If we cannot consistently will that everyone would do some type of action, then that type of action is morally wrong. Kant argues, for example, that we cannot consistently will that everyone make lying promises, for the very institution of promising entails or depends on general adherence to keeping the promise or an intention to do so.

Kant offers a second formulation of the categorical imperative: "So act as to treat humanity, whether in your own person or in that of any other, in every case as an end and never as merely a means only." Each person by virtue of his or her reason has dignity and profound worth, which entails that he or she must never be exploited or manipulated or merely used as a means to our idea of what is for the general good. Kant thought that this formulation was substantively identical with the first, but his view is controversial.

(A biographical sketch of Kant appears on p. 150.)

Study Questions

1. What is the aim of Kant's work? Why does he want to reject empirical (e.g., sociological and anthropological) data in constructing a "pure moral philosophy"?

2. What is the only quality which is good without qualification? Analyze Kant's reasoning here. Is it cogent?

3. Why does Kant deprecate the role of reason in producing happiness? Is his view of the purposive function of a faculty (e.g., our rational capacity, our will) in line with standard evolutionary theory?

4. What is the relationship between duty and inclination? Do acts done out of good inclination have any moral worth?

5. What is the role of consequences in moral reasoning? According to Kant, should we ask ourselves what are the likely consequences before we decide what to do?

6. What is the categorical imperative?

7. What is the difference between a maxim and a principle of universal law?

8. How does Kant illustrate the moral law? Do you see any problems with his examples? Is it clear that none of them could be universalized?

9. What is Kant's second formulation of the moral law? Is it different from or similar to his first formulation?

The Good Will

NOTHING CAN POSSIBLY be conceived in the world, or even out of it, which can be called good, without qualification, except a Good Will. Intelligence, wit, judgment, and the other *talents* of the mind, however they may be named, or courage, resolution, perseverance, as qualities of temperament, are undoubtedly good and desirable in many respects; but these gifts of nature may also become extremely bad and mischievous if the will which is to make use of them, and which, therefore, constitutes what is called *character*, is not good. It is the same with the *gifts of fortune*. Power, riches, honour, even health, and the general well-being and contentment with one's conditions which is called *happiness*, inspire pride, and often presumption, if there is not a good will to correct the influence of these on the mind, and with this also to rectify the whole principle of acting, and adapt it to its end. The sight of a being who is not adorned with a single feature of a pure and good will, enjoying unbroken prosperity, can never give pleasure to an

Reprinted from The Foundations of the Metaphysic of Morals, *translated by T. K. Abbott (this translation first published in 1873).*

imperial rational spectator. Thus a good will appears to constitute the indispensable condition even of being worthy of happiness.

There are even some qualities which are of service to this good will itself, and may facilitate its action, yet which have no intrinsic unconditional value, but always presuppose a good will, and this qualifies the esteem that we justly have for them, and does not permit us to regard them as absolutely good. Moderation in the affections and passions, self-control, and calm deliberation are not only good in many respects, but even seem to constitute part of the intrinsic worth of the person; but they are far from deserving to be called good without qualification, although they have been so unconditionally praised by the ancients. For without the principles of a good will, they may become extremely bad; and the coolness of a villain not only makes him far more dangerous, but also directly makes him more abominable in our eyes than he would have been without it.

A good will is good not because of what it performs or effects, not by its aptness for the attainment of some proposed end, but simply by virtue of the volition, that is, it is good in itself, and considered by itself to be esteemed much higher than all that can be brought about by it in favour of any inclination, nay, even of the sum-total of all inclinations. Even if it should happen that, owing to special disfavour of fortune, or the niggardly provision of a step-motherly nature, this will should wholly lack power to accomplish its purpose, if with its greatest efforts it should yet achieve nothing, and there should remain only the good will (not, to be sure, a mere wish, but the summoning of all means in our power), then, like a jewel, it would still shine by its own light, as a thing which has its whole value in itself. Its usefulness or fruitlessness can neither add to nor take away anything from this value. It would be, as it were, only the setting to enable us to handle it the more conveniently in common commerce, or to attract to it the attention of those who are not yet connoisseurs, but not to recommend it to true connoisseurs, or to determine its value.

Why Reason Was Made to Guide the Will

There is, however, something so strange in this idea of the absolute value of the mere will, in which no account is taken of its utility, that notwithstanding the thorough assent of even common reason to the idea, yet a suspicion must arise that it may perhaps really be the product of mere high-blown fancy, and that we may have misunderstood the purpose of nature in assigning reason as the governor of our will. Therefore we will examine this idea from this point of view.

In the physical constitution of an organized being, that is, a being adapted suitably to the purposes of life, we assume it as a fundamental principle that no organ for any purpose will be found but what is also the fittest and best adapted for that purpose. Now in a being which has reason and a will, if the proper object of nature were its *conservatism,* its *welfare,* in a word, its *happiness,* then nature would have hit upon a very bad arrangement in selecting the reason of the creature to carry out this purpose. For all the actions which the creature has to perform with a view to this purpose, and the whole rule of its conduct, would be far more surely prescribed to it by instinct, and that end would have been attained thereby much more certainly than it ever can be by reason. Should reason have been communicated to this favoured creature over and above, it must only have served it to contemplate the happy constitution of its nature, to admire it, to congratulate itself thereon, and to feel thankful for it to the beneficent cause, but not that it should subject its desires to that weak and delusive guidance, and meddle bunglingly with the purpose of nature. In a word, nature would have taken care that reason should not break forth into *practical exercise,* nor have the presumption, with its weak insight, to think out for itself the plan of happiness, and of the means of attaining it. Nature would not only have taken on herself the choice of the ends, but also of the means, and with wise foresight would have entrusted both to instinct.

And, in fact, we find that the more a cultivated reason applies itself with deliberate purpose to the enjoyment of life and happiness, so much the more does the man fail of true satisfaction. And from this circumstance there arises in many, if they are candid enough to confess it, a certain degree of *misology,* that is, hatred of reason, especially in the case of those who are most experienced in the use of it, because after calculating all the advantages they derive, I do not say from the invention of all the arts of common luxury, but even from the sciences (which seem to them to be after all only a luxury of the understanding), they find that they have, in fact, only brought more trouble on their shoulders, rather than gained in happiness; and they end by envying, rather than despising, the more common stamp of men who keep closer to the guidance of mere instinct, and do not allow their reason much influence on their conduct. And this we must admit, that the judgment of those who would very much lower the lofty eulogies of the advantages which reason gives us in regard to the happiness and satisfaction of life, or who would even reduce them below zero, is by no means morose or ungrateful to the goodness with which the world is governed, but that there lies at the root of these judgments the idea that our existence has a different and far nobler end, for which, and not for happiness, reason is properly intended, and which must, therefore, be regarded as the supreme condition to which the private ends of man must, for the most part, be postponed.

For as reason is not competent to guide the will with certainty in regard to its objects and the satisfaction of all our wants (which it to some extent even multiplies), this being an end to which an implanted instinct would have led with much greater certainty; and since, nevertheless, reason is imparted to us as a practical faculty, *i.e.* as one which is to have influence on the will, therefore, admitting that nature generally in the distribution of her capacities has adapted the means to the end, its true destination must be to produce a *will,* not merely good as a *means* to something else, but *good in itself,* for which reason was absolutely necessary. This will then, though not indeed the sole and complete good, must be the supreme good and the condition of every other, even of the desire of happiness. Under these circumstances, there is nothing inconsistent with the wisdom of nature in the fact that the cultivation of the reason, which is requisite for the first and unconditional purpose, does in many ways interfere, at least in this life, with the attainment of the second, which is always conditional, namely, happiness. Nay, it may even reduce it to nothing, without nature thereby failing in her purpose. For reason recognizes the establishment of a good will as its highest practical destination, and in attaining this purpose is capable only of a satisfaction of its own proper kind, namely, that from the attainment of an end, which end again is determined by reason only, notwithstanding that this may involve many a disappointment to the ends of inclination.

The First Proposition of Morality
[An action must be done from a sense of duty, if it is to have moral worth]

We have then to develop the notion of a will which deserves to be highly esteemed for itself, and is good without a view to anything further, a notion which exists already in the sound natural understanding, requiring rather to be cleared up than to be taught, and which in estimating the value of our actions always takes the first place, and constitutes the condition of all the rest. In order to do this, we will take the notion of duty, which includes that of a good will, although implying certain subjective restrictions and hindrances. These, however, far from concealing it, or rendering it unrecognizable, rather bring it out by contrast, and make it shine forth so much the brighter.

I omit here all actions which are already recognized as inconsistent with duty although they may be useful for this or that purpose, for with these the question whether they are done *from duty* cannot arise at all, since they even conflict with it. I also set aside those actions which really conform to duty, but to which men have *no* direct *inclination,* performing them because they are impelled thereto by some other inclination. For in this case we can readily distinguish whether the action which agrees with duty is done *from duty,* or from a selfish view. It is much harder to make this distinction when the action accords with duty, and the subject has besides a *direct* inclination to it. For example, it is always a matter of duty that a dealer should not overcharge an inexperienced purchaser; and wherever there is much commerce the prudent tradesman does not overcharge, but keeps a fixed price for everyone, so that a child buys of him as well as any other. Men are thus *honestly* served; but this is not enough to make us believe that the tradesman has so acted from duty and from principles of honesty: his own advantage required it; it is out of the question in this case to suppose that he might besides have a direct inclination in favour of the buyers, so that, as it were, from love he should give no advantage to one over another. Accordingly the action was done neither from duty nor from direct inclination, but merely with a selfish view.

On the other hand, it is a duty to maintain one's life; and, in addition, everyone has also a direct inclination to do so. But on this account the often anxious care which most men take for it has no intrinsic worth, and their maxim has no moral import. They preserve their life *as duty requires,* no doubt, but not *because duty requires.* On the other hand, if adversity and hopeless sorrow have completely taken away the relish for life; if the unfortunate one, strong in mind, indignant at his fate rather than desponding or dejected, wishes for death, and yet preserves his life without loving it—not from inclination or fear,

but from duty—then his maxim has a moral worth.

To be beneficent when we can is a duty; and besides this, there are many minds so sympathetically constituted that, without any other motive of vanity or self-interest, they find a pleasure in spreading joy around them, and can take delight in the satisfaction of others so far as it is their own work. But I maintain that in such a case an action of this kind, however proper, however amiable it may be, has nevertheless no true moral worth, but is on a level with other inclinations, *e.g.* the inclination to honour, which, if it is happily directed to that which is in fact of public utility and accordant with duty, and consequently honourable, deserves praise and encouragement, but not esteem. For the maxim lacks the moral import, namely, that such actions be done *from duty,* not from inclination. Put the case that the mind of that philanthropist was clouded by sorrow of his own, extinguishing all sympathy with the lot of others, and that while he still has the power to benefit others in distress, he is not touched by their trouble because he is absorbed with his own; and now suppose that he tears himself out of this dead insensibility, and performs the action without any inclination to it, but simply from duty, then first has his action its genuine moral worth. Further still; if nature has put little sympathy in the heart of this or that man; if he, supposed to be an upright man, is by temperament cold and indifferent to the sufferings of others, perhaps because in respect of his own he is provided with the special gift of patience and fortitude, and supposes, or even requires, that others should have the same—and such a man would certainly not be the meanest product of nature—but if nature had not specially framed him for a philanthropist, would he not still find in himself a source from whence to give himself a far higher worth than that of a good-natured temperament could be? Unquestionably. It is just in this that the moral worth of the character is brought out which is incomparably the highest of all, namely, that he is beneficent, not from inclination, but from duty.

To secure one's own happiness is a duty, at least indirectly; for discontent with one's condition, under a pressure of many anxieties and amidst unsatisfied wants, might easily become a great *temptation to transgression of duty*. But here again, without looking to duty, all men have already the strongest and most intimate inclination to happiness, because it is just in this idea that all inclinations are combined in one total. But the precept of happiness is often of such a sort that it greatly interferes with some inclinations, and yet a man cannot form any definite and certain conception of the sum of satisfaction of all of them which is called happiness. It is not then to be wondered at that a single inclination, definite both as to what it promises and as to the time within which it can be gratified, is often able to overcome such a fluctuating idea, and that a gouty patient, for instance, can choose to enjoy what he likes, and to suffer what he may, since, according to his calculation, on this occasion at least, he has [only] not sacrificed the enjoyment of the present moment to a possibly mistaken expectation of a happiness which is supposed to be found in health. But even in this case, if the general desire for happiness did not influence his will, and supposing that in his particular case health was not a necessary element in this calculation, there yet remains in this, as in all other cases, this law, namely, that he should promote his happiness not from inclination but from duty, and by this would his conduct first acquire true moral worth.

It is in this manner, undoubtedly, that we are to understand those passages of Scripture also in which we are commanded to love our neighbour, even our enemy. For love, as an affection, cannot be commanded, but beneficence for duty's sake may; even though we are not impelled to it by any inclination—nay, are even repelled by a natural and unconquerable aversion. This is *practical* love, and not *pathological**—a love which is seated in the will, and not in the propensions of sense—in principles of action and not of tender sympathy; and it is this love alone which can be commanded.

The Second Proposition of Morality

The second proposition is: That an action done from duty derives its moral worth, *not from the purpose* which is to be attained by it, but from the maxim by which it is determined, and therefore does not depend on the realization of the object of the action, but merely on the *principle of volition* by which the action has taken place, without regard to any object of desire. It is clear from what precedes that the purposes which we may have in view in our actions, or their effects regarded as ends and springs of the will, cannot give to actions any unconditional or moral worth. In what, then, can their worth lie, if it is not to consist in the will and in reference to its expected effect? It cannot lie anywhere but in the *principle of the will* without regard to the ends which can be attained by the action. For the will stands between its *à priori principle,* which is formal, and its *à posteriori* spring, which is material, as between two roads, and as it must be determined by something, it follows that it must be determined by the formal principle of volition when an action is done from duty, in which case every material principle has been withdrawn from it.

The Third Proposition of Morality

The third proposition, which is a consequence of the two preceding, I would express thus: *Duty is the necessity of acting from respect for the law*. I may have *inclination* for an object as the effect of my proposed action, but I cannot have *respect* for it, just for this reason, that it is an effect and not an energy of will. Similarly, I can-

* passional or emotional

not have respect for inclination, whether my own or another's; I can at most, if my own, approve it; if another's, sometimes even love it; *i.e.* look on it as favourable to my own interest. It is only what is connected with my will as a principle, by no means as an effect—what does not subserve my inclination, but overpowers it, or at least in case of choice excludes it from its calculation—in other words, simply the law of itself, which can be an object of respect, and hence a command. Now an action done from duty must wholly exclude the influence of inclination, and with it every object of the will, so that nothing remains which can determine the will except objectively the *law*, and subjectively *pure respect* for this practical law, and consequently the maxim that I should follow this law even to the thwarting of all my inclinations.

Thus the moral worth of an action does not lie in the effect expected from it, nor in any principle of action which requires to borrow its motive from this expected effect. For all these effects—agreeableness of one's condition, and even the promotion of the happiness of others—could have been also brought about by other causes, so that for this there would have been no need of the will of a rational being; whereas it is in this alone that the supreme and unconditional good can be found. The pre-eminent good which we call moral can therefore consist in nothing else than *the conception of law* in itself, *which certainly is only possible in a rational being*, in so far as this conception, and not the expected effect, determines the will. This is a good which is already present in the person who acts accordingly, and we have not to wait for it to appear first in the result.

The Supreme Principle of Morality: The Categorical Imperative

But what sort of law can that be, the conception of which must determine the will, even without paying any regard to the effect expected from it, in order that this will may be called good absolutely and without qualification? As I have deprived the will of every impulse which could arise to it from obedience to any law, there remains nothing but the universal conformity of its actions to law in general, which alone is to serve the will as a principle, *i.e.* I am never to act otherwise than so *that I could also will that my maxim should become a universal law.* Here, now, it is the simple conformity to law in general, without assuming any particular law applicable to certain actions, that serves the will as its principle, and must so serve it, if duty is not to be a vain delusion and a chimerical notion. The common reason of men in its practical judgments perfectly coincides with this, and always has in view the principle here suggested. Let the question be, for example: May I when in distress make a promise with the intention not to keep it? I readily distinguish here between the two significations which the question may have: Whether it is prudent, or whether it is right, to make a false promise? The former may undoubtedly often be the case. I see clearly indeed that it is not enough to extricate myself from a present difficulty by means of this subterfuge, but it must be well considered whether there may not hereafter spring from this lie much greater inconvenience than that from which I now free myself, and as, with all my supposed *cunning*, the consequences cannot be so easily foreseen but that credit once lost may be much more injurious to me than any mischief which I seek to avoid at present, it should be considered whether it would not be more *prudent* to act herein according to a universal maxim, and to make it a habit to promise nothing except with the intention of keeping it. But it is soon clear to me that such a maxim will still only be based on the fear of consequences. Now it is a wholly different thing to be truthful from duty, and to be so from apprehension of injurious consequences. In the first case, the very notion of the action already implies a law for me; in the second case, I must first look about elsewhere to see what results may be combined with it which would affect myself. For to deviate from the principle of duty is beyond all doubt wicked; but to be unfaithful to my maxim of prudence may often be very advantageous to me, although to abide by it is certainly safer. The shortest way, however, and an unerring one, to discover the answer to this question whether a lying promise is consistent with duty, is to ask myself, Should I be content that my maxim (to extricate myself from difficulty by a false promise) should hold good as a universal law, for myself as well as for others? and should I be able to say to myself, "Every one may make a deceitful promise when he finds himself in a difficulty from which he cannot otherwise extricate himself"? Then I presently become aware that while I can will the lie, I can by no means will that lying should be a universal law. For with such a law there would be no promises at all, since it would be in vain to allege my intention in regard to my future actions to those who would not believe this allegation, or if they over-hastily did so, would pay me back in my own coin. Hence my maxim, as soon as it should be made a universal law, would necessarily destroy itself.

I do not, therefore, need any far-reaching penetration to discern what I have to do in order that my will may be morally good. Inexperienced in the course of the world, incapable of being prepared for all its contingencies, I only ask myself: Canst thou also will that thy maxim should be a universal law? If not, then it must be rejected, and that not because of a disadvantage accruing from myself or even to others, but because it cannot enter as a principle into a possible universal legislation, and reason extorts from me immediate respect for such legislation. I do not indeed as yet *discern* on what this respect is based (this the philosopher may inquire), but at least I understand this, that it is an estimation of the worth which far outweighs all worth of what is recommended by inclination, and that the necessity of acting from *pure* respect for the practical law is what constitutes duty, to which every other motive must give place, because it is

the condition of a will being good *in itself,* and the worth of such a will is above everything.

Thus, then, without quitting the moral knowledge of common human reason, we have arrived at its principle. And although, no doubt, common men do not conceive it in such an abstract and universal form, yet they always have it really before their eyes, and use it as the standard of their decision. . . .

Nor could anything be more fatal to morality than that we should wish to derive it from examples. For every example of it that is set before me must be first itself tested by principles of morality, whether it is worthy to serve as an original example, *i.e.* as a pattern, but by no means can it authoritatively furnish the conception of morality. Even the Holy One of the Gospels must first be compared with our ideal of moral perfection before we can recognize Him as such; and so He says of Himself, "Why call ye Me [whom you see] good; none is good [the model of good] but God only [whom ye do not see]." But whence have we the conception of God as the supreme good? Simply from the *idea* of moral perfection, which reason frames *à priori,* and connects inseparably with the notion of a free will. Imitation finds no place at all in morality, and examples serve only for encouragement, *i.e.* they put beyond doubt the feasibility of what the law commands, they make visible that which the practical rule expresses more generally, but they can never authorize us to set aside the true original which lies in reason, and to guide ourselves by examples.

From what has been said, it is clear that all moral conceptions have their seat and origin completely *à priori* in the reason, and that, moreover, in the commonest reason just as truly as in that which is in the highest degree speculative; that they cannot be obtained by abstraction from any empirical, and therefore merely contingent knowledge; that it is just this purity of their origin that makes them worthy to serve as our supreme practical principle, and that just in proportion as we add anything empirical, we detract from their genuine influence, and from the absolute value of actions; that it is not only of the greatest necessity, in a purely speculative point of view, but is also of the greatest practical importance, to derive these notions and laws from pure reason, to present them pure and unmixed, and even to determine the compass of this practical or pure rational knowledge, *i.e.* to determine the whole faculty of pure practical reason; and, in doing so, we must not make its principles dependent on the particular nature of human reason, though in speculative philosophy this may be permitted, or may even at times be necessary; but since moral laws ought to hold good for every rational creature, we must derive them from the general concept of a rational being. In this way, although for its *application* to man morality has need of anthropology, yet, in the first instance, we must treat it independently as pure philosophy, *i.e.* as metaphysic, complete in itself (a thing which in such distinct branches of science is easily done); knowing well that unless we are in possession of this, it would not only be vain to determine the moral element of duty in right actions for purposes of speculative criticism, but it would be impossible to base morals on their genuine principles, even for common practical purposes, especially of moral instruction, so as to produce pure moral dispositions, and to engraft them on men's minds to the promotion of the greatest possible good in the world. . . .

The Rational Ground of the Categorical Imperative

. . . the question, how the imperative of *morality* is possible, is undoubtedly one, the only one, demanding a solution, as this is not at all hypothetical, and the objective necessity which it presents cannot rest on any hypothesis, as is the case with the hypothetical imperatives. Only here we must never leave out of consideration that we *cannot* make out *by any example*, in other words empirically, whether there is such an imperative at all; but it is rather to be feared that all those which seem to be categorical may yet be at bottom hypothetical. For instance, when the precept is: Thou shalt not promise deceitfully; and it is assumed that the necessity of this is not a mere counsel to avoid some other evil, so that it should mean: Thou shalt not make a lying promise, lest if it become known thou shouldst destroy thy credit, but that an action of this kind must be regarded as evil in itself, so that the imperative of the prohibition is categorical; then we cannot show with certainty in any example that the will was determined merely by the law, without any other spring of action, although it may appear to be so. For it is always possible that fear of disgrace, perhaps also obscure dread of other dangers, may have a secret influence on the will. Who can prove by experience the nonexistence of a cause when all that experience tells us is that we do not perceive it? But in such a case the so-called moral imperative, which as such appears to be categorical and unconditional, would in reality be only a pragmatic precept, drawing our attention to our own interests, and merely teaching us to take these into consideration.

We shall therefore have to investigate *à priori* the possibility of a categorical imperative, as we have not in this case the advantage of its reality being given in experience, so that [the elucidation of] its possibility should be requisite only for its explanation, not for its establishment. In the meantime it may be discerned beforehand that the categorical imperative alone has the purport of a practical law: all the rest may indeed be called *principles* of the will but not laws, since whatever is only necessary for the attainment of some arbitrary purpose may be considered as in itself contingent, and we can at any time be free from the precept if we give up the purpose: on the contrary, the unconditional command leaves the will no liberty to choose the opposite; consequently it alone carries with it that necessity which we require in a law.

Secondly, in the case of this categorical imperative or law of morality, the difficulty (of discerning its possibility) is a very profound one. It is an *à priori* synthetical practical proposition; and as there is so much difficulty in discerning the possibility of speculative propositions of this kind, it may readily be supposed that the difficulty will be no less with the practical.

First Formulation of the Categorical Imperative: Universal Law

In this problem we will first inquire whether the mere conception of a categorical imperative may not perhaps supply us also with the formula of it, containing the proposition which alone can be a categorical imperative; for even if we know the tenor of such an absolute command, yet how it is possible will require further special and laborious study, which we postpone to the last section.

When I conceive a hypothetical imperative, in general I do not know beforehand what it will contain until I am given the condition. But when I conceive a categorical imperative, I know at once what it contains. For as the imperative contains besides the law only the necessity that the maxims shall conform to this law, while the law contain no conditions restricting it, there remains nothing but the general statement that the maxim of the action should conform to a universal law, and it is this conformity alone that the imperative properly represents as necessary.

There is therefore but one categorical imperative, namely, this: *Act only on that maxim whereby thou canst at the same time will that it should become a universal law.*

Now if all imperatives of duty can be deduced from this one imperative as from their principle, then, although it should remain undecided whether what is called duty is not merely a vain notion, yet at least we shall be able to show what we understand by it and what this notion means.

Since the universality of the law according to which effects are produced constitutes what is properly called *nature* in the most general sense (as to form), that is the existence of things so far as it is determined by general laws, the imperative of duty may be expressed thus: *Act as if the maxim of thy action were to become by thy will a universal law of nature.*

Four Illustrations

We will now enumerate a few duties, adopting the usual division of them into duties to ourselves and to others, and into perfect and imperfect duties.

1. A man reduced to despair by a series of misfortunes feels wearied of life, but is still so far in possession of his reason that he can ask himself whether it would not be contrary to his duty to himself to take his own life. Now he inquires whether the maxim of his action could become a universal law of nature. His maxim is: From self-love I adopt it as a principle to shorten my life when its longer duration is likely to bring more evil than satisfaction. It is asked then simply whether this principle founded on self-love can become a universal law of nature. Now we see at once that a system of nature of which it should be a law to destroy life by means of the very feeling whose special nature it is to impel to the improvement of life would contradict itself, and therefore could not exist as a system of nature; hence that maxim cannot possibly exist as a universal law of nature, and consequently would be wholly inconsistent with the supreme principle of all duty.

2. Another finds himself forced by necessity to borrow money. He knows that he will not be able to repay it, but sees also that nothing will be lent to him, unless he promises stoutly to repay it in a definite time. He desires to make this promise, but he has still so much conscience as to ask himself: Is it not unlawful and inconsistent with duty to get out of a difficulty in this way? Suppose, however, that he resolves to do so, then the maxim of his action would be expressed thus: When I think myself in want of money, I will borrow money and promise to repay it, although I know that I never can do so. Now this principle of self-love or of one's own advantage may perhaps be consistent with my whole future welfare; but the question is, Is it

right? I change then the suggestion of self-love into a universal law, and state the question thus: How would it be if my maxim were a universal law? Then I see at once that it could never hold as a universal law of nature, but would necessarily contradict itself. For supposing it to be a universal law that everyone when he thinks himself in a difficulty should be able to promise whatever he pleases, with the purpose of not keeping his promise, the promise itself would become impossible, as well as the end that one might have in view in it, since no one would consider that anything was promised to him, but would ridicule all such statements as vain pretenses.

3. A third finds in himself a talent which with the help of some culture might make him a useful man in many respects. But he finds himself in comfortable circumstances, and prefers to indulge in pleasure rather than to take pains in enlarging and improving his happy natural capacities. He asks, however, whether his maxim of neglect of his natural gifts, besides agreeing with his inclination to indulgence, agrees also with what is called duty. He sees then that a system of nature could indeed subsist with such a universal law although men (like the South Sea islanders) should let their talents rest, and resolve to devote their lives merely to idleness, amusement, and propagation of their species—in a word, to enjoyment; but he cannot possibly *will* that this should be a universal law of nature, or be implanted in us as such by a natural instinct. For, as a rational being, he necessarily wills that his faculties be developed, since they serve him, and have been given him, for all sorts of possible purposes.

4. A fourth, who is in prosperity, while he sees that others have to contend with great wretchedness and that he could help them, thinks: What concern is it of mine? Let everyone be as happy as Heaven pleases, or as he can make himself; I will take nothing from him nor even envy him, only I do not wish to contribute anything to his welfare or to his assistance in distress! Now no doubt if such a mode of thinking were a universal law, the human race might very well subsist, and doubtless even better than in a state in which everyone talks of sympathy and good-will, or even takes care occasionally to put it into practice, but, on the other side, also cheats when he can, betrays the rights of men, or otherwise violates them. But although it is possible that a universal law of nature might exist in accordance with that maxim, it is impossible to *will* that such a principle should have the universal validity of a law of nature. For a will which resolved this would contradict itself, inasmuch as many cases might occur in which one would have need of the love and sympathy of others, and in which, by such a law of nature, sprung from his own will, he would deprive himself of all hope of the aid he desires.

These are a few of the many actual duties, or at least what we regard as such, which obviously fall into two classes on the one principle that we have laid down. We must be *able to will* that a maxim of our action should be a universal law. This is the canon of the moral appreciation of the action generally. Some actions are of such a character that their maxim cannot without contradiction be even *conceived* as a universal law of nature, far from it being possible that we should *will* that it *should* be so. In others this intrinsic impossibility is not found, but still it is impossible to *will* that their maxim should be raised to the universality of a law of nature, since such a will would contradict itself. It is easily seen that the former violate strict or rigorous (inflexible) duty; the latter only laxer (meritorious) duty. Thus it has been completely shown by these examples how all duties depend as regards the nature of the obligation (not the object of the action) on the same principle.

Second Formulation of the Categorical Imperative: Humanity as an End in Itself

. . . Now I say: man and generally any rational being *exists* as an end in himself, *not merely as a means* to be arbitrarily used by this or that will, but in all his actions, whether they concern himself or other rational beings, must be always regarded at the same time as an end. All objects of the inclinations have only a conditional worth; for if the inclinations and the wants founded on them did not exist, then their object would be without value. But the inclinations themselves being sources of want are so far from having an absolute worth for which they should be desired, that, on the contrary, it must be the universal wish of every rational being to be wholly free from them. Thus the worth of any object which is *to be acquired* by our action is always conditional. Beings whose existence depends not on our will but on nature's, have nevertheless, if they are nonrational beings, only a relative value as means, and are therefore called *things;* rational beings, on the contrary, are called *persons,* because their very nature points them out as ends in themselves, that is as something which must not be used merely as means, and so far therefore restricts freedom of action (and is an object of respect). These, therefore, are not merely subjective ends whose existence has a worth *for us* as an effect of our action, but *objective ends,* that is things whose existence is an end in itself: an end moreover for which no other can be substituted, which they should subserve *merely* as means, for otherwise nothing whatever would possess *absolute worth;* but if all worth were conditioned and therefore contingent, then there would be no supreme practical principle of reason whatever.

If then there is a supreme practical principle or, in respect of the human will, a categorical imperative, it must be one which, being drawn from the conception of that which is necessarily an end for everyone because it is *an end in itself,* constitutes an *objective* principle of will, and can therefore serve as a universal practical law. The foundation of this principle is: *rational nature exists as an end in itself.* Man necessarily conceives his own existence as being so: so far then this is a *subjective* principle of human actions. But every other rational being regards its existence similarly, just on the same rational principle that holds for me: so that it is at the same time an ob-

jective principle, from which as a supreme practical law all laws of the will must be capable of being deduced. Accordingly the practical imperative will be as follows: *So act as to treat humanity, whether in thine own person or in that of any other, in every case as an end withal, never as means only. . . .*

. . . Looking back now on all previous attempts to discover the principle of morality, we need not wonder why they all failed. It was seen that man was bound to laws by duty, but it was not observed that the laws to which he is subject are *only those of his own giving,* though at the same time they are *universal,* and that he is only bound to act in conformity with his own will; a will, however, which is designed by nature to give universal laws. For when one has conceived man only as subject to a law (no matter what), then this law required some interest, either by way of attraction or constraint, since it did not originate as a law from *his own* will, but his will was according to a law obliged by *something else* to act in a certain manner. Now by this necessary consequence all the labour spent in finding a supreme principle of *duty* was irrevocably lost. For men never elicited duty, but only a necessity of acting from a certain interest. Whether this interest was private or otherwise, in any case the imperative must be conditional, and could not by any means be capable of being a moral command. I will therefore call this the principle of *Autonomy* of the will, in contrast with every other which I accordingly reckon as *Heteronomy.*

The Kingdom of Ends

The conception of every rational being as one which must consider itself as giving in all the maxims of its will universal laws, so as to judge itself and its actions from this point of view—this conception leads to another which depends on it and is very fruitful, that of a *kingdom of ends.*

By a *kingdom* I understand the union of different rational beings in a system by common laws. Now since it is by laws that ends are determined as regards their universal validity, hence, if we abstract from the personal differences of rational beings, and likewise from all the content of their private ends, we shall be able to conceive all ends combined in a systematic whole (including both rational beings as ends in themselves, and also the special ends which each may propose to himself), that is to say, we can conceive a kingdom of ends, which on the preceding principles is possible.

For all rational beings come under the *law* that each of them must treat itself and all others *never merely as means,* but in every case *at the same time as ends in themselves.* Hence results a systematic union of rational beings by common objective laws, *i.e.,* a kingdom which may be called a kingdom of ends, since what these laws have in view is just the relation of these beings to one another as ends and means. . . .

For Further Reflection

1. Is Kant's philosophy merely a development of the Golden Rule: "Do unto others what you would have them do unto you"? If it is equivalent, does it make Kant's system more intuitively plausible? But does it also lead to problems with what Kant thought to be the implications of his system? For example, on the basis of the Golden Rule one might endorse certain instances of euthanasia, but Kant's discussion of suicide seems to rule this out.

2. Kant's ethics are called deontological (from the Greek word for "duty") because he believes that the value of an act is in the act itself rather than in its consequences (as teleologists hold). Deontological ethics have been criticized as being too rigid. Do you think that this is true? Should the notion of consequences be taken into consideration?

3. How would Kant deal with moral conflicts? When two universal principles conflict, how would Kant resolve the dilemma?

4. Kant's categorical imperative has also been criticized for being more wide open than he realized, for it doesn't limit what could be universalized. How would Kant respond to these counter-examples: (1) Everyone should tie his right shoe before his left shoe; (2) All retarded or senile people should be executed by the government (adding, if I should become retarded or senile, I should also undergo this fate).

VI.9   Utilitarianism Is the Correct Moral Theory

JOHN STUART MILL

John Stuart Mill (1806–1873), one of the most important British philosophers of the nineteenth century, was born in London and educated by his father, learning Greek at the age of three and Latin at the age of eight. By the time he was fourteen he had received a thorough classical education at home. He began work as a clerk for the East India Company at the age of seventeen and eventually became director of the company. He was elected to Parliament in 1865. A man of liberal ideas and a penetrating mind, he made significant contributions to logic, philosophy of science, philosophy of religion, political theory, and ethics. His principal works are *A System of Logic* (1843), *Utilitarianism* (1863), *On Liberty* (1859), and *The Subjection of Women* (1869).

Mill defends utilitarianism, a form of teleological ethics, against more rule-bound deontological systems, the sort of system we considered in the last selection, Kant's categorical imperative. *Teleological* is from the Greek "telos," which means "end" or "goal." That is, the standard of right or wrong action for the teleologists is the comparative consequences of the available actions. That act is right which produces the best consequences. Whereas the deontologist is concerned only with the rightness of the act itself, the teleologist asserts that there is no such thing as an act having intrinsic worth. While there is something intrinsically bad about lying for the deontologist, the only thing wrong with lying for the teleologist is the bad consequences it produces. If you can reasonably calculate that a lie will do even slightly more good than telling the truth, you have an obligation to lie.

The present selection was written against the background of a debate over Jeremy Bentham's hedonistic version of utilitarianism, which failed to differentiate between kinds and quality of pleasure, and so received the name of "pig philosophy." Mill meets this charge by substituting a more complex theory of happiness for Bentham's undifferentiated pleasure.

Study Questions

1. How does Mill define utilitarianism?
2. How does Mill reply to the charge that utilitarianism is a pig philosophy?
3. What test is there to distinguish the higher pleasures from the lower?
4. What is meant by "Better to be Socrates dissatisfied than a pig satisfied"?
5. Why do some people prefer the lower pleasures?
6. How can utilitarianism attain its end?
7. Why do some critics say that utilitarianism sets too high a standard for humanity?
8. What is Mill's "proof" of the truth of utilitarianism? Is it a clear and cogent argument?

What Utilitarianism Is

. . . THE CREED WHICH ACCEPTS as the foundation of morals, Utility, or the Greatest Happiness Principle, holds that actions are right in proportion as they tend to promote happiness, wrong as they tend to produce the reverse of happiness. By happiness is intended pleasure, and the absence of pain; by unhappiness, pain, and the privation of pleasure. To give a clear view of the moral standard set up by the theory, much more requires to be said; in particular, what things it includes in the ideas of pain and pleasure; and to what extent this is left an open question. But these supplementary explanations do not affect the theory of life on which this theory of morality is grounded—namely, that pleasure, and freedom from pain, are the only things desirable as ends; and that all desirable things (which are as numerous in the utilitarian as in any other scheme) are desirable either for the pleasure inherent in themselves, or as a means to the promotion of pleasure and the prevention of pain.

Now, such a theory of life excites in many minds, and among them in some of the most es-

From *John Stuart Mill*, Utilitarianism *(1861), chapters 2 and 4.*

timable in feeling and purpose, inveterate dislike. To suppose that life has (as they express it) no higher end than pleasure—no better and nobler object of desire and pursuit—they designate as utterly mean and grovelling; as a doctrine worthy only of swine, to whom the followers of Epicurus were, at a very early period, contemptuously likened; and modern holders of the doctrine are occasionally made the subject of equally polite comparisons by its German, French, and English assailants.

When thus attacked, the Epicureans have always answered, that it is not they, but their accusers, who represent human nature in a degrading light; since the accusation supposes human beings to be capable of no pleasures except those of which swine are capable. If this supposition were true, the charge could not be gainsaid, but would then be no longer an imputation; for if the sources of pleasure were precisely the same to human beings and to swine, the rule of life which is good enough for the one would be good enough for the other. The comparison of the Epicurean life to that of beasts is felt as degrading, precisely because a beast's pleasures do not satisfy a human being's conception of happiness. Human beings have faculties more elevated than the animal appetites, and when once made conscious of them, do not regard anything as happiness which does not include their gratification. I do not, indeed, consider the Epicureans to have been by an means faultless in drawing out their scheme of consequences from the utilitarian principle. To do this in any sufficient manner, many Stoic, as well as Christian elements require to be included. But there is no known Epicurean theory of life which does not assign to the pleasures of the intellect, of the feelings and imagination, and of the moral sentiments, a much higher value as pleasures than to those of mere sensation. It must be admitted, however, that utilitarian writers in general have placed the superiority of mental over bodily pleasures chiefly in the greater permanency, safety, uncostliness, etc., of the former—that is, in their

circumstantial advantages rather than in their intrinsic nature. And on all these points utilitarians have fully proved their case; but they might have taken the other, and, as it may be called, higher ground, with entire consistency. It is quite compatible with the principle of utility to recognise the fact, that some *kinds* of pleasure are more desirable and more valuable than others. It would be absurd that while, in estimating all other things, quality is considered as well as quantity, the estimation of pleasures should be supposed to depend on quantity alone.

If I am asked, what I mean by difference of quality in pleasures, or what makes one pleasure more valuable than another, merely as a pleasure, except its being greater in amount, there is but one possible answer. Of two pleasures, if there be one which all or almost all who have experience of both give a decided preference, irrespective of any feeling of moral obligation to prefer it, that is the more desirable pleasure. If one of the two is, by those who are competently acquainted with both, placed so far above the other that they prefer it, even though knowing it to be attended with a great amount of discontent, and would not resign it for any quantity of the other pleasure which their nature is capable of, we are justified in ascribing to the preferred enjoyment a superiority in quality, so far outweighing quantity as to render it, in comparison, of small account.

Now it is an unquestionable fact that those who are equally acquainted with, and equally capable of appreciating and enjoying, both, do give a most marked preference to the manner of existence which employs their higher faculties. Few human creatures would consent to be changed into any of the lower animals, for a promise of the fullest allowance of a beast's pleasures; no intelligent human being would consent to be a fool, no instructed person would be an ignoramus, no person of feeling and conscience would be selfish and base, even though they should be persuaded that the fool, the dunce, or the rascal is better satisfied with his lot than they are with theirs. They would not resign what they possess more than he for the most complete satisfaction of all the desires which they have in common with him. If they ever fancy they would, it is only in cases of unhappiness so extreme, that to escape from it they would exchange their lot for almost any other, however undesirable in their own eyes. A being of higher faculties requires more to make him happy, is capable probably of more acute suffering, and certainly accessible to it at more points, than one of an inferior type; but in spite of these liabilities, he can never really wish to sink into what he feels to be a lower grade of existence. We may give what explanation we please of this unwillingness; we may attribute it to pride, a name which is given indiscriminately to some of the most and to some of the least estimable feelings of which mankind are capable; we may refer it to the love of liberty and personal independence, an appeal to which was with the Stoics one of the most effective means for the inculcation of it; to the love of power, or to the love of excitement, both of which do really enter into and contribute to it: but its most appropriate appellation is a sense of dignity, which all human beings possess in one form or another, and in some, though by no means in exact, proportion to their higher faculties, and which is so essential a part of the happiness of those in whom it is strong, that nothing which conflicts with it could be, otherwise than momentarily, an object of desire to them. Whoever supposes that this preference takes place at a sacrifice of happiness—that the superior being, in anything like equal circumstances, is not happier than the inferior—confounds the two very different ideas, of happiness, and content. It is indisputable that the being whose capacities of enjoyment are low, has the greatest chance of having them fully satisfied; and a highly endowed being will always feel that any happiness which he can look for, as the world is constituted, is imperfect. But he can learn to bear its imperfections, if they are at all bearable; and they will not make him envy the being who is indeed unconscious of the imperfections, but only because he feels not at all the good which those imperfections qualify. It is better to be a human being dissatisfied than a pig satisfied; better to be Socrates dissatisfied than a fool satisfied. And if the fool, or the pig, are of a different opinion, it is because they only know their own side of the question. The other party to the comparison knows both sides.

It may be objected, that many who are capable of the higher pleasures, occasionally, under the influence of temptation, postpone them to the lower. But this is quite compatible with a full appreciation of the intrinsic superiority of the higher. Men often, from infirmity of character, make their election for the nearer good, though they know it to be the less valuable; and this no less when the choice is between two bodily pleasures, than when it is between bodily and mental. They pursue sensual indulgences to the injury of health, though perfectly aware that health is the greater good. It may be further objected, that many who begin with youthful enthusiasm for everything noble, as they advance in years sink into indolence and selfishness. But I do not believe that those who undergo this very common change, voluntarily choose the lower description of pleasures in preference to the higher. I believe that before they devote themselves exclusively to the one, they have already become incapable of the other. Capacity for the nobler feelings is in most natures a very tender plant, easily killed, not only by hostile influences, but by mere want of sustenance; and in the majority of young persons it speedily dies away if the occupations to which their position in life has devoted them, and the society into which it has thrown them, are not favourable to keeping that higher capacity in exercise. Men lose their high aspirations as they lose their intellectual tastes, because they have not time or opportunity for indulging them; and they addict themselves to inferior pleasures, not because they deliberately prefer them, but because they are either the only ones to which they have access, or the only ones which they are any longer capable of enjoying. It may be questioned whether any one who has remained equally susceptible to both classes of pleasures, ever knowingly and calmly preferred the lower; though many, in all ages, have broken down in an ineffectual attempt to combine both.

From this verdict of the only competent judges, I apprehend there can be no appeal. On a question which is the best worth having of two pleasures, or which of two modes of existence is the most grateful to the feelings, apart from its moral attributes and from its consequences, the judgment of those who are qualified by knowledge of both, or, if they differ, that of the majority among them, must be admitted as final. And there needs to be the less hesitation to accept this judgment respecting the quality of pleasures, since there is no other tribunal to be referred to even on the question of quantity. What means are there of determining which is the acutest of two pains, or the intensest of two pleasurable sensations, except the general suffrage of those who are familiar with both? Neither pains nor pleasures are homogeneous, and pain is always heterogeneous with pleasure. What is there to decide whether a particular pleasure is worth purchasing at the cost of a particular pain, except the feelings and judgment of the experienced? When, therefore, those feelings and judgment declare the pleasures derived from the higher faculties to be preferable *in kind*, apart from the question of intensity, to those of which the animal nature, disjoined from the higher faculties, is susceptible, they are entitled on this subject to the same regard.

I have dwelt on this point, as being a necessary part of a perfectly just conception of Utility or Happiness, considered as the directive rule of human conduct. But it is by no means an indispensable condition to the acceptance of the utilitarian standard; for that standard is not the agent's own greatest happiness, but the greatest amount of happiness altogether; and if it may possibly be doubted whether a noble character is always the happier for its nobleness, there can be

no doubt that it makes other people happier, and that the world in general is immensely a gainer by it. Utilitarianism, therefore, could only attain its end by the general cultivation of nobleness of character, even if each individual were only benefited by the nobleness of others, and his own, so far as happiness is concerned, were a sheer deduction from the benefit. But the bare enunciation of such an absurdity as this last, renders refutation superfluous.

According to the Greatest Happiness Principle, as above explained, the ultimate end, with reference to and for the sake of which all other things are desirable (whether we are considering our own good or that of other people), is an existence exempt as far as possible from pain, and as rich as possible in enjoyments, both in point of quantity and quality; the test of quality, and the rule for measuring it against quantity, being the preference felt by those who in their opportunities of experience, to which must be added their habits of self-consciousness and self-observation, are best furnished with the means of comparison. This, being, according to the utilitarian opinion, the end of human action, is necessarily also the standard of morality; which may accordingly be defined, the rules and precepts for human conduct, by the observance of which an existence such as has been described might be, to the greatest extent possible, secured to all mankind; and not to them only, but, so far as the nature of things admits, to the whole sentient creation. . . .

The objectors to utilitarianism cannot always be charged with representing it in a discreditable light. On the contrary, those among them who entertain anything like a just idea of its disinterested character, sometimes find fault with its standard as being too high for humanity. They say it is exacting too much to require that people shall always act from the inducement of promoting the general interests of society. But this is to mistake the very meaning of a standard of morals, and confound the rule of action with the motive of it. It is the business of ethics to tell us what are our duties, or by what test we may know them; but no system of ethics requires that the sole motive of all we do shall be a feeling of duty; on the contrary, ninety-nine hundredths of all our actions are done from other motives, and rightly so done, if the rule of duty does not condemn them. It is the more unjust to utilitarianism that this particular misapprehension should be made a ground of objection to it, inasmuch as utilitarian moralists have gone beyond almost all others in affirming that the motive has nothing to do with the morality of the action, though much with the worth of the agent. He who saves a fellow-creature from drowning does what is morally right, whether his motive be duty, or the hope of being paid for his trouble; he who betrays the friend that trusts him, is guilty of a crime, even if his object be to serve another friend to whom he is under greater obligation. But to speak only of actions done from the motive of duty, and in direct obedience to principle: it is a misapprehension of the utilitarian mode of thought, to conceive it as implying that people should fix their minds upon so wide a generality as the world, or society at large. The great majority of good actions are intended not for the benefit of the world, but for that of individuals, of which the good of the world is made up; and the thoughts of the most virtuous man need not on these occasions travel beyond the particular persons concerned, except so far as is necessary to assure himself that in benefiting them he is not violating the rights, that is, the legitimate and authorised expectations, of any one else. The multiplication of happiness is, according to the utilitarian ethics, the object of virtue: the occasions on which any person (except one in a thousand) has it in his power to do this on an extended scale, in other words to be a public benefactor, are but exceptional; and on these occasions alone is he called on to consider public utility; in every other case, private utility, the interest or happiness of some few persons, is all he has to attend to. Those alone the influence of whose actions extends to society in general, need

concern themselves habitually about so large an object. In the case of abstinences indeed—of things which people forbear to do from moral considerations, though the consequences in the particular case might be beneficial—it would be unworthy of an intelligent agent not to be consciously aware that the action is of a class which, if practised generally, would be generally injurious, and that this is the ground of the obligation to abstain from it. The amount of regard for the public interest implied in this recognition, is no greater than is demanded by every system of morals, for they all enjoin to abstain from whatever is manifestly pernicious to society. . . .

Chapter IV   Of What Sort of Proof the Principle of Utility Is Susceptible

It has already been remarked, that questions of ultimate ends do not admit of proof, in the ordinary acceptation of the term. To be incapable of proof by reasoning is common to all first principles; to the first premises of our knowledge, as well as to those of our conduct. But the former, being matters of fact, may be the subject of a direct appeal to the faculties which judge of fact—namely, our senses, and our internal consciousness. Can an appeal be made to the same faculties on questions of practical ends? Or by what other faculty is cognisance taken of them?

Questions abouts ends are, in other words, questions what things are desirable. The utilitarian doctrine is, that happiness is desirable, and the only thing desirable, as an end; all other things being only desirable as means to that end. What ought to be required of this doctrine—what conditions is it requisite that the doctrine should fulfil—to make good its claim to be believed?

The only proof capable of being given that an object is visible, is that people actually see it. The only proof that a sound is audible, is that people hear it: and so of the other sources of our experience. In like manner, I apprehend, the sole evidence it is possible to produce that anything is desirable, is that people do actually desire it. If the end which the utilitarian doctrine proposes to itself were not, in theory and in practice, acknowledged to be an end, nothing could ever convince any person that it was so. No reason can be given why the general happiness is desirable, except that each person, so far as he believes it to be attainable, desires his own happiness. This, however, being a fact, we have not only all the proof which the case admits of, but all which it is possible to require, that happiness is a good: that each person's happiness is a good to that person, and the general happiness, therefore, a good to the aggregate of all persons. Happiness has made out its title as *one* of the ends of conduct, and consequently one of the criteria of morality.

But it has not, by this alone, proved itself to be the sole criterion. To do that, it would seem, by the same rule, necessary to show, not only that people desire happiness, but that they never desire anything else. . . .

We have now, then, an answer to the question, of what sort of proof the principle of utility is susceptible. If the opinion which I have now stated is psychologically true—if human nature is so constituted as to desire nothing which is not either a part of happiness or a means of happiness, we can have no other proof, and we require no other, that these are the only things desirable. If so, happiness is the sole end of human action, and the promotion of it the test by which to judge of all human conduct; from whence it necessarily follows that it must be the criterion of morality, since a part is included in the whole.

And now to decide whether this is really so; whether mankind do desire nothing for itself but that which is a pleasure to them, or of which the absence is a pain; we have evidently arrived at a question of fact and experience, dependent, like all similar questions, upon evidence. It can only be determined by practised self-consciousness and self-observation, assisted by observation of others. I believe that these sources of evidence, impartially consulted, will declare that desiring a thing and finding it pleasant, aversion to it and thinking of it as painful, are phenomena entirely inseparable, or rather two parts of the same phenomenon; in strictness of language, two different modes of naming the same psychological fact: that to think of an object as desirable (unless for the sake of its consequences), and to think of it as pleasant, are one and the same thing; and that to desire anything, except in proportion as the idea of it is pleasant, is a physical and metaphysical impossibility.

For Further Reflection

1. To better grasp the difference between utilitarianism and deontological ethics, consider this example. Suppose a raft floating in the Pacific Ocean. On the raft are two men starving to death. One day they discover some food in an inner compartment of a box on the raft. They have reason to believe that the food will be sufficient to keep one of them alive until the raft reaches a certain island where help is available, but if they share the food, both will most likely die. Now, one of these men is a brilliant scientist who has in his mind the cure for cancer. The other man is undistinguished. Otherwise there is no relevant difference between the two. What is the morally right thing to do? Share the food and hope against the odds for a miracle? Flip a coin to see which man gets the food? Give the food to the scientist?

If you voted to flip a coin or share the food, you sided with the deontologist, but if you voted to give the food to the scientist, you sided with the teleologist, the utilitarian, who would calculate that there would be greater good accomplished as a result of the scientist getting the food and living than in any of the other likely outcomes.

It has often been admitted that utilitarianism could easily be misused. If people tried to "play God" and decide each case on the basis of what they thought would be the "best" consequences, chaos might result, so that some utilitarians have advocated keeping their doctrine a secret. What do you think of both the prediction of the anti-utilitarian consequences of widespread utilitarianism and the prescription of keeping the doctrine a secret?

2. John Rawls has argued that the fault of utilitarianism is that it makes a false inference from what one is allowed to do with one's own life to what one is allowed to do with other people's lives. We often have a right to forego some present enjoyment for the sake of a future personal higher goal, but, he argues, we have not the same right to restrict some other person from a present enjoyment for what you deem to be his higher future goal. That is, utilitarianism is a paternalistic violator of human rights. It treats rights as expendable. Do you agree with this criticism?

3. What do you see as the overall merits and liabilities of deontological and utilitarian systems? Where do you stand at this juncture?

4. Nietzsche wrote, "If we possess our *why* of life we can put up with almost any *how*— Man does not strive after happiness; only the Englishman does that" (Friedrich Nietzsche, *Twilight of the Idols*). Do you agree or disagree with Nietzsche on the unimportance of the search for happiness?

A Reconciliation of Two Systems of Ethics VI.10

WILLIAM FRANKENA

William Frankena was raised in a Dutch community in Michigan and graduated from Calvin College. He has recently retired from a long career as professor of philosophy at the University of Michigan. He is the author of several works in ethical theory, including *Ethics* (1963), one of the most helpful books in ethical theory, from which the present reading is taken.

Frankena argues that both utilitarianism and deontological ethics have strengths and weaknesses. Utilitarianism, among other things, has the fault of not respecting rights or the principle of justice. Deontological theories often fail to see that "morality is made for man, not man for morality," and become rigidly rule bound. Frankena opts for a compromise system with two principles: beneficence and justice, thus producing a system that is basically deontological but preserves the truth of utilitarianism.

Study Questions

1. Why must the two principles in Frankena's system be regarded as creating *prima facie* duties (see glossary) and not actual duties?

2. Does Frankena's system offer a decision-making formula for deciding which principle to use on every occasion of conflict?

3. What does Frankena mean by "morality is made for man, not man for morality"? Do you know the original saying of which this is a paraphrase? Does it throw light on Frankena's position?

4. What does Frankena mean by the principle of utility? What more general principle is presupposed by the principle of utility? Why does Frankena prefer it to the principle of utility?

5. What does Frankena mean by justice and why can't beneficence be derived from justice?

6. What is an "imperfect duty"?

7. Describe Frankena's principle of justice. Which of the competing views does Frankena choose?

8. How does Frankena deal with moral conflict of principles?

I. My Proposed Theory of Obligation

SO FAR IN THIS CHAPTER I have been trying to show that we cannot be satisfied with the principle of utility as our sole basic standard of right and wrong in morality, whether it is applied in AU, GU, or RU* style. In particular, I have contended that we should recognize a principle of justice to guide our distribution of good and evil that is independent of any principle about maximizing the balance of good over evil in the world. It may still be, of course, that we should recognize other independent principles as well, as deontologists like Ross think, e.g., that of keeping promises. Now I shall try to present the theory of obligation that seems to me most satisfactory from the moral point of view.

What precedes suggests that perhaps we should recognize two basic principles of obligation, the principle of utility and some principle of justice. The resulting theory would be a deontological one, but it would be much closer to utilitarianism than most deontological theories; we might call it a *mixed deontological theory*. It might maintain that all of our more specific rules of obligation, like that of keeping promises, and all of our judgments about what to do in particular situations can be derived, directly or indirectly, from its two principles. It might even insist that we are to determine what is right or wrong in particular situations, normally at least, by consulting rules such as we usually associate with morality, but add that the way to tell what rules to live by is to see which rules best fulfill the joint requirements of utility and justice (not, as in RU,

the requirements of utility alone). This view is still faced with the problem of measuring and balancing amounts of good and evil, and, since it recognizes two basic principles, it must also face the problem of possible conflict between them. This means that it must regard its two principles as principles of prima facie, not of actual duty; and it must, if our above argument is correct, allow that the principle of justice may take precedence over that of utility, at least on some occasions, though perhaps not always. However, it may not be able to provide any formula saying when justice takes precedence and when it does not.

Should we adopt this theory of obligation? To my mind, it is close to the truth but not quite right. Let us begin, however, by asking whether we should recognize the principle of utility at all. It seems to me we must at least recognize something like it as one of our basic premises. Whether we have even a prima facie obligation to maximize the balance of good over evil depends, in part, on whether it makes sense to talk about good and evil in quantitative terms. Assuming that it makes at least rough sense, it is not easy to deny, as pure deontologists do, that one of the things we ought to do, other things being equal, is to bring about as much of a balance of good over evil as we can, which even Ross, Carritt, and perhaps Butler, allow. I find it hard to believe that any action or rule can be right, wrong, or obligatory in the moral sense, if there is no good or evil connected with it in any way, directly or indirectly. This does not mean that there are no other factors affecting their rightness or wrongness, or that our only duty is to pile up the biggest possible stockpile of what is good, as utilitarians think; but it does imply that

* [Act Utilitarianism, General Utilitarianism, and rule Utilitarianism—ed. note]

From Ethics, *second edition* © *1973, pp. 43–53. Reprinted by permission of Prentice-Hall, Inc. and the author.*

we do have, at least as one of our prima facie obligations, that of doing something about the good and evil in the world.

In fact, I wish to contend that we do not have any moral obligations, prima facie or actual, to do anything that does not, directly or indirectly, have some connection with what makes somebody's life good or bad, better or worse. If not our particular actions, then at least our rules must have some bearing on the increase of good or decrease of evil or on their distribution. Morality was made for man, not man for morality. Even justice is concerned about the distribution *of good and evil*. In other words, all of our duties, even that of justice, *presuppose* the existence of good and evil and some kind of concern about their existence and incidence. To this extent, and only to this extent, is the old dictum that love is what underlies and unifies the rules of morality correct. It is the failure to recognize the importance of this point that makes so many deontological systems unsatisfactory.

To say this is to say not only that we have no obligations except when some improvement or impairment of someone's life is involved but also that we have a prima facie obligation *whenever* this is involved. To quote William James's inimitable way of putting it:

Take any demand, however slight, which any creature, however weak, may make. Ought it not, for its own sole sake, to be satisfied? If not, prove why not. [1]

II. The Principle of Beneficence

If this is so, then we must grant that the utilitarians have hold of an important part of the truth, and that we must recognize something like the principle of utility as one of our basic premises. Still, I do not think that we can regard the principle of utility itself as a basic premise, and my reason is that something more basic underlies it. By the principle of utility I have meant and shall continue to mean, quite strictly, the principle that we ought to do the act or follow the practice or rule that will or probably will bring about *the*

greatest possible balance of good over evil in the universe. It seems clear, however, that this principle presupposes another one that is more basic, namely, that we ought to do good and to prevent or avoid doing harm. If we did not have this more basic obligation, we could have no duty to try to realize the greatest balance of good over evil. In fact, the principle of utility represents a compromise with the ideal. The ideal is to do only good and not to do any harm (omitting justice for the moment). But this is often impossible, and then we seem forced to try to bring about the best possible balance of good over evil. If this is so, then the principle of utility presupposes a more basic principle—that of producing good as such and preventing evil. We have a prima facie obligation to maximize the balance of good over evil only if we have a *prior* prima facie obligation to do good and prevent harm. I shall call this prior principle the *principle of beneficence*. The reason I call it the principle of *beneficence* and not the principle of *benevolence* is to underline the fact that it asks us actually to do good and not evil, not merely to want or will to do so.

It might be thought that the principle of utility not only presupposes the principle of beneficence but follows from it. This, however, is not the case. The principle of utility is stated in quantitative terms and presupposes that goods and evils can be measured and balanced in some way. The principle of beneficence does not deny this, of course, but neither does it imply this. In applying it in practice one hopes that goods and evils can to a considerable extent at least be measured and balanced, but the principle of beneficence does not itself require that this be always possible; it is, for example, compatible with Mill's insistence that pleasures and pains, and hence goods and evils, differ in quality as well as quantity. I take this to be an advantage of the principle of beneficence over that of utility as I have stated it. There is another advantage. Suppose we have two acts, A and B, and that A produces 99 units of good and no evil, while B produces both good and evil but has a net balance of 100 units of good over evil. In this case, act-utilitarianism requires us to say that B is the right thing to do. But some of us would surely think that act A is the right one, and the principle of beneficence permits one to say this, though it does not require us to do so.

I propose, then, that we take as the basic premises of our theory of right and wrong two principles, that of beneficence and some principle of just distribution. To this proposal it might be objected that, although the principle of justice cannot be derived from that of beneficence, it is possible to derive the principle of beneficence from that of justice. For, if one does not increase the good of others and decrease evil for them when one can do so and when no conflicting obligations are present, then one is being unjust. Hence, justice implies beneficence (when possible and not ruled out by other considerations). In reply, I want to agree that in some sense beneficence is *right* and failure to be beneficent *wrong* under the conditions specified, but I want to deny that they are, respectively, just or unjust, properly speaking. Not everything that is right is just, and not everything that is wrong is unjust. Incest, even if it is wrong, can hardly be called unjust. Cruelty to children may be unjust, if it involves treating them differently from adults, but it is surely wrong anyway. Giving another person pleasure may be right, without its being properly called just at all. The area of justice is a part of morality but not the whole of it. Beneficence, then, may belong to the other part of morality, and this is just what seems to me to be the case. Even Mill makes a distinction between justice and the other obligations of morality, and puts charity or beneficence among the latter. So does Portia when she says to Shylock,

And earthly power doth then show likest God's
When mercy seasons justice.

It has been contended, nevertheless, that we do not have, properly speaking, a duty or obligation to be beneficent. From this point of view, being beneficent is considered praiseworthy and

virtuous, but is beyond the call of moral *duty*. All that morality can demand of us is justice, keeping promises, and the like, not beneficence. There is some truth in this. It is not always strictly wrong not to perform an act of beneficence even when one can, for example, not giving someone else one's concert ticket. Not giving him the ticket is only strictly wrong if he has a *right* to my beneficence, and this he does not always have. It may still be, however, that in some wider sense of "ought," I ought to be beneficent, perhaps even to give my ticket to another who needs it more. Kant made a similar point by saying that beneficence is an "imperfect" duty; one ought to be beneficent, he thought, but one has some choice about the occasions on which to do good. In any case, it is certainly wrong, at least prima facie, to inflict evil or pain on anyone, and to admit this is to admit that the principle of beneficence is partly correct.

A point about our use of terms may help here. The terms "duty," "obligation," and "ought to be done" are often used interchangeably, especially by philosophers, for example, in this book. This is true even to some extent in ordinary discourse. But in our more careful ordinary discourse we tend to use "duty" when we have in mind some rule like "Tell the truth" or some role or office like that of a father or secretary, and to use "obligation" when we have in mind the law or some agreement or promise. In these cases we tend to think that one person has a duty or obligation and another has a correlative right. The expression "ought to do," however, is used in a wider sense to cover things we would not regard as strict duties or obligations or think another person has a right to. Thus, it is natural to say that one ought to go the second mile, not so natural to say one has a duty or obligation to do this, and quite unnatural to say that the other person has a right to expect one to do it. This will help to explain why some assert and others deny that beneficence is a requirement of morality. The matter, it should be observed, is made all the more difficult by two further facts: on the one hand, that "right" sometimes means "ought to be done" and sometimes means only "not wrong," and on the other, that "wrong" is used as the opposite of all the other expressions mentioned, and so has somewhat different forces in different contexts.

One more remark is worth making. Even if one holds that beneficence is not a *requirement* of morality but something supererogatory and morally *good,* one is still regarding beneficence as an important part of morality—as desirable if not required.

What does the principle of beneficence say? Four things, I think:

1. One ought not to inflict evil or harm (what is bad).
2. One ought to prevent evil or harm.
3. One ought to remove evil.
4. One ought to do or promote good.

These four things are different, but they may appropriately be regarded as parts of the principle of beneficence. Of the four, it is most plausible to say that (4) is not a duty in the strict sense. In fact, one is inclined to say that in some sense (1) takes precedence over (2), (2) over (3), and (3) over (4), other things being equal. But all are, at any rate, principles of prima facie duty. By adding "to or for anyone" at the end of each of them one makes the principle of beneficence universalistic, by adding "to or for others" one makes it altruistic. What one does here depends on whether he is willing to say that one has moral duties to oneself or not. For example, does one have a moral duty not to sacrifice any of one's own happiness for that of another? We shall look at this question again later.

It is tempting to think that, since the first four parts of the principle of beneficence may come into conflict with one another in choice situations, say, between actions both of which do some good and some evil, we should regard it as having a fifth part that instructs us, in such cases, to do what will bring about the greatest balance of good over evil. This would, however, presup-

pose that good and evil can always be measured in some way and lose the advantages ascribed to the principle of beneficence over the principle of utility; in fact, it would make the former equivalent to the latter in practice, since we are always choosing between two courses of action, even if one of them is called "inaction." Even so, we may perhaps follow this instruction—or the principle of utility—as a heuristic maxim in conflict situations involving only the principle of beneficence, at least insofar as the goods and evils involved are susceptible of some kind of measuring and balancing, though remembering its limitations.

There are many rules of prima facie right, wrong, or obligation, to be used in determining our actual duties, which can be derived from the principle of beneficence. Wherever one can form a general statement about what affects the lives of people for better or for worse, there one has a valid principle of prima facie duty, for example, "One ought not to kick people in the shin" or "We ought to promote knowledge." Most of the usual rules—keeping promises, telling the truth, showing gratitude, making reparation, not interfering with liberty, etc.—can be seen on this basis to be valid prima facie rules. For instance, given the principle of beneficence and the fact that knowing the truth is a good (in itself or as a means), it follows that telling the truth is a prima facie duty.

Thus, some of our rules of prima facie duty follow directly from the principle of beneficence. The rule of telling the truth can probably be defended also (perhaps with certain built-in exceptions) on the ground that its adoption makes for the greatest general good—as rule-utilitarians hold.

However, not all of our prima facie obligations can be derived from the principle of beneficence any more than from that of utility. For the principle of beneficence does not tell us how we are to distribute goods and evils; it only tells us to produce the one and prevent the other. When conflicting claims are made upon us, the most it could do (and we saw it cannot strictly even do this) is to instruct us to promote the greatest balance of good over evil and, as we have already seen, we need something more. This is where a principle of justice must come in.

III. The Principle of Justice: Equality

We have seen that we must recognize a basic principle of justice. But which one? What is justice? We cannot go into the whole subject of social justice here, but we must at least complete our outline of a normative theory of moral obligation, in which the principle of justice plays a crucial role. We are talking here about *distributive justice,* justice in the distribution of good and evil. There is also *retributive justice* (punishment, etc.), about which a little will be said in Chapter 4. Distributive justice is a matter of the *comparative treatment* of individuals. The paradigm case of injustice is that in which there are two similar individuals in similar circumstances and one of them is treated better or worse than the other. In this case, the cry of injustice rightly goes up against the responsible agent or group; and unless that agent or group can establish that there is some relevant dissimilarity after all between the individuals concerned and their circumstances, he or they will be guilty as charged. This is why Sidgwick suggested his formula, according to which justice is the similar and injustice the dissimilar treatment of similar cases. This formula does give a necessary condition of justice; similar cases are to be treated similarly so far as the requirements of justice are concerned, although these requirements may be outweighed by other considerations. But Sidgwick's formula is not sufficient. All it really says is that we must act according to rules if we mean to be just. Although this formula is correct as far as it goes, it tells us nothing about what the rules are to be, and this is what we want to know, since we have already seen that rules themselves may be unjust. If this were not so, there could be no unjust laws or practices, for laws and practices are rules. Much depends, as we shall see, on which

similarities and dissimilarities of individuals are taken as a basis for similarity or dissimilarity of treatment.

The question remaining to be answered is how we are to tell what rules of distribution or comparative treatment we are to act on. We have seen that these rules cannot be determined on the basis of beneficence alone (as I think the rules of not injuring anyone and of keeping covenants can be). A number of criteria have been proposed by different thinkers: (1) that justice is dealing with people according to their *deserts* or *merits;* (2) that it is treating human beings as *equals* in the sense of distributing good and evil equally among them, excepting perhaps in the case of punishment; (3) that it is treating people according to their *needs,* their *abilities,* or both. An example of the first is the classical *meritarian* criterion of justice as found in Aristotle and Ross. According to this view, the criterion of desert or merit is virtue, and justice is distributing the good (e.g., happiness) in accordance with virtue. One might, of course, adopt some other criterion of merit, for example, ability, contribution, intelligence, blood, color, social rank, or wealth, and then justice would consist in distributing good and evil in accordance with this criterion. The second criterion is the *equalitarian* one that is characteristic of modern democratic theory. The third is also a modern view, and may take various forms; its most prominent form today is the Marxist dictum, "From each according to his ability, to each according to his needs." I shall argue for the second view.

Some of the criteria of merit mentioned seem to be palpably nonmoral or even unjust, for example, the use of blood, color, intelligence, sex, social rank, or wealth as a basis for one's rules of distribution. Use of ability as a basis would give us a form of the third view. This leaves moral and/or nonmoral virtue as possible criteria of merit. Should we adopt a meritarian theory of this Aristotle-Ross sort? It seems to me that virtue, moral or nonmoral, cannot be our basic criterion in matters of distributive justice, because a recognition of any kind of virtue as a basis of distribution is justified only if every individual has an equal chance of achieving all the virtue of that kind he is capable of (and it must not be assumed that they have all had this chance, for they have not). If the individuals competing for goods, positions, and the like have not had an equal chance to achieve all the virtue they are capable of, then virtue is not a fair basis for distributing such things among them. If this is so, then, before virtue can reasonably be adopted as a basis of distribution, there must first be a prior *equal* distribution of the conditions for achieving virtue, at least insofar as this is within the control of human society. This is where equality of opportunity, equality before the law, and equality of access to the means of education come in. In other words, recognition of virtue as a basis of distribution is reasonable only against the background of an acknowledgment of the principle of equality. The primary criterion of distributive justice, then, is not merit in the form of virtue of some kind or other, but equality.

One might object here that there is another kind of merit, namely, effort, and that effort made should be taken as a basis of distribution in at least certain kinds of cases. This is true, but again, it does seem to me that effort cannot serve as our *basic* criterion of distribution, and that recognition of it in any defensible way presupposes the general notion that we should all be treated equally.

We certainly must consider abilities and needs in determining how we are to treat others. This is required by the principle of beneficence, for it asks us to be concerned about the goodness of their lives, which involves catering to their needs and fostering and making use of their abilities. But is it required by the principle of justice? More particularly, does the principle of justice require us to help people in proportion to their needs or to call on them in proportion to their abilities? It is wrong to ask more of people than they can do or to assign them tasks out of proportion to their ability, but this is because "ought" implies "can." Justice asks us to do something about cases of special need; for example, it asks us

to give special attention to people with certain kinds of handicaps, because only with such attention can they have something comparable to an equal chance with others of enjoying a good life. But does it always ask us, at least prima facie, to *proportion* our help to their needs and our demands to their abilities? Are we always prima facie unjust if we help A in proportion to his needs but not B, or if we make demands of C in proportion to his abilities but not of D? It seems to me that the basic question is whether or not in so doing we are showing an equal concern for the goodness of the lives of A and B or of C and D. Whether we should treat them in proportion to their needs and abilities depends, as far as *justice* is concerned, on whether doing so helps or hinders them equally in the achievement of the best lives they are capable of. If helping them in proportion to their needs is necessary for making an equal contribution to the goodness of their lives, then and only then is it unjust to do otherwise. If asking of them in proportion to their abilities is necessary for keeping their chances of a good life equal, then and only then is it unjust to do otherwise. In other words, the basic standard of distributive justice is *equality* of treatment. That, for instance, is why justice calls for giving extra attention to handicapped people.

If this is correct, then we must adopt the equalitarian view of distributive justice. In other words, the principle of justice lays upon us the prima facie obligation of treating people equally. Here we have the answer to our question. This does not mean that it is prima facie unjust to treat people of the same color differently or to treat people of different heights similarly. Color and height are not morally relevant similarities or dissimilarities. Those that are relevant are the ones that bear on the goodness or badness of people's lives, for example, similarities or dissimilarities in ability, interest, or need. Treating people equally does not mean treating them identically; justice is not so monotonous as all that. It means making the same relative contribution to the goodness of their lives (this is equal help or helping according to need) or asking the same relative sacrifice (this is asking in accordance with ability).

Treating people equally in this sense does not mean making their lives equally good or maintaining their lives at the same level of goodness. It would be a mistake to think that justice requires this. For, though people are equally capable of some kind of good life (or least bad one), the kinds of life of which they are capable are not equally good. The lives of which some are capable simply are better, nonmorally as well as morally, than those of which others are capable. In this sense men are not equal, since they are not equal in their capacities. They are equal only in the sense that they ought prima facie to be treated equally, and they ought to be treated equally only in the sense that we ought prima facie to make proportionally the same contribution to the goodness of their lives, once a certain minimum has been achieved by all. This is what is meant by the equal intrinsic dignity or value of the individual that is such an important concept in our culture.

We must remember that this equality of treatment, though it is a basic obligation, is only a prima facie one, and that it may on occasion (and there is no formula for determining the occasions) be overruled by the principle of beneficence. We may claim, however, that in distributing goods and evils, help, tasks, roles, and so forth, people are to be treated equally in the sense indicated, except when unequal treatment can be justified by considerations of beneficence (including utility) or on the ground that it will promote greater equality in the long run. Unequal treatment always requires justification and only certain kinds of justification suffice.

It is in the light of the preceding discussion, it seems to me, that we must try to solve such social problems as education, economic opportunity, racial integration, and aid to underdeveloped countries, remembering always that the principle of beneficence requires us to respect the liberty of others. Our discussion provides only the most general guide lines for solving such problems, of course, but most of what is needed in addition is good will, clarity of thought, and knowledge of the relevant facts.

Summary of My Theory of Obligation

We have now arrived at a mixed deontological theory of obligation somewhat different from the one tentatively sketched earlier. It takes as basic the principle of beneficence (not that of utility) and the principle of justice, now identified as equal treatment. Must we recognize any other basic principles of right and wrong? It seems to me that we need not. As far as I can see, we can derive all of the things we may wish to recognize as duties from our two principles, either directly as the crow flies or indirectly as the rule-utilitarian does. From the former follow various more specific rules of prima facie obligation, for example, those of not injuring anyone, and of not interfering with another's liberty. From the latter follow others like equality of consideration and equality before the law. Some, like telling the truth or not being cruel to children, may follow separately from both principles, which may give them a kind of priority they might not otherwise have. Others, like keeping promises and not crossing university lawns, may perhaps be justified in rule-utilitarian fashion on the basis of the two principles taken jointly, as being rules whose general acceptance and obedience is conducive to a state of affairs in which a maximal balance of good over evil is as equally distributed as possible (the greatest good of the greatest number).

The Problem of Conflict

Several problems facing this theory remain to be discussed. One is the problem of possible conflict between its two principles. I see no way out of this. It does seem to me that the two principles may come into conflict, both at the level of individual action and at that of social policy, and I know of no formula that will always tell us how to solve such conflicts or even how to solve conflicts between their corollaries. It is tempting to say that the principle of justice always takes precedence over that of beneficence: do justice though the heavens fall. But is a small injustice never to be preferred to a great evil? Perhaps we should lean over backwards to avoid committing injustice, but are we never justified in treating people unequally? One might contend that the principle of equal treatment always has priority at least over the fourth or positive part of the principle of beneficence, but is it never right to treat people unequally when a considerable good is at stake? The answer to these questions, I regret to say, does not seem to me to be clearly negative, and I am forced to conclude that the problem of conflict that faced the pluralistic deontological theories discussed earlier is still with us. One can only hope that, if we take the moral point of view, become clearheaded, and come to know all that is relevant, we will also come to agree on ways of acting that are satisfactory to all concerned.

The following reflection may be encouraging in this respect. It seems to me that everyone who takes the moral point of view can agree that the ideal state of affairs is one in which everyone has the best life he or she is capable of. Now, in such a state of affairs, it is clear that the concerns of both the principle of justice or equality and the principle of beneficence will be fulfilled. If so, then we can see that the two principles are in some sense ultimately consistent, and this seems to imply that increasing insight may enable us to know more and more how to solve the conflicts that trouble us now when we know so little about realizing the ideal state of affairs in which the principles are at one. Then, while Ross is right in saying that we must finally appeal to "perception," we can at least give an outline of what that perception is supposed to envision.

NOTE

1. *Essays in Pragmatism,* A. Castell, ed. (New York: Hafner Publishing Co., 1948), p. 73.

For Further Reflection

1. What do you see as the strengths and weaknesses of Frankena's compromise? Is it an attractive way of negotiating between the claims of deontologists, on the one hand, and utilitarians, on the other?

2. Is Frankena's system unduly intuitive? If you have two variables (e.g., justice and beneficence) relevant to a moral situation, can you ever have a clear decision-making process? How does one know which principle wins out in the end? Does Frankena offer any help here?

3. Is the problem of conflict of principles endemic to moral decision-making, so that ethics can never become a science (with a clear, unequivocal decision-making procedure)?

Existentialist Ethics   VI.11

JEAN-PAUL SARTRE

Jean-Paul Sartre (1905–1980) was born in Paris and was a teacher in a French high school. He served in the French army during World War II, was captured by the Germans, and spent time in a prison camp reading German philosophers (especially Hegel, Husserl, and Heidegger). After the war, Sartre's plays, novels, and philosophical work, especially *Being and Nothingness* (1943), set him apart as Europe's premier existentialist. Later he combined existentialism with Marxism, though he never joined the Communist party.

Here is Paul Johnson's description of the impact of Sartre and the essay we are about to read on French society:

> [On October 29, 1945 shortly after the end of the war], at the Club Maintenant, Jean-Paul Sartre delivered a lecture, "Existentialism is a Humanism." Here was the new Paris. This occasion . . . was packed. Men and women fainted, fought for chairs, smashing thirty of them, shouted and barracked. It coincided with the launching of Sartre's new review, *Les Temps Modernes,* in which he argued that literary culture, plus the haute couture of the fashion shops, were the only things France now had left—a symbol of Europe, really— and he produced Existentialism to give people a bit of dignity and to preserve their individuality in the midst of degradation and absurdity. The response was overwhelming. As his consort, Simone de Beauvoir, put it, "We were astounded by the furore we caused." Existentialism was remarkably un-Gallic; hence perhaps, its attractiveness. Sartre was half-Alsacian (Albert Schweitzer was his cousin) and he was brought up in the house of his grandfather, Karl Schweitzer. His culture was as much German as French. He was essentially a product of the Berlin school and especially Heidegger, from whom most of his ideas derived. . . . Thus Existentialism was a French cultural import, which Paris then re-exported to Germany, its country of origin, in a sophisticated and vastly more attractive guise. (Paul Johnson, *Modern Times,* Harper & Row, 1983, p. 575f)

In this essay Sartre sets forth the principles of atheistic existentialism: that we are completely free; that since there is no God to give us an essence, we must create our own essence; that we are completely responsible for our actions, and are responsible for everyone else too; that because of the death of God and the human predicament, which leaves us totally free to create our values and our world, we must exist in anguish, forlornness, and despair. Yet there is a certain celebration and optimism in knowing that we are creators of our own values.

In this essay you will come across Sartre's notion that "essence precedes existence." This is a difficult idea, but he seems to mean something like the following. If you have an idea of something in your mind first and then create it, we would say that the idea (essence) of the thing preceded the actuality or existence of the thing. But if the thing existed before any idea of it, then its existence preceded its essence. If there were a God who created us, who had us in mind, we would have an essence (in terms of a function or purpose) and our existence would succeed our essence, but since, according to Sartre, there is no God to create us, we simply find ourselves existing and must create our own essence (i.e., give ourselves a function or purpose). This is a start at getting at the meaning of this difficult phrase. Perhaps you can improve on this explanation.

Study Questions

1. What are the two meanings of "subjectivism" in this essay?

2. What does Sartre mean by saying that responsibility for our actions involves being responsible for everyone? How does he answer those who deny this thesis? Has Sartre begged the question against them?

3. Describe Sartre's notion of anguish. Why must we experience it? Is his argument cogent?

4. Describe Sartre's notion of forlornness. Why must we experience it? Is his argument clear and plausible?

5. What does Sartre mean by saying that we are "condemned to be free"?

6. Examine the case of the student who finds himself in a moral dilemma. Is Sartre correct that there are no objective principles to help him make his decision, but he must make a leap of faith?

WHAT IS MEANT by the term *existentialism?*

Most people who use the word would be rather embarrassed if they had to explain it, since, now that the word is all the rage, even the work of a musician or painter is being called existentialist. . . . It seems that for want of an advance-guard doctrine analogous to surrealism, the kind of people who are eager for scandal and flurry turn to this philosophy which in other respects does not at all serve their purposes in this sphere.

Actually, it is the least scandalous, the most austere of doctrines. It is intended strictly for specialists and philosophers. Yet it can be defined easily. What complicates matters is that there are two kinds of existentialists; first, those who are Christian, among whom I would include Jaspers and Gabriel Marcel, both Catholic; and on the other hand, the atheistic existentialists, among whom I class Heidegger, and then the French existentialists and myself. What they have in common is that they think that existence precedes essence, or, if you prefer, that subjectivity must be the starting point.

Just what does that mean? Let us consider some object that is manufactured, for example, a book or a paper-cutter: here is an object which has been made by an artisan whose inspiration came from a concept. He referred to the concept of what a paper-cutter is and likewise to a known method of production, which is part of the concept, something which is, by and large, a routine. Thus, the paper-cutter is at once an object produced in a certain way and, on the other hand, one having a specific use; and one cannot

postulate a man who produces a paper-cutter but does not know what it is used for. Therefore, let us say that, for the paper-cutter, essence—that is, the ensemble of both the production routines and the properties which enable it to be both produced and defined—precedes existence. Thus, the presence of the paper-cutter or book in front of me is determined. Therefore, we have here a technical view of the world whereby it can be said that production precedes existence.

When we conceive God as the Creator, He is generally thought of as a superior sort of artisan. Whatever doctrine we may be considering, whether one like that of Descartes or that of Leibnitz, we always grant that will more or less follows understanding or, at the very least, accompanies it, and that when God creates He knows exactly what He is creating. Thus, the concept of man in the mind of God is comparable to the concept of paper-cutter in the mind of the manufacturer, and, following certain techniques and a conception, God produces man, just as the artisan, following a definition and a technique, makes a paper-cutter. Thus, the individual man is the realization of a certain concept in the divine intelligence.

In the eighteenth century, the atheism of the *philosophes* discarded the idea of God, but not so much for the notion that essence precedes existence. To a certain extent, this idea is found everywhere; we find it in Diderot, in Voltaire, and even in Kant. Man has a human nature; this human nature, which is the concept of the human, is found in all men, which means that each

Source: Jean-Paul Sartre, Existentialism, *trans. by Bernard Frechtman (New York, 1947). Reprinted by permission of the Philosophical Library, Inc.*

man is a particular example of a universal concept, man. In Kant, the result of this universality is that the wild-man, the natural man, as well as the bourgeois, are circumscribed by the same definition and have the same basic qualities. Thus, here too the essence of man precedes the historical existence that we find in nature.

Atheistic existentialism, which I represent, is more coherent. It states that if God does not exist, there is at least one being in whom existence precedes essence, a being who exists before he can be defined by any concept, and that this being is man, or, as Heidegger says, human reality. What is meant here by saying that existence precedes essence? It means that, first of all, man exists, turns up, appears on the scene, and, only afterwards, defines himself. If man, as the existentialist conceives him, is indefinable, it is because at first he is nothing. Only afterward will he be something, and he himself will have made what he will be. Thus, there is no human nature, since there is no God to conceive it. Not only is man what he conceives himself to be, but he is also only what he wills himself to be after this thrust toward existence.

Man is nothing else but what he makes of himself. Such is the first principle of existentialism. It is also what is called subjectivity, the name we are labeled with when charges are brought against us. But what do we mean by this, if not that man has a greater dignity than a stone or table? For we mean that man first exists, that is, that man first of all is the being in the future. Man is at the start a plan which is aware of itself, rather than a patch of moss, a piece of garbage, or a cauliflower; nothing exists prior to this plan; there is nothing in heaven; man will be what he will have planned to be. Not what he will want to be. Because by the word "will" we generally mean a conscious decision, which is subsequent to what we have already made of ourselves. I may want to belong to a political party, write a book, get married; but all that is only a manifestation of an earlier, more spontaneous choice that is called "will." But if existence really does precede essence, man is responsible for what he is. Thus, existentialism's first move is to make every man aware of what he is and to make the full responsibility of his existence rest on him. And when we say that a man is responsible for himself, we do not only mean that he is responsible for his own individuality, but that he is responsible for all men.

The word subjectivism has two meanings, and our opponents play on the two. Subjectivism means, on the one hand, that an individual chooses and makes himself; and, on the other, that it is impossible for man to transcend human subjectivity. The second of these is the essential meaning of existentialism. When we say that man chooses his own self, we mean that every one of us does likewise; but we also mean by that that in making this choice he also chooses all men. In fact, in creating the man that we want to be, there is not a single one of our acts which does not at the same time create an image of man as we think he ought to be. To choose to be this or that is to affirm at the same time the value of what we choose, because we can never choose evil. We always choose the good, and nothing can be good for us without being good for all.

If, on the other hand, existence precedes essence, and if we grant that we exist and fashion our image at one and the same time, the image is valid for everybody and for our whole age. Thus, our responsibility is much greater than we might have supposed, because it involves all mankind. If I am a workingman and choose to join a Christian trade-union rather than be a communist, and if by being a member I want to show that the best thing for man is resignation, that the kingdom of man is not of this world, I am not only involving my own case—I want to be resigned for everyone. As a result, my action has involved all humanity. To take a more individual matter, if I want to marry, to have children; even if this marriage depends solely on my own circumstances or passion or wish, I am involving all humanity in monogamy and not merely myself. Therefore, I am responsible for myself and for everyone else. I am creating a certain image of man of my own choosing. In choosing myself, I choose man.

This helps us understand what the actual content is of such rather grandiloquent words as anguish, forlornness, despair. As you will see, it's all quite simple.

First, what is meant by anguish? The existentialists say at once that man is anguish. What that means is this: the man who involves himself and who realizes that he is not only the person he chooses to be, but also a law-maker who is, at the same time, choosing all mankind as well as himself, cannot help escape the feeling of his total and deep responsibility. Of course, there are many people who are not anxious; but we claim that they are hiding their anxiety, that they are fleeing from it. Certainly, many people believe that when they do something, they themselves are the only ones involved, and when someone says to them, "What if everyone acted that way?" they shrug their shoulders and answer, "Everyone doesn't act that way." But really, one should always ask himself, "What would happen if everybody looked at things that way?" There is no escaping this disturbing thought except by a kind of double-dealing. A man who lies and makes excuses for himself by saying "not everybody does that," is someone with an uneasy conscience, because the act of lying implies that a universal value is conferred upon the lie.

Anguish is evident even when it conceals itself. This is the anguish that Kierkegaard called the anguish of Abraham. You know the story: an angel has ordered Abraham to sacrifice his son; if it really were an angel who has come and said, "You are Abraham, you shall sacrifice your son," everything would be all right. But everyone might first wonder, "Is it really an angel, and am I really Abraham? What proof do I have?" . . .

Now, I'm not being singled out as an Abraham, and yet at every moment I'm obliged to perform exemplary acts. For every man, everything happens as if all mankind had its eyes fixed on him and were guiding itself by what he does.

And every man ought to say to himself, "Am I really the kind of man who has the right to act in such a way that humanity might guide itself by my actions?" And if he does not say that to himself, he is masking his anguish.

There is no question here of the kind of anguish which would lead to quietism, to inaction. It is a matter of a simple sort of anguish that anybody who has had responsibilities is familiar with. For example, when a military officer takes the responsibility for an attack and sends a certain number of men to death, he chooses to do so, and in the main he alone makes the choice. Doubtless, orders come from above, but they are too broad; he interprets them, and on this interpretation depend the lives of ten or fourteen or twenty men. In making a decision he cannot help having a certain anguish. All leaders know this anguish. That doesn't keep them from acting; on the contrary, it is the very condition of their action. For it implies that they envisage a number of possibilities, and when they choose one, they realize that it has value only because it is chosen. We shall see that this kind of anguish, which is the kind that existentialism describes, is explained, in addition, by a direct responsibility to the other men whom it involves. It is not a curtain separating us from action, but is part of action itself.

When we speak of forlornness, a term Heidegger was fond of, we mean only that God does not exist and that we have to face all the consequences of this. The existentialist is strongly opposed to a certain kind of secular ethics which would like to abolish God with the least possible expense. About 1880, some French teachers tried to set up a secular ethics which went something like this: God is a useless and costly hypothesis; we are discarding it; but meanwhile, in order for there to be an ethics, a society, a civilization, it is essential that certain values be taken seriously and that they be considered as having an *a priori* existence. It must be obligatory, *a priori*, to be honest, not to lie, not to beat your wife, to have children, etc., etc. So we're going to try a little device which will make it possible to show that values exist all the same, inscribed in a heaven of ideas, though otherwise God does not exist. In other words—and this, I believe, is the tendency of everything called reformism in France—nothing will be changed if God does not exist. We shall find ourselves with the same norms of honesty, progress, and humanism, and we shall have made of God an outdated hypothesis which will peacefully die off by itself.

The existentialist, on the contrary, thinks it very distressing that God does not exist, because all possibility of finding values in a heaven of ideas disappears along with Him; there can be no longer an *a priori* Good, since there is no infinite and perfect consciousness to think it. Nowhere is it written that the Good exists, that we must be honest, that we must not lie; because the fact is we are on a plane where there are only men. Dostoievsky said, "If God didn't exist, everything would be possible." That is the very starting point of existentialism. Indeed, everything is permissible if God does not exist, and as a result man is forlorn, because neither within him nor without does he find anything to cling to. He can't start making excuses for himself.

If existence really does precede essence, there is no explaining things away by reference to a fixed and given human nature. In other words, there is no determinism, man is free, man is freedom. On the other hand, if God does not exist, we find no values or commands to turn to which legitimize our conduct. So, in the bright realm of values, we have no excuse behind us, no justification before us. We are alone, with no excuses.

That is the idea I shall try to convey when I say that man is condemned to be free. Condemned, because he did not create himself, yet, in other respects is free; because, once thrown into the world, he is responsible for everything he does. The existentialist does not believe in the power of passion. He will never agree that a sweeping passion is a ravaging torrent which fatally leads a man to certain acts and is therefore an excuse. He thinks that man is responsible for his passion.

The existentialist does not think that man is going to help himself by finding in the world some omen by which to orient himself. Because he thinks that man will interpret the omen to suit himself. Therefore, he thinks that man, with no support and no aid, is condemned every moment to invent man. Ponge, in a very fine article, has said, "Man is the future of man." That's exactly it. But if it is taken to mean that this future is recorded in heaven, that God sees it, then it is false, because it would really no longer be a future. If it is taken to mean that, whatever a man may be, there is a future to be forged, a virgin future before him, then this remark is sound. But then we are forlorn.

To give you an example which will enable you to understand forlornness better, I shall cite the case of one of my students who came to see me under the following circumstances: his father was on bad terms with his mother, and, moreover, was inclined to be a collaborationist; his older brother had been killed in the German offensive of 1940, and the young man, with somewhat immature but generous feelings, wanted to avenge him. His mother lived alone with him, very much upset by the half-treason of her husband and the death of her older son; the boy was her only consolation.

The boy was faced with the choice of leaving for England and joining the Free French Forces—that is, leaving his mother behind—or remaining with his mother and helping her to carry on. He was fully aware that the woman lived only for him and that his going-off—and perhaps his death—would plunge her into despair. He was also aware that every act that he did for his mother's sake was a sure thing, in the sense that it was helping her to carry on, whereas every effort he made toward going off and fighting was an uncertain move which might run aground and prove completely useless; for example, on his way to England he might, while passing through Spain, be detained indefinitely in a Spanish camp; he might reach England or Algiers and be stuck in an office at a desk job. As a result, he was faced with two very different kinds of action: one, concrete, immediate, but concerning only one individual; the other concerned an incomparably vaster group, a national collectivity, but for that very reason was dubious, and might be interrupted en route. And, at the same time, he was wavering between two kinds of ethics. On the one hand, an ethics of sympathy, of personal devotion; on the other, a broader ethics, but one whose efficacy was more dubious. He had to choose between the two.

Who could help him choose? Christian doctrine? No. Christian doctrine says, "Be charitable, love your neighbor, take the more rugged path, etc., etc." But which is the more rugged path? Whom should he love as a brother? The fighting man or his mother? Which does the greater good, the vague act of fighting in a group, or the concrete one of helping a particular human being to go on living? Who can decide *a priori?* Nobody. No book of ethics can tell him. The Kantian ethics says, "Never treat any person as a means, but as an end." Very well, if I stay with my mother, I'll treat her as an end and not as a means; but by virtue of this very fact, I'm running the risk of treating the people around me who are fighting, as means; and, conversely, if I go to join those who are fighting, I'll be treating them as an end, and, by doing that, I run the risk of treating my mother as a means.

If values are vague, and if they are always too broad for the concrete and specific case that we are considering, the only thing left for us is to trust our instincts. That's what this young man tried to do; and when I saw him, he said, "In the end, feeling is what counts. I ought to choose whichever pushes me in one direction. If I feel that I love my mother enough to sacrifice everything else for her—my desire for vengeance, for action, for adventure—then I'll stay with her. If, on the contrary, I feel that my love for my mother isn't enough, I'll leave."

But how is the value of a feeling determined? What gives his feeling for his mother value? Precisely the fact that he remained with her. I may say that I like so-and-so well enough to sacrifice a certain amount of money for him, but I may

say so only if I've done it. I may say, "I love my mother well enough to remain with her" if I have remained with her. The only way to determine the value of this affection is, precisely, to perform an act which confirms and defines it. But, since I require this affection to justify my act, I find myself caught in a vicious circle. . . .

As for despair, the term has a very simple meaning. It means that we shall confine ourselves to reckoning only with what depends upon our will, or on the ensemble of probabilities which make our action possible. When we want something, we always have to reckon with probabilities. I may be counting on the arrival of a friend. The friend is coming by rail or street-car; this supposes that the train will arrive on schedule, or that the street-car will not jump the track. I am left in the realm of possibility; but possibilities are to be reckoned with only to the point where my action comports with the ensemble of these possibilities, and no further. The moment the possibilities I am considering are not rigorously involved by my action, I ought to disengage myself from them, because no God, no scheme, can adapt the world and its possibilities to my will. When Descartes said, "Conquer yourself rather than the world," he meant essentially the same thing.

The Marxists to whom I have spoken reply, "You can rely on the support of others in your action, which obviously has certain limits because you're not going to live forever. That means: rely on both what others are doing elsewhere to help you, in China, in Russia, and what they will do later on, after your death, to carry on the action and lead it to its fulfillment, which will be the revolution. You even *have* to rely upon that, otherwise you're immortal." I reply at once that I will always rely on fellow fighters insofar as these comrades are involved with me in a common struggle, in the unity of a party or a group in which I can more or less make my weight felt; that is, one whose ranks I am in as a fighter and whose movements I am aware of at every moment. In such a situation, relying on the unity and will of the party is exactly like counting on the fact that the train will arrive on time or that the car won't jump the track. But, given that man is free and that there is no human nature for me to depend on, I cannot count on men whom I do not know by relying on human goodness or man's concern for the good of society. I don't know what will become of the Russian revolution; I may make an example of it to the extent that at the present time it is apparent that the proletariat plays a part in Russia that it plays in no other nation. But I can't swear that this will inevitably lead to a triumph of the proletariat. I've got to limit myself to what I see.

Given that men are free, and that tomorrow they will freely decide what man will be, I cannot be sure that, after my death, fellow fighters will carry on my work to bring it to its maximum perfection. Tomorrow, after my death, some men may decide to set up Fascism, and the others may be cowardly and muddled enough to let them do it. Fascism will then be the human reality, so much the worse for us.

Actually, things will be as man will have decided they are to be. Does that mean that I should abandon myself to quietism? No. First, I should involve myself; then, act on the old saw, "Nothing ventured, nothing gained." Nor does it mean that I shouldn't belong to a party, but rather that I shall have no illusions and shall do what I can. For example, suppose I ask myself, "Will socialization, as such, ever come about?" I know nothing about it. All I know is that I'm going to do everything in my power to bring it about. Beyond that, I can't count on anything. Quietism is the attitude of people who say, "Let others do what I can't do." The doctrine I am presenting is the very opposite of quietism, since it declares, "There is no reality except in action." Moreover, it goes further, since it adds, "Man is nothing else than his plan; he exists only to the extent that he fulfills himself; he is, therefore, nothing else than the ensemble of his acts, nothing else than his life."

For Further Reflection

1. How are existentialist ethics different from other theories we have studied? What are its strengths and weaknesses?

2. Has Sartre gotten to the heart of the matter with his example of the student who must choose between his mother and the war effort? Could we object that he is making an exception to the norm? In normal situations we know perfectly well the right thing to do. For example, suppose that there was no war; then, wouldn't it be automatically right to take care of the mother? Does existentialism have a response to this criticism?

3. Sartre believes that it makes all the difference in the world whether God exists. If God does not exist, all things are morally permissible, there is no right or wrong, but thinking makes it so. Is this correct?

VI.12   The Ethics of Nobility

FRIEDRICH NIETZSCHE

Friedrich Nietzsche (1844–1900) was a German existentialist who has played a major role in contemporary intellectual development. Descended through both of his parents from Christian ministers, Nietzsche was brought up in a pious German Lutheran home and was known as "the little Jesus" by his schoolmates. He studied theology at the University of Bonn and philology at Leipzig, becoming an atheist in the process. At the age of twenty-four he was appointed professor of classical philology at the University of Basel in Switzerland, where he taught for ten years until forced by ill health to retire. Eventually he became mentally ill. He died on August 25, 1900.

Nietzsche believes that the fundamental creative force that motivates all creation is the will to power. We all seek to affirm ourselves, to flourish and dominate. Since we are essentially unequal in ability, it follows that the fittest will survive and be victorious in the contest with the weaker and the baser. There is great aesthetic beauty in the noble spirit coming to fruition, but this process is hampered by Judeo-Christian morality, which Nietzsche labels "slave morality." Slave morality, which is the invention of jealous priests, envious and resentful of the power of the noble, prescribes that we give up the will to power and excellence and become meek and mild, that we believe the lie of all humans having equal worth. In our reading, Nietzsche also refers to this as the ethics of resentment.

Nietzsche's ideas of inegalitarian ethics are based on his notion of the death of God. God plays no vital role in our culture—except as a protector of the slave morality, including the idea of equal worth of all persons. If we recognize that there is no rational basis for believing in God, we will see that the whole edifice of slave morality must crumble and with it the notion of equal worth. In its place will arise the morality of the noble person based on the virtues of the high courage, discipline, and intelligence, in the pursuit of self-affirmation and excellence.

We begin this section with Nietzsche's famous description of the madman who announces the death of God and then turn to selections from *Beyond Good and Evil, The Genealogy of Morals,* and *The Twilight of the Idols.*

Study Questions

1. What does Nietzsche mean by the idea that God is dead?
2. What is the cause of slave morality?
3. What is the difference between noble or master morality and slave morality?
4. What is Nietzsche's justification for exploitation of the lower types of humanity?
5. What does Nietzsche mean by "good" and "evil"?

The Madman and the Death of God

HAVE YOU EVER HEARD OF THE MADMAN who on a bright morning lighted a lantern and ran to the market-place calling out unceasingly: "I seek God! I seek God!"—As there were many people standing about who did not believe in God, he caused a great deal of amusement. Why! is he lost? said one. Has he strayed away like a child? said another. Or does he keep himself hidden? Is he afraid of us? Has he taken a sea-voyage? Has he emigrated?—the people cried out laughingly, all in a hubbub. The insane man jumped into their midst and transfixed them with his glances. "Where is God gone?" he called out. "I mean to tell you! *We have killed him,—* you and I! We are all his murderers! But how have we done it? How were we able to drink up

Reprinted from The Complete Works of Nietzsche, *ed. Oscar Levy, vols. 10 and 11 (T. N. Foulis, 1910). I have paraphrased a few difficult passages.*

the sea? Who gave us the sponge to wipe away the whole horizon? What did we do when we loosened this earth from its sun? Whither does it now move? Whither do we move? Away from all suns? Do we not dash on unceasingly? Backwards, sideways, forewards, in all directions? Is there still an above and below? Do we not stray, as through infinite nothingness? Does not empty space breathe upon us? Has it not become colder? Does not night come on continually, darker and darker? Shall we not have to light lanterns in the morning? Do we not hear the noise of the grave-diggers who are burying God? Do we not smell the divine putrefaction?—for even Gods putrefy! God is dead! God remains dead! And we have killed him! How shall we console ourselves, the most murderous of all murderers? The holiest and the mightiest that the world has hitherto possessed, has bled to death under our knife,—who will wipe the blood from us? With what water could we cleanse ourselves? What lustrums, what sacred games shall we have to devise? Is not the magnitude of this deed too great for us? Shall we not ourselves have to become Gods, merely to seem worthy of it? There never was a greater event,—and on account of it, all who are born after us belong to a higher history than any history hitherto!"—Here the madman was silent and looked again at his hearers; they also were silent and looked at him in surprise. At last he threw his lantern on the ground, so that it broke in pieces and was extinguished. "I come too early," he then said, "I am not yet at the right time. This prodigious event is still on its way, and is travelling,—it has not yet reached men's ears. Lightning and thunder need time, the light of the stars needs time, deeds need time, even after they are done, to be seen and heard. This deed is as yet further from them than the furthest star,—*and yet they have done it!*"—It is further stated that the madman made his way into different churches on the same day, and there intoned his *Requiem aeternam deo.* When led out and called to account, he always gave the reply: "What are these churches now, if they are not the tombs and monuments of God?"— . . .

What Is Noble?

Every elevation of the type "man," has hitherto been the work of an aristocratic society and so it will always be—a society believing in a long scale of gradations of rank and differences of worth among human beings, and requiring slavery in some form or other. Without the *pathos of distance,* such as grows out of the incarnated difference of classes, out of the constant outlooking and downlooking of the ruling caste on subordinates and instruments, and out of their equally constant practice of obeying and commanding, of keeping down and keeping at a distance—that other more mysterious pathos could never have arisen, the longing for an ever new widening of distance within the soul itself, the formation of ever higher, rarer, further, more extended, more comprehensive states, in short, just the elevation of the type "man," the continued "self-surmounting of man," to use a moral formula in a supermoral sense. To be sure, one must not resign oneself to any humanitarian illusions about the history of the origin of an aristocratic society (that is to say, of the preliminary condition for the elevation of the type "man"): the truth is hard. Let us acknowledge unprejudicedly how ever higher civilisation hitherto has *originated!* Men with a still natural nature, barbarians in every terrible sense of the word, men of prey, still in possession of unbroken strength of will and desire for power, threw themselves upon weaker, more moral, more peaceful races (perhaps trading or cattle-rearing communities), or upon old mellow civilisations in which the final vital force was flickering out in brilliant fireworks of wit and depravity. At the commencement, the noble caste was always the barbarian caste: their superiority did not consist first of all in their physical, but in their psychical power—they were more *complete* men (which at every point also implies the same as "more complete beasts").

Corruption—as the indication that anarchy threatens to break out among the instincts, and that the foundation of the emotions, called "life," is convulsed—is something radically different according to the organisation in which it manifests itself. When, for instance, an aristocracy like that of France at the beginning of the Revolution, flung away its privileges with sublime disgust and sacrificed itself to an excess of its moral sentiments, it was corruption:—it was really only the closing act of the corruption which had existed for centuries, by virtue of which that aristocracy had abdicated step by step its lordly prerogatives and lowered itself to a *function* of royalty (in the end even to its decoration and parade-dress). The essential thing, however, in a good and healthy aristocracy is that it should *not* regard itself as a function either of the kingship or the commonwealth, but as the *significance* and highest justification thereof—that it should therefore accept with a good conscience the sacrifice of a legion of individuals, who, *for its sake,* must be suppressed and reduced to imperfect men, to slaves and instruments. Its fundamental belief must be precisely that society is *not* allowed to exist for its own sake, but only as a foundation and scaffolding, by means of which a select class of beings may be able to elevate themselves to their higher duties, and in general to a higher *existence:* like those sun-seeking climbing plants in Java—they are called *Sipo Matador,*—which encircle an oak so long and so often with their arms, until at last, high above it, but supported by it, they can unfold their tops in the open light, and exhibit their happiness.

To refrain mutually from injury, from violence, from exploitation, and put one's will on a par with that of others: this may result in a certain rough sense in good conduct among individuals when the necessary conditions are given (namely, the actual similarity of the individuals in amount of force and degree of worth, and their co-relation within one organisation). As soon, however, as one wished to take this principle more generally, and if possible even as *the fundamental principle of society,* it would immediately disclose what it really is—namely, a Will to the *denial* of life, a principle of dissolution and decay. Here one must think profoundly to

the very basis and resist all sentimental weakness: life itself is *essentially* appropriation, injury, conquest of the strange and weak, suppression, severity, obtrusion of peculiar forms, incorporation, and at the least, putting it mildest, exploitation;—but why should one for ever use precisely these words on which for ages a disparaging purpose has been stamped? Even the organisation within which, as was previously supposed, the individuals treat each other as equal—it takes place in every healthy aristocracy—must itself, if it be a living and not a dying organisation, do all that towards other bodies, which the individuals within it refrain from doing to each other: it will have to be the incarnated Will to Power, it will endeavour to grow, to gain ground, attract to itself and acquire ascendency—not owing to any morality or immorality, but because it *lives,* and because life *is* precisely Will to Power. On no point, however, is the ordinary consciousness of Europeans more unwilling to be corrected than on this matter; people now rave everywhere, even under the guise of science, about coming conditions of society in which "the exploiting character" is to be absent:—that sounds to my ears as if they promised to invent a mode of life which should refrain from all organic functions. "Exploitation" does not belong to a depraved, or imperfect and primitive society: it belongs to the *nature* of the living being as a primary organic function; it is a consequence of the intrinsic Will to Power, which is precisely the Will to Life.— Granting that as a theory this is a novelty—as a reality it is the *fundamental fact* of all history: let us be so far honest towards ourselves!

MASTER AND SLAVE MORALITY

In a tour through the many finer and coarser moralities which have hitherto prevailed or still prevail on the earth, I found certain traits recurring regularly together, and connected with one another, until finally two primary types revealed themselves to me, and a radical distinction was brought to light. There is *master-morality* and *slave-morality;*—I would at once add, however, that in all higher and mixed civilisations, there are also attempts at the reconciliation of the two moralities; but one finds still oftener the confusion and mutual misunderstanding of them, indeed, sometimes their close juxtaposition—even in the same man, within one soul. The distinctions of moral values have either originated in a ruling caste, pleasantly conscious of being different from the ruled—or among the ruled class, the slaves and dependents of all sorts. In the first case, when it is the rulers who determine the conception "good," it is the exalted, proud disposition which is regarded as the distinguishing feature, and that which determines the order of rank. The noble type of man separates from himself the beings in whom the opposite of this exalted, proud disposition displays itself: he despises them. Let it at once be noted that in this first kind of morality the antithesis "good" and "bad" means practically the same as "noble" and "despicable";—the antithesis "good" and "*evil*" is of a different origin. The cowardly, the timid, the insignificant, and those thinking merely of narrow utility are despised; moreover, also, the distrustful, with their constrained glances, the self-abasing, the dog-like kind of men who let themselves be abused, the mendicant flatterers, and above all the liars:—it is a fundamental belief of all aristocrats that the common people are untruthful. "We truthful ones"—the nobility in ancient Greece called themselves. It is obvious that everywhere the designations of moral value were at first applied to *men,* and were only derivatively and at a later period applied to *actions;* it is a gross mistake, therefore, when historians of morals start with questions like, "Why have sympathetic actions been praised?" The noble type of man regards *himself* as a determiner of values; he does not require to be approved of; he passes the judgment: "What is injurious to me is injurious in itself"; he knows that it is he himself only who confers honour on things; he is a *creator of values*. He honours whatever he recognises in himself: such morality is self-glorification. In the foreground there is the feeling of plenitude, of power, which seeks to overflow, the happiness of high tension, the consciousness of a wealth which would fain give and bestow:—the noble man also helps the unfortunate, but not—or scarcely—out of pity, but rather from an impulse generated by the super-abundance of power. The noble man honours in himself the powerful one, him also who has power over himself, who knows how to speak and how to keep silence, who takes pleasure in subjecting himself to severity and hardness, and has reverence for all that is severe and hard. "Wotan placed a hard heart in my breast," says an old Scandinavian Saga: it is thus rightly expressed from the soul of a proud Viking. Such a type of man is even proud of *not* being made for sympathy; the hero of the Saga therefore adds warningly: "He who has not a hard heart when young, will never have one." The noble and brave who think thus are the furthest removed from the morality which sees precisely in sympathy, or in acting for the good of others, or in *désintéressement,* the characteristic of the moral; faith in oneself, pride in oneself, a radical enmity and irony towards "selflessness," belong as definitely to noble morality, as do a careless scorn and precaution in presence of sympathy and the "warm heart."—It is the powerful who *know* how to honour, it is their art, their domain for invention. The profound reverence for age and for tradition—all law rests on this double reverence,—the belief and prejudice in favour of ancestors and unfavourable to newcomers, is typical in the morality of the powerful; and if, reversely, men of "modern ideas" believe almost instinctively in "progress" and the "future," and are more and more lacking in respect for old age, the ignoble origin of these "ideas" has complacently betrayed itself thereby. A morality of the ruling class, however, is more especially foreign and irritating to present-day taste in the sternness of its principle that one has duties only to one's equals; that one may act towards beings of a lower rank, towards all that is foreign, just as seems good to one, or "as the heart desires," and in any case "beyond good and evil": it is here that sympathy and similar sentiments can have a place. The ability and obligation to exercise prolonged gratitude and prolonged revenge—both only within the circle of equals,—artfulness in retaliation, *raffinement* of the idea in friendship, a certain necessity to have enemies (as outlets for the emotions of envy, quarrelsomeness, arrogance—in fact, in order to be a good *friend*): all these are typical characteristics of the noble morality, which, as has been pointed out, is not the morality of "modern ideas," and is therefore at present difficult to realise and also to unearth and disclose.—It is otherwise with the second type of morality, *slave-morality*. Supposing that the abused, the oppressed, the suffering, the unemancipated, the weary, and those uncertain of themselves, should moralise, what will be the common element in their moral estimates? Probably a pessimistic suspicion with regard to the entire situation of man will find expression, perhaps a condemnation of man, together with his situation. The slave has an unfavourable eye for the virtues of the powerful; he has a scepticism and distrust, a *refinement* of distrust of everything "good" that is there honoured—he would fain persuade himself that the very happiness there is not genuine. On the other hand, *those* qualities which serve to alleviate the existence of sufferers are brought into prominence and flooded with light; it is here that sympathy, the kind, helping hand, the warm heart, patience, diligence, humility, and friendliness attain to honour; for here these are the most useful qualities, and almost the only means of supporting the burden of existence. Slave-morality is essentially the morality of utility. Here is the seat of the origin of the famous antithesis "good" and "evil":—power and dangerousness are assumed to reside in the evil, a certain dreadfulness, subtlety, and strength, which do not admit of being despised. According to slave-morality, therefore, the "evil" man arouses fear; according to master-morality, it is precisely the "good" man who arouses fear and seeks to arouse it, while the bad man is regarded as the despicable being. The contrast attains its maximum when, in accordance with the logical consequences of slave-morality, a shade of depreciation—it may be slight and well-intentioned—at last attaches itself to the "good" man of this morality; because, according to the servile mode of thought, the good man must in any case be the *safe* man: he is good-natured, easily deceived, perhaps a little stupid, *un bonhomme*. Everywhere that slave-morality gains the ascendency, language shows a tendency to approximate the significations of the words "good" and "stupid."—A last fundamental difference: the desire for *freedom*, the instinct for happiness and the refinements of the feeling of liberty belong as necessarily to slave-morals and morality, as artifice and enthusiasm in reverence and devotion are the regular symptoms of an aristocratic mode of thinking and estimating.—Hence we can understand without further detail why love *as a passion*—it is our European specialty—must absolutely be of noble origin; as is well known, its invention is due to the Provençal poet-cavaliers, those brilliant, ingenious men of the "*gai saber*," to whom Europe owes so much, and almost owes itself. . . .

There is an *instinct for rank,* which more than anything else is already the sign of a *high* rank; there is a *delight* in the *nuances* of reverence which leads one to infer noble origin and habits. The refinement, goodness, and loftiness of a soul are put to a perilous test when something passes by that is of the highest rank, but is not yet protected by the awe of authority from obtrusive touches and incivilities: something that goes its way like a living touchstone, undistinguished, undiscovered, and tentative, perhaps voluntarily veiled and disguised. He whose task and practice it is to investigate souls, will avail himself of many varieties of this very art to determine the ultimate value of a soul, the unalterable, innate order of rank to which it belongs: he will test it by its *instinct for reverence. Différence engendre haine* [Difference engenders hate.—ED.]: the vulgarity of many a nature spurts up suddenly like dirty water, when any holy vessel, any jewel from closed shrines, any book bearing the marks of great destiny, is brought before it; while on the other hand, there is an involuntary silence, a hesitation of the eye, a cessation of all gestures, by which it is indicated that a soul *feels* the nearness of what is worthiest of respect. . . .

The revolt of the slaves in morals begins in the very principle of *resentment* becoming creative and giving birth to values—a resentment experienced by creatures who, deprived as they are of the proper outlet of action, are forced to find their compensation in an imaginary revenge. While every aristocratic morality springs from a triumphant affirmation of its own demands, the slave morality says "no" from the very outset to what is "outside itself," "different from itself," and "not itself": and this "no" is its creative deed. This reversal of the valuing standpoint—this *inevitable* gravitation to the objective instead of back to the subjective—is typical of "resentment": the slave-morality requires as the condition of its existence an external and objective world, to employ physiological terminology, it requires objective stimuli to be capable of action at all—its action is fundamentally a reaction. The contrary is the case when we come to the aristocrat's system of values: it acts and grows spontaneously, it merely seeks its antithesis in order to pronounce a more grateful and exultant "yes" to its own self;—its negative conception, "low," "vulgar," "bad," is merely a pale late-born foil in comparison with its positive and fundamental conception (saturated as it is with life and passion), of "we aristocrats, we good ones, we beautiful ones, we happy ones."

When the aristocratic morality goes astray and commits sacrilege on reality, this is limited to that particular sphere with which it is *not* sufficiently acquainted—a sphere, in fact, from the real knowledge of which it disdainfully defends itself. It misjudges, in some cases, the sphere which it despises, the sphere of the common vulgar man and the low people: on the other hand,

due weight should be given to the consideration that in any case the mood of contempt, of disdain, of superciliousness, even on the supposition that it *falsely* portrays the object of its contempt, will always be far removed from that degree of falsity which will always characterise the attacks—in effigy, of course—of the vindictive hatred and revengefulness of the weak in onslaughts on their enemies. In point of fact, there is in contempt too strong an admixture of nonchalance, of casualness, of boredom, of impatience, even of personal exultation, for it to be capable of distorting its victim into a real caricature or a real monstrosity. Attention again should be paid to the almost benevolent *nuances* which, for instance, the Greek nobility imports into all the words by which it distinguishes the common people from itself; note how continuously a kind of pity, care, and consideration imparts its honeyed *flavour,* until at last almost all the words which are applied to the vulgar man survive finally as expressions for "unhappy," "worthy of pity" . . .—and how, conversely, "bad," "low," "unhappy" have never ceased to ring in the Greek ear with a tone in which "unhappy" is the predominant note: this is a heritage of the old noble aristocratic morality, which remains true to itself even in contempt. . . . The "well-born" simply *felt* themselves the "happy"; they did not have to manufacture their happiness artificially through looking at their enemies, or in cases to talk and lie themselves into happiness (as is the custom with all resentful men); and similarly, complete men as they were, exuberant with strength, and consequently *necessarily* energetic, they were too wise to dissociate happiness from action—activity becomes in their minds necessarily counted as happiness (that is the etymology of $\varepsilon\grave{v}\ \pi\rho\acute{\alpha}\tau\tau\varepsilon\iota\nu$)—all in sharp contrast to the "happiness" of the weak and the oppressed, with their festering venom and malignity, among whom happiness appears essentially as a narcotic, a deadening, a quietude, a peace, a "Sabbath," an enervation of the mind and relaxation of the limbs,—in short, a purely *passive* phenomenon. While the aristocratic man lived in confidence and openness with himself (γεν-ναῖος, "noble-born," emphasises the nuance "sincere," and perhaps also "naïf"), the resentful man, on the other hand, is neither sincere nor naïf, nor honest and candid with himself. His soul *squints;* his mind loves hidden crannies, tortuous paths and backdoors, everything secret appeals to him as *his* world, *his* safety, *his* balm; he is past master in silence, in not forgetting, in waiting, in provisional self-depreciation and self-abasement. A race of such *resentful* men will of necessity eventually prove more *prudent* than any aristocratic race, it will honour prudence on quite a distinct scale, as, in fact, a paramount condition of existence, while prudence among aristocratic men is apt to be tinged with a delicate flavour of luxury and refinement; so among them it plays nothing like so integral a part as that complete certainty of function of the governing *unconscious* instincts, or as indeed a certain lack of prudence, such as a vehement and valiant charge, whether against danger or the enemy, or as those ecstatic bursts of rage, love, reverence, gratitude, by which at all times noble souls have recognised each other. When the resentment of the aristocratic man manifests itself, it fulfils and exhausts itself in an immediate reaction, and consequently instils no *venom:* on the other hand, it never manifests itself at all in countless instances, when in the case of the feeble and weak it would be inevitable. An inability to take seriously for any length of time their enemies, their disasters, their *misdeeds*—that is the sign of the full strong natures who possess a superfluity of moulding plastic force, that heals completely and produces forgetfulness: a good example of this in the modern world is Mirabeau, who had no memory for any insults and meannesses which were practised on him, and who was only incapable of forgiving because he forgot. Such a man indeed shakes off with a shrug many a worm which would have buried itself in another; it is only in characters like these that we see the possibility (supposing,

of course, that there is such a possibility in the world) of the real "*love* of one's enemies." What respect for his enemies is found, forsooth, in an aristocratic man—and such a reverence is already a bridge to love! He insists on having his enemy to himself as his distinction. He tolerates no other enemy but a man in whose character there is nothing to despise and *much* to honour! On the other hand, imagine the "enemy" as the resentful man conceives him—and it is here exactly that we see his work, his creativeness; he has conceived "the evil enemy," the "evil one," and indeed that is the root idea from which he now evolves as a contrasting and corresponding figure a "good one," himself—his very self!

The method of this man is quite contrary to that of the aristocratic man, who conceives the root idea "good" spontaneously and straight away, that is to say, out of himself, and from that material then creates for himself a concept of "bad"! This "bad" of aristocratic origin and that "evil" out of the cauldron of unsatisfied hatred—the former an imitation, an "extra," an additional nuance; the latter, on the other hand, the original, the beginning, the essential act in the conception of a slave-morality—these two words "bad" and "evil," how great a difference do they mark, in spite of the fact that they have an identical contrary in the idea "good." But the idea "good" is *not* the same: much rather let the question be asked, "Who is really evil according to the meaning of the morality of resentment?" In all sternness let it be answered thus:—*just* the good man of the other morality, just the aristocrat, the powerful one, the one who rules, but who is distorted by the venomous eye of resentfulness, into a new colour, a new signification, a new appearance. This particular point we would be the last to deny: the man who learnt to know those "good" ones only as enemies, learnt at the same time not to know them only as "*evil enemies,*" and the same men who . . . were kept so rigorously in bounds through convention, respect, custom, and gratitude, though much more through mutual vigilance and jealousy, . . . these men who in their relations with each other find so many new ways of manifesting consideration, self-control, delicacy, loyalty, pride, and friendship, these men are in reference to what is outside their circle (where the foreign element, a *foreign* country, begins), not much better than beasts of prey, which have been let loose. They enjoy there freedom from all social control, they feel that in the wilderness they can give vent with impunity to that tension which is produced by enclosure and imprisonment in the peace of society, they *revert* to the innocence of the beast-of-prey conscience, like jubilant monsters, who perhaps come from a ghostly bout of murder, arson, rape, and torture, with bravado and a moral equanimity, as though merely some wild student's prank had been played, perfectly convinced that the poets have now an ample theme to sing and celebrate. It is impossible not to recognise at the core of all these aristocratic races the beast of prey; the magnificent *blonde brute,* avidly rampant for spoil and victory; this hidden core needed an outlet from time to time, the beast must get loose again, must return into the wilderness—the Roman, Arabic, German, and Japanese nobility, the Homeric heroes, the Scandinavian Vikings, are all alike in this need. It is the aristocratic races who have left the idea "Barbarian" on all the tracks in which they have marched; nay, a consciousness of this very barbarianism, and even a pride in it, manifests itself even in their highest civilisation (for example, when Pericles says to his Athenians in that celebrated funeral oration, "Our audacity has forced a way over every land and sea, rearing everywhere imperishable memorials of itself for *good* and for *evil*"). This audacity of aristocratic races, mad, absurd, and spasmodic as may be its expression; the incalculable and fantastic nature of their enterprises, . . . their nonchalance and contempt for safety, body, life, and comfort, their awful joy and intense delight in all destruction, in all the ecstasies of victory and cruelty,—all these features become crystallised, for those who suffered thereby in the picture of the "barbar-

ian," of the "evil enemy," perhaps of the "Goth" and of the "Vandal." The profound, icy mistrust which the German provokes, as soon as he arrives at power,—even at the present time,—is always still an aftermath of that inextinguishable horror with which for whole centuries Europe has regarded the wrath of the blonde Teuton beast. . . .

. . . One may be perfectly justified in being always afraid of the blonde beast that lies at the core of all aristocratic races, and in being on one's guard: but who would not a hundred times prefer to be afraid, when one at the same time admires, than to be immune from fear, at the cost of being perpetually obsessed with the loathsome spectacle of the distorted, the dwarfed, the stunted, the envenomed? And is that not our fate? What produces to-day our repulsion towards "man"?—for we *suffer* from "man," there is no doubt about it. It is not fear; it is rather that we have nothing more to fear from men; it is that the worm "man" is in the foreground and pullulates; it is that the "tame man," the wretched mediocre and unedifying creature, has learnt to consider himself a goal and a pinnacle, an inner meaning, an historic principle, a "higher man"; yes, it is that he has a certain right so to consider himself, in so far as he feels that in contrast to that excess of deformity, disease, exhaustion, and effeteness whose odour is beginning to pollute present-day Europe, he at any rate has achieved a relative success, he at any rate still says "yes" to life.

Goodness and the Will to Power

What is good?—All that enhances the feeling of power, the Will to Power, and the power itself in man. What is bad?—All that proceeds from weakness. What is happiness?—The feeling that power is increasing—that resistance has been overcome.

Not contentment, but more power; not peace at any price but war; not virtue, but competence (virtue in the Renaissance sense, *virtu,* free from all moralistic acid). The first principle of our humanism: The weak and the failures shall perish. They ought even to be helped to perish.

What is more harmful than any vice?—Practical sympathy and pity for all the failures and all the weak: Christianity.

Christianity is the religion of pity. Pity opposes the noble passions which heighten our vi-

tality. It has a depressing effect, depriving us of strength. As we multiply the instances of pity we gradually lose our strength of nobility. Pity makes suffering contagious and under certain conditions it may cause a total loss of life and vitality out of all proportion to the magnitude of the cause. . . . Pity is the practice of nihilism.

For Further Reflection

1. What do you make of the parable of God's death? What is its significance for ethics?

2. A good exercise for getting a grip on the radicality of Nietzsche's ethics is to read Jesus' Sermon on the Mount (Matthew 5–7) after reading Nietzsche. Discuss the contrast.

3. Compare Nietzsche's ethics with Aristotle's ethics of virtue. What are the similarities and differences? How might Aristotle respond to the charge that his ethics are really a "gentleman's" version of Nietzsche's more shocking ideas?

Suggestions for Further Reading

GENERAL WORKS

Baier, Kurt. *The Moral Point of View.* Cornell University Press, 1958.

Beauchamp, Tom L. *Philosophical Ethics.* McGraw-Hill, 1982. A good blend of analysis with readings.

Brandt, Richard. *Ethical Theory.* Englewood Cliffs, NJ: Prentice-Hall, 1959. A solid, comprehensive work on ethical theory.

Feldman, Fred. *Introductory Ethics.* Englewood Cliffs, NJ: Prentice-Hall, 1978. An excellent expression of analytic method applied to ethical theory.

Harris, C. E. *Applying Moral Theories.* Belmont, CA: Wadsworth, 1986.

MacIntyre, A. *A Short History of Ethics.* Macmillan, 1966.

Mackie, J. L. *Ethics: Inventing Right and Wrong.* Penguin, 1977.

Pojman, Louis, ed. *Ethical Theory: Classical and Contemporary.* Belmont, CA: Wadsworth, 1989.

Rachels, James. *The Elements of Moral Philosophy.* New York: Random House, 1986. An elementary, succinct introduction.

Taylor, Paul. *Principles of Ethics.* Dickenson, 1975.

ETHICAL RELATIVISM

Copp, David, and David Zimmerman, eds. *Morality, Reason and Truth: New Essays on the Foundations of Ethics.* Rowman & Allanheld, 1984.

Gewirth, Alan. *Reason and Morality.* Chicago: University of Chicago Press, 1978.

Gillispie, Norman, ed. *Moral Realism (Southern Journal of Philosophy,* vol. XXIV, Supplement), 1986. This volume contains an excellent collection of essays on moral realism, including a bibliography on the subject by Geoffrey Sayre-McCord.

Ladd, John, ed. *Ethical Relativism*. Belmont, CA: Wadsworth, 1973.

Stace, W. T. *The Concept of Morals*. Macmillan, 1937.

Wellman, Carl. "The Ethical Implications of Cultural Relativity." *Journal of Philosophy,* LX, 1963.

Werner, Richard. "Ethical Realism." *Ethics,* vol. 93, 1983.

Westermarck, Edward. *Ethical Relativity*. Humanities Press, 1960.

Williams, Bernard. *Morality*. Harper Torchbooks, 1972.

Wong, David. *Moral Relativity*. University of California Press, 1985.

MORALITY AND SELF INTEREST

Gauthier, David, ed. *Morality and Rational Self-Interest*. Englewood Cliffs, NJ: Prentice-Hall, 1970.

Gauthier, David. *Morality by Agreement*. Clarendon Press, 1986.

MacIntyre, Aladair. "Egoism and Altruism" in *The Encyclopedia of Philosophy,* ed. Paul Edwards. Macmillan, 1967.

Sidgwick, Henry. *The Methods of Ethics*. Seventh ed. Hackett, 1981.

Slote, Michael. "An Empirical Basis for Psychological Egoism." *Journal of Philosophy,* vol. 61.

ETHICAL THEORIES

Aristotle. *Nicomachean Ethics,* trans. Terence Irwin. Hackett, 1985.

Becker, Lawrence. *On Justifying Moral Arguments,* chap. 19. London: Routledge & Kegan Paul, 1973.

Cooper, John. *Reason and the Human Good in Aristotle*. Harvard University Press, 1975.

Aristotle. *Nicomachean Ethics,* trans. Terence Irwin. Hackett, 1985.

Donagan, Alan. *The Theory of Morality*. Chicago: University of Chicago Press, 1977.

Hare, Richard. *Reason and Freedom*. Oxford University Press, 1961.

Kant, Immanuel. *Fundamental Principles of the Metaphysics of Morals,* trans. Lewis Beck. Bobbs-Merrill, 1949.

Kruschwitz, Robert, and Robert Roberts, eds. *The Virtues*. Belmont, CA: Wadsworth, 1987. An excellent up-to-date anthology.

MacIntyre, Alasdair. *After Virtue*. University of Notre Dame Press, 1981.

Mill, John Stuart. *Utilitarianism*. Bobbs-Merrill, 1957.

Singer, Peter. *The Expanding Circle*. Oxford University Press, 1983. A nice job of integrating sociobiology with moral theory.

Smart, J. J. C. and Bernard Williams. *Utilitarianism: For and Against*. Cambridge University Press, 1973. A classic debate.

Sommers, Christina Hoff, ed. *Vice and Virtues in Everyday Life*. Harcourt Brace Jovanovich, 1985.

Taylor, Richard. *Good and Evil*. Macmillan, 1970.

Taylor, Richard. *Ethics, Faith and Reason*. Englewood Cliffs, NJ: Prentice-Hall, 1985.

Warnock, G. J. *The Object of Morality*. Methuen, 1971.

Part VII

Political Philosophy

In heaven, there is laid up a pattern of the Ideal City, methinks, which he who desires may behold, and beholding, may set his own house in order. But whether such an one exists, or ever will exist in fact, is no matter: for he will live after the manner of that city, having nothing to do with any other.

PLATO, *Republic* IX, 592, trans. Jowett

Y OU ARE FILLING OUT your yearly federal income tax forms and become irritated at the large sum of money that you are going to have to pay, $5,000. If that weren't bad enough, you don't believe in the programs for which most of the money will be spent. You ask yourself, what right does the government have to demand payment of me? But you don't like the likely consequences of not paying—a prison sentence—so you very reluctantly write out a check for $5,000, realizing that you will not be able to afford needed house repairs or a vacation this year.

So you put your forms with a check inside an envelope and go out to mail your income tax at the nearest mailbox. On your way home a man accosts you with a gun. "Your money or your life," he roughly demands. You open your wallet and hand him the $100 therein. You continue home, beaten in spirit, feeling twice robbed, and wondering which is the greater robber, the gunman or the government?

You ask yourself if that feeling is justified. Is the government, with its laws, only a gunman who observes reliable rituals and procedures and, unlike the robber, warns you in advance that it will take a percentage of your money at a certain time every year? You've always been a law-abiding citizen, but now you wonder, by what right does the government demand my obedience? Why should I obey the State? What is the justification of government?

Why Should I Obey the Government?
What Is the Justification of Political Authority?

Many answers have been given to these questions, some emphasizing the need for protection and orderly process as the justification of government, others emphasizing the promotion of the spiritual or cultural aspects of the people, and still others emphasizing the economic well-being, which in turn is seen as the foundation for all other values.

In our readings in this part of our book we find five different answers to these questions: (1) the Hobbesian answer, which says that the state of nature without political security is so dangerous, barbarous, and impoverished that it is rational to give up significant freedom to the State in order to obtain peace and security; (2) the Lockean answer, which agrees with Hobbes that we contract with the State to give up some freedom for security, but disagrees with Hobbes on the degree of the surrender. We do not give up our natural rights to life, property, representation, and other goods—better a state of nature, which is not as bad as Hobbes makes out, than slavery to the State! (3) the utilitarian answer developed by John Stuart Mill that the function of government is to protect individuals from "the tyranny of the majority," so that they can fulfil themselves in their own particular ways; (4) the libertarian answer, represented in our readings by John Hospers, founder of the Libertarian party in the United States, which goes further than Locke or Mill in honoring freedom, especially our right to own property, and in insisting that the only function of the State is to protect us from external and internal enemies—otherwise, the government that governs least, governs best; and (5) the Marxist answer, which is diametrically opposite the libertarian position and argues that property should belong to the State so that it might make use of it for human good, taking from each as he or she is able and giving to each as he or she has need. In other words, the function which justifies political authority is that of justice: of justly distributing the goods of the society in a radical egalitarian manner. Because capitalist societies fail to promote this state of justice, the proletariat is justified in overthrowing the State by revolutionary means.

The Absolutist Answer: The Justification of the State Is the Security It Affords

VII.1

THOMAS HOBBES

Thomas Hobbes (1588–1679) is the greatest English political philosopher, who gave classic expression to the idea that morality and politics arise out of a social contract. He was born in the year of the Spanish Armada, was educated at Oxford University, and lived through an era of political revolutions as a scholar and tutor (he was tutor to Prince Charles II of England). He was widely travelled and was in communication with most of the intellectual luminaries of his day, both on the continent (Galileo, Gassendi, and Descartes) and in England (Francis Bacon, Ben Johnson, and William Harvey), and was regarded as a brilliant, if somewhat unorthodox and controversial, intellectual.

Hobbes is known today primarily for his masterpiece in political theory, *Leviathan* (1651), a book that was suppressed in his own day for its controversial ideas. In this book, from which our selection is taken, he develops a moral and political theory based on psychological egoism. Hobbes argues that people are all egoists who always act in their own self-interest, to obtain gratification and avoid harm. However, we cannot obtain any of the basic goods because of the inherent fear and insecurity in an unregulated "state of nature," in which life is "solitary, poor, nasty, brutish, and short." We cannot relax our guard, for everyone is constantly in fear of everyone else. In this state of anarchy the prudent person concludes that it really is in all our self-interest to make a contract to keep to a minimal morality of respecting human life, keeping covenants made, and obeying the society's laws. This minimal morality, which Hobbes refers to as "the laws of nature," is nothing more than a set of maxims of prudence. In order to ensure that we all obey this covenant Hobbes proposes a strong sovereign or "Leviathan" to impose severe penalties on those who disobey the laws, for "covenants without the sword are but words."

Study Questions

1. According to Hobbes, in what sense are all persons equal?
2. What is the natural relationship between people in the state of nature? Describe the state of nature. Are Hobbes' examples appropriate?
3. Does the notion of justice have any application in the state of nature? Why or why not?
4. What is necessary in order to establish morality and law?
5. What is the difference between the right of nature and the law of nature?
6. What is a contract, according to Hobbes?
7. How does Hobbes define good and evil?
8. What is the solution to the horrible state of nature?
9. What is the Leviathan? Why does Hobbes use this image?

Of the Natural Condition of Mankind as Concerning Their Felicity, and Misery

NATURE HATH MADE men so equal, in the faculties of the body, and mind; as that though there be found one man sometimes manifestly stronger in body, or of quicker mind than another; yet when all is reckoned together, the difference between man, and man, is not so considerable, as that one man can thereupon claim to himself any benefit, to which another may not pretend, as well as he. For as to the strength of body, the weakest has strength enough to kill the strongest, either by secret machination, or by confederacy with others, that are in the same danger with himself.

And as to the faculties of the mind, setting aside the arts grounded upon words, and especially that skill of proceeding upon general, and infallible rules, called science; which very few have, and but in few things; as being not a native faculty, born with us; nor attained, as prudence, while we look after somewhat else, I find yet a greater equality amongst men, than that of strength. For prudence, is but experience; which

equal time, equally bestows on all men, in those things they equally apply themselves unto. That which may perhaps make such equality incredible, is but a vain conceit of one's own wisdom, which almost all men think they have in a greater degree, than the vulgar; that is, than all men but themselves, and a few others, whom by fame, or for concurring with themselves, and a few others, whom by fame, or for concurring with themselves, they approve. For such is the nature of men, that howsoever they may acknowledge many others to be more witty, or more eloquent, or more learned; yet they will hardly believe there be many so wise as themselves; for they see their own wit at hand, and other men's at a distance. But this proveth rather that men are in that point equal, than unequal. For there is not ordinarily a greater sign of the equal distribution of any thing, than that every man is contented with his share.

From this equality of ability, ariseth equality of hope in the attaining of our ends. And therefore if any two men desire the same thing, which nevertheless they cannot both enjoy, they become enemies; and in the way to their end,

From Leviathan, *1651*.

which is principally their own conservation, and sometimes their delectation only, endeavour to destroy, or subdue one another. And from hence it comes to pass, that where an invader hath no more to fear, than another man's single power; if one plant, sow, build, or possess a convenient seat, others may probably be expected to come prepared with forces united, to dispossess, and deprive him, not only of the fruit of his labour, but also of his life, or liberty. And the invader again is in the like danger of another.

And from this diffidence of one another, there is no way for any man to secure himself, so reasonable, as anticipation; that is, by force, or wiles, to master the persons of all men he can, so long, till he see no other power great enough to endanger him: and this is no more than his own conservation requireth, and is generally allowed. Also because there be some, that taking pleasure in contemplating their own power in the acts of conquest, which they pursue farther than their security requires; if others, that otherwise would be glad to be at ease within modest bounds, should not by invasion increase their power, they would not be able, long time, by standing only on their defence, to subsist. And by consequence, such augmentation of dominion over men being necessary to a man's conservation, it ought to be allowed him.

Again, men have no pleasure, but on the contrary a great deal of grief, in keeping company, where there is no power able to over-awe them all. For every man looketh that his companion should value him, at the same rate he sets upon himself: and upon all signs of contempt, or undervaluing, naturally endeavours, as far as he dares, (which amongst them that have no common power to keep them in quiet, is far enough to make them destroy each other), to extort a greater value from his contemners, by damage; and from others, by the example.

So that in the nature of man, we find three principal causes of quarrel. First, competition; secondly, diffidence; thirdly, glory.

The first, maketh men invade for gain; the second, for safety; and the third, for reputation. The first use violence, to make themselves masters of other men's persons, wives, children, and cattle; the second, the defend them; the third, for trifles, as a word, a smile, a different option, and any other sign of undervalue, either direct in their persons, or by reflection in their kindred, their friends, their nation, their profession, or their name.

Hereby it is manifest, that during the time men live without a common power to keep them all in awe, they are in that condition which is called war; and such a war, as is of every man, against every man. For war, consisteth not in battle only, or the act of fighting; but in a tract of time, wherein the will to contend by battle is sufficiently known: and therefore the notion of *time,* is to be considered in the nature of war; as it is in the nature of weather. For as the nature of foul weather, lieth not in the shower or two of rain; but in an inclination thereto of many days together: so the nature of war, consisteth not in actual fighting; but in the known disposition thereto, during all the time there is no assurance to the contrary. All other time is PEACE.

Whatsoever therefore is consequent to a time of war, where every man is enemy to every man; the same is consequent to the time, wherein men live without other security, than what their own strength, and their own invention shall furnish them withal. In such condition, there is no place for industry; because the fruit thereof is uncertain: and consequently no culture of the earth; no navigation, nor use of the commodities that may be imported by sea; no commodious building; no instruments of moving, and removing, such things as require much force; no knowledge of the face of the earth; no account of time; no arts; no letters; no society; and which is worst of all, continual fear, and danger of violent death; and the life of man, solitary, poor, nasty, brutish, and short.

It may seem strange to some man, that has not well weighed these things; that nature should thus dissociate, and render men apt to invade, and destroy one another: and he may therefore, not trusting to this inference, made from the passions, desire perhaps to have the same confirmed by experience. Let him therefore consider with himself, when taking a journey, he arms himself, and seeks to go well accompanied; when going to sleep, he locks his doors; when even in his house he locks his chests; and this when he knows there be laws, and public officers, armed, to revenge all injuries shall be done him; what opinion he has of his fellow-subjects, when he rides armed; of his fellow citizens, when he locks his doors; and of his children, and servants, when he locks his chests. Does he not there as much accuse mankind by his actions, as I do by my words? But neither of us accuse man's nature in it. The desires, and other passions of man, are in themselves no sin. No more are the actions, that proceed from those passions, till they know a law that forbids them: which till laws be made they cannot know: nor can any law be made, till they have agreed upon the person that shall make it.

It may peradventure be thought, there was never such a time, nor condition of war as this; and I believe it was never generally so, over all the world: but there are many places, where they live so now. For the savage people in many places of America, except the government of small families, the concord whereof dependeth on natural lust, have no government at all; and live at this day in that brutish manner, as I said before. Howsoever, it may be perceived what manner of life there would be, where there were no common power to fear, by the manner of life, which men that have formerly lived under a peaceful government, use to degenerate into, in a civil war.

But though there had never been any time, wherein particular men were in a condition of war one against another; yet in all times, kings, and persons of sovereign authority, because of their independency, are in continual jealousies, and in the state and posture of gladiators; having their weapons pointing, and their eyes fixed on one another; that is, their forts, garrisons, and guns upon the frontiers of their kingdoms; and continual spies upon their neighbours; which is a posture of war. But because they uphold thereby, the industry of their subjects; there does not follow from it, that misery, which accompanies the liberty of particular men.

To this war of every man, against every man, this also is consequent; that nothing can be unjust. The notions of right and wrong, justice and injustice have there no place. Where there is no common power, there is no law: where no law, no injustice. Force, and fraud, are in war the two cardinal virtues. Justice, and injustice are none of the faculties neither of the body, nor mind. If they were, they might be in a man that were alone in the world, as well as his senses, and passions. They are qualities, that relate to men in society, not in solitude. It is consequent also to the same condition, that there be no propriety, no dominion, no *mine* and *thine* distinct; but only that to be every man's, that he can get; and for so long, as he can keep it. And thus much for the ill condition, which man by mere nature is actually placed in; though with a possibility to come out of it, consisting partly in the passions, partly in his reason.

The passions that incline men to peace, are fear of death; desire of such things as are necessary to commodious living; and a hope by their industry to obtain them. And reason suggesteth convenient articles of peace, upon which men may be drawn to agreement. These articles, are they, which otherwise are called the Laws of Nature: whereof I shall speak more particularly, in the two following chapters.

Of the First and Second Natural Laws, and of Contracts

The right of nature, which writers commonly call *jus naturale,* is the liberty each man hath, to use his own power, as he will himself, for the preservation of his own nature; that is to say, of his own life; and consequently, of doing any thing, which in his own judgment, and reason, he shall conceive to be the aptest means thereunto.

By LIBERTY, is understood, according to the proper signification of the word, the absence of external impediments: which impediments, may oft take away part of a man's power to do what he would; but cannot hinder him from using the power left him, according as his judgment, and reason shall dictate to him.

A LAW OF NATURE, *lex naturalis,* is a precept or general rule, found out by reason, by which a man is forbidden to do that, which is destructive of his life, or taketh away the means of preserving the same; and to omit that, by which he thinketh it may be best preserved. For though they that speak of this subject, use to confound *jus,* and *lex, right* and *law:* yet they ought to be distinguished; because RIGHT, consisteth in liberty to do, or to forbear; whereas LAW, determineth, and bindeth to one of them: so that law, and right, differ as much, as obligation, and liberty; which in one and the same matter are inconsistent.

And because the condition of man, as hath been declared in the precedent chapter, is a condition of war of every one against every one; in which case every one is governed by his own reason; and there is nothing he can make use of, that may not be a help unto him, in preserving his life against his enemies; it followeth, that in such a condition, every man has a right to every thing; even to one another's body. And therefore, as long as this natural right of every man to every thing endureth, there can be no security to any man, how strong or wise soever he be, of living out the time, which nature ordinarily alloweth men to live. And consequently it is a precept, or general rule of reason, *that every man, ought to endeavour peace, as far as he has hope of obtaining it; and when he cannot obtain it, that he may seek, and use, all helps, and advantages of war.* The first branch of which rule, containeth the first, and fundamental law of nature; which is, *to seek peace, and follow it.* The second, the sum of

the right of nature; which is, *by all means we can, to defend ourselves.*

From this fundamental law of nature, by which men are commanded to endeavour peace, is derived this second law; *that a man be willing, when others are so too, as far-forth, as for peace, and defence of himself he shall think it necessary, to lay down this right to all things; and be contented with so much liberty against other men, as he would allow other men against himself.* For as long as every man holdeth this right, of doing any thing he liketh; so long are all men in the condition of war. But if other men will not lay down their right, as well as he; then there is no reason for any one, to divest himself of his: for that were to expose himself to prey, which no man is bound to, rather than to dispose himself to peace. This is that law of the Gospel; *whatsoever you require that others should do to you, that do ye to them.* And that law of all men, *quod tibi fieri non vis, alteri ne feceris.* *

To *lay down* a man's *right* to any thing, is to *divest* himself of the *liberty,* of hindering another of the benefit of his own right to the same. For he that renounceth, or passeth away his right, giveth not to any other man a right which he had not before; because there is nothing to which every man had not right by nature: but only standeth out of his way, that he may enjoy his own original right, without hindrance from him; not without hindrance from another. So that the effect which redoundeth to one man, by another man's defect of right, is but so much diminution of impediments to the use of his own right original.

Right is laid aside, either by simply renouncing it; or by transferring it to another. By *simply* RENOUNCING; when he cares not to whom the benefit thereof redoundeth. By TRANSFERRING; when he intendeth the benefit thereof to some certain person, or persons. And when a man hath in either manner abandoned, or granted

*["What you do not want done to you, do not do to others."—ed. note]

away his right; then is he said to be OBLIGED, or BOUND, not to hinder those, to whom such right is granted, or abandoned, from the benefit of it: and that he *ought,* and it is his DUTY, not to make void that voluntary act of his own: and that such hindrance is INJUSTICE, and INJURY, as being *sine jure,** the right being before renounced, or transferred. So that *injury, or injustice,* in the controversies of the world, is somewhat like to that, which in the disputations of scholars is called *absurdity.* For as it is there called an absurdity, to contradict what one maintained in the beginning: so in the world, it is called injustice, and injury, voluntarily to undo that, which from the beginning he had voluntarily done. The way by which a man either simply renounceth, or transferreth his right, is a declaration, or signification, by some voluntary and sufficient sign, or signs, that he doth so renounce, or transfer; or hath so renounced, or transferred the same, to him that accepteth it. And these signs are either words only, or actions only; or, as it happeneth most often, both words, and actions. And the same are the BONDS, by which men are bound, and obliged: bonds, that have their strength, not from their own nature, for nothing is more easily broken than a man's word, but from fear of some evil consequence upon the rupture.

Whensoever a man transferreth his right, or renounceth it; it is either in consideration of some right reciprocally transferred to himself; or for some other good he hopeth for thereby. For it is a voluntary act: and of the voluntary acts of every man, the object is some *good to himself.* And therefore there be some rights, which no man can be understood by any words, or other signs, to have abandoned, or transferred. At first a man cannot lay down the right of resisting them, that assault him by force, to take away his life; because he cannot be understood to aim thereby, at any good to himself. The same may be said of wounds, and chains, and imprisonment; both because there is no benefit conse-

quent to such patience; as there is to the patience of suffering another to be wounded, or imprisoned: as also because a man cannot tell, when he seeth men proceed against him by violence, whether they intend his death or not. And lastly the motive, and end for which this renouncing, and transferring of right is introduced, is nothing else but the security of a man's person, in his life, and in the means of so preserving life, as not to be weary of it. And therefore if a man by words, or other signs, seem to despoil himself of the end, for which those signs were intended; he is not to be understood as if he meant it, or that it was his will; but that he was ignorant of how such words and actions were to be interpreted.

The mutual transferring of right, is that which men call CONTRACT.

There is a difference between transferring of right to the thing; and transferring, or tradition, that is delivery of the thing itself. For the thing may be delivered together with the translation of the right; as in buying and selling with ready-money; or exchange of goods, or lands: and it may be delivered some time after.

Again, one of the contractors, may deliver the thing contracted for on his part, and leave the other to perform his part as some determinate time after, and in the mean time be trusted; and then the contract on his part, is called PACT, or COVENANT: or both parts may contract now, to perform hereafter: in which cases, he that is to perform in time to come, being trusted, his performance is called *keeping of promise,* or faith; and the failing of performance, if it be voluntary, *violation of faith.*

When the transferring of right, is not mutual: but one of the parties transferreth, in hope to gain thereby friendship, or service from another, or from his friends; or in hope to gain the reputation of charity, or magnanimity; or to deliver his mind from the pain of compassion; or in hope of reward in heaven, this is not contract, but GIFT, FREE-GIFT, GRACE: which words signify one and the same thing.

Signs of contract, are either *express,* or *by inference.* Express, are words spoken with under-

---

*[that is, without right.—ed. note]

standing of what they signify: and such words are either of the time *present*, or *past*; as, *I give, I grant, I have given, I have granted, I will that this be yours:* or of the future; as, *I will give, I will grant:* which words of the future are called PROMISE.

If a covenant be made, wherein neither of the parties perform presently, but trust one another; in the condition of mere nature, which is a condition of war of every man against every man, upon any reasonable suspicion, it is void: but if there be a common power set over them both, with right and force sufficient to compel performance, it is not void. For he that performeth first, has no assurance the other will perform after; because the bonds of words are too weak to bridle men's ambition, avarice, anger, and other passions, without the fear of some coercive power; which in the condition of mere nature, where all men are equal, and judges of the justness of their own fears, cannot possibly be supposed. And therefore he which performeth first, does but betray himself to his enemy; contrary to the right, he can never abandon, of defending his life, and means of living.

But in a civil estate, where there is a power set up to constrain those that would otherwise violate their faith, that fear is no more reasonable: and for that cause, he which by the covenant is to perform first, is obliged so to do.

The cause of fear, which maketh such a covenant invalid, must be always something arising after the covenant made; as some new fact, or other sign of the will not to perform: else it cannot make the covenant void. For that which could not hinder a man from promising, ought not to be admitted as a hindrance of performing.

Of Other Laws of Nature

From that law of nature, by which we are obliged to transfer to another, such rights, as being retained, hinder the peace of mankind, there followeth a third; which is this, *that men perform their covenants made:* without which, covenants are in vain, and but empty words; and the right of all men to all things remaining, we are still in the condition of war.

And in this law of nature, consisteth the fountain and original of JUSTICE. For where no covenant hath preceded, there hath no right been transferred, and every man has right to every thing; and consequently, no action can be unjust. But when a covenant is made, then to break it is *unjust:* and the definition of INJUSTICE, is no other than *the not performance of covenant.* And whatsoever is not unjust, is *just.*

But because covenants of mutual trust, where there is a fear of not performance on either part, as hath been said in the former chapter, are invalid; though the original of justice be the making of covenants; yet injustice actually there can be none, till the cause of such fear be taken away; which while men are in the natural condition of war, cannot be done. Therefore before the names of just, and unjust can have place, there must be some coercive power, to compel men equally to the performance of their covenants, by the terror of some punishment, greater than the benefit they expect by the breach of their covenant; and to make good that propriety, which by mutual contract men acquire, in recompense of the universal right they abandon: and such power there is none before the erection of a commonwealth. And this is also to be gathered out of the ordinary definition of justice in the Schools: for they say, that *justice is the constant will of giving to every man his own,* and therefore where there is no *own,* that is, no propriety, there is no injustice; and where there is no coercive power erected, that is, where there is no commonwealth, there is no propriety; all men having right to all things: therefore where there is no commonwealth, there nothing is unjust. So that the nature of justice, consisteth in keeping of valid covenants: but the validity of covenants begins not but with the constitution of a civil power, sufficient to compel men to keep them: and then it is also that propriety begins. . . .

And because, though men be never so willing to observe these laws, there may nevertheless arise questions concerning a man's action; first, whether it were done, or not done; secondly, if done, whether against the law, or not against the law; the former whereof, is called a question *of fact;* the latter a question *of right,* therefore unless the parties to the question, covenant mutually to stand to the sentence of another, they are as far from peace as ever. This other to whose sentence they submit is called an ARBITRATOR. And therefore it is of the law of nature, *that they that are at controversy, submit their right to the judgment of an arbitrator.*

And seeing every man is presumed to do all things in order to his own benefit, no man is a fit arbitrator in his own cause; and if he were never so fit; yet equity allowing to each party equal benefit, if one be admitted to the judge, the other is to be admitted also; and so the controversy, that is, the cause of war, remains, against the law of nature.

For the same reason no man in any cause ought to be received for arbitrator, to whom greater profit, or honour, or pleasure apparently ariseth out of the victory of one party, than of the other: for he hath taken, though an unavoidable bribe, yet a bribe; and no man can be obliged to trust him. And thus also the controversy, and the condition of war remaineth, contrary to the law of nature.

And in a controversy of *fact,* the judge being to give no more credit to one, than to the other, if there be no other arguments, must give credit to a third; or to a third and fourth; or more: for else the question is undecided, and left to force, contrary to the law of nature.

These are the laws of nature, dictating peace, for a means of the conservation of men in multitudes; and which only concern the doctrine of civil society. There be other things tending to the destruction of particular men; as drunkenness, and all other parts of intemperance; which may therefore also be reckoned amongst those things which the law of nature hath forbidden; but are not necessary to be mentioned, nor are pertinent enough to this place.

And though this may seem too subtle a deduction of the laws of nature, to be taken notice of by all men; whereof the most part are too busy in getting food, and the rest too negligent to understand; yet to leave all men inexcusable, they have been contracted into one easy sum, intelligible even to the meanest capacity; and that is, *Do not that to another, which thou wouldest not have done to thyself;* which sheweth him, that he has no more to do in learning the laws of nature, but, when weighing the actions of other men with his own, they seem too heavy, to put them into the other part of the balance, and his own into their place, that his own passions, and self-love, may add nothing to the weight; and then there is none of these laws of nature that will not appear unto him very reasonable.

The laws of nature oblige *in foro interno;** that is to say, they bind to a desire they should take place: but *in foro externo,*† that is, to the putting them in act, not always. For he that should be modest, and tractable, and perform all he promises, in such time, and place, where no man else should do so, should but make himself a prey to others, and procure his own certain ruin, contrary to the ground of all laws of nature, which tend to nature's preservation. And again, he that having sufficient security, that others shall observe the same laws towards him, observes them not himself, seeketh not peace, but war; and consequently the destruction of his nature by violence.

And whatsoever laws bind *in foro interno,* may be broken, not only by a fact contrary to the law, but also by a fact according to it, in case a man think it contrary. For though his action in this case, be according to the law; yet his purpose was against the law; which, where the obligation is *in foro interno,* is a breach.

The laws of nature are immutable and eternal; for injustice, ingratitude, arrogance, pride, iniquity, acception of persons, and the rest, can never be made lawful. For it can never be that war shall preserve life, and peace destroy it.

* [literally, "in the internal forum"—that is, in a person's mind or conscience.—ed. note]
† [literally, "in the external forum"—that is, in the public world of action.—ed. note]

The same laws, because they oblige only to a desire, and endeavour, I mean an unfeigned and constant endeavour, are easy to be observed. For in that they require nothing but endeavour, he that endeavoureth their performance, fulfilleth them; and he that fulfilleth the law, is just.

And the science of them, is the true and only moral philosophy. For moral philosophy is nothing else but the science of what is *good*, and *evil*, in the conversation, and society of mankind. *Good*, and *evil*, are names that signify our appetites, and aversions; which in different tempers, customs, and doctrines of men, are different: and divers men, differ not only in their judgment, on the sense of what is pleasant, and unpleasant to the taste, smell, hearing, touch, and sight; but also of what is conformable, or disagreeable to reason, in the actions of common life. Nay, the same man, in divers times, differs from himself; and one time praiseth, that is, calleth good, what another time he dispraiseth, and called evil: from whence arise disputes, controversies, and at last war. And therefore so long as a man is in the condition of mere nature, which is a condition of war, as private appetite is the measure of good, and evil: and consequently all men agree on this, that peace is good, and therefore also the way, or means of peace, which, as I have shewed before, are *justice, gratitude, modesty, equity, mercy,* and the rest of the laws of nature, are good; that is to say; *moral virtues;* and their contrary *vices,* evil. Now the science of virtue and vice, is moral philosophy; and therefore the true doctrine of the laws of nature, is the true moral philosophy. But the writers of moral philosophy, though they acknowledge the same virtues and vices; yet not seeing wherein consisted their goodness; nor that they come to be praised, as the means of peaceable, sociable, and comfortable living, place them in a mediocrity of passions: as if not the cause, but the degree of daring, made fortitude; or not the cause, but the quantity of a gift, made liberality.

These dictates of reason, men used to call by the name of laws, but improperly: for they are but conclusions, of theorems concerning what conduceth to the conservation and defence of themselves; whereas law, properly, is the word of him, that by right hath command over others. But yet if we consider the same theorems, as delivered in the word of God, that by right commandeth all things; then are they properly called laws.

Of the Causes, Generation, and Definition of a Commonwealth

The final cause, end, or design of men, who naturally love liberty, and dominion over others, in the introduction of that restraint upon themselves, in which we see them live in commonwealths, is the foresight of their own preservation, and of a more contented life thereby; that is to say, of getting themselves out from that miserable condition of war, which is necessarily consequent, as hath been shown in chapter XIII, to the natural passions of men, when there is no visible power to keep them in awe, and tie them by fear of punishment to the performance of their covenants, and observation of those laws of nature set down in the fourteenth and fifteenth chapters.

For the laws of nature, as *justice, equity, modesty, mercy,* and, in sum, *doing to others, as we would be done to,* of themselves, without the terror of some power, to cause them to be observed, are contrary to our natural passions, that carry us to partiality, pride, revenge, and the like. And covenants, without the sword, are but words, and of no strength to secure a man at all. Therefore notwithstanding the laws of nature, which every one hath then kept, when he has the will to keep them, when he can do it safely, if there be no power erected, or not great enough for our security; every man will, and may lawfully rely on his own strength and art, for caution against all other men. And in all places, where men have lived by small families, to rob and spoil one another, has been a trade, and so far from being reputed against the law of nature, that the greater spoils they gained, the greater was their honour; and men observed no other laws therein, but the laws of honour; that is, to abstain from cruelty, leaving to men their lives, and instruments of husbandry. And as small families did then; so now do cities and kingdoms which are but greater families, for their own security, enlarge their dominions, upon all pretences of danger, and fear of invasion, or assistance that may be given to invaders, and endeavour as much as they can, to subdue, or weaken their neighbours, by open force, and secret arts, for want of other caution, justly; and are remembered for it in after ages with honour.

It is true, that certain living creatures, as bees, and ants, live sociably one with another, which are therefore by Aristotle numbered amongst political creatures; and yet have no other direction, than their particular judgments and appetites; nor speech, whereby one of them can signify to another, what he thinks expedient for the common benefit: and therefore some man may perhaps desire to know, why mankind cannot do the same. To which I answer,

First, that men are continually in competition for honour and dignity, which these creatures are not; and consequently amongst men there ariseth on that ground, envy and hatred, and finally war; but amongst these not so.

Secondly, that amongst these creatures, the common good differeth not from the private; and being by nature inclined to their private, they procure thereby the common benefit. But man, whose joy consisteth in comparing himself with other men, can relish nothing but what is eminent.

Thirdly, that these creatures, having not, as man, the use of reason, do not see, nor think they see any fault, in the administration of their common business; whereas amongst men, there are very many, that think themselves wiser, and abler to govern the public, better than the rest; and these strive to reform and innovate, one this way, another that way; and thereby bring it into distraction and civil war.

Fourthly, that these creatures, though they have some use of voice, in making known to one another their desires, and other affections; yet they want that art of words, by which some men can represent to others, that which is good, in the likeness of evil; and evil, in the likeness of good; and augment, or diminish the apparent greatness of good and evil; discontenting men, and troubling their peace at their pleasure.

Fifthly, irrational creatures cannot distinguish between *injury,* and *damage;* and therefore as long as they be at ease, they are not offended with their fellows: whereas man is then most troublesome, when he is most at ease: for then it is that he loves to shew his wisdom, and control the actions of them that govern the commonwealth.

Lastly, the agreement of these creatures is natural; that of men, is by covenant only, which is artificial: and therefore it is no wonder if there be somewhat else required, besides covenant, to make their agreement constant and lasting; which is a common power, to keep them in awe, and to direct their actions to the common benefit.

The only way to erect such a common power, as may be able to defend them from the invasion of foreigners, and the injuries of one another, and thereby to secure them in such sort, as that by their own industry, and by the fruits of the earth, they may nourish themselves and live contentedly; is, to confer all their power and strength upon one man, or upon one assembly of men, that may reduce all their wills, by plurality of voices, unto one will: which is as much as to say, to appoint one man, or assembly of men, to bear their person; and every one to own, and acknowledge himself to be author of whatsoever he that so beareth their person, shall act, or cause to be acted, in those things which concern the common peace and safety; and therein to submit their wills, every one to his will, and their judgments, to his judgment. This is more than consent, or concord; it is a real unity of them all, in one and the same person, made by covenant of every man with every man, in such manner, as if every man should say to every man, *I authorize and give up my right of governing myself, to this man, or to this assembly of men, on this condition, that thou give up they right to him, and authorize all his actions in like manner.* This done, the multitude so united in one person, is called a COMMONWEALTH, in Latin CIVITAS. This is the generation of that great LEVIATHAN, or rather, to speak more reverently, of that *mortal god,* to which we owe under the *immortal God,* our peace and defence. For by this authority, given him by every particular man in the commonwealth, he hath the use of so much power and strength conferred on him, that by terror thereof, he is enabled to perform the wills of them all, to peace at home, and mutual aid against their enemies abroad. And in him consisteth the essence of the commonwealth; which, to define it, is *one person, of whose acts a great multitude, by mutual covenants one with another, have made themselves every one the author, to the end he may use the strength and means of them all, as he shall think expedient, for their peace and common defence.*

And he that carrieth this person, is called SOVEREIGN, and said to have *sovereign* power; and every one besides, his SUBJECT.

For Further Reflection

1. Hobbes wrote, "The utility of morality and civil philosophy is to be estimated, not so much by the commodities we have by knowing these sciences, as by the calamities we receive from not knowing them." What does he mean by this, and does the selection above illustrate it?

2. Is Hobbes' view of human nature accurate? Do we always act out of the motivations of fear and distrust? Are people entirely self-interested egoists? Is psychological egoism, the view that we always do what we perceive to be in our best interest, too bleak and one-sided?

3. Hobbes thought that only an absolute sovereign could establish or ensure peace and civil society. Is he correct? What would his estimation of democracy be? Could democratic society make use of his analysis? How would democrats modify Hobbes' theory?

4. David Hume criticized the idea that contract theories provide a justification of political authority. First of all, there is no evidence of an original contract ever being made and, secondly, even if our ancestors did sign an original contract, why should that give us any reason for obeying the laws of the state? Even as we are not bound by the marriage or business contracts of our ancestors, why should we be obligated by their political contracts?

The Democratic Answer: The Justification of the State Is Its Promotion of Security and Natural Human Rights

VII.2

JOHN LOCKE

With the Restoration of the Catholic royalty in 1660, after the English Civil War, Locke joined those who sought to limit the power of the King and give greater power to Parliament. After the Glorious Revolution of 1688, in which Locke's hopes were realized, he published two long essays on the justification of political authority. The second of these essays, the *Second Treatise of Civil Government*, is the most important single work on constitutional democracy and greatly influenced the formation of the United States Constitution.

Regarding human nature and the state of nature, Locke is not so pessimistic as Hobbes. Whereas Hobbes saw the state of nature as one in which life was "solitary, poor, nasty, brutish, and short," "a war of all against all," Locke sees it as an inferior state due to lack of adequate cooperation and common laws, but still one in which our natural rights are enjoyed. Humans are not all as egoist or innately cruel as Hobbes would make out. Government arises through a social contract in which individuals agree to be bound by the laws of a central authority which represents the will of the majority. It is the will of the majority together with natural rights to life, liberty, and property which limit the government. The government loses its legitimacy if it ceases to represent the will of the people and becomes tyrannical. In that case revolution is warranted.

There were those in Locke's day who rejected the contract theory of government (as set forth by Hobbes and others) on the basis that there was no record of an original social contract and that even if there were, it would not be binding on us. To this charge Locke responds that each of us upon reaching adulthood *implicitly* subscribes to the social contract by remaining in the country, living under its laws, and benefiting from its structure and security.

(A biographical note on Locke appears on p. 119.)

Study Questions

1. What is the natural state of human beings?
2. How does government come into existence?
3. How should decisions be made within the State?
4. How do we dissolve our relation to the State as individuals?
5. Why will people surrender some of their freedom in order to join the State? What do they gain thereby?
6. What two powers in the state of nature do we give up in joining the State?
7. When are we justified in dissolving the government? How do we dissolve the government?
8. What is the purpose of government?

Of the Beginning of Political Societies

MEN BEING BY NATURE ALL FREE, equal, and independent, no one can be put out of his estate and subjected to the political power of another without his own consent, which is done by agreeing with other men, to join and unite into a community for their comfortable, safe, and peaceful living, one amongst another, in a secure enjoyment of their properties, and a greater security against any that are not of it. This any number of men may do, because it injures not the freedom of the rest; they are left, as they were, in the liberty of the state of nature. When any number of men have so consented to make one community or government, they are thereby

From Second Treatise on Civil Government *(1690)*.

presently incorporated, and make one body politic, wherein the majority have a right to act and [include] the rest.

For, when any number of men have, by the consent of every individual, made a community, they have thereby made that community one body, with a power to act as one body, which is only by the will and determination of the majority. . . .

And thus every man, by consenting with others to make one body politic under one government, puts himself under an obligation to everyone of that society to submit to the determination of the majority, and to be [included] by it; or else this original compact, whereby he with others incorporates into one society, would signify nothing, and be no compact if he be left free and under no other ties than he was in before in the state of nature. For what appearance would there be of any compact? . . . For where the majority cannot include the rest, there they cannot act as one body, and consequently will be immediately dissolved again.

Whosoever therefore out of a state of nature unite into a community, must be understood to give up all the power necessary to the ends for which they unite society to the majority of the community, unless they expressly agreed in any number greater than the majority. And this is done by barely agreeing to unite into one political society, which is all the compact that is, or needs be, between the individuals that enter into or make up a commonwealth. And thus, that which begins and actually constitutes any political society is nothing but the consent of any number of freemen capable of a majority, to unite and incorporate into such a society. And this is that, and that only, which did or could give beginning to any lawful government in the world. . . .

Every man that hath any possession of enjoyment of any part of the dominions of any government doth thereby give his tacit consent, and is as far forth obliged to obedience to the laws of that government, during such enjoyment, as any

one under it, whether this his possession be of land to him and his heirs for ever, or a lodging only for a week; or whether it be barely travelling freely on the highway; and, in effect, it reaches as far as the very being of anyone within the territories of that government.

To understand this better, it is fit to consider that every man when he at first incorporates himself into any commonwealth, he, by his uniting himself thereunto, annexes also, and submits to the community those possessions which he has, or shall acquire, that do not already belong to any other government. For it would be a direct contradiction for anyone to enter into society with others for the securing and regulating of property, and yet to suppose his land, whose property is to be regulated by the laws of the society, should be exempt from the jurisdiction of that government to which he himself, the proprietor of the land, is subject. By the same act, therefore, whereby anyone unites his person, which was before free, to any commonwealth, by the same he unites his possessions, which were before free, to it also; and they become, both of them, person and possession, subject to the government and dominion of that commonwealth as long as it hath a being. Whoever therefore from thenceforth, by inheritance, purchase, permission, or otherwise enjoys any part of the land so annexed to, and under the government of that commonwealth, must take it with the condition it is under; that is, of submitting to the government of the commonwealth, under whose jurisdiction it is, as far forth as any subject of it.

But since the government has a direct jurisdiction only over the land and reaches the possessor of it (before he has actually incorporated himself in the society) only as he dwells upon and enjoys that, the obligation anyone is under by virtue of such enjoyment to submit to the government begins and ends with the enjoyment; so that whenever the owner, who has given nothing but such a tacit consent to the government, will, by donation, sale or otherwise, quit the said possession, he is at liberty to go and incorporate himself into any other commonwealth, or agree with others to begin a new one in any part of the world they can find free and unpossessed; whereas he that has once, by actual agreement and any express declaration, given his consent to be of any commonweal, is perpetually and indispensably obliged to be, and remain unalterably a subject to it, and can never be again in the liberty of the state of nature, unless by any calamity the government he was under comes to be dissolved; or else by some public act cuts him off from being any longer a member of it.

But submitting to the laws of any country, living quietly, and enjoying privileges and protection under them makes not a man a member of that society; this is only a local protection and homage due to and from all those who, not being in a state of war, come within the territories belonging to any government, to all parts whereof the force of its law extends. But this no more makes a man a member of that society than it would make a man a subject to another in whose family he found it convenient to abide for some time. . . . Nothing can make any man [a citizen] but his actually entering into it by positive engagement and express promise and compact.

Of the Ends of Political Society and Government

If man in the state of nature be so free as has been said; if he be absolute lord of his own person and possessions; equal to the greatest and subject to no body, why will he part with his freedom? Why will he give up this empire, and subject himself to the dominion and control of any other power? To which 'tis obvious to answer, that though in the state of nature he hath such a right, yet the enjoyment of it is very uncertain and constantly exposed to the invasion of others; for all being kings as much as he, every man his equal, and the greater part no strict ob-

servers of equity and justice, the enjoyment of the property he has in this state is very unsafe, very unsecure. This makes him willing to quit this condition which, however free, is full of fears and continual dangers; and 'tis not without reason that he seeks out and is willing to join in society with others who are already united, or have a mind to unite for the mutual preservation of their lives, liberties, and estates, which I call by the general name, property.

The great and chief end therefore, of men's uniting into commonwealths, and putting themselves under government, is the preservation of their property; to which in the state of nature there are many things wanting.

First, There wants an established, settled, known law, received and allowed by common consent to be the standard of right and wrong, and the common measure to decide all controversies between them. For though the law of nature be plain and intelligible to all rational creatures, yet men, being biased by their interest, as well as ignorant for want of study of it, are not apt to allow of it as a law binding to them in the application of it to their particular cases.

Secondly, In the state of nature there wants a known and indifferent judge, with authority to determine all differences according to the established law. For everyone in that state being both judge and executioner of the law of nature, men being partial to themselves, passion and revenge is very apt to carry them too far, and with too much heat in their own cases, as well as negligence and unconcernedness, make them too remiss in other men's.

Thirdly, In the state of nature there often wants power to back and support the sentence when right, and to give it due execution. They who by any injustice offended, will seldom fail where they are able by force to make good their injustice. Such resistance many times makes the punishment dangerous, and frequently destructive to those who attempt it.

Thus mankind, notwithstanding all the privileges of the state of nature, being but in an ill condition while they remain in it, are quickly driven into society. Hence it comes to pass, that we seldom find any number of men live any time together in this state. The inconveniences that they are therein exposed to by the irregular and uncertain exercise of the power every man has of punishing the transgressions of others, make them take sanctuary under the established laws of government, and therein seek the preservation of their property. 'Tis this makes them so willingly give up every one his single power of punishing to be exercised by such alone as shall be appointed to it amongst them, and by such rules as the community, or those authorized by them to that purpose, shall agree on. And in this we have the original right and rise of both the legislative and executive power as well as of the governments and societies themselves.

For in the state of nature to omit the liberty he has of innocent delights, a man has two powers.

The first is to do whatsoever he thinks fit for the preservation of himself and others within the permission of the law of nature; by which law, common to them all, he and all the rest of mankind are one community, make up one society distinct from all other creatures and were it not for the corruption and viciousness of degenerate men, there would be no need of any other, no necessity that men should separate from this great and natural community, and associate into less combinations.

The other power a man has in the state of nature is the power to punish the crimes committed against that law. Both these he gives up when he joins in a private, if I may so call it, or particular political society, and incorporates into any commonwealth separate from the rest of mankind.

The first power, *viz.* of doing whatsoever he thought fit for the preservation of himself and the rest of mankind, he gives up to be regulated by laws made by the society, so far forth as the preservation of himself and the rest of that society shall require; which laws of the society in many things confine the liberty he had by the law of nature.

Secondly, the power of punishing he wholly gives up, and engages his natural force (which he might before employ in the execution of the law of nature, by his own single authority, as he thought fit) to assist the executive power of the society as the law thereof shall require. For being now in a new state, wherein he is to enjoy many conveniences from the labour, assistance, and society of others in the same community, as well as protection from its whole strength, he is to part also with as much of his natural liberty, in providing for himself, as the good, prosperity, and safety of the society shall require, which is not only necessary but just, since the other members of the society do the like.

But though men when they enter into society give up the equality, liberty, and executive power they had in the state of nature into the hands of the society, to be so far disposed of by the legislative as the good of the society shall require, yet it being only with an intention in everyone the better to preserve himself, his liberty and property (for no rational creature can be supposed to change his condition with an intention to be worse), the power of the society or legislative constituted by them can never be supposed to extend farther than the common good, but is obliged to secure everyone's property by providing against those three defects above-mentioned that made the state of nature so unsafe and uneasy. And so, whoever has the legislative or supreme power of any commonwealth, is bound to govern by established standing laws, promulgated and known to the people, and not by extemporary decrees, by indifferent and upright judges, who are to decide controversies by those laws; and to employ the force of the community at home only in the execution of such laws, or abroad to prevent or redress foreign injuries and secure the community from inroads and invasion. And all this to be directed to no other end but the peace, safety, and public good of the people. . . .

Of the Extent of the Legislative Power

These are the bounds which the trust that is put in them by the society and the law of God and nature have set to the legislative power of every commonwealth, in all forms of government.

First, They are to govern by promulgated established laws, not to be varied in particular cases, but to have one rule for rich and poor, for the favourite at Court, and the countryman at plough.

Secondly, These laws also ought to be designed for no other end ultimately but the good of the people.

Thirdly, They must not raise taxes on the property of the people without the consent of the people given by themselves or their deputies. And this properly concerns only such governments where the legislative is always in being, or at least where the people have not reserved any part of the legislative to deputies, to be from time to time chosen by themselves.

Fourthly, The legislative neither must nor can transfer the power of making laws to anybody else, or place it anywhere but where the people have. . . .

The Legitimacy of Revolution

The reason why men enter into society is the preservation of their property; and the end why they choose and authorize a legislative is that there may be laws made and rules set as guards and fences to the properties of all the members of the society to limit the power and moderate the dominion of every part and member of the society; for since it can never be supposed to be the will of the society that the legislative should have a power to destroy that which every one designs to secure by entering into society, and for which the people submitted themselves to legislators of their own making. Whenever the legislators endeavor to take away and destroy the property of the people, or to reduce them to slavery under arbitrary power, they put themselves into a state of war with the people who are thereupon absolved from any further obedience, and are left to the common refuge which God has provided for all men against force and violence. Whensoever, therefore, the legislative shall transgress this fundamental rule of society, and either by ambition, fear, folly, or corruption, endeavor to grasp themselves, or put into the hands of any other, an absolute power over the lives, liberties, and estates of the people, by this breach of trust they forfeit the power the people had put into their hands for quite contrary ends, and it devolves to the people, who have a right to resume their original liberty and, by the establishment of a new legislative, such as they shall think fit, provide for their own safety and security, which is the end for which they are in society. What I have said here concerning the legislative in general holds true also concerning the supreme executor, who having a double trust put in him—both to have a part in the legislative and the supreme execution of the law—acts against both when he goes about to set up his own arbitrary will as the law of the society. . . .

Here, it is like, the common question will be made: Who shall be judge whether the prince or legislative act contrary to their trust? This, perhaps, ill-affected and factious men may spread amongst the people, when the prince only makes use of his due prerogative. To this I reply: The people shall be judge; for who shall be judge whether his trustee or deputy acts well and according to the trust reposed in him but he who deputes him and must, by having deputed him, have still a power to discard him when he fails in his trust? If this be reasonable in particular cases of private men, why should it be otherwise in that of the greatest moment where the welfare of millions is concerned, and also where the evil, if not prevented, is greater and the redress very difficult, dear, and dangerous? . . .

To conclude, the power that every individual gave the society when he entered into it, can never revert to the individuals again as long as the society lasts, but will always remain in the community, because without this there can be no community, no commonwealth, which is contrary to the original agreement; so also when the society hath placed the legislative in any assembly of men to continue in them and their successors, with direction and authority for providing such successors, the legislative can never revert to the people whilst that government lasts, because having provided a legislative with power to continue for ever, they have given up their political power to the legislative and cannot resume it. But if they have set limits to the duration of their legislative, and made this supreme power in any person or assembly only temporary; or else when by the miscarriages of those in authority it is forfeited; upon the forfeiture, or at the determination of the time set, it reverts to the society, and the people have a right to act as supreme, and continue the legislative in themselves; or place it in a new form, or new hands as they think good.

For Further Reflection

1. Locke justifies his notion of obedience to the State in terms of a Social Contract, saying that it is implicit and binding since if we don't like it, we can leave the country. Is this a realistic solution?

2. Compare Hobbes' account of the social contract with Locke's account. Which do you think is more accurate?

3. What would Locke say about the rights of unpopular minorities? What if a majority of a community voted that pornography should not be allowed into the community, so that it was illegal for individuals to view certain forms of art in the privacy of their homes? Would Locke's theory permit the community to limit individual liberty in this way?

The Utilitarian Answer: Government Must Promote Freedom   VII.3

JOHN STUART MILL

Although Mill (1806–1873) agrees with Locke in favoring representational democracy, he does not accept the notion of natural rights. Typically utilitarians follow Jeremy Bentham in viewing the idea of natural rights as "nonsense on stilts." We should promote a democracy dedicated to individual liberty because that will maximize happiness. Furthermore, Mill disagrees with Locke's majoritarian emphasis and warns of a new form of tyranny, the "tyranny of the majority." Every educated adult must be free to do what he or she desires. The only grounds for interfering with individuals is to protect others from harm.

(A biographical sketch of John Stuart Mill appears on page 370.)

Study Questions

1. What is the subject of this essay?
2. How did the concern of the patriots to set limits to power arise in society?
3. In what two ways was this limiting of political power attempted in the past?
4. What is the main problem which popular government conceals from observation?
5. What sorts of tyrannies must the individual be protected against?
6. What is the sole justification of society's interfering in the lives of its members? What are some unjustified reasons?
7. Does the principle of liberty apply to all people everywhere? Explain.
8. Does Mill base his principle of liberty on a basic natural right to liberty? If so, why? If not, why not?
9. What are the areas of life covered by the principle of liberty?
10. What is the peculiar evil of silencing unpopular expressions of opinion?
11. What does Mill say about different life styles?

Chapter I. Introductory

THE SUBJECT OF THIS ESSAY is not the so-called Liberty of the Will, so unfortunately opposed to the misnamed doctrine of Philosophical Necessity; but Civil, or Social Liberty: the nature and limits of the power which can be legitimately exercised by society over the individual. A question seldom stated, and hardly ever discussed, in general terms, but which profoundly influences the practical controversies of the age by its latent presence, and is likely soon to make itself recognised as the vital question of the future. It is so far from being new, that, in a certain sense, it has divided mankind, almost from the remotest ages; but in the stage of progress into which the more civilised portions of the species have now entered, it presents itself under new conditions, and requires a different and more fundamental treatment.

The struggle between Liberty and Authority is the most conspicuous feature in the portions of history with which we are earliest familiar, particularly in that of Greece, Rome, and England. But in old times this contest was between subjects, or some classes of subjects, and the Government. By liberty, was meant protection against the tyranny of the political rulers. The rulers were conceived (except in some of the popular governments of Greece) as in a necessarily antagonistic position to the people whom they ruled. They consisted of a governing One, or a governing tribe or caste, who derived their authority from inheritance or conquest, who, at all events, did not hold it at the pleasure of the governed, and whose supremacy men did not venture, perhaps did not desire, to contest, whatever precautions might be taken against its oppressive exercise. Their power was regarded as necessary, but also as highly dangerous; as a weapon which they would attempt to use against their subjects, no less than against external enemies. To prevent the weaker members of the community from being preyed upon by innumerable vultures, it was needful that there should be an animal of prey stronger than the rest, commissioned to keep them down. But as the king of the vultures would be no less bent upon preying on the flock than any of the minor harpies, it was indispensable to be in a perpetual attitude of defence against his beak and claws. The aim, therefore, of patriots was to set limits to the power which the ruler should be suffered to exercise over the community; and this limitation was

From On Liberty *(1859)*.

what they meant by liberty. It was attempted in two ways. First, by obtaining a recognition of certain immunities, called political liberties or rights, which it was to be regarded as a breach of duty in the ruler to infringe, and which if he did infringe, specific resistance, or general rebellion, was held to be justifiable. A second, and generally a later expedient, was the establishment of constitutional checks, by which the consent of the community, or of a body of some sort, supposed to represent its interests, was made a necessary condition to some of the more important acts of the governing power. To the first of these modes of limitation, the ruling power, in most European countries, was compelled, more or less, to submit. It was not so with the second; and, to attain this, or when already in some degree possessed, to attain it more completely, became everywhere the principal object of the lovers of liberty. And so long as mankind were content to combat one enemy by another, and to be ruled by a master, on condition of being guaranteed more or less efficaciously against his tyranny, they did not carry their aspirations beyond this point.

A time, however, came, in the progress of human affairs, when men ceased to think it a necessity of nature that their governors should be an independent power, opposed in interest to themselves. It appeared to them much better that the various magistrates of the State should be their tenants or delegates, revocable at their pleasure. In that way alone, it seemed, could they have complete security that the powers of government would never be abused to their disadvantage. By degrees this new demand for elective and temporary rulers became the prominent object of the exertions of the popular party, wherever any such party existed; and superseded, to a considerable extent, the previous efforts to limit the power of rulers. As the struggle proceeded for making the ruling power emanate from the periodical choice of the ruled, some persons began to think that too much importance had been attached to the limitation of

the power itself. *That* (it might seem) was a resource against rulers whose interests were habitually opposed to those of the people. What was now wanted was, that the rulers should be identified with the people; that their interest and will should be the interest and will of the nation. The nation did not need to be protected against its own will. There was no fear of its tyrannising over itself. Let the rulers be effectually responsible to it, promptly removable by it, and it could afford to trust them with power of which it could itself dictate the use to be made. Their power was but the nation's own power, concentrated, and in a form convenient for exercise. This mode of thought, or rather perhaps of feeling, was common among the last generation of European liberalism, in the Continental section of which it still apparently predominates. Those who admit any limit to what a government may do, except in the case of such governments as they think ought not to exist, stand out as brilliant exceptions among the political thinkers of the Continent. A similar tone of sentiment might by this time have been prevalent in our own country, if the circumstances which for a time encouraged it, had continued unaltered.

But, in political and philosophical theories, as well as in persons, success discloses faults and infirmities which failure might have concealed from observation. The notion, that the people have no need to limit their power over themselves, might seem axiomatic, when popular government was a thing only dreamed about, or read of as having existed at some distant period of the past. Neither was that notion necessarily disturbed by such temporary aberrations as those of the French Revolution, the worst of which were the work of a usurping few, and which, in any case, belonged, not to the permanent working of popular institutions, but to a sudden and convulsive outbreak against monarchical and aristocratic despotism. In time, however, a democratic republic came to occupy a large portion of the earth's surface, and made itself felt as one of the most powerful members of the community of nations; and elective and responsible government became subject to the observations and criticisms which wait upon a great existing fact. It was now perceived that such phrases as 'self-government,' and 'the power of the people over themselves,' do not express the true state of the case. The 'people' who exercise the power are not always the same people with those over whom it is exercised; and the 'self-government' spoken of is not the government of each by himself, but of each by all the rest. The will of the people, moreover, practically means the will of the most numerous or the most active *part* of the people; the majority, or those who succeed in making themselves accepted as the majority; the people, consequently *may* desire to oppress a part of their number; and precautions are as much needed against this as against any other abuse of power. The limitation, therefore, of the power of government over individuals loses none of its importance when the holders of power are regularly accountable to the community, that is, to the strongest party therein. This view of things, recommending itself equally to the intelligence of thinkers and to the inclination of those important classes in European society to whose real or supposed interests democracy is adverse, has had no difficulty in establishing itself; and in political speculations 'the tyranny of the majority' is now generally included among the evils against which society requires to be on its guard.

Like other tyrannies, the tyranny of the majority was at first, and is still vulgarly, held in dread, chiefly as operating through the acts of the public authorities. But reflecting persons perceived that when society is itself the tyrant—society collectively over the separate individuals who compose it—its means of tyrannising are not restricted to the acts which it may do by the hands of its political functionaries. Society can and does execute its own mandates: and if it issues wrong mandates instead of right, or any mandates at all in things with which it ought not to meddle, it practises a social tyranny more for-midable than many kinds of political oppression, since, though not usually upheld by such extreme penalties, it leaves fewer means of escape, penetrating much more deeply into the details of life, and enslaving the soul itself. Protection, therefore, against the tyranny of the magistrate is not enough: there needs protection also against the tyranny of the prevailing opinion and feeling; against the tendency of society to impose, by other means than civil penalties, its own ideas and practices as rules of conduct on those who dissent from them; to fetter the development, and, if possible, prevent the formation, of any individuality not in harmony with its ways, and compels all characters to fashion themselves upon the model of its own. There is a limit to the legitimate interference of collective opinion with individual independence: and to find that limit, and maintain it against encroachment, is as indispensable to a good condition of human affairs, as protection against political despotism.

The object of this Essay is to assert one very simple principle, as entitled to govern absolutely the dealings of society with the individual in the way of compulsion and control, whether the means used be physical force in the form of legal penalties, or the moral coercion of public opinion. That principle is, that the sole end for which mankind are warranted, individually or collectively, in interfering with the liberty of action of any of their number, is self-protection. That the only purpose for which power can be rightfully exercised over any member of a civilised community, against his will, is to prevent harm to others. His own good, either physical or moral, is not a sufficient warrant. He cannot rightfully be compelled to do or forbear because it will be better for him to do so, because it will make him happier, because, in the opinions of others, to do so would be wise, or even right. These are good reasons for remonstrating with him, or reasoning with him, or persuading him, or entreating him, but not for compelling him, or visiting him with any evil in case he do otherwise. To justify that, the conduct from which it is desired to deter him must be calculated to produce evil to some one else. The only part of the conduct of any one, for which he is amenable to society, is that which concerns others. In the part which merely concerns himself, his independence is, of right, absolute. Over himself, over his own body and mind, the individual is sovereign.

It is, perhaps, hardly necessary to say that this doctrine is meant to apply to human beings in the maturity of their faculties. We are not speaking of children, or of young persons below the age which the law may fix as that of manhood or womanhood. Those who are still in a state to require being taken care of by others, must be protected against their own actions as well as against external injury. For the same reason, we may leave out of consideration those backward states of society in which the race itself may be considered as in its nonage. The early difficulties in the way of spontaneous progress are so great, that there is seldom any choice of means for overcoming them; and a ruler full of the spirit of improvement is warranted in the use of any expedients that will attain an end, perhaps otherwise unattainable. Despotism is a legitimate mode of government in dealing with barbarians, provided the end be their improvement, and the means justified by actually effecting does not harm them, even though they should think our conduct foolish, perverse, or wrong. Thirdly, from this liberty of each individual, follows the liberty, within the same limits, of combination among individuals; freedom to unite, for any purpose not involving harm to others: the persons combining being supposed to be of full age, and not forced or deceived.

No society in which these liberties are not, on the whole, respected, is free, whatever may be its form of government; and none is completely free in which they do not exist absolute and unqualified. The only freedom which deserves the name, is that of pursuing our own good in our own way, so long as we do not attempt to deprive others of theirs, or impede their efforts to obtain it. Each is the proper guardian of his own

health, whether bodily, *or* mental and spiritual. Mankind are greater gainers by suffering each other to live as seems good to themselves, than by compelling each to live as seems good to the rest.

Though this doctrine is anything but new, and, to some persons, may have the air of a truism, there is no doctrine which stands more directly opposed to the general tendency of existing opinion and practice. Society has expended fully as much effort in the attempt (according to its lights) to compel people to conform to its notions of personal as of social excellence. . . .

Chapter II. Of the Liberty of Thought and Discussion

The time, it is to be hoped, is gone by, when any defence would be necessary of the 'liberty of the press' as one of the securities against corrupt or tyrannical government. No argument, we may suppose, can now be needed, against permitting a legislature or an executive, not identified in interest with the people, to prescribe opinions to them, and determine what doctrines or what arguments they shall be allowed to hear. This aspect of the question, besides, has been so often and so triumphantly enforced by preceding writers, that it needs not be specially insisted on in this place. Though the law of England, on the subject of the press, is as servile to this day as it was in the time of the Tudors, there is little danger of its being actually put in force against political discussion, except during some temporary panic, when fear of insurrection drives ministers and judges from their propriety; and, speaking generally, it is not, in constitutional countries, to be apprehended, that the government, whether completely responsible to the people or not, will often attempt to control the expression of opinion, except when in doing so it makes itself the organ of the general intolerance of the public. Let us suppose, therefore, that the government is entirely at one with the people, and never thinks of exerting any power of coercion unless in agreement with what it conceives to be their voice. But I deny the right of the people to exercise such coercion, either by themselves or by their government. The power itself is illegitimate. The best government has no more title to it than the worst. It is as noxious, or more noxious, when exerted in accordance with public opinion, than when in opposition to it. If all mankind minus one were of one opinion, and only one person were of the contrary opinion, mankind would be no more justified in silencing that one person, than he, if he had the power, would be justified in silencing mankind. Were an opinion a personal possession of no value except to the owner; if to be obstructed in the enjoyment of it were simply a private injury, it would make some difference whether the injury was inflicted only on a few persons or on many. But the peculiar evil of silencing the expression of an opinion is, that it is robbing the human race; posterity as well as the existing generation; those who dissent from the opinion, still more than those who hold it. If the opinion is right, they are deprived of the opportunity of exchanging error for truth: if wrong, they lose, what is almost as great a benefit, the clearer perception and livelier impression of truth, produced by its collision with error. . . .

As it is useful that while mankind are imperfect there should be different opinions, so is it that there should be different experiments of living; that free scope should be given to varieties of character, short of injury to others; and that the worth of different modes of life should be proved practically, when any one thinks fit to try them. It is desirable, in short, that in things which do not primarily concern others, individuality should assert itself. Where, not the person's own character, but the traditions or customs of other people are the rule of conduct, there is wanting one of the principal ingredients of human happiness, and quite the chief ingredient of individual and social progress.

In maintaining this principle, the greatest difficulty to be encountered does not lie in the appreciation of means towards an acknowledged end, but in the indifference of persons in general to the end itself. If it were felt that the free development of individuality is one of the leading essentials of wellbeing; that it is not only a coordinate element with all like that is designated by the terms civilization, instruction, education, culture, but is itself a necessary part and condition of all those things; there would be no danger that liberty should be undervalued, and the adjustment of the boundaries between it and social control would present no extraordinary difficulty. But the evil is, that individual spontaneity is hardly recognized by the common modes of thinking, as having any intrinsic worth, or deserving any regard on its own account. . . .

He who lets the world, or his own portion of it, choose his plan of life for him, has no need of any other faculty than the ape-like one of imitation. He who chooses his plan for himself, employs all his faculties. He must use observation to see, reasoning and judgment to foresee, activity to gather materials for decision, discrimination to decide, and when he has decided, firmness and self-control to hold to his deliberate decision. And these qualities he requires and exercises exactly in proportion as the part of his conduct which he determines according to his own judgment and feelings is a large one. It is possible that he might be guided in some good path, and kept out of harm's way, without any of these things. But what will be his comparative worth as a human being? It really is of importance, not only what men do, but also what manner of men they are that do it. Among the works of man, which human life is rightly employed in perfecting and beautifying, the first in importance surely is man himself. Supposing it were possible to get houses built, corn grown, battles fought, causes tried, and even churches erected and prayers said, by machinery—by automatons in human form—it would be a considerable loss to exchange for these automatons even the men and women who at present inhabit the more civilized parts of the world, and who

assuredly are but starved specimens of what nature can and will produce. Human nature is not
a machine to be built after a model, and set to do
exactly the work prescribed for it, but a tree,

which requires to grow and develop itself on all
sides, according to the tendency of the inward
forces which make it a living thing. . . .

For Further Reflection

1. Do you agree with Mill that the principle of liberty can be justified only by utilitarian
considerations? Is he correct in rejecting the notion of natural rights?

2. Do you agree with Mill's formulation of the principle of liberty? Should we sometimes
act paternalistically even with educated adults? How would Mill's principle apply to someone
using drugs? Should we intervene? Would Mill advocate legalizing drugs—and thereby taking
the criminal and profit motive out of the drug abuse?

3. Mill wrote, "It is not useful, but hurtful, that the constitution of the country should
declare ignorance to be entitled to as much political power as knowledge," and called for
weighted voting rights in which the votes of higher intelligence would count for more than
the uninformed and less intelligent. Do you agree with Mill?

The Libertarian Answer: The Justification of the State Is the Preservation of Freedom   VII.4

JOHN HOSPERS

Hospers argues that freedom is the highest political value. Every person is owner of
his or her own life, so every human being has the right to act in accordance with his or
her own choices, unless those actions infringe on the liberty of others. The government's function is to protect human rights, especially this right to liberty. No other
function is justified. The government has no justification to protect people from themselves—if they want to harm themselves, that's their business, not the government's,
nor has it the right to require people to help others, to rob Peter to pay Paul.

(A biographical sketch of Hospers appears on p. 157.)

Study Questions

1. What is the basic idea of libertarianism?
2. What are the three theses of libertarianism?
3. What is involved in the right to property?
4. What does Hospers think about the abolition of property, that everyone should own
everything?

5. What is the proper role of government?

6. Why is government the most dangerous institution in history?

7. What does Hospers think about the welfare state in which the well-off are taxed to provide for the poor and unemployed?

8. What is Hospers' alternative to the welfare state?

The Libertarian Manifesto

THE POLITICAL PHILOSOPHY that is called libertarianism (from the Latin *libertas,* liberty) is the doctrine that every person is the owner of his own life, and that no one is the owner of anyone else's life: and that consequently every human being has the right to act in accordance with his own choices, unless those actions infringe on the equal liberty of other human beings to act in accordance with their choices.

There are several other ways of stating the same libertarian thesis:

1. *No one is anyone else's master, and no one is anyone else's slave.* Since I am the one to decide how my life is to be conducted just as you decide about yours, I have no right (even if I had the power) to make you my slave and be your master, nor have you the right to become the master by enslaving me. Slavery is *forced* servitude, and since no one owns the life of anyone else, no one has the right to enslave another. Political theories past and present have traditionally been concerned with who should be the master (usually the king, the dictator, or government bureaucracy) and who should be the slaves, and what the extent of the slavery should be. Libertarianism holds that no one has the right to use force to enslave the life of another, or any portion or aspect of that life.

2. *Other men's lives are not yours to dispose of.* I enjoy seeing operas; but operas are expensive to produce. Opera-lovers often say, "The state (or the city, etc.) should subsidize opera, so

that we can all see it. Also it would be for people's betterment, cultural benefit, etc." But what they are advocating is nothing more or less than legalized plunder. They can't pay for the productions themselves, and yet they want to see opera, which involves a large number of people and their labor; so what they are saying in effect is, "Get the money through legalized force. Take a little bit more out of every worker's paycheck every week to pay for the operas we want to see." But I have no right to take by force from the workers' pockets to pay for what I want.

Perhaps it would be better if he *did* go to see opera—then I should try to convince him to go voluntarily. But to take the money from him forcibly, because in my opinion it would be good for *him,* is still seizure of his earnings, which is plunder.

Besides, if I have the right to force him to help pay for my pet projects, hasn't he equally the right to force me to help pay for his? Perhaps he in turn wants the government to subsidize rock-and-roll, or his new car, or a house in the country? If I have the right to milk him, why hasn't he the right to milk me? If I can be a moral cannibal, why can't he too?

We should beware of the inventors of utopias. They would remake the world according to their vision—with the lives and fruits of the labor of *other* human beings. Is it someone's utopian vision that others should build pyramids to beautify the landscape? Very well, then other men should provide the labor; and if he is in a position of political power, and he can't get men to do it voluntarily, then he must

From The Liberation Alternative, *ed. Tibor Machan* ©*1974 Tibor Machan. Reprinted by permission of Nelson-Hall Publishing.*

compel them to "cooperate"—i.e. he must enslave them. . . .

3. *No human being should be a nonvoluntary mortgage on the life of another.* I cannot claim your life, your work, or the products of your effort as mine. The fruit of one man's labor should not be fair game for every freeloader who comes along and demands it as his own. The orchard that has been carefully grown, nurtured, and harvested by its owner should not be ripe for the plucking for any bypasser who has a yen for the ripe fruit. The wealth that some men have produced should not be fair game for looting by government, to be used for whatever purposes its representatives determine, no matter what their motives in so doing may be. The theft of your money by a robber is not justified by the fact that he used it to help his injured mother.

It will already be evident that libertarian doctrine is embedded in a view of the rights of man. Each human being has the right to live his life as he chooses, compatibly with the equal right of all other human beings to live their lives as they choose.

All man's rights are implicit in the above statement. Each man has the right to life: any attempt by others to take it away from him, or even to injure him, violates this right, through the use of coercion against him. Each man has the right to liberty: to conduct his life in accordance with the alternatives open to him without coercive action by others. And every man has the right to property: to work to sustain his life (and the lives of whichever others he chooses to sustain, such as his family) and to retain the fruits of his labor.

People often defend the rights of life and liberty but denigrate property rights, and yet the right to property is as basic as the other two: indeed, without property rights no other rights are possible. Depriving you of property is depriving you of the means by which you live. . . .

I have no right to decide how *you* should spend your time or your money. I can make that decision for myself, but not for you, my neighbor. I may deplore your choice of life-style, and I may talk with you about it provided you are willing to listen to me. But I have no right to use force to change it. Nor have I the right to decide how you should spend the money you have earned. I may appeal to you to give it to the Red Cross, and you may prefer to go to prizefights. But that is your decision, and however much I may chafe about it I do not have the right to interfere forcibly with it, for example by robbing you in order to use the money in accordance with *my* choices. (If I have the right to rob you, have you also the right to rob me?)

When I claim a right, I carve out a niche, as it were, in my life, saying in effect, "This activity I must be able to perform without interference from others. For you and everyone else, this is off limits." And so I put up a "no trespassing" sign, which marks off the area of my right. Each individual's right is his "no trespassing" sign in relation to me and others. I may not encroach on his domain any more than he upon mine, without my consent. Every right entails a duty, true—but the duty is only that of *forebearance*—that is, of *refraining* from violating the other person's right. If you have a right to life, I have no right to take your life; if you have a right to the products of your labor (property), I have no right to take it from you without your consent. The nonviolation of these rights will not guarantee you protection against natural catastrophes such as floods and earthquakes, but it will protect you against the aggressive activities *of other men*. And rights, after all, have to do with one's relations to other human beings, not with one's relations to physical nature.

Nor were these rights created by government; governments—some governments, obviously not all—*recognize* and *protect* the rights that individuals already have. Governments regularly forbid homicide and theft; and, at a more advanced stage, protect individuals against such things as libel and breach of contract. . . .

The *right to property* is the most misunderstood and unappreciated of human rights, and it is one most constantly violated by governments. "Property" of course does not mean only real estate; it includes anything you can call your own— your clothing, your car, your jewelry, your books and papers. . . .

"But why have *individual* property rights? Why not have lands and houses owned by everybody together?" Yes, this involves no violation of individual rights, as long as everybody consents to this arrangement and no one is forced to join it. The parties to it may enjoy the communal living enough (at least for a time) to overcome certain inevitable problems: that some will work and some not, that some will achieve more in an hour than others can do in a day, and still they will all get the same income. The few who do the most will in the end consider themselves "workhorses" who do the work of two or three or twelve, while the others will be "freeloaders" on the efforts of these few. But as long as they can get out of the arrangement if they no longer like it, no violation of rights is involved. They got in voluntarily, and they can get out voluntarily; no one has used force.

"But why not say that everybody owns everything? That we *all* own everything there is?"

To some this may have a pleasant ring—but let us try to analyze what it means. If everybody owns everything, then everyone has an equal right to go everywhere, do what he pleases, take what he likes, destroy if he wishes, grow crops or burn them, trample them under, and so on. Consider what it would be like in practice. Suppose you have saved money to buy a house for yourself and your family. Now suppose that the principle, "everybody owns everything," becomes adopted. Well then, why shouldn't every itinerant hippie just come in and take over, sleeping in your beds and eating in your kitchen and not bothering to replace the food supply or clean up the mess? After all, it belongs to all of us, doesn't it? So we have just as much right to it as you, the buyer, have. What happens if we *all* want to sleep in the bedroom and there's not room for all of us? Is it the strongest who wins?

What would be the result? Since no one would be responsible for anything, the property would soon be destroyed, the food used up, the facilities nonfunctional. Beginning as a house that *one* family could use, it would end up as a house that *no one* could use. And if the principle continued to be adopted, no one would build houses any more—or anything else. What for? They would only be occupied and used by others, without remuneration. . . .

How can any of man's rights be violated? Ultimately, only by the use of force. I can make suggestions to you, I can reason with you, entreat you (if you are willing to listen), but I cannot *force* you without violating your rights; only by forcing you do I cut the cord between your free decisions and your actions. Voluntary relations between individuals involve no deprivation of rights, but murder, assault, and rape do, because in doing these things I make you the unwilling victim of my actions. A man's beating his wife involves no violation of rights if she *wanted* to be beaten. *Force is behavior that requires the unwilling involvement of other persons.*

According to libertarianism, the role of government should be limited to the retaliatory use of force against those who have initiated its use. It should not enter into any other areas, such as religion, social organization, and economics.

Government is the most dangerous institution known to man. Throughout history it has violated the rights of men more than any individual or group of individuals could do: it has killed people, enslaved them, sent them to forced labor and concentration camps, and regularly robbed and pillaged them of the fruits of their expended labor. Unlike individual criminals, government has the power to arrest and try; unlike individual criminals, it can surround and encompass a person totally, dominating every aspect of one's life, so that one has no recourse from it but to leave the country (and in totalitarian nations even that is prohibited). Government throughout history has a much sorrier record than any individual, even that of a ruthless mass murderer. The signs we see on bumper stickers are chillingly accurate: "Beware: the Government Is Armed and Dangerous."

The only proper role of government, according to libertarians, is that of the protector of the citizen against aggression by other individuals. The government, of course, should never initiate aggression; its proper role is as the embodiment of the *retaliatory* use of force against anyone who initiates its use.

If each individual had constantly to defend himself against possible aggressors, he would have to spend a considerable portion of his life in target practice, karate exercises, and other means of self-defenses, and even so he would probably be helpless against groups of individuals who might try to kill, maim, or rob him. He would have little time for cultivating those qualities which are essential to civilized life, nor would improvements in science, medicine, and the arts be likely to occur. The function of government is to take this responsibility off his shoulders: the government undertakes to defend him against aggressors and to punish them if they attack him. When the government is effective in doing this, it enables the citizen to go about his business unmolested and without constant fear for his life. To do this, of course, government must have physical power—the police, to protect the citizen from aggression within its borders, and the armed forces, to protect him from aggressors outside. Beyond that, the government should not intrude upon his life, either to run his business, or adjust his daily activities, or prescribe his personal moral code. . . .

What then should be the function of government? In a word, the *protection of human rights*.

1. *The right to life:* libertarians support all such legislation as will protect human beings against the use of force by others, for example, laws against killing, attempting killing, maiming, beating, and all kinds of physical violence.

2. *The right to liberty:* there should be no laws compromising in any way freedom of speech, of the press, and peaceable assembly. There should be no censorship of ideas, books, films, or of anything else by government.

3. *The right to property:* libertarians support legislation that protects the property rights of individuals against confiscation, nationalization, eminent domain, robbery, trespass, fraud and misrepresentation, patent and copyright, libel and slander. . . .

Laws may be classified into three types: (1) laws protecting individuals against themselves, such as laws against fornication and other sexual behavior, alcohol, and drugs; (2) laws protecting individuals against aggressions by other individuals, such as laws against murder, robbery, and fraud; (3) laws requiring people to help one another; for example, all laws which rob Peter to pay Paul, such as welfare.

Libertarians reject the first class of laws totally. Behavior which harms no one else is strictly the individual's own affair. Thus, there should be no laws against becoming intoxicated, since whether or not to become intoxicated is the individual's own decision: but there should be laws against driving while intoxicated, since the drunken driver is a threat to every other motorist on the highway (drunken driving falls into type 2). Similarly, there should be no laws against drugs (except the prohibition of sale of drugs to minors) as long as the taking of these drugs poses no threat to anyone else. Drug addiction is a psychological problem to which no present solution exists. Most of the social harm caused by addicts, other than to themselves, is the result of the thefts which they perform in order to continue their habit—and then the *legal* crime is the theft, not the addiction. The actual cost of heroin is about ten cents a shot; if it were legalized, the enormous traffic in illegal sale and purchase of it would stop, as well as the accompanying proselytization to get new addicts (to make more money for the pusher) and the thefts performed by addicts who often require eighty dollars a day just to keep up the habit. Addiction would not stop, but the crimes would: it is estimated that 75 percent of the burglaries in New York City today are performed by addicts, and all these crimes could be wiped out at one stroke through the legalization of drugs. (Only when the taking of drugs could be shown to constitute a threat to *others*, should it be prohibited by law. It is only laws protecting people against *themselves* that libertarians oppose.)

Laws should be limited to the second class only: aggression by individuals against other individuals. These are laws whose function is to protect human beings against encroachment by others; and this, as we have seen, is (according to libertarianism) the sole function of government.

Libertarians also reject the third class of laws totally: no one should be forced by law to help others, not even to tell them the time of day if requested, and certainly not to give them a portion of one's weekly paycheck. Governments, in the guise of humanitarianism, have given to some by taking from others (charging a "handling fee" in the process, which, because of the government's waste and inefficiency, sometimes is several hundred percent). And in so doing they have decreased incentive, violated the rights of individuals and lowered the standard of living of almost everyone.

All such laws constitute what libertarians call *moral cannibalism*. A cannibal in the physical sense is a person who lives off the flesh of other human beings. A *moral* cannibal is one who believes he has a right to live off the "spirit" of other human beings—who believes that he has a moral claim on the productive capacity, time, and effort expended by others.

It has become fashionable to claim virtually everything that one needs or desires as one's *right*. Thus, many people claim that they have a right to a job, the right to free medical care, to

free food and clothing, to a decent home, and so on. Now if one asks, apart from any specific context, whether it would be desirable if everyone had these things, one might well say yes. But there is a gimmick attached to each of them: *At whose expense?* Jobs, medical care, education, and so on, don't grow on trees. These are goods and services *produced only by men*. Who then is to provide them, and under what conditions? . . .

All those who demand this or that as a "free service" are consciously or unconsciously evading the fact that there is in reality no such thing as free services. All man-made goods and services are the result of human expenditure of time and effort. There is no such thing as "something for nothing" in this world. If you demand something free, you are demanding that other men give their time and effort to you without compensation. If they voluntarily choose to do this, there is no problem; but if you demand that they be *forced* to do it, you are interfering with their right not to do it if they so choose. "Swimming in this pool ought to be free!" says the indignant passerby. What he means is that others should build a pool, others should provide the material, and still others should run it and keep it in functioning order, so that *he* can use it without fee. But what right has he to the expenditure of *their* time and effort? To expect something "for free" is to expect it *to be paid for by others* whether they choose to or not.

Many questions, particularly about economic matters, will be generated by the libertarian account of human rights and the role of government. Should government have no role in assisting the needy, in providing social security, in legislating minimum wages, in fixing prices and putting a ceiling on rents, in curbing monopolies, in erecting tariffs, in guaranteeing jobs, in managing the money supply? To these and all similar questions the libertarian answers with an unequivocal no.

"But then you'd let people go hungry!" comes the rejoinder. This, the libertarian insists, is precisely what would not happen; with the restrictions removed, the economy would flourish as never before. With the controls taken off business, existing enterprises would expand and new ones would spring into existence satisfying more and more consumer needs; millions more people would be gainfully employed instead of subsisting on welfare, and all kinds of research and production, released from the stranglehold of government, would proliferate, fulfilling man's needs and desires as never before. It has always been so whenever government has permitted men to be free traders on a free market. But *why* this is so, and how the free market is the best solution to all problems relating to the material aspect of man's life, is another and far longer story.

For Further Reflection

1. Assess the strengths and weaknesses of Hospers' libertarianism. Do you agree with its high valuation of liberty and property rights? Do you think it exaggerates these rights against other rights?

2. Compare it with Hobbes and Locke. Is Hospers consistent with either of these? Note that Locke put limits on property holdings, determined by the involvement of the owner and the needs of others. Does Hospers put any constraints on how much property we may own?

3. Discuss his alternative to the welfare state. Do you think it is a viable solution?

4. Should we be taxed to help the less fortunate?

The Communist Answer: The Justification of the State Is Its Promotion of Radical Equality   VII.5

KARL MARX AND FRIEDRICH ENGELS

Friedrich Engels (1820–1895) was born the son of a German industrialist who moved to Manchester, England. He had considerable experience of the workings of British industry during the Industrial Revolution and was able to provide Marx with a first-hand insight of industrial realities. Harold Laski describes the co-founder of the Marxist movement as "always friendly, usually optimistic, with great gifts both for practical action and for getting on with others. . . . Widely read, with a very real talent for moving rapidly through a great mass of material, he was facile rather than profound. He was utterly devoid of jealousy or vanity. He had a happy nature which never agonised over the difficulty of thought. . . . It never occurred to him, during the friendship of forty years, marked only by one brief misunderstanding, to question his duty to serve Marx in every way he could." (Introduction to *The Communist Manifesto,* Random House, 1967)

Karl Marx (1818–1883) was born in Trier and educated in Catholic schools and at the University of Berlin, where he received his doctorate. He began his career in 1842 as a journalist for the liberal *Rheinische Zeitung* and soon distinguished himself as a brilliant and radical thinker. He was described as follows: "He combines the deepest philosophical seriousness with the most biting wit. Imagine Rousseau, Voltaire, Holbach, Lessing, Heine, and Hegel fused into one person—I say fused, not juxtaposed—and you have Dr. Marx." (cited in David McClellen's *Karl Marx,* Viking Press, 1975, p. 3) He played the dominant role in founding the Marxist movement. His principal works are *Economic and Philosophical Manuscripts of 1844,* the *Communist Manifesto* (with Friedrich Engels, 1848), and *Capital* (3 volumes, 1867, 1885, 1895).

Marx wrote as a young man, "Hitherto, the various philosophies have only interpreted the world in various ways; the point is to change it." The message of our selection from the *Communist Manifesto* embodies that thesis. It combines socio-economic analysis of the class struggle with a plan of action for overthrowing the existing oppressive conditions. It argues that the struggle between classes is the essential catalyst of historical change, but whereas in earlier times the structure of society was a complicated arrangement of hierarchical classes, in the present period of the bourgeoisie the social structure is developing towards a simple division of two classes: the bourgeoisie, owners of the means of production and ruling class, and the proletariat, the worker-slaves. The proletariat are fast becoming self-conscious of their exploited state and an international drama is unfolding in which they will create a violent revolution, throwing off their chains and, as new dictators, inaugurating a new era of justice, a classless society in which everyone freely and equally participates, "in which the free development of each is the condition for the free development of all."

Study Questions

1. How do Marx and Engels divide all previous societies?
2. How do they characterize their own epoch? How is it different from previous times?
3. Describe the bourgeoisie. How is it in the process of self-destruction?
4. Who are the proletariat? What is their condition?
5. What do Marx and Engels predict as the future course of the class struggle?
6. What is the relationship between the Communist party and the proletariat?
7. What will be the result of the proletariat revolution?
8. What are some of the specific social changes that will occur in the most advanced countries? To what degree have their predictions been realized?

I. Bourgeois and Proletarians

THE HISTORY OF ALL hitherto existing society is the history of class struggles.

Freeman and slave, patrician and plebeian, lord and serf, guildmaster and journeyman, in a word, oppressor and oppressed, stood in constant opposition to one another, carried on an uninterrupted, now hidden, now open fight, a fight that each time ended, either in a revolutionary re-constitution of society at large, or in the common ruin of the contending classes.

From Karl Marx and Friedrich Engels, Manifesto of the Communist Party, *trans. by Samuel Moore in 1888 from the original German text of 1848 and edited by Frederick Engels (Progress Publishers, Moscow).*

In the earlier epochs of history, we find almost everywhere a complicated arrangement of society into various orders, a manifold gradation of social rank. In ancient Rome we have patricians, knights, plebeians, slaves; in the Middle Ages, feudal lords, vassals, guild-masters, journeymen, apprentices, serfs; in almost all of these classes, again, subordinate gradations.

The modern bourgeois society that has sprouted from the ruins of feudal society has not done away with class antagonisms. It has but established new classes, new conditions of oppression, new forms of struggle in place of the old ones.

Our epoch, the epoch of the bourgeoisie, possesses, however, this distinctive feature: it has simplified the class antagonisms. Society as a whole is more and more splitting up into two great hostile camps, into two great classes directly facing each other: Bourgeoisie and Proletariat.

From the serfs of the Middle Ages sprang the chartered burghers of the earliest towns. From the burgesses the first elements of the bourgeoisie were developed.

The discovery of America, the rounding of the Cape, opened up fresh ground for the rising bourgeoisie. The East-Indian and Chinese markets, the colonisation of America, trade with the colonies, the increase in the means of exchange and in commodities generally, gave to commerce, to navigation, to industry, an impulse never before known, and thereby, to the revolutionary element in the tottering feudal society, a rapid development.

The feudal system of industry, under which industrial production was monopolised by closed guilds, now no longer sufficed for the growing wants of the new markets. The manufacturing system took its place. The guild-masters were pushed on one side by the manufacturing middle class; division of labour between the different corporate guilds vanished in the face of division of labour in each single workshop.

Meantime the markets kept ever growing, the demand ever rising. Even manufacture no longer sufficed. Thereupon, steam and machinery revolutionised industrial production. The place of manufacture was taken by the giant, Modern Industry, the place of the industrial middle class, by industrial millionaires, the leaders of whole industrial armies, the modern bourgeois.

Modern industry has established the world market, for which the discovery of America paved the way. This market has given an immense development to commerce, to navigation, to communication by land. This development has, in its turn, reacted on the extension of industry; and in proportion as industry, commerce, navigation, railways extended, in the same proportion the bourgeoisie developed, increased its capital, and pushed into the background every class handed down from the Middle Ages.

We see, therefore, how the modern bourgeoisie is itself the product of a long course of development, of a series of revolutions in the modes of production and of exchange. . . .

The bourgeoisie, wherever it has got the upper hand, has put an end to all feudal, patriarchal, idyllic relations. It has pitilessly torn asunder the motley feudal ties that bound man to his "natural superiors", and has left remaining no other nexus between man and man than naked self-interest, than callous "cash payment". It has drowned the most heavenly ecstasies of religious fervour, of chivalrous enthusiasm, of philistine sentimentalism, in the icy water of egotistical calculation. It has resolved personal worth into exchange value, and in place of the numberless indefeasible chartered freedoms, has set up that single, unconscionable freedom—Free Trade. In one word, for exploitation, veiled by religious and political illusions, it has substituted naked, shameless, direct, brutal exploitation.

The bourgeoisie has stripped of its halo every occupation hitherto honoured and looked up to with reverent awe. It has converted the physician, the lawyer, the priest, the poet, the man of science, into its paid wage-labourers.

The bourgeoisie has torn away from the family its sentimental zeal and has reduced the family relation to a mere money relation. . . .

The bourgeoisie cannot exist without constantly revolutionising the instruments of production, and thereby the relations of production, and with them the whole relations of society. Conservation of the old modes of production in unaltered form, was, on the contrary, the first condition of existence for all earlier industrial classes. Constant revolutionising of production, uninterrupted disturbance of all social conditions, everlasting uncertainty and agitation distinguished the bourgeois epoch from all earlier ones. All fixed, fast-frozen relations, with their train of ancient and venerable prejudices and opinions are swept away, all new-formed ones become antiquated before they can ossify. All that is solid melts into air, all that is holy is profaned, and man is at last compelled to face with sober senses, his real conditions of life, and his relations with his kind.

The need of a constantly expanding market for its products chases the bourgeoisie over the whole surface of the globe. It must nestle everywhere, settle everywhere, establish connexions everywhere.

The bourgeoisie has through its exploitation of the world market given a cosmopolitan character to production and consumption in every country. To the great chagrin of Reactionists, it has drawn from under the feet of industry the national ground on which it stood. All old-established national industries have been destroyed or are daily being destroyed. They are dislodged by new industries, whose introduction becomes a life and death question for all civilized nations, by industries that no longer work up indigenous raw material, but raw material drawn from the remotest zones; industries whose products are consumed, not only at home, but in every quarter of the globe. In place of the old wants, satisfied by the productions of the country, we find new wants, requiring for their satisfaction the products of distant lands and climes. In place of the old local and national seclusion and self-sufficiency, we have intercourse in every direction, universal inter-dependence of nations. And as in material, so also in intellectual production. The

intellectual creations of individual nations become common property. National one-sidedness and narrow-mindedness become more and more impossible, and from the numerous national and local literatures there arises a world literature.

The bourgeoisie, by the rapid improvement of all instruments of production, by the immensely facilitated means of communication, draws all, even the most barbarian, nations into civilization. The cheap prices of its commodities are the heavy artillery with which it batters down all Chinese walls, with which it forces the barbarians' intensely obstinate hatred of foreigners to capitulate. It compels all nations, on pain of extinction, to adopt the bourgeois mode of production; it compels them to introduce what it calls civilization into their midst, *i.e.*, to become bourgeois themselves. In one word, it creates a world after its own image.

The bourgeoisie has subjected the country to the rule of the towns. It has created enormous cities, has greatly increased the urban population as compared with the rural, and has thus rescued a considerable part of the population from the idiocy of rural life. Just as it has made the country dependent on the towns, so it has made barbarian and semi-barbarian countries dependent on the civilized ones, nations of peasants on nations of bourgeois, the East on the West.

The bourgeoisie keeps more and more doing away with the scattered state of the population, of the means of production, and of property. It has agglomerated population, centralized means of production, and has concentrated property in a few hands. The necessary consequence of this was political centralization. Independent, or but loosely connected, provinces with separate interests, laws, governments and systems of taxation, became lumped together into one nation, with one government, one code of laws, one national class-interest, one frontier and one customs-tariff.

The bourgeoisie, during its rule of scarce one hundred years, has created more massive and more colossal productive forces than have all preceding generations together. Subjection of Nature's forces to man, machinery, application of chemistry to industry and agriculture, steam-navigation, railways, electric telegraphs, clearing of whole continents for cultivation, canalization of rivers, whole populations conjured out of the ground—what earlier century had even a presentiment that such productive forces slumbered in the lap of social labour?

We see then: the means of production and of exchange, on whose foundation the bourgeoisie built itself up, were generated in feudal society. At a certain stage in the development of these means of production and of exchange, the conditions under which feudal society produced and exchanged, the feudal organization of agriculture and manufacturing industry, in one word, the feudal relations of property became no longer compatible with the already developed productive forces; they became so many fetters. They had to be burst asunder; they were burst asunder.

Into their place stepped free competition, accompanied by a social and political constitution adapted to it, and by the economical and political sway of the bourgeois class.

A similar movement is going on before our own eyes. Modern bourgeois society with its relations of production, of exchange and of property, a society that has conjured up such gigantic means of production and of exchange, is like the sorcerer, who is no longer able to control the powers of the nether world whom he has called up by his spells. For many a decade past the history of industry and commerce is but the history of the revolt of modern productive forces against modern conditions of production, against the property relations that are the conditions for the existence of the bourgeoisie and of its rule. It is enough to mention the commercial crises that by their periodical return put on its trial, each time more threateningly, the existence of the entire bourgeois society. In these crises a great part not only of the existing products, but also of the previously created productive forces, are periodically destroyed. In these crises there breaks

out an epidemic that, in all earlier epochs, would have seemed an absurdity—the epidemic of over-production. Society suddenly finds itself put back into a state of momentary barbarism; it appears as if a famine, a universal war of devastation had cut off the supply of every means of subsistence; industry and commerce seem to be destroyed; and why? Because there is too much civilization, too much means of subsistence, too much industry, too much commerce. The productive forces at the disposal of society no longer tend to further the development of the conditions of bourgeois property; on the contrary, they have become too powerful for these conditions, by which they are fettered, and so soon as they overcome these fetters, they bring disorder into the whole of bourgeois society, endanger the existence of bourgeois property. The conditions of bourgeois society are too narrow to compromise the wealth created by them. And how does the bourgeoisie get over these crises? On the one hand by enforced destruction of a mass of productive forces; on the other, by the conquest of new markets, and by the more thorough exploitation of the old ones. That is to say, by paving the way for more extensive and more destructive crises, and by diminishing the means whereby crises are prevented.

The weapons with which the bourgeoisie felled feudalism to the ground are now turned against the bourgeoisie itself.

But not only has the bourgeoisie forged the weapons that bring death to itself; it has also called into existence the men who are to wield those weapons—the modern working class—the proletarians.

In proportion as the bourgeoisie, *i.e.*, capital, is developed, in the same proportion is the proletariat, the modern working class, developed—a class of labourers who live only so long as they find work, and who find work only so long as their labour increases capital. The labourers, who must sell themselves piecemeal, are a commodity, like every other article of commerce, and are consequently exposed to all the vicissitudes of competition, to all the fluctuations of the market.

Owing to the extensive use of machinery and to division of labour, the work of the proletarians has lost all individual character, and, consequently, all charm for the workman. He becomes an appendage of the machine, and it is only the most simple, most monotonous, and most easily acquired knack, that is required of him. Hence, the cost of production of a workman is restricted, almost entirely, to the means of subsistence that he requires for his maintenance, and for the propagation of his race. But the price of a commodity, and therefore also of labour, is equal to its cost of production. In proportion, therefore, as the repulsiveness of the work increases, the wage decreases. Nay more, in proportion as the use of machinery and division of labour increases, in the same proportion the burden of toil also increases, whether by prolongation of the working hours, by increase of the work exacted in a given time or by increased speed of the machinery, etc.

Modern industry has converted the little workshop of the patriarchal master into the great factory of the industrial capitalist. Masses of labourers, crowded into the factory, are organized like soldiers. As privates of the industrial army they are placed under the command of a perfect hierarchy of officers and sergeants. Not only are they slaves of the bourgeois class, and of the bourgeois State; they are daily and hourly enslaved by the machine, by the overlooker, and, above all, by the individual bourgeois manufacturer himself. The more openly this despotism proclaims gain to be its end and aim, the more petty, the more hateful and more embittering it is.

The less the skill and exertion of strength implied in manual labour, in other words, the more modern industry becomes developed, the more is the labour of men superseded by that of women. Differences of age and sex have no longer any distinctive social validity for the working class.

All are instruments of labour, more or less expensive to use, according to their age and sex.

No sooner is the exploitation of the labourer by the manufacturer, so far, at an end, that he receives his wages in cash, than he is set upon by the other portions of the bourgeoisie, the landlord, the storekeeper, the pawnbroker, etc.

The lower strata of the middle class—the small tradespeople, shopkeepers, and retired tradesmen generally, the handicraftsmen and peasants—all these sink gradually into the proletariat, partly because their diminutive capital does not suffice for the scale on which Modern Industry is carried on, and is swamped in the competition with the large capitalists, partly because their specialized skill is rendered worthless by new methods of production. Thus the proletariat is recruited from all classes of the population.

The proletariat goes through various stages of development. With its birth begins its struggle with the bourgeoisie. At first the contest is carried on by individual labourers, then by the workpeople of a factory, then by the operatives of one trade, in one locality, against the individual bourgeois who directly exploits them. They direct their attacks not against the bourgeois conditions of production, but against the instruments of production themselves; they destroy imported wares that compete with their labour, they smash to pieces machinery, they set factories ablaze, they seek to restore by force the vanished status of the workman of the Middle Ages.

At this stage the labourers still form an incoherent mass scattered over the whole country, and broken up by their mutual competition. If anywhere they unite to form more compact bodies, this is not yet the consequence of their own active union, but of the union of the bourgeoisie, which class, in order to attain its own political ends, is compelled to set the whole proletariat in motion, and is moreover yet, for a time, able to do so. At this stage, therefore, the proletarians do not fight their enemies, but the enemies of their enemies, the remnants of absolute monarchy, the landowners, the non-industrial bourgeois, the petty bourgeoisie. Thus the whole historical movement is concentrated in the hands of the bourgeoisie; every victory so obtained is a victory for the bourgeoisie.

But with the development of industry the proletariat not only increases in number; it becomes concentrated in greater masses, its strength grows, and it feels that strength more. The various interests and conditions of life within the ranks of the proletariat are more and more equalized, in proportion as machinery obliterates all distinctions of labour, and nearly everywhere reduces wages to the same low level. The growing competition among the bourgeois, and the resulting commercial crises, make the wages of the workers ever more fluctuating. The unceasing improvement of machinery, ever more rapidly developing, makes their livelihood more and more precarious; the collisions between individual workmen and individual bourgeois take more and more the character of collisions between two classes. Thereupon the workers begin to form combinations (Trades' Unions) against the bourgeois; they club together in order to keep up the rate of wages; they found permanent associations in order to make provision beforehand for these occasional revolts. Here and there the contest breaks out into riots.

Now and then the workers are victorious, but only for a time. The real fruit of their battles lies, not in the immediate result, but in the everexpanding union of the workers. This union is helped on by the improved means of communication that are created by modern industry and that place the workers of different localities in contact with one another. It was just this contact that was needed to centralize the numerous local struggles, all of the same character, into one national struggle between classes. But every class struggle is a political struggle. . . .

This organization of the proletarians into a class, and consequently into a political party, is continually being upset again by the competition between the workers themselves. But it ever rises up again, stronger, firmer, mightier. It compels legislative recognition of particular interests of the workers, by taking advantage of the divisions among the bourgeoisie itself. . . .

Altogether, collisions between the classes of the old society further, in many ways, the course of development of the proletariat. The bourgeoisie finds itself involved in a constant battle. At first with the aristocracy; later on, with those portions of the bourgeoisie itself, whose interests have become antagonistic to the progress of industry; at all times, with the bourgeoisie of foreign countries. In all these battles it sees itself compelled to appeal to the proletariat, to ask for its help, and thus, to drag it into the political arena. The bourgeoisie itself, therefore, supplies the proletariat with its own elements of political and general education, in other words, it furnishes the proletariat with weapons for fighting the bourgeoisie.

Further, as we have already seen, entire sections of the ruling classes are, by the advance of industry, precipitated into the proletariat, or are at least threatened in their conditions of existence. These also supply the proletariat with fresh elements of enlightenment and progress.

Finally, in times when the class struggle nears the decisive hour, the process of dissolution going on within the ruling class, in fact within the whole range of old society, assumes such a violent, glaring character, that a small section of the ruling class cuts itself adrift, and joins the revolutionary class, the class that holds the future in its hands. Just as, therefore, at an earlier period, a section of the nobility went over to the bourgeoisie, so now a portion of the bourgeoisie goes over to the proletariat, and in particular, a portion of the bourgeoisie ideologists, who have raised themselves to the level of comprehending theoretically the historical movement as a whole.

Of all the classes that stand face to face with the bourgeoisie today, the proletariat alone is a really revolutionary class. The other classes decay and finally disappear in the face of modern industry; the proletariat is its special and essential product.

The lower middle class, the small manufacturer, the shopkeeper, the artisan, the peasant, all these fight against the bourgeoisie, to save from extinction their existence as fractions of the middle class. They are therefore not revolutionary, but conservative. Nay more, they are reactionary, for they try to roll back the wheel of history. If by chance they are revolutionary, they are so only in view of their impending transfer into the proletariat, they thus defend not their present, but their future interests, they desert their own standpoint to place themselves at that of the proletariat. . . .

In the conditions of the proletariat, those of old society at large are already virtually swamped. The proletarian is without property; his relation to his wife and children has no longer anything in common with the bourgeoisie family relations; modern industrial labour, modern subjection to capital, the same in England as in France, in America as in Germany, has stripped him of every trace of national character. Law, morality, religion, are to him so many bourgeois prejudices, behind which lurk in ambush just as many bourgeois interests.

All the preceding classes that got the upper hand, sought to fortify their already acquired status by subjecting society at large to their conditions of appropriation. The proletarians cannot become masters of the productive forces of society, except by abolishing their own previous mode of appropriation, and thereby also every other previous mode of appropriation. They have nothing of their own to secure and to fortify; their mission is to destroy all previous securities for, and insurances of, individual property.

All previous historical movements were movements of minorities, or in the interest of minorities. The proletarian movement is the self-conscious, independent movement of the immense majority, in the interest of the immense majority. The proletariat, the lowest stratum of our present society, cannot stir, cannot raise itself up, without the whole superincumbent strata of official society being sprung into the air.

Though not in substance, yet in form, the struggle of the proletariat with the bourgeoisie is at first a national struggle. The proletariat of each country must, of course, first of all settle matters with its own bourgeoisie.

In depicting the most general phases of the development of the proletariat, we traced the more or less veiled civil war, raging within existing society, up to the point where that war breaks out into open revolution, and where the violent overthrow of the bourgeoisie lays the foundation for the sway of the proletariat.

Hitherto, every form of society has been based, as we have already seen, on the antagonism of oppressing and oppressed classes. But in order to oppress a class, certain conditions must be assured to it under which it can, at least, continue its slavish existence. The serf, in the period of serfdom, raised himself to membership in the commune, just as the petty bourgeois, under the yoke of feudal absolutism, managed to develop into a bourgeois. The modern labourer, on the contrary, instead of rising with the progress of industry, sinks deeper and deeper below the conditions of existence of his own class. He becomes a pauper, and pauperism develops more rapidly than population and wealth. And here it becomes evident that the bourgeoisie is unfit any longer to be the ruling class in society, and to impose its conditions of existence upon society as an overriding law. It is unfit to rule because it is incompetent to assure an existence to its slave within his slavery, because it cannot help letting him sink into such a state, that it has to feed him, instead of being fed by him. Society can no longer live under this bourgeoisie, in other words, its existence is no longer compatible with society.

The essential condition for the existence, and for the sway of the bourgeois class, is the formation and augmentation of capital; the condition for capital is wage labour. Wage labour rests exclusively on competition between the labourers. The advance of industry, whose involuntary promoter is the bourgeoisie, replaces the isolation of the labourers, due to competition, by their revolutionary combination, due to association. The development of Modern Industry, therefore, cuts from under its feet the very foundation on which the bourgeoisie produces and appropriates products. What the bourgeoisie, therefore, produces, above all, is its own gravediggers. Its fall and the victory of the proletariat are equally inevitable.

II. Proletarians and Communists

In what relation do the Communists stand to the proletarians as a whole?

The Communists do not form a separate party opposed to other working-class parties.

They have no interests separate and apart from those of the proletariat as a whole.

They do not set up any sectarian principles of their own, by which to shape and mould the proletarian movement.

The Communists are distinguished from the other working-class parties by this only: 1. In the national struggles of the proletarians of the different countries, they point out and bring to the front the common interests of the entire proletariat, independently of all nationality. 2. In the various stages of development which the struggle of the working class against the bourgeoisie has to pass through, they always and everywhere represent the interests of the movement as a whole.

The Communists, therefore, are on the one hand, practically, the most advanced and resolute section of the working-class parties of every country, that section which pushes forward all others; on the other hand, theoretically, they have over the great mass of the proletariat the advantage of clearly understanding the line of march, the conditions, and the ultimate general results of the proletarian government.

The immediate aim of the Communists is the same as that of all the other proletarian parties: formation of the proletariat into a class, overthrow of the bourgeois supremacy, conquest of political power by the proletariat. . . .

The proletariat will use its political supremacy to wrest, by degrees, all capital from the bourgeoisie, to centralize all instruments of production in the hands of the State, *i.e.,* of the proletariat organized as the ruling class; and to increase the total of productive forces as rapidly as possible.

Of course, in the beginning, this cannot be effected except by means of despotic inroads on the rights of property, and on the conditions of bourgeois production; by means of measures, therefore, which appear economically insufficient and untenable, but which, in the course of the movement, outstrip themselves, necessitate further inroads upon the old social order, and are unavoidable as a means of entirely revolutionizing the mode of production.

These measures will of course be different in different countries.

Nevertheless in the most advanced countries, the following will be pretty generally applicable.

1. Abolition of property in land and application of all rents of land to public purposes.

2. A heavy progressive or graduated income tax.

3. Abolition of all right of inheritance.

4. Confiscation of the property of all emigrants and rebels.

5. Centralization of credit in the hands of the State by means of a national bank with State capital and an exclusive monopoly.

6. Centralization of the means of communication and transport in the hands of the State.

7. Extension of factories and instruments of production owned by the State; the bringing

into cultivation of waste-lands, and the improvement of the soil generally in accordance with a common plan.

8. Equal liability of all to labour. Establishment of industrial armies, especially for agriculture.

9. Combination of agriculture with manufacturing industries; gradual abolition of the distinction between town and country, by a more equable distribution of the population over the country.

10. Free education for all children in public schools. Abolition of children's factory labour in its present form. Combination of education with industrial production. . . .

When, in the course of development, class distinctions have disappeared, and all production has been concentrated in the hands of a vast association of the whole nation, the public power will lose its political character. Political power, properly so called, is merely the organized power of one class for oppressing another. If the proletariat during its contest with the bourgeoisie is compelled, by the force of circumstances, to organize itself as a class, if, by means of a revolution, it makes itself the ruling class, and, as such, sweeps away by force the old conditions of production, then it will, along with these conditions, have swept away the conditions for the existence of class antagonisms and of classes generally, and will thereby have abolished its own supremacy as a class.

In place of the old bourgeois society, with its classes and class antagonisms, we shall have an association, in which the free development of each is the condition for the free development of all. . . .

The Communists disdain to conceal their views and aims. They openly declare that their ends can be attained only by the forcible overthrow of all existing social conditions. Let the ruling classes tremble at a Communistic revolution. The proletarians have nothing to lose but their chains. They have a world to win.

WORKING MEN OF ALL COUNTRIES, UNITE!

For Further Reflection

1. Do you agree with Engels and Marx that the cultural values, including moral ideals and laws, of a society are always the reflection of the ruling class? Does this make all values relative?

2. What are the strengths and weaknesses of Marxist political philosophy?

3. Compare Marx and Engels' philosophy with Hospers' version of libertarianism. Which view is closer to the truth?

Suggestions for Further Reading

Barker, Ernest, ed. *Social Contract: Essays by Locke, Hume and Rousseau*. Oxford University Press, 1971.

Bedau, Hugo, ed. *Civil Disobedience*. Pegasus, 1969.

Benn, S. I., and R. Peters. *Social Principles and Democratic State*. London: Allen & Unwin, 1959.

Bowie, Norman, and Robert Simon. *The Individual and the Political Order*. Prentice-Hall, 1977.

Brown, Alan. *Modern Political Philosophy*. Penguin Books, 1986.

Feinberg, Joel. *Social Philosophy*. Englewood Cliffs, NJ: Prentice-Hall, 1973.

Hospers, John *Libertarianism*. Los Angeles: Nash, 1971.

Marx, Karl. *Karl Marx: Selected Writings,* ed. David McClellan. New York: Oxford University Press, 1977.

Mill, John Stuart. *On Liberty*. Indianapolis, IN: Bobbs-Merrill, 1956.

Nozick, Robert. *Anarchy, State and Utopia*. New York: Basic Books, 1974.

Plato. *The Republic,* trans. G.M.A. Grube. Indianapolis, IN: Hackett, 1974.

Rawls, John. *A Theory of Justice*. Harvard University Press, 1971.

Wolff, Robert P. *In Defense of Anarchism*. Harper & Row, 1970.

Part VIII

What Is the Meaning of Life?

To lose one's life is a little thing and I shall have the courage to do so if it is necessary; but to see the meaning of this life dissipated, to see our reason for existing disappear, that is what is unbearable. One cannot live without meaning.

ALBERT CAMUS

What is missing in my life is an understanding of what I must do, *not what I must know—except, of course, that a certain amount of knowledge is presupposed in every action. I need to understand the purpose of my life, and this means that I must find a truth which is true for me, that I must discover* that Idea for which I can live and die. *For what is truth but to live and die for an Idea?*

SØREN KIERKEGAARD as a twenty-two-year-old university student. An entry in his journal August 1, 1835.

I N HIS AUTOBIOGRAPHY Tolstoy tells the story of a traveller fleeing an infuriated animal. Attempting to save himself from the beast, the man runs towards a well and begins to climb down, when to his distress he spies a dragon at the bottom. The dragon is waiting with open jaws, ready to eat him. The poor fellow is caught in a dilemma. He dare not drop into the well for fear of the dragon, but he dare not climb out of the well for fear of the beast. So he clutches a branch of a bush growing in the cleft of the well and hangs onto it for dear life. His hands grow weak, and he feels that soon he shall have to give in to his grim fate, but he still holds on desperately. As he grasps the branch for his salvation, he notices that two mice, one white and one black, are nibbling away at the main trunk of the branch onto which he is clinging. Soon they will dislodge the branch.

The traveller is you and I, and his plight is your plight and mine, the danger of our demise on every hand. The white mouse represents our days and the black our nights. Together they are nibbling away at the three-score years and ten which make up our branch of life. Inevitably all will be over, and what have we to show for it? Is this all there is? Can this brief moment in the history of the universe have significance? What gives life importance?

The certainty of death heightens the question of the meaning of life. Like a prisoner sentenced to death or a patient with terminal illness, we know that, in a sense, we are all sentenced to death and terminally ill, but we flee the thought in a thousand ways. What is the purpose of life?

Our readings represent some of the classic responses to this question. Epicurus advises moderate pleasure in a life that accepts mortality without tears. Camus argues that life is meaningless, and to illustrate his view he tells the story of Sisyphus rolling a stone up a hill for eternity. Walker finds the essence of a purposeful life in religion. W. T. Stace tries to reason through to an acceptance of the loss of Meaning (an objective, overall purpose) in which we come to terms with our mortality and create our own meaning to life.

VIII.1   Epicurean Philosophy

EPICURUS

Epicurus (341–271 B.C.) was a Greek philosopher who was born on the isle of Samos but lived much of his life in Athens, where he founded his very successful school of philosophy. He was influenced by the materialist Democritus (460–370 B.C.), who is the first philosopher known to believe that the world is made up of atoms. Only a few fragments of Epicurus' writings are extant.

Epicurus identified good with pleasure and evil with pain. This doctrine (repeated later in Bentham) is called *hedonism* (from the Greek word for pleasure). But contrary to popular opinion, Epicurus was not what "Epicureanism" sometimes has been taken to mean: a sensuous, profligate life. He believed that the true life of pleasure consisted in an attitude of imperturbable emotional calm which needed only simple pleasures, a good diet, health, a prudent moral life, and good friends. Since only good or bad sensations (pleasure or pain) should concern us, and death is not a sensation, we should not fear death.

Study Questions

1. Does Epicurus believe in God? What sort of theology does he have?
2. What counsel does he give about death? What is his argument? Is it plausible?
3. What should the wise person seek? That is, what is the good?
4. What is the relationship between pleasure and pain? Describe his philosophy of life. What does he mean by the complete life?
5. What is his view of morality (justice)?

Letter to Menoeceus

LET NO ONE WHEN YOUNG delay to study philosophy, nor when he is old grow weary of his study. For no one can come too early or too late to secure the health of his soul. And the man who says that the age for philosophy has either not yet come or has gone by is like the man who says that the age for happiness is not yet come to him, or has passed away. Wherefore both when young and old a man must study philosophy, that as he grows old he may be young in blessings through the grateful recollection of what has been, and that in youth he may be old as well, since he will know no fear of what is to come. We must then meditate on the things that make our happiness, seeing that when that is with us we have all, but when it is absent we do all to win it.

The things which I used unceasingly to commend to you, these do and practise, considering them to be the first principles of the good life.

First of all believe that god is a being immortal and blessed, even as the common idea of a god is engraved on men's minds, and do not assign to him anything alien to his immortality or illsuited to his blessedness: but believe about him everything that can uphold his blessedness and immortality. For gods there are, since the knowledge of them is by clear vision. But they are not such as the many believe them to be: for indeed they do not consistently represent them as they believe them to be. And the impious man is not he who denies the gods of the many, but he who attaches to the gods the beliefs of the many. For the statements of the many about the gods are not conceptions derived from sensation, but false suppositions, according to which the greatest misfortunes befall the wicked and the greatest blessings the good by the gift of the gods. For men being accustomed always to their own virtues welcome those like themselves, but regard all that is not of their nature as alien.

Become accustomed to the belief that death is

nothing to us. For all good and evil consists in sensation, but death is deprivation of sensation. And therefore a right understanding that death is nothing to us makes the mortality of life enjoyable, not because it adds to it an infinite span of time, but because it takes away the craving for immortality. For there is nothing terrible in life for the man who has truly comprehended that there is nothing terrible in not living. So that the man speaks but idly who says that he fears death not because it will be painful when it comes, but because it is painful in anticipation. For that which gives no trouble when it comes, is but an empty pain in anticipation. So death, the most terrifying of ills, is nothing to us, since so long as we exist, death is not with us; but when death comes, then we do not exist. It does not then concern either the living or the dead, since for the former it is not, and the latter are no more.

But the many at one moment shun death as the greatest of evils, at another yearn for it as a respite from the evils in life. But the wise man neither seeks to escape life nor fears the cessation of life, for neither does life offend him nor does the absence of life seem to be any evil. And just as with food he does not seek simply the larger share and nothing else, but rather the most pleasant, so he seeks to enjoy not the longest period of time, but the most pleasant.

And he who counsels the young man to live well, but the old man to make a good end, is foolish, not merely because of the desirability of life, but also because it is the same training which teaches to live well and to die well. Yet much worse still is the man who says it is good not to be born, but

'once born make haste to pass the gates of Death'.

For if he says this from conviction why does he not pass away out of life? For it is open to him to do so, if he had firmly made up his mind to this. But if he speaks in jest, his words are idle among men who cannot receive them.

We must then bear in mind that the future is neither ours, nor yet wholly not ours, so that we may not altogether expect it as sure to come, nor abandon hope of it, as if it will certainly not come.

We must consider that of desires some are natural, others vain, and of the natural some are necessary and others merely natural; and of the necessary some are necessary for happiness, others for the repose of the body, and others for very life. The right understanding of these facts enables us to refer all choice and avoidance to the health of the body and the soul's freedom from disturbance, since this the aim of the life of blessedness. For it is to obtain this end that we always act, namely, to avoid pain and fear. And when this is once secured for us, all the tempest of the soul is dispersed, since the living creature has not to wander as though in search of something that is missing, and to look for some other thing by which he can fulfil the good of the soul and the good of the body. For it is then that we have need of pleasure, when we feel pain owing to the absence of pleasure; but when we do not feel pain, we no longer need pleasure. And for this cause we call pleasure the beginning and end of the blessed life. For we recognize pleasure as the first good innate in us, and from pleasure we begin every act of choice and avoidance, and to pleasure we return again, using the feeling as the standard by which we judge every good.

And since pleasure is the first good and natural to us, for this very reason we do not choose every pleasure, but sometimes we pass over many pleasures, when greater discomfort accrues to us as the result of them: and similarly we think many pains better than pleasures, since a greater pleasure comes to us when we have endured pains for a long time. Every pleasure then because of its natural kinship to us is good, yet not every pleasure is to be chosen: even as every pain also is an evil, yet not all are always of a nature to be avoided. Yet by a scale of comparison and by the consideration of advantages and disadvantages we must form our judgement on all these matters. For the good on certain occasions we treat as bad, and conversely the bad as good.

And again independence of desire we think a great good—not that we may at all times enjoy but a few things, but that, if we do not possess many, we may enjoy the few in the genuine persuasion that those have the sweetest pleasure in luxury who least need it, and that all that is natural is easy to be obtained, but that which is superfluous is hard. And so plain savours bring us pleasure equal to a luxurious diet, when all the pain due to want is removed; and bread and water produce the highest pleasure, when one who needs them puts them to his lips. To grow accustomed therefore to simple and not luxurious diet gives us health to the full, and makes a man alert for the needful employments of life, and when after long intervals we approach luxuries, disposes us better towards them, and fits us to be fearless of fortune.

When, therefore, we maintain that pleasure is the end, we do not mean the pleasures of profligates and those that consist in sensuality, as is supposed by some who are either ignorant or disagree with us or do not understand, but freedom from pain in the body and from trouble in the mind. For it is not continuous drinkings and revellings, nor the satisfaction of lusts, nor the enjoyment of fish and other luxuries of the wealthy table, which produce a pleasant life, but sober reasoning, searching out the motives for all choice and avoidance, and banishing mere opinions, to which are due the greatest disturbance of the spirit.

Of all this the beginning and the greatest good is prudence. Wherefore prudence is a more precious thing even than philosophy: far from prudence are sprung all the other virtues, and it teaches us that it is not possible to live pleasantly without living prudently and honourably and justly, nor, again, to live a life of prudence, honour, and justice without living pleasantly. For the virtues are by nature bound up with the pleasant life, and the pleasant life is inseparable from them. For indeed who, think you, is a better

man than he who holds reverent opinions concerning the gods, and is at all times free from fear of death, and has reasoned out the end ordained by nature? He understands that the limit of good things is easy to fulfil and easy to attain, whereas the course of ills is either short in time or slight in pain: he laughs at destiny, whom some have introduced as the mistress of all things. He thinks that with us lies the chief power in determining events, some of which happen by necessity and some by chance, and some are within our control; for while necessity cannot be called to account, he sees that chance is inconstant, but that which is in our control is subject to no master, and to it are naturally attached praise and blame. For, indeed, it were better to follow the myths about the gods than to become a slave to the destiny of the natural philosophers: for the former suggests a hope of placating the gods by worship, whereas the latter involves a necessity which knows no placation. As to chance, he does not regard it as a god as most men do (for in a god's acts there is no disorder), nor as an uncertain cause of all things: for he does not believe that good and evil are given by chance to man for the framing of a blessed life, but that opportunities for great good and great evil are afforded by it. He therefore thinks it better to be unfortunate in reasonable action than to prosper in unreason. For it is better in a man's actions that what is well chosen should fail, rather than that what is ill chosen should be successful owing to chance.

Meditate therefore on these things and things akin to them night and day by yourself, and with a companion like to yourself, and never shall you be disturbed waking or asleep, but you shall live like a god among men. For a man who lives among immortal blessings is not like to a mortal being.

PRINCIPAL DOCTRINES

I. The blessed and immortal nature knows no trouble itself nor causes trouble to any other, so that it is never constrained by anger or favour. For all such things exist only in the weak.

II. Death is nothing to us: for that which is dissolved is without sensation; and that which lacks sensation is nothing to us.

III. The limit of quantity in pleasures is the removal of all that is painful. Wherever pleasure is present, as long as it is there, there is neither pain of body nor of mind, nor of both at once.

IV. Pain does not last continuously in the flesh, but the acutest pain is there for a very short time, and even that which just exceeds the pleasure in the flesh does not continue for many days at once. But chronic illnesses permit a predominance of pleasure over pain in the flesh.

V. It is not possible to live pleasantly without living prudently and honourably and justly, nor again to live a life of prudence, honour, and justice without living pleasantly. And the man who does not possess the pleasant life, is not living prudently and honourably and justly, and the man who does not possess the virtuous life, cannot possibly live pleasantly.

VI. To secure protection from men anything is a natural good, by which you may be able to attain this end.

VII. Some men wished to become famous and conspicuous, thinking that they would thus win for themselves safety from other men. Wherefore if the life of such men is safe, they have obtained the good which nature craves; but if it is not safe, they do not possess that for which they strove at first by the instinct of nature.

VIII. No pleasure is a bad thing in itself: but the means which produce some pleasures bring with them disturbances many times greater than the pleasures.

IX. If every pleasure could be intensified so that it lasted and influenced the whole organism or the most essential parts of our nature, pleasures would never differ from one another.

X. If the things that produce the pleasures of profligates could dispel the fears of the mind about the phenomena of the sky and death and its pains, and also teach the limits of desires and of pains, we should never have cause to blame them: for they would be filling themselves full with pleasures from every source and never have pain of body or mind, which is the evil of life.

XI. If we were not troubled by our suspicions of the phenomena of the sky and about death, fearing that it concerns us, and also by our failure to grasp the limits of pains and desires, we should have no need of natural science.

XII. A man cannot dispel his fear about the most important matters if he does not know what is the nature of the universe but suspects the truth of some mythical story. So that without natural science it is not possible to attain our pleasures unalloyed.

XIII. There is no profit in securing protection in relation to men, if things above and things beneath the earth and indeed all in the boundless universe remain matters of suspicion.

XIV. The most unalloyed source of protection from men, which is secured to some extent by a certain force of expulsion, is in fact the immunity which results from a quiet life and the retirement from the world.

XV. The wealth demanded by nature is both limited and easily procured; that demanded by idle imaginings stretches on to infinity.

XVI. In but few things chance hinders a wise man, but the greatest and most important matters reason has ordained and throughout the whole period of life does and will ordain.

XVII. The just man is most free from trouble, the unjust most full of trouble.

XVIII. The pleasure in the flesh is not increased, when once the pain due to want is removed, but is only varied: and the limit as regards pleasure in the mind is begotten by the reasoned understanding of these very pleasures and of the emotions akin to them, which used to cause the greatest fear to the mind.

XIX. Infinite time contains no greater pleasure than limited time, if one measures by reason the limits of pleasure.

XX. The flesh perceives the limits of pleasure as unlimited and unlimited time is required to supply it. But the mind, having attained a reasoned understanding of the ultimate good of the flesh and its limits and having dissipated the fears concerning the time to come, supplies us with the complete life, and we have no further need of infinite time: but neither does the mind shun pleasure, nor, when circumstances begin to bring about the departure from life, does it approach its end as though it fell short in any way of the best life.

XXI. He who has learned the limits of life knows that that which removes the paid due to want and makes the whole of life complete is easy to obtain; so that there is no need of actions which involve competition.

XXII. We must consider both the real purpose and all the evidence of direct perception, to which we always refer the conclusions of opinion; otherwise, all will be full of doubt and confusion.

XXIII. If you fight against all sensations, you will have no standard by which to judge even those of them which you say are false.

XXIV. If you reject any single sensation and fail to distinguish between the conclusion of opinion as to the appearance awaiting confirmation and that which is actually given by the sensation or feeling, or each intuitive apprehension of the mind, you will confound all other sensations as well with the same groundless opinion, so that you will reject every standard of judgement. And if among the mental images created by your opinion you affirm both that which awaits confirmation and that which does not, you will not escape error, since you will have preserved the whole cause of doubt in every judgement between what is right and what is wrong.

XXV. If on each occasion instead of referring your actions to the end of nature, you turn to some other nearer standard when you are making a choice or an avoidance, your actions will not be consistent with your principles.

XXVI. Of desires, all that do not lead to a sense of pain, if they are not satisfied, are not

necessary, but involve a craving which is easily dispelled, when the object is hard to procure or they seem likely to produce harm.

XXVII. Of all the things which wisdom acquires to produce the blessedness of the complete life, far the greatest is the possession of friendship.

XXVIII. The same conviction which has given us confidence that there is nothing terrible that lasts for ever or even for long, has also seen the protection of friendship most fully completed in the limited evils of this life.

XXIX. Among desires some are natural and necessary, some natural but not necessary, and others neither natural nor necessary, but due to idle imagination.

XXX. Wherever in the case of desires which are physical, but do not lead to a sense of pain, if they are not fulfilled, the effort is intense, such pleasures are due to idle imagination, and it is not owing to their own nature that they fail to be dispelled, but owing to the empty imaginings of the man.

XXXI. The justice which arises from nature is a pledge of mutual advantage to restrain men from harming one another and save them from being harmed.

XXXII. For all living things which have not been able to make compacts not to harm one another or be harmed, nothing ever is either just or unjust; and likewise too for all tribes of men which have been unable or unwilling to make compacts not to harm or be harmed.

XXXIII. Justice never is anything in itself, but in the dealings of men with one another in any place whatever and at any time it is a kind of compact not to harm or be harmed.

XXXIV. Injustice is not an evil in itself, but only in consequence of the fear which attaches to the apprehension of being unable to escape those appointed to punish such actions.

XXXV. It is not possible for one who acts in secret contravention of the terms of the compact not to harm or be harmed, to be confident that he will escape detection, even if at present he escapes a thousand times. For up to the time of death it cannot be certain that he will indeed escape.

XXXVI. In its general aspect justice is the same for all, for it is a kind of mutual advantage in the dealings of men with one another: but with reference to the individual peculiarities of a country or any other circumstances the same thing does not turn out to be just for all.

XXXVII. Among actions which are sanctioned as just by law, that which is proved on examination to be of advantage in the requirements of men's dealings with one another, has the guarantee of justice, whether it is the same for all or not. But if a man makes a law and it does not turn out to lead to advantage in men's dealings with each other, then it no longer has the essential nature of justice. And even if the advantage in the matter of justice shifts from one side to the other, but for a while accords with the general concept, it is none the less just for that period in the eyes of those who do not confound themselves with empty sounds but look to the actual facts.

XXXVIII. Where, provided the circumstances have not been altered, actions which were considered just, have been shown not to accord with the general concept in actual practice, then they are not just. But where, when circumstances have changed, the same actions which were sanctioned as just no longer lead to advantage, there they were just at the time when they were of advantage for the dealings of fellow-citizens with one another; but subsequently they are no longer just, when no longer of advantage.

XXXIX. The man who has best ordered the element of disquiet arising from external circumstances has made those things that he could akin to himself and the rest at least not alien: but with all to which he could not do even this, he has refrained from mixing, and has expelled from his life all which it was of advantage to treat thus.

XL. As many as possess the power to procure complete immunity from their neighbours, these also live most pleasantly with one another, since they have the most certain pledge of security, and after they have enjoyed the fullest intimacy, they do not lament the previous departure of a dead friend, as though he were to be pitied.

For Further Reflection

1. Epicureanism is often thought of as a shallow, gluttonous, profligate life of undifferentiated pleasure, whose motto has been "Eat, drink, and be merry, for tomorrow we die" ("the pig philosophy"). Does one get this impression from Epicurus' writings?

2. Consider his view towards the fact of death: You ought not fear what never touches you. Death never touches you, for when you are, it is not; and when it is, you are not. Is this a reasonable argument against the fear of death? Why do we consider death an evil? What is the proper attitude towards death and why?

3. In the Hindu scripture *Bhagavad Gita,* Dharma, the personification of Duty, asks the young prince Yudhistira, "Of all the world's wonders, which is the most wonderful?" Yudhistira replies, "That no man, though he sees others dying all around him, believes that he himself will die." Is this applicable to Epicureanism? Is it a telling criticism?

4. How important is pleasure for the good life? What makes the "complete life" that Epicurus wrote about?

Life Is Absurd   VIII.2

ALBERT CAMUS

Albert Camus (1913–1960) was born in French colonial Algeria, into a poor working-class family. He was a French journalist, novelist, and philosopher who fought in the French underground during World War II and fought for courage and integrity in public life. He is most famous for his novels *The Stranger* (1942), *The Plague* (1947), and *The Fall* (1957), for which he received a Nobel Prize for literature. He was killed in a car crash in 1960. His rival existentialist, Jean-Paul Sartre, fittingly called it "an absurd death."

In this selection we see Camus' overall assessment that life is absurd, meaningless. The only important philosophical question is, why not commit suicide? Life is compared to the myth of Sisyphus, wherein that man is condemned by the gods to roll a huge stone up a mountain, watch it roll back down, and retrieve it, only to repeat the process again, endlessly.

Study Questions

1. What is the only important philosophical question and why is it important?
2. What is the "Absurd"? What does it mean to say that life is absurd? How does this feeling arise?
3. What is the only important thing in life? Is Camus' notion of value clear?
4. What does Camus mean by living "without appeal"?
5. Why do the gods condemn Sisyphus to his awful fate?
6. What does Sisyphus symbolize?

Absurdity and Suicide

THERE IS BUT ONE TRULY SERIOUS philosophical problem, and that is suicide. Judging whether life is or is not worth living amounts to answering the fundamental question of philosophy. All the rest—whether or not the world has three dimensions, whether the mind has nine or twelve categories—comes afterwards. These are games; one must first answer. And if it is true, as Nietzsche claims, that a philosopher, to deserve our respect, must preach by example, you can appreciate the importance of that reply, for it will precede the definitive act. These are facts the heart can feel; yet they call for careful study before they become clear to the intellect.

If I ask myself how to judge that this question is more urgent than that, I reply that one judges by the actions it entails. I have never seen anyone die for the ontological argument. Galileo, who held a scientific truth of great importance, abjured it with the greatest of ease as soon as it endangered his life. In a certain sense, he did right.* That truth was not worth the stake. Whether the earth or the sun revolves around the other is a matter of profound indifference. To tell the truth, it is a futile question. On the other hand, I see many people die because they judge that life is not worth living. I see others paradoxically getting killed for the ideas or illusions that give them a reason for living (what is called a reason for living is also an excellent reason for dying). I therefore conclude that the meaning of life is the most urgent of questions. How to answer it? On all essential problems (I mean thereby those that run the risk of leading to death or those that intensify the passion of living) there are probably but two methods of thought: the method of La Palisse and the method of Don Quixote. Solely the balance between evidence and lyricism can allow us to achieve simultaneously emotion and lucidity. In a subject at once so humble and so heavy with emotion, the learned and classical dialectic must yield, one can see, to a more modest attitude of mind deriving at one and the same time from common sense and understanding.

Suicide has never been dealt with except as a social phenomenon. On the contrary, we are concerned here, at the outset, with the relationship between individual thought and suicide. An act like this is prepared within the silence of the heart, as is a great work of art. The man himself is ignorant of it. One evening he pulls the trigger or jumps. Of an apartment-building manager who had killed himself I was told that he had lost his daughter five years before, that he had changed greatly since, and that that experience had "undermined" him. A more exact word cannot be imagined. Beginning to think is beginning to be undermined. Society has but little connection with such beginnings. The worm is in man's heart. That is where it must be sought.

---

*From the point of view of the relative value of truth. On the other hand, from the point of view of virile behavior, this scholar's fragility may well make us smile.

One must follow and understand this fatal game that leads from lucidity in the face of existence to flight from light. . . .

But it is hard to fix the precise instant, the subtle step when the mind opted for death, it is easier to deduce from the act itself the consequences it implies. In a sense, and as in melodrama, killing yourself amounts to confessing. It is confessing that life is too much for you or that you do not understand it. Let's not go too far in such analogies, however, but rather return to everyday words. It is merely confessing that that "is not worth the trouble." Living, naturally, is never easy. You continue making the gestures commanded by existence for many reasons, the first of which is habit. Dying voluntarily implies that you have recognized, even instinctively, the ridiculous character of that habit, the absence of any profound reason for living, the insane character of that daily agitation, and the uselessness of suffering.

What, then, is that incalculable feeling that deprives the mind of the sleep necessary to life? A world that can be explained even with bad reasons is a familiar world. But, on the other hand, in a universe suddenly divested of illusions and lights, man feels an alien, a stranger. His exile is without remedy since he is deprived of the memory of a lost home or the hope of a promised land. This divorce between man and his life, the actor and his setting, is properly the feeling of absurdity. All healthy men having thought of their own suicide, it can be seen, without further explanation, that there is a direct connection between this feeling and the longing for death.

The subject of this essay is precisely this relationship between the absurd and suicide, the exact degree to which suicide is a solution to the absurd. The principle can be established that for a man who does not cheat, what he believes to be true must determine his action. Belief in the absurdity of existence must then dictate his conduct. It is legitimate to wonder, clearly and without false pathos, whether a conclusion of this importance requires forsaking as rapidly as possible an incomprehensible condition. I am speaking, of course, of men inclined to be in harmony with themselves. . . .

All great deeds and all great thoughts have a ridiculous beginning. Great works are often born on a street-corner or in a restaurant's revolving door. So it is with absurdity. The absurd world more than others derives its nobility from that abject birth. In certain situations, replying "nothing" when asked what one is thinking about may be pretense in a man. Those who are loved are well aware of this. But if that reply is sincere, if it symbolizes that odd state of soul in which the void becomes eloquent, in which the chain of daily gestures is broken, in which the heart vainly seeks the link that will connect it again, then it is as it were the first sign of absurdity.

It happens that the stage sets collapse. Rising, streetcar, four hours in the office or the factory, meal, streetcar, four hours of work, meal, sleep, and Monday Tuesday Wednesday Thursday Friday and Saturday according to the same rhythm—this path is easily followed most of the time. But one day the "why" arises and everything begins in that weariness tinged with amazement. "Begins"—this is important. Weariness comes at the end of the acts of a mechanical life, but at the same time it inaugurates the impulse of consciousness. It awakens consciousness and provokes what follows. What follows is the gradual return into the chain or it is the definitive awakening. At the end of the awakening comes, in time, the consequence: suicide or recovery. In itself weariness has something sickening about it. Here, I must conclude that it is good. For everything begins with consciousness and nothing is worth anything except through it. . . .

But what does life mean in such a universe? Nothing else for the moment but indifference to the future and a desire to use up everything that is given. Belief in the meaning of life always implies a scale of values, a choice, our preferences. Belief in the absurd, according to our definitions, teaches the contrary. But this is worth examining.

Knowing whether or not one can live *without*

appeal is all that interests me. I do not want to get out of my depth. This aspect of life being given me, can I adapt myself to it? Now, faced with this particular concern, belief in the absurd is tantamount to substituting the quantity of experiences for the quality. If I convince myself that this life has no other aspect than that of the absurd, if I feel that its whole equilibrium depends on that perpetual opposition between my conscious revolt and the darkness in which it struggles, if I admit that my freedom has no meaning except in relation to its limited fate, than I must say that what counts is not the best of living but the most living. . . .

On the one hand the absurd teaches that all experiences are unimportant, and on the other it urges toward the greatest quantity of experiences. How, then, can one fail to do as so many of those men I was speaking of earlier—choose the form of life that brings us the most possible of that human matter, thereby introducing a scale of values that on the other hand one claims to reject?

But again it is the absurd and its contradictory life that teaches us. For the mistake is thinking that that quantity of experiences depends on the circumstances of our life when it depends solely on us. Here we have to be over-simple. To two men living the same number of years, the world always provides the same sum of experiences. It is up to us to be conscious of them. Being aware of one's life, one's revolt, one's freedom, and to the maximum, is living, and to the maximum. Where lucidity dominates, the scale of values becomes useless. . . .

The Myth of Sisyphus

The gods had condemned Sisyphus to ceaselessly rolling a rock to the top of a mountain, whence the stone would fall back of its own weight. They had thought with some reason that there is no more dreadful punishment than futile and hopeless labor.

If one believes Homer, Sisyphus was the wisest and most prudent of mortals. According to another tradition, however, he was disposed to practice the profession of highwayman. I see no contradiction in this. Opinions differ as to the reasons why he became the futile laborer of the underworld. To begin with, he is accused of a certain levity in regard to the gods. He stole their secrets. Ægina, the daughter of Æsopus, was carried off by Jupiter. The father was shocked by that disappearance and complained to Sisyphus. He, who knew of the abduction, offered to tell about it on condition that Æsopus would give water to the citadel of Corinth. To the celestial thunderbolts he preferred the benediction of water. He was punished for this in the underworld. Homer tells us also that Sisyphus had put Death in chains. Pluto could not endure the sight of his deserted, silent empire. He dispatched the god of war, who liberated Death from the hands of her conqueror.

It is said also that Sisyphus, being near to death, rashly wanted to test his wife's love. He ordered her to cast his unburied body into the middle of the public square. Sisyphus woke up in the underworld. And there, annoyed by an obedience so contrary to human love, he obtained from Pluto permission to return to earth in order to chastise his wife. But when he had seen again the face of this world, enjoyed water and sun, warm stones and the sea, he no longer wanted to go back to the infernal darkness. Recalls, signs of anger, warnings were of no avail. Many years more he lived facing the curve of the gulf, the sparkling sea, and the smiles of earth. A decree of the gods was necessary. Mercury came and seized the impudent man by the collar and, snatching him from his joys, led him forcibly back to the underworld, where his rock was ready for him.

You have already grasped that Sisyphus is the absurd hero. He *is*, as much through his passions as through his torture. His scorn of the gods, his hatred of death, and his passion for life won him that unspeakable penalty in which the whole being is exerted toward accomplishing nothing. This is the price that must be paid for the passions of this earth. Nothing is told us about Sisy-

phus in the underworld. Myths are made for the imagination to breathe life into them. As for this myth, one sees merely the whole effort of a body straining to raise the huge stone, to roll it and push it up a slope a hundred times over; one sees the face screwed up, the cheek tight against the stone, the shoulder bracing the clay-covered mass, the foot wedging it, the fresh start with arms outstretched, the wholly human security of two earth-clotted hands. At the very end of his long effort measured by skyless space and time without depth, the purpose is achieved. Then Sisyphus watches the stone rush down in a few moments toward that lower world whence he will have to push it up again toward the summit. He goes back down to the plain.

It is during that return, that pause, that Sisyphus interests me. A face that toils so close to stones is already stone itself! I see that man going back down with a heavy yet measured step toward the torment of which he will never know the end. That hour like a breathing-space which returns as surely as his suffering, that is the hour of consciousness. At each of those moments when he leaves the heights and gradually sinks toward the lairs of the gods, he is superior to his fate. He is stronger than his rock.

If this myth is tragic, that is because its hero is conscious. Where would his torture be, indeed, if at every step the hope of succeeding upheld him? The workman of today works every day in his life at the same tasks, and this fate is no less absurd. But it is tragic only at the rare moments when it becomes conscious. Sisyphus, proletarian of the gods, powerless and rebellious, knows the whole extent of his wretched condition: it is what he thinks of during his descent. The lucidity that was to constitute his torture at the same time crowns his victory. There is no fate that cannot be surmounted by scorn.

If the descent is thus sometimes performed in sorrow, it can also take place in joy. This word is not too much. Again I fancy Sisyphus returning toward his rock, and the sorrow was in the beginning. When the images of earth cling too tightly to memory, when the call of happiness becomes too insistent, it happens that melancholy rises in man's heart: this is the rock's victory, this is the rock itself. The boundless grief is too heavy to bear. These are our nights of Gethsemane. But crushing truths perish from being acknowledged. Thus, Œdipus at the outset obeys fate without knowing it. But from the moment he knows, his tragedy begins. Yet at the same moment, blind and desperate, he realizes that the only bond linking him to the world is the cool hand of a girl. Then a tremendous remark rings out: "Despite so many ordeals, my advanced age and the nobility of my soul make me conclude that all is well." Sophocles' Œdipus, like Dostoevsky's Kirilov, thus gives the recipe for the absurd victory. Ancient wisdom confirms modern heroism.

One does not discover the absurd without being tempted to write a manual of happiness. "What! by such narrow ways—?" There is but one world, however. Happiness and the absurd are two sons of the same earth. They are inseparable. It would be a mistake to say that happiness necessarily springs from the absurd discovery. It happens as well that the feeling of the absurd springs from happiness. "I conclude that all is well," says Œdipus, and that remark is sacred. It echoes in the wild and limited universe of man. It teaches that all is not, has not been, exhausted. It drives out of this world a god who had come into it with dissatisfaction and a preference for futile sufferings. It makes of fate a human matter, which must be settled among men.

All Sisyphus' silent joy is contained therein.

His fate belongs to him. His rock is his thing. Likewise, the absurd man, when he contemplates his torment, silences all the idols. In the universe suddenly restored to its silence, the myriad wondering little voices of the earth rise up. Unconscious, secret calls, invitations from all the faces, they are the necessary reverse and price of victory. There is no sun without shadow, and it is essential to know the night. The absurd man says yes and his effort will henceforth be unceasing. If there is a personal fate, there is no higher destiny, or at least there is but one which he concludes is inevitable and despicable. For the rest, he knows himself to be the master of his days. At that subtle moment when man glances backward over his life, Sisyphus returning toward his rock, in that slight pivoting he contemplates that series of unrelated actions which becomes his fate, created by him, combined under his memory's eye and soon sealed by his death. Thus, convinced of the wholly human origin of all that is human, a blind man eager to see who knows that the night has no end, he is still on the go. The rock is still rolling.

I leave Sisyphus at the foot of the mountain! One always finds one's burden again. But Sisyphus teaches the higher fidelity that negates the gods and raises rocks. He too concludes that all is well. This universe henceforth without a master seems to him neither sterile nor futile. Each atom of that stone, each mineral flake of that night-filled mountain, in itself forms a world. The struggle itself toward the heights is enough to fill a man's heart. One must imagine Sisyphus happy.

For Further Reflection

1. Is life absurd, as Camus insists? Does Camus give good reasons for this claim? What leads him to this pessimistic conclusion?

2. Is Camus being irreverent in asking such an outrageous question as "Why not commit suicide"?

3. Why does Camus say that Sisyphus must be imagined to be happy?

4. Compare Camus with Kierkegaard. Do they agree on the nature of existence, its essential absurdity? What is the difference between them?

VIII.3 Religion Gives Meaning to Life

LOIS HOPE WALKER

Lois Hope Walker is the pen name for an author who wishes to remain anonymous. In this essay Walker argues that religion, specifically theistic religion, gives special meaning to life, unavailable in secular world views. Furthermore, the autonomy that secularists prize (sometimes value it beyond its worth) is not significantly diminished by religious faith.

Study Questions

1. What are the two theses that the atheist holds and how does Walker argue against them?
2. What are her definitions of "meaning" and "autonomy"?
3. What is the relationship of meaning to freedom or autonomy?
4. Which of Walker's eight theses on the value of religious faith do you agree with and which do you disagree with?

SEVERAL YEARS AGO during a class break, I was discussing the significance of religion in our society with a few students in the college lounge. I, at that time an agnostic, was conceding to a devout Christian that it would be nice if theism were true, for then the world would not be simply a matter of chance and necessity, a sad tale with a sadder ending. Instead, "the world would be personal, a gift from our heavenly Father, who provides a basis for meaning and purpose." A mature woman from another class, whom I knew to be an atheist, overheard my remarks, charged through a group of coffee drinkers and angrily snapped at me, "That is the most disgusting thing I've ever heard!" I inquired why she thought this, and she replied, "Religion keeps humans from growing up. We don't need a big Daddy in the sky. We need to grow up and become our own parents."

I recalled Nietzsche's dictum that now that "God is dead," now that we have killed the Holy One, we must ourselves become gods to seem worthy of the deed. The atheist woman was prizing autonomy over meaning and claiming that religion did just the opposite.

In other words, she held two theses:

(1) It is more important to be free or autonomous than to have a grand meaning or purpose to life.

(2) Religion provides a grand meaning or purpose to life, but it does not allow humans to be free or autonomous.

I've thought a lot about that woman's response over the years. I think that she is wrong on both counts. In this essay I will defend religion against her two theses and try to show that meaning and autonomy are both necessary or important ingredients for an ideal existence and that they are compatible within a religious framework.

Let me begin with the first thesis, that it is more important to be free than that there be meaning in life. First let us define our terms. By "autonomy" I mean self-governing, the ability to make choices on the basis of good reasons rather than being coerced by threats or forces from without.

By "meaning" in life I mean that life has a purpose. There is some intrinsic rationale or plan to it. Now this purpose can be good, bad, or indifferent. An example of something with a bad purpose is the activity of poisoning a reservoir on which a community depends for its sustenance. An example of something with an indifferent purpose might be pacing back and forth to pass the time of day (it is arguable that this is bad or good depending on the options and context, and if you think that then either choose your own example or dismiss the category of indifferent purpose). An example of a good purpose is digging a well in order to provide water to a community in need of water.

Now it seems to be the case that, as a value, autonomy is superior to indifferent and bad purposes, since it has positive value but these other two categories do not. Autonomy may be more valuable to us than some good purposes, but it does not seem to be superior to *all* good purposes. While it may be more valuable to be free than to have this or that incidental purpose in life, freedom cannot really be understood apart from the notion of purposiveness. To be free is to be able to do some act *A,* when you want to, in order to reach some goal *G.* So the two ideas are related.

But the atheist woman meant more than this. She meant that if she had to choose whether to have free will or to live in a world that had a governing providential hand, she would choose the former. But this seems to make two mistakes. (1) It makes autonomy into an unjustified absolute and (2) it creates a false dilemma.

(1) Consider two situations: In situation A you are as free as you are now (say you have 100 units of autonomy—call these units "autono-

toms") but are deeply miserable because you are locked in a large and interesting room which is being slowly filled with poisonous gas. You can do what ever you want for five more minutes but then you will be dead. In situation B, however, you have only 95 autonotoms (that is, there are a few things that you are unable to do in this world—say commit adultery or kill your neighbor) but the room is being filled with sunshine and fresh air. Which world would you choose? I would choose situation B, for autonomy, it seems to me, is not the only value in the universe, nor is it always the overriding value. I think most of us would be willing to give up a few autonotoms for an enormous increase in happiness. And I think that a world with a good purpose would be one in which we would be willing to give up a few bits of freedom. If we were told that we could eliminate poverty, crime, and great suffering in the world by each sacrificing one autonotom, wouldn't we do this? If so, then autonomy is not an absolute which always overrides every other value. It is one important value among others.

I turn to the atheist's second thesis, that religion always holds purpose as superior to autonomy. I think that this is a misunderstanding of what the best types of religion try to do. As Jesus said in John 8:32, "Ye shall know the truth and the truth shall set you free." Rather than seeing freedom and meaning as opposites, theism sees them as inextricably bound together. Since it claims to offer us the truth about the world, and since having true beliefs is important in reaching one's goals, it follows that our autonomy is actually heightened in having the truth about the purpose of life. If we know why we are here and what the options in our destiny really are, we will be able to choose more intelligently than the blind who lead the blind in ignorance.

Indeed theistic religion (I have in mind Judaism, Christianity, and Islam, but this could apply to many forms of Hinduism and African religions as well) claims to place before us options of the greatest importance, so that if it is true the world is far better (infinitely better?) than if it is not.

Let me elaborate on this point. If theism is true and there is a benevolent supreme being governing the universe, the following eight theses are true:

1. We have a satisfying explanation of the origin and sustenance of the universe. We are the product not of chance and necessity or an impersonal Big Bang, but of a Heavenly Being who cares about us. As William James says, if religion is true, "the universe is no longer a mere *It* to us, but a *Thou* . . . and any relation that may be possible from person to person might be possible here." We can take comfort in knowing that the visible world is part of a more spiritual universe from which it draws its meaning and that there is, in spite of evil, an essential harmonious relation between our world and the transcendent reality.

2. Good will win out over evil—we're not fighting alone, but God is on our side in the battle. So, you and I are not fighting in vain—we'll win eventually. This thought of the ultimate victory of Goodness gives us confidence to go on in the fight against injustice and cruelty when others calculate that the odds against righteousness are too great to fight against.

3. God loves and cares for us—His love compels us (II Corinthians 5:7), so that we have a deeper motive for morally good actions, including high altruism. We live deeply moral lives because of deep gratitude to One who loves us and whom we love. Secularism lacks this sense of cosmic love, and it is, therefore, no accident that it fails to produce moral saints like Jesus, St. Francis, Gandhi, Martin Luther King, and Mother Teresa. You need special love to leave a world of comfort in order to go to a desolate island to minister to lepers, as Father Damian did.

4. We have an answer to the problem why be moral—it's clearly in your interest. Secular ethics has a severe problem with the question, Why be moral when it is not in your best interest, when you can profitably advance yourself by an egoistic act? But such a dilemma does not arise in religious ethics, for Evil really is bad for you and the Good good for you.

5. Cosmic Justice reigns in the universe. The scales are perfectly balanced so that everyone will get what he or she deserves, according to their moral merit. There is no moral luck (unless you interpret the grace which will finally prevail as a type of "luck"), but each will be judged according to how one has used one's talents (Matthew, chapter 25).

6. All persons are of equal worth. Since we have all been created in the image of God and are His children, we are all brothers and sisters. We are family and ought to treat each other benevolently as we would family members of equal worth. Indeed, modern secular moral and political systems often assume this equal worth of the individual without justifying it. But without the Parenthood of God it makes no sense to say that all persons are innately of equal value. From a perspective of intelligence and utility, Aristotle and Nietzsche are right, there are enormous inequalities, and why shouldn't the superior persons use the baser types to their advantage? In this regard, secularism, in rejecting inegalitarianism, seems to be living off of the interest of a religious capital which it has relinquished.

7. Grace and forgiveness—a happy ending for all. All's well that ends well (the divine comedy). The moral guilt which we experience, even for the most heinous acts, can be removed, and we can be redeemed and given a new start. This is true moral liberation.

8. There is life after death. Death is not the end of the matter, but we shall live on, recognizing each other in a better world. We have eternity in our souls and are destined for a higher existence. (Of course, hell is a problem here—which vitiates the whole idea somewhat, but many variations of theism [e.g., varieties of theistic Hinduism and the Christian theologians Origen (in the second century), F. Maurice, and Karl Barth] hold to universal salvation in the end. Hell is only a temporary school in moral education—I think that this is a plausible view.) So if Hebraic-Christian theism is true, the world is

a friendly home in which we are all related as siblings in one family, destined to live forever in cosmic bliss in a reality in which good defeats evil.

If theism is false and secularism is true, then there is no obvious basis for human equality, no reason to treat all people with equal respect, no simple and clear answer to the question, Why be moral even when it is not in my best interest? no sense of harmony and purpose in the universe, but "Whirl has replaced Zeus and is king" (Sophocles).

Add to this the fact that theism doesn't deprive us of any autonomy that we have in non-theistic systems. We are equally free to choose the good or the evil whether or not God exists (assuming that the notions of good and evil make sense in a non-theistic universe)—then it seems clear that the world of the theist is far better and more satisfying to us than one in which God does not exist.

Of course, the problem is that we probably do not know if theism, let alone our particular religious version of it, is true. Here I must use a Pascalean argument to press my third point that we may have an obligation or, at least, it may be a good thing, to live *as if* theism is true. That is, unless you think that theism is so improbable that we should not even consider it as a candidate for truth, we should live in such a way as to allow the virtues of theism to inspire our lives and our culture. The theistic world view is so far superior to the secular that—even though we might be agnostics or weak atheists—it is in our interest to live as though it were true, to consider each person as a child of God, of high value, to work as though God is working with us in the battle of Good over evil, and to build a society based on these ideas. It is good then to gamble on God. Religion gives us a purpose to life and a basis for morality that is too valuable to dismiss lightly. It is a heritage that we may use to build a better civilization and one which we neglect at our own peril.

For Further Reflection

1. Does Walker exaggerate the importance of religion for a meaningful life? How would a secularist respond?

2. Karl Marx said that religion was the opium of the people. It deludes them into thinking that all will be well with the world, leading to passive acceptance of evil and injustice. Is there some truth in Marx's dictum? How would Walker respond to this?

There Is Meaning in Absurdity   VIII.4

WALTER T. STACE

In this reading Stace considers how modern human beings may deal with the loss of the religious vision ("the Grand Illusion") which gave meaning to countless generations of humans. He agrees with Dostoevsky and Kierkegaard that with the disappearance of God from the sky all has changed and we appear to be living in a dead universe where darkness is ubiquitous. He describes how this situation came about and offers advice on how the situation can be ameliorated, enabling us to live with sufficient purpose to make life meaningful.

(A biographical sketch of Stace appears on p. 271.)

Study Questions

1. What do both the Roman Catholic bishops and the French existentialist Jean-Paul Sartre agree is the major cause of the confusion and loss of meaning in the modern world?
2. What has caused the decay of faith?
3. What does the rejection of "final causes" have to do with the decline of faith? How has it "killed religion"? Do you agree with Stace?
4. What is the essence of the "modern mind"?
5. What are the further deleterious consequences to values of the "ruin of the religious vision"?
6. What are the prospects for a successful secular ethics?
7. How does the demise of religion affect belief in free will?
8. What can philosophy do to remedy the tragic situation of modern existence?
9. Is science the answer to our troubles? Why or why not?
10. What must we do to ameliorate our predicament?

THE CATHOLIC BISHOPS OF AMERICA once issued a statement in which they said that the chaotic and bewildered state of the modern world is due to man's loss of faith, his abandonment of God and religion. I agree with this statement though I do not accept the religious beliefs of most bishops. It is no doubt an oversimplification to speak of *the* cause of so complex a state of affairs as the tortured condition of the world today. Its causes are doubtless multitudinous. Yet allowing for some element of oversimplification, I say that the bishops' assertion is substantially true.

M. Jean-Paul Sartre, the French existentialist philosopher, labels himself an atheist. Yet his views seem to me plainly to support the statement of the bishops. So long as there was believed to be a God in the sky, he says, men could regard him as the source of their moral ideals. The universe, created and governed by a fatherly God, was a friendly habitation for man. We could be sure that, however great the evil in the world, good in the end would triumph and the forces of evil would be routed. With the disappearance of God from the sky all this has changed. Since the world is not ruled by a spiritual being, but rather by blind forces, there cannot be any ideals, moral or otherwise, in the universe outside us. Our ideals, therefore, must proceed only from our own minds; they are our own inventions. Thus the world which surrounds us is nothing but an immense spiritual emptiness. It is a dead universe. We do not live in a universe which is on the side of our values. It is completely indifferent to them.

Years ago Mr. Bertrand Russell, in his essay "A Free Man's Worship," said much the same thing.

Such in outline, but even more purposeless, more void of meaning, is the world which Science presents for our belief. Amid such a world,

From Walter T. Stace, "Man Against Darkness," The Atlantic Monthly, September, 1948. Copyright © 1948, 1976, by The Atlantic Monthly Company, Boston, Mass.

if anywhere, our ideals henceforward must find a home. . . . Blind to good and evil, reckless of destruction, omnipotent matter rolls on its relentless way; for man, condemned today to lose his dearest, tomorrow himself to pass through the gate of darkness, it remains only to cherish, ere yet the blow falls, the lofty thoughts that ennoble his little day; . . . to worship at the shrine his own hands have built; . . . to sustain alone, a weary but unyielding Atlas, the world that his own ideals have fashioned despite the trampling march of unconscious power.

It is true that Mr. Russell's personal attitude to the disappearance of religion is quite different from either that of M. Sartre or the bishops or myself. The bishops think it a calamity. So do I. M. Sartre finds it "very distressing." And he berates as shallow the attitude of those who think that without God the world can go on just the same as before, as if nothing had happened. This creates for mankind, he thinks, a terrible crisis. And in this I agree with him. Mr. Russell, on the other hand, seems to believe that religion has done more harm than good in the world, and that its disappearance will be a blessing. But his picture of the world, and of the modern mind, is the same as that of M. Sartre. He stresses the *purposelessness* of the universe, the facts that man's ideals are his own creations, that the universe outside him in no way supports them, that man is alone and friendless in the world.

Mr. Russell notes that it is science which has produced this situation. There is no doubt that this is correct. But the way in which it has come about is not generally understood. There is a popular belief that some particular scientific discoveries or theories, such as the Darwinian theory of evolution, or the views of geologists about the age of the earth, or a series of such discoveries, have done the damage. It would be foolish to deny that these discoveries have had a great effect in undermining religious dogmas. But this account does not at all go to the root of the matter. Religion can probably outlive any scientific discoveries which could be made. It can accommodate itself to them. The root cause of the decay of faith has not been any particular discovery of science, but rather the general spirit of science and certain basic assumptions upon which modern science, from the seventeenth century onwards, has proceeded.

It was Galileo and Newton—notwithstanding that Newton himself was a deeply religious man—who destroyed the old comfortable picture of a friendly universe governed by spiritual values. And this was effected, not by Newton's discovery of the law of gravitation nor by any of Galileo's brilliant investigations, but by the general picture of the world which these men and others of their time made the basis of the science, not only of their own day, but of all succeeding generations down to the present. That is why the century immediately following Newton, the eighteenth century, was notoriously an age of religious skepticism. Skepticism did not have to wait for the discoveries of Darwin and the geologists in the nineteenth century. It flooded the world immediately after the age of the rise of science. Neither the Copernican hypothesis nor any of Newton's or Galileo's particular discoveries were the real causes. Religious faith might well have accommodated itself to the new astronomy. The real turning point between the medieval age of faith and the modern age of unfaith came when the scientists of the seventeenth century turned their backs upon what used to be called "final causes." The final cause of a thing or event meant the purpose which it was supposed to serve in the universe, its cosmic purpose. What lay back of this was the presupposition that there is a cosmic order or plan and that everything which exists could in the last analysis be explained in terms of its place in this cosmic plan, that is, in terms of its purpose.

Plato and Aristotle believed this, and so did the whole medieval Christian world. For instance, if it were true that the sun and the moon were created and exist for the purpose of giving light to man, then this fact would explain why the sun and the moon exist. We might not be able to discover the purpose of everything, but everything must have a purpose. Belief in final causes thus amounted to a belief that the world is governed by purposes, presumably the purposes of some overruling mind. This belief was not the invention of Christianity. It was basic to the whole of Western civilization, whether in the ancient pagan world or in Christendom, from the time of Socrates to the rise of science in the seventeenth century.

The founders of modern science—for instance, Galileo, Kepler, and Newton—were mostly pious men who did not doubt God's purposes. Nevertheless they took the revolutionary step of consciously and deliberately expelling the idea of purpose as controlling nature from their new science of nature. They did this on the ground that inquiry into purposes is useless for what science aims at: namely, the prediction and control of events. To predict an eclipse, what you have to know is not its purpose but its causes. Hence science from the seventeenth century onwards became exclusively an inquiry into causes. The conception of purpose in the world was ignored and frowned on. This, though silent and almost unnoticed, was the greatest revolution in human history, far outweighing in importance any of the political revolutions whose thunder has reverberated through the world.

For it came about in this way that for the past three hundred years there has been growing up in men's minds, dominated as they are by science, a new imaginative picture of the world. The world, according to this new picture, is purposeless, senseless, meaningless. Nature is nothing but matter in motion. The motions of matter are governed, not by any purpose, but by blind forces and laws. Nature in this view, says Whitehead—to whose writings I am indebted in this part of my essay—is "merely the hurrying of material, endlessly, meaninglessly." You can draw a sharp line across the history of Europe dividing it into two epochs of very unequal length. The line passes through the lifetime of Galileo. European man before Galileo—whether ancient pagan or more recent Christian—thought of the world as controlled by plan and purpose. After Galileo European man thinks of it as utterly purposeless. This is the great revolution of which I spoke.

It is this which has killed religion. Religion could survive the discoveries that the sun, not the earth, is the center; that men are descended from simian ancestors; that the earth is hundreds of millions of years old. These discoveries may render out of date some of the details of older theological dogmas, may force their restatement in new intellectual frameworks. But they do not touch the essence of the religious vision itself, which is the faith that there is plan and purpose in the world, that the world is a moral order, that in the end all things are for the best. This faith may express itself through many different intellectual dogmas, those of Christianity, of Hinduism, of Islam. All and any of these intellectual dogmas may be destroyed without destroying the essential religious spirit. But that spirit cannot survive destruction of belief in a plan and purpose of the world, for that is the very heart of it. Religion can get on with any sort of astronomy, geology, biology, physics. But it cannot get on with a purposeless and meaningless universe. If the scheme of things is purposeless and meaningless, then the life of man is purposeless and meaningless too. Everything is futile, all effort is in the end worthless. A man may, of course, still pursue disconnected ends, money, fame, art, science, and may gain pleasure from them. But his life is hollow at the center. Hence the dissatisfied, disillusioned, restless, spirit of modern man.

The picture of a meaningless world, and a meaningless human life is, I think, the basic theme of much modern art and literature. Certainly it is the basic theme of modern philosophy. According to the most characteristic philosophies of the modern period from Hume in the eighteenth century to the so-called positivists of today, the world is just what it is, and that is the end of all inquiry. There is no *reason* for its being what it is. Everything might just as well have been quite different, and there would have been no reason for that either. When you have stated what things are, what things the world contains, there is nothing more which could be said, even by an omniscient being. To ask any question about *why* things are thus, or what purpose their being so serves, is to ask a senseless question, because they serve no purpose at all. For instance, there is for modern philosophy no such thing as the ancient problem of evil. For this once famous question presupposes that pain and misery, though they seem so inexplicable and irrational to us, must ultimately subserve some rational purpose, must have their places in the cosmic plan. But this is nonsense. There is no such overruling rationality in the universe. Belief in the ultimate irrationality of everything is the quintessence of what is called the modern mind.

It is true that, parallel with these philosophies which are typical of the modern mind, preaching the meaninglessness of the world, there has run a line of idealistic philosophies whose contention is that the world is after all spiritual in nature and that moral ideals and values are inherent in its structure. But most of these idealisms were simply philosophical expressions of romanticism, which was itself no more than an unsuccessful counterattack of the religious against the scientific view of things. They perished, along with romanticism in literature and art, about the beginning of the present century, though of course they still have a few adherents. At the bottom these idealistic systems of thought were rationalizations of man's wishful thinking. They were born of the refusal of men to admit the cosmic darkness. They were comforting illusions within the warm glow of which the more tenderminded intellectuals sought to shelter themselves from the icy winds of the universe. They lasted a little while. But they are shattered now, and we return once more to the vision of a purposeless world.

Along with the ruin of the religious vision there went the ruin of moral principles and in-

deed of all values. If there is a cosmic purpose, if there is in the nature of things a drive towards goodness, then our moral systems will derive their validity from this. But if our moral rules do not proceed from something outside us in the nature of the universe—whether we say it is God or simply the universe itself—then they must be our own inventions. Thus it came to be believed that moral rules must be merely an expression of our own likes and dislikes. But likes and dislikes are notoriously variable. What pleases one man, people, or culture displeases another. Therefore morals are wholly relative. This obvious conclusion from the idea of a purposeless world made its appearance in Europe immediately after the rise of science, for instance in the philosophy of Hobbes. Hobbes saw at once that if there is no purpose in the world there are no values either. "Good and evil," he writes, "are names that signify our appetites and aversions; which in different tempers, customs, and doctrines of men are different. . . . Every man calleth that which pleaseth him, good; and that which displeaseth him, evil."

This doctrine of the relativity of morals, though it has recently received an impetus from the studies of anthropologists, was thus really implicit in the whole scientific mentality. It is disastrous for morals because it destroys their entire traditional foundation. That is why philosophers who see the danger signals, from the time at least of Kant, have been trying to give to morals a new foundation, that is, a secular or nonreligious foundation. This attempt may very well be intellectually successful. Such a foundation, independent of the religious view of the world, might well be found. But the question is whether it can ever be a *practical* success, that is, whether apart from its logical validity and its influence with intellectuals, it can ever replace among the masses of men the lost religious foundation. On that question hangs perhaps the future of civilization. But meanwhile disaster is overtaking us.

The widespread belief in "ethical relativity" among philosophers, psychologists, ethnologists, and sociologists is the theoretical counterpart of the repudiation of principle which we see all around us, especially in international affairs, the field in which morals have always had the weakest foothold. No one any longer effectively believes in moral principles except as the private prejudices either of individual men or of nations or cultures. This is the inevitable consequence of the doctrine of ethical relativity, which in turn is the inevitable consequence of believing in a purposeless world.

Another characteristic of our spiritual state is loss of belief in the freedom of the will. This also is a fruit of the scientific spirit, though not of any particular scientific discovery. Science has been built up on the basis of determinism, which is the belief that every event is completely determined by a chain of causes and is therefore theoretically predictable beforehand. It is true that recent physics seems to challenge this. But so far as its practical consequences are concerned, the damage has long ago been done. A man's actions, it was argued, are as much events in the natural world as is an eclipse of the sun. It follows that men's actions are as theoretically predictable as an eclipse. But if it is certain now that John Smith will murder Joseph Jones at 2:15 P.M. on January 1, 2000 A.D., what possible meaning can it have to say that when that time comes John Smith will be *free* to choose whether he will commit the murder or not? And if he is not free, how can he be held responsible?

It is true that the whole of this argument can be shown by a competent philosopher to be a tissue of fallacies—or at least I claim that it can. But the point is that the analysis required to show this is much too subtle to be understood by the average entirely unphilosophical man. Because of this, the argument against free will is generally swallowed whole by the unphilosophical. Hence the thought that man is not free, that he is the helpless plaything of forces over which he has no control, has deeply penetrated the modern mind. We hear of economic determinism, cultural determinism, historical determinism. We are not responsible for what we do because our glands control us, or because we are the products of environment or heredity. Not moral self-control, but the doctor, the psychiatrist, the educationist, must save us from doing evil. Pills and injections in the future are to do what Christ and the prophets have failed to do. Of course I do not mean to deny that doctors and educationists can and must help. And I do not mean in any way to belittle their efforts. But I do wish to draw attention to the weakening of moral controls, the greater or less repudiation of personal responsibility which, in the popular thinking of the day, result from these tendencies of thought.

What, then, is to be done? Where are we to look for salvation from the evils of our time? All the remedies I have seen suggested so far are, in my opinion, useless. Let us look at some of them.

Philosophers and intellectuals generally can, I believe, genuinely do something to help. But it is extremely little. What philosophers can do is to show that neither the relativity of morals nor the denial of free will really follows from the grounds which have been supposed to support them. They can also try to discover a genuine secular basis for morals to replace the religious basis which has disappeared. Some of us are trying to do these things. But in the first place philosophers unfortunately are not agreed about these matters, and their disputes are utterly confusing to the non-philosophers. And in the second place their influence is practically negligible because their analyses necessarily take place at a level on which the masses are totally unable to follow them.

The bishops, of course, propose as remedy a return to belief in God and in the doctrines of the Christian religion. Others think that a new religion is what is needed. Those who make these proposals fail to realize that the crisis in man's spiritual condition is something unique in history for which there is no sort of analogy in the past. They are thinking perhaps of the collapse of the ancient Greek and Roman religions. The vacuum then created was easily filled by Christianity, and it might have been filled by Mithraism if Christianity had not appeared. By analogy they think that Christianity might now be replaced by a new religion, or even that Christianity itself, if revivified, might bring back health to men's lives.

But I believe that there is no analogy at all between our present state and that of the European peoples at the time of the fall of paganism. Men had at that time lost their belief only in particular dogmas, particular embodiments of the religious view of the world. It had no doubt become incredible that Zeus and the other gods were living on the top of Mount Olympus. You could go to the top and find no trace of them. But the imaginative picture of a world governed by purpose, a world driving towards the good—which is the inner spirit of religion—had at that time received no serious shock. It had merely to re-embody itself in new dogmas, those of Christianity or some other religion. Religion itself was not dead in the world, only a particular form of it.

But now the situation is quite different. It is not merely that particular dogmas, like that of the virgin birth, are unacceptable to the modern mind. That is true, but it constitutes a very superficial diagnosis of the present situation of religion. Modern skepticism is of a wholly different order from that of the intellectuals of the ancient world. It has attacked and destroyed not merely the outward forms of the religious spirit, its particularized dogmas, but the very essence of that spirit itself, belief in a meaningful and purposeful world. For the founding of a new religion a new Jesus Christ or Buddha would have to appear, in itself a most unlikely event and one for which in any case we cannot afford to sit and wait. But even if a new prophet and a new religion did appear, we may predict that they would fail in the modern world. No one for long would believe in them, for modern men have lost the vision, basic to all religion, of an ordered plan and purpose of the world. They have before their minds the picture of a purposeless universe, and such a world-picture must be fatal to any religion at all, not merely to Christianity.

We must not be misled by occasional appearances of a revival of the religious spirit. Men, we are told, in their disgust and disillusionment at the emptiness of their lives, are turning once more to religion, or are searching for a new message. It may be so. We must expect such wistful yearnings of the spirit. We must expect men to wish back again the light that is gone, and to try to bring it back. But however they may wish and try, the light will not shine again—not at least in the civilization to which we belong.

Another remedy commonly proposed is that we should turn to science itself, or the scientific spirit, for our salvation. Mr. Russell and Professor Dewey both made this proposal, though in somewhat different ways. Professor Dewey seemed to believe that discoveries in sociology, the application of scientific method to social and political problems, will rescue us. This seems to me to be utterly naive. It is not likely that science, which is basically the cause of our spiritual troubles, is likely also to produce the cure for them. Also it lies in the nature of science that, though it can teach us the best means for achieving our ends, it can never tell us what ends to pursue. It cannot give us any ideals. And our trouble is about ideals and ends, not about the means for reaching them.

No civilization can live without ideals, or to put it in another way, without a firm faith in moral ideas. Our ideals and moral ideas have in the past been rooted in religion. But the religious basis of our ideals has been undermined, and the superstructure of ideals is plainly tottering. None of the commonly suggested remedies on examination seems likely to succeed. It would therefore look as if the early death of our civilization were inevitable.

Of course we know that it is perfectly possible for individual men, very highly educated men, philosophers, scientists, intellectuals in general, to live moral lives without any religious convictions. But the question is whether a whole civilization, a whole family of peoples, composed almost entirely of relatively uneducated men and women, can do this. It follows, of course, that if we could make the vast majority of men as highly educated as the very few are now, we might save the situation. And we are already moving slowly in that direction through the techniques of mass education. But the critical question seems to concern the time-lag. Perhaps in a hundred years most of the population will, at the present rate, be sufficiently highly educated and civilized to combine high ideals with an absence of religion. But long before we reach any such stage, the collapse of our civilization may have come about. How are we to live through the intervening period?

I am sure that the first thing we have to do is to face the truth, however bleak it may be, and then next we have to learn to live with it. Let me say a word about each of these two points. What I am urging as regards the first is complete honesty. Those who wish to resurrect Christian dogmas are not, of course, consciously dishonest. But they have that kind of unconscious dishonesty which consists in lulling oneself with opiates and dreams. Those who talk of a new religion are merely hoping for a new opiate. Both alike refuse to face the truth that there is, in the universe outside man, no spirituality, no regard for values, no friend in the sky, no help or comfort for man of any sort. To be perfectly honest in the admission of this fact, not to seek shelter in new or old illusions, not to indulge in wishful dreams about this matter, this is the first thing we shall have to do.

I do not urge this course out of any special regard for the sanctity of truth in the abstract. It is not self-evident to me that truth is the supreme value to which all else must be sacrificed. Might not the discoverer of a truth which would be fatal to mankind be justified in suppressing it, even in teaching men a falsehood? Is truth more valu-

able than goodness and beauty and happiness? To think so is to invent yet another absolute, another religious delusion in which Truth with a capital T is substituted for God. The reason why we must now boldly and honestly face the truth that the universe is non-spiritual and indifferent to goodness, beauty, happiness, or truth is not that it would be wicked to suppress it, but simply that it is too late to do so, so that in the end we cannot do anything else but face it. Yet we stand on the brink, dreading the icy plunge. We need courage. We need honesty.

Now about the other point, the necessity of learning to live with the truth. This means learning to live virtuously and happily, or at least contentedly, without illusions. And this is going to be extremely difficult because what we have now begun dimly to perceive is that human life in the past, or at least human happiness, has almost wholly depended upon illusions. It has been said that man lives by truth, and that the truth will make us free. Nearly the opposite seems to me to be the case. Mankind has managed to live only by means of lies, and the truth may very well destroy us. If one were a Bergsonian one might believe that nature deliberately puts illusions into our souls in order to induce us to go on living.

The illusions by which men have lived seem to be of two kinds. First, there is what one may perhaps call the Great Illusion—I mean the religious illusion that the universe is moral and good, that it follows a wise and noble plan, that is gradually generating some supreme value, that goodness is bound to triumph in it. Secondly, there is a whole host of minor illusions on which human happiness nourishes itself. How much of human happiness notoriously comes from the illusions of the lover about his beloved? Then again we work and strive because of the illusions connected with fame, glory, power, or money. Banners of all kinds, flags, emblems, insignia, ceremonials, and rituals are invariably symbols of some illusion or other. The British Empire, the connection between mother country and dominions, used to be partly kept going by illusions surrounding the notion of kingship. Or think of the vast amount of human happiness which is derived from the illusion of supposing that if some nonsense syllable, such as "sir" or "count" or "lord" is pronounced in conjunction with our names, we belong to a superior order of people.

There is plenty of evidence that human happiness is almost wholly based upon illusions of one kind or another. But the scientific spirit, or the spirit of truth, is the enemy of illusions and therefore the enemy of human happiness. That is why it is going to be so difficult to live with the truth. There is no reason why we should have to give up the host of minor illusions which render life supportable. There is no reason why the lover should be scientific about the loved one. Even the illusions of fame and glory may persist. But without the Great Illusion, the illusion of a good, kindly, and purposeful universe, we shall *have* to learn to live. And to ask this is really no more than to ask that we become genuinely civilized beings and not merely sham civilized beings.

I can best explain the difference by a reminiscence. I remember a fellow student in my college days, an ardent Christian, who told me that if he did not believe in a future life, in heaven and hell, he would rape, murder, steal and be a drunkard. That is what I call being a sham civilized being. On the other hand, not only could a Huxley, a John Stuart Mill, a David Hume, live great and fine lives without any religion, but a great many others of us, quite obscure persons, can at least live decent lives without it. To be genuinely civilized means to be able to walk straightly and to live honorably without the props and crutches of one or another of the childish dreams which have so far supported men. That such a life is likely to be ecstatically happy I will not claim. But that it can be lived in quiet content, accepting resignedly what cannot be helped, not expecting the impossible, and being thankful for small mercies, this I would maintain. That it will be difficult for men in general to learn this lesson I do not deny. But that it will be impossible I would not admit since so many have learned it already.

Man has not yet grown up. He is not adult. Like a child he cries for the moon and lives in a world of fantasies. And the race as a whole has perhaps reached the great crisis of its life. Can it grow up as a race in the same sense as individual men grow up? Can man put away childish things and adolescent dreams? Can he grasp the real world as it actually is, stark and bleak, without its romantic or religious halo, and still retain his ideals, striving for great ends and noble achievements? If he can, all may yet be well. If he cannot, he will probably sink back into the savagery and brutality from which he came, taking a humble place once more among the lower animals.

For Further Reflection

1. Is Stace accurate in his description of the human predicament? Do you think he is right on target, too pessimistic, or too optimistic? Does he dismiss religion too quickly without sufficient argument? Or does he underestimate how futile our predicament without a religious orientation is?

2. How would you relate the thesis of the first reading of this book, that the unexamined life is not worth living, with this article? Does Stace make you doubt that judgment (ignorance is bliss), or is he correct, that we must learn to live gracefully with the truth—even when it is not what we might wish it to be?

VIII.5   Reflections on Suffering

BERTRAND RUSSELL

A philosopher whom we have studied at length in this work is Bertrand Russell, someone who thought deeply about the question of the meaning of life. Russell says in his *Autobiography* that his youth was very unhappy and only the love of mathematics kept him from committing suicide. Gradually, he learned to find happiness. In these two short selections from his *Autobiography,* Russell first tells of an experience which greatly affected his life and then goes on to summarize what gives him meaning in life.
    (A biographical sketch of Russell appears on p. 18.)

Study Questions

1. Describe the situation in the first part of this essay.
2. What sort of feelings and thoughts did Russell experience in the face of the suffering he witnessed?
3. What are the three passions that have dominated Russell's life?

Spring 1901

WHEN WE CAME HOME, we found Mrs. W undergoing an unusually severe bout of pain. She seemed cut off from everyone and everything by walls of agony, and the sense of the solitude of each human soul suddenly overwhelmed me. Ever since my marriage, my emotional life had been calm and superficial. I had forgotten all the deeper issues, and had been content with flippant cleverness. Suddenly the ground seemed to give way beneath me, and I found myself in quite another region. Within five minutes I went thru some such reflections as the following: the loneliness of the human soul is unendurable; nothing can penetrate it except the highest intensity of the sort of love that religious teachers have preached; whatever does not spring from this motive is harmful, or at best useless; it follows that war is wrong, that a public school edu-

cation is abominable, that the use of force is to be deprecated, and that in human relations one should penetrate to the core of loneliness in each person and speak to that. [The writer then describes his sudden awareness of Mrs. W's three year old son with whom he then and there found an affinity.] . . . At the end of those five minutes, I had become a completely different person. For a time, a sort of mystic illumination possessed me. I felt that I knew the inmost thoughts of everybody that I met in the street, and though this was, no doubt, a delusion, I did in actual fact find myself in *far closer* touch than previously with all my friends, and many of my acquaintances. Having been an Imperialist, I became during those five minutes . . . a Pacificist. Having for years cared only for exactness and analysis, I found myself filled with semi-mystical feelings about beauty, and with an intense interest in children and with a desire almost as profound

From The Autobiography of Bertrand Russell, *v. I, p. 146. Reprinted by permission of Unwin Hyman Ltd.*

as that of the Buddha to find some philosophy which should make human life endurable. A strange excitement possessed me, containing intense pain but also some element of triumph through the fact that I could dominate pain, and make it, as I thought, a gateway to wisdom. The mystic insight which I then imagined myself to possess has largely faded, and the habit of analysis has reasserted itself. But something of what I thought I saw in that moment has remained always with me, *causing* my attitude during the first war, my interest in my children, my indifference to minor misfortunes and a certain emotional tone in all my human relations.

Epilogue

LOVE, KNOWLEDGE, AND PITY

Three passions, simple but overwhelmingly strong, have governed my life: the longing for love, the search for knowledge, and unbearable pity for the suffering of mankind. These passions, like great winds, have blown me hither and thither, in a wayward course, over a deep ocean of anguish, reaching to the very verge of despair.

I have sought love, first, because it brings ecstasy—ecstasy so great that I would often have sacrificed all the rest of life for a few hours of this joy. I have sought it, next, because it relieves loneliness—that terrible loneliness in which one shivering consciousness looks over the rim of the world into the cold unfathomable lifeless abyss. I have sought it, finally, because in the union of love I have seen, in a mystic miniature, the prefiguring vision of the heaven that saints and poets have imagined. This is what I sought, and though it might seem too good for human life, this is what—at last—I have found.

With equal passion I have sought knowledge. I have wished to understand the hearts of men. I have wished to know why the stars shine. And I have tried to apprehend the Pythagorean power by which number holds sway above the flux. A little of this, but not much, I have achieved.

Love and knowledge, so far as they were possible, led upward toward the heavens. But always pity brought me back to earth. Echoes of cries of pain reverberate in my heart. Children in famine, victims tortured by oppressors, helpless old people a hated burden to their sons, and the whole world of loneliness, poverty, and pain make a mockery of what human life should be. I long to alleviate the evil, but I cannot, and I too suffer.

This has been my life. I have found it worth living, and would gladly live it again if the chance were offered me.

For Further Reflection

1. Compare the first selection with the second. Do you see any differences?
2. How does your set of values compare with Russell's? Do you think that Russell's philosophy of life is adequate for happiness and the good life? Compare it with the other readings in this part.

Suggestions for Further Reading

Barrett, William. *Irrational Man.* Doubleday, 1958.
Bretall, Robert, ed. *A Kierkegaard Anthology.* Princeton University, 1946.
Camus, Albert. *The Myth of Sisyphus and Other Essays,* trans. J. O. O'Brien. Random House, 1955.

Camus, Albert. *The Plague*. Random House, 1948.

Frankl, Victor. *Man's Search for Meaning*. Beacon Press, 1963.

Kaufmann, Walter. *Existentialism from Dostoevsky to Sartre*. New American Library, 1975.

Kaufmann, Walter, ed. and trans. *A Portable Nietzsche*. Viking, 1954.

Kierkegaard, Søren. *Fear and Trembling*, trans. Walter Lowrie. Princeton University, 1954.

Klemke, E. D. *The Meaning of Life*. Oxford University, 1981.

Nietzsche, Friedrich. *The Will to Power*. Random House, 1967.

Russell, Bertrand. *The Conquest of Happiness*. New American Library, 1930.

Sanders, Steven and David Cheney, eds. *The Meaning of Life*. Englewood Cliffs, NJ: Prentice-Hall, 1980.

Sartre, Jean-Paul. *Existentialism and Human Emotions*. Philosophical Library, 1948.

Schopenhauer, Arthur. *The Will to Live: Selected Writings of Arthur Schopenhauer*, ed. Richard Taylor. Ungar, 1967.

Tolstoy, Leo. *My Confessions*, trans. Leo Wiener. Dent, 1905.

Part IX

Ethics in Action

What is the use of studying philosophy if all that it does for you is enable you to talk with some plausibility about some abstruse questions of logic, etc., and if it does not improve your thinking about the important questions of everyday life?

LUDWIG WITTGENSTEIN

S EVERAL MORAL ISSUES are tearing our society apart; among the most prominent are abortion, euthanasia, racism, reverse discrimination, the death penalty, and the status of animals. Can philosophical analysis throw light on these issues? Can philosophy have practical implications?

While this introduction to philosophy concentrates on the classical problems of philosophy, the topics covered in Parts I through VIII, it is hoped that this short section will provide examples of how philosophical reasoning can illuminate contemporary issues. I have chosen three that have special interest to students: abortion, capital punishment, and animal rights.

Is Abortion Morally Permissible?

> Abortion during the first two or three months of gestation is morally equivalent to removal of a piece of tissue from the woman's body. [philosopher Thomas Szasz]

> Every unborn child must be regarded as a human person with all the rights of a human person, from the moment of conception. [*Ethical and Religious Directives for Catholic Hospitals*]

One of the major social issues before us today, one that divides our nation as no other issue does, is that of the moral and legal status of the human fetus and the corresponding question of the moral permissibility of abortion. On the one hand, such organizations as the Roman Catholic Church and the Right to Life movement, appalled by the more than 1.5 million abortions that take place in this country each year, have exerted significant political pressure toward introducing a constitutional amendment that would grant full legal rights to fetuses. These movements have in some cases made the abortion issue the single issue in political campaigns. On the other hand, pro-choice groups such as the National Organization of Women (NOW), the National Abortion Rights Action League (NARAL), and feminist organizations have exerted enormous pressure on politicians to support pro-abortion legislation. The Republican and Democrat political platforms of the last two elections took diametrically opposite sides on this issue.

Why is abortion a moral issue? Take a fertilized egg, a zygote, a tiny sphere of cells. By itself, it is hard to see what is so important about such an inconspicuous piece of matter. It is virtually indistinguishable from other clusters of cells, or the zygotes of other animals. On the other hand, take an adult human being, a class of beings that we all intuitively feel to be worthy of high respect, having rights, including the right to life. To kill an innocent human being is an act of murder and universally condemned. However, no obvious line of division separates that single-cell zygote from the adult it will become. Hence, the problem of abortion.

474

It is with this sort of analysis that John Noonan begins his argument against abortion. He argues that since it is always wrong to kill innocent human beings and since fetuses are innocent human beings, it is wrong to kill fetuses. He makes an exception when the mother's life is in danger, since something of comparable worth is at stake. Noonan argues that conception is the only nonarbitrary cut-off place between nonpersonhood and personhood.

Mary Anne Warren argues against Noonan that fetuses are not persons since persons must have such characteristics as self-consciousness and rationality and fetuses do not have these.

Abortion Is Not Morally Permissible   IX.1

JOHN T. NOONAN, JR.

John T. Noonan, Jr., is professor of law at the University of California, Berkeley. He is a Roman Catholic philosopher who has written several works on moral issues, including *Contraception: A History of Its Treatment by the Catholic Theologians and Canonists* (1965) and *A Private Choice: Abortion in America in the Seventies* (1979). In this selection Noonan defends the conservative view that an entity becomes a person at conception and that abortion, except to save the mother's life, is morally wrong. He uses an argument from probabilities to show that his criterion of humanity is objectively based.

Study Questions

1. What is the most fundamental question in the history of thought on abortion?
2. How did theologians answer that question?
3. What are four rival answers to the question, When does a fetus become a human being? Why does Noonan reject each of them?
4. What does Noonan say about the relevance of probabilities in the assessment of whether a fetus will become a fully formed human being?

THE MOST FUNDAMENTAL QUESTION involved in the long history of thought on abortion is: How do you determine the humanity of a being? To phrase the question that way is to put in comprehensive humanistic terms what the theologians either dealt with as an explicitly theological question under the heading of "ensoulment" or dealt with implicitly in their treatment of abortion. The Christian position as it originated did not depend on a narrow theological or philosophical concept. It had no relation to theories of infant baptism. It appealed to no special theory of instantaneous ensoulment. It took the world's view on ensoulment as that view changed from Aristotle to Zacchia. There was, indeed, theological influence affecting the theory of ensoulment finally adopted, and, of course, ensoulment itself was a theological concept, so that the position was always explained in theological terms. But the theological notion of ensoulment could easily be translated into humanistic language by substituting "human" for "rational soul"; the problem of knowing when a man is a man is common to theology and humanism.

If one steps outside the specific categories used by the theologians, the answer they gave can be analyzed as a refusal to discriminate among human beings on the basis of their varying potentialities. Once conceived, the being was recognized as man because he had man's potential. The criterion for humanity, thus, was simple and all-embracing: if you are conceived by human parents, you are human.

The strength of this position may be tested by a review of some of the other distinctions offered in the contemporary controversy over legalizing abortion. Perhaps the most popular distinction is in terms of viability. Before an age of so many months, the fetus is not viable, that is, it cannot be removed from the mother's womb and live apart from her. To that extent, the life of the fetus is absolutely dependent on the life of the mother. This dependence is made the basis of denying recognition to its humanity.

There are difficulties with this distinction. One is that the perfection of artificial incubation may make the fetus viable at any time: it may be removed and artificially sustained. Experiments with animals already show that such a procedure is possible. This hypothetical extreme case relates to an actual difficulty: there is considerable elasticity to the idea of viability. Mere length of life is not an exact measure. The viability of the fetus depends on the extent of its anatomical and functional development. The weight and length of the fetus are better guides to the state of its development than age, but weight and length vary. Moreover, different racial groups have different ages at which their fetuses are viable. Some evidence, for example, suggests that Negro fetuses mature more quickly than white fetuses. If viability is the norm, the standard would vary with race and with many individual circumstances.

The most important objection to this approach is that dependence is not ended by viability. The fetus is still absolutely dependent on someone's care in order to continue existence; indeed a child of one or three or even five years of age is absolutely dependent on another's care for existence; uncared for, the older fetus or the younger child will die as surely as the early fetus detached from the mother. The unsubstantial lessening in dependence at viability does not seem to signify any special acquisition of humanity.

A second distinction has been attempted in terms of experience. A being who has had experience, has lived and suffered, who possesses memories, is more human than one who has not. Humanity depends on formation by experience. The fetus is thus "unformed" in the most basic human sense.

This distinction is not serviceable for the embryo which is already experiencing and reacting. The embryo is responsive to touch after eight weeks and at least at that point is experiencing. At an earlier stage the zygote is certainly alive and responding to its environment. The distinction may also be challenged by the rare case where aphasia has erased adult memory: has it erased humanity? More fundamentally, this distinction leaves even the older fetus or the younger child to be treated as an unformed inhuman thing. Finally, it is not clear why experience as such confers humanity. It could be argued that certain central experiences such as loving or learning are necessary to make a man human. But then human beings who have failed to love or to learn might be excluded from the class called man.

A third distinction is made by appeal to the sentiments of adults. If a fetus dies, the grief of the parents is not the grief they would have for a living child. The fetus is an unnamed "it" till birth, and is not perceived as personality until at least the fourth month of existence when movements in the womb manifest a vigorous presence demanding joyful recognition by the parents.

Yet feeling is notoriously an unsure guide to the humanity of others. Many groups of humans have had difficulty in feeling that persons of another tongue, color, religion, sex, are as human as they. Apart from reactions to alien groups, we mourn the loss of a 10-year-old boy more than the loss of his one-day-old brother or his 90-year-old grandfather. The difference felt and the grief expressed vary with the potentialities extinguished, or the experience wiped out; they do not seem to point to any substantial difference in the humanity of baby, boy, or grandfather.

Distinctions are also made in terms of sensation by the parents. The embryo is felt within the womb only after about the fourth month. The embryo is seen only at birth. What can be neither seen nor felt is different from what is tangible. If the fetus cannot be seen or touched at all, it cannot be perceived as man.

Yet experience shows that sight is even more untrustworthy than feeling in determining humanity. By sight, color became an appropriate index for saying who was a man, and the evil of racial discrimination was given foundation. Nor can touch provide the test; a being confined by sickness, "out of touch" with others, does not thereby seem to lose his humanity. To the extent that touch still has appeal as a criterion, it appears to be a survival of the old English idea of "quickening"—a possible mistranslation of the Latin *animatus* used in the canon law. To that extent touch as a criterion seems to be dependent on the Aristotelian notion of ensoulment, and to fall when this notion is discarded.

Finally, a distinction is sought in social visibility. The fetus is not socially perceived as human. It cannot communicate with others. Thus, both subjectively and objectively, it is not a member of society. As moral rules are rules for the behavior of members of society to each other, they cannot be made for behavior toward what is not yet a member. Excluded from the society of men, the fetus is excluded from the humanity of men.

By force of the argument from the consequences, this distinction is to be rejected. It is more subtle than that founded on an appeal to physical sensation, but it is equally dangerous in its implications. If humanity depends on social recognition, individuals or whole groups may be dehumanized by being denied any status in their society. Such a fate is fictionally portrayed in *1984* and has actually been the lot of many men in many societies. In the Roman empire, for example, condemnation to slavery meant the practical denial of most human rights; in the Chinese Communist world, landlords have been classified as enemies of the people and so treated as nonpersons by the state. Humanity does not depend on social recognition, though often the failure of society to recognize the prisoner, the alien, the heterodox as human had led to the destruction of human beings. Anyone conceived by a man and a woman is human. Recognition of this condition by society follows a real event in the objective order, however imperfect and halting the recognition. Any attempt to limit humanity to exclude some group runs the risk of furnishing authority and precedent for excluding other groups in the name of the consciousness or perception of the controlling group in the society.

A philosopher may reject the appeal to the humanity of the fetus because he views "humanity" as a secular view of the soul and because he doubts the existence of anything real and objective which can be identified as humanity. One answer to such a philosopher is to ask how he reasons about moral questions without supposing that there is a sense in which he and the others of whom he speaks are human. Whatever group is taken as the society which determines who may be killed is thereby taken as human. A second answer is to ask if he does not believe that there is a right and wrong way of deciding moral questions. If there is such a difference, experience may be appealed to: to decide who is human on the basis of the sentiment of a given society has led to consequences which rational men would characterize as monstrous.

The rejection of the attempted distinctions based on viability and visibility, experience and feeling, may be buttressed by the following considerations: Moral judgments often rest on distinctions, but if the distinctions are not to appear arbitrary fiat, they should relate to some real difference in probabilities. There is a kind of continuity in all life, but the earlier stages of the elements of human life possess tiny probabilities of development. Consider for example, the spermatozoa in any normal ejaculate: There are about 200,000,000 in any single ejaculate, of which one has a chance of developing into a zygote. Consider the oocytes which may become ova: there are 100,000 to 1,000,000 oocytes in a female infant, of which a maximum of 390 are ovulated. But once spermatozoon and ovum meet and the conceptus is formed, such studies as have been made show that roughly in only 20 percent of the cases will spontaneous abortion occur. In other words, the chances are about 4 out of 5 that this new being will develop. At this stage in the life of the being there is a sharp shift in probabilities, an immense jump in potentialities. To make a distinction between the rights of spermatozoa and the rights of the fertilized ovum is to respond to an enormous shift in possibilities. For about twenty days after conception the egg may split to form twins or combine with another egg to form a chimera, but the probability of either event happening is very small.

It may be asked, What does a change in biological probabilities have to do with establishing humanity? The argument from probabilities is not aimed at establishing humanity but at establishing an objective discontinuity which may be taken into account in moral discourse. As life itself is a matter of probabilities, as most moral reasoning is an estimate of probabilities, so it seems in accord with the structure of reality and the nature of moral thought to found a moral judgment on the change in probabilities at conception. The appeal to probabilities is the most commonsensical of arguments, to a greater or smaller degree all of us base our actions on probabilities, and in morals, as in law, prudence and negligence are often measured by the account one has taken of the probabilities. If the chance is 200,000,000 to 1 that the movement in the bushes into which you shoot is a man's, I doubt if many persons would hold you careless in shooting; but if the chances are 4 out of 5 that the movement is a human being's, few would acquit you of blame. Would the argument be different if only one out of ten children conceived came to term? Of course this argument would be different. This argument is an appeal to probabilities that actually exist, not to any and all states of affairs which may be imagined.

The probabilities as they do exist do not show the humanity of the embryo in the sense of a demonstration in logic any more than the probabilities of the movement in the bush being a man demonstrate beyond all doubt that the being is a man. The appeal is a "buttressing" consideration, showing the plausibility of the standard adopted. The argument focuses on the decisional factor in any moral judgment and assumes that part of the business of a moralist is drawing lines. One evidence of the nonarbitrary character of the line drawn is the difference of probabilities on either side of it. If a spermatozoon is destroyed, one destroys a being which had a chance of far less than 1 in 200 million of developing into a reasoning being, possessed of the genetic code, a heart and other organs, and capable of pain. If a fetus is destroyed, one destroys a being already possessed of the genetic code, organs, and sensitivity to pain, and one which had an 80 percent chance of developing further into a baby outside the womb who, in time, would reason.

The positive argument for conception as the decisive moment of humanization is that at conception the new being receives the genetic code. It is this genetic information which determines his characteristics, which is the biological carrier of the possibility of human wisdom, which makes him a self-evolving being. A being with a human genetic code is man.

This review of current controversy over the humanity of the fetus emphasizes what a fundamental question the theologians resolved in asserting the inviolability of the fetus. To regard the fetus as possessed of equal rights with other humans was not, however, to decide every case where abortion might be employed. It did decide the case where the argument was that the fetus should be aborted for its own good. To say a being was human was to say it had a destiny to decide for itself which could not be taken from it by another man's decision. But human beings with equal rights often come in conflict with each other, and some decision must be made as whose claims are to prevail. Cases of conflict involving the fetus are different only in two respects: the total inability of the fetus to speak for itself and the fact that the right of the fetus regularly at stake is the right to life itself.

The approach taken by the theologians to these conflicts was articulated in terms of "direct" and "indirect." Again, to look at what they were doing from outside their categories, they may be said to have been drawing lines or "balancing values." "Direct" and "indirect" are spatial metaphors; "line-drawing" is another. "To weigh" or "to balance" values is a metaphor of a more complicated mathematical sort hinting at the process which goes on in moral judgments. All the metaphors suggest that, in the moral judgments made, comparisons were necessary, that no value completely controlled. The principle of double effect was no doctrine fallen from

heaven, but a method of analysis appropriate where two relative values were being compared. In Catholic moral theology, as it developed, life even of the innocent was not taken as an absolute. Judgments on acts affecting life issued from a process of weighing. In the weighing, the fetus was always given a value greater than zero, always a value separate and independent from its parents. This valuation was crucial and fundamental in all Christian thought on the subject and marked it off from any approach which considered that only the parents' interests needed to be considered.

Even with the fetus weighed as human, one interest could be weighed as equal or superior: that of the mother in her own life. The casuists between 1450 and 1895 were willing to weigh this interest as superior. Since 1895, that interest was given decisive weight only in the two special cases of the cancerous uterus and the ectopic pregnancy. In both of these cases the fetus itself had little chance of survival even if the abortion were not performed. As the balance was once struck in favor of the mother whenever her life was endangered, it could be so struck again. The balance reached between 1895 and 1930 attempted prudentially and pastorally to forestall a multitude of exceptions for interests less than life.

The perception of the humanity of the fetus and the weighing of fetal rights against other human rights constituted the work of the moral analysts. But what spirit animated their abstract judgments? For the Christian community it was the injunction of Scripture to love your neighbor as yourself. The fetus as human was a neighbor; his life had parity with one's own. The commandment gave life to what otherwise would have been only rational calculation.

The commandment could be put in humanistic as well as theological terms: Do not injure your fellow man without reason. In these terms, once the humanity of the fetus is perceived, abortion is never right except in self-defense. When life must be taken to save life, reason alone cannot say that a mother must prefer a child's life to her own. With this exception, now of great rarity, abortion violates the rational humanist tenet of the equality of human lives.

For Christians the commandment to love had received a special imprint in that the exemplar proposed of love was the love of the Lord for his disciples. In the light given by this example, self-sacrifice carried to the point of death seemed in the extreme situations not without meaning. In the less extreme cases, preference for one's own interests to the life of another seemed to express cruelty or selfishness irreconcilable with the demands of love.

For Further Reflection

1. Do you agree with Noonan in drawing the line between the human and nonhuman at conception? Explain your answer.

2. Has Noonan successfully argued that abortion is almost always immoral? Should he take cases of rape and incest into consideration? What would Noonan say to the suggestion that a rape victim should be allowed to have an abortion?

3. Some have compared our practice of abortion to Hitler's Holocaust. A friend wrote, "With reference to abortion the world is upside down. When a criminal is sentenced to death, the whole world is dismayed because it goes against human rights. But when an unborn baby is sentenced to death, the world approves of it because the 'rights' of the mother take precedence over the rights of the child. But how is this different from the Nazi Holocaust, where Mother Germany sent 12 million innocent lives to the gas chamber? Haven't we sent over 30 million innocent lives to their death?" Do you agree with this comparison? Explain.

IX.2   Abortion Is Morally Permissible

MARY ANNE WARREN

Mary Anne Warren teaches philosophy at San Francisco State University and has written in the area of feminism, including *The Nature of Woman: An Encyclopedia and Guide to the Literature* (1980). In this paper she defends the liberal view that abortion is always morally permissible. She attacks Noonan's argument on the basis of an ambiguity in the use of the term *human being,* showing that the term has a biological and moral sense. What is important is the moral sense, which presupposes certain characteristics, such as self-consciousness and rationality, and which a fetus does not have. At the end of her article, she addresses the issue of infanticide.

Study Questions

1. What is the question which we must answer in order to solve the problem of whether abortion is morally permissible?

2. How is the term *human being* ambiguous?

3. How does this ambiguity undermine the conservative argument for the humanity of the fetus?

4. According to Warren, what characteristics make an entity a person? Which are the most important characteristics in this set?

5. Does potentiality for personhood grant a fetus a right to life? How does Warren illustrate her answer?

6. According to Warren, when does a woman have a right to an abortion?

7. What are Warren's views on infanticide?

THE QUESTION WHICH WE MUST answer in order to produce a satisfactory solution to the problem of the moral status of abortion is this: How are we to define the moral community, the set of beings with full and equal moral rights, such that we can decide whether a human fetus is a member of this community or not? What sort of entity, exactly, has the inalienable rights to life, liberty, and the pursuit of happiness? Jefferson attributed these rights to all *men,* and it may or may not be fair to suggest that he intended to attribute them *only* to men. Perhaps he ought to have attributed them to all human beings. If so, then we arrive, first, at Noonan's problem of defining what makes a being human, and, second, at the equally vital question which Noonan does not consider, namely, What reason is there for identifying the moral community with the set of all human beings, in whatever way we have chosen to define that term?

1. On the Definition of "Human"

One reason why this vital second question is so frequently overlooked in the debate over the moral status of abortion is that the term "human" has two distinct, but not often distinguished, senses. This fact results in a slide of meaning, which serves to conceal the fallaciousness of the traditional argument that since (1) it is wrong to kill innocent human beings, and (2) fetuses are innocent human beings, then (3) it is

wrong to kill fetuses. For if "human" is used in the same sense in both (1) and (2) then, whichever of the two senses is meant, one of these premises is question-begging. And if it is used in two different senses then of course the conclusion doesn't follow.

Thus, (1) is a self-evident moral truth,[1] and avoids begging the question about abortion, only if "human being" is used to mean something like "a full-fledged member of the moral community." (It may or may not also be meant to refer exclusively to members of the species *Homo sapiens.*) We may call this the *moral* sense of "human." It is not to be confused with what we will call the *genetic* sense, i.e., the sense in which *any* member of the species is a human being, and no member of any other species could be. If (1) is acceptable only if the moral sense is intended, (2) is nonquestion-begging only if what is intended is the genetic sense.

In "Deciding Who Is Human," Noonan argues for the classification of fetuses with human beings by pointing to the presence of the full genetic code, and the potential capacity for rational thought.[2] It is clear that what he needs to show, for his version of the traditional argument to be valid, is that fetuses are human in the moral sense, the sense in which it is analytically true that all human beings have full moral rights. But, in the absence of any argument showing that whatever is genetically human is also morally human, and he gives none, nothing more

Reprinted from The Monist, *vol. 57, no. 1 (January 1973), with the permission of the author and the publisher.*

than genetic humanity can be demonstrated by the presence of the human genetic code. And, as we will see, the *potential* capacity for rational thought can at most show that an entity has the potential for *becoming* human in the moral sense.

2. Defining the Moral Community

Can it be established that genetic humanity is sufficient for moral humanity? I think that there are very good reasons for not defining the moral community in this way. I would like to suggest an alternative way of defining the moral community, which I will argue for only to the extent of explaining why it is, or should be, self-evident. The suggestion is simply that the moral community consists of all and only *people,* rather than all and only human beings;[3] and probably the best way of demonstrating its self-evidence is by considering the concept of personhood, to see what sorts of entity are and are not persons, and what the decision that a being is or is not a person implies about its moral rights.

What characteristics entitle an entity to be considered a person? This is obviously not the place to attempt a complete analysis of the concept of personhood, but we do not need such a fully adequate analysis just to determine whether and why a fetus is or isn't a person. All we need is a rough and approximate list of the most basic criteria of personhood, and some idea of which, or how many, of these an entity must satisfy in order to properly be considered a person.

In searching for such criteria, it is useful to look beyond the set of people with whom we are acquainted, and ask how we would decide whether a totally alien being was a person or not. (For we have no right to assume that genetic humanity is necessary for personhood.) Imagine a space traveler who lands on an unknown planet and encounters a race of beings utterly unlike any he has ever seen or heard of. If he wants to be sure of behaving morally toward these beings, he has to somehow decide whether they are people, and hence have full moral rights,

or whether they are the sort of thing which he need not feel guilty about treating as, for example, a source of food.

How should he go about making this decision? If he has some anthropological background, he might look for such things as religion, art, and the manufacturing of tools, weapons, or shelters, since these factors have been used to distinguish our human from our prehuman ancestors, in what seems to be closer to the moral than the genetic sense of "human." And no doubt he would be right to consider the presence of such factors as good evidence that the alien beings were people, and morally human. It would, however, be overly anthropocentric of him to take the absence of these things as adequate evidence that they were not, since we can imagine people who have progressed beyond, or evolved without ever developing, these cultural characteristics.

I suggest that the traits which are most central to the concept of personhood, or humanity in the moral sense, are, very roughly, the following:

> 1. consciousness (of objects and events external and/or internal to the being), and in particular the capacity to feel pain;
> 2. reasoning (the *developed* capacity to solve new and relatively complex problems);
> 3. self-motivated activity (activity which is relatively independent of either genetic or direct external control);
> 4. the capacity to communicate, by whatever means, messages of an indefinite variety of types, that is, not just with an indefinite number of possible contents, but on indefinitely many possible topics;
> 5. the presence of self-concepts, and self-awareness, either individual or racial, or both.

Admittedly, there are apt to be a great many problems involved in formulating precise definitions of these criteria, let alone in developing universally valid behavioral criteria for deciding when they apply. But I will assume that both we and our explorer know approximately what

(1)–(5) mean, and that he is also able to determine whether or not they apply. How, then, should he use his findings to decide whether or not the alien beings are people? We needn't suppose that an entity must have *all* of these attributes to be properly considered a person; (1) and (2) alone may well be sufficient for personhood, and quite probably (1)–(3) are sufficient. Neither do we need to insist that any one of these criteria is *necessary* for personhood, although once again (1) and (2) look like fairly good candidates for necessary conditions, as does (3), if "activity" is construed so as to include the activity of reasoning.

All we need to claim, to demonstrate that a fetus is not a person, is that any being which satisfies *none* of (1)–(5) is certainly not a person. I consider this claim to be so obvious that I think anyone who denied it, and claimed that a being which satisfied none of (1)–(5) was a person all the same, would thereby demonstrate that he had no notion at all of what a person is—perhaps because he had confused the concept of a person with that of genetic humanity. If the opponents of abortion were to deny the appropriateness of these five criteria, I do not know what further arguments would convince them. We would probably have to admit that our conceptual schemes were indeed irreconcilably different, and that our dispute could not be settled objectively.

I do not expect this to happen, however, since I think that the concept of a person is one which is very nearly universal (to people), and that it is common to both proabortionists and antiabortionists, even though neither group has fully realized the relevance of this concept to the resolution of their dispute. Furthermore, I think that on reflection even the antiabortionists ought to agree not only that (1)–(5) are central to the concept of personhood, but also that it is a part of this concept that all and only people have full moral rights. The concept of a person is in part a moral concept; once we have admitted that *x* is a person we have recognized, even if we have not

agreed to respect, *x*'s right to be treated as a member of the moral community. It is true that the claim that *x is a human being* is more commonly voiced as part of an appeal to treat *x* decently than is the claim that *x* is a person, but this is either because "human being" is here used in the sense which implies personhood, or because the genetic and moral senses of "human" have been confused.

Now if (1)–(5) are indeed the primary criteria of personhood, then it is clear that genetic humanity is neither necessary nor sufficient for establishing that an entity is a person. Some human beings are not people, and there may well be people who are not human beings. A man or woman whose consciousness has been permanently obliterated but who remains alive is a human being which is no longer a person; defective human beings, with no appreciable mental capacity, are not and presumably never will be people; and a fetus is a human being which is not yet a person, and which therefore cannot coherently be said to have full moral rights. Citizens of the next century should be prepared to recognize highly advanced, self-aware robots or computers, should such be developed, and intelligent inhabitants of other worlds, should such be found, as people in the fullest sense, and to respect their moral rights. But to ascribe full moral rights to an entity which is not a person is as absurd as to ascribe moral obligations and responsibilities to such an entity.

3. Fetal Development and the Right to Life

Two problems arise in the application of these suggestions for the definition of the moral community to the determination of the precise moral status of a human fetus. Given that the paradigm example of a person is a normal adult human being, then (1) How like this paradigm, in particular how far advanced since conception, does a human being need to be before it begins to have a right to life by virtue, not of being fully a person as of yet, but of being *like* a person? and

(2) To what extent, if any, does the fact that a fetus has the *potential* for becoming a person endow it with some of the same rights? Each of these questions requires some comment.

In answering the first question, we need not attempt a detailed consideration of the moral rights of organisms which are not developed enough, aware enough, intelligent enough, etc., to be considered people, but which resemble people in some respects. It does seem reasonable to suggest that the more like a person, in the relevant respects, a being is, the stronger is the case for regarding it as having a right to life, and indeed the stronger its right to life is. Thus we ought to take seriously the suggestion that, insofar as "the human individual develops biologically in a continuous fashion . . . the rights of a human person might develop in the same way."[4] But we must keep in mind that the attributes which are relevant in determining whether or not an entity is enough like a person to be regarded as having some of the same moral rights are no different from those which are relevant to determining whether or not it is fully a person— i.e., are no different from (1)–(5)—and that being genetically human, or having recognizably human facial and other physical features, or detectable brain activity, or the capacity to survive outside the uterus, are simply not among these relevant attributes.

Thus it is clear that even though a seven- or eight-month fetus has features which make it apt to arouse in us almost the same powerful protective instinct as is commonly aroused by a small infant, nevertheless it is not significantly more personlike than is a very small embryo. It is *somewhat* more personlike; it can apparently feel and respond to pain, and it may even have a rudimentary form of consciousness, insofar as its brain is quite active. Nevertheless, it seems safe to say that it is not fully conscious, in the way that an infant of a few months is, and that it cannot reason, or communicate messages of indefinitely many sorts, does not engage in self-motivated activity, and has no self-awareness. Thus,

in the *relevant* respects, a fetus, even a fully developed one, is considerably less personlike than is the average mature mammal, indeed the average fish. And I think that a rational person must conclude that if the right to life of a fetus is to be based upon its resemblance to a person, then it cannot be said to have any more right to life than, let us say, a newborn guppy (which also seems to be capable of feeling pain), and that a right of that magnitude could never override a woman's right to obtain an abortion, at any stage of her pregnancy.

There may, of course, be other arguments in favor of placing legal limits upon the stage of pregnancy in which an abortion may be performed. Given the relative safety of the new techniques of artificially inducing labor during the third trimester, the danger to the woman's life or health is no longer such an argument. Neither is the fact that people tend to respond to the thought of abortion in the later stages of pregnancy with emotional repulsion, since mere emotional responses cannot take the place of moral reasoning in determining what ought to be permitted. Nor, finally, is the frequently heard argument that legalizing abortion, especially late in the pregnancy, may erode the level of respect for human life, leading, perhaps, to an increase in unjustified euthanasia and other crimes. For this threat, if it is a threat, can be better met by educating people to the kinds of moral distinctions which we are making here than by limiting access to abortion (which limitation may, in its disregard for the rights of women, be just as damaging to the level of respect for human rights).

Thus, since the fact that even a fully developed fetus is not personlike enough to have any significant right to life on the basis of its personlikeness shows that no legal restrictions upon the stage of pregnancy in which an abortion may be performed can be justified on the grounds that we should protect the rights of the older fetus, and since there is no other apparent justification for such restrictions, we may conclude that they are entirely unjustified. Whether or not it would be *indecent* (whatever that means) for a woman in her seventh month to obtain an abortion just to avoid having to postpone a trip to Europe, it would not, in itself, be *immoral,* and therefore it ought to be permitted.

4. Potential Personhood and the Right to Life

We have seen that a fetus does not resemble a person in any way which can support the claim that it has even some of the same rights. But what about its *potential,* the fact that if nurtured and allowed to develop naturally it will very probably become a person? Doesn't that alone give it at least some right to life? It is hard to deny that the fact that an entity is a potential person is a strong prima facie reason for not destroying it; but we need not conclude from this that a potential person has a right to life, by virtue of that potential. It may be that our feeling that it is better, other things being equal, not to destroy a potential person is better explained by the fact that potential people are still (felt to be) an invaluable resource, not to be lightly squandered. Surely, if every speck of dust were a potential person, we would be much less apt to conclude that every potential person has a right to become actual.

Still, we do not need to insist that a potential person has no right to life whatever. There may well be something immoral, and not just imprudent, about wantonly destroying potential people, when doing so isn't necessary to protect anyone's rights. But even if a potential person does have some prima facie right to life, such a right could not possibly outweigh the right of a woman to obtain an abortion, since the rights of any actual person invariably outweigh those of any potential person, whenever the two conflict. Since this may not be immediately obvious in the case of a human fetus, let us look at another case.

Suppose that our space explorer falls into the hands of an alien culture, whose scientists decide to create a few hundred thousand or more human beings, by breaking his body into its component cells, and using these to create fully developed human beings, with, of course, his genetic code. We may imagine that each of these newly created men will have all of the original man's abilities, skills, knowledge, and so on, and also have an individual self-concept, in short that each of them will be a bona fide (though hardly unique) person. Imagine that the whole project will take only seconds, and that its chances of success are extremely high, and that our explorer knows all of this, and also knows that these people will be treated fairly. I maintain that in such a situation he would have every right to escape if he could, and thus to deprive all of these potential people of their potential lives; for his right to life outweighs all of theirs together, in spite of the fact that they are all genetically human, all innocent, and all have a very high probability of becoming people very soon, if only he refrains from acting.

Indeed, I think he would have a right to escape even if it were not his life which the alien scientists planned to take, but only a year of his freedom, or, indeed, only a day. Nor would he be obligated to stay if he had gotten captured (thus bringing all these people-potentials into existence) because of his own carelessness, or even if he had done so deliberately, knowing the consequences. Regardless of how he got captured, he is not morally obligated to remain in captivity for *any* period of time for the sake of permitting any number of potential people to come into actuality, so great is the margin by which one actual person's right to liberty outweighs whatever right to life even a hundred thousand potential people have. And it seems reasonable to conclude that the rights of a woman will outweigh by a similar margin whatever right to life a fetus may have by virtue of its potential personhood.

Thus, neither a fetus's resemblance to a person, nor its potential for becoming a person provides any basis whatever for the claim that it has any significant right to life. Consequently, a woman's right to protect her health, happiness, freedom, and even her life,[5] by terminating an unwanted pregnancy, will always override whatever right to life it may be appropriate to ascribe to a fetus, even a fully developed one. And thus, in the absence of any overwhelming social need for every possible child, the laws which restrict the right to obtain an abortion, or limit the period of pregnancy during which an abortion may be performed, are a wholly unjustified violation of a woman's most basic moral and constitutional rights.[6]

Postscript on Infanticide

Since the publication of this article, many people have written to point out that my argument appears to justify not only abortion, but infanticide as well. For a newborn infant is not significantly more personlike than an advanced fetus, and consequently it would seem that if the destruction of the latter is permissible so too must be that of the former. Inasmuch as most people, regardless of how they feel about the morality of abortion, consider infanticide a form of murder, this might appear to represent a serious flaw in my argument.

Now, if I am right in holding that it is only people who have a full-fledged right to life, and who can be murdered, and if the criteria of personhood are as I have described them, then it obviously follows that killing a newborn infant isn't murder. It does *not* follow, however, that infanticide is permissible, for two reasons. In the first place, it would be wrong, at least in this country and in this period of history, and other things being equal, to kill a newborn infant, because even if its parents do not want it and would not suffer from its destruction, there are other people who would like to have it, and would, in all probability, be deprived of a great deal of pleasure by its destruction. Thus, infanticide is wrong for reasons analogous to those which make it wrong to wantonly destroy natural resources, or great works of art.

Secondly, most people, at least in this country, value infants and would much prefer that they be preserved, even if foster parents are not immediately available. Most of us would rather be taxed to support orphanages than allow unwanted infants to be destroyed. So long as there are people who want an infant preserved, and who are willing and able to provide the means of caring for it, under reasonably humane conditions, it is *ceteris paribus,* wrong to destroy it.

But, it might be replied, if this argument shows that infanticide is wrong, at least at this time and in this country, doesn't it also show that abortion is wrong? After all, many people value fetuses, are disturbed by their destruction, and would much prefer that they be preserved, even at some cost to themselves. Furthermore, as a potential source of pleasure to some foster family, a fetus is just as valuable as an infant. There is, however, a crucial difference between the two cases: so long as the fetus is unborn, its preservation, contrary to the wishes of the pregnant woman, violates her rights to freedom, happiness, and self-determination. Her rights override the rights of those who would like the fetus preserved, just as if someone's life or limb is threatened by a wild animal, his right to protect himself by destroying the animal overrides the rights of those who would prefer that the animal not be harmed.

The minute the infant is born, however, its preservation no longer violates any of its mother's rights, even if she wants it destroyed, because she is free to put it up for adoption. Consequently, while the moment of birth does not mark any sharp discontinuity in the degree to which an infant possesses the right to life, it does mark the end of its mother's right to determine its fate. Indeed, if abortion could be performed without killing the fetus, she would never possess the right to have the fetus destroyed, for the same reasons that she has no right to have an infant destroyed.

On the other hand, it follows from my argument that when an unwanted or defective infant is born into a society which cannot afford and/or is not willing to care for it, then its destruction is permissible. This conclusion will, no doubt, strike many people as heartless and immoral; but remember that the very existence of people who feel this way, and who are willing and able to provide care for unwanted infants, is reason enough to conclude that they should be preserved.

NOTES

1. Of course, the principle that it is (always) wrong to kill innocent human beings is in need of many other modifications, e.g., that it may be permissible to do so to save a greater number of other innocent hu-man beings, but we may safely ignore these complications here.

2. John Noonan, "Deciding Who Is Human," *Natural Law Forum*, 13 (1968), 135.

3. From here on, we will use "human" to mean genetically human since the moral sense seems closely connected to, and perhaps derived from, the assumption that genetic humanity is sufficient for membership in the moral community.

4. Thomas L. Hayes, "A Biological View," *Commonweal*, 85 (March 17, 1967), 677–78; quoted by Daniel Callahan, in *Abortion: Law, Choice and Morality* (London: Macmillan & Co., 1970).

5. That is, insofar as the death rate, for the woman, is higher for childbirth than for early abortion.

6. My thanks to the following people, who were kind enough to read and criticize an earlier version of this paper. Herbert Gold, Gene Glass, Anne Lauter-bach, Judith Thomson, Mary Mothersill, and Timothy Binkley.

For Further Reflection

1. Has Warren successfully refuted Noonan's argument against abortion? Are there any aspects of Noonan's argument that she has not successfully answered?

2. Examine Warren's postscript on infanticide. Does Warren's analysis of the morality of abortion lead to the justification of infanticide? Does it lead to justification of killing the severely retarded, mentally ill, and senile?

3. Is there a middle ground between Noonan's conservatism and Warren's liberalism on abortion?

Is the Death Penalty Morally Permissible?

The day before I wrote this introduction (August 15, 1990), A. D., age 19, was sentenced in the Bronx for the murder of an Israeli immigrant who had employed one of his friends. After strangling the man with a shoelace and stabbing him, A. D. and four friends donned Halloween masks to rob, beat, and gang-rape the man's wife and 16-year-old daughter. The women were then sexually tortured while the man's 3-year-old daughter watched from her crib.

A. D. already had been convicted of burglary four times before he was 16. A. D.'s lawyer, Paul Auerbach, said that A. D. was an honest boy forced by poverty to do bad things. A. D. was sentenced to 38⅓ years to life on thirteen counts of murder, robbery, burglary, and conspiracy. His accomplice, V. S., aged twenty-one, who worked for the murdered man and planned the murder, had already been sentenced to fifteen years to life.[1]

As I write, the National Center of Health Statistics has reported that the homicide rate for young men in the United States is four to seventy-three times the rate of other industrial countries. Whereas killings per 100,000 for men 15 through 24 years old in 1986 or 1987 was 0.3 in Austria and 0.5 in Japan, it was 21.9 in the United States and as high as 232 for blacks in some states.

Crimes bring out deep emotions in all of us, and heinous acts of violence, such as A. D.'s crime, fill us with rage. We instinctively feel that violent criminals should be severely punished. While attention must be given by society to the social and psychological causes of crime, so long as we presume people to be free and responsible for their actions, the subject of punishment, including capital punishment, will deserve special treatment.

Traditionally, there have been two main theories of punishment: retributivism and deterrence. Retributivism is typically held by deontologists, such as Kant, who treat punishment as a just desert. Justice demands that the criminal be punished in proportion to the gravity of his or her offence. Retributive theories are *backward* looking, focusing on the evil deed rather than on future consequences of the punishment. Deterrent theories are generally held by utilitarians, who focus on *future* considerations, using punishment to correct, deter, or prevent future crimes. The proper amount of punishment to be inflicted on the offender is that amount which will do the most good to all those who will be affected by it.

The death penalty has been used widely throughout history for just about every crime imaginable. In the seventh century B.C., Draco's Athenian code prescribed the death penalty for stealing fruit salad. Later Athenians were executed for making misleading public speeches. The criminal code of the Holy Roman Empire and later of Europe punished sorcery, arson, blasphemy, sodomy, and counterfeiting by burning at the stake.

Most of us are appalled by this indiscriminate use of the death penalty, and many abolitionists argue that all uses of the death penalty are barbaric, "cruel and unusual" punishments that only degrade humankind.

Proponents of capital punishment attempt to justify it either from a retributive or a utilitarian framework. One can, of course, use both theories for a combined justification. Abolitionists—those who oppose capital punishment—deny that these arguments for capital punishment are valid. They argue that the sanctity of human life which gives each person a right to life is inconsistent with the practice of putting criminals to death.

In our first reading, I use retributive considerations to argue that the death penalty is morally permissible. I also use a version of the deterrent argument, the best-bet argument, to support my position. In our second reading, Hugo Bedau argues that the deterrent argument is not sound and the retributivist argument does not support capital punishment.

NOTE

1. *New York Times,* August 16, 1990.

Yes, the Death Penalty Is Morally Permissible   IX.3

LOUIS P. POJMAN

In this article I defend the practice of capital punishment, using versions of the retributive and deterrent argument. I then answer three typical objections to the use of the death penalty. In the article, I refer to the *lex talionis* (lit. "law of the claw"). This refers to the law of retaliation, mentioned in the Bible (Exod. 21:23), which says the offender should be punished: "An eye for an eye, a tooth for a tooth, and a life for a life."

Study Questions

1. What is the retributivist position as set forth by Kant?
2. How does the abolitionist respond to retributive justifications for the death penalty?
3. According to the article, what two mistakes does the abolitionist make?
4. Does Pojman believe we should always punish criminals in exact proportion to gravity of their crimes?
5. Is there evidence that capital punishment deters?
6. What is the best-bet argument?
7. Is capital punishment really a thirst for revenge?
8. What does Pojman say about the danger of executing innocent people?
9. Does the death penalty deny the wrongdoers essential humanity?

IN THIS PAPER, I ARGUE that there are moral reasons to apply the death penalty to those who commit first-degree murder. I use both retributivist and a type of deterrence argument to support my position. At the end of the paper, I meet three important objections to the use of the death penalty.

A classic expression of the retributivist position on capital punishment is Kant's statement that if an offender "has committed murder, he must *die*. In this case, no possible substitute can satisfy justice. For there is no *parallel* between death and even the most miserable life, so that there is no equality of crime and retribution unless the perpetrator is judicially put to death (at all events without any maltreatment which might make humanity an object of horror in the person of the sufferer)."

Kant illustrates his doctrine of exact retribution:

> Even if a civil society were to dissolve itself with the consent of all its members (for example, if a people who inhabited an island decided to separate and disperse to other parts of the world), the last murderer in prison would first have to be executed in order that each should receive his just deserts and that the people should not bear the guilt of a capital crime through failing to insist on its punishment; for if they do not do so, they can be re-

garded as accomplices in the public violation of justice. (*The Metaphysics of Morals*, p. 156)

For Kant, the death penalty was a conclusion of the argument for justice, just recompense to the victim and just punishment to the offender. As a person of dignity the victim deserves to have his offender harmed in proportion to the gravity of the crime and as a person of high worth and responsibility, the offender shows himself deserving of capital punishment.

Let us expand on the retributivist argument. Each person has a right to life. But criminal C violates an innocent victim V's right to life by threatening it or by killing V. The threat to V constitutes a grave offense, but taking V's life constitutes a capital offense. C deserves to be put to death for his offense.

But the abolitionist responds, "No, putting C to death only compounds evil. If killing is an evil, then the State actually doubles the evil by executing the murderer. The State violates C's right to life."

But the abolitionist is mistaken on two counts. First, the State does not violate C's right to life. C has already forfeited any right he had to life in murdering V. The right to life is not an absolute right that can never be overridden. It is a serious prima facie right that can be jettisoned only by a more weighty moral reason. In this case, the violating of V's right is sufficient reason for overriding C's right to life. Secondly, while killing C may be an evil, it is a lesser of evils and may be justified. Not to right a wrong, not to punish the criminal, may be a worse evil than harming him.

I said that the criminal *forfeits* his or her right to life by deliberately murdering his victim. But forfeiture does not tell the whole story. Not only does he forfeit his life, but he positively deserves his punishment. If he has committed a capital offense, he deserves a capital punishment. If first-degree murder is on the level of the worst types of crimes, as we think it is, then we are justified in imposing the worst type of punishments on the murderer. Death would seem to be the fit-

ting punishment—anything less would seem to lessen the seriousness of the offense.

Of course, we know of worse crimes than murder—torturing a victim over a long period of time and driving him insane is worse than murdering him. It might well be that society should torture the torturer and the rapist (it would be too repulsive to rape him). *Lex talionis* with a vengeance! For most of us, death seems an adequate punishment for the worst types of crimes—though strictly speaking it may not be anywhere near to the proportion of suffering or evil done by the criminal. How could we punish Hitler in proportion to the gravity of his offense? There are limits to punishment. Nothing more than death seems right. The question is whether something less than death would do as well—say long-term prison sentences?

A moderate retributivist (like myself) might well allow mercy to enter the picture earlier. If society is secure, it might well opt to show mercy and not execute murderers. It may be that utilitarian reasons enter into the calculation. Retributivism may be mitigated by utilitarian considerations. Not because the criminal doesn't deserve the death penalty but because a secure society isn't threatened as a whole by occasional murders, heinous though they be. In a secure society (Scandinavian or Swiss societies, with crime rates a tiny fraction of that of the United States, come to mind) capital offenses are not tearing away at the very fabric of the social order.

The utilitarian argument for capital punishment is that it deters would-be offenders from committing first-degree murder. The evidence for this is very weak. There is a lack of evidence that capital punishment deters, but this should not be construed as evidence for the lack of deterrence. There is no such evidence for non-deterrence. We simply don't know. Statistics are hard to read, though common sense would seem to give some credence to the idea. Arthur Lewis, a British member of Parliament, was converted from abolitionism to supporting the death penalty. Here is an account of his change of mind:

One reason that has stuck in my mind, and which has proved to me beyond question, is that there was once a professional burglar in [my] constituency who consistently boasted of the fact that he had spent about one-third of his life in prison. . . . He said to me, "I am a professional burglar. Before we go out on a job we plan it down to every detail. Before we go into the boozer to have a drink we say, 'Don't forget, no shooters'"—shooters being guns. He adds "We did our job and didn't have shooters because at that time there was capital punishment. Our wives, girlfriends and our mums said, 'Whatever you do, do not carry a shooter because if you are caught you might be topped.' If you do away with capital punishment they will all be carrying shooters."[1]

However, it is difficult to know how widespread such reasoning is. Perhaps it is mainly confined to a certain class of professional burglars or middle-class people who are tempted to kill their enemies. We simply don't know how much capital punishment deters or whether the deterrence is negligible.

John Stuart Mill admitted that capital punishment does not inspire terror in hardened criminals, but it may well make an impression on prospective murderers. "As for what is called the failure of the death punishment, who is able to judge of that? We partly know who those are whom it has not deterred; but who is there who knows whom it has deterred, or how many human beings it has saved who would have lived to be murderers if that awful association had not been thrown round the idea of murder from their earliest infancy."[2]

In this regard the best argument for capital punishment is Ernest van den Haag's best-bet argument.[3] Ernest van den Haag has argued that even though we don't know for certain whether the death penalty deters or prevents other murders, we should bet that it does. Actually, due to our ignorance, any social policy we take is a gamble. Not to choose capital punishment for first-degree murder is as much a bet that capital punishment doesn't deter as choosing the policy is a bet that it does. There is a significant difference in the betting, however, in that to bet against capital punishment is to bet against the innocent, while to bet for it is to bet against the murderer and for the innocent.

Suppose that we choose a policy of capital punishment for capital crimes. In this case we are betting that the death of some murderers will be more than compensated by the lives of some innocents not being murdered (either by these murderers or others who would have murdered—for example, Lewis' burglar). If we're right, we have saved the lives of the innocent. If we're wrong, unfortunately, we've sacrificed the lives of some murderers. But say we choose not to have a social policy of capital punishment. If capital punishment doesn't work as a deterrent, we've come out ahead, but if it does, then we've missed an opportunity to save innocent lives. If we value the saving of innocent lives more highly than the loss of the guilty, then it is rational to bet on a policy of capital punishment. The reasoning for this is shown in the table at the bottom of the page (CP stands for capital punishment).

	CP works	*CP doesn't work*
We bet on CP	a. We win: some murderers die and some innocents are saved.	b. We lose: some murderers die for no purpose.
We bet vs. CP	c. We lose: murderers live and some innocents die needlessly.	d. We win: murderers live and the lives of others are unaffected.

Suppose that we estimate that the utility value of a murderer's life is 5 and that the value of an innocent's life is 10 (it's at least twice the value of the murderer's life). The sums work out this way:

A murderer saved	+5
A murderer executed	−5
An innocent saved	+10
An innocent murdered	−10

Suppose that for each execution only two innocent lives are spared. Then the sums read as follows:

a. −5 + 20 = +15
b. −5
c. +5 −10 = −15
d. +5

If all the possibilities are roughly equal, we can sum the results like this:

If we bet on CP, we get (a) and (b), or +10
If we bet against CP, we get (c) and (d), or −10

So it turns out that it is a good bet to execute convicted murderers. It is a bad bet to choose to abolish the death penalty. We unnecessarily put the innocent at risk.

Even if we value the utility of an innocent life only slightly more than that of the murderers, it is still rational to execute convicted murderers. As van den Haag writes, "Though we have no proof of the positive deterrence of the penalty, we also have no proof of zero or negative effectiveness. I believe we have no right to risk additional future victims of murder for the sake of sparing convicted murderers; on the contrary, our moral obligation is to risk the possible ineffectiveness of executions."[4]

Objections to Capital Punishment

Objection 1: Capital punishment is a morally unacceptable thirst for revenge. As former British Prime Minister Edward Heath put it, "The real point which is emphasized to me by many constituents is that even if the death penalty is not a deterrent, murderers deserve to die. This is the question of revenge. Again, this will be a matter of moral judgment for each of us. I do not believe in revenge. If I were to become the victim of terrorists, I would not wish them to be hanged or killed in any other way for revenge. All that would do is deepen the bitterness which already tragically exists in the conflicts we experience in society, particularly in Northern Ireland."[5]

Response: Retributivism is not to be equated with revenge, although the motifs are often intermixed in practice. Revenge is a personal response to someone for an injury. Retribution is an impartial and impersonal response to an offender for an offense done against someone. It is not possible to want revenge for the harm of someone whom you are indifferent to. Revenge always involves personal concern for the victim. Retribution is not personal but based on objective factors—the criminal has deliberately harmed an innocent party and so *deserves* to be punished—whether I wish it or not. I would agree that I or my son or daughter *deserve* to be punished—whether I wish it or not. I would agree that I or my son or daughter *deserve* to be punished for our crimes—but I don't wish any vengeance on myself or my son or daughter.

Furthermore, while revenge often leads us to exact more suffering from the offender than the offense warrants, retribution stipulates that the offender be punished in proportion to the gravity of the offense. In this sense, the *lex talionis* ("an eye for an eye, a tooth for a tooth, a life for a life") that we find in the Old Testament is actually a progressive rule, where retribution replaces revenge as the mode of punishment. It says that there are limits to what one can do to the offender. Revenge demands a life for an eye or a tooth, but Moses gives a rule that exacts a penalty equal to the harm done by the offender.

Objection 2: Capital punishment is to be rejected because of human fallibility in convicting innocent parties and sentencing them to death. While some compensation is available to those unjustly imprisoned, the death sentence is irrevocable. We can't compensate the dead. As John Maxton, a member of the British Parliament, puts it, "If we allow one innocent person to be executed, morally we are committing the same, or, in some ways, a worse crime than the person who committed the murder."[6]

Response: Maxton is incorrect in saying that mistaken judicial execution is morally the same or worse than murder, for in a murder there is a deliberate intention to kill the innocent, whereas in wrongful capital punishment there is no such intention.

The fact that we can err in applying the death penalty should give us pause and cause us to build an appeals process into the judicial system. Such a process is already in the American and British legal systems. The fact that occasional error may be made, regrettable though this is, is not a sufficient reason for us to refuse to use the death penalty, if on balance it serves a just and useful function.

Objection 3: The death penalty constitutes a denial of the wrongdoer's essential dignity as a human being. No matter how bad a person becomes, no matter how terrible his deed, we must never cease to regard him as an end in himself, as someone with inherent dignity. Capital punishment violates that dignity. As Thurgood Marshall wrote in *Gregg* vs. *Georgia,*

> The Eighth Amendment demands more than that a challenged punishment be acceptable to contemporary society. To be sustained under the Eighth Amendment, the death penalty must [comport] with the basic concept of human dignity at the core of the Amendment; the objective in imposing it must be [consistent] with our respect for the dignity of [other] men. Under these standards, the taking of life "because the wrongdoer deserves it" surely must fail, for such a punishment has as its very basis the total denial of the wrongdoer's dignity and worth. The death penalty, unnecessary to promote the goal of deterrence or to further any legitimate notion of retribution, is an excessive penalty forbidden by the Eighth and Fourteenth Amendments (United State Supreme Court, 428 U.S. 153 [1976]).

Margaret Falls argues eloquently that treating people as moral agents prohibits us from executing them. "Holding an offender responsible necessarily includes demanding that she respond as only moral agents can: by reevaluating her behavior. If the punishment meted out makes reflective response to it impossible, then it is not a demand for response as a moral agent. Death is not a punishment to which reflective moral response is possible. . . . Death terminates the possibility of moral reform."[7]

Response: Actually, rather than being a violation of the wrongdoer's dignity, capital punishment may constitute a recognition of human dignity. As we noted in discussing Kant's view of retribution, the use of capital punishment respects the worth of the victim in calling for an equal punishment to be exacted from the offender, and it respects the dignity of the offender in treating him as a free agent who must be respected for his decisions and who must bear the cost of his acts as a responsible agent.

First, it respects the worth of the victim. Columnist Mike Royko bluntly put it this way:

> When I think of the thousands of inhabitants of Death Rows in the hundreds of prisons in this country, I don't react the way the kindly souls do—with revulsion that the state would take these lives. My reaction is: What's taking us so long? Let's get that electrical current flowing. Drop the pellets now!
>
> Whenever I argue this with friends who have opposite views, they say that I don't have enough regard for that most marvelous of miracles—human life.
>
> Just the opposite: It's because I have so much regard for human life that I favor capital punishment. Murder is the most terrible crime there is. Anything less than the death penalty is an insult to the victim and society. It says, in effect, that we don't value the victim's life enough to punish the killer fully.[8]

It is just because the *victim's* life is sacred that the death penalty is a fitting punishment for first-degree murder.

Secondly, it's just because the murderer is an autonomous, free agent, that we regard his act of murder as his own and hold him responsible for it. Not to hold him responsible for his crime is to treat him as less than autonomous. Just as we praise and reward people in proportion to the merit of their good deeds, so we blame and punish them in proportion to the evil of their bad deeds. If there is evidence that the offender did not act freely, we would mitigate his sentence. But if he did act of his own free will, he bears the responsibility for his actions and deserves to be punished accordingly.

To Meg Falls' argument that the death penalty makes moral reform impossible, two things must be said: (1) It's false and (2) it's not an argument for the complete abolition of capital punishment.

(1) It's false. The criminal may be given to repent of his or her offense before execution. It is hard to know when the murderer has truly repented and has been rehabilitated—faking it is in his self-interest—but even if he does repent, the heinousness of the deed remains and he should receive his just deserts.

(2) Even if some offenders are suitably rehabilitated, and even if we have a policy of showing mercy to those who give strong evidence of having been morally reformed, many criminals may be and probably are incurable—given our present means for rehabilitation and moral reform. At present, rehabilitation programs are not very successful.

I have not argued for an absolute duty to execute first-degree murderers. The principle that the guilty should suffer in proportion to the harm they caused, and that this sometimes entails the death penalty, is not absolute. I can be overridden by mercy. But it must be a judicious expression of mercy, serving the public good.

No doubt we should work toward the day when capital punishment is no longer necessary, when the murder rate becomes a tiny fraction of what it is today, when a civilized society can safely incarcerate the relatively few violent criminals in its midst, and where moral reform of the criminal is a reality. I for one regret the use of the death penalty. I am against capital punishment. I would vote for its abolition in an instant if only one condition were met—that those contemplating murder would set an example for me. Otherwise, it is better that the murderer perish than that innocent victims be cut down by the murderer's knife or bullet.

NOTES

1. British *Parliamentary Debates* fifth series, vol 23, issue 1243, House of Commons, 11 May 1982. Quoted in Tom Sorell, *Moral Theory and Capital Punishment* (Blackwell, 1987), p. 36.

2. *Parliamentary Debates,* third series, 21 April 1868. Reprinted in Peter Singer, ed., *Applied Ethics* (Oxford University Press), pp. 97–104.

3. Ernest van den Haag, "On Deterrence and the Death Penalty," *Ethics,* 78 (July 1968).

4. Op. cit.

5. British *Parliamentary Debates,* 1982 quoted in Sorell, op. cit., p. 43.

6. Op. cit., p. 47.

7. Margaret Falls, "Against the Death Penalty: A Christian Stance in a Secular World" in the *Christian Century,* December 10, 1986, pp. 1118, 1119.

8. Mike Royko, *Chicago Sun-Times,* September 1983.

For Further Reflection

1. Assess the strengths of Pojman's arguments in favor of capital punishment. Can you think of objections to his notion of retribution or the best-bet argument? Should we use a gambling metaphor when talking about taking another person's life?

2. Has Pojman dealt fairly with the objections to capital punishment?

3. If moral wrong should be the basis of punishment, as Pojman seems to suppose, should people be punished for their *intentions* to do wrong as well as for their actual deeds? If John attempts to kill Mary but fails (through no fault of his own), should he receive the punishment fitting the actual crime?

No, the Death Penalty Is Not Morally Permissible   IX.4

HUGO ADAM BEDAU

Hugo Adam Bedau is professor of philosophy at Tufts University and past president of the American League to Abolish Capital Punishment. He has been a leading spokesman for the abolitionist movement and is the editor of *The Death Penalty in America* (1982) and the author of *The Courts, the Constitution and Capital Punishment* (1977).

In this selection Bedau first draws an analogy between self-defense and the death penalty. Just as in defending ourselves we are to use no more force than is necessary to prevent harm, so in punishing criminals we are to use no more violence than is necessary to adequately punish the criminal. Bedau then argues that neither the deterrence nor the retributive argument for capital punishment is a good argument. He thinks that the literal application of the *lex talionis* is barbaric and that long-term imprisonment is adequate punishment.

Study Questions

1. What is the analogy between self-defense and capital punishment?
2. When does the law impose "a duty to retreat"?
3. According to Bedau, how much violence may justifiably be used to ward off aggression?
4. How does Bedau apply this idea of resentment to the issue of punishment for crime?
5. Does Bedau think that the threat of the death penalty deters would-be murderers better than the threat of long-term prison sentences?
6. Would Bedau oppose the death penalty if there was good evidence that it did deter?
7. What are the two principles of retributive justice relevant to the death penalty controversy?
8. Why, according to Bedau, aren't we consistent in our application of the principle of retribution (the *lex talionis*)?
9. In what way does Bedau thinks that the application of the death penalty is biased? Why does this unfairness occur?

The Analogy with Self-Defense

CAPITAL PUNISHMENT, it is sometimes said, is to the body politic what self-defense is to the individual. If the latter is not morally wrong, how can the former be morally wrong? In order to assess the strength of this analogy, we need to inspect rather closely the morality of self-defense.

Except for the absolute pacifists, who believe it is morally wrong to use violence even to defend themselves or others from unprovoked and undeserved aggression, most of us believe that it is not morally wrong and may even be our moral duty to use violence to prevent aggression. The law has long granted persons the right to defend themselves against the unjust aggressions of others, even to the extent of killing a would-be assailant. It is very difficult to think of any convincing argument that would show it is never rational to risk the death of another in order to prevent death or grave injury to oneself or to others. Certainly self-interest dictates the legitimacy of self-defense. So does concern for the well-being of others. So also does justice. If it is unfair for one person to attempt violence on another, then it is hard to see why morality compels the victim to acquiesce in the attempt by another to hurt him or her, rather than to resist it, even if that resistance may involve injury to the assailant.

The foregoing account assumes that the person acting in self-defense is innocent of any provocation of the assailant. It also assumes that there is no alternative to victimization except resistance. In actual life, both assumptions—especially the second—are often false, because there may be a third alternative: escape, or removing oneself from the scene of danger and imminent aggression. Hence, the law imposes on us the so-called "duty to retreat." Before we use violence to resist aggression, we must try to get out of the way, lest unnecessary violence be used to resist aggression. Now suppose that unjust aggression is imminent, and there is no path open for escape. How much violence may justifiably be used to ward off aggression? The answer is: No more violence than is necessary to prevent the aggressive assault. Violence beyond that is unnecessary and therefore unjustified. We may restate the principle governing the use of violence in self-defense in terms of the use of "deadly force" by the police in the discharge of their duties. The rule is this: Use of deadly force is justified only to prevent loss of life in immediate jeopardy where a lesser use of force cannot reasonably be expected to save the life that is threatened.

In real life, violence in self-defense in excess of the minimum necessary to prevent aggression is often excusable. One cannot always tell what will suffice to deter or prevent becoming a victim, and the law looks with a certain tolerance upon the frightened and innocent would-be victim who turns upon a vicious assailant and inflicts a fatal injury even though a lesser injury would have been sufficient. What is not justified is deliberately using far more violence than is necessary to prevent becoming a victim. It is the deliberate, not the impulsive, use of violence that is relevant to the death-penalty controversy, since the death penalty is enacted into law and carried out in each case only after ample time to weigh alternatives. Notice that we are assuming that the act of self-defense is to protect one's person or that of a third party. The reasoning outlined here does not extend to the defense of one's property. Shooting a thief to prevent one's automobile from being stolen cannot be excused or justified in the way that shooting an assailant charging with a knife pointed at one's face can be. In terms of the concept of "deadly force," our criterion is that deadly force is never justified to prevent crimes against property or other violent crimes not immediately threatening the life of a person.

The rationale for self-defense as set out above illustrates two moral principles of great importance to our discussion. One is that if a life is to be risked, then it is better that it be the life of someone who is guilty (in our context, the initial assailant) rather than the life of someone who is not (the innocent potential victim). It is not fair to expect the innocent prospective victim to run the added risk of severe injury or death in order to avoid using violence in self-defense to the extent of possibly killing his assailant. It is only fair that the guilty aggressor run the risk.

The other principle is that taking life deliberately is not justified so long as there is any feasible alternative. One does not expect miracles, of course, but in theory, if shooting a burglar through the foot will stop the burglary and enable one to call the police for help, then there is no reason to shoot to kill. Likewise, if the burglar is unarmed, there is no reason to shoot at all. In actual life, of course, burglars are likely to be shot at by aroused householders because one does not know whether they are armed, and prudence may dictate the assumption that they are. Even so, although the burglar has no right to commit a felony against a person or a person's property, the attempt to do so does not give the chosen victim the right to respond in whatever way he or she pleases in retaliation, and then to excuse or justify such conduct on the ground that he or she was "only acting in self-defense." In these ways the law shows a tacit regard for the life of even a felon and discourages the use of unnecessary violence even by the innocent; morality can hardly do less.

The Death Penalty as a Crime Deterrent

Determining whether the death penalty is an effective deterrent is even more difficult than determining its effectiveness as a crime preventive. In general, our knowledge about how penalties deter crimes and whether in fact they do—whom they deter, from which crimes, and under what conditions—is distressingly inexact. Most people nevertheless are convinced that punishments do deter, and that the more severe a punishment is the better it will deter. For more than a generation, social scientists have studied the question of whether the death penalty is a deterrent and of whether it is a better deterrent than the alternative of imprisonment. Their verdict, while not unanimous, is fairly clear. Whatever may be true about the deterrence of lesser crimes by other penalties, the deterrence achieved by the death penalty for murder is not measurably greater than the deterrence achieved by long-term imprisonment. In the nature of the case, the evidence is quite indirect. No one can identify for certain any crimes that did not occur because the would-be offender was deterred by the threat of the death penalty and that would not have been deterred by a lesser threat. Likewise, no one can identify any crimes that did occur because the offender was not deterred by the threat of prison even though he would have been deterred by the threat of death. Nevertheless, such

evidence as we have fails to show that the more severe penalty (death) is really a better deterrent than the less severe penalty (imprisonment) for such crimes as murder.

If the conclusion stated above is correct, and the death penalty and long-term imprisonment are equally effective (or ineffective) as deterrents to murder, then the argument for the death penalty on grounds of deterrence is seriously weakened. One of the moral principles identified earlier comes into play and requires us to reject the death penalty on moral grounds. This is the principle that unless there is a good reason for choosing a more rather than a less severe punishment for a crime, the less severe penalty is to be preferred. This principle obviously commends itself to anyone who values human life and who concedes that, all other things being equal, less pain and suffering is always better than more. Human life is valued in part to the degree that it is free of pain, suffering, misery, and frustration, and in particular that it is free of such experiences when they serve no purpose. If the death penalty is not a more effective deterrent than imprisonment, then its greater severity than imprisonment is gratuitous, purposeless suffering and deprivation.

A Cost/Benefit Analysis of the Death Penalty

A full study of the costs and benefits involved in the practice of capital punishment would not be confined solely to the question of whether it is a better deterrent or preventive of murder than imprisonment. Any thoroughgoing utilitarian approach to the death-penalty controversy would need to examine carefully other costs and benefits as well, because maximizing the balance of social benefits over social costs is the sole criterion of right and wrong according to utilitarianism. Let us consider, therefore, some of the other costs and benefits to be calculated. Clinical psychologists have presented evidence to suggest that the death penalty actually incites some persons of unstable mind to murder others, either because they are afraid to take their own lives and hope that society will punish them for murder by putting them to death, or because they fancy that they, too, are killing with justification, analogous to the justified killing involved in capital punishment. If such evidence is sound, capital punishment can serve as a counterpreventive or an incitement to murder, and these incited murders become part of its social cost. Imprisonment, however, has not been known to incite any murders or other crimes of violence in a comparable fashion. (A possible exception might be found in the imprisonment of terrorists, which has inspired other terrorists to take hostages as part of a scheme to force the authorities to release their imprisoned comrades.) The risks of executing the innocent are also part of the social cost. The historical record is replete with innocent persons indicted, convicted, sentenced, and occasionally legally executed for crimes they did not commit, not to mention the guilty persons unfairly convicted, sentenced to death, and executed on the strength of perjured testimony, fraudulent evidence, subornation of jurors, and other violations of the civil rights and liberties of the accused. Nor is this all. The high costs of a capital trial, of the inevitable appeals, the costly methods of custody most prisons adopt for convicts on "death row," are among the straightforward economic costs that the death penalty incurs. No scientifically valid cost/benefit analysis of capital punishment has ever been conducted, and it is impossible to predict exactly what such a study would show. Nevertheless, based on such evidence as we do have, it is quite possible that a study of this sort would favor abolition of all death penalties rather than their retention.

What If Executions Did Deter?

From the moral point of view, it is quite important to determine what one should think about capital punishment if the evidence clearly showed that the death penalty is a distinctly superior method of social defense by comparison with less severe alternatives. Kantian moralists, as we have seen, would have no use for such knowledge, because their entire case for the morality of the death penalty rests on the way it is thought to provide just retribution, not on the way it is thought to provide social defense. For a utilitarian, however, such knowledge would be conclusive. Those who follow Locke's reasoning would also be gratified, because they defend the morality of the death penalty both on the ground that it is retributively just and on the ground that it provides needed social defense.

What about the opponents of the death penalty, however? To oppose the death penalty in the face of incontestable evidence that it is an effective method of social defense seems to violate the moral principle that where grave risks are to be run, it is better that they be run by the guilty than by the innocent. Consider in this connection an imaginary world in which by executing a murderer the victim is invariably restored to life, whole and intact, as though the murder had never occurred. In such a miraculous world, it is hard to see how anyone could oppose the death penalty on moral grounds. Why shouldn't a murderer die if that will infallibly bring the victim back to life? What could possibly be morally wrong with taking the murderer's life under such conditions? It would turn the death penalty into an instrument of perfect restitution, and it would give a new and better meaning to *lex talionis,* "a life for a life." The whole idea is fanciful, of course, but it shows better than anything else how opposition to the death penalty cannot be both moral and wholly unconditional. If opposition to the death penalty is to be morally responsible, then it must be conceded that there are conditions (however unlikely) under which that opposition should cease.

But even if the death penalty were known to be a uniquely effective social defense, we could still imagine conditions under which it would be reasonable to oppose it. Suppose that in addition to being a slightly better preventive and deterrent than imprisonment, executions also have a slight incitive effect (so that for every ten murders an execution prevents or deters, it also incites another murder). Suppose also that the administration of criminal justice in capital cases is inefficient, unequal, and tends to secure convictions of murderers who least "deserve" to be sentenced to death (including some death sentences and a few executions of the innocent). Under such conditions, it would still be reasonable to oppose the death penalty, because on the facts supposed more (or not fewer) innocent lives are being threatened and lost by using the death penalty than would be risked by abolishing it. It is important to remember throughout our evaluation of the deterrence controversy that we cannot ever apply the principle that advises us to risk the lives of the guilty in order to save the lives of the innocent. Instead, the most we can do is weigh the risk for the general public against the execution of those who are *found* guilty by an imperfect system of criminal justice. These hypothetical factual assumptions illustrate the contingencies upon which the morality of opposition to the death penalty rests. And not only the morality of opposition; the morality of any defense of the death penalty rests on the same contingencies. This should help us understand why, in resolving the morality of capital punishment one way or the other, it is so important to know, as well as we can, whether the death penalty really does deter, prevent, or incite crime, whether the innocent really are ever executed, and whether any of these things are likely to occur in the future.

How Many Guilty Lives Is One Innocent Life Worth?

The great unanswered question that utilitarians must face concerns the level of social defense that executions should be expected to achieve before it is justifiable to carry them out. Consider three possible situations: (1) At the level of a hundred executions per year, each additional execution of a convicted murderer reduces the number of murder victims by ten. (2) Executing every convicted murderer reduces the number of murders to 5,000 victims annually, whereas executing only one out of ten reduces the number to 5,001. (3) Executing every convicted murderer reduces the murder rate no more than does executing one in a hundred and no more than a random pattern of executions does.

Many people contemplating situation (1) would regard this as a reasonable trade-off: The execution of each further guilty person saves the lives of ten innocent ones. (In fact, situation (1) or something like it may be taken as a description of what most of those who defend the death penalty on grounds of social defense believe is true.) But suppose that, instead of saving 10 lives, the number dropped to 0.5, i.e., one victim avoided for each two additional executions. Would that be a reasonable price to pay? We are on the road toward the situation described in situation (2), where a drastic 90 percent reduction in the number of persons executed causes the level of social defense to drop by only 0.0002 percent. Would it be worth it to execute so many more murderers at the cost of such a slight decrease in social defense? How many guilty lives is one innocent life worth? In situation (3), of course, there is no basis for executing all convicted murderers, since there is no gain in social defense to show for each additional murderer executed after the first out of each hundred murderers has been executed. How, then, should we determine which out of each hundred convicted murderers is the unlucky one to be put to death?

It may be possible, under a complete and thoroughgoing cost/benefit analysis of the death penalty, to answer such questions. But an appeal merely to the moral principle that if lives are to be risked then let it be the lives of the guilty rather than the lives of the innocent will not suffice. . . . Nor will it suffice to agree that society deserves all the crime prevention and deterrence it can get by inflicting severe punishments. These principles are consistent with too many different policies. They are too vague by themselves to resolve the choice on grounds of social defense when confronted with hypothetical situations like those proposed above.

Since no adequate cost/benefit analysis of the death penalty exists, there is no way to resolve these questions from this standpoint at the present time. Moreover, it can be argued that we cannot have such an analysis without already establishing in some way or other the relative value of innocent lives versus guilty lives. Far from being a product of a cost/benefit analysis, this comparative evaluation of lives would have to be brought into any such analysis. Without it, no cost/benefit analysis can get off the ground. Finally, it must be noted that we have no knowledge at present that begins to approximate anything like the situation described above in (1), whereas it appears from the evidence we do have that we achieve about the same deterrent and preventive effects whether we punish murder by death or by imprisonment. Therefore, something like the situation in (2) or in (3) may be correct. If so, this shows that the choice between the two policies of capital punishment and life imprisonment for murder will probably have to be made on some basis other than social defense; on that basis the two policies are equivalent and therefore equally acceptable.

Capital Punishment and Retributive Justice

. . . There are two leading principles of retributive justice relevant to the capital-punishment controversy. One is the principle that crimes should be punished. The other is the principle that the severity of a punishment should be proportional to the gravity of the offense. (A corollary to the latter principle is the judgment that nothing so fits the crime of murder as the punishment of death.) Although these principles do not seem to stem from any concern over the worth, value, dignity, or rights of persons, they are moral principles of recognized weight and

no discussion of the morality of capital punishment would be complete without them. Leaving aside all questions of social defense, how strong a case for capital punishment can be made on the basis of these principles? How reliable and persuasive are these principles themselves?

Crime Must Be Punished

Given [a general rationale for punishment], there cannot be any dispute over this principle. In embracing it, of course, we are not automatically making a fetish of "law and order," in the sense that we would be if we thought that the most important single thing society can do with its resources is to punish crimes. In addition, this principle is not likely to be in dispute between proponents and opponents of the death penalty. Only those who completely oppose punishment for murder and other erstwhile capital crimes would appear to disregard this principle. Even defenders of the death penalty must admit that putting a convicted murderer in prison for years is a punishment of that criminal. The principle that crime must be punished is neutral to our controversy, because both sides acknowledge it and comply with it.

It is the other principle of retributive justice that seems to be a decisive one. Under the principle of retaliation, *lex talionis,* it must always have seemed that murderers ought to be put to death. Proponents of the death penalty, with rare exceptions, have insisted on this point, and it seems that even opponents of the death penalty must give it grudging assent. The strategy for opponents of the death penalty is to show either (a) that this principle is not really a principle of justice after all, or (b) that although it is, other principles outweigh or cancel its dictates. As we shall see, both these objections have merit.

Is Murder Alone to Be Punished by Death?

Let us recall, first, that not even the Biblical world limited the death penalty to the punishment of murder. Many other nonhomicidal crimes also carried this penalty (e.g., kidnapping, witchcraft, cursing one's parents). In our own recent history, persons have been executed for aggravated assault, rape, kidnapping, armed robbery, sabotage, and espionage. It is not possible to defend any of these executions (not to mention some of the more bizarre capital statutes, like the one in Georgia that used to provide an optional death penalty for desecration of a grave) on grounds of just retribution. This entails that either such executions are not justified or that they are justified on some ground other than retribution. In actual practice, few if any defenders of the death penalty have ever been willing to rest their case entirely on the moral principle of just retribution as formulated in terms of "a life for a life." Kant seems to have been a conspicuous exception. Most defenders of the death penalty have implied by their willingness to use executions to defend limb and property, as well as life, that they did not place much value on the lives of criminals when compared to the value of both lives and things belonging to innocent citizens.

Are All Murders to Be Punished by Death?

Our society for several centuries has endeavored to confine the death penalty to some criminal homicides. Even Kant took a casual attitude toward a mother's killing of her illegitimate child. ("A child born into the world outside marriage is outside the law . . . , and consequently it is also outside the protection of the law.")[1] In our society, the development nearly 200 years ago of the distinction between first- and second-degree murder was an attempt to narrow the class of criminal homicides deserving of the death penalty. Yet those dead owing to manslaughter, or to any kind of unintentional, accidental, unpremeditated, unavoidable, unmalicious killing are just as dead as the victims of the most ghastly murder. Both the law in practice and moral reflection show how difficult it is to identify all and only the criminal homicides that are appropri-

ately punished by death (assuming that any are). Individual judges and juries differ in the conclusions they reach. The history of capital punishment for homicides reveals continual efforts, uniformly unsuccessful, to identify before the fact those homicides for which the slayer should die. Benjamin Cardozo, a justice of the United State Supreme Court fifty years ago, said of the distinction between degrees of murder that it was

> . . . so obscure that no jury hearing it for the first time can fairly be expected to assimilate and understand it. I am not at all sure that I understand it myself after trying to apply it for many years and after diligent study of what has been written in the books. Upon the basis of this fine distinction with its obscure and mystifying psychology, scores of men have gone to their death.[2]

Similar skepticism has been registered on the reliability and rationality of death-penalty statutes that give the trial court the discretion to sentence to prison or to death. As Justice John Marshall Harlan of the Supreme Court observed a decade ago,

> Those who have come to grips with the hard task of actually attempting to draft means of channeling capital sentencing discretion have confirmed the lesson taught by history. . . . To identify before the fact those characteristics of criminal homicide and their perpetrators which call for the death penalty, and to express these characteristics in language which can be fairly understood and applied by the sentencing authority, appear to be tasks which are beyond present human ability.[3]

The abstract principle that the punishment of death best fits the crime of murder turns out to be extremely difficult to interpret and apply.

If we look at the matter from the standpoint of the actual practice of criminal justice, we can only conclude that "a life for a life" plays little or no role whatever. Plea bargaining (by means of which one of the persons involved in a crime agrees to accept a lesser sentence in exchange for testifying against the others to enable the prosecutor to get them all convicted), even where murder is concerned, is widespread. Studies of criminal justice reveal that what the courts (trial or appellate) decide on a given day is first-degree murder suitably punished by death in a given jurisdiction could just as well be decided in a neighboring jurisdiction on another day either as second-degree murder or as first-degree murder but without the death penalty. The factors that influence prosecutors in determining the charge under which they will prosecute go far beyond the simple principle of "a life for a life." Nor can it be objected that these facts show that our society does not care about justice. To put it succinctly, either justice in punishment does not consist of retribution, because there are other principles of justice; or there are other moral considerations besides justice that must be honored; or retributive justice is not adequately expressed in the idea of "a life for a life."

Is Death Sufficiently Retributive?

Given the reality of horrible and vicious crimes, one must consider whether is not a quality of unthinking arbitrariness in advocating capital punishment for murder as the retributively just punishment. Why does death in the electric chair or the gas chamber or before a firing squad or on a gallows meet the requirements of retributive justice? When one thinks of the savage, brutal, wanton character of so many murders, how can retributive justice be served by anything less than equally savage methods of execution for the murderer? From a retributive point of view, the oft-heard exclamation, "Death is too good for him!" has a certain truth. Yet few defenders of the death penalty are willing to embrace this consequence of their own doctrine.

The reason they do not and should not is that, if they did, they would be stooping to the methods and thus to the squalor of the murderer. Where criminals set the limits of just methods of punishment, as they will do if we attempt to give exact and literal implementation to *lex talionis*, society will find itself descending to the cruelties

and savagery that criminals employ. But society would be deliberately authorizing such acts, in the cool light of reason, and not (as is often true of vicious criminals) impulsively or in hatred and anger or with an insane or unbalanced mind. Moral restraints, in short, prohibit us from trying to make executions perfectly retributive. Once we grant the role of these restraints, the principle of "a life for a life" itself has been qualified and no longer suffices to justify the execution of murderers.

Other considerations take us in a different direction. Few murders, outside television and movie scripts, involve anything like an execution. An execution, after all, begins with a solemn pronouncement of the death sentence from a judge, is followed by long detention in maximum security awaiting the date of execution, various appeals, perhaps a final sanity hearing, and then "the last mile" to the execution chamber itself. As the French writer Albert Camus remarked,

> For there to be an equivalence, the death penalty would have to punish a criminal who had warned his victim of the date at which he would inflict a horrible death on him and who, from that moment onward, had confined him at his mercy for months. Such a monster is not encountered in private life.[4]

Differential Severity Does Not Require Executions

What, then, emerges from our examination of retributive justice and the death penalty? If retributive justice is thought to consist in *lex talionis*, all one can say is that this principle has never exercised more than a crude and indirect effect on the actual punishments meted out. Other principles interfere with a literal and single-minded application of this one. Some murders seem improperly punished by death at all; other murders would require methods of execution too horrible to inflict; in still other cases any possible execution is too deliberate and monstrous given the nature of the motivation culminating in the murder. Proponents of the death penalty rarely confine themselves to reliance on this principle of just retribution and nothing else, since they rarely confine themselves to supporting the death penalty only for all murders.

But retributive justice need not be thought to consist of *lex talionis*. One may reject that principle as too crude and still embrace the retributive principle that the severity of punishments should be graded according to the gravity of the offense. Even though one need not claim that life imprisonment (or any kind of punishment other than death) "fits" the crime of murder, one can claim that this punishment is the proper one for murder. To do this, the schedule of punishments accepted by society must be arranged so that this mode of imprisonment is the most severe penalty used. Opponents of the death penalty need not reject this principle of retributive justice, even though they must reject a literal *lex talionis*.

Equal Justice and Capital Punishment

During the past generation, the strongest practical objection to the death penalty has been the inequities with which it has been applied. As Supreme Court Justice William O. Douglas once observed, "One searches our chronicles in vain for the execution of any member of the affluent strata of this society."[5] One does not search our chronicles in vain for the crime of murder committed by the affluent. Every study of the death penalty for rape has confirmed that black male rapists (especially where the victim is a white female) are far more likely to be sentenced to death (and executed) than white male rapists. Half of all those under death sentence during 1976 and 1977 were black, and nearly half of all those executed since 1930 were black. All the sociological evidence points to the conclusion that the death penalty is the poor man's justice; as the current street saying has it, "Those without the capital get the punishment."

Let us suppose that the factual basis for such a criticism is sound. What follows for the morality of capital punishment? Many defenders of the death penalty have been quick to point out that since there is nothing intrinsic about the crime of murder or rape that dictates that only the poor or racial-minority males will commit it, and since there is nothing overtly racist about the statutes that authorize the death penalty for murder or rape, it is hardly a fault in the idea of capital punishment if in practice it falls with unfair impact on the poor and the black. There is, in short, nothing in the death penalty that requires it to be applied unfairly and with arbitrary or discriminatory results. It is at worst a fault in the system of administering criminal justice (and some, who dispute the facts cited above, would deny even this).

Presumably, both proponents and opponents of capital punishment would concede that it is a fundamental dictate of justice that a punishment should not be unfairly—inequitably or unevenly—enforced and applied. They should also be able to agree that when the punishment in question is the extremely severe one of death, then the requirement to be fair in using such a punishment becomes even more stringent. Thus, there should be no dispute in the death penalty controversy over these principles of justice. The dispute begins as soon as one attempts to connect these principles with the actual use of this punishment.

In this country, many critics of the death penalty have argued, we would long ago have got rid of it entirely if it had been a condition of its use that it be applied equally and fairly. In the words of the attorneys who argued against the death penalty in the Supreme Court during 1972, "It is a freakish aberration, a random extreme act of violence, visibly arbitrary and discriminatory—a penalty reserved for unusual application because, if it were usually used, it would affront universally shared standards of public decency."[6] It is difficult to dispute this judgment, when one considers that there have been in the United

States during the past fifty years about half a million criminal homicides but only about 4,000 executions (all but 50 of which were of men).

We can look at these statistics in another way to illustrate the same point. If we could be assured that the 4,000 persons executed were the worst of the worst, repeated offenders without exception, the most dangerous murderers in captivity—the ones who had killed more than once and were likely to kill again, and the least likely to be confined in prison without imminent danger to other inmates and the staff—then one might accept half a million murders and a few thousand executions with a sense that rough justice had been done. But the truth is otherwise. Persons are sentenced to death and executed not because they have been found to be uncontrollably violent, hopelessly poor parole and release risks, or for other reasons. Instead, they are executed for entirely different reasons. They have a poor defense at trial; they have no funds to bring sympathetic witnesses to court; they are immigrants or strangers in the community where they were tried; the prosecuting attorney wants the publicity that goes with "sending a killer to the chair"; they have inexperienced or overworked counsel at trial; there are no funds for an appeal or for a transcript of the trial record; they are members of a despised racial minority. In short, the actual study of why particular persons have been sentenced to death and executed does not show any careful winnowing of the worst from the bad. It shows that the executed were usually the unlucky victims of prejudice and discrimination, the losers in an arbitrary lottery that could just as well have spared them as killed them, the victims of the disadvantages that almost always go with poverty. A system like this does not enhance respect for human life; it cheapens and degrades it. However heinous murder and other crimes are, the system of capital punishment does not compensate for or erase those crimes. It only tends to add new injuries of its own to the catalogue of our inhumanity to each other.

NOTES

1. Immanuel Kant, *The Metaphysical Elements of Justice* (1797), tr. John Ladd, p. 106.
2. Benjamin Cardozo, "What Medicine Can Do for Law" (1928), reprinted in Margaret E. Hall, ed., *Selected Writings of Benjamin Nathan Cardozo* (1947), p. 204.
3. *McGautha v. California*, 402 U.S. 183 (1971), at p. 204.
4. Albert Camus, *Resistance, Rebellion, and Death* (1961), p. 199.
5. *Furman v. Georgia*, 408 U.S. 238 (1972), at pp. 251–252.
6. NAACP Legal Defense and Educational Fund, Brief for Petitioner in *Aikens v. California*, O.T. 1971, No. 68-5027, reprinted in Philip English Mackey, ed., *Voices Against Death: American Opposition to Capital Punishment, 1787–1975* (1975), p. 288.

For Further Reflection

1. Is the death penalty "cruel and unusual punishment," thus meriting prohibition under the Eighth Amendment?
2. Do you agree with Bedau that the death penalty "only tends to add new injuries of its own to the catalogue of our inhumanity to each other"?
3. Do you think that long-term imprisonment is an adequate punishment for first-degree murder? Some people think that long-term imprisonment is worse punishment than execution. Do you agree? Explain.

Do Animals Have Rights?

Every minute of the day, 24 hours a day, 100 animals are killed in laboratories in the United States. Fifty million animals used in experiments are put to death each year. Some die in the testing of industrial and cosmetic products, some are killed after being force fed or after being tested for pharmaceutical drugs. Product testing on animals is required by government before the products are allowed for use by human beings.

Legal requirements that animals be anesthetized are circumvented in many experiments. Recently, at a major university, baboons were strapped down in boxlike vises and had specially designed helmets cemented to their skulls. Then a pneumatic device delivered calibrated blows to the helmet to determine its strength. The blows continued until the baboon's skull was fractured and the animal was brain damaged. Dogs are driven insane with electric shocks so that scientists can study the effects of insanity. Cats are deprived of sleep until they die. Primates have been restrained for months in steel chairs allowing no movement, and elephants have been given LSD to study aggression. Legs have been cut off mice to study how they walk on the stumps, and polar bears have been drowned in vats of crude oil to study the effect of oil spills in polar regions.

Kittens have been blinded, castrated, and rendered deaf in order to see what effect these incapacities would have on their sexual development. Civet cats are placed in small cages in dark rooms where the temperature is 110°F, and confined there until they die. The musk that is scraped from their genitals once a day for as long as they can survive makes the scent of perfume last a bit longer after each application.

Neither is all well down on the farm. Factory farming with high-tech machinery has replaced free-range agriculture. Farmer McDonald doesn't visit his hens in barns in order to pick an egg from the comfortable nest. Now, as soon as chicks are hatched, they are placed in small cages. Between five and nine chickens are pressed close together in cages about 18 inches by 10 inches where they cannot move around, with thin wire-mesh floors that hurt their feet. They are painfully debeaked so that they cannot attack each other in these unnatural quarters. In other chicken factories the chickens are hung by their feet from conveyer belts that transport them through automatic throat-slicing machines. Three billion chickens are killed in the United States each year. Likewise, pigs and veal calves are kept in pens so small they cannot move or turn around and develop muscles. They are separated from their mothers so they cannot be suckled and are fed a diet low in iron so they will produce very tender meat.

Do animals have rights? In the light of the practices described above, do we have a responsibility to improve our behavior toward the animal kingdom? No one disagrees that we should not cause animals *unnecessary* suffering, but those who defend animal factories and animal experimentation argue that human need justifies these practices. On the other side of the controversy, animal rights advocates argue that animals should be accorded equal consideration with humans—that their specific needs should be taken seriously. If this were done, we would become vegetarians, cease to use leather, and cease all (or almost all) animal experimentation.

In our first reading, Peter Singer, the torchbearer of animal liberation, argues that animals should be treated with equal consideration as human beings. Singer says that if a nonhuman and a human are suffering, and we have only enough painkiller for one, it is not clear who should get the painkiller.

Carl Cohen argues in our second reading that the idea of rights does not apply to animals since "rights" is a concept appropriate only to members of the moral community and animals cannot make moral decisions. Humans are of far greater value than animals. Cohen readily admits that gratuitous suffering should be prohibited, but animal experimentation is needed to ameliorate human suffering, and, as such, it is justified.

IX.5   The Case for Animal Liberation

PETER SINGER

Peter Singer is a member of the philosophy department at La Trobe University in Australia. His book, *Animal Liberation* (1975), from which this selection is taken, is one of the most influential books ever written on the subject and inaugurated the contemporary animal rights movement. Singer argues that animal liberation today is analogous to racial and gender justice in the past. Just as people once thought it incredible that women should be treated as equal to men, or blacks as equal to whites, so now "speciesists" mock the idea that all animals should be given equal consideration. Singer defines "speciesism" as the prejudice (unjustified bias) that favors one's own species over every other. That which equalizes all sentient beings is our ability to suffer. In that, we and animals are equal and deserve equal respect.

Study Questions

1. What is the relationship between the women's rights movement, the civil rights movement, and the animal rights movement?
2. How does Singer define "speciesism"?
3. What is the basis of equality in humans and nonhumans?
4. Does equal consideration mean that we should treat animals exactly as we treat humans?
5. What changes would have to be made in our behavior if we took animal rights seriously?

THIS [VIEWPOINT] IS about the tyranny of human over nonhuman animals. This tyranny has caused and today is still causing an amount of pain and suffering that can only be compared with that which resulted from the centuries of tyranny by white humans over black humans.

Reprinted from Animal Liberation *(New York Review of Books, 1975)*.

The struggle against this tyranny is a struggle as important as any of the moral and social issues that have been fought over in recent years.

Most readers will take what they have just read to be a wild exaggeration. Five years ago I myself would have laughed at the statements I have now written in complete seriousness. Five years ago I did not know what I know today. . . .

Changing Prejudicial Attitudes

A liberation movement demands an expansion of our moral horizons. Practices that were previously regarded as natural and inevitable come to be seen as the result of an unjustifiable prejudice. Who can say with any confidence that none of his or her attitudes and practices can legitimately be questioned? If we wish to avoid being numbered among the oppressors, we must be prepared to rethink all our attitudes to other groups, including the most fundamental. . . .

I believe that our present attitudes are based on a long history of prejudice and arbitrary discrimination. I argue that there can be no reason—except the selfish desire to preserve the privileges of the exploiting group—for refusing to extend the basic principle of equality of consideration to members of other species. I ask you to recognize that your attitudes to members of other species are a form of prejudice no less objectionable than prejudice about a person's race or sex. . . .

"Animal Liberation" may sound more like a parody of other liberation movements than a serious objective. The idea of "The Rights of Animals" actually was once used to parody the case for women's rights. When Mary Wollstonecraft, a forerunner of today's feminists, published her *Vindication of the Rights of Women* in 1792, her views were widely regarded as absurd, and before long an anonymous publication appeared entitled *A Vindication of the Rights of Brutes*. The author of this satirical work (now known to have been Thomas Taylor, a distinguished Cambridge philosopher) tried to refute Mary Wollstonecraft's arguments by showing that they could be carried one stage further. If the argument for equality was sound when applied to women, why should it not be applied to dogs, cats, and horses? The reasoning seemed to hold for these "brutes" too; yet to hold that brutes had rights was manifestly absurd; therefore the reasoning by which this conclusion had been reached must be unsound, and if unsound when applied to brutes, it must also be unsound when applied to women, since the very same arguments had been used in each case. . . .

One way in which we might reply is by saying that the case for equality between men and women cannot validly be extended to nonhuman animals. Women have a right to vote, for instance, because they are just as capable of making rational decisions about the future as men are; dogs, on the other hand, are incapable of understanding the significance of voting, so they cannot have the right to vote. There are many other obvious ways in which men and women resemble each other closely, while humans and animals differ greatly. So, it might be said, men and women are similar beings and should have similar rights, while humans and nonhumans are different and should not have equal rights.

Equal Consideration of Rights

The reasoning behind this reply to Taylor's analogy is correct up to a point, but it does not go far enough. There *are* important differences between humans and other animals, and these differences must give rise to *some* differences in the rights that each has. Recognizing this obvious fact, however, is no barrier to the case for extending the basic principle of equality to nonhuman animals. The differences that exist between men and women are equally undeniable, and the supporters of Women's Liberation are aware that these differences may give rise to different rights. Many feminists hold that women have the right to an abortion on request. It does not follow that since these same feminists are campaigning for equality between men and women they must support the right of men to have abortions too. Since a man cannot have an abortion, it is meaningless to talk of his right to have one. Since a dog can't vote, it is meaningless to talk of its right to vote. There is no reason why either Women's Liberation or Animal Liberation should get involved in such nonsense. The extension of the basic principle of equality from one group to another does not imply that we must treat both groups in exactly the same way, or grant exactly the same rights to both groups. Whether we should do so will depend on the nature of the members of the two groups. The basic principle of equality does not require equal or identical *treatment*; it requires equal *consideration*. Equal consideration for different beings may lead to different treatment and different rights. . . .

The Basis of Equality

Although, it may be said, humans differ as individuals there are no differences between the races and sexes *as such*. From the mere fact that a person is black or a woman we cannot infer anything about that person's intellectual or moral capacities. This, it may be said, is why racism and sexism are wrong. The white racist claims that whites are superior to blacks, but this is false—although there are differences among individuals, some blacks are superior to some whites in all of the capacities and abilities that could conceivably be relevant. The opponent of sexism would say the same: a person's sex is no guide to his or her abilities, and this is why it is unjustifiable to discriminate on the basis of sex. . . .

It is an implication of this principle of equality that our concern for others and our readiness to consider their interests ought not to depend on what they are like or on what abilities they may possess. Precisely what this concern or consideration requires us to do may vary according

to the characteristics of those affected by what we do: concern for the well-being of a child growing up in America would require that we teach him to read; concern for the well-being of a pig may require no more than that we leave him alone with other pigs in a place where there is adequate food and room to run freely. But the basic element—the taking into account of the interests of the being, whatever those interests may be—must, according to the principle of equality, be extended to all beings, black or white, masculine or feminine, human or nonhuman. . . .

When in the 1850s the call for women's rights was raised in the United States, a remarkable black feminist named Sojourner Truth [spoke] . . . at a feminist convention:

> They talk about this thing in the head; what do they call it? ["Intellect," whispered someone near by.] That's it. What's that got to do with women's rights or Negroes' rights? If my cup won't hold but a pint and yours holds a quart, wouldn't you be mean not to let me have my little half-measure full?

It is in accordance with this principle that the attitude that we may call "speciesism," by analogy with racism, must also be condemned. Speciesism—the word is not an attractive one, but I can think of no better term—is a prejudice or attitude of bias toward the interest of members of one's own species and against those members of other species. . . .

Many philosophers and other writers have proposed the principle of equal consideration of interests, in some form or other, as a basic moral principle; but not many of them have recognized that this principle applies to members of other species as well as to our own. Jeremy Bentham was one of the few who did realize this. In a forward-looking passage written at a time when black slaves had been freed by the French but in the British dominions were still being treated in the way we now treat animals, Bentham wrote:

> The day *may* come when the rest of the animal creation may acquire those rights which never

could have been withholden from them but by the hand of tyranny. The French have already discovered that the blackness of the skin is no reason why a human being should be abandoned without redress to the caprice of a tormentor. It may one day come to be recognized that the number of the legs, the villosity of the skin, or the termination of the *os sacrum* are reasons equally insufficient for abandoning a sensitive being to the same fate. What else is it that should trace the insuperable line? Is it the faculty of reason, or perhaps the faculty of discourse? But a full-grown horse or dog is beyond comparison a more rational, as well as a more conversable animal, than an infant of a day or week or even a month, old. But suppose they were otherwise, what would it avail. The question is not, Can they *reason?* nor Can they *talk?* but, *Can they suffer?*

In this passage Bentham points to the capacity for suffering as the vital characteristic that gives a being the right to equal consideration. The capacity for suffering—or more strictly, for suffering and/or enjoyment or happiness—is not just another characteristic like the capacity for language or higher mathematics. Bentham is not saying that those who try to mark "the insuperable line" that determines whether the interests of a being should be considered happen to have chosen the wrong characteristic. By saying that we must consider the interests of all beings with the capacity for suffering or enjoyment Bentham does not arbitrarily exclude from consideration any interests at all—as those who draw the line with reference to the possession of reason or language do. The capacity for suffering and enjoyment is *a prerequisite for having interests at all,* a condition that must be satisfied before we can speak of interests in a meaningful way. It would be nonsense to say that it was not in the interests

of a stone to be kicked along the road by a schoolboy. A stone does not have interests because it cannot suffer. Nothing that we can do to it could possibly make any difference to its welfare. A mouse, on the other hand, does have an interest in not being kicked along the road, because it will suffer if it is.

No Excuse for Ignoring Suffering

If a being suffers there can be no moral justification for refusing to take that suffering into consideration. No matter what the nature of the being, the principle of equality requires that its suffering be counted equally with the like suffering—in so far as rough comparisons can be made—of any other being. If a being is not capable of suffering, or of experiencing enjoyment or happiness, there is nothing to be taken into account. So the limit of sentience (using the term as a convenient if not strictly accurate shorthand for the capacity to suffer and/or experience enjoyment) is the only defensible boundary of concern for the interests of others. To mark this boundary by some other characteristic like intelligence or rationality would be to mark it in an arbitrary manner. Why not choose some other characteristic, like skin color?

The racist violates the principle of equality by giving greater weight to the interests of members of his own race when there is a clash between their interests and the interests of those of another race. The sexist violates the principle of equality by favoring the interests of his own sex. Similarly the speciesist allows the interests of his own species to override the greater interests of members of other species. The pattern is identical in each case.

For Further Reflection

  1. Has Singer convinced you that animals have rights equal to humans not to suffer needlessly? If Singer is correct, how should we change our social practices?
  2. What are the broader implications of Singer's proposal? How far should we go with

equal treatment of all animals? Should we kill bacteria or call the exterminator when termites are making a meal of our house? Does his theory lead to a reverence for all life in the manner of Albert Schweitzer?

Albert Schweitzer (1875–1965), the missionary doctor and Nobel Peace Prize winner, combined a Christian and animist view in advocating what he called "Reverence for Life."

> I am life which wills to live, and I exist in the midst of life which wills to live. . . . A living world—and life view, informing all the facts of life, gushes forth from it continually, as from an eternal spring. A mystically ethical oneness with existence grows forth from it unceasingly. . . . Ethics thus consists in this, that I experience the necessity of practising the same reverence for life toward all will-to-live, as toward my own. Therein I have already the needed fundamental principle of morality. It is *good* to maintain and cherish life; it is evil to destroy and to check life. A man is really ethical only when he obeys the constraint laid on him to help all life which he is able to succour, and when he goes out of his way to avoid injuring anything living. He does not ask how far this or that life deserves sympathy as valuable in itself, nor how far it is capable of feeling. To him life as such is sacred. . . . He tears no leaf from its tree, breaks off no flower, and is careful not to crush any insect as he walks. If he works by lamplight on a summer evening, he prefers to keep the window shut and to breathe stifling air, rather than to see insect after insect fall on his table with singed and sinking wings.
>
> If he goes out into the street after a rainstorm and sees a worm which has strayed there, he reflects that it will certainly dry up in the sunshine, if it does not quickly regain the damp soil into which it can creep, and so he helps it back from the deadly paving stones into the lush grass. Should he pass by an insect which has fallen into a pool, he spares the time to reach it a leaf or stalk on which it may clamber and save itself.
>
> Ethics is, in its unqualified form, extended responsibility with regard to everything that has life.

How do you react to this passage? Is it consistent with Singer's idea of liberation? If the ideas are not exactly the same, where do they differ? What do you think of the reverence for life principle?

IX.6   The Case Against Animal Rights

CARL COHEN

Carl Cohen is a professor at the University of Michigan. Cohen argues that while humans have a duty to treat animals humanely, animals cannot have rights. The idea of rights does not apply to animals since "rights" is a concept appropriate only to members of the moral community and animals cannot make moral decisions. Humans are of far greater value than animals, and the result of not using animals for medical experimentation would be greater human suffering.

Study Questions

1. Why don't animals have rights? What does one need to have in order to have moral rights?
2. What are some philosophical views on the attributes necessary for moral capability?
3. What does Kant say that makes humans members of the moral community?
4. Why does Cohen defend speciesism?
5. What are the "absurd consequences" of the animal rights position?

USING ANIMALS as research subjects in medical investigations is widely condemned on two grounds: first, because it wrongly violates the *rights* of animals, and second, because it wrongly imposes on sentient creatures much avoidable *suffering*. Neither of these arguments is sound. The first relies on a mistaken understanding of rights; the second relies on a mistaken calculation of consequences. Both deserve definitive dismissal.

Why Animals Have No Rights

A right, properly understood, is a claim, or potential claim, that one party may exercise against another. The target against whom such a claim may be registered can be a single person, a group, a community, or (perhaps) all humankind. The content of rights claims also varies greatly: repayment of loans, nondiscrimination by employers, noninterference by the state, and so on. To comprehend any genuine right fully, therefore, we must know *who* holds the right, *against whom* it is held, and *to what* it is a right.

Alternative sources of rights add complexity. Some rights are grounded in constitution and law (e.g., the right of an accused to trial by jury); some rights are moral but give no legal claims (e.g., my right to your keeping the promise you gave me); and some rights (e.g., against theft or assault) are rooted both in morals and in law.

The differing targets, contents, and sources of rights, and their inevitable conflict, together weave a tangled web. Notwithstanding all such complications, this much is clear about rights in general: they are in every case claims, or potential claims, within a community of moral agents. Rights arise, and can be intelligibly defended, only among beings who actually do, or can, make moral claims against one another. Whatever else rights may be, therefore, they are necessarily human; their possessors are persons, human beings.

The attributes of human beings from which this moral capability arises have been described variously by philosophers, both ancient and modern: the inner consciousness of a free will (Saint Augustine); the grasp, by human reason, of the binding character of moral law (Saint Thomas Aquinas); the self-conscious participation of human beings in an objective ethical order (G. W. F. Hegel); human membership in an organic moral community (F. H. Bradley); the development of the human self through the consciousness of other moral selves (G. H. Mead); and the underivative, intuitive cognition of the rightness of an action (H. A. Prichard). Most influential has been Immanuel Kant's emphasis on the universal human possession of a uniquely moral will and the autonomy its use entails. Humans confront choices that are purely moral; humans—but certainly not dogs or mice—lay down moral laws, for others and for themselves. Human beings are self-legislative, morally *auto-nomous*.

Animals (that is, nonhuman animals, the ordinary sense of that word) lack this capacity for

Reprinted from The New England Journal of Medicine *vol. 315, pp. 864–870 by permission of the editor.*

free moral judgment. They are not beings of a kind capable of exercising or responding to moral claims. Animals therefore have no rights, and they can have none. This is the core of the argument about the alleged rights of animals. The holders of rights must have the capacity to comprehend rules of duty, governing all including themselves. In applying such rules, the holders or rights must recognize possible conflicts between what is in their own interest and what is just. Only in a community of beings capable of self-restricting moral judgments can the concept of a right be correctly invoked.

Humans have such moral capacities. They are in this sense self-legislative, are members of communities governed by moral rules, and do possess rights. Animals do not have such moral capacities. They are not morally self-legislative, cannot possibly be members of a truly moral community, and therefore cannot possess rights. In conducting research on animal subjects, therefore, we do not violate their rights, because they have none to violate. . . .

Genuinely moral acts have an internal as well as an external dimension. Thus, in law, an act can be criminal only when the guilty deed, the actus reus, is done with a guilty mind, mens rea. No animal can ever commit a crime; bringing animals to criminal trial is the mark of primitive ignorance. The claims of moral rights are similarly inapplicable to them. Does a lion have a right to eat a baby zebra? Does a baby zebra have a right not to be eaten? Such questions, mistakenly invoking the concept of right where it does not belong, do not make good sense. Those who condemn biomedical research because it violates "animal rights" commit the same blunder.

In Defense of Speciesism

Abandoning reliance on animal rights, some critics resort instead to animal sentience—their feelings of pain and distress. We ought to desist from the imposition of pain insofar as we can. Since all or nearly all experimentation on animals does impose pain and could be readily forgone, say these critics, it should be stopped. The ends sought may be worthy, but those ends do not justify imposing agonies on humans, and by animals the agonies are felt no less. The laboratory use of animals (these critics conclude) must therefore be ended—or at least very sharply curtailed.

Argument of this variety is essentially utilitarian, often expressly so; it is based on the calculation of the net product, in pains and pleasures, resulting from experiments on animals. Jeremy Bentham, comparing horses and dogs with other sentient creatures, is thus commonly quoted: "The question is not, Can they reason? nor Can they talk? but, Can they suffer?"

Biomedical Research Must Still Proceed

Animals certainly can suffer and surely ought not to be made to suffer needlessly. But in inferring, from these uncontroversial premises, that biomedical research causing animal distress is largely (or wholly) wrong, the critic commits two serious errors.

The first error is the assumption, often explicitly defended, that all sentient animals have equal moral standing. Between a dog and a human being, according to this view, there is no moral difference; hence the pains suffered by dogs must be weighed no differently from the pains suffered by humans. To deny such equality, according to this critic, is to give unjust preference to one species over another; it is "speciesism." The most influential statement of this moral equality of species was made by Peter Singer:

> The racist violates the principle of equality by giving greater weight to the interests of members of his own race when there is a clash between their interests and the interests of those of another race. The sexist violates the principle of equality by favoring the interests of his own sex. Similarly the speciesist allows the interests of his own species to override the greater interests of members of other species. The pattern is identical in each case.

This argument is worse than unsound; it is atrocious. It draws an offensive moral conclusion from a deliberately devised verbal parallelism that is utterly specious. Racism has no rational ground whatever. Differing degrees of respect or concern for humans for no other reason than that they are members of different races is an injustice totally without foundation in the nature of the races themselves. Racists, even if acting on the basis of mistaken factual beliefs, do grave moral wrong precisely because there is no morally relevant distinction among the races. The supposition of such differences has led to outright horror. The same is true of the sexes, neither sex being entitled by right to greater respect or concern than the other. No dispute here.

Between species of animate life, however— between (for example) humans on the one hand and cats or rats on the other—the morally relevant differences are enormous, and almost universally appreciated. Humans engage in moral reflection; humans are morally autonomous; humans are members of moral communities, recognizing just claims against their own interest. Human beings do have rights; theirs is a moral status very different from that of cats or rats.

Speciesism Is Necessary

I am a speciesist. Speciesism is not merely plausible; it is essential for right conduct, because those who will not make the morally relevant distinctions among species are almost certain, in consequence, to misapprehend their true obligations. The analogy between speciesism and racism is insidious. Every sensitive moral judgment requires that the differing natures of the beings to whom obligations are owed be considered. If all forms of animate life—or vertebrate animal life—must be treated equally, and if therefore in evaluating a research program the pains of a rodent count equally with the pains of a human, we are forced to conclude (1) that neither humans nor rodents possess rights, or (2) that rodents possess all the rights that humans possess.

Both alternatives are absurd. Yet one or the other must be swallowed if the moral equality of all species is to be defended. . . .

Those who claim to base their objection to the use of animals in biomedical research on their reckoning of the net pleasures and pains produced make a second error, equally grave. Even if it were true—as it is surely not—that the pains of all animate beings must be counted equally, a cogent utilitarian calculation requires that we weigh all the consequences of the use, and of the nonuse, of animals in laboratory research. Critics relying (however mistakenly) on animal rights may claim to ignore the beneficial results of such research, rights being trump cards to which interest and advantage must give away. But an argument that is explicitly framed in terms of interest and benefit for all over the long run must attend also to the disadvantageous consequences of not using animals in research, and to all the achievements attained and attainable only through their use. The sum of the benefits of their use is utterly beyond quantification. The elimination of horrible disease, the increase of longevity, the avoidance of great pain, the saving of lives, and the improvement of the quality of lives (for humans and for animals) achieved through research using animals is so incalculably great that the argument of these critics, systematically pursued, establishes not their conclusion but its reverse: to refrain from using animals in biomedical research is, on utilitarian ground, morally wrong.

When balancing the pleasures and pains resulting from the use of animals in research, we must not fail to place on the scales the terrible pains that would have resulted, would be suffered now, and would long continue had animals not been used. Every disease eliminated, every vaccine developed, every method of pain relief devised, every surgical procedure invented, every prosthetic device implanted—indeed, virtually every modern medical therapy is due, in part or in whole, to experimentation using animals. Nor may we ignore, in the balancing process, the predictable gains in human (and animal) well-being that are probably achievable in the future but that will not be achieved if the decision is made now to desist from such research or to curtail it. . . .

The Absurd Consequences of Animal Rights

Finally, inconsistency between the profession and the practice of many who oppose research using animals deserves comment. This frankly ad hominem observation aims chiefly to show that a coherent position rejecting the use of animals in medical research imposes costs so high as to be intolerable even to the critics themselves.

One cannot coherently object to the killing of animals in biomedical investigations while continuing to eat them. Anesthetics and thoughtful animal husbandry render the level of actual animal distress in the laboratory generally lower than that in the abattoir. So long as death and discomfort do not substantially differ in the two contexts, the consistent objector must not only refrain from all eating of animals but also protest as vehemently against others eating them as against others experimenting on them. No less vigorously must the critic object to the wearing of animal hides in coats and shoes, to employment in any industrial enterprise that uses animal parts, and to any commercial development that will cause death or distress to animals. . . .

Scrupulous vegetarianism, in matters of food, clothing, shelter, commerce, and recreation, and in all other spheres, is the only fully coherent position the critic may adopt. At great human cost, the lives of fish and crustaceans must also be protected, with equal vigor, if speciesism has been forsworn. A very few consistent critics adopt this position. It is the reductio ad absurdum of the rejection of moral distinctions between animals and human beings.

For Further Reflection

1. Compare Cohen's argument against animal rights with Singer's argument for animal rights? Which, in your opinion, is closer to the truth? Explain?

2. Examine Cohen's "absurd consequences." How absurd do you think they really are?

3. Cohen doesn't address the problem of suffering caused by factory farming. Given his assumptions, how might he respond to the facts itemized in the introduction to this section? How do you react to them?

Suggestions for Further Reading

Bedau, Hugo A. and Charles M. Pierce, eds. *Capital Punishment in the United States*. NY: AMS Press, 1976.

Bender, David, Bruce Leone, and Janelle Rohr, eds. *Animal Rights*. San Diego: Greenhaven Press, 1989. A comprehensive anthology setting forth both sides of the debate.

Divine, Philip. *The Ethics of Homicide*. Ithaca: Cornell University Press, 1978. A cogent analysis of moral issues related to taking life from a conservative perspective.

Feinberg, Joel, ed. *The Problem of Abortion*. Belmont, CA: Wadsworth Publishing Co., 1973. Probably the best anthology on the subject.

Frey, R. G. *Interests and Rights: The Case Against Animals*. New York: Oxford University Press, 1980. A critique of the notion that animals have rights.

Glover, Jonathan. *Causing Death and Saving Lives.* NY: Penguin, 1977. A clear and cogent analysis of life and death issues from a utilitarian perspective.

Mappes, Thomas and Jane Zembaty, eds. *Social Ethics,* 3rd ed. NY: McGraw-Hill, 1987. An excellent anthology with good introductions.

Mason, Jim and Peter Singer. *Animal Factories.* New York: Crown Publishers, 1980. A exposé of the manufacturing of food in the USA.

Murphy, Jeffrie, ed. *Punishment and Rehabilitation.* Belmont: Wadsworth Publishing Co., 1973. One of the best collections of articles on the topic.

Regan, Tom, ed. *Matters of Life and Death.* Random House, 1980. One of the best collections of articles on applied ethics, covering euthanasia, suicide, violence and war, capital punishment, abortion, animal rights, famine relief, and environmental ethics.

Regan, Tom and Peter Singer, eds. *Animal Rights and Human Obligation.* Englewood Cliffs, NJ: Prentice-Hall, 1976. Contains classical and contemporary articles in favor of animal rights.

Singer, Peter. *Animal Liberation.* NY: Avon Books, 1975. A vigorous defense of animal rights.

Sterba, James. *Morality in Practice,* 3rd ed. Belmont, CA: Wadsworth Publishing Company, 1991. An excellent, updated anthology, covering eleven important issues.

Appendix I

How to Read and Write
a Philosophy Paper

> Nothing worthwhile was ever accomplished without great difficulty.
> PLATO, *The Republic*

Just about everyone who comes to philosophy—usually in college—feels a sinking sensation in his or her stomach when first encountering this very strange material, involving a different sort of style and method from anything else they have ever dealt with. It was certainly my first reaction as a student. Lured by questions such as "Is there a God? What can I truly know? What is the meaning of life? How shall I live my life?" I began to read philosophy on my own. My first book was Bertrand Russell's *History of Western Philosophy,* which is much more than a history of the subject, being also Russell's own analysis and evaluation of major themes in the history of Western philosophy. Although it is not a terribly difficult text, most of the ideas and arguments were new to me. Since he opposed many of the beliefs that I had been brought up with, I felt angry with him. But since he seemed to argue so persuasively, my anger gave way to confusion and then to a sense of defeat and despair. Yet I felt compelled to go on with this "forbidden fruit," finishing Russell's long work and going on to read Plato's *Republic,* René Descartes' *Meditations,* David Hume's *Dialogues on Natural Religion,* selected writings of Immanuel Kant, William James' *Will to Believe,* and finally contemporary readings by Antony Flew, R. M. Hare, John Hick, and Ludwig Wittgenstein. Gradually, I became aware that on every issue on which I disagreed with Hume or Russell, Kant or Hick, someone else had a plausible counterargument. Eventually, I struggled to the place where I could see weaknesses in arguments (sometimes in the arguments of those figures with whom I had agreed) and finally I came to the point where I could write out arguments of my own. The pain of the process slowly gave way to joy—almost addictive joy, let me warn you—so that I decided to go to graduate school to get an advanced degree in philosophy.

As I mentioned earlier, it was a gnawing worry about fundamental questions of existence that drew me to philosophy. Is there a God? What can I know for sure? Do I have a soul that will live forever? Am I truly free, or simply determined by my heredity and environment? What is it to live a moral life? If you have asked these questions and pondered alternative responses, most of the essays in this book will make sense to you. But if you haven't spent a lot of time thinking about this sort of subject matter, you might ask yourself whether or not these questions are important and you might out-

Reprinted from Introduction to Philosophy: Classical and Contemporary Readings *by Louis P. Pojman* (Belmont, Calif.: Wadsworth, 1991).

line your own present responses to them. For unless you've asked the question, the proposed answers may sound like only one end of a telephone conversation.

This textbook is meant to suggest responses in order to stimulate you to work out your own position on the questions addressed herein. This text, offering readings on alternative sides of each issue, along with a teacher to serve as a guide—and, I hope, some fellow students with whom to discuss the material—should challenge you to begin to work out your own philosophy of life.

However, neither the textbook nor the teacher will be sufficient to save you from a sense of disorientation and uncertainty in reading and writing about philosophy, so let me offer a few tips from my experience as a student and as a teacher of philosophy.

Suggestions on Reading a Philosophy Text

The styles and methods of philosophy are different from other subjects with which you have been acquainted since grammar school: English, history, psychology, and science. Of course, there are many methods, and some writings—for example, those of the existentialists: Søren Kierkegaard, Friedrich Nietzsche, Albert Camus, and Jean-Paul Sartre—do resemble what we encounter in literature more than more typical essays in philosophical analysis. In some ways philosophy resembles mathematics, since it usually strives to develop a deductive argument much like a mathematical proof, only the premises of the argument are usually in need of a lot of discussion and objections need to be considered. Sometimes I think of arguing about a philosophical problem as a kind of legal reasoning before a civil court. Each side presents its evidence and gives reasons for accepting its conclusion rather than the opponent's. For example, suppose you believe in freedom of the will and I believe in determinism. We each set forth the best reasons we have for accepting our respective conclusions. The difference between philosophical argument and the court case is that we are also the jury. We can change our minds on hearing the evidence and even change sides by hearing our opponent make a persuasive case.

Suggestions on Writing a Philosophy Paper

Talking about philosophy and writing philosophy are excellent ways to improve your understanding of the content and process of the subject as well as to improve your philosophical reasoning skill. Writing an essay on a philosophical issue focuses your mind and forces you to concentrate on the essential arguments connected with the issue. The process is hard, but it's amazing how much progress one can make—some faster than others, but in my experience some of those who have the hardest time at first end up doing the deepest, most thorough work.

First of all, identify a *problem* you want to shed light on or solve or a *thesis* you want to defend. Be sure that you have read at least a few good articles on different sides of the issue and can put the arguments in your own words.

Now you are ready to begin to write. Here are some suggestions that may help you.

1. Identify the problem you want to analyze. For example, you might want to show that W. T. Stace (in Part V) has put forth an unsound argument for the thesis that free will and determinism are compatible.

2. As clearly as possible, state the problem and what you intend to show (for example, "I intend to analyze Stace's argument for compatibilism and show that he has misconstrued the issue. His argument for compatibilism is unsound").

3. Set forth your argument in logical order, supporting your own premises with reasons. It may help to illustrate your points with examples or to point out counterexamples to the opposing points of view.

4. Consider alternative points of view from your own and objections to your position. Try to meet these charges and to show why your position is more plausible.

5. End your paper with a summary and a conclusion: review your argument and show its implications for other issues.

6. You will probably need to write at least two drafts before you have a working copy. It helps to have another philosophy student go over the preliminary draft before you write a final draft. Make sure that your argument is well constructed and that your paper as a whole is coherent.

7. Regarding style, write *clearly,* in an active voice, put other people's ideas in your own words as much as possible, and give credit in the text and in bibliographic notes wherever you have used someone else's idea or quoted someone.

8. Include a bibliography at the end of your paper, listing all the sources you used for your paper.

When you have a serious problem, do not hesitate to contact your teacher. That is what he or she is there for: to help you make progress in doing philosophical reasoning.

Good luck and I hope you come to enjoy the philosophical quest for truth and wisdom as much as I have.

Appendix II

A Little Bit of Logic

Philosophy is centered in the analysis and construction of *arguments*. We call the study of arguments *logic*. So let us devote a little time to the rudiments of logic. By "argument," we do not mean a verbal fight, but the process of supporting a thesis (called the *conclusion*) with reasons (called *logic*). An argument consists of at least two declarative sentences (sometimes called *propositions*), one of which (the conclusion) logically follows from the others (the premises). There are two main kinds of arguments, *deductive* and *inductive*. A *valid deductive argument* is one that follows a correct logical form, so that if the premises are true, the conclusion must also be true. If the form is not a good one, the argument is invalid. We say that a valid deductive argument *preserves truth*. It does so in much the same way as a good refrigerator preserves food. If the food is good, a good refrigerator will preserve it, but if it is already spoilt, the refrigerator will not make it good. Likewise with premises of a valid argument. If the statements are true and the form is correct, the conclusion will be true; but if the premises are not true, a valid argument will not guarantee a true conclusion.

A classic example of a valid argument is the following:

1. Socrates is a man.
2. All men are mortal.
3. Therefore Socrates is mortal.

In order to identify the form, let us look at the conclusion (3) and identify the two major components: a subject (S) and a predicate (P). "Socrates" is the subject term and "mortal" is the predicate term. Now go back to the two premises and identify these two terms in them. We discover that the two terms are connected by a third term "man" (or the plural "men"). We call this the *middle term*.

The form of the argument is as follows:

1. S is M.
2. All M is P.
3. Therefore S is P.

This is an example of a valid deductive form. If Premises 1 and 2 are true, we will always get a true conclusion by using this form. But note how easy it would be to get an invalid form. Change the order of the second premise to read "All P are M." Let the first premise read, "My roommate is a mammal," and let the second premise read, "All dogs are mammals." What do you get? The following:

Reprinted from Introduction to Philosophy: Classical and Contemporary Readings *by Louis P. Pojman (Belmont, Calif.: Wadsworth, 1991).*

1. My roommate, Sam Smith, is a mammal. (premise)
2. All dogs are mammals. (premise)
3. Therefore my roommate is a dog. (conclusion)

Regardless of how badly you might treat your roommate, the argument has improper form and cannot yield a valid conclusion. By seeking to find counterexamples for argument forms, we can discover which forms are correct. (A full study of this process, however, would have to wait for a course in logic.)

But validity is not the only concept we need to examine. *Soundness* is also important. An argument can be valid but still *unsound*. An argument is sound if it has a valid form and all its premises are true. If at least one premise is false, the argument is unsound. Here is an example of a sound argument:

1. If Mary is a mother, she must be a woman.
2. Mary is a mother, for she has just given birth to a baby boy.
3. Therefore, Mary is a woman.

If Mary hasn't given birth, then Premise 2 is false and the argument is unsound.

There are four other deductive argument forms of which you should be aware: *modus ponens* (affirming the antecedent), *modus tollens* (denying the consequent), *disjunctive syllogisms* (denying the disjunct), and *reductio ad absurdum* (reducing to a contradiction). Here are their forms:

Modus Ponens	Modus Tollens
1. If P, then Q.	1. If P, then Q.
2. P.	2. Not Q.
3. Therefore Q.	3. Therefore not P.

Note that in a hypothetical proposition ("If P, then Q") the first term (the proposition P) is called the *antecedent* and the second term (Q), the *consequent*. Both affirming the antecedent and denying the consequent yield valid forms.

Disjunctive Syllogism	Reductio ad Absurdum
1. Either P or Q.	1. Suppose A (which you want to refute).
2. Not Q.	2. If A, then B.
3. Therefore P.	3. If B, then C.
	4. If C, then not A.
	5. Therefore A *and* "Not A."
	6. But since a contradiction cannot be true, A must be false and "Not A" must be true.

We have already given an example of *modus ponens*:

1. If Mary is a mother, she must be a woman.
2. Mary is a mother, for she has just given birth to a baby boy.
3. Therefore, Mary is a woman.

Here is an example of *modus tollens:*

   1. If Leslie is a mother, she is a woman.
   2. Leslie is not a woman (but a man).
   3. Therefore Leslie is not a mother.

Here is an example of a disjunctive syllogism (sometimes called "denying the disjunct"—a *disjunct* is a proposition with an "or" statement in it, such as "P or Q").

   1. John is either a bachelor or a married man.
   2. We know for certain that John is not married.
   3. Therefore John is a bachelor.

Here is an example of *reductio ad absurdum.* It is a little more complicated than the other forms but it is important especially in reference to the ontological argument (see Part II). Suppose someone denies that there is such a thing as a self, and you wish to refute the assertion. You might argue in the following manner:

   1. Suppose that you're correct and there is no such thing as a self. ("Not A")
   2. But if there is no such thing as a self, then no one ever acts. ("If not A, then not B")
   3. But if no one ever acts, then no one can utter meaningful statements. ("If not B, then not C")
   4. But you have purported to utter a meaningful statement in saying that there is no such thing as a self, so there is at least one meaningful statement. (C)
   5. Therefore, according to your argument there is and there is not at least one meaningful statement. (C *and* Not C)
   6. Therefore it must be false that there is no such thing as a self. ("Not, Not A"—which by double negation yields A).

So we have proved by *reductio ad absurdum* that there *is* such a thing as a self.

Before we leave the realm of deductive argument, we must point out two invalid forms that often give students trouble. In order to understand them, look back at *modus ponens* and *modus tollens,* which respectively argue by affirming the antecedent and denying the consequent. But note that two other forms are possible. You can also deny the antecedent and affirm the consequent as follows:

Denying the Antecedent	**Affirming the Consequent**
1. If P, then Q.	1. If P, then Q.
2. Not P.	2. Q.
3. Therefore Not Q.	3. Therefore P.

Are these valid forms? Remember, a valid form must always yield true conclusions if the premises are true. Try to find a counterexample that will show that these two forms are invalid. You might let 1 (If P, then Q) be represented by the proposition "If

Mary is a mother, then she is a woman." First deny the antecedent. Does it necessarily yield a true conclusion?

1. If Mary is a mother, she is a woman.
2. Mary is not a mother.
3. Therefore Mary is not a woman.

It says that Mary is not a woman, which is false. There are lots of women who are not mothers. So denying the antecedent is an invalid form.

Now take the same initial proposition and affirm the consequent "Mary is a woman." Does this in itself yield the conclusion that she is a mother? Of course not. She could be a woman without being a mother.

1. If Mary is a mother, she is a woman.
2. She is a woman.
3. Therefore Mary is a mother.

So while *modus ponens* and *modus tollens* are valid forms, denying the antecedent and affirming the consequent are not.

These are just simple examples of deductive argument forms. Often, alas, it is difficult to state exactly what the author's premises are.

Let's turn our attention to *inductive arguments*. Unlike their counterpart valid deductive arguments, inductive arguments do not preserve truth. That is, they do not guarantee that if we have true premises we will obtain a true conclusion. They bring only *probability*. But in most of life that is the best we can hope for. Thus Hume says that "Probability is the guide of life." Wise people guide their lives by the best evidence available, always realizing that one could be mistaken. We usually do not speak of inductive arguments as being invalid, and sound or unsound, but as being strong or weak. In inductive arguments, the premises are *evidence* for the conclusion or hypothesis. An inductive argument has the following form:

1. A_1 is a B.
2. A_2 is a B.
3. A_3 is a B.
4. So probably the next A we encounter (A_4) will also be a B.

For example, suppose that you are somewhere in the Pacific Ocean, surrounded by four islands. You examine all the trees on three of the islands but can't reach the fourth. Nevertheless you might make some predictions on the basis of your experience on the first three islands. For example, you note that all the trees on Island A are coconut palms and all the trees on Island B are coconut palms and all the trees on Island C are coconut palms. From this you predict that there are coconut palms on Island D, and probably that's the only kind of tree found there.

We learn by induction. After a few experiences of getting burnt by fire (or by people of a certain type), we learn to avoid fire (or such people). The human species has learned by inductive experience that cooperation generally produces more benefits than noncooperation, so we advocate cooperative ventures.

Sometimes we generalize or make predictions from an inadequate sample. When we should know better, we call this type of malformed induction *prejudice*. If a child infers from only six bad experiences with people from Podunkville that all people in Podunkville are bad, that might be acceptable, but if an adult, who could easily have evidence that a lot of good people live in Podunkville, still generalizes about the people of Podunkville and acts accordingly, we label this an irrational bias, a *prejudice*.

Let us apply these brief lessons of logic to reading philosophy. Since the key to philosophy is the argument, you will want to concentrate and even outline the author's reasoning. Find his or her thesis or conclusion. Usually, it is stated quite early. In this anthology, I have identified it in the introductions to each reading. Hereafter, identify the premises that support or lead to the conclusion. For example, Thomas Aquinas (Part II) concludes that God exists. He argues for this conclusion in five different ways. In the second argument, he uses such premises as (1) there is motion and (2) there cannot be motion without something initiating the motion to reach his conclusion.

It helps to outline the premises of the argument. For example, here's how we might set forth Aquinas' second argument mentioned earlier:

1. Some things are in motion. (premise)
2. Nothing in the world can move itself, but must be moved by another. (premise)
3. There cannot be an infinite regress of motions. (premise)
4. Therefore, there must be a first mover who is responsible for all other motion. (conclusion of Premises 1–3, which in turn becomes a premise for the rest of the argument)
5. This first mover is what we call God (explanation of the meaning of God). (premise)
6. Therefore God exists. (conclusion of second part of the argument, Premises 4 and 5)

After identifying the premises and conclusion, analyze them, looking for mistakes in the reasoning. Sometimes arguments are weak or unsound, but not obviously so. Then one needs to stretch one's imagination and think of possible counterexamples to the claims of the author. I found this process almost impossible at first, but gradually it became second nature.

Because philosophical arguments are often complex and subtle (and because philosophers do not always write as clearly as they should), a full understanding of an essay is not readily available after a single reading. So read it two or even three times. The first time I read a philosophy essay, I read for understanding. I want to know where the author is coming from and what he or she is trying to establish. After the first reading, I leave the essay for some time, ruminating on it. Sometimes objections to the arguments awaken me at night or pop up while I am working at something else. Then a day or so later I read the essay again, this time trying to determine its soundness.

A few pointers: Some students find it helpful to keep a notebook on their reflections on the readings. If you own this book, I suggest that you make notes in the margins—initially in pencil, since you may want to revise your impressions after a second reading. Finally, practice charity. Give the author the best possible interpretation, in order to see if the argument has merit. Always try to deal with the most generous version of the argument, especially if you don't agree with its conclusion. The exercise will broaden your horizons and help you develop sharper reasoning skills.

Glossary

Absolute. A moral absolute is a principle that is universally binding. It can never be overridden by another principle. Utilitarianism is a type of system that has only one ethical absolute principle: Do that action which maximizes utility. Kant's system has several absolutes, whereas other deontological systems may have only a few broad absolutes, such as "Never cause unnecessary harm." Sometimes *ethical absolutism* refers to the notion that there is only one correct answer to every moral problem. Diametrically opposed to ethical absolutism is ethical relativism (cf. *relativism,* below), which says that the validity of ethical principles is dependent on social acceptance. Between these polar opposites is ethical objectivism (cf. *objectivism,* below).

Ad hoc. A proposition added to a theory to save it from being considered logically impossible or implausible. As *ad hoc,* the proposition itself may have little or no support itself, but simply serve to stave off rejection of the original theory.

Agnosticism. The view that we do not know whether God exists. It is contrasted with theism, the belief in God, and atheism, the belief that there is no such being.

Anthropomorphism. From the Greek "form of humanity." The tendency to see the divine as having human properties. David Hume and Kai Nielsen (in Part II) accuse theists of viewing God as a super-human being, rather than as something infinitely beyond humanity.

A posteriori. From the Latin "the later." Knowledge that is obtained only from experience, such as sense perceptions or pain sensations.

A priori. From the Latin "preceding." Knowledge that is not based on sense experience but is innate or known simply by the meaning of words or definitions. Hume limited the term to "relations of ideas," referring to analytic truths and mathematics.

Aretaic ethics (Greek, *arete,* virtue). The theory, first presented by Aristotle, that the basis of ethical assessment is character. Rather than seeing the heart of ethics in actions or duties, it focuses on the character and dispositions of the agent. Whereas *deontological* and *teleological* ethical systems emphasize *doing,* aretaic or virtue ethics emphasize *being,* being a certain type of person who will no doubt manifest his or her being in appropriate actions. See Part VI.

Atheism. The view that there is no such being as God (see *agnosticism* and *theism*).

Bourgeoisie. In Marxism the bourgeoisie are the capitalists, who own the means of production, the machines and factories, and thus control the lives of the workers, the proletariat.

Categorical imperative. The categorical imperative commands actions which are necessary of themselves without reference to other ends. This is contrasted with *hypothetical imperative* (cf. below), which commands actions not for their own sakes but for some other good. For Kant, moral duties command categorically. They represent the injunctions of reason, which endows them with universal validity and objective necessity.

Communism. The political-economic philosophy developed in its most famous form by Karl Marx and Friedrich Engels in the nineteenth century, which holds to (1) economic determinism—that the way a society produces its wealth determines all else; and (2) the notion of a class struggle in which the working class will eventually overthrow the bourgeoisie and establish a proletariat dictatorship.

Compatibilism. The view that an act may be entirely determined and yet be free in the sense that it was done voluntarily and not under external coercion. Stace represents this position in reading V.3. It is sometimes referred to as "soft determinism."

527

Contingent. A proposition is contingent if its denial is logically possible. Its denial is not contradictory. A being is contingent if it is not logically necessary.

Deductive argument. An argument is a sound deductive argument if it follows a valid form and has true premises. In that case, the truth of its conclusion is guaranteed. A deductive argument is valid (but not necessarily sound) if it follows an approved form that would guarantee the truth of the conclusion if the premises were true.

Deism. The view that God exists but takes no interest in human affairs. He wound up the world as a clock and then left it to run itself down.

Deontological ethics. Deontological (from the Greek *deon,* which means "duty") ethical systems see certain features in the moral act itself as having intrinsic value. These are contrasted with *teleological* systems (see below), which see the ultimate criterion of morality in some non-moral value that results from actions. For example, for the deontologist there is something right about truth-telling even when it may cause pain or harm, and there is something wrong about lying even when it may produce good consequences. Cf. Part VI.

Determinism. The theory that every event and state of affairs in the world, including human actions, is caused. There are two versions of determinism: hard determinism, which states that because every event is caused, no one is responsible for his or her actions, and soft determinism, or compatibilism, which states that rational creatures can still be held accountable for their actions insofar as they acted voluntarily.

Dualism or **dualistic interactionism.** The view that there are two types of substances or realities in conscious beings—mind and matter—and that these interact with one another, the body producing mental events and the mind leading to physical action.

Egoism. There are two types of egoism. Psychological egoism is a *descriptive* theory about human motivation which holds that people always act to satisfy their perceived best interest. Ethical egoism is a *prescriptive* or normative theory about how people *ought* to act. They ought to act according to their perceived best interests. See Part VI.

Emergentism. The emergent property view says that in nature the whole is often greater than the sum of its parts. Nature exhibits a hierarchy of systems—subatomic particles, atoms, molecules, cells, organs, and organisms. Each whole manifests properties that its parts lack. For example, water has the property wetness, which its parts, H_2O molecules, lack. Likewise, the mind is a whole, which has the property of consciousness, which its individual parts lack. This view is related to *epiphenomenalism* (see below). See Part IV.

Empiricism. The school of philosophy which asserts that the source of all knowledge is experience. John Locke stated that our minds were like blank slates (*tabula rasa*) on which experience writes her messages. There are no innate ideas. Empiricism is contrasted with rationalism, which holds that there are innate ideas so that the mind can discover important metaphysical truth through reason alone. In our readings, Hume and Russell are empiricists.

Epiphenomenalism. A version of dualism which holds that bodily events cause mental events, but mental events do not cause bodily events. The action is one way only, from body to mind.

Epistemology. The study of the nature, origin, and validity of knowledge and belief. See Part III.

Existentialism. The philosophical method that studies human existence from the inside of the subject's experience rather than the outside. It takes a first-person or subjective approach to the ultimate questions rather than a third-person or objective approach. Examples of this view are found in our readings by Jean-Paul Sartre and Albert Camus.

Hedonic (Greek *hedone,* pleasure). Possessing pleasurable or painful quality. Sometimes *hedon* is used to stand for a quantity of pleasure.

Hedonism. Psychological hedonism is the theory that motivation is to be explained exclusively in terms of desire for pleasure and aversion from pain. Ethical hedonism is the theory that pleasure is the only intrinsic positive value and pain or "unpleasant consciousness" the only thing which has negative intrinsic value or intrinsic disvalue. All other values are derived from these two. See Part VIII.

Hedonistic paradox. This is the apparent contradiction arising from the doctrine that pleasure is the only thing worth seeking and the fact that whenever one seeks pleasure, it is not found. Pleasure normally arises as an accompaniment of satisfaction of desire whenever one reaches one's goal.

Heteronomy of the will. This is Kant's term for the determination of the will on nonrational grounds. It is contrasted with *autonomy of the will,* where the will is guided by reason.

Hypothetical imperative. Hypothetical imperatives command actions because they are useful for the attainment of some end which one may or may not desire to obtain. Ethicists who view moral duties to be dependent on consequences would view moral principles as hypothetical imperatives. They have the form: If you want *X,* do action *A* (for example, if you want to live in peace, do all in your power to prevent violence). This is contrasted with the *categorical impera-tive* (above).

Indeterminism. The view that some events are uncaused. Some versions state that some events are uncaused because they happen by chance. Others hold the minimal thesis that some events or states of being (e.g., the self) are uncaused, so that free will is consistent with the position. This view is contrasted with *determinism* (above).

Inductive argument. An argument in which the premises support the truth of the conclusion but do not guarantee it (as a valid deductive argument would).

Innate ideas. The theory that appears in Descartes (reading III.1) that states that all humans are born with certain knowledge.

Intentionality. The view that consciousness is always *about* or *of* something. One never finds mere consciousness existing all by itself. Mental states have objects. I have a belief *about* the president, a thought *of* getting a good grade, a desire *for* friendship.

Intuitionism. This is the ethical theory that the good or the right thing to do can be known directly via the intuition. G. E. Moore is an intuitionist about the good, defining it as a simple, unanalyzable property. William Frankena holds to a version of this doctrine (reading VI.10).

Lex talionis. Literally, the law of the claw. The theory of retaliation, stemming from the biblical passage (Exod. 21:23f), which says that the punishment for a crime shall be "a life for a life, an eye for an eye, a tooth for a tooth, hand for hand, foot for foot, burning for burning, wound for wound, stripe for stripe."

Libertarianism. The theory that humans have free will in the sense that given the same antecedent conditions, one can do otherwise. That is, the self is undetermined by causes and is itself the determining cause of action. This view is represented by William James and Susan Anderson in Part V. Contrasted with *compatibilism* and *determinism* (see above).

Metaphysics. "Beyond physics." The study of ultimate reality, that which is not readily accessible through ordinary empirical experience. Metaphysics includes within its domain such topics as free will, causality, the nature of matter, immortality, and the existence of God.

Monism. The theory that reality is all of one substance, rather than two or more. Examples are materialist monism, which holds that matter is the single substance that makes up all there is, and idealism, which holds that all reality is spiritual or made up of ideas. Lucretius, Democritus, Bertrand Russell, and Richard Taylor all hold to materialistic monism. Spinoza, Berkeley, and Hinduism are examples of proponents of idealism.

Naturalism. The theory that ethical terms are defined through factual terms in that ethical terms refer to natural properties. Ethical hedonism is one version of ethical naturalism, for it states that the good which is the basis of all ethical judgment refers to the experience of pleasure. Other naturalists like Geoffrey Warnock speak of the content of morality in terms of promoting human flourishing or ameliorating the human predicament.

Natural theology. The view that knowledge of God can be obtained through the use of reason. Strong versions hold that we can prove the existence of God. It is contrasted with revealed theology, which holds that all knowledge of God must come from a revelation of God.

Necessary truth. One that cannot be false, such as analytic propositions (e.g., "All bachelors are male").

Noncognitivism. This is the theory that ethical judgments have no truth value but express attitudes or prescriptions.

Objectivism. This is the view that moral principles have objective validity whether or not people recognize them as such; that is, moral rightness or wrongness does not depend on social approval but on independent considerations. Objectivism differs from absolutism in that it allows that all or many of its principles are overridable in given situations. See Part VI.

Occam's Razor. Sometimes called "the principle of parsimony." Named after William of Occam (1290–1349), this states that "entities are not to be multiplied beyond necessity." The razor metaphor connotes that useless or unnecessary material should be cut away from any explanation and the simplest hypothesis accepted.

Pantheism. The view that God is everything and everything is God.

Physicalism. The view that everything (or every substance) in the universe is physical and subject to the laws of science. Related to the mind/body problem. The physicalist says that even our mental states are physical states. We have no separate soul or mind.

Pragmatism. The theory set forth by C. S. Peirce and William James that interprets the meaning of a statement in terms of its practical consequences. They usually go on to say, as James does in Part III, that a proposition is true or false according to its results.

Prima facie. The Latin word that means "at first glance." It signifies an initial status of an idea or principle. In ethics, beginning with W. D. Ross, it stands for a duty that has a presumption in its favor but may be overridden by another duty. *Prima facie* duties are contrasted with *actual duties* or *all-things-considered duties.*

Proposition. A sentence or statement that must either be true or false. Every statement that "states" how the world is a proposition. Questions and imperatives are not propositions. "Would you open the door" and "Please, open the door," are not propositions, but "The door is open" is since it claims to describe a situation.

Rationalism. The school of philosophy that holds that there are important truths which can be known by the mind even though we have never experienced them. The rationalist generally believes in innate knowledge (or ideas), so that we can have certainty about metaphysical truth. Plato and Descartes are two classic examples of rationalists.

Relativism. There are two main types of relativism: cultural and ethical. Cultural relativism is a descriptive thesis, stating that there is enormous variety of moral beliefs across cultures. It is neutral as to whether this is the way things ought to be. Ethical relativism, on the other hand, is an evaluative thesis which holds that the truth of a moral judgment depends on whether a culture recognizes the principle in question. See readings VI.2 and VI.3.

Retributivism. The view on punishment that the criminal (or moral offender) deserves to be punished in proportion to the seriousness of the offense. Kant held this view. See Part IX.

Skepticism. The view that we can have no knowledge. Universal skepticism holds that we cannot know anything at all, whereas local, or particular, skepticism holds that there are important realms in which we are ignorant (e.g., Hume regarding metaphysics).

Speciesism. The view first put forth by Peter Singer (reading IX.5) that just as one may have a prejudice in favor of one's own race, one may have a prejudice in favor of one's own species.

Supererogatory (from the Latin *supererogatus*—beyond the call of duty). A supererogatory act is one that is not required by moral principles but contains enormous value. Supererogatory acts are those that are beyond the call of duty, such as risking one's life to save a stranger. Although most moral systems allow for the possibility of supererogatory acts, some theories (most versions of classical utilitarianism) deny that there can be such acts.

Teleological ethics. Teleological ethical theories place the ultimate criterion of morality in some nonmoral value (for example, happiness or welfare) that results from acts. Whereas *deontological* ethical theories (above) ascribe intrinsic value to features of the acts themselves, teleological theories see only instrumental value in the acts but intrinsic value in the consequences of those acts. Both ethical egoism and utilitarianism are teleological theories. Cf. Part VI.

Theism. The belief that a personal God exists and is providentially involved in human affairs. It is to be contrasted with atheism, which believes that no such being exists, and deism, which holds that God exists but he is not providentially concerned with human affairs.

Theodicy. This view holds that evil can be explained in the light of an overall plan of God and that, rightly understood, this world is the best of all possible worlds. John Hick holds to a version of this doctrine in Part II.

Universalizability. This principle, found explicitly in Kant's and R. M. Hare's philosophy and implicitly in most ethicists' work, states that if some act is right (or wrong) for one person in a situation, it is right (or wrong) for any relevantly similar person in that kind of a situation. It is a principle of consistency, which aims to eliminate irrelevant considerations from ethical assessment.

Utilitarianism. The theory that the right action is that which maximizes utility. Sometimes utility is defined in terms of *pleasure* (Jeremy Bentham), *happiness* (J. S. Mill), *ideals* (G. E. Moore and H. Rashdall), or *interests* (R. B. Perry). Its motto, which characterizes one version of utilitarianism, is "the greatest happiness for the greatest number." Utilitarians further divide into *act* and *rule* utilitarians. Act utilitarians hold that the right act in a situation is that which results (or is most likely to result) in the best consequences, whereas rule utilitarians hold that the right act is that which conforms to the set of rules which in turn will result in the best consequences (relative to other sets of rules) (cf. reading VI.9).